lonely planet

Norway

The Far North
p314

Nordland
p272

Svalbard
p351

Trøndelag
p255

**The Western
Fjords**
p209

**Central
Norway**
p124

**Bergen &
the Southwestern
Fjords** p154

Oslo
p46

**Southern
Norway**
p94

Anthony Ham,
Oliver Berry, Donna Wheeler

PLAN YOUR TRIP

ON THE ROAD

KIEV.VICTOR/SHUTTERSTOCK ©

OSLO P46

ANDREY ARMYAGOV/SHUTTERSTOCK ©

GEIRANGERFJORD P240

Contents

COVID-19

We have re-checked every business in this book before publication to ensure that it is still open after the COVID-19 outbreak. However, the economic and social impacts of COVID-19 will continue to be felt long after the outbreak has been contained, and many businesses, services and events referenced in this guide may experience ongoing restrictions. Some businesses may be temporarily closed, have changed their opening hours and services, or require bookings; some unfortunately could have closed permanently. We suggest you check with venues before visiting for the latest information.

Right: Svalbard
(p351)

WELCOME TO
Norway

The first time I stood on the waterfront at Aurland and contemplated the fjords, I was utterly convinced that there was no more beautiful country on earth. On my many Norwegian journeys since then, in winter and in summer, I've never lost that feeling. Even more than the fjords and the high country, I now find myself drawn to the gravitas of Svalbard, to the perfect juxtaposition of water, rock and human habitation in the Lofoten Islands, and to the far horizons and Sami encampments of Norway's Arctic North.

By Anthony Ham, Writer
For more about our writers, see p448

Norway

N 0 ——— 200 km
0 ——— 100 miles

RUSSIA

FINLAND

Tromsø
Enjoy this vibrant northern city (p315)

Lofoten Islands
Explore Scandinavia's most beautiful islands (p291)

Kystriksveien Coastal Route
Take the slow road into the Arctic (p281)

Ålesund
Admire coastal art-nouveau architecture (p244)

Svalbard
Savour the high Arctic (p351)

NORWEGIAN SEA

Svalbard (550km) (see inset)

Knivskjelodden (71s1I'08"N)

Batsfjord
Vadsø
Kirkenes
Honningsvåg
Repvåg
Kjøllefjord
Lakselv
Karasjok
Kautokeino
Hammerfest
Hasvik
Afta
Skibotn
Lyngseidet
Finnsnes
Ringvassøy
Tromsø
Gryllefjord
Andenes
Harstad
Vesterålen
Narvik
Lofoten
Vestvågøy
Loplingen
Svolvær
Moskenesøy
Værøy
Fauske
Vedøya
Bodø
Ørnes
Saltfjellet-Svartisen National Park
Mo i Rana
Mosjøen
Sandnessjøen
Brønnøysund
Rørvik

Arctic Circle

70°N

65°N

5°W   0° (Greenwich)   5°E   10°E   15°E   20°E   25°E   30°E

Jan Mayen (1200km)

Svalbard inset

80°E   10°E   15°E   20°E   25°E   30°E   35°E

Svalbard
Kvitøya
Storøya
Nordaustlandet
Erik Eriksenstretet
Kong Karls Land
Svenskøya
Barentsøya
Edgeøya
Olgastretet
Storfjorden
Spitsbergen
Magdalenefjord
Prins Karls Forlandet
Longyearbyen

0 ——— 100 km
0 ——— 50 miles

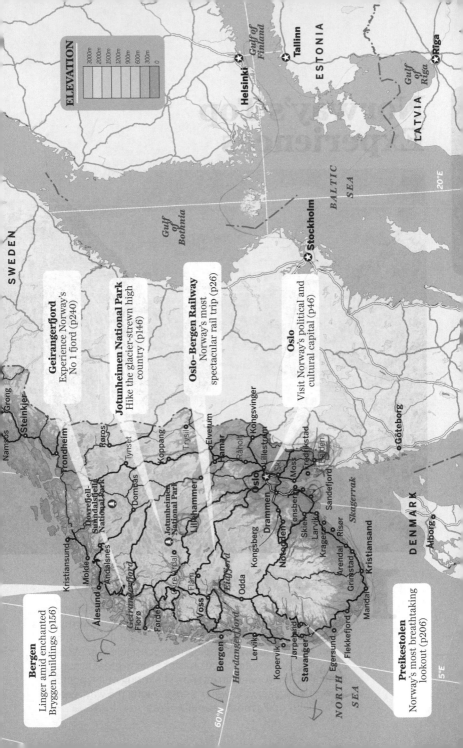

ELEVATION
3000m
2000m
1500m
1200m
900m
600m
300m
0

Geirangerfjord
Experience Norway's
No 1 fjord (p240)

Jotunheimen National Park
Hike the glacier-strewn high
country (p146)

Oslo–Bergen Railway
Norway's most
spectacular rail trip (p26)

Oslo
Visit Norway's
political and
cultural capital (p46)

Bergen
Linger amid enchanted
Bryggen buildings (p156)

Preikestolen
Norway's most breathtaking
lookout (p206)

SWEDEN

Gulf of
Finland

Helsinki

Tallinn

ESTONIA

Gulf
of
Riga

Riga

LATVIA

BALTIC
SEA

20°E

Gulf
of
Bothnia

Stockholm

Nampos
Grong
Steinkjer

Trondheim

Røros

Tynset

Koppang

Trysil

Elverum
Hamar
Råholt
Kongsvinger
Lillestrøm

Dovrefjell-
Sunndalsfjella
National Park

Dombås

Jotunheimen
National Park

Lillehammer

Kristiansund
Molde
Ålesund
Åndalsnes

Geirangerfjord

Florø
Førde
Voss

Øre Vidal

Flåm

Odda

Kongsberg

Drammen

Notodden
Skien
Larvik

Oslo
Moss
Fredrikstad
Halden

Sandefjord

Skagerrak

Krager
Risør
Arendal
Grimstad
Mandal
Kristiansand

Göteborg

DENMARK

Ålborg

Lervik

Kopervik

Jørpeland
Stavanger

Egersund
Flekkefjord

Bergen

Hardangerfjord

Eidfjord

NORTH
SEA

60°N

5°E

Norway's Top Experiences

1 FABULOUS FJORDS

Carved by glaciers in eons past, Norway's fjords surely rank among the world's most spectacular natural landforms. This is a world as filled with drama as it is beautiful, a realm of sheer rock walls, lonely and barely accessible homesteads and vertiginous water-filled chasms. These great fissures run deep into the Norwegian interior, sheltering quiet, postcard-perfect villages by the water's edge. Along the way, expect some of Europe's most beautiful views. Above: Geirangerfjord (p240)

Geirangerfjord

The 20km chug along Geirangerfjord (pictured left and right), a Unesco World Heritage site, must rank as the world's loveliest ferry journey. Long-abandoned farmsteads still cling to the fjord's cliffs while ice-cold cascades tumble, twist and gush down to emerald-green waters. p240

Hardangerfjord

At once a gateway to the interior and a glorious world unto itself, Hardangerfjord is the kind of place you'll want to spend days exploring. Hardanger villages like Ulvik and Eidfjord rank among Norway's loveliest, while Hardangerfjord is also known for its fresh-fruit orchards and for its easy proximity to Bergen. p177

Above: Trolltunga (p192)

Nærøyfjord

If you're thinking of a jaw-dropping Norwegian fjord, chances are you're thinking of Unesco World Heritage-listed Nærøyfjord. The views here are simply extraordinary, filled with classic fjord scenery, from the impossibly-sited villages and kilometres-high rock walls, to the villages that sit by the water's edge. p216

2 EXQUISITE ARCTIC ISLANDS

Norway's islands are quite literally breathtaking. From the soulful Lofoten Islands to the sub-polar Svalbard (Spitsbergen) archipelago, these Arctic isles are simply astonishing. They're also important bastions of coastal cultures whose fortunes are intimately tied to the sea.

Above: Hamnøy, Lofoten Islands (p304)

IZHAIRGUNS/GETTY IMAGES ©

JUSTIN FOULKES/LONELY PLANET ©

RISTO RAUNIO/SHUTTERSTOCK ©

Lofoten Islands

The jagged ramparts of this astonishing island chain (pictured above left) rise abruptly from the sea in summer greens and yellows or the stark blue and white of winter, their razor-sharp peaks stabbing at a clear, cobalt sky or shrouded mysteriously in swirling mists. Gorgeous villages with wooden *rorbuer* (fishing huts) cling to the shoreline, while the A-frame racks for drying fish tell of a land intimately entwined with the sea. p291

Svalbard

Deliciously remote Svalbard (pictured above) is Europe's most evocative slice of the polar north and one of the continent's last great wilderness areas. Shapely peaks, massive ice fields (60% of Svalbard is covered by glaciers) and Arctic wildlife that includes walruses and polar bears) provide the perfect backdrops for activities that get you out amid the ringing silence of the snows. p351

3 ARCTIC EXPLORATION

Exploring Norway's Arctic realm should be high on your list of must-dos when you visit Norway. The further north you travel, the lighter the traffic and the smaller the towns, the more you'll appreciate the crystalline light of Norway's north. In summer, you can explore almost without limits. In winter, this place of other-worldly beauty comes into its own, with dog-sledding, encounters with the Sami, and, yes, the northern lights.

Below: Northern lights over the Lofoten Islands (p291)

Northern Lights

There is no more uplifting natural phenomenon than the aurora borealis, or northern lights. Visible throughout the long night of the Arctic winter from October to March, they dance across the sky in green or white curtains of light, shifting in intensity and taking on forms that seem to spring from a child's vivid imagination. p380

Dog-Sledding

There's no finer way to explore the wilderness than on a sled pulled by huskies. Dog-sledding immerses you into the trackless world of Norway's far north in the eerily beautiful light of the Arctic winter. p36

Sami Culture

Even as the world changes, Sami culture lives on and is increasingly accessible to visitors, especially in Karasjok and Kautokeino; in the former, the Sami Parliament is a masterpiece of traditional design in mellow wood. p396

Above right: a woman in traditional Sami dress

4 UNIQUE ARCHITECTURE

Of all the arts, Norway's architecture has the most distinctively Norwegian cast. Wooden waterfront warehouses line small harbours, elaborate stave churches rise from southern forests, and cities like Ålesund have a uniform style that, when combined with the backdrop, has become all its own. Norway has also been at the centre of contemporary architecture's new wave, with Oslo's Opera House one of the finest examples among many.

Bergen's Bryggen

Bergen is one of Europe's most beautiful cities. Its Unesco World Heritage–listed waterfront district of Bryggen (pictured below) is an archaic tangle of tilted and colourful wooden buildings that now shelter artisan boutiques and traditional restaurants. p156

ANDREY KRUPENKO/SHUTTERSTOCK ©

Stave Churches

All over southern and central Norway, fairy-tale wooden stave churches are adorned with fantastically carved creatures. There's none more beautiful than spectacular Heddal Stave Church (pictured above; p116). p403

Art Nouveau in Ålesund

Rebuilt after a fire a century ago, Ålesund (pictured right) was reborn, a brand new town rich in ornamentation, with turrets, spires, gargoyles and other fanciful elements based on local motifs. p244

5 CITY LIFE

NANISIMOVA/GETTY IMAGES ©

GRISHA BRUEV/SHUTTERSTOCK ©

TATIANA POPOVA/SHUTTERSTOCK ©

Norway's cities are very Scandinavian, as stylish as they are brim-full of life. Each has its own character, from student-fuelled Tromsø, to oil-rich Stavanger, and Oslo, the country's seat of power. Elsewhere, Bergen and Ålesund overflow with architectural treasures. Add in fine museums and art galleries, waterfront markets, and so many scenes of culinary excellence, and you may just want to plan your itinerary around these cities. Above: Oslo Opera House (p49), designed by Snøhetta

Oslo

Oslo is fast becoming a world-renowned centre of art and culture. Already boasting top-notch museums, art galleries and an opera house, it has reimagined its waterfront district with daring architecture, a modern-art gallery, new restaurants and even a beach. p46

Tromsø

Tromsø is northern Norway's most significant city and is one of the country's liveliest. In summer, Tromsø's a base for round-the-clock, 24-hour daylight activity. Once the first snows fall, head out of town to ski and gaze skywards for a glimpse of the Northern Lights. p315

Stavanger

Stavanger is filled with museums and has a pretty old quarter with historic wooden buildings that press close around a horse-shoe-shaped harbour. You'll eat and drink well while you're in this buzzing town, and the location is excellent for exploring some of Norway's prettiest corners. p199

6 BEAUTIFUL VILLAGES

Where to start? Norway's small, isolated settlements have, for centuries, been the lifeblood of Norwegian existence, from fishing villages and fjord-side hamlets to former mining settlements deep in the interior. Lofoten has so many candidates, from Henningsvær to Reine to Å and back again. In fjord country, there's Utne, Solvorn, Eidfjord, Ulvik, and Aurland. Down south, Sogndalstrand is the face of a thousand tourist brochures. Why not visit them all?

Below: Nusfjord (p302)

Røros

Unesco World Heritage–listed Røros (pictured right) is a former mining settlement with splendid wooden buildings. Wander out to the mines for marvellous village views or down the two picturesque main streets. p133

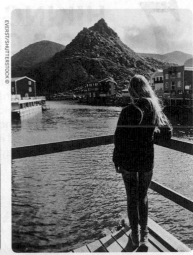

Nyksund

On a windswept northern cove along a remote stretch of the Vesterålen coast, this once-abandoned fishing village (pictured above) has been transformed into an artists' colony in a hauntingly beautiful setting. p307

Nusfjord

Folded around a narrow harbour in a secluded valley of the Lofoten Islands, Nusfjord (pictured left) is an artsy village that captures the islands' spirit, and showcases its red-hued, fishing-village architecture. p302

7 HIKING THE HIGH COUNTRY

You could spend an entire summer hiking across the roof of Norway, one of Europe's most rewarding hiking destinations. Jotunheimen and the hike up to Preikestolen are undoubtedly the picks of a very exciting bunch. But the trails of Hardangervidda, Rondane, and elsewhere are similarly magnificent. The short window of fine weather and ice-free trails means some tracks can be crowded, but nothing can take away from Norway's big, beautiful views.

PE3K/SHUTTERSTOCK ©

Preikestolen

As lookouts go, Preikestolen (Pulpit Rock; pictured above) has few peers. Perched atop an almost perfectly sheer cliff that hangs more than 600m above gorgeous Lysefjord, Preikestolen is one of Norway's signature images and most eye-catching sights. The hike to reach it is simply wonderful. p206

Jotunheimen National Park

Of all Norway's hiking destinations, Jotunheimen (pictured top right and bottom right) rises above all others. With 60 glaciers and 275 summits over 2000m, Jotunheimen is exceptionally beautiful and home to iconic trails such as Besseggen, Hurrungane and those around Galdhøpiggen, Norway's highest peak. p146

8 SCENIC JOURNEYS

MARIUS DOBILAS/SHUTTERSTOCK ©

Norway has so many routes that defy superlatives. Whether you're travelling by rail, road, or coastal boat, you'll find it hard to take your eyes off the views. The iconic Hurtigruten is widely considered one of the most spectacular coastal journeys on earth, the Oslo–Bergen Railway (pictured above) holds a similar place in the hearts of railway enthusiasts, and there are almost as many scenic road trips in Norway as there are roads.

Hurtigruten Coastal Ferry

Travelling daily between Bergen and Kirkenes, the Hurtigruten dips into coastal fjords, docks at isolated villages barely accessible by road, draws near to dramatic headlands and crosses the Arctic Circle. p423

Kystriksveien Coastal Route

The coastal route through Nordland is an experience of rare and staggering beauty. Even a sample (preferably from Sandnessjøen to Storvik) is all but mandatory if you're travelling north. p281

Oslo–Bergen Railway

The Oslo–Bergen railway traverses some of Norway's best scenery. It passes through southern Norwegian forests, climbs to the horizonless Hardangervidda plateau, and then continues down through fjord country into Bergen. p26

Need to Know

For more information, see Survival Guide (p409)

Currency
Norwegian kroner (kr)

Language
Norwegian

Visas
Generally not required for stays of up to 90 days (nor for members of EU or Schengen countries). Some nationalities need a Schengen visa.

Money
ATMs are widely available, and credit cards are accepted in most hotels, restaurants, taxis, ferries and shops.

Mobile Phones
Local SIM cards are widely available and can be used in most international mobile phones. There's mobile coverage in all but wilderness areas.

Time
Central European Time (GMT/UTC plus one hour)

When to Go

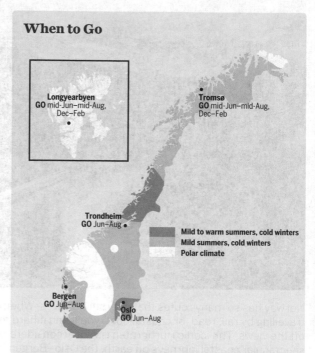

Longyearbyen
GO mid-Jun–mid-Aug, Dec–Feb

Tromsø
GO mid-Jun–mid-Aug, Dec–Feb

Trondheim
GO Jun–Aug

Bergen
GO Jun–Aug

Oslo
GO Jun–Aug

- Mild to warm summers, cold winters
- Mild summers, cold winters
- Polar climate

High Season
(mid-Jun–mid-Aug)

➡ Accommodation and transport often booked out in advance.

➡ Accommodation prices at their lowest (except in Lofoten).

➡ No guarantees with the weather – can be warm and sunny or cool and rainy.

Shoulder
(May–mid-Jun & mid-Aug–Sep)

➡ A good time to travel, with generally mild, clear weather and fewer crowds.

➡ Accommodation prices can be high, except on weekends.

➡ Book accommodation well ahead for festivals.

Low Season
(Oct–Apr)

➡ Can be bitterly cold and many attractions may be closed.

➡ Northern lights tourism can create mini high seasons in the far north.

➡ Short days, especially in the far north.

➡ Seasonal accommodation deals often available.

Useful Websites

Visit Norway (www.visitnorway.com) Tourist Board site ranging from practical to inspirational. Check out its excellent apps.

Fjord Norway (www.fjordnorway.com) Focused on Norway's star attractions.

Lonely Planet (www.lonelyplanet.com/norway) Destination information, hotel bookings, traveller forum and more.

Northern Norway (www.nordnorge.com) Everything you need to know about northern Norway.

Lofoten (www.lofoten.info) Comprehensive resource for visiting the islands.

Important Numbers

From outside Norway, dial your international access code, Norway's country code, then the number.

Directory assistance	☏180
International access code	☏00
Norway's country code	☏47
Ambulance	☏113
Police	☏112

Exchange Rates

Australia	A$1	6.48kr
Canada	C$1	7.00kr
Europe	€1	10.35kr
Japan	¥100	8.00kr
New Zealand	NZ$1	6.20kr
UK	UK£1	12.20kr
USA	US$1	8.80kr

For current exchange rates, see www.xe.com.

Daily Costs

Budget:
Less than €160

➡ Dorm bed: from €35

➡ Hut or cabin: from €55

➡ Double in B&B or guesthouse: up to €80

➡ Excellent supermarkets and cheaper lunch specials: up to €14

➡ Book ahead for *minipris* (discounted) train tickets

Midrange: €160–240

➡ Double room in midrange hotel (weekends and high season): €80–150

➡ Lunch or dinner in decent local restaurant: €14–22

➡ Car rental: from €90 per day

Top end:
More than €240

➡ Double room in top-end hotel: €150 and up

➡ Lunch or dinner in decent local restaurant: from €22 per person

Opening Hours

These standard opening hours are for high season (mid-June to mid-August) and tend to decrease outside that time.

Banks 8.15am to 3pm Monday to Wednesday and Friday, to 5pm Thursday

Central Post Offices 8am to 8pm Monday to Friday, 9am to 6pm Saturday; otherwise 9am to 5pm Monday to Friday, 10am to 2pm Saturday

Restaurants noon to 3pm and 6pm to 11pm; some don't close between lunch and dinner

Shops 10am to 5pm Monday to Wednesday and Friday, to 7pm Thursday, to 2pm Saturday

Supermarkets 9am to 9pm Monday to Friday, to 6pm Saturday

Arriving in Norway

Gardermoen International Airport (Oslo) Trains connect the airport to the city centre (19 to 26 minutes, 90kr) up to six times hourly from around 4am to midnight. Buses (adult/child 160/80kr) take 40 minutes. Taxis cost 750kr to 1150kr (30 minutes to one hour).

Flesland Airport (Bergen) Airport bus connects the airport with downtown Bergen (adult one way/return 90/160kr, 45 minutes) up to four times hourly from 3.50am to just after midnight.

Getting Around

Train Trains reach as far north as Bodø, with an additional branch line connecting Narvik with Sweden further north. Book in advance for considerably cheaper *minipris* tickets.

Car Roads are in good condition, but travel times can be slow thanks to winding roads, heavy summer traffic with few overtaking lanes, and ferries.

Bus Services along major routes are fast and efficient. Services to smaller towns can be infrequent, sometimes with no services at all on weekends.

Air SAS and Norwegian have extensive domestic networks. Widerøe services small towns.

Boat Ferries, many of which will take cars, connect offshore islands to the mainland, while the Hurtigruten sails from Bergen to Kirkenes and back every day of the year.

For much more on **getting around**, see p421

Month by Month

January

Despite bitterly cold temperatures, January is good for snowmobiling, dog-sledding and seeing the northern lights. By the end of January, the sun has returned to much of mainland Norway.

◉ Northern Lights

The aurora borealis, one of the natural world's most astonishing phenomena, is reason enough to visit northern Norway in winter. Visit Tromsø in late January for the Northern Lights Festival. (p321)

February

Generally Norway's coldest month, February is ideal for viewing the northern lights, joining winter activities and experiencing two celebrations that capture the spirit of the Norwegian winter. Booking ahead is recommended, especially in northern Norway.

☆ Polar Jazz

Held deep in the months-long Arctic night, Svalbard's Polar Jazz festival is the world's northernmost jazz festival and serves as a rhythmic reminder that life goes on even in the depths of the polar winter. Held in early February. (p358)

Rørosmartnan

Norway's largest winter festival, in Røros, dates back centuries and runs from Tuesday to Saturday in the second-last week of February. It's the perfect tonic for the long Norwegian winter with cultural programs, markets and live entertainment. (p136)

Sami Week

No one endures the Arctic winter quite like the Sami, the indigenous inhabitants of Norway's north. During Sami Week in early February, Tromsø's main street is the scene of the national reindeer sledge championship. (p321)

March

Days are lengthening as Norway awakes from its slumber with a full program of festivals (celebrating either winter's end or traditional Norwegian activities). It's one of the most popular months for visiting Svalbard.

Finnmarksløpet

Alta's Borealis Alta winter festival in March has concerts and other cultural events aimed at saying good riddance to winter. The festival also marks the beginning of Europe's longest dog-sled endurance race, the epic Finnmarksløpet. (p328)

☆ Sami Easter

Easter among the indigenous Sami people in Kautokeino sees celebrations to mark the end of the polar night, with weddings, reindeer racing, the Sami Grand Prix (actually a *yoik* – a rhythmic-poem contest) and other traditional events. (p349)

Sunfest

The inhabitants of Longyearbyen in the high-Arctic archipelago of Svalbard must withstand the winter darkness longer than any other Norwegians. Their week-long Sunfest, in early March, is celebrated with special fervour. (p358)

April

April has surprisingly few festivals of note and represents something of a breathing space between the end-of-winter celebrations and action-packed Norwegian summers. The weather is improving and few tourists are around.

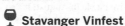 Stavanger Vinfest

Stavanger is a port city par excellence and its culinary culture is one of Norway's most varied. In mid-April, the local love of food and wine takes on special significance with the Stavanger Vinfest. (p202)

☆ Trondheim Blues

One of northern Europe's premier blues events, Trondheim's Nidaros Blues Festival is a shining light in an otherwise quiet month, with international and local acts taking the stage. (p262)

May

By May, Norway has a real spring in its step: the weather's warming up, Norway's renowned music festivals get under way and tourists have yet to arrive in great numbers.

☆ Alta Blues & Soul Festival

Close to the end of May or in early June, the Alta Blues & Soul Festival is a worthy prelude to the summer-long

program of music festivals. Held in the far north, it draws a respected international cast of bands. (p328)

☆ Bergen International Festival

One of the biggest events on Norway's cultural calendar, this two-week Bergen festival, beginning in late May, showcases dance, music and folklore presentations. In a typically Bergen twist, it's at once international and a return to the city's roots. (p162)

Constitution Day

On 17 May Norway's most popular nationwide festival sees the country engulfed in a wave of patriotism during. It's celebrated with special fervour in Oslo, where locals descend on the Royal Palace dressed in the finery of their native districts.

Lofoten Cod

Henningsvær combines a celebration of local cod with cool music with Codstock in mid-May. It's one of the Lofoten's best festivals and is all the better for pre-dating the summer crowds. (p296)

☆ Night Jazz Festival (Nattjazz)

Norway's calendar is replete with world-renowned jazz festivals and this fine Bergen festival in late May is one of the happiest, with serious jazz to be heard as the city's large student population gets into the swing. (p162)

June

The main tourist season begins in earnest and it's always

worth booking ahead for accommodation. Some of Norway's best festivals take place and the weather can be mild and clear, although poor weather is possible.

Extreme Sports Festival

Adventure junkies from across the world converge on Voss in late June for a week of skydiving, paragliding, parasailing and base jumping; local and international music acts keep the energy flowing. (p175)

Middle Ages Festival

Locals in period costume and Gregorian chants in the glass cathedral of Hamar are the highlights of this popular local festival. Held in June, it provides an alternative slant on the long-distant Norwegian past in a fantastic setting. (p132)

Midnight Sun Marathon

A midnight marathon could only happen in Norway, and Tromsø is the place to try the world's northernmost 42km road race. It's held in June and is possibly the only marathon in the world where the participants are still straggling in at 5am. (p321)

☆ Norwegian Wood

One of Oslo's best music festivals among many, Norwegian Wood draws local and international acts to an appreciative audience in an especially good mood with summer just around the corner. (p67)

🏹 Viking Festival

The southwest is Norway's Viking heartland and in early or mid-June, Karmøy island provides a focal point for this fascinating history with Viking feasts, processions and saga evenings. (p199)

🏊 Whale Watching in Vesterålen

Although it may be possible to go whale watching from Andenes or Stø in late May or even earlier, daily departures are guaranteed in June. Sperm whales are the big prize, although pilot whales are also around. (p309)

July

July is the peak tourist season throughout most of Norway, with the year's best weather and cheapest prices for hotels. Tourist sights can be crowded and we strongly recommend advance reservations for accommodation.

☆ Kongsberg Jazz Festival

Kongsberg's Jazz Festival, Norway's second largest, begins in early July, lasts four days and pulls in some of the biggest international names. As it precedes the Moldejazz festival, this is a great season for jazz-lovers. (p115)

☆ Moldejazz

Norway has a fine portfolio of jazz festivals, but Molde's version in mid-July is the most prestigious. With 100,000 spectators, world-class performers and a reputation for consistently

high-quality music, it's easily one of Norway's most popular festivals. (p249)

🏹 St Olav Festival

This nationwide commemoration of Norway's favourite saint in late July is celebrated with special gusto in Trondheim, with processions, medieval markets, Viking dress-ups, concerts and a local food festival. In Stiklestad the saint is celebrated with a prestigious five-day pageant. (p262)

August

August is the scene of musical festivals across all genres. The weather should be fine and cheaper high-season prices continue, although in some cases only until the middle of the month. Book ahead.

☆ International Chamber Music Festival

Most Norwegian music festivals cater more to a young and energetic audience, but Stavanger in early August provides an antidote with this stately festival; some concerts take place in the architecturally distinguished Stavanger Cathedral. (p202)

☆ Norwegian Film

The highlight of the year for Norway's small but respected film industry, the Norwegian International Film Festival in Haugesund showcases innovative new works and coincides with the national film awards. It's held in mid- to late August. (p197)

☆ Notodden Blues Festival

This outstanding blues festival held in early August offers proof that even smaller Norwegian towns play their part in the country's festival obsession. You'll find it in nondescript Notodden; it draws a massive international crowd. (p116)

☆ Oslo International Jazz Festival

A worthy member of Norway's coterie of terrific jazz festivals, this one takes over Oslo for six days of live music in August. It's so popular that many locals plan their summer holidays to be back in town for this event. (p67)

☆ Rauma Rock

If Norway's regular diet of jazz and blues festivals doesn't suit your musical tastes, Central Norway's largest musical gathering is held in Åndalsnes over two days in early August, with everything from indie to hard rock. (p238)

☆ Varanger-festivalen

It may lie well beyond well-travelled tourist trails but Vadsø runs one of northern Norway's oldest music festivals, Varangerfestivalen, with jazz, rock and world music sharing a stage. (p340)

☆ West Coast Jazz

Norway has a fabulous array of jazz festivals, but Silda Jazz in Haugesund is one of the country's most underrated jam sessions. Respected enough to draw big names but far enough off traveller routes to draw a predominantly local crowd, Silda Jazz is worth the trip out west. (p197)

☆ Øya Festival

Norway's largest rock and indie music festival takes place in Oslo and is one of Europe's finest such festivals. It's also one of the greenest with impeccable environmental credentials. Hedonism without the guilt – it's a terrific combination. (p67)

September

The crowds have largely disappeared, but so have most of the cheaper summer deals; in some areas, many hotels and restaurants actually close down. In short, it's a quieter but often more expensive time to visit.

☆ Dyrsku'n Festival

Seljord's premier annual festival centres on Norway's largest traditional market and cattle show, and is one of the best ways to get a feel for traditional Norwegian culture. Held in the second week of September, it attracts 60,000 visitors annually. (p121)

October

Summer is a distant memory and by the end of October the months-long polar night begins in

Svalbard. Temperatures have begun to drop and business travellers far outnumber those travelling for pleasure.

☆ Bergen International Film Festival

Arguably Norway's most important film festival, Bergen becomes a film-lover's paradise with subtitled movies in cinemas across the city in mid- to late October. Unlike Haugesund's August film festival, the focus is resolutely international. (p162)

☆ Dark Season Blues

In late October, with the long polar night just around the corner, Longyearbyen hosts a well-regarded blues festival, with scheduled concerts and improvised jam sessions. (p358)

☆ Lillehammer Jazz Festival

This former Olympic city farewells the now-distant summer with the last major jazz festival of the Norwegian year; like any ski town, Lillehammer rocks (so to speak) during festival time, which is sometimes late September but more often October. (p129)

☆ UKA

Norway's largest cultural festival involves three weeks of concerts, plays

and general celebration led by Trondheim's 25,000-strong university-student population. It takes place in odd-numbered years, beginning in October and not stopping until well into November. (p262)

November

A quiet month for tourism in Norway with the winter chill starting to bite and the daylight hours getting shorter but many winter activities are still yet to begin.

☆ Tromsø Whale Watching

November is usually the month when whales begin arriving in the waters around Norway's northern city. Humpbacks and orcas are usually possible, with other species also around until January or February. (p319)

December

Winter is very much under way with a Christmas–New Year peak season for travellers looking to spend their Christmas holidays in the north – advance bookings are required. Most winter activities are in full swing.

Itineraries

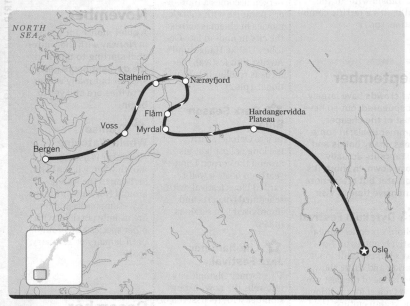

NORTH SEA

Stalheim
Nærøyfjord
Flåm
Hardangervidda Plateau
Voss
Myrdal
Bergen
Oslo

1 WEEK **Norway in Microcosm**

Even with only a week to spare, you can still see the best that Norway has to offer. This itinerary begins with **Oslo's** considerable charms, traverses the drama of Norway's high country and precipitous fjords, and ends up in beautiful Bergen. This journey can just as easily be done in reverse.

After a couple of days exploring the fine galleries and museums of Oslo, take the scenic Oslo–Bergen railway, one of the most spectacular rail journeys on earth. From Oslo, the line climbs gently through forests, plateaus and ski centres to the beautifully desolate **Hardangervidda Plateau**, home to Norway's largest herd of wild reindeer and numerous hiking trails. At **Myrdal**, take the Flåmsbana railway down to **Flåm**, from where fjord cruises head up the incomparable **Nærøyfjord**. Travel via Gudvangen, sleep overnight in **Stalheim**, and then continue on to **Voss**, where thrill-seekers love the easily accessible activities on offer. Trains then carry you on to **Bergen**, arguably Norway's prettiest city – wander its historic wooden waterfront, climb the surrounding mountains for sweeping views or soak up the atmosphere of the bars and restaurants that so distinguish this cosmopolitan city.

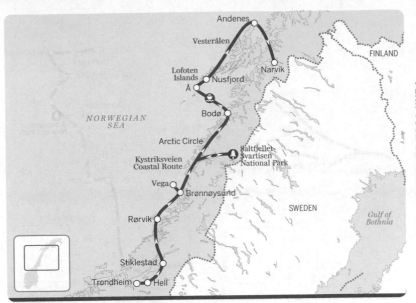

(2 WEEKS) The Norwegian Coast

The coastline between Trondheim and the Lofoten Islands takes you across the Arctic Circle along a shoreline fissured with deep inlets, shadowed by countless offshore islands and populated by quiet fishing villages. You'll need a car to make the most of this route; also consider the Hurtigruten coastal ferry for a leg or two.

Begin in **Trondheim** and linger for a couple of days in one of Norway's most agreeable cities. Heading north, via **Hell**, stop off in **Stiklestad**, a site of great historical significance for Norwegians. Overnight here or continue on **Rørvik**, where a fascinating multimedia display is the perfect introduction to coastal life.

The Rv17 travels north to picturesque **Brønnøysund**, and don't miss the offshore detour to the fascinating, Unesco World Heritage–listed island of **Vega**; count on a couple of nights in Brønnøysund and Vega. Back on the mainland, the extraordinary **Kystriksveien coastal route** hugs the coastline. A candidate for Norway's most spectacular drive, this road passes an estimated 14,000 islands. It can be slow going with all the ferries and inlet-hugging stretches of road, but it is unquestionably worth it. The entire route could be done in a couple of days, but four or five is far more enjoyable. Factor in time as well for a detour to the **Saltfjellet-Svartisen National Park**, home to Norway's second-largest icefield and accessible glacier tongues. The most beautiful section of the Kystriksveien route is between Sandnessjøen and Storvik, and it's along this section that you'll cross the **Arctic Circle**.

The primary appeal of **Bodø** is as the gateway (by ferry) to the **Lofoten Islands**. Unlike any other landscape in Norway, the Lofoten could easily occupy a week of your time, although it can be experienced much more rapidly for those in a hurry – make three days a minimum. All of the islands and villages are worth visiting, but on no account miss **Nusfjord** and **Å**, a charmingly preserved village at the southern tip of Moskenesøy. Like Lofoten but with far fewer visitors, **Vesterålen** is wild and beautiful and worth two days, including summer whale-watching off **Andenes**, before you head on to your journey's end at **Narvik**.

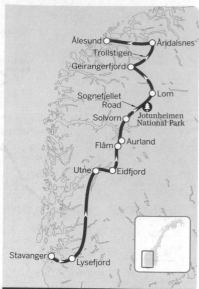

(5 DAYS) A Bergen Long Weekend

Bergen is one of northern Europe's most popular short-break trips, with good reason. While there's more than enough to keep you occupied for five days in Bergen itself, the city's hinterland might entice you to consider a two-night excursion to see what all the fuss is about out in the fjords.

Bergen is the reason you came here and you've a busy time ahead of you if you hope to pack it all into two very full days of museums, wining and dining, shopping and simply wandering the postcard-perfect streets.

Although ranging beyond Bergen can be done using public transport, we recommend renting a car and driving on your third day through **Norheimsund**, the peaceful gateway to the stirring panoramas of the Hardangerfjord network. Pause in **Øystese** long enough to enjoy an unlikely contemporary-art fix, then overnight in dramatic **Eidfjord**. The next morning, after a detour to **Kjeåsen Farm**, drive to gorgeous **Ulvik** for extraordinary views, stop for lunch in **Voss**, then drive to **Stalheim** for more spectacular views. Go for a hike in the morning, then drive back to Bergen in time for your flight home.

(2 WEEKS) Best of the Fjords

Few natural attractions have come to define a country quite like the Norway's fjords. This meandering route through Norway's fjord country, with a detour up and over the roof of Norway, is one of Europe's most beautiful. You'll need your own vehicle. Take as long as you can.

Begin in the far south, in **Stavanger**. After a day or two, take a day trip to **Lysefjord**, including the hike up to the signature lookout of Preikestolen (Pulpit Rock). A long day's drive north brings you to Hardangerfjord, and a string of villages you'll never want to leave, among them **Utne** and **Eidfjord**. Overnight in the latter, then continue on to **Flåm**; if you've still enough left in the tank, make for far lovelier **Aurland** for a couple of nights surrounded by extraordinary views. Wind your way north to pretty **Solvorn** on Lustrafjord, climb up and over the **Sognefjellet Road** through **Jotunheimen National Park**, then overnight in **Lom**, with its perfectly sited stave church. Then it's on to peerless **Geirangerfjorden**, up another breathtaking mountain road, the **Trollstigen**, down to **Åndalsnes** and then follow the coast to quiet and lovely **Ålesund**.

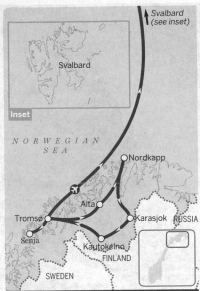

2 WEEKS The Arctic North

The mystique of the extreme north has drawn explorers for centuries. Here is a horizonless world seemingly without end, a frozen wilderness that inspires the awe reserved for the great empty places of our earth. If you're really lucky, you might see a polar bear.

Tromsø is a university town par excellence. Its Polar Museum captures the spirit of Arctic exploration, its Arctic Cathedral wonderfully evokes the landscapes of the north, while the surrounding peaks host a wealth of summer and winter activities. You could also visit lovely **Senja** from here. Next head east for the rock carvings of **Alta**, then **Nordkapp**: as far north as you can go in Norway without setting out to sea. Then head inland to **Karasjok** and **Kautokeino**, to the heartland of the Sami people. No exploration of the Arctic North would be complete without **Svalbard**. Return to Tromsø and catch a flight deep into the polar regions, where the Svalbard archipelago is one of Europe's last great wildernesses. Allow at least five days to tap into the many activities that get you out into the wilderness.

1 WEEK The Heart of Norway

The high country of central Norway is simply spectacular and, provided you're willing to rent a car for part of the time, it offers some unparalleled opportunities to explore the region's quiet back roads; serious cyclists could also follow many of the same routes.

After a couple of days in **Oslo**, it's a short trip to **Lillehammer**, which hosted the 1994 Winter Olympics and remains one of central Norway's most pleasing spots; it has a wealth of Olympic sites and a lovely setting. Continuing north after a night in Lillehammer, **Ringebu** has one of Norway's prettiest stave churches. Having a car enables you to take the quiet Rv27, which draws near to the precipitous massifs of the **Rondane National Park**, before continuing northeast to Unesco World Heritage-listed **Røros**, one of Norway's most enchanting villages, with painted timber houses and old-world charm. After one or two nights in Røros, it's an easy detour north to **Trondheim**, a delightful coastal city with a stunning cathedral, a large student population and an engaging cultural scene; it's worth a two- or three-night stay.

HENRYK WELLE / GETTY IMAGES ©

Above: Northern lights, Longyearbyen (p353)

Left: Lofoten Islands (p291)

Plan Your Trip

Outdoor Activities

Norway's portfolio of activities is simply extraordinary, from Europe's best summer hiking to fabulous winter sports. Better still, it caters equally for first-timers leaving the car behind and hard-core adventurers who think nothing of leaping off a cliff. And whichever you choose, it'll be against an utterly magnificent backdrop.

Planning

When to Go

Norway has two major – and radically different – seasons for activities. Outside these periods, you'll probably find that the operators have simply shut up shop and, in many cases, followed their passion elsewhere in the world wherever the weather suits.

The summer season – when signature activities include hiking, kayaking, white-water rafting and high-thrill pursuits that usually have 'para' attached as a prefix (namely parasailing etc) – most reliably runs from mid-June until mid-August. That's when there are enough travellers around to ensure regular departures and hence a wider range of options that suit your schedule. Depending on the weather, operators, however, may open in May and/or remain open until the middle or end of September.

Winter – when skiing, snowmobiling and dog-sledding take over – usually runs from December (or late November) until late February or early March.

What to Take

There are few requirements for most summer activities, and operators who organise white-water rafting, kayaking, parasailing and other similar 'sports' will provide the necessary equipment.

Top Choices

Best Cycle Route
Cycle along the Rallarvegen from Finse to Flåm from mid-June to mid-August.

Best Extreme Sport
Para-bungee jumping in Voss from May to September, but anything in Voss is designed to thrill.

Best Salmon Fishing
Tana Bru in Eastern Finnmark from mid-June to mid-August.

Best Glacier Hike
Hardangerjøkulen on the Hardangervidda Plateau from mid-June to mid-August.

Best Hike
Besseggen in Jotunheimen National Park from mid-June to mid-August.

Best Dog-Sledding
Engholm's Husky in Karasjok from December to March.

Best Winter Skiing
Olympic ski slopes at Lillehammer from December to March.

The major exception is hiking. Most hikers head to the trail under their own steam, but even those who plan on joining an organised hike will usually need to bring their own equipment, including appropriate wind- and waterproof gear and hiking boots.

In winter you won't need much in the way of equipment for most of the activities – skis, etc can be rented at ski stations and there are no special requirements for snowmobiling or dog-sledding.

Summer Activities

The fresh air and stunning landscapes make Norway a summer paradise for outdoors lovers. There's a huge range of ways to explore: hiking, cycling, kayaking and sailing, to name a few, as well as more niche pastimes such as stand-up paddleboarding, deep-sea fishing and cold-water surfing. This is one place where it's really too gorgeous to spend too much time inside.

Cycling

Whether you're keen to take a two-wheeled amble around the flat shoreline of your favourite fjord or are a serious cyclist with your sights set on the ultimate Norwegian challenge, Norway won't disappoint.

For the ambler, many tourist offices, some hotels and most bicycle shops rent out bicycles and provide information on cycling trails in their local area.

Cycling Resources

For an excellent overview of what's possible, check out Syklist Velkommen (Cyclists Welcome; www.cyclingnorway.no). This excellent website has route descriptions, maps and other advice for some of the better long-distance cycling routes around the country. It can also link you up with guided and self-guided package cycling and mountain-bike tours.

For self-guided hiking tours, check out **Discover Norway** (☑917 25 200; www.discover-norway.no/sykkelturer-2).

Extreme Sports

Norway is gaining traction as a favoured destination for thrill-seekers thanks to its combination of highly professional operators and spectacular settings. Those who either have no fear or would simply love a bird's-eye view of some of Europe's most spectacular country have numerous possibilities, although they're almost exclusively centred on the fjord region in the western part of the country.

Voss in particular is arguably Norway's adventure capital and one of the world epicentres for extreme sports. Devotees of high-speed airborne pursuits converge on this lovely town in late June for the Extreme Sports Festival (p175).

Extreme Sports Destinations

Some of the best places to get the adrenaline flowing:

➔ **Voss** (p174) Paragliding, parasailing, a 180m-high bungee jump from a parasail (which claims to be Europe's highest bungee-jump) and skydiving.

➔ **Rjukan** (p118) Norway's highest land-based bungee jump (84m), located in the southern Norwegian interior.

➔ **Kjeragbolten, Lysefjord** (p207) BASE jumping from the sheer cliffs of Lysefjord close to the famous chock-stone of Kjeragbolten.

Fishing

Norway's rivers and lakes have drawn avid anglers since the 19th century and salmon fishing is the undisputed star attraction. Norway's salmon runs are still legendary and, in June and July, you can't beat the rivers of Finnmark. In addition to salmon, 41 other fish species inhabit the country's 200,000 rivers and lakes. In the south, you'll find the best fishing from June to September; and in the north, in July and August.

TOP FIVE CYCLING EXPERIENCES

➔ Sognefjellet Road (p147), through the Jotunheimen National Park.

➔ The exhilarating descent from Finse down to the shores of Aurlandsfjorden Flåm along the Rallarvegen (p153).

➔ Lofoten (p297), with its leisurely cycling through some wonderful, rugged scenery.

➔ Across the Hardangervidda Plateau (p120) near Rjukan.

➔ The steep and spectacular SnøVegen (p215) route above the fjords.

The 175-page book *Angling in Norway,* available from tourist offices for 200kr, details the best salmon- and trout-fishing areas, as well as fees and regulations, of which there are many.

Regulations vary between rivers but, generally, from mid-September to November, fish under 20cm must be thrown back. At other times between August and May, the limit is 30cm. Fishing is prohibited within 100m of fish farms, or cables and nets that are anchored or fastened to the shore, and fishing with live bait is illegal.

Anyone over 16 who wishes to fish in Norway needs to purchase an annual licence (260kr for salmon, trout and char), which is sold at post offices. Check out http://fiskeravgift.miljodirektoratet.no for more information on the fee. To fish on private land, you must also purchase a local licence (100kr to 550kr per day), which is available from sports shops, hotels, campgrounds and tourist offices. Some areas require a compulsory equipment disinfection certificate (150kr).

For fishing tours to Norway, check out the UK-based **Go Fishing Worldwide** (✆0208 742 1556; www.gofishingworldwide.co.uk).

Fishing Spots

➤ **Tana Bru** (p339) Legendary salmon fishing.

➤ **Lakselv** (p337) Fine salmon-fishing in the far north.

➤ **Stabbursnes** (p338) Another salmon centre.

➤ **Reisa National Park** (p349) Another good salmon venue.

➤ **Saltstraumen Maelstrom** (p290) Popular fishing where two fjords collide.

➤ **Moskenesøy** (p302) Deep-sea fishing off the Lofoten islands.

➤ **Gjesvær** (p336) Expeditions near Nordkapp.

➤ **Tromsø** (p319) Ice fishing in winter.

Glacier Hiking

Glacier hiking is one of Norway's most memorable summer pastimes, but you should only set out with an experienced local guide. Among our favourite places for a glacier hike are the following:

➤ **Hardangerjøkulen glacier on Hardangervidda** (p151) Said by some to be Norway's most breathtaking glacier hike.

➤ **Folgefonna National Park** (p194) One of Norway's largest icefields, with glacier hikes at various points around the perimeter.

➤ **Nigardsbreen** (p227) The pick of the accessible glaciers in the Jostedalsbreen area.

➤ **Saltfjellet-Svartisen National Park** (p277) Some of Europe's lowest-lying (and hence most easily accessible) glacier tongues just inside the Arctic Circle.

➤ **Svalbard** (p356) With 60% of Svalbard covered by glaciers, there are plenty of opportunities here, including some close to Longyearbyen.

Hiking

Norway has some of Europe's best hiking, including a network of around 20,000km of marked trails that range from easy strolls through the green zones around cities, to long treks through national parks and wilderness areas. Many of these trails are maintained by Den Norske Turistforening (p412) and are marked either with cairns or red Ts at 100m or 200m intervals.

The hiking season runs roughly from late May to early October, with a much shorter season in the higher mountain areas and the far north. In the highlands, the snow often remains until June and returns in September, meaning that many routes are only possible in July and August.

Hiking Resources

There are many excellent hiking books, including the folowing:

➤ *Mountain Hiking in Norway* (Erling Welle-Strand; 1993)

➤ *Walks and Scrambles in Norway* (Anthony Dyer et al; 2006)

➤ *Walking in Norway* (Constance Roos; 2014)

➤ *From Beaches to Mountains: 38 walks and hikes in the Stavanger Region* (Koninx Ute & Nicholson Rosslyn; 2016)

➤ *Norwegian Mountains on Foot* – the English edition of the Norwegian classic *Til Fots i Fjellet* (DNT).

Hiking Routes

The list of possibilities for hiking in Norway is almost endless, but if we had to list our top 10, it would be the following:

➤ **Jotunheimen National Park** (p146) The doyen of Norwegian hiking destinations, with countless routes and incomparable high country.

→ **Rondane National Park** (p142) Less-crowded trails than those of Jotunheimen, but arguably as beautiful.

→ **Hardangervidda Plateau** (p152) Trails criss-cross this magnificent plateau, the home of reindeer.

→ **Aurlandsdalen** (p215) Historic four-day hike following ancient trading routes from Geiteryggen to Aurland.

→ **Trollstigen** (p237) Some wonderful treks through the dramatic Trollstigen range.

→ **Dovrefjell-Sunndalsfjella National Park** (p141) Wildlife- and bird-rich park with the Knutshøene massif as a centrepiece.

PERSONAL HIKING EQUIPMENT CHECKLIST

Summer

☐ Sturdy hiking boots; if you're heading to Svalbard, knee-high rubber hiking boots are recommended.

☐ A high-quality sleeping bag – even in summer the weather can turn nasty at short notice.

☐ Warm clothing, including a jacket, jersey (sweater) or anorak (windbreaker) that can be added or removed, even in summer.

☐ A bed sheet – most huts charge extra for bed linen.

☐ A sturdy but lightweight tent.

☐ Mosquito repellent.

☐ A lightweight stove.

☐ Airline-style sleeping mask for light-filled Norwegian summer nights.

☐ Membership of Den Norske Turistforening (DNT).

☐ Good topographical maps.

Winter

☐ Warm boots (ideally with a thick insulation of wool) big enough to wear double socks and to move your toes inside.

☐ At least one long underwear top and bottom (not cotton, but preferably underwear made of polypropylene).

☐ Multiple pairs of light synthetic (polypropylene) socks and heavy wool socks (again, not cotton).

☐ Flannel or polypropylene shirts.

☐ Trousers for walking, preferably made from breathing waterproof (and windproof) material such as Gore-Tex.

☐ Fleece sweater.

☐ Windproof and waterproof jacket with hood that's big enough to let you wear a lot of clothes underneath.

☐ One knitted, fur or fleece hat (such as a balaclava) to protect your face and another windproof one to cover your head and ears.

☐ Long woollen scarf.

☐ Woollen mittens plus windproof and waterproof mittens.

☐ Air-filled sleeping pad.

☐ Arctic-strength sleeping bag filled with synthetics or down; only necessary if you're likely to be sleeping out overnight.

☐ Swiss Army knife.

☐ Torch (flashlight) with extra batteries or headlamp.

➜ **Stabbursdalen National Park** (p338)
Roadless park with tracks through glacial canyons and the world's northernmost pine forest.

➜ **Femundsmarka National Park** (p138) Lakes and forests with musk ox, close to the Swedish border and Røros.

➜ **Saltfjellet-Svartisen National Park** (p277) Icecaps and treeless uplands lend these trails an epic Arctic quality.

➜ **Trollheimen** (p139) Rolling mountains and high-altitude lakes make for memorable walking.

Kayaking

With all the hype surrounding hiking, white-water rafting and extreme summer sports, Norway's kayaking possibilities rarely receive the attention they deserve. And yet the chance to take to the water is a wonderful way to experience Norway's waterways without the crowds.

Kayaking Destinations

Norway's premier kayaking sites are clustered around (although by no means restricted to) the western fjords and there are numerous operators offering guided kayaking excursions. It's possible in many places to rent kayaks and the accompanying equipment from fjord-side campgrounds and tourist offices.

Top kayaking destinations include the following:

➜ **Jostedalsbreen National Park** (p224) Guided kayaking and hiking trips that get up close to a glacier.

➜ **Svalbard** (p356) and Lofoten Islands (p291) Paddle through the icy waters of the far, far north.

➜ **Langøya island, Vesterålen Islands** (p306) Introductory and more advanced courses around the time of the 170km Arctic Sea Kayak Race in July.

➜ **Voss** (p175) One- to three-day kayaking trips on gorgeous Nærøyfjord.

➜ **Flåm** (p212) Takes you away from the crowds on one of Norway's prettiest but busiest fjords.

➜ **Geiranger** (p241) Coastal kayaking trips from a spectacular base.

➜ **Lustrafjord** (p218) Four-hour kayaking tours on this lovely arm of Sognefjorden.

Rock Climbing & Mountaineering

Norway's astounding vertical topography is a paradise for climbers interested in rock, ice and alpine pursuits. In fact, outside the Alps, Norway is probably Europe's finest climbing venue, although Norway's climatic extremes mean that technical climbers face harsh conditions, short seasons and strict restrictions. The western fjords region in particular is all the rage among serious climbers.

Climbing Resources

In addition to the rock-climbers' classic *Climbing in the Magic Islands* by Ed Webster, which describes most of the feasible routes in Lofoten, look for *Ice Fall in Norway* by Sir Ranulph Fiennes, which describes a 1970 sojourn around Jostedalsbreen. The more practical *Scandinavian Mountains* by Peter Lennon introduces the country's finest climbing venues.

For more information on climbing in Norway, contact the **Norsk Tindeklub** (☑930 61 513; www.ntk.no). In the Lofoten, try the North Norwegian Climbing School (p296).

Climbing Destinations

The most popular alpine venues in Norway include the following. Ice climbers should head to Rjukan.

➜ **Trollveggen or Romsdalshorn, Åndalsnes** (p237) Norway's prime climbing routes. Åndalsnes also hosts a very popular mountaineering festival, Norsk Fjellfestival (p238), in early July.

➜ **Lyngen Alps** (p324) Remote climbing and mountaineering but only for the experienced and self-sufficient.

➜ **Uskedalen** (p196) A well-guarded but much-celebrated secret in the world climbing community, close to Rosendal.

➜ **Lofoten** (p296) Site of a good climbing school that organises expeditions on the islands' vertiginous rock walls.

Skiing

Numerous cross-country trails remain snow-bound throughout the year and a number of summer ski centres allow both cross-country (nordic) and downhill skiing. These include the following:

➡ **Stryn Summer Ski Centre** (p230) Norway's largest 'sommar skisenter' with good cross-country and downhill trails.

➡ **Fonna Glacier Ski Resort** (p194) A well-regarded centre high on the icefields of the southwestern fjord region.

➡ **Galdhøpiggen Summer Ski Centre** (p149) Sitting around 1850m above sea level but still in the shadow of Norway's highest peak, this is one of the prettiest places to ski at any time, although it's inaccessible in the depths of winter.

White-Water Rafting

The cascading, icy-black waters and white-hot rapids of central Norway are a rafter's paradise during the short season from mid-June to mid-August. A number of reputable operators offer trips, primarily in central Norway. These range from short, Class II doddles to Class III and IV adventures and rollicking Class V punishment. Rates include all requisite equipment and waterproofing.

Norges Padleforbund (☑21 02 98 35; www.padling.no; Sognsveien 73, Oslo) provides a list of rafting operators.

The best places to go rafting include the following:

➡ **Heidalen, Sjoa** (p142)

➡ **Setesdalen, Evje** (p122)

➡ **Drivadalen, Oppdal** (p138)

➡ **Voss** (p174)

➡ **Jostedalsbreen National Park** (p224)

Winter Activities

Skiing is the most popular winter activity (both as a leisure pursuit and a means of getting around), while snowmobiling serves a similar purpose in the far north and on the sub-polar archipelago of Svalbard. Dog-sledding is another major drawcard.

Dog-Sledding

Norwegians have been harnessing canine pulling-power since time immemorial, and there aren't many activities that feel quite as authentically Arctic as learning how to *mush-mush* your own dog-sled. Swishing through the snow, surrounded by silence and a winter wonderland as far as the eye can see – it doesn't get much more fun than this.

Expeditions can range from half-day tasters to multiday trips with overnight stays in remote forest huts (if you're really lucky, you might even spot the northern lights). With most operators, you'll have the option (depending on the number of travellers in your group) of *mushing* your own sled (after a brief primer course before setting out) or sitting atop the sled and watching the world pass by as someone else urges the dogs onwards.

There are several long-distance dog-sled races in Norway where you can see how the professionals do it. The longest is Finnmarksløpet (p328), which takes place in March, and involves more than 150 dog teams racing over 1000km of snow and ice in northern Norway.

ALLEMANNSRETTEN

Anyone considering camping or hiking in Norway should be aware of *allemannsretten* (every man's right, often referred to as 'right of access'). This 1000-year-old law, in conjunction with the modern Friluftsleven (Outdoor Recreation Act), entitles anyone to:

➡ camp anywhere for up to two days, as long as it's more than 150m from a dwelling (preferably further and out of sight);

➡ hike or ski across uncultivated wilderness areas, including outlying fields and pastures (except in fields with standing crops and close to people's houses);

➡ cycle or ride on horseback on all paths and roads; and

➡ canoe, kayak, row and sail on all rivers and lakes.

However, these freedoms come with responsibilities, among the most important of which are the prohibition against fires between 15 April and 15 September and the requirement that you leave the countryside, any wildlife and cultural sights as pristine as you found them.

Dog-Sledding Destinations

Although most of the dog-sledding possibilities are to be found in Norway's high Arctic, Røros, in central Norway, is another option.

➡ **Karasjok** (p347) Wonderful short and long expeditions run by Sven Engholm (who has won the Finnmarksløpet a record 11 times) and his team.

➡ **Øvre Dividal National Park** (p325) A growing number of options for multiday expeditions into remote country.

➡ **Svalbard** (p357) The most spectacular landscapes bar none that can be reached by husky.

➡ **Alta** (p328) Three-hour excursions to five-day expeditions not far from Alta.

➡ **Røros** (p134) From a few hours to a few days in one of Norway's coldest corners.

➡ **Tromsø** (p319) Up to four-day treks from Kvaløya island, south of town, with reindeer-sledding also possible.

➡ **Kirkenes** (p344) Mostly short-haul excursions but longer options are possible.

Skiing

'Ski' is a Norwegian word and thanks to aeons-old rock carvings depicting hunters travelling on skis, Norwegians make a credible claim to having invented the sport. Interest hasn't waned over the years and these days it's the national pastime.

Cross-Country Skiing

Most skiing is of the cross-country (nordic) variety, and Norway has thousands of kilometres of maintained cross-country ski trails. Visitors should only set off after closely studying the trails/routes (wilderness trails are identified by colour codes on maps and signposts) and ensuring that they have appropriate clothing, sufficient food and water, and emergency supplies, such as matches and a source of warmth. You can either bring your own equipment or hire it on site.

Most towns and villages provide some illuminated ski trails, but elsewhere it's still worth carrying a good torch, as winter days are very short and in the north there's no daylight at all in December and January. The ski season generally lasts from early December to April. Snow conditions vary greatly from year to year and region to region, but February and March,

as well as the Easter holiday period, tend to be the best (and busiest) times.

Downhill Skiing

Norway has dozens of downhill winter ski centres, although it can be an expensive pastime due to the costs of ski lifts, accommodation and the après-ski drinking sessions. The spring season lasts longer than in the Alps and the snow is of better quality, too.

Skiing Resources

The Norwegian Tourist Board (p418) publishes the useful *Skiing in Norway* brochure each year.

For more on epic cross-country skiing in Svalbard, contact **Exodus** (📞 UK 0203 131 6100; www.exodus.co.uk).

Skiing Destinations

Norway's better and more popular skiing locations include the following:

➡ **Lillehammer** (p125) The chance to ski the downhill slopes used in the 1994 Winter Olympics.

➡ **Trysil** (p133) The largest network of trails in the country, with something to suit every standard and style.

➡ **Holmenkollen, Oslo** (p64) Has 2400km of cross-country trails, many of them floodlit.

➡ **Geilo** (p152) The Oslo–Bergen railway line leaves you within sight of the ski lifts.

➡ **Voss** (p174) Good trails in the Stølsheimen mountains high above Voss.

➡ **Myrkdalen** (p176) One of Norway's newer ski resorts, close to Voss.

➡ **Hovden** (p123) A popular winter resort in the southern Norwegian interior.

THE TELEMARK MANOEUVRE

The Telemark region of Norway has lent its name to the graceful turn that has made nordic (cross-country) skiing popular around the world. Nordic ski bindings attach the boot at the toes, allowing free movement of the heel; to turn, one knee is dropped toward the ski while the other leg is kept straight. The skis are positioned one behind the other, allowing the skier to smoothly glide around the turn in the direction of the dropped knee.

WEATHER WARNING

Always check weather and other local conditions before setting out cross-country. This applies whenever traversing any exposed area, but is particularly an issue for hikers and cross-country skiers (two Scottish cross-country skiers died after being caught in snow and freezing fog in March 2007 on the Hardangervidda Plateau despite, according to some reports, being warned by local experts not to set out). At any time of the year, you should always be prepared for sudden inclement weather and stay aware of potential avalanche dangers, which are particularly rife in Jotunheimen but are a possibility anywhere in Norway's high country. Also, never venture onto glacial ice without the proper equipment and experience. And trust the advice of locals, who understand the conditions better than even the most experienced out-of-town hikers or skiers – if they say not to go, don't go.

➡ **Tromsø** (p319) The pick of the far north, with plenty of experienced operators.

Snowmobiling

While snowmobiling may have its critics as a less-than-environmentally sound means of getting around, life for many in the high Arctic would simply not be possible in winter without the snowmobile. For the traveller, snowmobiling also enables you to go much further than is possible with dog-sleds. In Norway's sub-polar north, on Svalbard, snowmobiling is the main way to get around in winter.

Most operators allow you to ride as a passenger behind an experienced driver or (usually for an additional charge) as the driver yourself; for the latter, a valid driving licence may be required.

Snowmobiling Destinations

Snowmobiling is generally restricted to the far north and Svalbard. Possibilities include the following:

➡ **Svalbard** (p357) Norway's premier snowmobiling location, with trails taking you deep into the main Spitsbergen island of this extraordinary place; there are some restrictions on where you can go.

➡ **Kirkenes** (p344) Day and night trips into the beautiful Pasvik Valley wedged between Finland and Russia.

➡ **Alta** (p328) One of the snowmobile hubs of mainland Norway.

➡ **Tromsø** (p319) Good trails close to Norway's northern capital.

Snowshoeing

Like most winter activities, strapping on a pair of snowshoes is a time-honoured way of getting around in snowbound regions and one that has morphed into a popular winter activity. That said, in our experience snowshoeing is something of a novelty to try for short distances rather than longer excursions – it can be exhausting and it takes a long time to get anywhere.

Throughout the Arctic North, hotels and operators who organise other winter activities rent out snowshoes and some also organise expeditions in Narvik (p279), Lofoten (p291) and Tromsø (p319).

Tour Operators
Norwegian Tour Operators

Many Norwegian tour operators offer activities and adventure expeditions. Although it is sometimes possible to simply turn up and join a tour, we always recommend that you make contact in advance, especially during the peak summer and winter seasons, to make sure that you don't turn up and find that all available places have been taken or that the departures don't fit within your travelling schedule.

Local operators can be reached via local tourist offices.

International Tour Operators

Many companies outside the country offer adventure- or activities-based tours to Norway. In most cases, tours are all-inclusive: the cost of your tour includes all accommodation, airfares, the cost of the activities and, in *some* cases, equipment. In short, what you lose in flexibility you gain in convenience.

Plan Your Trip
Travel with Children

Norway is a terrific destination in which to travel as a family. This is a country that has become world famous for creating family-friendly living conditions, and most hotels, restaurants and many sights are accordingly child-friendly. Remember, however, that distances are vast and careful planning is required.

Planning

As you'd expect, children's products such as baby food, infant formula, soy and cow's milk, and disposable nappies (diapers) are widely available in Norway (in supermarkets, pharmacies and more expensive convenience stores), but they're much more expensive than back home. You may want to bring a reasonable supply in order to keep costs down.

For all-round information and advice, check out Lonely Planet's book *Travel with Children*.

Accommodation

Hotels, hostels, campsites and other accommodation options often have 'family rooms' or cabins that accommodate up to two adults and two children. Although many hotels do have larger, dedicated family rooms, other places simply squeeze in cots and/or extra beds when space allows, always for an additional fee.

One hotel chain that makes a special effort to cater for families from mid-June to mid-August is Thon Hotels (www.thon hotels.no), where family rooms can cost as little as 1150kr – stunning value by Norwegian standards. Most Thon Hotels also have a small children's play area and nice touches such as children's check-in steps.

Best Regions for Kids

Oslo

Green parklands in abundance and a large array of museums, many with an interactive component, mean there's plenty to keep children happy, but be warned that not all sights and restaurants are that welcoming to younger travellers.

Central Norway

Lillehammer's (sometimes interactive) Winter Olympic sites may appeal, as will activities around Røros, and safaris that set off in search of elk and musk oxen.

Bergen & the Southwestern Fjords

Bergen and Stavanger have numerous child-oriented attractions, while elsewhere there are boat trips on the fjords, interactive museums, water-based activities and the occasional Viking landmark.

Nordland

Whale-watching is the main draw here, with ample opportunities on Vesterålen.

The Far North

Winter-based activities such as dog-sledding thrill travellers of any age, while the northern lights are something the kids will never forget.

Restaurants

Even in some upmarket restaurants, children will be made to feel welcome and, as a result, Norwegians are often seen eating out as a family group. Many restaurants offer children's menus with smaller portions and prices to match. And most of those that don't are willing to serve a smaller portion if you ask.

The high cost of meals can mean it's a challenge in Norway to ensure that your children eat well, but the general availability of hot dogs, hamburgers and pizzas do provide a fall-back option. Supermarkets are also good if you're stocking up for a family picnic and many have pre-made meals. Most restaurants have baby-change areas and a limited number of high chairs.

Transport

Norway's impressive public transport system is at once a comfortable means of getting from A to B and – given the variety, which spans trains, buses, tourist boats and ferries – may also carry considerable appeal for children.

On trains and buses, children under four generally travel for free (although they won't have a seat), while those aged between four and 15 (16 on the Hurtigruten coastal ferry) travel for 50% of the adult fare. Some long-distance trains have a special family carriage complete with a children's play area!

Car-rental firms hire out children's safety seats at a nominal cost, but it's essential that you book them in advance, especially in summer and on weekends when demand is high.

When to Go

Easily the best time to travel in Norway with children is the main tourist season, which runs from mid-June to mid-August – this is when hotels offer the best deals for families, all sights and attractions are open and the weather is more conducive to a happy family holiday.

If you've come to Norway for the northern lights or winter activities such as dog-sledding, don't be put off by the bitterly cold weather. It's all about coming prepared with the appropriate clothes (Norwegian families don't hide in their homes for 10 months of the year!), and winter can be a magical time to be here.

Children's Highlights

Museums

➡ **Vikingskipshuset, Oslo** (p57) Reconstructed Viking ships at the Viking Ship Museum.

➡ **Kon-Tiki Museum, Oslo** (p58) Guaranteed to inspire the inner explorer.

➡ **Natural History Museum, Oslo** (p60) Stuffed Arctic wildlife.

➡ **Archaeology Museum, Stavanger** (p201) Viking-themed activities in summer.

➡ **Norsk Oljemuseum, Stavanger** (p200) The Oil Museum is one of Norway's most interactive.

➡ **Norwegian Children's Museum, Stavanger** (p200) Wonderful indoor playground for younger kids.

➡ **Nordvegen Historiesenter, Karmøy** (p199) Part museum, part Viking farm.

➡ **Norwegian Glacier Museum, Fjærland** (p225) Hands-on exhibits of Norway's icefields.

➡ **Norsk Luftfartsmuseum, Bodø** (p287) Ideal for the aeroplane enthusiast.

Theme Parks & Aquariums

➡ **Kristiansand Dyrepark** (p107) Outstanding zoo and funfair in Norway's far south.

➡ **Hunderfossen Familiepark** (p131) Water rides, wandering trolls and fairy-tale palaces.

➡ **Atlanterhavsparken, Ålesund** (p246) Atlantic Ocean Park is one of northern Europe's best aquariums.

➡ **Akvariet i Bergen** (p160) Fantastic aquarium that you can reach by boat.

➡ **Lofoten Aquarium, Kabelvåg** (p298) Seals, sea otters and other marine creatures.

➡ **Olympic Park, Lillehammer** (p125) Everything from simulators to bobsled runs.

➡ **Senjatrollet, Senja** (p326) The world's biggest troll, with accompanying attractions.

➡ **Polar Park, Setermoen** (p325) An excellent animal park with Arctic species.

Activities

➡ **White-water rafting** Family-friendly trips in Sjoa (p143) and elsewhere.

➡ **Dog-sledding** Possible from Røros (p134) in central Norway to Tromsø (p319), Øvre Dividal National Park (p325), Karasjok (p347) and Svalbard (p351) in winter, with sleds on wheels in summer.

Gokstad ship, Vikingskipshuset (p57), Oslo

➡ **Skiing** Year-round skiing at centres used to catering for kids, including Lillehammer (p125), Trysil (p133), Voss (p174) and, in summer, Stryn (p230).

➡ **Kayaking** Shorter family-friendly trips in Voss (p174), Svalbard (p351) and across the fjords.

Wildlife-Watching

➡ **Whale-watching** See the giants of the sea off the northern coast from Andenes (p308), Stø (p306) and Tromsø (p319).

➡ **Musk-ox safaris** Search for this otherworldly beast in Dovrefjell-Sunndalsfjella National Park (p141), around Oppdal (p138) and elsewhere.

➡ **Elk safaris** Free-range moose in southern and central Norway, including from Oppdal (p138), Rjukan (p118) and Evje (p122).

➡ **Walrus, reindeer and Arctic foxes** Walrus safaris are an exciting addition to Svalbard's wildlife offering, while reindeer and (to a lesser extent) Arctic foxes are sometimes seen within Longyearbyen (p351) itself.

Other Highlights

➡ **Seljord** (p121) Troll-rich country home to Selma the Serpent.

➡ **Midnight sun** (p380) Endless days have huge novelty appeal.

➡ **Northern lights** (p380) One of the natural world's most mysterious phenomena.

➡ **Hurtigruten coastal ferry** (p423) Some kids' activities on board, and an alternative to long car journeys.

Regions at a Glance

⭐ Oslo

Museums & Galleries
Architecture
Activities

Norway's Cultural Home

If it happened in Norwegian history, there's probably a museum in Oslo dedicated to the event, from the Vikings to Thor Heyerdahl and beyond. Some of the towering icons of national culture have wall space here as well, while cultural giants such as Edvard Grieg and Henrik Ibsen also left their mark.

Beautiful Buildings

Oslo's growing architectural reputation was cemented with the opening of the award-winning Opera House in 2008, but there's plenty more to turn the head, from a 14th-century fortress to the distinctive parliament and contemporary-art gallery.

The Great Outdoors

Escape the pressures of city life and take to the stands of green that surround Oslo. Much of the activity on offer coalesces around the Holmenkollen Ski Jump and the Nordmarka woodland.

p46

Southern Norway

Festivals
Villages
Landscapes

Celebrations

The summer tourist season draws Norwegians to the southern coast in droves. Yes, they come partly for the beaches, but some of Norway's most popular festivals and celebrations of coastal life also loom large.

Seaside Hamlets

Southern Norway's seaside villages showcase the whitewashed timber architecture for which the region is famous. Grimstad, Lillesand and Risør are the prettiest among many.

Beyond Fjords

Coastal inlets of the kind that once sheltered Vikings are the topographical mainstay of the south, but there's drama aplenty in Jøssingfjord, the rolling hills of Setesdalen and the peak of Gausta.

p94

Central Norway

Hiking
Wildlife
Architecture

High-Country Hikes

Jotunheimen National Park has the most celebrated trails over the roof of Norway, although the parks of Hardangervidda and Rondane are every bit as good and the scenery just as dramatic.

Reindeer & Musk Oxen

There aren't many places where it's easier to see three signature species of the north: wild reindeer roam the Hardangervidda Plateau, the musk ox inhabits two central Norwegian national parks and the humble elk is easy to see.

History in Wood

The stave churches at Lom and Ringebu, the mining town of Røros and Lillehammer's Maihaugen Folk Museum take you on a journey through Norwegian architectural history.

p124

Bergen & the Southwestern Fjords

Scenery
Villages
Cities

Fantastic Fjords

Spectacular Hardangerfjord, its shorelines carpeted in fruit trees, is far less travelled by tourists than the fjords further north. To the south, Lysefjord is picture-perfect with two iconic vantage points.

Timeless Hamlets

Some of Norway's prettiest villages – Ulvik and Eidfjord to name just two – are at once worthy destinations in their own right and front-row seats for stunning fjord country.

Beautiful Bergen

There is no more picturesque city in northern Europe than Bergen, with its harbourside district, mountainous backdrop and vibrant cultural life. Stavanger, too, is filled with energy and charm.

p154

The Western Fjords

Fjords
Activities
Architecture

Best Fjords

Norway's western fjords region – home to Geirangerfjord, as well as Nærøyfjord, Aurlandsfjorden and the other vertiginous tributaries of the vast Sognefjorden – is one of the most beautiful places on earth.

Ice-Bound

Take to the water in a kayak or hike up a mountainside, but the main drawcard here is the chance to venture onto the glacier tongues of the epic Jostedalsbreen icefield.

Stave Churches & Art Nouveau

Norway's prettiest stave churches – including Stordal, Kaupanger, Borgund and Urnes – are set against a postcard-perfect backdrop of fjords and mountains. To the northeast, art-nouveau Ålesund is magnificent.

p209

Trøndelag

Hiking
Cities
History

Sacred Path

Few Norwegian hiking trails resonate so strongly with the sacred. The Pilgrims' Way is an ancient pilgrimage trail with Trondheim as its goal. The Bymarka wilderness also contains fine trails.

Terrific Trondheim

A worthy rival to Bergen for the title of Norway's most agreeable city, Trondheim boasts excellent museums, a thriving culinary and cultural scene, and a slew of architecturally distinguished buildings.

Medieval Echoes

Trøndelag is a mother lode for Norway's history. Trondheim's 12th-century Nidaros Cathedral is Scandinavia's largest medieval building. Stiklestad marks the site of St Olav's martyrdom and one of the most significant battles in Viking history.

p255

Nordland

Scenery
Islands
Nature

Enter the Arctic

Whether you choose the snaking Kystriksveien or the Arctic Highway (and we suggest both), there are no finer passages into the Arctic anywhere in the world. Along both, the Arctic Circle is a gateway to many scenes of intense, dramatic beauty.

Jagged Coast

More than 14,000 islands sit just off the Nordland coast. The Vega archipelago consists of low-lying skerries, Vesterålen is wild and untravelled, while Lofoten is arguably Europe's most spectacular island chain.

Whales & Glaciers

Norway's best whale-watching is to be found offshore from Andenes and Stø. Inland, Saltfjellet-Svartisen National Park is Norway's second-largest icefield.

p272

The Far North

Activities
The Sami
Landscapes

Arctic Winter

While the rest of Norway hibernates for winter, the far north takes to the snow aboard snowmobiles, skis and sleds pulled by teams of huskies.

Sami Homeland

The indigenous Sami are Arctic Norway's most enduring human inhabitants, and their emergence from centuries of persecution and an extreme climate is celebrated most powerfully in Karasjok and Kautokeino, now proud bastions of Sami culture.

Coast & Cathedrals

From the remote national parks of the interior to the coastal splendours of Senja, the Lyngen Alps and Nordkapp, Norway's high-Arctic landscapes inspire travellers and architects alike.

p314

Svalbard

Activities
Landscapes
Wildlife

Year-Round Adventure

Dog-sledding and snowmobiling in winter, hiking, cruises and kayaking in summer – there's not much you can't do here, and they're all fabulous ways to get out and explore the Svalbard wilderness.

Frozen Wilderness

Svalbard's natural beauty – ice-bound for much of the year – defies superlatives. Much of the archipelago ranks among Europe's most beautiful wilderness areas, with mountainous ramparts, epic icefields and lonely fjords.

Arctic Wildlife

Here be polar bears. And walruses. And whales, reindeer, Arctic foxes and more than 160 bird species. Svalbard offers a rare opportunity to see the inhabitants of this accessible slice of the polar north.

p351

On the Road

The Far North
p314

Svalbard
p351

Nordland
p272

Trøndelag
p255

The Western Fjords
p209

Central Norway
p124

Bergen & the Southwestern Fjords p154

Southern Norway
p94

✪ **Oslo**
p46

Oslo

POP 666,760

Best Places to Eat

➡ Brutus (p77)

➡ Bass (p75)

➡ Maaemo (p72)

➡ Sentralen Restaurant (p70)

Best Places to Stay

➡ Ellingsens Pensjonat (p69)

➡ The Thief (p68)

➡ PS: Hotell (p69)

➡ Hotel Grand Central (p68)

➡ Lysebu Hotel (p70)

Why Go?

Surrounded by mountains and the sea, this compact, cultured, caring and fun city is Europe's fastest-growing capital, with a palpable sense of reinvention. Oslo is also home to world-class museums and galleries to rival anywhere else on the European art trail.

But even here Mother Nature has managed to make her mark, and Oslo is fringed with forests, hills and lakes awash with opportunities for hiking, cycling, skiing and boating. Add to this mix a thriving cafe and bar culture, top-notch restaurants, nightlife options ranging from opera to indie rock, and a large and visible immigrant community who add their own colourful touch to the city, and the result is a thoroughly intoxicating place in which to forget about the fjords for a while.

When to Go
Oslo

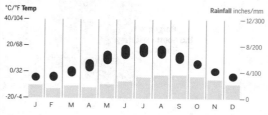

Apr–May Spring flowers fill the parks, and National Day brings crowds.

Jun The days are long and there's a packed cultural calendar.

Dec The first snow falls and Christmas markets and concerts bring seasonal magic.

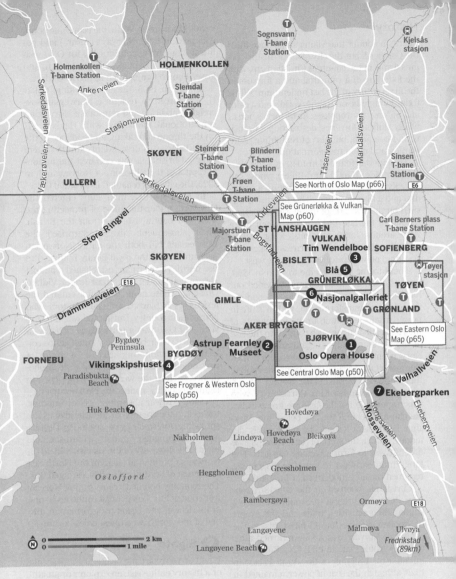

Oslo Highlights

1 Oslo Opera House (p49) Dreaming of operatic perfection while admiring Oslo Opera House.

2 Astrup Fearnley Museet (p49) Checking out the arresting artwork at this daring contemporary art museum.

3 Tim Wendelboe (p80) Going to the source of Norway's coffee obsession.

4 Vikingskipshuset (p57) Returning to the glorious Viking age at this remarkably intact longship museum.

5 Blå (p83) Getting to the heart of Oslo's pulsating nightlife.

6 Nasjonalgalleriet (p53) Screaming with delight at *The Scream* by Edvard Munch.

7 Ekebergparken (p61) Wandering through forested parkland with contemporary sculptures at every turn.

History

There's no doubt that viking ships once filled the Oslofjord, but the city of Oslo's history begins firmly in the country's Christian era, with the founding of a cathedral and a fortress in the first century of the last millennium. While today it might be one of the world's most calm and ordered metropolises, its history is one of wildly shifting fortunes, destruction, obscurity and conquest, but also of rebuilding, reinvention and rapid transformation.

The city was founded in 1049 by King Harald Hardråde (Harald Hard-Ruler), whose son Olav Kyrre (Olav the Peaceful) set up a cathedral and a bishopric here. This first town was sited on the east side of the Bjørvika inlet, although in the late 13th century, when there were around 3000 residents, King Håkon V built the Akershus Fortress (Akershus Festning) on its strategic point to the west.

The Bubonic plague came to Oslo in 1349, and, as it did around the country, wiped out half the population. After a period of economic and social transformation, with a shift in power from the Church to the merchants of the Hanseatic League. As a counter to the rise of this German trading organisation, in 1536 Norway entered a more formal coalition with Denmark. Oslo became but a symbolic capital, then, in 1624, it burned to the ground.

It was the Danish King Christian IV who was responsible for the Oslo we know today. He chose to rebuild the city below the Akershus Fortress so it could be more easily defended, and, in the spirit of (late) Renaissance order, it was to form a rectangular grid. The king, in an early act of brand management, renamed the new modern city Christiania.

Christiania boomed in the late 18th century, due to a thriving tree-milling industry, shipbuilding activities, trade and the export of wooden planks. Its official status as the capital of Norway was finally returned after the Napoleonic Wars in 1814. King Karl Johan initiated the building of the Royal Palace in 1825, although the seat of power remained in Stockholm. From this time on, many of the city's state institutions, such as its grandiose parliament building and the Bank of Norway, were constructed.

This newfound political stability and the country's industrialisation saw a stratospheric growth in population in the city, from around 10,000 in 1814 to 230,000 at the turn of the century. A building boom transformed the city centre and surrounding area, and the banks of the Akerselva became lined with various industries. While the economic boom collapsed in 1899, Norway's cultural and political blossoming continued, with Oslo residents Henrik Ibsen and Edvard Munch, and lesser-known figures such as Sigrid Undset.

Finally, in 1905, the Swedish king, Oskar II, was forced to recognise Norwegian sovereignty, abdicate and reinstate a Norwegian constitutional monarchy, with Haakon VII on the throne and taking up residence in the Royal Palace (his descendants still live there today). Christiania was declared the national capital of the Kingdom of Norway and, in 1925, the city was renamed its original Oslo.

In April 1940 German ships entered the Oslofjord, under the guise of protecting the then still neutral Norway from the British. Their subsequent advance surprised the Norwegians but both the entire Norwegian parliament and the royal family managed to flee north. The Germans established a puppet government under the fascist leader Vidkun Quisling, whose name thereafter entered the lexicon as a byword for collaborators who betray their country. During the war the University of Oslo was a particularly rich site of resistance, with both a key intelligence-collecting operation conducted by a group of its students and notable acts of civil disobedience, such as the wearing of paper clips to signify solidarity against the Nazi occupiers.

Oslo's postwar absorption of surrounding towns and the creation of suburbs give us the sprawling, forested city we see today. Despite growth it remained, for many, a hard-scrabble town. The discovery of the Ekofisk oilfield on Norway's Continental shelf, in the North Sea southwest of Stavanger in 1969, changed this. The economy boomed, transforming Norway from one of Europe's poorest countries to one of its richest, and Oslo's transformation into one of the world's wealthiest cities began.

⊙ Sights

Whether you're artistic or literary, a peacenik or a history enthusiast, an explorer or an athlete, the chances are there is a museum in Oslo tailor-made for you. Most are clustered around the city centre, but there a number of museums to be found on the Bygdøy Peninsula, and there are other important sights in Frogner and in Sofienberg too. The collections housed in the city often represent the best that the country has to offer, although they are joined by some amazing private art collections and fascinating and intimate house museums.

◉ Central Oslo

★ Oslo Opera House   ARCHITECTURE

(Den Norske Opera & Ballett; Map p50; ☎ 21 42 21 21; www.operaen.no; Kirsten Flagstads plass 1; foyer free; ⊙ foyer 10am-9pm Mon-Fri, 11am-9pm Sat, noon-9pm Sun; ☊ Sentralstasjonen) The centrepiece of the city's rapidly developing waterfront is the magnificent Opera House, one of the most iconic modern buildings of Scandinavia. Designed by Oslo-based architectural firm Snøhetta and costing around €500 million to build, the Opera House opened in 2008, and resembles a glacier floating in the waters of the Oslofjord. Its design is a meditation on the notion of monumentality, the dignity of cultural production, Norway's unique place in the world and the conversation between public life and personal experience.

It's worth spending some time here, but if you only have a short amount of time, make sure you tackle the roof, a broad luminous 'carpet' of marble patchwork, for one of those architectural experiences that are far more than the sum of their parts, not to mention wonderful views of the city.

To fully appreciate the building's interior, join one of the guided tours (p66).

While wandering around the building, it can be easy to forget that it's not just there to serve as eye candy for tourists, and that its prime role is to act as a showcase for top-notch opera and ballet performances. Upcoming performances are listed on the website and ticket prices vary from 100kr to 745kr.

Munchmuseet   GALLERY

(Munch Museum; Map p50; ☎ 23 49 35 00; www.munchmuseet.no; Edvard Munchs plass 1; adult/child 100kr/free; ⊙ 10am-4pm, to 5pm mid-Jun–late Sep; ☊ Sentralstasjonen) A monographic museum dedicated to Norway's greatest artist Edvard Munch (1863–1944), and housing the largest collection of his work in the world: 28,000 items including 1100 paintings and 4500 watercolours, many of which were gifted to the city by Munch himself – although his best-known pieces, including *The Scream*, are held in the Nasjonalgalleriet (p53).

★ Astrup Fearnley Museet   GALLERY

(Astrup Fearnley Museum; Map p56; ☎ 22 93 60 60; www.afmuseet.no; Strandpromenaden 2; adult/child 120kr/free; ⊙ noon-5pm Tue, Wed & Fri, to 7pm Thu, 11am-5pm Sat & Sun; ⛴ Aker brygge) Designed by Renzo Piano, this private contemporary art museum is housed in a wonderful building of silvered wood, with a sail-like glass roof that feels both maritime and at one with the Oslofjord landscape. While the museum's original collecting brief was conceptual American work from the '80s (with artists of the ilk of Jeff Koons, Tom Sachs, Cindy Sherman and Richard Prince well represented), it later broadened beyond that, with, for example, a room dedicated to Sigmar Polke and Anselm Kiefer.

Its most famous piece remains, however, the gilded ceramic sculpture *Michael Jackson and Bubbles*, by Koons, and there are also

---

OSLO IN...

Two Days...

Start your day at the **Nasjonalgalleriet** (p53) for a representative dose of artwork by Edvard Munch. Afterwards, try an alfresco, pier-side seafood lunch at one of the restaurant developments at Aker Brygge in **Central Oslo**. Take a ferry from here to Bygdøy Peninsula, and spend your afternoon learning about the exploits of Norway's greatest explorers at the **Polarship Fram Museum** (p58) or **Vikingskipshuset** (p57). On day two head to the breathtaking **Oslo Opera House**, timing your visit to coincide with one of the guided tours. Afterwards, explore the medieval **Akershus Festning & Slott** (p55) and then take a look at all that's cool and modern at the amazing **Astrup Fearnley Museet** (p49). Finally, if time allows, learn how to make the world a better place at the **Nobels Fredssenter** (p54).

Four Days...

If you have a couple of extra days, wander among the bold statues at **Vigelandsanlegget** (p56) and consider launching yourself off the enormous **Holmenkollen Ski Jump** (p61), although it's probably better to content yourself with a virtual attempt in the nearby simulator. The energetic might also spend a day walking, skiing or biking in the **Nordmarka** (p62); otherwise simply make a lazy day trip to pretty **Fredrikstad** (p89).

Central Oslo

OSLO

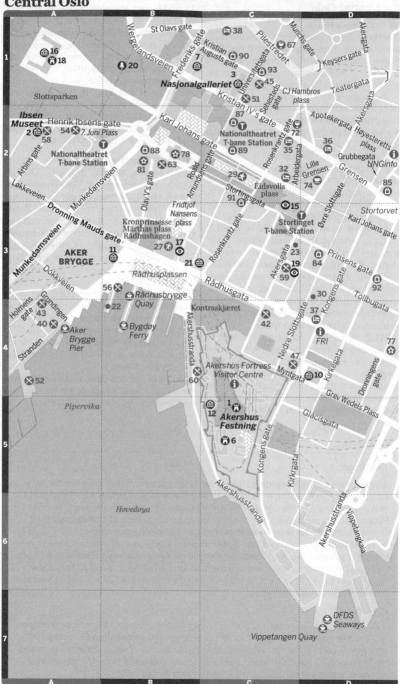

St Olavs gate

38

Pilestredet

67

Munchs gate

Akersgata

Keysers gate

Wergelandsveien

Kristian 90

Augusts gate

7

Frederiks gate

3

93

Universitetsgata

Kristian IV's gate

51

CJ Hambros plass

45

Teatergata

Akersgata

Slottsparken

Nasjonalgalleriet

87

Apotekergata

Høyesteretts plass

Ibsen
Museet

Henrik Ibsens gate

Arbins gate

54 58 7. Juni Plass

2

Karl Johans gate

Nationaltheatret
T-bane Station

72

36

UNGinfo

Nationaltheatret
T-bane Station

89

35

Grubbegata

Grensen

Rosenkrantz gate

Arbeidergata

Lille
Grensen

Løkkeveien

Munkedamsveien

88

78

81

63

Roald Amundsens gate

29

32

74

85

Olav V's gate

91

Stortingsgata

Eidsvolls plass

Øvre Slottsgate

Stortorvet

Dronning Mauds gate

Fridtjöf
Nansens
plass

Stortinget
T-bane Station

15

Karl Johans gate

Munkedamsveien

Kronprinsesse
Märthas plass
Rådhushagen

27

17

AKER
BRYGGE

11

Rosenkrantz gate

23

19

59

84

Prinsens gate

Kongens gate

Dokkveien

Rådhusplassen

21

Rådhusgata

Tollbugata

92

Holmens gate

Grundingen

56

Rådhusbrygge
Quay

Kontraskjæret

42

30

37

FRI

Nedre Slottsgate

43

40

Aker
Brygge
Pier

22

Bygdøy
Ferry

Akershusstranda

47

Myntgata

10

Kirkegata

Dronningens gate

77

Stranden

52

60

Akershus Fortress
Visitor Centre

Grev Wedels Plass

Pipervika

12

1

Akershus
Festning

Glacisgata

Kongens gate

Kirkgata

6

Hovedøya

Akershusstranda

Akershusstranda

Vippetangkaia

DFDS
Seaways

Vippetangen Quay

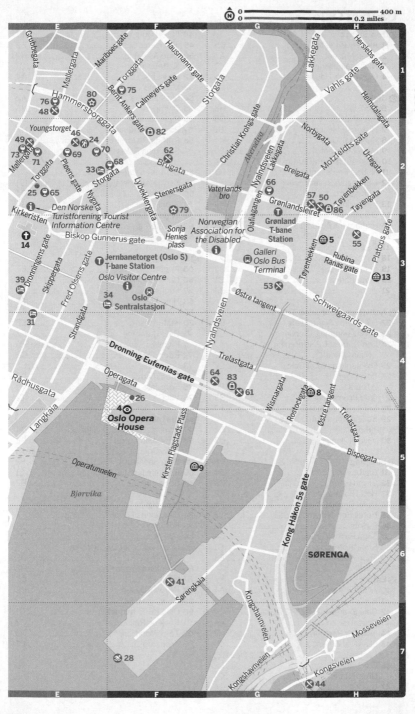

Central Oslo

◎ Top Sights
1 Akershus Festning C5
2 Ibsen Museet A2
3 Nasjonalgalleriet C1
4 Oslo Opera House F5

◎ Sights
5 1857...H3
6 Akershus Slott C5
7 Historisk Museum....................................B1
8 Kunsthall Oslo..H4
9 Munchmuseet...F5
10 Museet for Samtidskunst D4
11 Nobels Fredssenter B3
12 Norwegian Resistance
   Museum...C5
13 nyMusikk..H3
14 Oslo Cathedral..E3
15 Parliament Building C3
16 Queen Sonja Art Stable..........................A1
17 Rådhus...B3
18 Royal Palace..A1
19 Sentralen...C3
20 Slottsparken..B1
21 vi, vii..B3

◎ Activities, Courses & Tours
22 Båtservice Sightseeing...........................B4
23 Berlitz Language Services C3
24 Den Norske Turistforening
   Main Office..E2
25 Folkeuniversitetet Oslo E2
26 Oslo Opera House Guided
   Tours...F4
27 Oslo Promenade......................................B3
28 Sørenga Seapool......................................F7
29 Spikersuppa Outdoor Ice
   Rink...C2
30 Viking Biking D3

◎ Sleeping
31 Citybox Oslo..E4
32 Grand Hotel...C2
33 Hotel Folketeateret.................................E2
34 Hotel Grand Central................................F3
35 Hotell Bondeheimen................................C2
36 P-Hotel..D2
37 Saga Poshtel Oslo...................................D4
38 Smarthotel Oslo......................................C1
39 Thon Hotel Astoria..................................E3

◎ Eating
40 Albert Bistro..A4
41 Bun's Burger Bar F6
42 Café Skansen...C4
43 Delicatessen..A4
44 Ekeberg Restaurant.................................H7
45 Elias Mat & Sånt C1
   Far East..(see 82)
46 Fiskeriet...E2
   Grand Café ....(see 32)
47 Grosch...C4
48 Illegal Burgers E1
49 Justisen..E2
50 Kafe Asylet...H2
51 Kaffebrenneriet..C1
52 Ling Ling...A4
53 Maaemo..G3
54 Miss Sophie A2
55 Olympen...H3
56 Pipervika..B3
57 Punjab Tandoori.......................................H2
58 Ruffino Ristorante A2
   Sanguine Brasserie &
   Bar...(see 4)
59 Sentralen Cafeteria C3
   Sentralen Restaurant...................(see 19)
60 Solsiden...B4
61 Stock..G4
62 Teddy's Soft Bar F2
63 Theatercafeen..B2
64 Vaaghals...G4

◎ Drinking & Nightlife
65 Angst..E2
66 Dattera Til Hagen....................................G2
67 Fuglen..C1
68 Himkok...F2
69 Internasjonalen E2
70 Kulturhuset..E2
71 Oslo Camping..E2
   Pigalle...(see 55)
72 Røør C2
73 Sosialen...E2
74 Stockfleths D2
75 Torggata Botaniske F1
76 Villa E1

◎ Entertainment
77 Filmens Hus D4
78 Nationaltheatret B2
   Oslo Opera House............................(see 4)
79 Oslo Spektrum F2
80 Rockefeller Music Hall.............................E1
81 Saga Kino B2

◎ Shopping
82 Cappelens Forslag....................................F2
83 Foto.no..G4
84 FWSS D3
85 Glasmagasinet Department
   Store...D2
86 Grønland Bazaar......................................H2
87 Norli...C2
88 Norway Designs.......................................B2
89 Norwegian Rain.......................................C2
90 Oslo Kunsthandel....................................C1
91 Råkk og Rålls C2
92 Tom Wood D3
93 Tronsmo...C1

large works by Damien Hirst. The temporary shows range from the monographic, say Matthew Barney or young Norwegian artist Matias Faldbakken, to thematically tight curated surveys such as New Norwegian Abstraction or Chinese conceptual work. There are tours at 2pm each Sunday (50kr).

Tjuvholmen Sculpture Park   SCULPTURE
(Map p56; http://afmuseet.no/en/om-museet/skulpturparken; Tjuvholmen; ⊙24hr; 🚃 Aker brygge) FREE Like the Astrup Fearnley Museet that it surrounds, this sculpture park is designed by Renzo Piano and is also dedicated to international contemporary art. Don't miss Louise Bourgeois' magnificent and rather cheeky *Eyes* (1997), Ugo Rondinone's totemic and enchanting *Moonrise east. november* (2006) and Franz West's bright and tactile *Spalt* (2003). There are also works by Antony Gormley, Anish Kapoor, Ellsworth Kelly, and Peter Fischli and David Weiss. Along with the artwork there are canals and a small child-pleasing pebble beach.

⭐**Ibsen Museet**   MUSEUM
(Ibsen Museum; Map p50; 🗷40 02 36 30; www.ibsenmuseet.no; Henrik Ibsens Gate 26; adult/child 115/30kr; ⊙11am-6pm May-Sep, to 4pm Oct-Apr, guided tours hourly; 🚃Slottsparken) While downstairs houses a small and rather idiosyncratic museum, it's Ibsen's former apartment, which you'll need to join a tour to see, that is unmissable. This was the playwright's last residence and his study remains exactly as he left it, as does the bedroom where he uttered his famously enigmatic last words, *'Tvert imot!'* ('To the contrary!'), before dying on 23 May 1906.

Rooms have been restored and refurnished but the place feels totally and genuinely of its era. The guides are excellent, beautifully conjuring both Ibsen and wife Suzannah's daily life as well as the Oslo of the era.

⭐**Nasjonalgalleriet**   GALLERY
(National Gallery; Map p50; 🗷21 98 20 00; www.nasjonalmuseet.no; Universitetsgata 13; adult/child 100kr/free, Thu free; ⊙10am-6pm Tue, Wed & Fri, to 7pm Thu, 11am-5pm Sat & Sun; 🚃Tullinløkka) The gallery houses the nation's largest collection of traditional and modern art and many of Edvard Munch's best-known creations are on permanent display, including his most renowned work, *The Scream*. There's also an impressive collection of European art, with works by Gauguin, Claudel, Picasso and El Greco, plus Impressionists such as Manet, Degas, Renoir, Matisse, Cézanne and Monet. Nineteenth-century Norwegian artists have a strong showing too, including key figures such as JC Dahl and Christian Krohg.

At the time of writing, the gallery was closed pending its move to the new National Museum site.

Royal Palace   PALACE
(Det Kongelige Slott; Map p50; 🗷81 53 31 33; www.royalcourt.no; Slottsparken 1; palace tours adult/child 135/105kr, with Queen Sonja Art Stable 200kr; ⊙guided tours in English noon, 2pm, 2.20pm & 4pm Jun–mid-Aug; 🚃Slottsparken) The Norwegian royal family's seat of residence emerges from the wood-like **Slottsparken** (Map p50; Slottsparken; ⊙24hr; 🚃Slottsparken) FREE, a relatively modest, pale buttercup neoclassical pile. Built for the Swedish (in fact, French) king Karl Johan, the palace was never continuously occupied before King Haakon VII and Queen Maud were installed in 1905.

Construction of the 173-room palace originally began in 1825 but wasn't completed until 1849, five years after Karl Johan's death. His son, Oscar I, and daughter-in-law, Josephine, became the first royals to move in. The palace has been greatly modernised under the current monarch, King Harald V.

What's remarkable about this palace, and the royal family in general, is how approachable it is: children play and tourists pose for photos just metres from the main entrance door – quite a contrast to some other European royal seats.

In summer, one-hour guided tours of the interior are available. Tours visit a dozen rooms including the Cabinet Cloakroom, Mirror Room, Banqueting Hall and the Palace Chapel. Tickets can be bought at the gate (at the rear of the palace), but it's wise to pre-purchase by phone, at 7-Eleven stores or from www.ticketmaster.no as only limited spaces are available on the day.

Museet for Samtidskunst   GALLERY
(National Museum of Contemporary Art; Map p50; www.nasjonalmuseet.no) The highly regarded National Museum of Contemporary Art is keeper of the National Gallery's collections of post-WWII Scandinavian and international art. The gallery is also known for its cutting-edge temporary exhibitions. At time of writing it had closed its doors at Bankplassen in preparation for reopening in the new National Museum complex in 2022.

Damstredet
AREA

(Map p60; 🚇54) The quirky 18th-century wooden homes of the Damstredet district and the nearby Telthusbakken are a nice change of pace from the modern architecture of the city centre. Once an impoverished shanty town, Damstredet has become a popular residential neighbourhood for artists. To get there, walk north on Akersgata and turn right on Damstredet gate. Telthusbakken is a little further up Akersgata, also on the right.

Don't miss Vår Frelsers (Æreslunden; Map p60; Akersbakken 32; ⊙24hr; 🚇37), the graveyard where Ibsen, Munch and author Bjørnstjerne Bjørnson are buried.

Historisk Museum
MUSEUM

(Map p50; ✐22 85 19 00; www.khm.uio.no; Frederiks gate 2, University of Oslo; adult/child 50kr/free, includes entrance to Vikingskipmuseet; ⊙10am-5pm Tue-Sun; 🚇Tullinløkka) The Historical Museum is actually three museums under one roof. Most interesting is the ground-floor **National Antiquities Collection** (Oldsaksamlingen), which has displays of Viking-era coins, jewellery and ornaments, and includes the only complete Viking helmet ever found. Look out for the 9th-century **Hoen treasure** (2.5kg), the largest such find in Scandinavia. A section on medieval religious art includes the doors and richly painted ceiling of the Ål stave church (built around 1300).

The 2nd level has an **Arctic exhibit** and the Myntkabinettet, a collection of the earliest Norwegian coins from as far back as AD 995. Also on the 2nd level, and continuing on the top floor, is the **Ethnographic Museum**, with changing exhibits on Asia, Africa and the Americas.

Oslo Cathedral
CATHEDRAL

(Domkirke; Map p50; Stortorvet 1; ⊙24hr; 🚇Stortorvet) FREE The highlights of a visit to Oslo Cathedral, which dates from 1697, are the elaborate stained-glass windows by Emanuel Vigeland (brother of Gustav) and the painted ceiling, completed between 1936 and 1950. The exceptional altarpiece, a 1748 model of *The Last Supper and the Crucifixion* by Michael Rasch, was an original feature of the church (from 1700), but it was moved all over the country before being returned from Prestnes church in Majorstue in 1950.

The bazaar halls, around the back of the church, date from 1858 and are currently used by summer handicraft sales outlets and cafes.

Rådhus
ARCHITECTURE

(Map p50; Fridtjof Nansens plass; ⊙9am-6pm, guided tours 10am, noon & 2pm Jun–mid-Jul; 🚇Kontraskjæret) FREE This twin-towered town hall, completed in 1950 to commemorate Oslo's 900th anniversary, houses the city's political administration and is filled with mid-century tributes to Norwegian cultural and working life. Something of an Oslo landmark, the bombast of its red-brick functionalist exterior is polarising, if unmissable. It's here that the Nobel Peace Prize is awarded on 10 December each year.

Nobels Fredssenter
MUSEUM

(Nobel Peace Center; Map p50; ✐48 30 10 00; www.nobelpeacecenter.org; Rådhusplassen 1; adult/student 100/65kr; ⊙10am-6pm; 🚇Aker brygge) Norwegians take pride in their role as international peacemakers, and the Nobel Peace Prize is their gift to the men and women judged to have done the most to promote world peace over the course of the previous year. This state-of-the-art museum celebrates the lives and achievements of the winners with an array of digital displays that offer as much or as little information as you feel like taking in.

The changing exhibitions focus on vastly different aspects of the prize and its winners each year. Don't miss the Nobel Book on the 2nd floor, the theatre streaming films on the history of the prize and its winners, and the shop selling merchandise that manages to be both respectful and amusing.

Parliament Building
NOTABLE BUILDING

(Stortinget; Map p50; ✐23 31 33 33; www.stortinget. no; Karl Johans gate 22; ⊙guided tours in English 10am & 1pm Jul & Aug, Sat rest of year; 🚇Øvre Slottsgate) FREE Built in 1866, Norway's yellow-brick parliament building is one of Europe's more charming parliaments. If you find yourself really hooked on Norwegian political debate, you can tune into the live action through the Stortinget website.

vi, vii
GALLERY

(Map p50; ✐906 75 993; www.vivii.no; Tordenskiolds gate 12; ⊙1-5pm Thu & Fri, noon-4pm Sat; 🚇Kontraskjæret) An independent gallery with a good reputation for interesting shows from up-and-coming artists, housed in an interesting 1930s building.

Queen Sonja Art Stable
GALLERY

(Queen Sonja KunstStall; Map p50; www.royalcourt. no; adult 100kr; ⊙11am-5pm Thu-Sun; 🚇Slottsparken) The former palace stables, used for half a century as storage, were reopened as a public gallery space by Queen Sonja on her 80th birthday. The charming 19th-century building hosts yearly exhibitions as well as a permanent collection of fascinating photographs both by and collected by the late Queen Maud (1869–1938).

Sentralen   NOTABLE BUILDING
(Map p50; ☑22 33 33 22; www.sentralen.no; Øvre Slottsgate 3; ☐Øvre Slottsgate) If you're not here for the restaurant, the cafe, the bars or the live-music venues, it's still worth popping in for a poke around both the spectacular mash of contemporary and traditional architecture, along with installations by six Norwegian artists, including some surprising interventions by Hanne Friis and Vanessa Baird.

Kunsthall Oslo   GALLERY
(Map p50; ☑21 69 69 39; www.kunsthalloslo.no; Rostockgata 2-4; ☺11am-5pm Wed-Fri, from noon Sat & Sun; ☐Jernbanetorget) This nonprofit art space presents a very interesting program of both international and Norwegian contemporary artists, including special commissions.

Nobel Institute   NOTABLE BUILDING, LIBRARY
(Map p56; ☑22 12 93 00; www.nobelpeaceprize.org; Henrik Ibsens gate 51; ☺8am-3pm Mon-Fri; ☐Solli) FREE It is unclear why Alfred Nobel chose Norway to administer the Peace Prize, but whatever the reason, it is a committee of five Norwegians, appointed for six-year terms by the Norwegian Storting (parliament), that chooses the winner each year, and their meetings are held here behind closed doors. You can, however, visit the library, which contains some 200,000 volumes on international history and politics, peace studies and economics.

◉ Akershus Festning & Slott

★Akershus Festning   FORTRESS
(Akershus Fortress; Map p50; ☺6am-9pm; ☐Christiania Square) FREE When Oslo was named capital of Norway in 1299, King Håkon V ordered the construction of Akershus, strategically located on the eastern side of the harbour, to protect the city from external threats. It has, over the centuries, been extended, modified and had its defences beefed up a number of times. Still dominating the Oslo harbourfront, the sprawling complex consists of a medieval castle, Akershus Slot, a fortress and assorted other buildings, including still-active military installations.

Entry is through a gate at the end of Akersgata or over a drawbridge spanning Kongens gate at the southern end of Kirkegata. After 6pm in winter, use the Kirkegata entrance.

The **Akershus Fortress Information Centre** (Map p50; ☑23 09 39 17; Akershus Slott; guided tours adult/child 60/30kr; ☺11am-5pm Jul & Aug, 11-4pm Mon-Fri, noon-5pm Sat & Sun Sep-Jun; ☐Christiania Square), inside the main gate, has permanent exhibits recounting the history of the complex, as well as temporary exhibits highlighting aspects of Oslo's history. Staff can organise guided tours. At 1.30pm you can watch the changing of the guard at the fortress.

Akershus Slott   CASTLE
(Akershus Castle; Map p50; ☑22 41 25 21; www. nasjonalefestningsverk.no; Kongens gate; adult/child 60/30kr, with Oslo Pass free; ☺11am-4pm Mon-Sat, noon-5pm Sun; ☐Christiania Square) In the 17th century Christian IV renovated Akershus Castle into a Renaissance palace, although the front remains decidedly medieval. In its dungeons you'll find dark cubbyholes where outcast nobles were kept under lock and key, while the upper floors contained sharply contrasting lavish banquet halls and staterooms.

The castle chapel is still used for army events, and the crypts of King Håkon VII and Olav V lie beneath it. The guided tours are led by university students in period dress and, while not compulsory, they do offer an entertaining anecdotal history of the place that you won't get by wandering around on your own. Ask at the ticket office for tour information. Hours are extended in July and August.

Norwegian Resistance Museum   MUSEUM
(Norges Hjemmefront Museet; Map p50; ☑23 09 31 38; www.forsvaretsmuseer.no; adult/child 60/30kr; ☺10am-5pm Mon-Sat, from 11am Sun Jun-Aug, 10am-4pm Mon-Fri, from 11am Sat & Sun Sep-May; ☐Christiania Square) Within the Akershus Fortress complex the Norwegian Resistance Museum stands adjacent to a memorial for resistance fighters executed on this spot during WWII. The small but worthwhile museum covers the dark years of German occupation, as well as the jubilant day of 9 May 1945 when peace was declared. Artefacts include underground newspapers, numerous maps and photographs, and, most intriguingly, a set of dentures that belonged to a Norwegian prisoner of war in Poland that were wired to receive radio broadcasts.

Frogner & Western Oslo

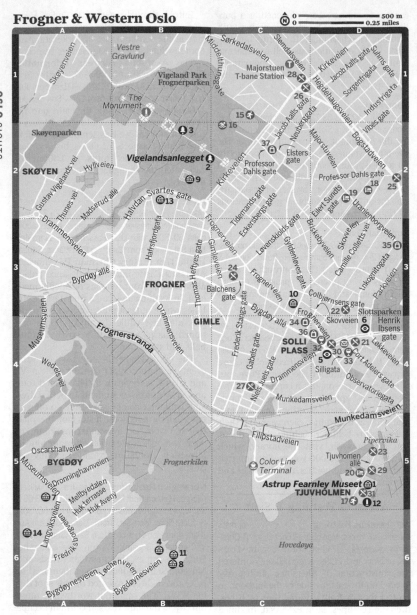

⊙ Frognerparken & Vigeland Park

★ Vigelandsanlegget   PARK
(Vigeland Sculpture Park; Map p56; www.vige
land.museum.no/no/vigelandsparken; Nobels gate

32; ⊙ Tue-Sun noon-4pm; T Borgen) The centre-piece of Frognerparken is an extraordinary open-air showcase of work by Norway's best-loved sculptor, Gustav Vigeland. Statistically one of the top tourist attractions in Norway, Vigeland Park is brimming with 212 gran-

Frogner & Western Oslo

OSLO SIGHTS

ite and bronze Vigeland works. His highly charged oeuvre includes entwined lovers, tranquil elderly couples, bawling babies and contempt-ridden beggars. Speaking of bawling babies, his most famous work here, *Sinataggen (Little Hot-Head)*, portrays a child in a mood of particular ill humour.

Frognerparken   PARK
(Map p56; T Borgen) Frognerparken attracts westside locals with its lawns, ponds, stream and rows of shady trees for picnics, strolling or lounging on the grass. It also contains Vigelandsanlegget (p55), a sprawling sculpture-park-within-a-park. To get here, take tram 12 to Vigelandsparken from the city centre.

Vigeland Museum   GALLERY
(Map p56; www.vigeland.museum.no; Nobelsgata 32; adult/child 60/30kr, with Oslo Pass free; ⊙10am-5pm Tue-Sun May-Aug, noon-4pm Tue-Sun rest of year; 🚌20, 🚌12, 🚌N12, T Borgen) For a more in-depth look at Gustav Vigeland's work, this museum is just opposite the southern entrance to Frognerparken. It was built by the city in the 1920s as a home and studio for the sculptor in exchange for the donation of a significant proportion of his life's work. It contains his early collection of statuary and monuments to public figures, as well as plaster moulds, woodblock prints and sketches.

When he died in 1943, Vigeland's ashes were deposited in the tower and the museum was opened to the public four years later. Guided tours are available (in English), with prior notice, from 1000kr per group; sketching (pencil only) is encouraged and you can borrow sketching boards and folding chairs. In addition to the works of Vigeland, the museum also has a very good program of seasonal contemporary shows.

Oslo City Museum   MUSEUM
(Oslo Bymuseet; Map p56; 🕿23 28 41 70; www.oslomuseum.no; Frognerveien 67; ⊙11am-4pm Tue-Sun; 🚊Solli) **FREE** Near the southern entrance to Vigeland Park, this charming museum is housed in the 18th-century Frogner Manor, built on the site of a Viking-era great house. It's a lovely snapshot of traditional bourgeois Norwegian life of the era and there are other exhibitions about Oslo's urban history.

◉ Bygdøy Peninsula

Vikingskipshuset   MUSEUM
(Viking Ship Museum; Map p56; 🕿22 13 52 80; www.khm.uio.no; Huk Aveny 35; adult/child 80kr/free; ⊙9am-6pm May-Sep, 10am-4pm Oct-Apr; 🚌91) Around 1100 years ago, Vikings dragged up two longships from the shoreline and used them as the centrepiece for grand ceremonial burials, most likely for important

ℹ OSLO PASS

Oslo Pass (www.visitoslo.com/en/activities-and-attractions/oslo-pass; 1/2/3days adult 395/595/745kr, child 210/295/370kr), sold at the tourist office, is a good way of cutting transport and ticket costs around the city. The majority of the city's museums are free with the pass, as is public transport within the city limits (barring late-night buses). Other perks include restaurant and tour discounts.

If you're planning to visit just the city-centre museums and galleries, it's worth checking which on your list are free before buying a pass.

chieftains or nobles. Along with the ships, they buried many items for the afterlife: food, drink, jewellery, furniture, carriages, weapons, and even a few dogs and servants for companionship. Discovered in Oslofjord in the late 19th century, the ships are beautifully restored and offer an evocative, emotive insight into the world of the Vikings.

There are three ships in total, all named after their places of discovery: *Oseberg*, *Gokstad* and *Tune*. The most impressive and ostentatious of the three is the *Oseberg*, plus the burial chamber beneath it held the largest collection of Viking-age artefacts ever uncovered in Scandinavia, though it had been looted of its jewellery. As daunting as the ship appears, it was probably only ever intended as a royal pleasure craft. The sturdier 24m-long *Gokstad*, built around 890, is the finest remaining example of a Viking longship, but when it was unearthed its corresponding burial chamber had also been looted and few artefacts were uncovered. There is also the third, smaller, boat, the *Tune*, which is fragmentary but what remains is incredibly well preserved.

Polarship Fram Museum   MUSEUM

(Frammuseet; Map p56; 🕿 23 28 29 50; www.frammuseum.no; Bygdøynesveien 36; adult/child 100/40kr, with Oslo Pass free; ☉ 9am-6pm Jun-Aug, 10am-5pm May & Sep, to 4pm Oct-May; 🚌 91) This museum is dedicated to one of the most enduring symbols of early polar exploration, the 39m schooner *Fram* (meaning 'Forward'). You can wander the decks, peek inside the cramped bunk rooms and imagine life at sea and among the polar ice. There are detailed exhibits complete with maps, pictures and artefacts of various expeditions, from Nansen's attempt to ski across the North Pole to Amundsen's discovery of the Northwest Passage.

Launched in 1892, the polar ship *Fram*, at the time the strongest ship ever built, spent much of its life trapped in the polar ice. From 1893 to 1896 Fridtjof Nansen's North Pole expedition took the schooner to Russia's New Siberian Islands, passing within a few degrees of the North Pole on their return trip to Norway.

In 1910 Roald Amundsen set sail in the *Fram*, intending to be the first explorer to reach the North Pole, only to discover en route that Robert Peary had beaten him to it. Not to be outdone, Amundsen turned the *Fram* around and, racing Robert Falcon Scott all the way, became the first man to reach the South Pole. Otto Sverdrup also sailed the schooner around southern Greenland to Canada's Ellesmere Island between 1898 and 1902, travelling over 18,000km.

In addition to the *Fram*, the museum also houses the *Gjøa*, the first ship to successfully navigate the Northwest Passage.

Kon-Tiki Museum   MUSEUM

(Map p56; 🕿 23 08 67 67; www.kon-tiki.no; Bygdøynesveien 36; adult/child 100/40kr, with Oslo Pass free; ☉ 9.30am-6pm Jun-Aug, 10am-5pm Mar-May, Sep & Oct, 10am-4pm Nov-Feb; 🚌 91) A favourite among children, this worthwhile museum is dedicated to the balsa raft *Kon-Tiki*, which Norwegian explorer Thor Heyerdahl sailed from Peru to Polynesia in 1947. The museum also displays the totora-reed boat *Ra II*, built by Aymara people on the Bolivian island of Suriqui in Lake Titicaca. Heyerdahl used it to cross the Atlantic in 1970.

Norwegian Maritime Museum   MUSEUM

(Map p56; www.marmuseum.no; Bygdøynesveien 37; adult/child 100/30kr, with Oslo Pass free; ☉ 10am-5pm mid-May–Aug, to 4pm rest of year; 🚌 91) Author Roald Dahl once said that in Norway everyone seems to have a boat, and the theory seems like quite a good one at the Norsk Maritime Museum. The museum depicts Norway's relationship with the sea, including the fishing and whaling industries, the seismic fleet (which searches for oil and gas), shipbuilding, wreck salvaging and pleasure craft.

Norsk Folkemuseum   MUSEUM

(Norwegian Folk Museum; Map p56; 🕿 22 12 37 00; www.norskfolkemuseum.no; Museumsveien 10; adult/child 130/40kr, with Oslo Pass free; ☉ 10am-6pm mid-May–mid-Sep, 11am-3pm Mon-Fri, 11am-4pm Sat & Sun mid-Sep–mid-May; 🚌 91) This folk museum is Norway's largest open-air museum and one of Oslo's most popular attractions. The museum includes more than 140 buildings, mostly from the 17th and 18th centuries, gathered from around the country, rebuilt and organised according to region of origin. Paths wind past old barns, elevated *stabbur* (raised storehouses) and rough-timbered farmhouses with sod roofs sprouting wildflowers. Little people will be entertained by the numerous farm animals, horse and cart rides, and other activities.

◉ Frogner & Western Oslo

Oslo Contemporary   GALLERY
(Map p56; ☑23 27 06 76; www.oslcontemporary.com; Haxthausens gate 3; ☉noon-5pm Tue-Fri, to 4pm Sat; ⬚Niels Juels gate) The westside's best commercial gallery. Set in a former garage, it represents an interesting line-up of emerging and established conceptual artists, mostly from Norway.

Nasjonalbiblioteket   LIBRARY
(National Library; Map p56; ☑23 27 60 11; www.nb.no; Henrik Ibsens gate 110; ☉9am-6pm Jun-Sep, 8.30am-3.30pm Mon-Fri Oct-May; ⬚Solli) **FREE** A thoroughly modern library where you can view important documents of Norway's cultural heritage, from 13th-century manuscripts to magazines, films and Norwegian musical scores. There are also temporary exhibitions highlighting various aspects of the collection.

◉ Grünerløkka & Vulkan

★Rod Bianco   GALLERY
(Map p60; ☑997 87 475; http://rodbianco.com; Waldemar Thranes gate 84c; ☉noon-5pm Tue-Fri, to 4pm Sat; ⬚30) Rod Bianco's white cube space, hidden behind an unmarked black door in a courtyard occupied by auto workshops and warehouses, has always-boundary-pushing work from both Norwegian and international contemporary artists. Oslo's own NYC-based bad boy artist Bjarne Melgaard regularly shows here.

Galleri 69   GALLERY
(Map p60; ☑22 38 00 28; http://lufthavna.no/galleri-69/; Toftes gate 69; ⬚Schous plass) Part of the Grünerløkka Lufthavn artists' studio and rehearsal space complex, this artist-run gallery has a monthly calendar of shows, with site-specific work produced exclusively for it. Check the website for opening hours.

Standard   GALLERY
(Map p60; ☑22 60 13 10; http://standardoslo.no; Waldemar Thranes gate 86; ☉noon-5pm Tue-Fri, to 4pm Sat; ⬚30) A decade-plus player in Oslo's contemporary art scene, Standard has two exhibition spaces in an industrial block. It shows a range of Norwegian and northern European artists, including current Oslo darling Matias Faldbakken.

Akerselva River   RIVER
(Map p60; ⬚54) Running from Maridalsvannet to the Oslofjord, this fast-flowing river was once the centre of Oslo's industry and then, until the late 20th century, abandoned and unloved. Today it's one of the city's favourite places to relax, an 8km swath of forested rapids, waterfalls, running tracks, picnic grounds, swimming holes and fishing spots. The falls at Beier Bridge are an inner-urban wonder.

Studio Schaeffers Gate 5   GALLERY
(Map p60; ☑452 18 078; www.schaeffersgate5.no; Schaeffers Gate 5; ☉4-7pm Thu & Fri, from 1pm Sat & Sun; ⬚Schous plass) An independent artist-run space that hosts regular shows as well as events and performances. Check the website for details of seasonal shows.

◉ Sofienberg, Grønland & Tøyen

1857   GALLERY
(Map p50; ☑22 17 60 50; http://1857.no; Tøyenbekken 12; ☉noon-5pm Wed-Fri, to 4pm Sat & Sun; ⓣGrønland) Stian Eide Kluge and Steffen Håndlykken began this artist-run space in a former timberyard in 2010 and it's one of the city's most respected and enduring. They are especially known for their collaborative curatorial efforts between young Norwegian artists and those from Europe and beyond. Openings are also some of the city's most fun.

nyMusikk   GALLERY
(Map p50; ☑21 99 68 00; http://nymusikk.no/; Platous gate 18; ☉office 10am-3pm; ⓣGrønland) Part gallery, part office, part library and part performance space, nyMusikk hosts a program of sound-focused art shows, performances and festivals. Even if there's nothing on, staff are happy for you to come in and browse the music magazines and literature and to chat about what's going on in the city.

Kampen   AREA
(Map p65; ⬚60, ⓣTøyen) This once-working-class neighbourhood retains a unique village-like atmosphere with pretty painted wooden buildings. It's a lovely place for a stroll, with a top view back down to the city from its central hill.

Grünerløkka & Vulkan

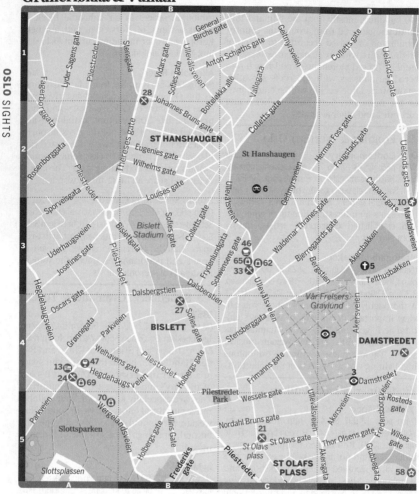

Botanical Garden   GARDENS
(Botanisk Hage; Map p65; Sars gate 1; ⏱7am-9pm mid-Mar–Sep, to 5pm rest of year; Ⓣ Tøyen) FREE Oslo's 6.5-hectare Botanical Garden – the oldest in Norway – has a beautiful arboretum, a sublime scent garden, a mini-mountain landscape and a collection of rare specimens from the Oslo fjords, including four that are almost extinct in nature. Look out also for the woven sculptures by British artist Tom Hare or just come for a walk, loll under a tree or grab a coffee from Handwerk (p77) cafe.

Natural History Museum   MUSEUM
(Naturhistorisk Museum; Map p65; www.nhm.uio.no; Sars gate 1; adult/child 50/25kr; ⏱11am-4pm Tue-Sun; Ⓣ Tøyen) Under the trees of Oslo's Botanical Garden, the university's serious-looking Natural History Museum comprises two collections: the Zoological Museum, which, as you might guess, is stuffed full of stuffed (excuse the pun) native wildlife; and the geological-palaeontological collection. The admission fee also allows you to get green-fingered with the tropical plants inside the greenhouses.

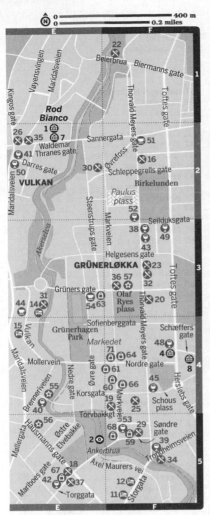

St Olafs Plass, Bislett & St Hanshaugen

St Hanshaugen Park   VIEWPOINT

(Map p60; Geitmyrsveien 31; 🚌37) This huge park is a favourite with the locals and, from its top, a very pleasant place to get a view of the city. The neighbourhood's name – a reference to 'midsummer hill' – comes from the park, not the other way around, as it was a popular spot for midsummer bonfires.

Gamle Aker Kirke   CHURCH

(Map p60; Akersbakken 26; ⊙noon-2pm Mon-Sat; 🚌37) This medieval stone church, located north of the centre on Akersbakken, dates from 1080 and is Oslo's oldest building. Take bus 37 from Jernbanetorget to Akersbakken, then walk up past the churchyard.

⊙ Greater Oslo

★**Ekebergparken**   PARK

(Ekeberg Sculpture Park; ☎21 42 19 19; https://ekebergparken.com; Kongsveien 23; ⊙24hr; 🚋Ekebergparken) **FREE** Opened to much controversy in 2013, Ekebergparken cemented Oslo's reputation as a contemporary-art capital and, in particular, one devoted to sculpture. A vast forested public park overlooking the city and the Oslofjord is dotted with work from the collection of property developer and art collector Christian Ringnes, with artists represented including Louise Bourgeois, Marina Abramović, Jenny Holzer, Tony Oursler, Sarah Lucas, Tony Cragg and Jake and Dinos Chapman, and a few traditional works from Rodin, Maillol and Vigeland.

You'll need at least half a day to explore properly, and expect your visit to unfold more as a treasure hunt than a usual museum experience. While seeking out the various installations, make sure you visit the **Ekeberg Stairs**, a historic as well as breathtaking viewpoint, and the **Munch Spot**, the view that inspired *The Scream* (as well as a 2013 Abramović work). There are children's activities held in the Swiss-chalet-style **Lund's House**, where you'll also find a museum exploring the geological and natural world of the park, as well as an art and design shop.

Holmenkollen Ski Jump   MOUNTAIN

(Map p66; ☎916 71 947; www.holmenkollen.com; adult/child 130/65kr, with Oslo Pass free; ⊙9am-8pm Jun-Aug, 10am-5pm May & Sep, 10am-4pm rest of year; 🚋Holmen) The Holmenkollen Ski Jump, perched on a hilltop overlooking Oslo, offers a panoramic view of the city and doubles as a concert venue. During Oslo's annual ski festival, held in March, it draws the world's best ski jumpers. Even if you're not a dare-devil ski jumper, the complex is well worth a visit thanks to its ski museum (p63) and a couple of other attractions.

Admission also includes entrance to the ski museum and the **ski-jump tower**. Part of the route to the top of the tower is served by a lift, but you're on your own for the final 114 steep

Grünerløkka & Vulkan

steps. To get to the museum, take T-bane line 1 to Holmenkollen and follow the signs uphill.

Nordmarka   FOREST
(Map p66; T Holmen) Oslo's beloved woodland sits to the north of the Holmenkollen Ski Jump and is a prime destination for hiking, mountain biking, sledding and skiing. In the summer, the **Tryvannstårnet observation tower** is a good place to start a hike or a bike trip; or head to the Oslo Vinterpark (p64) for skiing in winter. From the Holmenkollen

T-bane station, take the scenic ride to the end of the line at Frognerseteren and look for the signposted walking route.

It's also the geographical centre of the city, which must make Oslo, quite appropriately, about the only capital in the world to have a wild forest at its heart. Make sure you take a container for picking blueberries in summer.

Henie-Onstad Art Centre   MUSEUM
(Henie-Onstad Kunstsenter; ☑ 67 84 48 80; www. hok.no; Høvikodden; adult/child 100kr/free; ⊙ 11am-

5pm Tue-Sun; Blommenholm) This private art museum contains works by Joan Miró and Pablo Picasso, as well as assorted impressionist, abstract, expressionist and contemporary Norwegian works. It hosts big-name temporary contemporary shows too, as well as housing the largest collection of Kurt Schwitters' work outside of Germany, including much of the work he made while living in Norway during WWII. It's a 15-minute drive from the centre or you can take bus 160 to Høvikodden, from the Oslo Bus Terminal.

Emanuel Vigeland Museum   MUSEUM
(Map p66; ☑22 14 57 88; www.emanuelvigeland. museum.no; Grimelundsveien 8; adult/child 50kr/free; ☺noon-5pm Sun May-Sep, to 4pm Oct-Apr; ⓣSmestad) Emanual Vigeland, brother to the more famous Gustav, began construction on this large, vaulted space in 1926, with plans to make it a museum. The dimly lit space is today covered in a figurative work that depicts the cycle of life and the libidinous urge that is at its centre. Vigeland's work is in turns highly erotic, moving and disturbing; the 20-year fresco project was intended as his own tomb (his ashes indeed do rest here, in a characteristically symbolic egg-shaped urn).

TusenFryd   AMUSEMENT PARK
(Map p90; ☑64 97 64 97; www.tusenfryd.no; Vinterbro; adult/child/family 409/339/1799kr; ☺10.30am-7pm mid-Jun–Aug, shorter hours rest of year; ⓠ500) TusenFryd, an amusement park 10km south of the city, is enormously popular with kids from all over the Oslo region. The park offers carousels, a fantasy farm and an excellent wooden roller coaster, which creates zero gravity 12 times each circuit. You'll find it just off the E6. The TusenFryd bus (bus 546) departs from the corner of Fred Olsens gate and Prinsens gate roughly hourly between 10am and 4pm.

Ski Museum   MUSEUM
(Map p66; Kongeveien 5; incl Holmenkollen Ski Jump adult/child 130/65kr, with Oslo Pass free; ☺9am-8pm Jun-Aug, 10am-5pm May & Sep, 10am-4pm rest of year; ⓣHolmen) The Ski Museum, part of the Holmenkollen Ski Jump (p61) complex, leads you through the 4000-year history of nordic and downhill skiing in Norway. There are exhibits featuring the Antarctic expeditions of Amundsen and Scott, as well as Fridtjof Nansen's slog across the Greenland icecap (you'll see the boat he constructed from his sled and canvas tent to row the final 100km to Nuuk).

Norwegian Science & Technology Museum   MUSEUM
(Norsk Teknisk Museum & Telemuseum; Map p66; ☑22 79 60 00; www.tekniskmuseum.no; Kjelsåsveien 143; adult/child 150/100kr, with Oslo Pass free; ☺11am-6pm daily late Jun-late Aug, 9am-4pm Mon-Fri, 11am-6pm Sat & Sun rest of year; ⓠKjelsås) A popular rainy-day distraction near Lake Maridal, Norwegian Science & Technology Museum has Norway's first car and tram, water wheels, clocks and enough gadgetry to keep the whole family busy for hours.

🏃 Activities
Avid skiers, hikers and sailors, Oslo residents will do just about anything to get outside. That's not too hard given that there are over 240 sq km of woodland, 40 islands and 343 lakes within the city limits. And you can jump on a train with your skis and be on the slopes in less than 30 minutes.

Climbing
The best local climbing is on the pre-bolted faces of Kolsåstoppen, which is accessible on T-bane line 3 to Kolsås.

Vulkan Climbing Centre   CLIMBING
(Map p60; ☑22 11 28 90; www.kolsaas.no; Maridalsveien 17; adult/child from 80/65kr; ☺10am-10pm Mon-Thu, to 9pm Fri, to 8pm Sat & Sun; ⓠ54) Indoor climbing centre with challenges for all skill levels. The centre has climbing walls and bouldering walls. Open afternoons only during the week from June to August.

Cycling
Mountain bikers will find plenty of trails on which to keep themselves occupied in the Oslo hinterland. The tourist office has free cycling maps, with *Sykkelkart Oslo* tracing the bicycle lanes and paths throughout the city, and *Idrett og friluftsliv i Oslo* covering the Oslo hinterland. It also has a pamphlet called *Opplevelsesturer i Marka,* which contains six possible cycling and/or hiking itineraries within reach of Oslo.

Two especially nice rides within the city, which are also suitable to do on an Oslo City Bike (p88), are along the Akerselva up to Lake Maridal (Maridalsvannet; 11km), and in the woods around Bygdøy. The trip to Maridal passes several waterfalls and a number of converted factories at the edge of Grünerløkka and crosses several of Oslo's more unique bridges, including the Anker, or *eventyr* (fairy-tale), bridge. Cyclists should be sure to stop for coffee and a waffle at Hønse-Louisas

Hus (p75). This can also be done on foot by taking the T-bane to Kjesås and following the path back into the city. Cycling, or walking, around Bygdøy is far more pastoral and provides ample opportunity for swimming breaks. There is a bike rack in front of the Norwegian Folk Museum. For more serious cycling, take T-bane line 1 to Frognerseteren and head into the Nordmarka.

Syklistenes Landsforening CYCLING

(☑22 47 30 30; www.slf.no; Østensjøveien 29; ☺10am-5pm Mon-Fri; ⓉBrynseng) The main contact point for Norway's cycling clubs is useful for information on long-distance cycling routes and tunnels. It also sells *Sykkelruter i Norge* (120kr); it's only available in Norwegian, but the English-text Sykkelguide series of booklets with maps are available for 125kr each and include Lofoten, Rallarvegen, the North Sea Cycleway from the Swedish border at Svinesund to Bergen, and other routes.

Hiking

A network of 1200km of trails leads into Nordmarka from Frognerseteren (at the end of T-bane line 1), including a good trail down to Sognsvann lake, 6km northwest of the centre at the end of T-bane line 5. If you're walking in August, be sure to take a container for blueberries, and a swimsuit to cool off in the lake (bathing is allowed in all the woodland lakes around Oslo except Maridalsvannet and Skjersjøen lakes, which are drinking reservoirs). The pleasant walk around Sognsvann itself takes around an hour, or for a more extended trip, try hiking to the cabin at Ullevålseter (p78), a pleasant old farmhouse that serves waffles and coffee. The return trip (about 11km) takes around three hours.

The Ekeberg woods to the southeast of the city centre is another nice place for a stroll. During summer weekends it's a popular spot for riding competitions and cricket matches, and there's an Iron Age heritage path through the woods. To get to the woods, take bus 34 or 46 from Jernbanetorget to Ekeberg Camping (p69). For a piece of architectural history, don't miss the Ekeberg Restaurant (p77), one of the earliest examples of functionalism. On the way down, stop at the Valhall Curve to see the view that inspired Edvard Munch to paint *The Scream*.

The DNT office (p86), which maintains several mountain huts in the Nordmarka region, can provide information and maps covering longer-distance hiking routes throughout Norway.

Oslo Promenade WALKING

(Map p50; ☑22 42 70 20; www.guideservice.no; adult/child 200kr/free, with Oslo Pass free; ☺end May-Sep; ⓇRådhusplassen) Oslo Guide Service conducts a 1½-hour evening city walk starting from in front of the Rådhus (town hall) at 5.30pm; no booking required. The guides are knowledgeable and entertaining, making this a good option for getting an insider's view of Oslo. They also offer personalised city tours for groups of 10 or more, which have to be booked in advance.

Ice Skating

There are several ice-skating rinks in and around the city, including the outdoor winter-only one at **Frogner** (Map p56; ☑910 05 955; www.frognerstadion.no; Middelthunsgate 26; adult/child 40/15kr; ☺11am-10pm Mon-Thu, to 9pm Fri, to 6pm Sat & Sun Dec-Mar; ⓉBorgen).

Spikersuppa Outdoor Ice Rink ICE SKATING

(Map p50; Karl Johans gate; ⓇØvre Slottsgate) **FREE** The most central, and romantic, ice skating in Oslo can be found at the Spikersuppa outdoor ice rink, where you can skate for free whenever it's cold enough to freeze over (around November to March). The rink often closes at around 3pm to allow for ice preparation. Skates can be hired from the ice rink for 100kr.

Skiing

Oslo's ski season runs roughly from December to March. There are over 2400km of prepared nordic tracks (1000km in Nordmarka alone), many of them floodlit, as well as a ski resort within the city limits. Easy-access tracks begin at the end of T-bane lines 1 and 5. The **Skiservice Centre** (Map p66; ☑22 13 95 00; www.skiservice.no; Tryvannsveien 2; ☺10am-8pm; ⓉHolmen), at Voksenkollen station, one T-bane stop before Frognerseteren, hires out snowboards and nordic skis. The downhill slopes at **Oslo Vinterpark** (Map p66; ☑404 62 700; www.oslovinterpark.no; ☺10am-10pm Mon-Fri, to 5pm Sat & Sun Dec–mid-Apr; ⓉHolmen) are open in the ski season. Check out www.holmenkollen.com for more ski-related info.

Holmenkollen Ski Jump Simulator SKIING

(Map p66; ☑900 12 046; www.skisimulator.no; adult/child 95/55kr; ☺9am-8pm Jun-Aug, 10am-5pm May & Sep, 10am-4pm rest of year; ⓉHolmen) With its use of aeronautical flight simulator technology, you can hurtle down 130km of slopes. It's a fast and furious, if totally safe, experience and perhaps best avoided if you have a weak stomach.

Korketrekkeren   SNOW SPORTS
(Map p66; www.akeforeningen.no; Holmenkollen; adult/child hire per day 150/80kr; ⊙9am-9pm Mon-Sat, 10am-6pm Sun winter; ⓣ Holmen) In the winter, try sledding down the 'legendary' Korketrekkeren (corkscrew) toboggan run. The 2km-long track drops 255m and began its life as a bobsledding run for the 1952 Olympics. Sleds can be rented at the Akerforeningen, next to the Frognerseteren restaurant. To get here, take the T-bane to Frognerseteren and follow the signs downhill.

Swimming
Oslo has two rather charming outdoor municipal swimming pools, the **Tøyenbadet** (Map p65; ✆23 30 44 70; Helgesens gata 90; adult/child 98/48kr; ⊙9am-7pm; ⓣ Tøyen) and the **Frognerbadet** (Map p56; ✆23 27 54 50; Middelthuns gate 28; adult/child 98/48kr; ⊙7am-7.30pm Mon-Thu, to 8pm Fri-Sun Jun–mid-Aug; ⓣ Borgen) in the Frognerparken. There are also several fjord and river swimming spots, including spots up along the Akerselva past the art school, and the **Sørenga Seapool** (Map p50; Sørengkaia 69; ⌂ Bjørvika) FREE on the Bjørvika inlet.

Islands & Beaches
When (or perhaps, if) the weather heats up, there are a few reasonable beaches within striking distance of central Oslo. Ferries to half a dozen islands in the Oslofjord region leave from Vippetangen Quay (p87), southeast of Akershus Fortress. Boats to Hovedøya and Langøyene are relatively frequent in summer (running at least hourly), while other islands are served less often. The last ferry leaves Vippetangen at 6.45pm in winter and 9.05pm in summer.

The southwestern shore of otherwise rocky Hovedøya, the nearest island to the mainland, is popular with sunbathers. The island is ringed with walking paths to old cannon emplacements and the 12th-century **Cistercian monastery ruins**.

South of Hovedøya lies the undeveloped island of **Langøyene**, which has superb swimming from rocky or sandy beaches (one on the southeastern shore is designated for nude bathing). Boat 94 will get you there, but it only runs during the summer.

The Bygdøy Peninsula has two popular beaches, **Huk** and **Paradisbukta**, which can be reached on bus 30 from Jernbanetorget

Eastern Oslo

Eastern Oslo

⊙ Sights
1 Botanical Garden.............................. A1
2 Kampen... B2
3 Natural History Museum................... A1

⊙ Activities, Courses & Tours
4 Tøyenbadet Swimming Pool............. A1

⊗ Eating
5 Brutus... A2
6 Gràdi... A2
7 Handwerk... A1
8 Smia Galleri..................................... B3

to its last stop. While there are some sandy patches, most of Huk comprises grassy lawns and large smooth rocks ideal for sunbathing. Separated into two beaches by a small cove, the beach on the northwestern side is open to nude bathing. If Huk seems too crowded, a 10-minute walk through the woods north of the bus stop leads to the more secluded Paradisbukta.

Finally, just in front of the Astrup Fearnley Museum and bang in the heart of Oslo, there's a tiny, **man-made pebble beach** with very safe swimming that's popular with local families.

North of Oslo

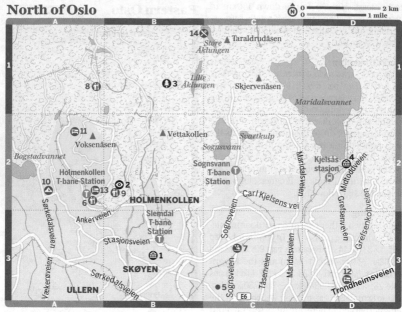

OSLO TOURS

North of Oslo

The waters around Oslo *can* get surprisingly warm – up to 22°C isn't unusual. So pack your swimming costume!

Tjuvholmen City Beach　　　　BEACH
(Map p56; Tjuvholmen; 🚇 Aker brygge) Backed by a sprawling, lush and sculpture-dotted lawn, this tiny beach is often crowded with little Osloites splashing like there's no tomorrow, but it's still a delight.

☞ Tours

Oslo has the usual range of guided tours that can offer greater cultural and historical insight into what is an easy-to-explore and super-well-organised destination, but one

with a back story that's not as well known as major world capitals. Along with these there are boat trips that include various sights along the waterfront and on the Bygdøy Peninsula as well as specialist tours for those interested in architecture, Norwegian crime fiction or the work of Henrik Ibsen or Edvard Munch. The Oslo Visitor Centre (p86) has details of them all, both online and in the office.

Oslo Opera House
English Guided Tours　　　　TOUR
(Map p50; ☎ 21 42 21 21; Kirsten Flagstads plass 1; adult/child 100/60kr; ⊙ 11am, noon & 1pm daily Jul-early Aug, 11am, noon & 1pm Mon-Fri, noon & 1pm Sat, 1pm Sun early Aug-31 Aug, 1pm Sun-Fri,

noon Sat rest of year; Ⓣ Jernbanetorget) In both English and Norwegian, these tours take you into some of the building's 1100 rooms. The guide will explain much of the spacial symbolism of the building, and reveal something of life behind the scenes at the Opera House. In high season it's a good idea to book in advance.

Viking Biking   CYCLING
(Map p50; ✆ 412 66 496; www.vikingbikingos lo.com; Nedre Slottsgate 4; 3hr tour adult/child 350/200kr; ⊕ 9.30am-6pm; 🚲 Øvre Slottsgate) This excellent outfit is a great place to head if you want to explore Oslo on two wheels. It runs a range of guided bike tours, including a three-hour 'City Highlights' route through some of Oslo's parks and backstreets, plus a 'River Tour' along the path beside the Akerselva River, both designed to avoid traffic wherever possible.

Båtservice Sightseeing   BOATING
(Map p50; ✆ 23 35 68 90; www.boatsightseeing. com; Pier 3, Rådhusbrygge; per person 215-650kr; 🚲 Aker brygge) For a watery view of Oslo and the Oslofjord, Båtservice Sightseeing offers a whole array of tours aboard either a traditional wooden schooner or a more up-to-date motorboat. There's a hop-on, hop-off service from May to September (24-hour ticket 215kr).

Norway in a Nutshell   TOURS
(Fjord Tours; ✆ 81 56 82 22; www.norwaynutshell. com) For maximum sights in minimal time. From Oslo, the typical route includes a train across Hardangervidda to Myrdal, descent along the dramatic Flåmbanen, cruise along Nærøyfjorden to Gudvangen, bus to Voss, connecting train to Bergen for a short visit, then an overnight return rail trip to Oslo (including a sleeper compartment); the return tour costs 2790kr.

You can also do one-way tours to Bergen (1890kr). Book at tourist offices or train stations.

✴ Festivals & Events

Holmenkollen Ski Festival   SPORTS
(✆ 22 92 32 00; http://skifest.no/; Kongeveien 5; ⊕ early Mar) One of the world's most revered ski festivals. Its penultimate day is so loved by locals it's dubbed 'second National Day'.

Inferno Metal Festival   MUSIC
(www.infernofestival.net; ⊕ Easter) This festival, held over Easter, lets the dark lords of heavy metal loose on the good people of Oslo.

OverOslo   MUSIC
(www.overoslo.no; Grefsenkollveien 100; ⊕ Jun) A three-day event with a broad range of acts set in a stunning natural amphitheatre with views all the way down to the Oslofjord.

Norwegian Wood Festival   MUSIC
(www.norwegianwood.no; ⊕ Jun) Oslo plays host to dozens of music festivals, but this is one of the most highly regarded and always includes a good selection of Norwegian acts as well as international headliners.

Øya Festival   MUSIC
(www.oyafestivalen.com; Tøyenparken; day passes 950kr; ⊕ early Aug; Ⓣ Tøyen) 🏖 Øya Festival, the largest rock and indie music festival in Norway, is a green example. The four festival stages are powered through renewable energy, all rubbish is recycled, and – maybe most impressively – the sewage generated by the 16,000 festival-goers is converted into bio-fuel to fuel the buses taking people between central Oslo and the festival grounds.

The Øya Festival attracts some of the biggest names in the rock and indie scene, with performers at the 2017 festival including the Pixies, Lana del Ray, Feist, Mac de Marco, Roy Ayers and Young MA, as well as many others. In addition, there are all the normal festival sideshows.

Oslo International Jazz Festival   MUSIC
(www.oslojazz.no; ⊕ mid-Aug) Jazz and Oslo's long summer evenings go well together, and the festival brings big names to venues across the city.

Oslo Opera Festival   PERFORMING ARTS
(www.operafestival.no; ⊕ Sep/Oct) Live opera fills the concert halls – and the streets – of Oslo.

🛏 Sleeping

Oslo has plenty of accommodation, including a growing number of small B&Bs and private rentals that offer more character than the chain hotels. Hotels are usually well run and comfortable, but tend towards the bland, and – yes, you guessed it – you'll pay a lot more for what you get compared with other countries. Most hotels have wi-fi access.

🛏 Central Oslo

★ Saga Poshtel Oslo   HOSTEL $$
(Map p50; ✆ 23 10 08 00; www.sagahoteloslocentral. no; Kongens gate 7; dm/d 520/1100; 🖥; 🚲 Øvre Slottsgate) A crossover hostel-hotel (posh-tel, if you didn't already get it), smartly designed

OSLO SLEEPING

and very central, with a big social lounge with decent wi-fi. Rooms are basic but spotless; there are lots of doubles, plus four- and six-bunk-bed dorms, all with en suites.

Citybox Oslo
HOTEL $$

(Map p50; ☑21 42 04 80; www.citybox.no/oslo; Prinsens gate 6; s/d 920/1045kr; ☞; ☒Dronningens Gate) This functional city chain comes to Oslo with its trademark brand of no-frills, bare-bones rooms at bargain prices (well, at least for Norway). But don't expect prison-block chic – it's surprisingly smart, with plain all-white rooms, Scandi-style furniture, free wi-fi and an on-site cafe, as well as a great downtown location. Plush: no; practical: very.

Hotel Folketeateret
HOTEL $$

(Map p50; ☑22 00 57 00; www.choiceno; Storgata 21-23; s/d half-board 2200/2400kr; ☞; ☒Kirkeristen) The rooms here are smart, large and decorated in a fabulously idiosyncratic style with more character than most Oslo hotels. It's located within the always buzzing theatre complex with Youngstorget at the other side. Comfortable public spaces, from a lounge to a dining room where a complimentary dinner is served each night, give it a friendly vibe.

Smarthotel Oslo
HOTEL $$

(Map p50; ☑415 36 500; www.smarthotel.no; St Olavs gate 26; s/d 835/935kr; ☞; ☒Tullinløkka) If you're after a no-fuss city-centre crash-pad, this efficient business hotel is a decent bet. It's just around the corner from the Slottsparken, albeit on quite a busy road, and offers pod-like rooms with minimal creature comforts. There's also a cafe downstairs.

Thon Hotel Astoria
HOTEL $$

(Map p50; ☑24 14 55 50; www.thonhotels.com; Dronningens gate 21; s/d 695/920kr; ☞; ☒Kirkeristen) This might be marketed as a Thon 'budget' hotel, but if it weren't for the small bathroom and the lack of a minibar, there would be nothing to distinguish its smart rooms from more-expensive options. It's well positioned close to the train station, but the only nearby parking is on the street.

Do note that single rooms can be very small indeed.

P-Hotel
HOTEL $$

(Map p50; ☑23 31 80 00; www.p-hotels.com; Grensen 19; s/d 799/1149kr; ☞; ☒Stortorvet) Traditional in style, with wooden furniture, carpets and floral curtains, this is a reliable, if not particularly glamorous, central choice. Breakfast in a bag is delivered to your door each morning.

★ The Thief
BOUTIQUE HOTEL $$$

(Map p56; ☑24 00 40 00; www.thethief.com; Landgangen 1; d 2900-4000kr; ☞☒; ☒Aker brygge) Overlooking the Astrup Fearnley Museum, Oslo's best design hotel is more dark glamour than Scandinavian sparse, though is packed with playful touches from beautiful artisan objects to video art. Views from many of the rooms, and the rooftop bar, are stunning.

Hotell Bondeheimen
HOTEL $$$

(Map p50; ☑23 21 41 00; www.bondeheimen.com; Rosenkrantz gate 8; s/d 950/2500kr; ☞; ☒Tinghuset) ✐ This century-old hotel, which has spacious, colourful rooms with smart, simple furnishings, started life as a boarding house for rural folk coming down to the big city and was owned by an organisation promoting Norwegian culture. The rooms have some lovely original architecture and an attention to detail that comes from a long history of hospitality.

Hotel Grand Central
HOTEL $$$

(Map p50; ☑22 98 28 00; www.choice.no; Jernanetorget 1; d 1350-2200kr; ☞; ☒Jernbanetorget) A no-fuss hotel that's within the beautiful old bones of the train station and sits above its modern food hall Østbanehallen. Sparse but comfortable design-forward rooms vary wildly between those with original-height ceilings and mansards that can feel a little pokey, but staff are delightful and it's perfectly positioned for easy train and airport access.

Grand Hotel
HISTORIC HOTEL $$$

(Map p50; ☑23 21 20 00; www.grand.no; Karl Johans gate 31; d 1890-2800kr; ℗☞☒; ⓣStortinget) While the lobby and downstairs restaurant brim with period character, the Grand's rooms are pared back, with a soothing simple elegance. Luxury touches include beautifully upholstered headboards and sofas, and beds strewn with cushions and throws and a choice between floorboards and carpeting. The suites are individually decorated, from a pretty pink one to a more formal beige and navy.

Despite its venerable status, it's contemporary in outlook and a good deal if you book ahead and/or out of season.

⌨ Frogner & Western Oslo

Cochs Pensjonat
PENSION $

(Map p60; ☑23 33 24 00; www.cochspensjonat.no; Parkveien 25; s/d with kitchenette from 710/940kr, without bathroom 540/750kr; ☞; ☒17B) Opened as a guesthouse for bachelors in the 1920s, this lovely old yellow-brick hotel offers simply furnished rooms, some with kitchenettes and all with floorboards and big windows. It's ideally located behind the Royal Palace, although it's on a busy intersection, so expect some noise. The rear rooms overlooking the Slottsparken are especially spacious; budget rooms share corridor bathrooms.

★ **Saga Hotel Oslo** BOUTIQUE HOTEL **$$**

(Map p56; ☑ 22 55 44 90; www.sagahoteloslo.no; Eilert Sundts gate 39; s/d from 995/1395kr; �; ⋒ Rosenborg) In a quiet, leafy street right behind the Royal Palace, this smart 46-room hotel occupies a grand corner building from the 1890s. Rooms and public spaces make the most of the elegant 19th-century bones with a restrained modern fit-out and lots of smart monochromes. There's a highly regarded sushi restaurant, Fangst, in the basement too.

★ **Ellingsens Pensjonat** PENSION **$$**

(Map p56; ☑ 22 60 03 59; www.ellingsenspensjonat. no; Holtegata 25; s/d 700/1050kr, without bathroom 590/800kr, apt s/d 850/1300kr; �; ⋒ Rosenborg) Located in a quiet, pleasant neighbourhood, this warm B&B offers one of the best deals in the capital. The building dates from 1890 and many of the original features (high ceilings, rose designs) remain. Rooms are bright, airy and smartly decorated, with fridges and kettles, and there's a small garden to lounge about in on sunny days.

It's very popular, so book ahead.

⌕ Grünerløkka & Vulkan

Anker Hostel HOSTEL **$**

(Map p60; ☑ 22 99 72 00; www.ankerhostel.no; Storgata 55; dm 260-300kr, s/d 620/900kr; �; ⋒ 54) This huge traveller-savvy hostel boasts an international atmosphere, sterile but neat rooms, a laundry, a luggage room, kitchens and a small bar. Breakfast isn't included, linen is 70kr extra and parking 230kr per 24 hours. The location isn't very scenic, but it's very convenient, with Grünerløkka and the city centre only a five-minute walk either way.

PS: Hotell DESIGN HOTEL **$$**

(Map p60; ☑ 23 15 65 00; www.pshotell.no; Maridalsveien 13c; s/d/ste 975/1390/1500kr; �; ⋒ 54) Taking inspiration from Vulkan's former industrial role, there are cool, grey-toned rooms that are small but well designed, with large windows. There are single and family rooms with bunk beds, and top-floor one-bedroom suites with dining tables and sofas.

Anker Hotel HOTEL **$$**

(Map p60; ☑ 22 99 75 00; www.anker-hotel.no; Storgata 55; s/d 1200/1350kr; �; ⋒ Hausmanns gate) A budget business-style hotel with simple rooms, many with floorboards and views. A huge breakfast spread is included and the downstairs lobby bar has a nice atmosphere.

★ **Scandic Vulkan** HOTEL **$$$**

(Map p60; ☑ 21 05 71 00; www.scandichotels.com; Maridalsveien 13; d 1395-1700kr; ⋒ 54) Floorboards and rough-hewn bedheads give this contemporary chain hotel a warmth and tactility that you might not expect from the exterior architecture; some rooms even come with quirks like a vintage vinyl collection tacked to the wall. The lobby is lots of fun and you're right by Mathallen for all-day drinking and eating too.

⌕ Greater Oslo

Ekeberg Camping CAMPGROUND **$**

(☑ 22 19 85 68; www.ekebergcamping.no; Ekebergveien 65; 2-/4-person tent 220/330kr; ☺ Jun-Aug; P; ⋒ Ekebergparken) Nestled on a scenic knoll southeast of the city, Ekeberg Camping provides one of the best vistas over Oslo. It can get seriously crowded, and if you're travelling with children note that it's on quite a steep slope. But oh what a view. Take bus 34 or 46 from Jernbanetorget to Ekeberg Camping (10 minutes).

Bogstad Camping CAMPGROUND **$**

(Map p66; ☑ 22 51 08 00; www.bogstadcamping.no; Ankerveien 117; tent with/without car from 330/240kr, cabins 590-1400kr; ☺ year-round; P; ⋒ 32) Located at the edge of the Nordmarka, sprawling Bogstad Camping is an ideal base for enjoying Oslo outdoors. The facilities include showers and communal kitchen, and there is a nearby kiosk and restaurant. It's 9km north of the city centre. To get here, take bus 32 from Oslo S (about 30 minutes).

If you don't have a tent or camper, there are cabins as well as furnished glamping-style tents.

Oslo Vandrerhjem Haraldsheim HOSTEL **$**

(Map p66; ☑ 22 22 29 65; www.haraldsheim.no; Haraldsheimveien 4; incl breakfast dm with/without bathroom 350/290kr, d with/without bathroom 660/560kr; @�; ⋒ Sinsenkrysset) A pleasant, if hard to find, hostel 4km from the city centre. It has 24-hour reception and 268 beds, in clean four-bed dorms or private rooms (some of the ones in the new building have balconies). There are kitchen and laundry facilities. Linen costs 50kr. Take tram 12, 15 or 17, or bus 31 or 32 to Sinsenkrysset, then walk five minutes uphill.

Scanic Holmenkollen Park
HISTORIC HOTEL $$

(Map p66; ☑22 92 20 00; www.holmenkollenpark hotel.no; Kongeveien 26; s/d 1400/1650; [P][⊡][≋]; [T]Holmen) Founded in 1891 as a sanatorium by Dr Ingebrigt Christian Lund, this fairy-tale-feeling hotel offers luxury, history and great views. If that weren't enough, you also get a vast breakfast buffet, complete with organic produce.

Lysebu Hotel
RESORT $$$

(Map p66; ☑21 51 10 00; www.lysebu.no; Lysebu-veien 12; s/d 1900/2300kr; [P][⊡][≋]; [T]Voksenkol-len) A gorgeous Norwegian-folk-style building from 1916 with easy access to the wilds of Nordmarka. Rooms are decorated in a clean, classical style that's comfortable but far from twee, with spectacular views. Facilities are super and the hotel also has a very interesting collection of mid-century Norwegian and Danish abstract painting, on permanent loan from the Henie-Onstad Art Centre (p62).

✕ Eating

Oslo's food scene has come into its own in recent years, attracting curious culinary-minded travellers who've eaten their way round Copenhagen or Stockholm and are looking for new sensations. Dining out here can involve a Michelin-starred restaurant, a hot-dog stand, peel-and-eat shrimp, innovative New Nordic small plates or a convincingly authentic Japanese, Italian, French, Indian or Mexican dish.

✕ Central Oslo

Illegal Burgers
BURGERS $

(Map p50; ☑22 20 33 02; Møllergata 23; burgers 96-142kr; ◷2-11pm Mon-Thu, to 1am Fri & Sat; ⬚37) Well-priced burgers with large char-grilled patties, interesting gourmet variations and chunky fries.

Sentralen Cafeteria
CAFE, PIZZA $

(Map p50; ☑22 33 33 22; Akersgata 2; meals 90-160kr; ◷7.30am-midnight Mon-Fri, from 10am Sat, 11am-5pm Sun; ⬚Øvre Slottsgate) At the heart of the Sentralen complex, this day-to-evening place really is a cafeteria for the area's many freelancers and creative industry workers. Join them for a morning coffee and pastry or sandwich (both care of the Handwerk bakery), eat in or take away healthy lunch dishes

or stay for wood-fired sourdough pizza and beer from 4pm on weekdays or from noon on weekends.

Kaffebrenneriet
CAFE $

(Map p50; www.kaffebrenneriet.no; Universtets-gata 1; snacks 35-105kr; ◷7am-7pm Mon-Fri, 9am-6pm Sat & Sun; ⬚Tullinløkka) Opposite the National Gallery, this relaxed branch of one of Norway's best cafe chains has good espresso and filter coffee, packets of coffee to take away, pastries and a good selection of filled rolls.

★ Sentralen Restaurant
NEW NORDIC $$

(Map p50; ☑22 33 33 22; www.sentralen.no; Øvre Slottsgate 3; small plates 85-195kr; ◷11am-10pm Mon-Sat; ⬚Øvre Slottsgate) One of Oslo's best dining experiences is also its most relaxed. A large dining room with a bustling open kitchen, filled with old social club chairs and painted in tones of deep, earthy green, draws city workers, visitors and natural-wine-obsessed locals in equal measure. Small-plate dining makes it easy to sample across the appealing New Nordic menu.

Dishes are mostly riffs on Norwegian standards, and use Norwegian products, but also work in international influences in subtle and surprising ways. Combinations may be bold but there's a lightness and prettiness to it all. The wine list is one of the city's most interesting and the friendly, knowledgeable staff are happy to walk you through it.

★ Grand Café
NORWEGIAN $$

(Map p50; ☑23 21 20 18; www.grand.no; Karl Johans gate 31; mains 145-295kr; ◷11am-11pm Mon-Fri, from noon Sat, noon-9pm Sun; ⬚Stortinget) At 11am sharp, Henrik Ibsen would leave his apartment and walk to Grand Café for a lunch of herring, beer and one shot of aquavit (an alcoholic drink made from potatoes and caraway liquor). His table is still here. Don't worry, though, today you can take your pick from perfectly plated, elegantly sauced cod and mussels, spelt risotto with mushrooms or cured lamb and potato.

★ Vingen
NEW NORDIC $$

(Map p56; ☑901 51 595; http://vingenbar.no; Strandpromenaden 2; mains 145-240kr; ◷10am-9pm Sun-Wed, to midnight Thu-Sat; ⬚Aker brygge) While honouring its role as museum cafe for Astrup Fearnley (p49) and a super-scenic pit stop, Vingen is so much more. Do drop in for excellent coffee, but also come for lunch or dinner with small, interesting menus subtly themed in homage to the museum's current temporary show. Nightfall brings cocktails, and sometimes DJs and dancing in the museum lobby and, in summer, on the waterfront terrace.

Justisen
NORWEGIAN, BURGERS $$

(Map p50; ☑ 22 42 24 72; www.justisen.no; Møllergata 15; mains 135-240kr; ဩ Brugata) A pubby people-pleaser, this incredibly charming and atmospheric place dates back to 1820. There's a large Norwegian menu to try, but you can't beat the happy-hour burger and drink deal for 255kr, especially if enjoyed in the all-weather beer garden.

Fiskeriet
SEAFOOD $$

(Map p50; ☑ 22 42 45 40; http://fiskeriet.com; Youngstorget 2; mains 165-249kr; ⊙ 11am-9pm Mon-Fri, from noon Sat, noon-8pm Sun, shop 10am-6pm Mon-Sat; ဩ Brugata) You'd be forgiven for thinking that you're actually dining in a fish shop, as this seafood-serving powerhouse is also one of Oslo's best places to pick up market-fresh produce. And, yes, it makes for a fun and atmospheric lunch or dinner. The menu is delightfully predictable with fish and chips, traditional fish soup, Mediterranean-style *baccala* (salt cod), seafood casserole and fish cakes.

It does well-priced takeaway too.

Miss Sophie
EUROPEAN $$

(Map p50; ☑ 21 09 78 79; www.misssophierestau rant.no; Henrik Ibsens gate 4; mains 175-275kr, brunch dishes 65-175kr; ⊙ 5pm-1am Tue-Fri, noon-2am Sat, to 6pm Sun; ဩ Slottsparken) A pretty corner shop opposite the park does all-day dining in glamorous surrounds. There are simple, if rather luxurious, pan-European standards such as steak frites, rösti done with sweet potato, or pasta with truffles on offer, although the super-popular weekend brunch is less so, with omelettes vying for attention with more Instagram-friendly dishes such as chia pudding, pancakes, banana bread and eggs Benedict.

Grosch
INTERNATIONAL $$

(Map p50; ☑ 22 42 12 12; www.groschbistro.no; Bankplassen 3; lunch dishes 95-165kr; ⊙ 11am-5pm Mon-Wed & Fri, to 7pm Thu, noon-5pm Sat & Sun; ဩ Øvre Slottsgate) Located in the pretty surrounds of the Nasjonalmuseet's Arkitektur building, this museum cafe serves up burgers, tapas, soups, sandwiches and sweet things. Count on Scandinavian designer chairs too.

OSLO EATING

ON TREND

Oslo locals have adventurous palates and an increasingly global food scene. What's hot right now?

New Nordic Traditional dishes are done with a twist: heritage ingredients (chicken hearts, cod tongue, blood sausage, slow-cooked beets, fresh cheese, rhubarb, barley) feature heavily. Not exclusively Norwegian, so often incorporate Icelandic, Danish or other culinary elements.

Pizza Norway is known for its love of frozen pizza, though in Oslo expect proper Neapolitan or thin-crust pizza made with top-quality ingredients.

Omakase With some of the freshest fish in the world, sushi is big in Oslo; this is how cashed-up locals like to do it – chef's menu style.

Natural Wine Oslo's sommeliers are some of the most dedicated to the minimal intervention, small producers from France, Italy, Austria and Germany.

Pipervika
SEAFOOD $$

(Map p50; www.pipervika.no; Rådhusbrygge 4; mains 175-250kr, shrimp per kg 130kr; ⊙ 7am-11pm; ဩ Aker brygge) If the weather is nice, nothing beats a shrimp lunch, with fresh shrimp on a baguette with mayonnaise and a spritz of lemon eaten dockside. The revamped fisherman's co-op still does takeaway peel-and-eat shrimp by the kilo, but you can now also relax with a sushi plate, oysters or a full seafood menu including fish burger on brioche or killer fish and chips.

Everything is prepared with daily bounty from the Oslofjord.

Delicatessen
TAPAS $$

(Map p50; http://delicatessen.no; Holmens gate 2; tapas 68-149kr; ⊙ 11am-midnight Sun-Wed, to 1am Thu-Sat; ဩ Aker brygge) This Grünerløkka favourite brings some welcome east-side cool to an industrial space in Akker Brygge, not to mention some of the city's best tapas. The large tapas menu takes in small dishes like saffron and chorizo croquettes and meatballs, plates of well-sourced Spanish *jamon* (ham) and artisan *manchego* (Spanish cheese), and larger plates of grilled octopus or chicken.

There's a pared-down menu and toasted sandwiches at lunch.

Ling Ling CANTONESE $$
(Map p50; ☑ 24 13 38 00; http://lingling.hakkasan. com; Stranden 30; mains 155-385kr; ⊘ 5-10pm Sun-Thu, to 11pm Fri & Sat; ☒ Aker brygge) Aker Brygge's culinary reputation has had a boost with the opening of this contemporary Asian restaurant and bar. Drawing inspiration from the Japanese *izakaya* food-pub concept, but serving Cantonese sharing plates, the dishes here are meant to be convivial and encourage sampling from the cocktail menu or beer or wine list.

King crab dumplings, reindeer puffs and scallop with glass vermicelli noodles all use locally sourced produce too.

Bun's Burger Bar BURGERS $$
(Map p50; http://bunsburger.no; Sørengkaia 71; burgers 140-180kr; ⊘ 11am-10pm Mon-Fri, from noon Sat & Sun; ☒ Bjørvika) Huge classic burgers compete with tuna steak and vegetarian options here and you can really go to town with the cheese-loaded or truffled fries. Great views and, if you're a fjord dipper, easy access to the beach.

Elias Mat & Sånt BISTRO $$
(Map p50; ☑ 22 20 22 21; www.cafeelias.no; Kristian Augusts gate 14; lunch mains 109-179kr, dinner mains 184-269kr; ⊘ 5-11pm Sun & Mon, from 11am Tue-Sat; ☒ Tullinløkka) A good bet for simple dishes in the city centre, and dead handy after a jaunt around the National Gallery. Tempting traditional options include pollack fish fillet with baby potatoes, or rich reindeer stew with a brown cheese sauce and mashed potatoes, served in a cosy little space. Lunch dishes such as fish soup or mussels are good value.

Maaemo NEW NORDIC $$$
(Map p50; ☑ 22 17 99 69; https://maaemo.no; Schweigaards gate 15; menu 2600kr; ⊘ 6pm-midnight Wed & Thu, from noon Sat & Sun; ☒ Bussterminalen Grønland) This is not a meal to be taken lightly: firstly, you'll need to book many months in advance, and secondly, there will, for most of us, be the indenting of funds. But go if you can, not for the three Michelin star accolades but for Esben Holmboe Bang's 20 or so courses that are one of the world's most potent culinary experiences and a sensual articulation of what it means to be Norwegian.

You'll share your meal with only a handful of other diners, either upstairs at the six-person chef's table, or downstairs in the glass-and-steel dining room, which has eight tables below the dreamlike, Norse-mythology-

conjuring photos of Christian Houge. Service and wine are, as you'd imagine, flawless. Wine pairings are 1800kr, or you can do juice pairing for 950kr.

★ **Vaaghals** NORWEGIAN $$$
(Map p50; ☑ 920 70 999; www.vaaghals.com; Dronning Eufemias gate 8; lunch mains 179-199kr, dinner 7-course menu 695kr; ⊘ 11am-10pm Mon-Fri, from 4.30pm Sat; ☒ Bjørvika) There's a lot of sharing going on at Vaaghals, but don't mention the 'sh' world. Here it's definitely *skifte*, a uniquely Norwegian way of communal dining. This intriguing restaurant combines a resolutely contemporary address and surroundings with rustic, quintessentially Norwegian ingredients, including dry-aged meats, lots of offal, wild fish and foraged herbs and vegetables.

Theatercafeen NORWEGIAN $$$
(Map p50; ☑ 22 82 40 50; Stortingsgata 24/26; mains 229-380kr; ⊘ noon-11pm Mon-Sat, 3-10pm Sun; ☒ Nationaltheatret) A favourite with Norwegian families during Christmas and on 17 May (Constitution Day), the Theatercafeen, located directly across from the National Theatre, presents Norwegian classics in Viennese surroundings that have been wowing them since 1900. The menu conjures Norway's wild and stormy seas and its dark forests, in dishes such as turbot with caviar cream or halibut with asparagus and mushrooms.

Tjuvholmen Sjømagasin SEAFOOD $$$
(Map p56; ☑ 23 89 77 77; www.sjomagasinet.no; Tjuvholmen allé 14; mains 295-385kr; ⊘ 11.30am-midnight Mon-Fri, from 1pm Sat; ☒ Aker brygge) Fresh fish and seafood are beautifully prepared at this sleek, upmarket seafood place, with both traditional Norwegian (yes, it has fish soup) and international dishes (say, deep-sea turbot with fennel and burnt butter). There's also a shellfish bar where you can choose tank lobster or crab by the kilo, oysters or shrimp, or opt for a platter of them all (795kr per person).

Café Skansen MEDITERRANEAN $$$
(Map p50; ☑ 24 20 13 11; www.cafeskansen.no; Rådhusgata 32; mains 205-248kr; ⊘ 11am-midnight Mon-Fri, noon-midnight Sat, noon-11pm Sun; ☒ Kontraskjæret) A dark wood and tiled dining room makes for an atmospheric change from Aker Brygge's stringent contemporary architecture and the menu here is in keeping with its surrounds, with lots of traditional seafood dishes, lamb and steaks. The Danish sausages with red wine gravy are a great 4pm dinner if you've been out exploring the Oslofjord and need warming sustenance.

Note that this restaurant offers whale steaks.

Albert Bistro
FRENCH $$$

(Map p50; ☑21 02 36 30; www.albertbistro. no; Stranden 3, Aker Brygge; mains 185-355kr; ☺7.30am-11pm Mon-Fri, 9am-11pm Sat & Sun; ⛴Aker brygge) Francophiles rejoice: you can get your French fix, from early-morning *croque monsieurs* and omelettes to a wide range of well-prepared bistro classics such as *carré d'agneau* (lamb cutlet), *moule frite* (mussels and chips) and *entrecôte* (steak). The space is no-surprises contemporary bistro-by-numbers but delightfully stylish and bright at that.

Sanguine Brasserie & Bar
NORWEGIAN $$$

(Map p50; Kirsten Flagstads plass 1, Oslo Opera House; mains 205-305kr, 2-/3-/4-course menu 410/525/585kr; ☺11am-9pm Mon-Sat, noon-8pm Sun; ⛴Bjørvika) A lovely airy space facing the Oslofjord, this is the Opera House's less formal dining option and a great place to enjoy the architecture at leisure with a glass in hand. The menu offers Norwegian standards and a few international dishes done in a fresh and elegant manner, with excellent produce and pretty plating.

The kitchen stays open until 11pm on the nights of evening performances. There's a very simple but well-priced kids' menu (hot dogs, pasta or pizza; 65kr to 112kr), and staff will be happy to do a kid-sized main from the regular menu too.

Stock
INTERNATIONAL $$$

(Map p50; ☑21 09 03 09; www.stockoslo.no; Dronning Eufemias gate 14; lunch mains 175-225kr, dinner mains 255-320kr, 3-course menu 295kr; ☺11am-midnight Mon-Fri, from 3pm Sat; ⛴Bjørvika) A warm and casually glamorous space, with large glass windows but warming use of wood and decorative tiles. Come for its smart menu of produce-driven modern Norwegian dishes, such as venison sausage with turnip and kale, glazed pork cheek with root celery puree, cabbage and yellow beets, or mackerel with deep-fried Jerusalem artichoke and pickled kohlrabi. The bar menu is equally thoughtful.

Oysters are from Brittany and sardines are done Spanish-style, but there are also local favourites smoked sausage and dark bread (45kr to 70kr). A daily lunch special dish (185kr) is a good option if you're on a budget.

Solsiden
SEAFOOD $$$

(Map p50; ☑22 33 36 30; www.solsiden.no; Søndre Akershus Kai 34; mains 295-315kr; ☺4.30-10pm Mon-Sat, to 9pm Sun; ⛴Kontraskjæret) Nestled beneath Oslo's fortress, looking out to Aker Brygge, Solsiden serves up some of the city's best-loved seafood dishes in an old warehouse that's airy and atmospheric (and a maritime-kitsch-free zone). You can do simple shell-on shrimps by the half-kilo (265kr) or really go to town with a platter of lobster, shrimps, scallops, snow crab, mussels and crayfish (755kr per person).

In summer the outside terrace is open from 3pm.

Ruffino Ristorante
ITALIAN $$$

(Map p50; ☑22 55 32 80; www.ruffino.no; Arbins gate 1; pasta 170-199kr, mains 300kr; ☺4-11pm Mon-Sat; 🐾; ⛴Slottsparken) An upmarket, traditional place where locals go to eat Italian standards including a large range of housemade pasta and seafood dishes. As befits such a family-friendly place, it's happy to do half-serves for kids.

Bølgen & Moi
SEAFOOD $$$

(Map p56; ☑22 44 10 20; www.bolgenogmoi.no; Tjuvholmen allé 5; mains 189-285kr; ☺11am-10pm Mon-Sat, 3-9pm Sun; ⛴Aker brygge) National chain Bølgen & Moi occupies a prime position overlooking the docks and is a good place for a summer-evening burger, pasta or fish soup and a drink.

✗ Frogner & Western Oslo

Åpent Bakeri
CAFE $

(Map p56; ☑22 04 96 67; Inkognito terrasse 1; snacks 45-129kr; ☺7.30am-5pm Mon-Fri, 9am-4pm Sat & Sun; ⛴Inkognitogata) A neighbourhood cafe that serves coffee in deep, cream-coloured bowls and has unbeatable breads and pastries. A freshly baked roll topped with homemade *røre syltetøy* (stirred jam) and enjoyed on the bakery's patio makes for one of Oslo's most atmospheric breakfasts.

Fyr Bistronomi
NEW NORDIC $$

(Map p56; www.fyrbistronomi.no; Underhaugsveien 28; mains 140-240kr, set menus 550-695kr; ☺6-11pm Tue-Sat, lounge from 11.30am; ⛴Vigelandsparken) Westside well-to-do your fellow diners may be, but this is a delightfully casual place with a focus on grilled meats, from lobster and prawns to wagyu and pork neck. That said, it's definitely not a BBQ joint, with a light and artful hand with accompaniments, saucing, sides and snacks. The wine list is elegant, as are the cocktails.

LOCAL KNOWLEDGE

NEW NORDIC KIDS ON THE BLOCK

For a while there it seemed that the Nordic cooking scene that the world had fallen in love with had passed Norway by, with no global super-star chef like Copenhagen's René Redzepi or the Swedish wildman Magnus Nilsson. Come to Oslo today, though, and you'll be spoilt for choice, with globally known Michelin-starred places such as Maaemo and Kontrast joined by a startling number of boundary-pushing but highly accessible bistros serving up serious and supremely local food in good-times surrounds. These often employ a small-plate approach, will have something ironic or provocative on the stereo (probably vinyl), and will have a sommelier who knows the guys producing the wine by name.

Villa Paradiso PIZZA $$
(Map p56; ☑ 917 67 639; www.villaparadisofrogner.com; Sommerragata 17; mains 239-310kr, pizza 105-195kr; ⏰ 11am-11pm Mon-Fri, from noon Sat & Sun; ☑ 30, 31, N12, N30, ☑ Solli) One of Solliplass' big drawcards is this eastside transplant. The space is even more atmospheric than the original, with beautiful tile work and lofty ceilings, and the pizzas are as legendary as the Grünerløkka originals. As well as the pizza, it does some good simple meat and fish dishes and pasta.

★Hos Thea NORWEGIAN $$$
(Map p56; ☑ 22 44 68 74; www.hosthea.no; Gabelsgata 11; mains 340kr, 4-/6-course menu 555/755kr; ⏰ 5-10pm Sun-Thu, to 10.30pm Fri & Sat; ☑ Skillebekk) Hos Thea manages to be both a reminder of that first bloom of gastronomic cooking in the capital (it's been going strong since 1987) and a friendly, warm locals' favourite for special occasion nights out. Set in a former butcher's shop, its flavourful dishes have the odd French flourish (brioche, foie gras) or Italian base (risotto, ravioli) but remain quintessentially Norwegian.

Alex Sushi SUSHI $$$
(Map p56; ☑ 22 43 99 99; www.alexsushi.no; Cort Adelers gate 2; set menus 495-1150kr; ⏰ 4-11pm; ☑ Solli) Sit around the elegant oval bar for what's widely considered Oslo's best sushi.

You can order à la carte, but most regulars go the *omakase* route (the chef's selection; 1150kr); whichever you decide, expect perfection if not innovation. Dishes feature the very best of Norwegian seafood prepared simply alongside signature dishes such as the tempura salad and au gratin lobster.

Park 29 INTERNATIONAL $$$
(Map p56; ☑ 481 70 000; www.park29.no; Parkveien 29; mains 295-335kr; ☑ Riddervolds plass) Set in one of Oslo's oldest remaining wooden villas (once the home of composer Halfdan Kjerulf and later a legendary car dealer) and with a summer dining lawn, this must be one of Oslo's prettiest restaurants. A menu of simply if carefully done international and Norwegian classics is attractively plated and the upmarket wine list is a treat to sample.

Feinschmecker NORWEGIAN $$$
(Map p56; ☑ 22 12 93 80; www.feinschmecker.no; Balchens gate; mains 325-425kr, 4-/7-course menus 895/1395kr; ⏰ 5-9pm Mon-Sat; ☑ Elisenberg) While no longer bearing a Michelin star, this gastronomic place is a firm neighbourhood favourite with a menu of modern Norwegian dishes using excellent local produce. Despite its venerable status, you're more than welcome to drop in for a glass of wine and there's no pressure to make the set menu commitment.

Gate of India INDIAN $$$
(Map p56; ☑ 22 69 09 33; www.gateofindia.no; Bogstadveien 66a; mains 179-249kr; ⏰ 3-11pm Mon-Sat, from 2pm Sun; ☑ Majorstuen) This upmarket Indian does flavourful dishes made with quality ingredients.

🍴 Grünerløkka & Vulkan

★Syverkiosken HOT DOGS $
(Map p60; ☑ 967 08 699; Maridalsveien 45; hot dogs from 20kr; ⏰ 9am-11.30pm Mon-Fri, from 11am Sat & Sun; ☑ 34) It might look like a hipster replica, but this hole-in-the-wall *pølser* (hot dogs) place is absolutely authentic and one of the last of its kind in Oslo. Dogs can be had in a potato bread wrap in lieu of the usual roll, or with both, and there's a large range of old-school accompaniments beyond sauce and mustard.

Wünderburger BURGERS $
(Map p60; Torggata 37; burgers 90-120kr; ⏰ 11am-10pm Mon-Thu, to 3am Fri, noon-3am Sat, 1-11pm Sun;

34) You'll find excellent Oslo burgers here, using free-range Lofoten beef, brioche buns and build-your-own choices. The veggie burgers are also good, and the gluten-free buns better than the usual.

Munchies
BURGERS $

(Map p60; http://munchies.no; Thorvald Meyers gate 36; burgers 92-115kr; ⊙11am-10pm Sun-Wed, to midnight Thu, to 3am Fri & Sat; Schous plass) Munchies might be perpetually crowded and those extras can add up, but its burgers and fries definitely put it in the city's best burger options. Grab a window stool and sample its craft beers too.

Liebling
CAFE $

(Map p60; 24 02 23 02; Øvrefoss 4; plates 125kr, sandwiches 65-85kr; ⊙8am-8pm Tue-Fri, from 10am Sat-Mon; Birkelunden) One of the nearby KHiO (Oslo National Academy of the Arts) kids' cafes of choice, this 'Berlin-style' corner gem is a great place to kick back with your laptop and a late, late breakfast. There's a huge range of pastries and cakes, including raw and gluten-free options; coffee is care of Supreme Roastworks, and there's beer and German and Austrian wines.

Kasbah
MIDDLE EASTERN $

(Map p60; 21 94 90 99; www.thekasbah.no; Kingos gate 1b; mains 98-165kr, meze dishes 47-79kr; ⊙11am-1am Mon-Fri; Biermanns gate) A basement hang-out specialising in filling falafels, filled pittas and mezze platters. It's as relaxing as throwing on a pair of Moroccan slippers, with sofas to lounge around on, reggae on the stereo and thrift-store decor to match.

Hønse-Louisas Hus
CAFE $

(Map p60; www.honselovisashus.no; Sandakerveien 2; snacks 80-135kr; ⊙11am-4pm; Biermanns gate) Stop for coffee and a waffle at Hønse-Louisas Hus, attached to an atmospheric little theatre.

Teddy's Soft Bar
AMERICAN $

(Map p50; 22 17 36 00; Brugata 3a; mains 95-120kr; ⊙11am-1am Mon-Sat; Brugata) The jukebox in the corner gives Teddy's Soft Bar a flavour of 1950s USA. It's something of a local institution that has scarcely changed in decades. Its burgers go well with that other 1950s American favourite – milkshakes – though it's as much a place for a beer as a meal.

Hotel Havana
SPANISH $

(Map p60; 23 23 03 23; www.hotelhavana. no; Thorvald Meyers gate 38; mains 80-120kr; ⊙10am-midnight Sun-Wed, to 1am Thu, to 2am Fri & Sat; Brugata) With blue-and-white Andalucian tiles, this little place models itself on a Spanish bar. The food is likewise Spanish but with a Norwegian twist, such as a Bergen-style fish soup popping up for lunch. There's also a basic tapas list for soaking up the jugs of sangria.

Far East
ASIAN $

(Map p50; 22 20 56 28; Bernt Ankers gate 4; mains 80-120kr; ⊙1pm-midnight; Brugata) Come for light and fresh Thai and Vietnamese curries, soups and noodles at this simple and very popular little place.

★ Bass
NEW NORDIC $$

(Map p60; 482 41 489; http://bassoslo. no; Thorvald Meyers gate 26; dishes 70-175kr; ⊙5pm-1am Tue-Sat, 3-8pm Sun; Birkelunden) In what could be yet another Grünerløkka corner cafe, you'll find one of the city's best small-plate dining options, served beneath vintage seascapes on classic Norwegian ceramics by jovial Løkka locals. Most dishes are what might be called contemporary Norwegian-meets-international – from fried chicken and potato pancakes to deep-sea cod in sorrel butter and death-by-chocolate cake.

There's also an impressive wine list, many of which can be had by the glass.

★ Mathallen Oslo
FOOD HALL $$

(Map p60; www.mathallenoslo.no; Maridalsveien 17, Vulkan; ⊙8am-1am Tue-Fri, from 9.30am Sat & Sun; 54) Down by the river, this former industrial space is now a food court dedicated to showcasing the very best of Norwegian regional cuisine, as well as some excellent internationals. There are dozens of delis, cafes and miniature restaurants, and the place buzzes throughout the day and well into the evening.

Eating here is a casual affair where strangers find themselves eating and chatting together, while families grab their preferences from different stalls. Various places within keep different opening hours, with most of the restaurants open until at least 8pm and the bars much later. Check the website for special culinary festivals held each month.

Kamai
ASIAN $$

(Map p60; 23 89 79 66; www.kamai.no; Korsgata 25; dishes 129-175kr, 4-course meal 485kr, bao and sushi 70-210kr; ⊙restaurant 5pm-1am Wed-Sun, takeaway 3-9pm Mon-Fri, 11am-11pm Sat; Schous plass) You get two restaurants here for the price of one: a shopfront casual canteen and takeaway doing sushi and *bao* (steam buns); and a restaurant hidden across the courtyard upstairs, serving elegant Nordic-Asian fusion small plates such as smoked reindeer heart, eel and potato, or salmon with wasabi and cabbage.

Villa Paradiso
PIZZA $$

(Map p60; 22 35 40 60; www.villaparadiso.no; Olaf Ryes plass 8; pizza 154-194kr; 8am-11pm Mon-Fri, from 10am Sat & Sun; Olaf Ryes plass) Overlooking Grünerløkka's central park, with summertime al fresco dining next to an old Italian car, this place is rated by many as serving some of the best pizza in the capital – no minor feat in a city obsessed with pizza. Always full, always happy.

Dr Kneipp's Vinbar
NORWEGIAN $$

(Map p60; 22 37 22 97; www.markveien.no; Torvbakkgt 12; mains 175-265kr; 4pm-1am Mon-Sat; Schous plass) The casual little sibling to Markveien Mat & Vinhus (p77), Dr Kneipp's is the place for sipping wines by the glass (there are around 400 wines to choose from) accompanied by light, snacky dishes such as cured mackerel or an Italian-style *carne crudo* (raw beef), or dishes from Markveien's menu. The baked cheesecake is legendary.

Nighthawk Diner
BURGERS $$

(Map p60; 966 27 327; www.nighthawkdiner.com; Seilduksgata 15; mains 159-269kr; 7am-11pm Mon-Thu, to 1am Fri, 10am-1am Sat, 10am-11pm Sun; Birkelunden) An all-American diner homage à la Edward Hopper, right down to the booth seats, jukebox, ketchup caddies and art-deco-style mirrored bar. Nighthawk serves burgers, shakes and hot dogs, and uses locally sourced beef and homemade sauces.

Mucho Mas
MEXICAN $$

(Map p60; 22 37 16 09; www.muchomas.no; Thorvald Meyers gate 36; mains 95-210kr; noon-midnight Mon-Thu, to 3am Fri & Sat; ; Olaf Ryes plass) What it lacks in Mexican authenticity, Mucho Mas more than makes up for in cheese and portion size. The full Tex-Mex repertoire is on offer, including tacos, nachos and burritos (which are enormous); all dishes are offered in meat or vegetarian versions. Well-priced beer helps put out the fire.

Café Sara
INTERNATIONAL $$

(Map p60; 22 03 40 00; www.cafesara.no; Hausmanns gate 29; mains 129-179kr; 11am-3.30am Mon-Sat, 1pm-3.30am Sun; Hausmanns gate)

Despite the light and airy name, this is a dark but warm English-style pub serving a hearty, unfussy mix of Norwegian dishes as well as pizza, Turkish and Tex-Mex. The house special is a meat stew with corn, rice and potatoes – perfect for a cold winter's night.

Fru Hagen
CAFE $$

(Map p60; 454 91 904; www.fruhagen.no; Thorvald Meyers gate 40; mains 165-199kr; 11am-midnight Mon-Thu, to 2am Fri & Sat, noon-11pm Sun; Olaf Ryes plass) The low-key and always full Fru Hagen (Mrs Garden) serves snacks, light meals and appealing mains such as local sausage with mushrooms and onion. Its location facing Olaf Ryes plass also makes it good for people-watching.

Kontrast
NEW NORDIC $$$

(Map p60; 21 60 01 01; www.restaurant-kontrast.no; Maridalsveien 15a; 6/10 courses 950/1250kr, small plates 135-225kr; 6pm-midnight Tue-Sat; 54) A minimalist, industrial space makes a dramatic backdrop for beautifully presented, seasonal dishes that combine a pure simplicity and honed technique. Peak season, organic and ethically sourced produce is used, including free-range or wild animals. It has a Michelin star, which means you'll need to book well in advance.

Bon Lio
SPANISH, GASTRONOMIC $$$

(Map p60; 467 77 212; http://bonlio.no; Fredensborgveien 42; menu 795kr; 6pm-12.30am Tue-Fri, from 5pm Sat; 34) You might expect some cultural dissonance between a Spanish gastronomic kitchen and a sweetly Norwegian wooden house, but it all comes together in a convivial and rather sexy manner. Bon Lio eschews formality but requires commitment: booking is mandatory, as is the tasting menu. Submit, and a multicourse feast of Mediterranean technique, Norwegian produce and occasional Asian flourishes will ensue.

Le Benjamin
FRENCH $$$

(Map p60; 22 35 79 44; www.lebenjamin.no; Søndre gate 6; mains 248-310kr; 4-11pm Tue-Sun; Schous plass) *Mais oui*, it's proper French bistro dining here, refined but relaxed, with classics such as fried sardines, poached pigeon, salt-baked turbot, beef marrow on toast and of course a *plat du jour*. There's a very good wine list heavy on French vintages too. Book ahead for a table or come early for an almost-Parisian terrace seat.

Markveien Mat & Vinhus   NORWEGIAN $$$
(Map p60; ☑ 22 37 22 97; www.markveien.no; Torvbakkgt 12; mains 280-325kr, 3/5 courses 455/615kr; ⊘ 4pm-1am Mon-Sat; 🚇 Heimdalsgata) For a cosy, traditional Norwegian dining room, this lovely spot on the southern edge of Grünerløkka is hard to better. Settle in at one of the candlelit tables and tuck into hearty, traditional (and sometimes international) dishes, such as lamb shank with root vegetables, confit duck leg with lentils or monkfish with radish and summer cabbage.

Süd Øst   INTERNATIONAL $$$
(Map p60; ☑ 23 35 30 70; www.sudost.no; Trondheimsveien 5; mains 165-299kr; ⊘ 11am-11pm Sun-Thu, to 1am Fri & Sat; 🚇 Heimdalsgata) With a large outdoor terrace overlooking the river for summer sunseekers, this upmarket place specialises in Southeast Asian fusion flavours. You can also just pop in for its Asian-influenced cocktails.

✕ Sofienberg, Grønland & Tøyen

★ Handwerk   CAFE, BAKERY $
(Map p65; ☑ 22 60 85 00; http://handwerk.no/Botaniske.html; Sarsgate 1; daily special 135-145kr, sandwiches 75kr; ⊘ 10am-4pm; 🚋 Tøyen) If you can't make it out into the countryside, come and find this beautiful cafe in the centre of the Botanical Garden. Set in a historic farm building, its pale-blue interior is lined with exquisite floral artworks, rows of candles and pendant lights. Windows reveal viridian (or snowy) views of the gardens all around while all is cosy within.

★ Punjab Tandoori   INDIAN $
(Map p50; ☑ 22 17 20 86; www.punjabtandoori.no; Grønlandsleiret 24; lunch deal 80-90kr, mains 80-135kr; ⊘ 11am-11pm Mon-Sat, noon-10pm Sun; 🚋 Grønland) This simple canteen-style affair serves spot-on northern Indian curries that are rich and highly flavoured. It's a real neighbourhood institution for the local Asian community and Norwegians in the know, and is as authentic an Indian restaurant as you'll get in Europe.

Gràdi   INTERNATIONAL $
(Map p65; ☑ 978 80 544; www.facebook.com/gradirestaurantogbar; Sørligata 40; mains 90-140kr; ⊘ 11am-1am Tue-Sat, to midnight Sun; 🚋 Tøyen) In a sweet corner spot looking back down the hill towards Sofienberg, Gràdi gives the locals what they really want: smart, flexible Norwegian fusion dishes, local beer and good cocktails at unusually reasonable

prices. Service is far from glossy, but there's a warm welcome and the room is an airy, pretty escape any time, especially during the day.

★ Brutus   NEW NORDIC $$
(Map p65; ☑ 22 38 00 88; www.barbrutus.no; Eiriks gate 2; dishes 85-255kr, snacks 55-90kr; ⊘ 5pm-1am; 🚇 Munkegata) With some of the biggest names in wine involved in this casual Tøyen corner spot, you could easily call Brutus a wine bar and not be wrong. But that would overlook that the cooking is some of the most exciting, and accessible, in the city. The space is pure Oslo: earthy, knowing, whimsical, rock and roll.

Think raw bricks, lushly painted wood cladding, simple vintage chairs, salon-hung contemporary art. The dishes that emerge from the open kitchen (where staff are uniformed in black metal-style Brutus T-shirts) are flavour bombs that highlight unusual local ingredients and incorporate pan-Nordic influences. The wine list features some of Europe's superstar natural producers and you can indeed come here to just drink and snack.

Olympen   NORWEGIAN $$
(Map p50; ☑ 24 10 19 99; www.olympen.no; Grønlandsleiret 15; mains 140-260kr; ⊘ 11am-midnight Sun-Tue, to 1am Wed & Thu, to 3.30am Fri & Sat; 🚇 37) Murals of the local streetscapes from the 1920s combine with dark wood panelling and chandeliers to make the easy-to-like, affordable Norwegian pub grub (steaks, suckling pig, mackerel) here something out of the ordinary. Known universally as Lompa, as a beer hall it also serves more than 100 beers, and is a beloved part of Grønland history.

★ Ekeberg Restaurant   NORWEGIAN $$$
(Map p50; ☑ 23 24 23 00; www.ekebergrestaurant en.com; Kongsveien 15; mains 295-310kr, set menu 650kr, terrace mains 170-190kr; ⊘ 11am-midnight Mon-Sat, noon-10pm Sun; 🚇 Ekebergparken) Lars Backer's early Oslofunkis (functionalist) masterpiece from 1929 fell into disrepair in the 1980s but happily is again here for all to enjoy, with a New Nordic dining room known for its simple, careful and elegant cooking. There's also a summertime eyrie terrace serving burgers, mussels and fries, and prawn sandwiches.

Even if you're not interested in Modernist architecture, come for the Oslofjord and city views.

OSLO EATING

Asylet

NORWEGIAN $$$

(Map p50; 📞22 17 09 39; www.asylet.no; Grønland 28; mains 245-270kr; ☺11am-11.30pm Mon & Tue, to 12.30am Wed-Fri, noon-12.30am Sat, to 10.30pm Sun; 🇹 Grønland) This classic hostelry dating from 1730 nestles in Grønland's multicultural heart. Head through the archway into the cobbled courtyard, surrounded by wooden galleries, then head inside to the low-ceilinged, half-timbered pub, complete with flagstones, beams and a decidedly wonky-looking fireplace. The food is filling and traditional – it's particularly known for its *smørbrød* (open-faced sandwiches).

Smia Galleri

NORWEGIAN $$$

(Map p65; 📞22 19 59 20; Opplandsgata 19; mains 205-280kr; ☺2-10pm Tue-Fri, noon-10pm Sat & Sun; 🇹 Grønland) An old bakery has been transformed into a cosy candlelit space that serves posh Norwegian and international dishes. The leafy patio is perfect in summer and you can linger until midnight. Check the website for its jazz evenings too.

It takes about 15 minutes to get here: from Oslo S, take bus 37 towards Helsfyr T-bane station and get off at Vålerenga.

🍴 St Olafs Plass, Bislett & St Hanshaugen

★ Kafe Oslo

CAFE $$

(Litteraturhuset; Map p60; 📞21 54 85 71; www.kafeoslo.no; Wergelandsveien 29; mains 155-245kr; ☺10am-12.30pm Mon-Thu, 10am-2pm Fri & Sat, noon-8pm Sun; 🚇17B) Litteraturhuset is one of the state-run organisations dedicated to the arts and here it is all about the promotion of literature, with frequent workshops, talks and debates, not all of them in Norwegian. It's also a lovely place to come and rest weary feet, with a cafe and bar serving a menu of Norwegian soul food tasty enough to attract the odd princess from the neighbouring Royal Palace.

At lunch the salads, patties and Oslo pots – a daily student-friendly casserole, served with as much bread you can eat – are good value. There's also a well-stocked bookshop and frequent screenings of arthouse films.

★ Kolonialen

GASTRONOMIC $$$

(Map p60; 📞401 03 578; www.kolonialenbislett.no; Sofiesgate 16; mains 240-290kr; 🚇37) When a venture is led by the ex-Maaemo owner, you can guess the food will be extraordinary, and

it is. The short menu is a mix of pan-European dishes done with a contemporary playfulness that stops short of quirky, care of the Australian chef.

Happolati

ASIAN, GASTRONOMIC $$$

(Map p60; 📞479 78 087; www.happolati.no; St Olavs plass 2; dishes 105-145kr, menu 650kr; ☺4.30-10pm Mon-Fri; 🚇37) Oslo restaurateur Nevzat Arikan's latest offering has an extremely beautiful, highly crafted fit-out that speaks to both the contemporary Asian menu on offer and the beautiful, soulful and very Norwegian space it occupies. Calm as it all may be, there's a dynamism to the many small Japanese, Chinese and Southeast Asian–style dishes and to the super staff.

Smalhans

NORWEGIAN $$$

(Map p60; 📞22 69 60 00; www.smalhans.no; Ullevålsveien 43; 3-/6-course menu 450/650kr; ☺11am-1pm Tue-Sun; 🚇37) If you want to really capture the St Hanshaugen spirit, come to this busy restaurant-bar-cafe for its daily early meal – *husmannskost* – between 4pm and 6pm (175kr, though you can ask for a half portion) or its legendary big or small (*smalhans* = frugal, *krøsus* = cashed-up) dinners, where an ever-changing rota of rustic Norwegian dishes is served sharing-style.

L'ardoise

BAKERY, WINE BAR $$$

(Map p60; 📞22 11 09 65; www.lardoise.no; Thereses gate 20; mains 225-295kr; ☺11am-midnight Mon-Sat, to 6pm Sun; 🚇37) There's a concise traditional menu of French standards in the pretty dining room here for lunch and dinner, but it's the pastries – including the city's best croissants and some very credible macarons – that keep most of the locals coming back.

🍴 Greater Oslo

Ullevålseter

WAFFLES $

(Map p66; www.ullevalseter.no; Maridalen; waffles 35-59kr; ☺10am-4pm Tue-Fri, 9am-7pm Sat & Sun) This pleasant old farmhouse serves waffles and coffee.

🍷 Drinking & Nightlife

The locals definitely don't seem to mind the high price of alcohol: Oslo has a ridiculously rich nightlife scene, with a huge range of bars and clubs, and most open until 3am or later on weekends. The compact nature of the city and its interconnecting inner neighbourhoods means bar crawling is a joy, if an expensive one.

☺ Central Oslo

★Kulturhuset   BAR, PUB
(Map p50; http://kulturhusetioslo.no; Youngs gate 6; ☺8am-3.30am Mon-Fri, from 11am Sat & Sun; ⓐBrugata) The Norwegian notion of culture being an interactive, collective enterprise combines here with their exceptional ability to have a good time. The city's 'culture house' moved into this beautiful, rambling old four-storey building in 2017, but it feels as if it's been part of the Oslo fabric for years.

Come for a coffee or a drink but wander upstairs for a game of shuffleboard, or end up out the back at a concert, club night, debate or lecture.

Oslo Camping   BAR
(Map p50; http://oslo-camping.no; Møllergata 12; minigolf 105kr; ☺1pm-1am Mon-Thu, to 3am Fri & Sat, to midnight Sun; ⓐBrugata) Norwegians like to have a pub activity on hand for those potentially awkward moments before the social lubrication kicks in. Here the activity is an 18-hole minigolf course. Cheap beer, metal clubs and small hard balls – what could go wrong? Nothing in fact, with lots of happy, minigolfing fun to be had, DJs on weekends and toast if you're hungry.

Røør   BEER HALL
(Map p50; Rosenkrantz gate 4; ☺1pm-3am; ⓐTinghuset) Craft-beer credentials (check out that blackboard list!) meet Norwegian fun with shuffleboard, an excellent vinyl collection and vending-machine snacks over two floors. There's around 70 beers on tap alone and a not-so-shabby selection of ciders and wine by the glass too.

Internasjonalen   COCKTAIL BAR
(Map p50; ☏468 25 240; www.internasjonalen.no; Youngstorget 2; ☺10am-1am Mon, to 3am Tue-Sat, 4pm-1am Sun; ⓐBrugata) One of the city's cocktail veterans, the decor here is Cold War kitsch, which is a nice fit for its Oslo Funkis (functionalist) style building, also home to the Norwegian Labour Party, Arbeiderpartiets. There are seats facing the square, a more intimate space upstairs for DJs and concerts, and you'll share bar stools with students, politicians, trade unionists and artists.

Angst   BAR
(Map p50; http://angstbar.blogspot.com; Torggata 11; ☺noon-11pm Mon & Tue, to 1.30am Wed & Thu, to 3am Fri & Sat, 2-11pm Sun; ⓐBrugata) Dark, yes, but otherwise far from angsty, this is one of Oslo's favourite small bars. Staff are friendly, there are passageway tables for summer, and a happy, cool crowd. Bonus: if you want to bar crawl or the post-11pm weekend queues are too long, there are many other options packed into Strøget passage.

Himkok   COCKTAIL BAR, BEER GARDEN
(Map p50; ☏22 42 22 02; www.facebook.com/HIMKOK.OSLO; Storgata 27; ☺5pm-3am Sun-Wed, from 3pm Thu-Sat; ⓐBrugata) First things first: be aware that the door is unmarked, save for a small, decorative 'H'. It's also good to know that the crew behind Himkok are the inventors of the 'taptail' – quality cocktails on tap. This also happens to be a distillery, so the vodka and gin in your expertly mixed drink has been made on the premises.

During the warmer months there is a courtyard restaurant, Munnsjenk, serving snacks. Whether or not you're up for imbibing spirits, it's an intriguing space, with much of its original atmosphere retained.

Sosialen   PUB
(Map p50; ☏22 41 50 06; http://sosialen.com; Møllergata 13; ☺4pm-midnight Mon & Tue, to 2am Wed & Thu, 3pm-3.30am Fri & Sat; ⓐStortinget) A good choice if you're not sure if you want to go out for a drink or have something to eat and kick on. There's a menu of Norwegian and international favourites to be had in the nicely industrial front room, or stay on for drinks and DJs.

Stockfleths   CAFE
(Map p50; www.stockfleths.as; Lille Grensen; ☺7am-6pm Mon-Fri, 10am-5pm Sat; ⓣStortinget) Founded in 1895, the award-winning Stockfleths is one of Oslo's oldest coffee shops. It also serves wholegrain bread with brown cheese, pastries and smoothies.

☺ Frogner & Western Oslo

Champagneria   WINE BAR
(Map p56; ☏21 08 09 09; www.champagneria.com; Frognerveien 2; ☺4pm-1am Mon-Wed, to 3am Thu & Fri, 1pm-3am Sat, 4-11pm Sun; ⓐSolli) Yes, it has Champagne – a very detailed and long list, in fact – but also Spanish cava and Italian prosecco. Spread over two floors, this is a busy after-work option, with a short tapas selection of tummy liners too.

LOCAL KNOWLEDGE

NIGHTLIFE HOT SPOTS

The city's best neighbourhood bar scene is along Thorvald Meyers gate and the surrounding streets in Grünerløkka and the Torggata strip after the bridge across the Akerselva. The Young-storget area has some of the most popular places close to the city centre and the developments around Aker Brygge have brought more after-dark life to the waterfront, while the Grønland and Tøyen neighbourhoods have an alternative feel. St Hanshaugen has a nice little collection of low-key, quietly cool places around Ullevålsveien.

Palace Bar
BAR

(Map p56; Solligata 2; ⊙6-10pm Mon-Sat; ⌂Solli) The place where the well-heeled crowd of Oslo West can be found sipping cocktails or downing beers. Its over-the-top back bar is covered with black and silver graffiti, with snakes, dolls and old phones preserved in bottles lining the shelves. The seven-table restaurant at the front does a 10-course daily menu, if you feel like making an evening of it.

🍺 Grünerløkka & Vulkan

★Torggata Botaniske
COCKTAIL BAR

(Map p50; ⌾980 17 830; Torggata 17b; ⊙5pm-1am Sun-Wed, to 2am Thu, 2pm-3am Fri & Sat; ⌂Brugata) This is the greenhouse effect done right, with a lush assortment of indoor plants (including a warm herb-growing area) as well as beautiful mid-century light fittings and chairs, chandeliers, and lots of marble and mirrors. If you're not already seduced by the decor, the drinks will do it, with a list that features the bar's own produce, fresh fruit and good-quality spirits.

★Territoriet
WINE BAR

(Map p60; http://territoriet.no/; Markveien 58; ⊙4pm-1am Mon-Fri, from noon Sat & Sun; ⌂Schous plass) A true neighbourhood wine bar that's also the city's most exciting. The grape-loving owners offer up more than 300 wines by the glass and do so without a list. Talk to the staff about your preferences and – yes, this is Norway – your budget, and they'll find something you'll adore. Ordering beer or gin and tonic won't raise an eyebrow, we promise.

There's vinyl on the decks (often something that's ironically nostalgic), arresting photographic works on the moodily dark walls and often not a chair or stool to spare.

★Tim Wendelboe
CAFE

(Map p60; ⌾400 04 062; www.timwendelboe.no; Grüners gate 1; ⊙8.30am-6pm Mon-Fri, 11am-5pm Sat & Sun; ⌂Schous plass) Tim Wendelboe is often credited with kick-starting the Scandinavian coffee revolution and his eponymous cafe and roastery is both a local freelancers' hang-out and an international coffee-fiend pilgrimage site. All the beans are, of course, self-sourced and hand-roasted (the roaster is part of the furniture), and all coffees – from an iced pour-over to a regular cappuccino – are world-class.

Supreme Roastworks
COFFEE

(Map p60; ⌾22 71 42 02; www.srw.no; Thorvald Meyers gate 18a; ⊙7am-5pm; ⌂Birkelunden) Run by award-winning barista Odd-Steinar Tøllefsenis, named the World Brewers Cup Champion in Sweden in 2015, this friendly cafe and micro-roastery offers espresso-based coffees, drip or hand-filters (J60 or Chemex), and you can watch the beans being roasted while you drink.

Oslovelo
BAR

(Map p60; ⌾23 23 05 53; www.oslovelo.com; Seilduksgata 23; ⊙10am-3.30am Mon-Fri, from 9am Sat, 10am-1am Sun; ⌂Birkelunden) Celebrate cycling at this light and friendly cafe and bar. It does all-day breakfast with coffee from Supreme and serves all manner of beers, including those from the Grünerløkka Brewery, with DJs later in the evening. If you're travelling with your bike, it's also somewhere you can get repairs or buy parts.

Crowbar & Brewery
BREWERY

(Map p60; ⌾21 38 67 57; http://crowbryggeri.com/; Torggata 32; ⊙3pm-3am; ⌂34) Huge, rustic industrial brewery spread over two floors. They brew their own as well as pouring brews from Haandbryggeriet, Lindheim, Amundsen and Voss, along with some interesting Danish, Swedish and New World beers.

Hytta
BAR

(Map p60; ⌾45 40 55 52; Thorvald Meyers gate 70; ⊙2pm-3am; ⌂Schous plass) So many Løkka bars, so little time. This one will grab your attention for its happy intimacy and towering bar stools, as well as Zeppelin on the turntable. For something that swings a little prog rock, the wine by the glass is rather good.

Bortenfor
BAR

(Map p60; ☑922 66 683; http://ingensteds.no; Brenneriveien 7; ☺4pm-1am Tue-Sun; ☐54) The only sign Bortenfor is there is the gate on Brenneriveien, so if you're lost best head for the bridge by stalwart club-bar Blå, but instead turn right and keep going. Along with the riverside beauty you'll get a cosy, cultured atmosphere, good music, Norwegian-themed cocktails and very decent wine by the glass.

Hendrix Ibsen
COFFEE

(Map p60; ☑457 97 150; http://hendrixibsen. rocks; Vulkan 20; ☺Mon-Thu 8am-11pm, to 3.30pm Fri & Sat, 10am-1pm Sun; ☐54) Perfect place to grab a takeaway coffee for Akerselva wandering, but you'll probably be tempted to linger over the racks of vintage vinyl or to pick up a bag of an interesting local roast coffee or hang out for an early-evening DJ performance.

Bettola
COCKTAIL BAR

(Map p60; www.facebook.com/bettolacocktailbar; Trondheimsveien 2; ☺4pm-1am Mon-Thu, to 3am Fri & Sat) Mid-century furniture, a pretty tiled floor and friendly bar staff give this corner bar a welcoming vibe. It does one of the city's best negronis, and both the cocktail and wine lists are very well priced.

Mir
BAR

(Map p60; ☑22 37 39 70; http://lufthavna.no; Toftes gate 69; ☺6pm-1am; ☐Schous plass) Part of the Grünerløkka Lufthavn complex – a collective cultural centre set around a typical garden courtyard and home to many local artists, performers and musicians – Mir is pure Grünerløkka good times with space-station decor (they'll even lend you a space helmet), craft beers, house-blend chilli vodka, and daily entertainment such as electronic acts, improv jazz, DJs and quiz nights.

Paul's Boutique
BAR

(Map p60; ☑483 87 730; www.facebook.com/ PaulsBoutiqueOslo; Darres gate 1; ☺2pm-12.30am Sun-Thu, to 3am Fri & Sat; ☐54) The Beastie Boys homage moniker might give you a clue as to this bar's ambience and older (though never old) hipster crowd. Parkside beers by day, simple, strong and well-made cocktails by night and ping pong in the basement whenever the hell you feel like it.

Grünerløkka Brygghus
PUB

(Map p60; www.brygghus.no; Thorvald Meyers gate 30; ☺3pm-1am Mon & Tue, to 2am Wed & Thu, to 3am Fri, noon-3am Sat, to midnight Sun; ☐Olaf Ryes plass)

This atmospheric alehouse and microbrewery does a range of house brews from pilsners to *Weißbiers*. Bottled beers include rarities such as sour *surøls* and Scandinavian Christmas beers. Stomach liners – burgers, bangers and mash, and fish and chips – can be ordered at the bar. Streetside benches are at a premium but worth trying to snare.

Villa
CLUB

(Map p50; www.thevilla.no; Møllergata 23; ☺11pm-3am Fri & Sat; ☐Brugata) With arguably the best sound system in the city, this is a diehard house- and electro-music club. In addition to Friday and Saturday, check for the occasional special Thursday gigs.

Bar Boca
BAR

(Map p60; ☑22 04 13 77; Thorvald Meyers gate 30; ☺11am-1am Sun-Thu, to 3am Fri & Sat; ☐Olaf Ryes plass) A proper local's hang-out with an '80s-dive-bar vibe and super-welcoming staff. Beers go down well here, but they're also quite skilled with classic cocktails. It gets very busy at weekends and will be full when nowhere else is. A Grünerløkka must.

Colonel Mustard
PUB

(Map p60; ☑21 95 05 00; http://colonelmustard. no; Darres gate 2; ☺11am-1am Sun-Thu, to 3am Fri & Sat; ☐54) Large vintage-furniture-filled pub named for a character from the boardgame Cluedo. There's a large range of beers on tap, lots of cosy nooks to settle into and Cluedo to play. If you're hungry, the fish-and-chip, risotto or osso buco dinners are good bets.

Tea Lounge
BAR

(Map p60; www.tealounge.no; Thorvald Meyers gate 33b; ☺11am-1am Mon-Wed, to 3am Thu-Sat, noon-1am Sun; ☐Birkelunden) During the day this split-personality bar is a teashop with a small range of leafy brews and a chilled-out soundtrack, but in the dark of night it transforms itself into a bar

---

❶ AGE LIMITS & DRESS CODES

Note that many Oslo nightspots have an unwritten dress code that expects patrons to be relatively well turned out – at the very least, don't show up in grubby gear and hiking boots. Many clubs, especially those serving spirits, impose a higher age limit.

Sofienberg, Grønland & Tøyen

Pigalle
CLUB, BAR

(Map p50; 24 10 19 99; www.olympen.no; Grøn-landsleiret 15; 4pm-1am Tue & Wed, to 3am Thu-Sat; 37) As unexpected as it might be in this street of grocers and curry places, Pigalle's most recent incarnation feels like a set from a Luc Besson movie from the '80s, with an organic curved oak-veneer roof, a conservatory, palm trees, lots of black and green, and mirrors galore. If you're lost, it's upstairs from the restaurant Olympen.

Dattera Til Hagen
BAR

(Map p50; www.dattera.no; Grønland 10; 11am-1am Mon-Wed, to 2am Thu, to 3.30am Fri & Sat, noon-mid-night Sun; Grønland) A rambling, defiantly bohemian bar with a backyard beer garden that goes off in summer. DJs and live music make for even more lively days or nights.

St Olafs Plass, Bislett & St Hanshaugen

★ Fuglen
COCKTAIL BAR, CAFE

(Map p50; www.fuglen.com; Universitetsgaten 2; 7.30am-10pm Mon & Tue, to 1am Wed & Thu, to 3am Fri, 11am-3am Sat, to 10pm Sun; 17B) Fuglen and its crew of merry, young entrepreneurs are part of Oslo's door-to-dreamily cool reinvention. Since taking over a traditional cafe, they've launched a coffee and Norwegian design mini-empire in Japan, while in their home city they continue to roast and brew as well as mix some of the best cocktails around.

Drinks are made with local spirits where possible and are often muddled with foraged ingredients (spruce tips, seaweed from the North Sea, forest flowers). There's a jukebox and iconic mid-century Norwegian furniture to sit on, or come during the day for always-perfect coffee on a footpath stool with a Norwegian wool rug for chillier days.

★ Rouleurs of Oslo
WINE BAR, CAFE

(Map p60; http://rosl.no; Ullevålsveien 16; noon-1am Mon-Thu, to 2am Fri & Sat, to 12.30am Sun; 37) An elegant Francophile of a bar that happens also to be part of a bike-repair workshop? Hello St Hanshaugen. Come here for daytime coffees (and bike repairs), or in the evening for a pre-dinner cocktail or Chablis. If you don't want to leave (the wine list *is* that good), don't, and make a meal of its duck rillettes, pâté or charcuterie plates.

Kunstnernes Hus
BAR, PIZZA

(Map p60; 22 85 34 10; http://kunstnerneshus. no; Wergelandsveien 17; 11am-10pm Tue-Thu, to 3am Fri, noon-3am Sat, noon-8pm Sun; 17B) One of the city's various artist-run cultural institutions, Kunstnernes Hus is set in a spectacular 1929 functionalist building with a broad terrace overlooking the green of Slottsparken. It's a supremely laid-back and scenic place to have a spritz, wine or beer; the crowd is an interesting mix of the city's creatives; and there are always excellent tunes playing on the decks.

There's also a program of occasional exhibitions and lectures, and it has a number of artist studios. The pizza is good too.

Java Espressobar
CAFE

(Map p60; http://javaoslo.no; Ullevålsveien 47; 7am-6pm Mon-Fri, from 8am Sat, from 9am Sun; 37) Even if you're not in the neighbourhood, if you're a coffee fanatic it's worth the trip to pay homage to Java, which along with Tim Wendelboe and Fuglen revolutionised coffee in Norway. It's also a lovely light and high-ceilinged space to linger.

Lorry
BEER GARDEN, PUB

(Map p60; http://lorry.no; Parkveien 12; 11am-1am Mon, to 3.30am Tue-Sat, noon-1am Sun; 17B) There's nothing New Nordic about Lorry: just ask the fictional Harry Hole of the Jo Nesbø detective novels. But it's a great place for an atmospheric old-school beer either inside or out, and you can, of course, make like Harry and eat here, with a menu of traditional Norwegian favourites.

☆ Entertainment

Oslo has a thriving live-music scene – it's said that the city hosts more than 5000 gigs a year. Its venues are spread across the city but concentrate on Møllegata and in Vulkan, Grünerløkka and Grønland. World-class opera or ballet performances are held at the Oslo Opera House. Book ahead or try for the last-minute 100kr standing seats.

☆ Central Oslo

Oslo Opera House
OPERA

(Den Norske Opera & Ballett; Map p50; www.oper aen.no; Kirsten Flagstads plass 1; tickets 100-795kr; Sentralstasjonen) Apart from being one of Norway's most impressive examples of contemporary architecture, Oslo Opera House is also the venue for world-class opera and ballet performances.

Nationaltheatret THEATRE
(National Theatre; Map p50; www.national
theatret.no; Stortingsgata 15; tickets 160-480kr;
Nationaltheatret) Norway's showcase theatre, with its lavish hall, was constructed specifically as a venue for the works
of Norwegian playwright Henrik Ibsen,
whose works are still performed here. Its
historicist style dates from 1899 and is care
of Oslo's Henrik Bull.

Saga Kino CINEMA
(Map p50; ☑22 83 23 75; www.oslokino.no;
Stortingsgata 28; Nationaltheatret) The six-
screen Saga Kino cinema shows first-run
movies, including Hollywood fare, in their
original language; the entrance is on Olav
V's gate.

Filmens Hus CINEMA
(Map p50; ☑22 47 45 00; www.nfi.no; Dronningens gate 16; Dronningens gate) Filmens Hus
screens old classics and international festival
winners.

☆ Grünerløkka & Vulkan

★ Kafe Hærverk LIVE MUSIC
(Map p60; ☑930 95 357; www.kafe-haerverk.com;
Hausmanns gate 34; ⊙6pm-3.30am Mon-Fri, from
4pm Sat & Sun; 54) A friendly, intimate and
rather stylish live venue that also has excellent
craft beers and natural wines to drink. There's
a summer courtyard for hanging between sets
too. Expect electronic or indie acts, as well as
some culty international acts like the Necks
from Australia.

★ Blå LIVE MUSIC, DANCE
(Map p60; www.blaaoslo.no; Brenneriveien 9c;
⊙1pm-4am; 54) Blå is all things to everyone, with DJs (it happens to be the city's
best spot for hip-hop), live gigs and jazz. On
Sundays there is a live big band that's been
playing every afternoon for years. Or just
come early for a drink at one of the pretty
riverside tables.

Parkteatret LIVE MUSIC
(Map p60; ☑22 35 63 00; http://parkteatret.no; Olaf
Ryes plass 11; Olaf Ryes plass) Oslo's beloved
medium-sized venue, right on the lovely main
square. Come to see international acts such as
Shabazz Palaces or locals like Lindstrom and
Anna of the North.

Rockefeller Music Hall LIVE MUSIC
(Map p50; www.rockefeller.no; Torggata 16; Brugata) One of the city's best concert halls,

OSLO SHOPPING

Rockefeller Music Hall, once a bathhouse,
hosts a wide range of artists and events.

Revolver LIVE MUSIC
(Map p60; ☑22 20 22 32; www.revolveroslo.no;
Møllergata 32; ⊙6pm-3.30am; Brugata) Dark
and (ever so slightly) dirty rock-and-roll bar
with an attached band room. A great place
to see a local or interesting international act
or just to hang at the front bar with a musi-
cian-heavy crowd.

Oslo Spektrum LIVE MUSIC
(Map p50; www.oslospektrum.no; Sonja Henies plass
2; Oslo Spektrum) One of the city's largest
concert venues hosts a range of big-name international stars.

🔒 Shopping
Oslo's centre and its inner neighbourhoods
have a great selection of small shops, if
you're not into the malls. The city centre's
Kirkegaten, Nedre Slottsgate and Prinsens
gate are all home to a well-considered collection of Scandinavian and international
fashion and homewares shops, with Frogner and St Hanshaugen also having some
good upmarket choices. Grünerløkka is
great for vintage and Scandinavian fashion
also.

★ Norwegian Rain FASHION & ACCESSORIES
(Map p50; ☑996 03 411; http://norwegianrain.
com; Kirkegata 20; ⊙10am-6pm Mon-Fri, to 5pm
Sat; Nationaltheatret) Bergen comes to Oslo!
This west coast design superstar creates
what might be the world's most coveta-
ble raincoats. This Oslo outpost stocks the
complete range as well as creative director
T-Michael's woollen suits, detachable-collar
shirts, leather shoes and bags, not to mention limited editions of Kings of Convenience LPs.

★ Utopia Retro Modern VINTAGE, HOMEWARES
(Map p56; ☑408 60 460; www.utopiaretro
modern.com; Bygdøy allé 7; ⊙12.30-6pm Thu
& Fri, 1-4pm Sat; Solli) Take note of this

lovely 1929 functionalist shopfront before browsing the great mid-century design within; designed by Arne Korsmo and Sverre Aasland, it remains super-characteristic of the era. While you'll also find plenty of fantastic international pieces here, look out for the beautiful Norwegian design pieces, both original and reissued, from names like Torbjørn Afdal, Gunnar Sørlie and Sven Ivar Dysthe.

★ Cappelens Forslag   BOOKS
(Map p50; ☑ 908 81 106; www.cappelensforslag. no; Bernt Ankers gate 4; ☺ 11am-6pm Mon-Fri, to 4pm Sat; ☐ Brugata) Both a rare and cult lit dealer and cafe, this bookshop is set to be your new favourite. Make yourself at home on the front-room sofa with a good coffee and browse your way through its first editions and other gems, most of which are in English. It also hosts readings, book launches and concerts.

★ Chillout Travel Centre   BOOKS
(Map p60; ☑ 22 35 42 00; www.chillout.no; Markveien 55; ☺ 10am-7pm Mon-Sat, noon-6pm Sun; ☐ Schous plass) This is our kind of shop: good coffee, tasty dishes from around the world (dhal from India, snacks from Italy and cakes from...where else but Norway), loads of travel essentials such as bags and shoes, and a travel bookshop bursting with travel literature and guidebooks in Norwegian and English, including Lonely Planet guides.

Tronsmo   BOOKS
(Map p50; ☑ 22 99 03 99; www.tronsmo.no; Universitetsgata 12; ☺ 9am-5pm Mon-Wed, to 6pm Thu & Fri, 10am-4pm Sat; ☐ Tullinløkka) A social hub as much as a bookshop, come for its large range of English-language books and stay for a reading or performance. There's a large LGBTIQ+ section and a basement full of comics and graphic novels.

Gutta På Haugen   FOOD & DRINKS
(Map p60; ☑ 22 60 85 12; http://gutta.no/; Ullevålsveien 45; ☺ 8am-7pm; ☐ 37) For picnic or self-catering supplies, head to this well-stocked St Hanshaugen institution. There's a huge cheese selection with both Norwegian and European produce, a lovely array of local sausages and boxes of the must-try Norwegian flat bread. Its fresh produce is the best of the season and you can grab an excellent soft serve to take away at its ice-cream van across the road. Staff are happy to help with recommendations.

FWSS   FASHION & ACCESSORIES
(Fall Winter Spring Summer; Map p50; http://fallwinterspringsummer.com; Prinsens gate 22; ☺ 10am-7pm Mon-Fri, to 6pm Sat; ☐ Øvre Slottsgate) New flagship of this fast-growing Norwegian label, known for its easy basics as well as seasonal collections that combine Scandinavian simplicity with a pretty, playful edge.

Tom Wood   FASHION & ACCESSORIES
(Map p50; ☑ 919 06 226; http://tomwoodproject. com; Kirkegata 20; ☺ 11am-6pm Mon-Fri, 10am-4pm Sat; ☐ Dronningens gate) Oslo label Tom Wood's restrained monochromatic clothes are as Norwegian as you'll get, with their austere simplicity and high-quality natural materials. The silver jewellery will please fans of 20th-century Scandinavian design too.

Nomaden   BOOKS
(Map p56; ☑ 23 13 14 15; www.nomaden.no; Uranienborgveien 4; ☺ 10am-6pm Mon-Fri, to 5pm Sat; ☐ 17B) This is a classic travel bookshop where the shelves are bursting with guides, maps and travel literature that will have you dreaming of your next holiday in no time.

Gulating Grünerløkka   ALCOHOL
(Map p60; ☑ 958 42 611; www.facebook.com/GulatingOlutsalgGrunerlokka; Markveien 48; ☺ 10am-8pm Tue-Fri, to 6pm Sat, noon-6pm Mon; ☐ Schous plass) Beer-lovers' heaven with one of Norway's largest selections of beers from classics to the novel and the rare. Friendly staff make it a double pleasure.

Råkk og Rålls   MUSIC
(Map p50; ☑ 22 41 17 01; Stortingsgata 8; ☺ 11am-6pm Mon-Sat; ☐ Stortinget) Crate-digger heaven: a huge, rambling den of secondhand vinyl, mostly from the '70s and '80s, and much else besides.

Hevn   FASHION & ACCESSORIES
(Map p60; ☑ 400 62 430; https://hevn.no/; Torggata 36; ☺ 11am-7pm Mon-Sat; ☐ 34) Nordic noir or Norwegian black, call it what you will. This shop specialises in the pared-back, mildly Gothic brand of Scandinavian fashion. There's both menswear and womenswear, jewellery and bags and shoes. All clothing is made ethically and it stocks a large range of designers from Norway, Sweden and Denmark.

Oslo Kunsthandel   ART
(Map p50; ☑ 22 60 80 10; http://oslokunsthandel. no; Kristian Augusts gate 13; ☺ 11am-5pm Tue-Fri,

noon-4pm Sat & Sun; 🚇Tullinløkka) Whether you're in the market for museum-quality Modernist paintings and stunning mid-century furniture or not, this commercial gallery is a fabulous browse. It hosts good shows of emerging Norwegian artists at the front, while its resale pieces fill the rest of the large industrial space. These also include silver, glass, ceramics and rustic pieces as well as the previously mentioned modernist icons.

Ensemble   FASHION & ACCESSORIES
(Map p60; 📞414 60 566; http://ensemble.as; Nordre Gate 15; ⏱11am-6pm Mon-Fri, 10am-5pm Sat & Sun; 🚇Schous plass) Clean by Christina Ledang (a stellar local stylist) might be one of the few Norwegian labels here, but there's still a particularly 'northern' sensibility on display at this pretty shop. Garments by Danish label Norse Projects hang above shoes by Swedish shoemakers All Tomorrow's Parties, or find the racks of colourful cool Swede Rodebjer and lingerie and swimming costumes by Dutch darlings Love Stories.

Vestkanttorget Flea Market   MARKET
(Map p56; Amaldus Nilsens plass; ⏱10am-4pm Sat; 🚇Majorstuen) If you're happy sifting through heaps of, well, junk in search of an elusive vintage band T-shirt or mid-century ceramic coffee pot, take a chance here. It's at the plaza that intersects Professor Dahls gate, a block east of Vigeland Park, and it's a more than pleasant way to pass a Saturday morning.

Fara   SPORTS & OUTDOORS
(Map p60; www.rosl.no; Ullevålsveien 16; ⏱11-7pm Mon-Sat; 🚇37) Nordic minimalist design and Norwegian endurance (they're fjord-proof, we're told) combine in this new cycle design outfit from Stjordal up north. Part of Rouleurs (p82) next door, cycling devotees will like to check these beauties out. You can also ask about its program of local rides.

Torpedo   BOOKS
(Map p60; www.torpedobok.no; Wergelandsveien 17; ⏱11am-4pm Tue & Wed, to 6pm Thu & Fri, noon-6pm Sat & Sun; 🚇Bjørvika) An Oslo-based art publisher that stocks both its own publications as well as other Norwegian and international art books and journals. It also organises artist book-based shows at Kunsthall Oslo (p55).

Acne Studios
Archive   FASHION & ACCESSORIES
(Map p60; 📞22 60 93 00; www.acnestudios.com; Markveien 60; ⏱11am-7pm Mon-Fri, to 6pm Sat & Sun; 🚇Schous plass) The Swedish super-label has a handful of beautiful shops throughout Oslo, but this is the pick if you're after a bargain, with deep discounts on last year's stock. It's also worth a peek just for the beautiful photo murals of sculptor Gustav Vigeland's old studio.

Fransk Bazaar   VINTAGE
(Map p60; www.franskbazar.no; Grünersgate 5; ⏱noon-6pm Wed-Sat, 1-5pm Sun; 🚇Olaf Ryes plass) A local Francophile haunt run by a friendly Franco-Norwegian couple. Pour over the soulful French vintage homewares, objects and clothing in this delightfully jumbled and attractive shopfront.

Hasla   JEWELLERY
(Map p60; 📞922 78 777; http://hasla.no; Markveien 54; ⏱11am-6pm Mon-Fri, to 4pm Sat; 🚇Schous plass) Norwegian silversmiths handcraft simple designs inspired by nature as well as classic Scandinavian modern pieces.

Foto.no   PHOTOGRAPHY
(Map p50; 📞46 46 24 24; http://foto.no; Dronning Eufemias gate 12; ⏱10am-6pm Mon-Fri, to 4pm Sat; 🚇Bjørvika) A beautifully designed camera store with not only extensive new stock but also secondhand equipment. There is a lounge area for photography chat, casual lessons and trying out the merchandise.

Vinmonopolet   WINE
(Map p60; www.vinmonopolet.no; Nordre gate 16; ⏱10am-6pm Mon-Thu, 9am-6pm Fri, 9am-3pm Sat; 🚇Schous plass) This branch of the state wine and spirit chain has a good selection of French, Italian and Spanish wines, including well-priced French wine in plastic screw-cap bottles, excellent for picnicking by the river. Note: you must be least 20 years old to purchase, and there are usually long queues on Friday and Saturday afternoons.

Glasmagasinet
Department Store   DEPARTMENT STORE
(Map p50; www.glasmagasinet.no; Stortorvet 9; ⏱10am-7pm Mon-Fri, to 6pm Sat; 🚇Stortorvet) This iconic city department store dates back to 1899 and has a good range of Scandinavian brands you know you want.

Hassan og Den Dama FASHION & ACCESSORIES
(Map p56; http://dendama.com; Skovveien 4;
⊙10am-6pm Mon-Fri, to 2pm Sat; 🚇Solli) A Skovveien stalwart, this shop has clothing, shoes and jewellery produced by Scandinavian and international designers.

Marita Stiftelsen VINTAGE
(Map p60; 🖉22 38 19 20; http://marita.no; Markveien 67; ⊙11am-5pm; 🚇Biermanns gate) Heaven for those who like to rummage for treasures, this bric-a-brac charity shop has shelves packed with vintage china, old lamps, glassware and coffee pots, with a smaller section upstairs for books and records.

Norway Designs FASHION & ACCESSORIES
(Map p50; www.norwaydesigns.no; Stortingsgata 28; ⊙10am-6pm Mon-Wed & Fri, to 7pm Thu, to 4pm Sat; 🚇Nationaltheatret) Features designer clothing and beautiful glassware, stationery and watches within a stone's throw of the National Theatre.

Grønland Bazaar SHOPPING CENTRE
(Map p50; Tøyengata 2; ⊙10am-8pm Mon-Sat; 🚇37) A mostly Middle Eastern shopping centre, with a food court.

Tanum Bookshop CULTURAL CENTRE
(Litteraturhuset; Map p60; 🖉23 69 10 80; http://litteraturhuset.no/no/huset/bokhandel/; Wergelandsveien 29; ⊙11am-8pm Mon-Fri, 10am-5pm Sat, noon-4pm Sun; 🚇17B) Litteraturhuset's well-stocked bookshop is testament to the vibrancy of Norwegian publishing; it's a great place to pick up beautiful local children's books too.

Norli BOOKS
(Map p50; www.norli.no; Universitetsgata 20-24; ⊙10am-7pm Mon-Sat; 🚇Nationaltheatret) The largest bookshop in Norway stocks a good range of foreign-language titles as well as numerous travel guides and maps.

ℹ Information

MEDICAL SERVICES

Jernbanetorget Apotek (Fred Olsens gate; ⊙24hr; 🚇Jernbanetorget) Pharmacy opposite Oslo Central Station.

Oslo Kommunale Legevakten (Oslo Emergency Clinic; 🖉22 93 22 93; Storgata 40; ⊙24hr; 🚇Hausmanns gate) Casualty and emergency medical clinic; can provide a list of private doctors.

POST

Main Post Office (Map p50; 🖉23 14 90 00; cnr Prinsens gate & Kirkegata; 🚇Dronningens gate) As well as this main office, you'll also find convenient post office branches at Solliplass (Map p56; Solliplass; ⊙7am-5pm Mon-Fri; 🚇Solli), Oslo Sentralstasjon (Oslo S) and on Grensen (Map p50; Grensen; ⊙7am-5pm Mon-Fri; 🚇Nationaltheatret).

SAFE TRAVEL

Oslo is a very safe city; however, do keep your wits about you in the wee hours.

➡ East Oslo has a relatively dodgy reputation and its fair share of drug addicts and homeless people, but like the rest of the city is still reasonably danger-free at all hours of the night.

➡ If you're planning on taking to Oslo's waterways or hiking up in the hills, remember that the weather here can, even in summer, change rapidly.

➡ Although drugs may be readily available, they aren't in fact legal.

TOURIST INFORMATION

Den Norske Turistforening Tourist Information Centre (DNT, Norwegian Mountain Touring Club; Map p50; www.turistforeningen.no; Storget 3; ⊙10am-5pm Mon-Wed & Fri, to 6pm Thu, to 3pm Sat; 🚇Jernbanetorget) DNT provides information, maps and brochures on hiking in Norway and sells memberships that include discounted rates on mountain huts along the main hiking routes. You can also book some specific huts and pick up keys, as well as buy hiking gear.

Oslo Visitor Centre (Map p50; 🖉81 53 05 55; www.visitoslo.com; Jernbanetorget 1; ⊙9am-6pm; 🚇Sentralstasjon) Right beside the main train station. Sells transport tickets as well as the useful Oslo Pass (p58); publishes free guides to the city.

Use-It (Map p50; 🖉24 14 98 20; http://use-it.unginfo.oslo.no/; Møllergata 3; ⊙10am-5pm Mon-Fri, noon-5pm Sat; 🚇Brugata) The exceptionally helpful and savvy Ungdomsinformasjonen (Youth Information Office, better known as Use-It) is aimed at, but not restricted to, backpackers under the age of 26. It makes (free) bookings for inexpensive or private accommodation and provides information on anything from current events to possibilities for hitching (note: hitching is never entirely safe, so we don't recommend it).

ℹ Getting There & Away

Oslo is well linked to other European countries by air, with a usual flying time of two hours from London or Paris, and a little shorter from Berlin;

flights from Stockholm and Copenhagen are less than an hour. There are also regular bus and rail services to Oslo from neighbouring Sweden, with a three- to four-hour journey to Gothenburg. Regular car and passenger ferries also connect the city's ports with Denmark, Sweden and Germany.

Flights, cars and tours can be booked online at www.lonelyplanet.com/bookings.

AIR
Oslo Gardermoen International Airport

Oslo Gardermoen International Airport (Map p90; www.osl.no), the city's main airport, is 50km north of the city. It's used by international carriers, including Norwegian, SAS, Air France and British Airways. It's one of the world's most beautiful airports and has an amazing selection of places to eat and drink as well as Norwegian design shops alongside standard airport shopping.

Torp International Airport

Some budget flights, including those run by SAS Braathens, Widerøe and Ryanair, operate from Torp International Airport (www.trop.no) in Sandefjord, some 123km southwest of Oslo. Check carefully which airport your flight is going to. It has limited but good restaurants and bars and extensive parking facilities.

BOAT

Ferries operated by **DFDS Seaways** (Map p50; www.dfdsseaways.com; Vippetangen 2; 🚌 60) connect Oslo daily with Denmark from the **Vippetangen Quay** (Map p50) off Skippergata. Bus 60 stops within a couple of minutes' walk of the terminal.

In the summer **Color Line Ferries** (Map p56; www.colorline.no; Color Line Terminalen, Hjortnes; 🚌 33) run daily to/from Kiel (Germany); boats dock at Hjortneskaia, west of the central harbour. Take tram 13 from Oslo S, bus 33 or the Color Line bus, which leaves from platform 7 of the central bus terminal one hour before boat departures.

BUS

Long-distance buses arrive and depart from the **Galleri Oslo Bus Terminal** (Map p50; 🗐 23 00 24 00; Schweigaards gate 8; 🚆 Sentralstasjon). The train and bus stations are linked via a convenient overhead walkway for easy connections.

Nor-Way Bussekspress (🗐 81 54 44 44; www.nor-way.no) provides timetables and bookings. International services also depart from the bus terminal. Destinations include the following:

Bergen (522kr, 11 hours, three daily)

Stavanger (802kr, seven hours, usually one daily) Via Kristiansand.

ℹ TICKETS & PASSES

➡ In addition to single-trip tickets, one-day and transferable eight-trip tickets are also available.

➡ Children aged four to 16 and seniors over 67 pay half-price on all fares.

➡ You can download an app to buy tickets, although it doesn't always accept foreign credit cards.

➡ The Oslo Pass (p58) includes access to all public-transport options within the city, with the exception of late-night buses and trams, and most ferries around Oslofjord (including Ferry 91 to Bygdøy; p88).

CAR & MOTORCYCLE

The main highways into the city are the E6 from the north and south, and the E18 from the southeast and west. Each time you enter Oslo, you must pass through (at least) one of 19 toll stations and pay the 33kr toll.

TRAIN

All trains arrive and depart from **Oslo S** (Jernbanetorget 1) in the city centre. It has **reservation desks** (⊙ 6.30am-11pm; 🚆 Sentralstasjon) and an **information desk** (🗐 81 50 08 88; 🚆 Sentralstasjon) that provides details on routes and timetables throughout Norway.

There are frequent train services around Oslofjord (eg Drammen, Skien, Moss, Fredrikstad and Halden). Other major destinations:

DESTINATION	FARE (KR)	TIME (HR)	FREQUENCY (DAILY)
Bergen via Voss	950	6½-7½	four
Røros via Hamar	810	5	every 2hr
Stavanger via Kristiansand	997	7¾	six
Trondheim via Hamar & Lillehammer	965	6½-7½	six

ℹ Getting Around

All public transport is covered off by the Ruter (https://ruter.no/en/) ticketing system; schedules and route maps are available online or at **Trafikanten** (🗐 177; www.ruter.no; Jernbanetorget; ⊙ 7am-8pm Mon-Fri, 8am-6pm Sat & Sun).

Tram Oslo's tram network is extensive and runs 24 hours.

T-bane The six-line Tunnelbanen underground system, better known as the T-bane, is faster and extends further from the city centre than most city buses or tram lines.

Train Suburban trains and services to the Oslofjord where the T-bane doesn't reach.

BICYCLE

Oslo City Bike (☑ 915 89 700; https://oslobysykkel.no) gives you unlimited rides of 45-minute duration over 24 hours, three days or the whole season (45/99/299kr) from bicycle stands around the city. You can buy a pass via the website and your smartphone, via its app or by getting a pin from the website. The bikes are convenient and well maintained but are only available from 6am to midnight and only in the 'ice-free' season (generally from April to December).

BOAT

Ferries to the Oslofjord islands sail from Vippetangen Quay. **Ferry 91** (Map p50; ☑ 23 35 68 90; on board adult/child 50/25kr, from kiosks on departure jetty adult/child 30/15kr, with Oslo Pass free) to Bygdøy (March to October only) leaves from **Rådhusbrygge Quay** (Map p50).

Boat 62 connects Oslo with Drøbak (90kr, 1¼ hours, 10am weekdays, 10am and 3pm weekends) and other Oslofjord stops en route, including Håøya (45 minutes), a holiday spot offering fine swimming and camping. It departs from **Aker Brygge Pier** (Map p50).

A good number of the inner-island ferries are covered by the Ruter network too.

BUS

Bus and tram lines lace the city and extend into the suburbs. There's no central, local bus station, but most buses converge at Jernbanetorget in front of Oslo S. Most westbound buses, including those to Bygdøy and Vigeland Park, also stop immediately south of the National Theatre.

Service frequency drops dramatically at night, but on weekends the night buses N12, N14 and N18 follow the tram routes until 4am or later; there are also weekend night buses (201 to 218).

Ruter tickets for trips in zone 1 (most of the city centre) cost adult/child 33/17kr if bought from a sales point in advance (ticket machine, 7-Eleven, Narvesen and Trafikanten), or 55/28kr if bought on board. A day pass costs 90/45kr and a seven-day pass 240/120kr.

Oslo Pass (p58) holders can travel for free on all daytime lines in the city centre.

CAR & MOTORCYCLE

Oslo has its share of one-way streets, and is introducing no-parking zones within the city centre, which can complicate city driving. That said, the streets are rarely as congested as in most European cities.

Metered street parking, identified by a solid blue sign with a white 'P', can be found throughout the city. Payment is usually required from 8am to 5pm Monday to Friday, and until 3pm Saturday. At other times parking is free unless otherwise posted. The city centre also has 16 multistorey car parks, including those at Oslo City and Aker Brygge shopping centres. Parking fees in a public car park cost between 250kr and 290kr per 24-hour period, depending on the car park.

Note that the Oslo Pass (p58) includes parking at all municipal car parks; instructions for display come with the pass.

TAXI

There are taxi stands at Oslo S, shopping centres and city squares, but any taxi with a lit sign is available for hire. Otherwise, phone **Norgestaxi** (☑ 08000; www.norgestaxi.no) or **Oslo Taxi** (☑ 02323; www.oslotaxi.no), but note that the meter starts running at the point of dispatch and they are definitely not cheap. Oslo Taxis accept major credit cards.

T-BANE

All T-bane lines pass through the Nationaltheatret, Stortinget and Jernbanetorget (for Oslo S) stations. Ruter tickets for trips in zone 1 (most of the city centre) cost adult/child 33/167kr if bought in advance (from T-bane ticket machines, 7-Elevens, Narvesen and Trafikanten).

OSLOFJORD & ØSTFOLD

The beautiful Oslofjord, the northernmost part of the Skagerrak strait, stretches south from Oslo, and is dotted with picturesque towns and islands, while the eastern region of Østfold is a mix of forest, pastoral farmland and small seaside villages that carry great historical significance. It's an area that's popular with holidaying Norwegians, but is rarely visited by other travellers unless on the way to Sweden.

Drøbak

POP 11,510

Once Oslo's winter harbour, Drøbak is a cosy little village by the water's edge, home to enough clapboard timber buildings to warrant a happy day trip from the capital.

⊙ Sights

Oscarsborg Fortress   FORTRESS
(Map p92; www.oscarsborgfestning.no) FREE
Don't miss the imposing Oscarsborg For-

WORTH A TRIP

HVALER SKERRIES

Norwegian holidaymakers and artists love the Hvaler Skerries, an offshore archipelago of 833 forested islands and islets guarding the southern entrance to Oslofjord. The main islands of **Vesterøy**, **Spjærøy**, **Asmaløy** and **Kirkøy** are connected to the mainland by a toll road (59kr) and tunnel. Bus 365 (72kr) runs all the way from Fredrikstad to Skjærhalden, at the far end of Kirkøy.

Gamlebyen tourist office (p91) can point you in the direction of the numerous sights dotted around the islands. There are a couple of other seasonal tourist offices scattered around the islands.

Above the coastline of **Akerøy island**, accessible only by ferry (taxi boat) from Skjærhalden, clings a well-preserved 17th-century coastal **fortress**, renovated in the 1960s. Admission is free and it's always open.

The mid-11th-century **stone church** (Map 92; Skjærhalden; ⊙noon-4pm Jul, noon-4pm Sat late Jun & early Aug) on Kirkøy is one of the oldest in Norway.

Tourist offices have lists of fully equipped private houses and chalets in the Hvaler Skerries, which are available for between 450kr and 800kr per day.

tress, which lies on an offshore island and dates back to the 1600s. It was the Oscarsborg batteries that sank the German warship *Blücher* on 9 April 1940, an act that saved the king and the Norwegian government from being captured, and which is dramatically depicted in the film *The King's Choice*. **Ferries** (Map p92; www.oscarsborgfestning.no; adult/child 105/65kr) to the island depart every five minutes or so from Sundbrygga on the harbour in summer and less frequently the rest of the year.

⊖ Getting There & Away

The hourly bus 541 travels between Oslo and Drøbak. Alternatively, in July you can travel by boat.

Fredrikstad

POP 80,200

Fredrikstad is home to one of the best-preserved, and prettiest, fortress towns in Scandinavia: the Gamlebyen (Old Town), with the modern waterfront district just across the water. Fredrikstad was once an important trading centre between mainland Europe and western Scandinavia.

◉ Sights

★**Gamlebyen**   OLD TOWN

(Map p90) The timbered houses, moats, gates and drawbridge of the Fredrikstad Gamlebyen are simply enchanting. The perimeter walls, once defended by 200 cannons, now consist of grassy embankments that make for a very pleasant stroll. The narrow, cobbled streets have been similarly pre-

served and are still lined with picturesque 17th-century buildings, many of which remain occupied today.

Cathedral   CATHEDRAL

(Map p90; ☑ 69 95 98 00; Riddervoldsgate 5) Fredrikstad's 1880 cathedral reflects the town's 19th-century importance with its stained-glass work by Emanuel Vigeland. Norwegian practicality combines here with its piousness: bizarrely, the steeple contains a lighthouse, which still functions at night.

Isegran   ISLAND

(Map p90; www.isegran.no; with Fredrikstad Museum adult/child 75/30kr; ⊙noon-4pm Fri-Sun mid-Jun–late Aug) Norse sagas mention the 13th-century fortress of Isegran, an islet in the Glomma that became a further line of defence against Sweden in the mid-17th century. The **ruins** (Map p90) of a stone tower are visible at the eastern end of the island. It's also the site of a small **museum** on local boat building (from the time when boats were lovingly handcrafted from wood).

By road or on foot, access is from Rv108, about 600m south of Fredrikstad city centre.

Kongsten Festning   FORT

(Kongsten Fort; Map p90; ☑ 479 77 795; http://ostfoldmuseene.no; Blakstads gate) On what was once called 'Gallows Hill' stands the flower-festooned Kongsten Festning. Dating from 1685, it once served as a lookout and warning post for the troops at nearby Gamlebyen. Although it can get overrun on summer weekends, this otherwise lonely and appealingly intact is a fun place at which to

Fredrikstad

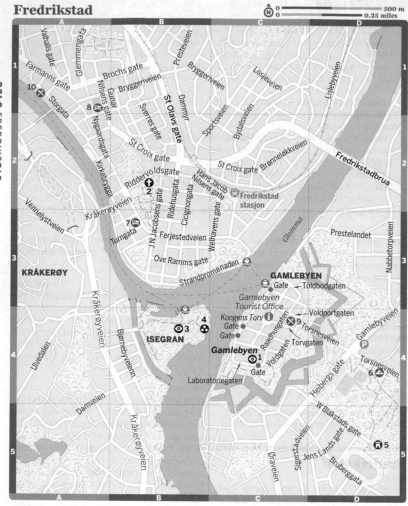

Fredrikstad

scramble around the turrets, embankments, walls and stockade, or just sit in the sun and soak up the quiet.

✨ Festivals & Events

Glomma Festival   MUSIC, FOOD
(www.glommafestivalen.no) The Glomma Festival runs in late June or early July. It's dedicated to

culinary delights and musical performances, ritual duels, a 'bathtub regatta' for creative vessels, and a veteran-sailing-ship exhibition. It's a very popular festival, so book ahead for accommodation.

🛏 Sleeping & Eating

Fredrikstad Motell & Camping　CAMPGROUND $
(Map p90; ☑ 69 32 03 15; www.fredrikstadmotel. no; Torsnesveien 16-18, Sarpsborg; campsite with/without car 250/200kr, motel s/d 450/550kr, cabins 900-1300kr; P 🐾) This comfortable if rather unscenic place is in the grounds of Kongsten Festning and most notable for its proximity to the Old Town. In summer there's a buffet breakfast for 90kr per person. From the centre, take any bus (eg 362) headed for Torsnes.

Hotel Victoria　HISTORIC HOTEL $$
(Map p90; ☑ 69 38 58 36; www.hotelvictoria.no; Turngaten 3, New Town; s/d 1195/1295kr; 🐾) The common areas of this century-old hotel are full of period trimmings and the rooms are plushed-up and cosy. Go for one with a pretty balcony and views to the trees and flowers of the neighbouring park. The staff are exceptionally helpful and friendly.

Quality Hotel Fredrikstad　HOTEL $$$
(Map p90; ☑ 69 39 30 00; www.qualityinn.com; Nygata 2-6, New Town; s/d from 1330/1490kr; 🐾) The business traveller's choice has super-smart, if rather functional, rooms enlivened by photographic art. Service is spot on and it couldn't be any more central.

Majoren's Stue og Kro　NORWEGIAN $$
(Map p90; ☑ 69 32 15 55; www.majoren.no; Voldportgata 73, Gamlebyen; mains 165-199kr; ☺ noon-8pm Mon-Thu, to 9pm Fri & Sat, to 7pm Sun) This rustic place specialises in Norwegian dishes cooked in a slow, old-fashioned manner that seems almost bang on trend again, along with more standard burgers and fish and chips, served either in the formal dining room or the back garden. An attached bar, with its own smart bar menu, is open for a few hours after the kitchen stops serving.

Riviera Fusion　ASIAN $$
(Map p90; ☑ 69 33 86 88; Storgata 13, Engelsviken, New Town; mains 125-215kr; ☺ 11am-10pm Mon-Thu, 11am-midnight Fri & Sat, noon-10pm Sun) This contemporary Asian-fusion place (think stir-frys, tempura and Thai curries alongside steaks and Italian seafood grills rather than actual fusion dishes) is set in a historic shopfront and has a summer terrace overlooking the waterfront.

ℹ Information

The helpful **Gamlebyen tourist office** (Map p90; ☑ 69 30 46 00; www.visitoslofjord.no; Kongens Torv; ☺ 9am-5pm Mon-Fri, 10am-4pm Sat, 11am-4pm Sun) is open year-round.

ℹ Getting There & Away

Intercity buses arrive and depart from the Fredrikstad Rutebilstasjon at the train station. There are regular **Flybussekspressen** (www.flybussekspressen.no) services from Fredrikstad to Oslo Gardermoen International Airport (307kr, 2¼ hours, every hour or two).

Fredrikstad lies on the **NSB** (www.nsb.no) rail line between Oslo and Göteborg. Trains to/from Oslo (221kr, one hour) run about 10 times daily, and also go to Sarpsborg and Halden, but note that southbound international trains require a mandatory seat reservation.

Drivers should follow the E6 south out of Oslo. Just after Råde, turn south on the 110 and follow it to Fredrikstad.

Halden

POP 30,550

The soporific but sweet border town of Halden, at the end of Iddefjord between steep rocky headlands, possesses a hugely significant history as a cornerstone of Norwegian defence through centuries of Swedish aggression. With a pretty little harbour filled with yachts, a looming fortress rising up behind the town and a sprinkling of decent restaurants, this place makes a worthwhile detour.

◉ Sights

**Fredriksten Fortress
& Museums**　FORTRESS
(Fredriksten Festning; Map p92; www.fredrikstenfestning.com; fortress free, adult/child all museums 60/20kr, guided tour 70/30kr; ☺ fortress 24hr, museums 11am-5pm daily mid-May–Aug, guided tours 2pm year-round) Crowning the hilltop behind Halden is the 1661 Fredriksten Fortress, which has resisted six Swedish sieges and never been captured. The fortress covers a large area, much of which is grassy expanses and tumble-down walls, but there are a couple of interesting museums, a restored cobbled street and great views. The whole place is brought entertainingly to life through the guided tours.

Oslofjord & Østfold

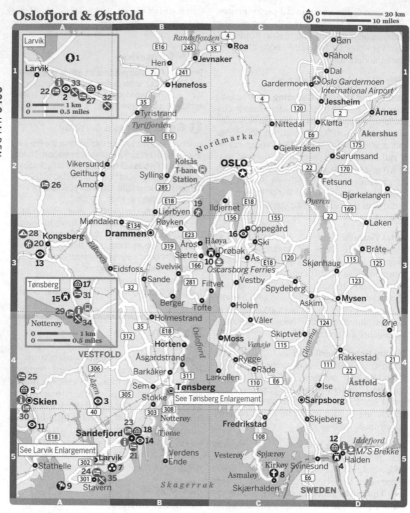

Rød Herregård

HISTORIC BUILDING

(Map p92; Herregårdsveien 10; tours adult/child 60/20kr; ⏱tours noon, 1pm & 2pm Mon-Sat, noon, 1pm, 2pm & 3pm Sun mid-Jun–mid-Aug, noon, 1pm & 2pm Sun May–mid-Jun & mid-Aug–Sep) Dating from at least 1690, Rød Herregård manor has fine interiors, which include notable collections of both weapons and art, as well as the mounted heads of many specimens of local wildlife. The formal gardens are some of the most pleasant in Norway. You'll find it 1.5km northwest of the town centre; it's well signposted.

🛏 Sleeping & Eating

Fredriksten Camping

CAMPGROUND $

(Map p92; ☎69 18 40 32; Fredriksten Festning; tent with car 275kr, 4-/5-bed cabins 490/790kr; ℗) Situated in a beautiful location amid the trees and adjacent to the fortress makes this well-run place a real winner. It also offers minigolf and, after the fortress closes and the crowds have disappeared, a quiet green spot to pitch a tent. There's an on-site restaurant selling various fried things.

Oslofjord & Østfold

OSLO HALDEN

Grand Hotell   HISTORIC HOTEL **$$**
(Map p92; ☑ 69 18 72 00; www.grandhotell.net; Jernbanetorget 1; r from 1310kr; P 🛜) The Grand Hotell, opposite the train station, is the oldest hotel in town and has a slightly forced old-world feel, but it's otherwise a very comfortable base.

★**Fredriksten Hotel**   HISTORIC HOTEL **$$$**
(Map p92; ☑ 69 02 10 10; www.fredrikstenhotell.no; Generalveien 25-27; s/d 1090/1545kr; P 🛜) A historic hotel with a very smart, contemporary style that has the best view in town. As well as its usual double and single rooms there are good number of family and six-bed rooms.

Kongens Brygge   PIZZA **$$**
(Map p92; ☑ 69 17 80 60; Gjesthavn; mains 135-190kr, pizzas 145-255kr; ☉1-11pm Sun-Tue & Thu, 1pm-2.30am Wed, noon-2.30am Fri & Sat) Right on the waterfront, this place has a cruisy atmos-phere and a wonderful pontoon terrace that's open in summer. The pizzas are expensive, but come in quite generous portions and are bound to fill hungry travellers. There are several similar places nearby.

ⓘ Information

The Halden **tourist office** (Map p92; ☑ 69 19 09 80; www.visithalden.com; Kongens Brygge 3; ☉9am-4.30pm Mon-Fri, 9am-noon Sat & Sun mid-Jun–mid-Aug, 9am-3.30pm Mon-Fri rest of year), just off Torget, has some useful information.

ⓘ Getting There & Away

Trains between Oslo and Halden (272kr, 1¾ hours) via Fredrikstad run hourly from Monday to Friday and every two hours on weekends. An average of four trains daily continue on to Göteborg and Malmö in Sweden. The long-distance bus terminal sits right on the harbour.

Southern Norway

Best Places to Eat

→ Bønder i Byen (p109)
→ Blom Restaurant (p103)
→ Tollboden (p101)
→ Kafe Strandhaven (p105)
→ Sanden (p99)

Best Places to Stay

→ Grand Hotell (p113)
→ Farris Bad (p99)
→ Lillesand Hotel Norge (p105)
→ Grand Hotell (p112)
→ Clarion Tyholmen Hotel (p103)

Why Go?

Come summer, the southern coastline draws Norwegian holidaymakers in droves. With a string of pristine coastal villages of whitewashed timber beside complex networks of bays and *skerries* (rocky islets) and a shimmering sea, it's not difficult to see why. For travellers, the 'Norwegian Riviera' offers a chance to experience a totally different destination from that of the fjords and high plateaus of the tourist brochures, one that is at once cosmopolitan and essentially Norwegian.

Venture inland and the scenery turns ever more dramatic. Deep in the region's interior is Rjukan, gateway to some of Norway's most scenic high country – the Hardangervidda National Park and the spectacularly formed mountain of Gausta. Elsewhere, scattered among a landscape smothered in forest and decorated in dark lakes filled with beavers, you'll discover idyllic, remote villages, wooden stave churches and a rich traditional culture.

When to Go
Kristiansand

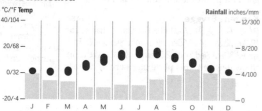

Feb–Mar Prime season for ice-climbing, skiing and dog-sledding in Rjukan.

Jul For south-coast beach towns at their most lively.

Aug–Sep Inland trails beckon as the autumn colours begin to appear.

THE COAST

You may have not come to Norway for the beaches, but plenty of Norwegians are drawn to the south coast by the lure of a paddle and a punt around its picturesque islands and *skerries*. The towns along the coast are almost all gorgeous, with town centres and harbourfront areas of whitewashed wooden cottages, and cafes, bars and restaurants all geared to seasonal holidaymakers. That it's appealing is never in doubt, and it's a wonderful way to experience Norwegian life at an even more gentle and relaxed pace than usual.

Tønsberg

POP 41,485

Tønsberg is the oldest town in Norway, although so distant are its origins that few interesting remnants remain. There are nonetheless a few Viking-era ruins and a decrepit castle that make the town worth a historical detour as you head along the coast.

◉ Sights

Tønsberg Castle   FORTRESS
(Castrum Tunsbergis; Map p92; ⊙ tower noon-5pm mid-Jun–mid-Aug, shorter hours rest of year) FREE Tønsberg Castle, spread across the hill behind the town, was the largest fortress in Norway in the 13th century. In 1503 the Swedes destroyed what they could, but nonetheless, the modern (1888), 17m-high **Slottsfjellstårnet tower** provides a good viewpoint over the ruins. Parts of the 600m-long outer wall remain intact, while the extant medieval stone foundations include **King Magnus Lagabøte's keep**, the 1191 **Church of St Michael**, the **hall of King Håkon Håkonsson** and various **guard towers**. The park is always open.

Vestfold County Museum   MUSEUM
(Vestfold Fylkesmuseum; Map p92; www.slottsfjells museet.no; Farmannsveien 30; adult/child 100/50kr, Tue free; ⊙ 11am-4pm mid-May–mid-Sep, shorter hours rest of year) At the foot of **Slottsfjellet** (Castle Rock) at the northern end of town, a five-minute walk northwest of the train station, this museum's highlights include displays on the excavation of the impressive *Oseberg* Viking ship (now shown in Oslo's Vikingskipshuset, p57), a collection of historic period-furnished farm buildings, and a section on Tønsberg's whaling history.

◉ Sleeping & Eating

Tønsberg Hostel   HOSTEL $
(Map p92; ☑ 33 31 21 75; tonsberg@hihostels.no; Dronning Blancasgata 22; dm 350kr, s/d with shared bathroom 750/850kr, d/q 895/1600kr; 🅿 🛜) This exceptionally well run and friendly hostel is well equipped, clean and tidy, and just a five-minute walk from the train station. The common areas would be the envy of many a fancy hotel. A good breakfast is served. The reception area is shut between noon and 3pm.

Thon Hotel Brygga   BUSINESS HOTEL $$
(Map p92; ☑ 33 34 49 00; www.thonhotels.no; Nedre Langgate 40; d 1215kr; @ 🛜) Inside a traditional wooden warehouse, this modern waterfront hotel has pleasant, if smallish, rooms and great breakfasts; it's popular with car-tripping families.

Roar I Bua   SEAFOOD $$
(www.roaribua.com; Nedre Langgate 42; sandwiches 80-99kr, mains 150-199kr; ⊙ 10am-10pm) This cute wooden shack is half-fishmonger and half-seafood cafe. However you choose to class it, the well-priced fish is so fresh it might well flop off your plate and back into the sea. If you're looking for picnic provisions, grab a slab of its smoked salmon to take away.

Restaurant Havariet   INTERNATIONAL $$
(Map p92; ☑ 33 35 83 90; www.havariet.no; Nedre Langgate 30e; mains 110-325kr; ⊙ 11am-2am) Arguably the most popular option along the waterfront, this place offers solid pub grub in a warm and inviting interior. It has good-value lunch deals and plenty of marine life on the menu, including some tasty, if sometimes over-burdened, salads.

ⓘ Information

Tourist Office (Map p92; ☑ 480 63 333; www.visittonsberg.com; Storgaten 38; ⊙ 9am-4.30pm Mon-Fri, 10am-2pm Sat mid-Jun–early Aug, 9am-2pm Mon-Fri rest of year) Just off the main square.

ⓘ Getting There & Around

The **Tønsberg Rutebilstasjon** (Map p92; ☑ 33 30 01 00; Jernbanegaten) is a block south of the train station. Nor-Way Bussekspress (p420) buses run to/from Kristiansand (437kr, 4½ hours, one to two daily) via most coastal towns en route, including Larvik (142kr, one hour, two daily). Nettbuss (p424) runs to Oslo (210kr, 1½ hours).

Intercity trains run hourly between Tønsberg and Oslo (237kr, 1½ hours) or south to Larvik (112kr, 34 minutes).

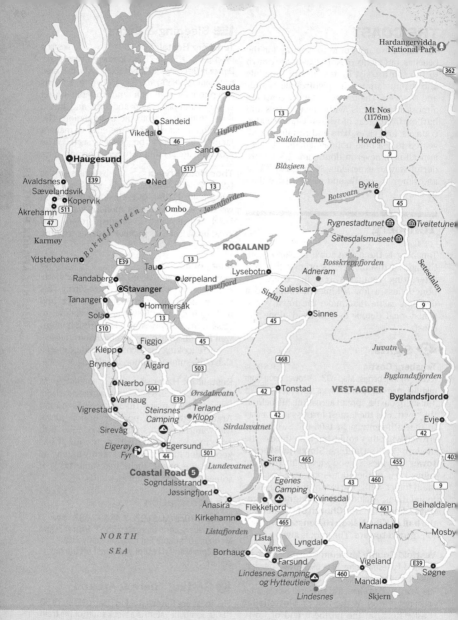

Southern Norway Highlights

1 Hardangervidda Plateau (p120) Striking out on foot across this haunting wilderness, home to Europe's largest herd of wild reindeer.

2 Dalen (p117) Boarding a slow boat down the Telemark Canal to this interior gem.

3 Gausta (p120) Summiting Norway's most beautiful mountain.

4 Stavern Festivalen (p100) Dancing the night away at this, just one of the coast's musical celebrations.

5 Coastal roads (p112) Driving the quiet, scenic route

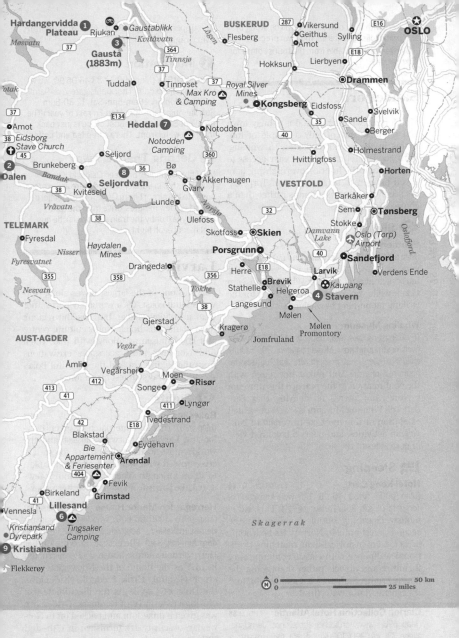

between Flekkefjord and Egersund.

6 Lillesand (p105) Strolling the evocative streets of this charming wooden 'white town'.

7 Heddal Stave Church (p116) Admiring the exquisite roof lines and paintings in this untouristed stave church.

8 Seljordvatn (p121) Scouring this brooding lake in search of Selma the Serpent.

9 Kristiansand (p105) Getting a cultural hit in between boating and swimming at the great museums of the coast's 'capital'.

Drivers with their own vehicles will be stung by automatic tolls for entering the town precincts.

Bike rental is available from the tourist office for 75kr per day.

Sandefjord

POP 61,220

This former whaling capital is a busy town and home to one of only a couple of museums in the world dedicated to whaling. With good hotel choices and easy access to the coast and the interior, overnighting here if you happen to be flying out of Torp, Oslo's second airport, is a bonus rather than a chore.

◉ Sights

Southern Actor   SHIP

(Map p90; ⊙ 9.30am-5pm late Jun-Aug) The 1950s whaleboat *Southern Actor* is moored at the harbour; entry is by your Whaling Museum ticket; while you're there, also look out for the striking monument to whalers.

Whaling Museum   MUSEUM

(Hvalfangst-museet; Map p90; ☑ 947 93 341; www. hvalfangstmuseet.no; Museumsgaten 39; adult/ child 70/50kr; ⊙ 10am-5pm late Jun-Aug, shorter hours rest of year) You might not agree with the continuation of the practice this museum explores, but there's no denying that Sandefjord's Whaling Museum is a well-presented exhibition of this most controversial of Norwegian activities, and offers a balanced view of both sides of the story.

🛏 Sleeping

Hotel Kong Carl   HISTORIC HOTEL $$

(Map p90; ☑ 33 46 31 17; www.kongcarl.no; Torggata 9; s/d 895/1195kr; 🅿 🛜) This ridiculously charming option is, allegedly, the second-oldest hotel in Norway. Its bedrooms are a kind of historical-light, matching traditional wallpaper with classic contemporary furniture and objects rather than going the antique route. Staff are kind and helpful and it's central, if not waterfront.

Clarion Collection Hotel Atlantic   HOTEL $$

(Map p90; www.nordicchoicehotels.no; Jernbanealleen 33; s/d 990/1090kr; 🅿 🛜) Occupying a beautiful building from 1914, three minutes' walk from the station, this Clarion boutique-style hotel is great value and one of the more atmospheric choices on this part of the coast. Rooms have a luxe aesthetic, though they're on the small side, and a light dinner,

or supper as they call it, is complimentary every night from 6pm.

ℹ Information

Tourist Office (Map p90; ☑ 33 46 05 90; www. visitsandefjord.com; Thor Dahls gate 7; ⊙ 9am-5.30pm Mon-Fri, 10am-5pm Sat, 12.30-5pm Sun Jul-Aug, 9am-4pm Mon-Fri rest of year) The excellent Sandefjord tourist office is just back from the waterfront. There's free tea and coffee.

ℹ Getting There & Away

Most buses running between Oslo and Kristiansand stop in Sandefjord and there are express buses to the airport from Oslo. Torp Sandefjord airport is a few minutes' drive from the town, either by taxi or by the train station shuttle bus that meets each flight.

Larvik

POP 43,900

Larvik is one of the largest towns along Norway's south coast. It's a workaday port rather than a holiday village, but has the region's most glamorous hotel, a new cultural centre and good museums. Along with that, you'll find Norway's most accessible excavations from the Viking era and the beautiful Bøkeskogen, Norway's largest beech forest.

◉ Sights

Bøkeskogen   FOREST

(Map p90) This sublime patch of green overlooking Larvik is Norway's largest and the world's most northerly beech tree forest. It is criss-crossed with walking trails, from 2.6km to 10km in length. There are stunning views over Lake Farris from its northwestern apex.

Herregården Manor House   HISTORIC BUILDING

(Map p90; ☑ 481 06 600; www.larvikmuseum.no; Herregårdsbakken; adult/child 50/30kr; ⊙ noon-4pm Jun–mid-Sep) The classic baroque timber Herregården manor house was constructed in 1677 as the home of the Norwegian Governor General, Ulrik Frederik Gyldenløve, the Duke of Larvik. As the illegitimate son of King Frederik IV of Denmark, Gyldenløve was given a dukedom and packed off to Norwegian obscurity. It's furnished in 17th- and 18th-century style.

Kaupang   ARCHAEOLOGICAL SITE

(Map p90; ☑ 906 22 744; www.vikingbyen.org; Kaupangveien 276; adult/child 60kr/free; ⊙ 10am-4pm mid-Jun–mid-Aug) Kaupang, 5km east of Larvik, was a former Viking town built around

AD 800 and occupied until 960. It is believed that up to 1000 people once lived here. Although most of the original artefacts are now in Oslo, the custodians of the site make the most of what they have with a small exhibition, four Viking tents and knowledgeable guides dressed as Vikings who can show you nearby Viking graves and explain Kaupang's past.

On Wednesday (family day) and weekends, they cook Viking soup and bread, and fire up the forge. The guides can also tell you where to find other Viking cemeteries in the Larvik area.

Bølgen   CULTURAL CENTRE
(Kulturhus; Map p90; www.kulturhusbolgen.no; Sanden 2; ⊙11am-10pm Mon-Sat, noon-10pm Sun) The town's impressive wave-shaped cultural centre houses a gallery that has an interesting curatorial calendar of contemporary Norwegian artists, concert halls and a cinema (screening original films), as well as the town's best cafe and bar, Sanden.

🏃 Activities

Farris Bad   SPA
(Map p90; ☑33 19 60 00; www.farrisbad.no; Fritzøe Brygge 2; ⊙7am-9pm Mon, Tue & Thu, to 11pm Wed & Fri, 8am-11pm Sat, 8am-9pm Sun) Larvik's spa is up there with Europe's better hotel spas, with an impressive collection of pools, steam rooms and saunas, a tantalising staircase down into the sea, lounges with spectacular sea views and a women-only sauna. There's 'obligatory textile-free' time on Wednesday nights and monthly Sunday afternoons.

🛏 Sleeping & Eating

Lysko Gjestegaard   GUESTHOUSE $$
(Map p90; ☑977 44 490; www.lysko-it.no; Kirkestredet 10; s/d from 840/1050kr; 🅿🛜) This quiet guesthouse occupies a lovely old timbered house opposite the Maritime Museum at the eastern end of the harbour. The rooms themselves are crammed with character via hand-decorated furniture and liberally applied colour on the walls and ceilings. There's a kitchen for guest use and an attached antique shop. Prices don't include breakfast.

★Farris Bad   HOTEL $$$
(Map p90; ☑33 19 60 00; www.farrisbad.no; Fritzøe Brygge 2; s/d 1560/2066kr) Along from the redeveloped dock precinct, built next to, and over, the town's nicest sandy beach, this full-service spa hotel has luxurious

rooms, many with views straight out to sea, as well as lavishly decorated public spaces. Outside high season and weekends, room prices, which always include complimentary entry to the gobsmackingly scenic spa, drop dramatically.

The hotel's restaurant has a beachside terrace and does a generous lunchtime seafood buffet (350kr) in summer.

Pakkhuset   PUB FOOD $$
(Map p90; ☑33 19 69 00; Storgata 19; mains 179-219kr, pizza 120-160kr; ⊙11am-9pm Sun-Thu, to midnight Fri & Sat, mid-May–mid-August) Part of the Quality Hotel Grand Farris, this bright, dockside restaurant is a fun, waterfront option for peel-and-eat shrimp, burgers or pizza. So fun, in fact, it turns into a club on Friday and Saturday nights.

Sanden   CAFE $$
(Map p90; www.bolgenkulturhus.no/sanden; Bølgen, Sanden 2; mains 165-245kr; ⊙11am-4pm Tue, to 8pm Wed & Thu, to 10pm Fri & Sat, to 5pm Sun, later for concerts) A bastion of cosmopolitan cool in Larvik. We could settle into Sanden's soaring waterfront space for hours. Coffee here is the best for miles around, with Oslo's Solberg & Hansen beans, and there's a burger menu that goes from basic to inspired ('Carla' has coriander and chilli mayo, 'Barbara' caramelised onion). It's open late as a bar for events; check ahead.

Georg Marius Larsen   FISH SHOP $$
(Map p90; ☑33 18 17 44; Dronningens gate 43; dishes 169-199kr; ⊙9am-4.30pm Mon-Fri, to 2.30pm Sat) An authentic fish deli that sells hot fish cakes, salads, pre-prepared meals such as seafood gratins, and fresh seafood.

ℹ Information

Tourist Office (Map p90; ☑33 69 71 00; www. visitlarvik.no; Bølgen, Sanden 2; ⊙1-8pm) This helpful tourist office is located inside the swish Bølgen cultural centre on the waterfront.

ℹ Getting There & Away

Nor-Way Bussekspress (p420) buses pass through Larvik en route between Seljord (292kr, 2¼ hours, up to three times daily) and Tønsberg (127kr, one hour). For other destinations along the coast, you may need to change at Tønsberg or Arendal. Local trains run hourly between Oslo S (Central Station) and Larvik (256kr to 322kr, two hours). The train and bus stations are side by side on Storgata.

Stavern

POP 5740

Stavern, located just south of Larvik, is set around a stunning fold of coastline; the ocean is full of granite outcrops, creating a maze of icy waterways, with the low-lying Brunlanes Peninsula and its strange rocky beaches and pleasant towns to the southwest. The village of Stavern itself is almost as pretty as the natural beauty surrounding it. Its pedestrian streets are lined with cafes, small private galleries and patinaed white houses, becoming Larvik's social club most summer nights. Highlights include the mid-18th-century fort **Fredriksvern Verft**, which is surrounded by block houses that once formed part of the fortress defences.

Activities

Coastal Walk WALKING

(Kyststien; Map p92) Stavern is the start of this beautiful, and very popular, 33km-long coastal walk to Ødegården on the western coast of Brunelanes. There's a route map on www.visitvestfold.com.

Festivals & Events

Stavern Festivalen MUSIC

(www.stavernfestivalen.no; pass 100kr; ☺ mid-Jul) Hugely atmospheric outdoor festival held between the shore and a forest. Features rock and pop acts, with great Scandinavian artists and international headliners.

Sleeping & Eating

Hotel Wassilioff HISTORIC HOTEL $$

(Map p92; ☑ 33 11 36 00; www.wassilioff.no; Havnegata 1; s/d 1195/1400kr; [P][🖥]) In operation since 1844, the Hotel Wassilioff has learned a thing or two about keeping guests happy and, thanks to touches such as old sepia photos of Norwegian royalty and vintage dining chairs, it has character in abundance. Rooms are a little less exciting than common areas. Its location, next to parkland and a pocket-sized beach, is delightful.

Smak av Stavern SPANISH $$

(Map p90; ☑ 948 78 832; http://smakavstavern.no; Strandveien 3; tapas 69-82kr, mains 172-189kr; ☺ 1pm-10pm Mon-Thu, noon-11pm Fri & Sat, to 10pm Sun) An archetypal Norwegian dining room, with all navy and red painted wooden chairs and bare tables decorated with candles, in a lovely dockside location, Smak does a surprising menu of tapas and paella, although there's also a fish soup and burgers if you don't want to go entirely Mediterranean.

ℹ Information

There's currently no actual office; www.visitvestfold.com has some useful information, as does the Larvik tourist office (p99).

ℹ Getting There & Away

To get to and from Larvik (45kr, 15 minutes, hourly), use bus 1.

Kragerø

POP 10,505

One of the favourite summer retreats for Norwegians, Kragerø has narrow streets and whitewashed houses climbing up from the water's edge. It's long served as a retreat for artists, and Edvard Munch spent a few restorative fishing holidays here, calling Kragerø 'the pearl of the coastal towns', though this coastal holiday cheer never showed up in his many seascapes. A statue of Munch stands on the spot where he painted a winter sun over the sea.

Sights & Activities

There's not much to see here; the offshore island of **Jomfruland** is Kragerø's most popular attraction. For a great view over the town and its *skerries*, climb from Kragerø Stadium to the lookout point on **Steinmann Hill**.

Seal Watching WILDLIFE WATCHING

(☑ 400 05 858; www.fjordbat.no; adult/child 250/200kr; ☺ 10.45am Tue, 3.25pm Fri, 11.10am Sat, 11.45am & 7.45pm Sun) M/S *Kragerø*, the same boat that runs ferry services to Jomfruland, offers a seal-watching package where you get return boat rides to Jomfruland, wildlife fact sheets and a take-home pair of binoculars. Seals are seen on around 50% of ferry crossings.

Sleeping & Eating

Kragerø Sportell Apartments APARTMENTS, HOTEL $

(☑ 35 98 57 00; www.kragerosportell.no; Lovisenbergveien 20; d/apt 750/1280kr; [P][@][🖥]) A former youth hostel, which is now privately owned, this place is an excellent deal with modern and comfortable, if plain, rooms and lovely waterfront apartments that sleep up to four and have their own kitchens. Breakfast is included in room rates unless you're staying in an apartment. To get here, follow the signs to the village of Kalstadkilen.

Victoria Hotel HISTORIC HOTEL **$$**
(☑35 98 75 25; www.victoria-kragero.no; PA Heuchtsgata 31; s/d 1100/1250kr; �) The rooms in the grand old Victoria all differ from one another and are the best in town. Some have little kitchenettes, while others have balconies overlooking the wharf. It's well run and nicely idiosyncratic.

Tollboden INTERNATIONAL, PIZZA **$$**
(www.tollboden.com; mains 150-225kr, pizza 175-220kr; � noon-9pm Mon-Fri, 11am-10pm Sat, 1-9pm Sun) Casual dining right by the water with burgers, sushi, fish soup, mussels and the like, and thin-crust pizzas. During summer there's a more formal place on the back garden terrace; it feels like you're attending a dinner party at a well-to-do friend's beach house (though with mains at 330kr to 385kr and caviar and Champagne for two at 2900kr).

ℹ Information

Tourist Office (☑35 98 23 88; www.visit-kragero.no; Tovgaten 1; �9am-6pm Mon-Sat, to 3pm Sun Jul–mid-Aug, 9am-4pm Mon-Fri May, Jun & mid-Aug–Sep) The exceptionally helpful tourist office is at the bus station.

ℹ Getting There & Away

Trains from Oslo or Kristiansand stop at Neslandsvatn, where most are met by a bus to Kragerø. Buses run up to five times daily to Oslo (335kr, 3½ hours) and Kristiansand (310kr, 2½ hours), although you may have to change in Tangen on the E18.

Risør

POP 6910

Snaking around the base of cliffs and hills and overlooking a moody ocean, the white-on-white town of Risør is one of southern Norway's prettiest. The focus of the town falls on the U-shaped harbour, full of colourful fishing boats and private yachts and surrounded by historic houses dating from as early as 1650.

WORTH A TRIP

MØLEN & DAMVANN

Mølen (Map p92) The Mølen Promontory, around 20 minutes' drive west of Stavern, is Norway's largest beach of rolling stones, and an austere, rather impressive sight. The 230 stone cairns and heaps of boulders, which are laid out in parallel rows, are all Iron Age burial mounds.

Damvann (Map p92) Some 20km north of Larvik is the beautiful, haunting lake of Damvann, surrounded by forests. Popular legend claims it to be the home of a witch called Huldra, who is of such exquisite beauty that any man who looks upon her is doomed. Access is difficult without a car; the nearest bus stop is at Kvelde (6km from the lake) on Numendalslågen Rd.

✪ Festivals & Events

Risør Chamber Music Festival MUSIC
(www.kammermusikkfest.no; � Jun) Held in the last week of June across several venues, this festival has a growing cast of local and international performers in attendance.

Risør Wooden Boat Festival SPORTS
(Trebåtfestival; www.trebatfestivalen.no; � Aug) Held over the first weekend in August, this festival (known as Trebåtfestival) encompasses boat races, concerts and kids' activities. Finding accommodation at this time can be difficult.

🛏 Sleeping & Eating

Sorlandet Feriesenter CAMPGROUND **$**
(☑900 26 168; www.sorlandet-feriesenter.no; Sandnes; campsites 210kr, cabins 600-1800kr) This delightful waterside campground, on the peninsula south of Risør, has a range of very well equipped cabins alongside lots of trees under which you can plonk a tent. Children will love all the activities and facilities on offer (boat rides, playgrounds, 'elephant' showers, giant bouncing balloons and so on).

Det Lille Hotell APARTMENT **$$$**
(☑37 15 14 95; www.detlillehotel.no; Storgata 5; apt per night 1400-2200kr; P�) Superb-value, self-catering suites and apartments are dotted around town under the umbrella host. Most are in delightfully restored homes with

WORTH A TRIP

THE SKERRIES OFF ARENDAL

The 260-hectare island of **Merdø**, just off Arendal, has been inhabited since at least the 16th century and was recorded as an outport as early as 1300. One nice maritime peculiarity is that the island bears the remnants of vegetable species introduced from the ballast of early sailing vessels. There's a couple of small, protected beaches on the harbour-side of the island and some lovely picnic spots.

Other favoured bathing sites are on **Tromøy**, **Spornes**, **Hisøy** and **Hove**. For Spornes, take the bus marked 'Tromøy Vest/Øst'; it's a 15-minute walk from the stop. Alternatively, take a bike on the M/S *Skilsø* ferry (adult/child 30/22kr, 10 minutes), which sails frequently between Arendal and the western end of Tromøy. Tromøy also has some enjoyable and easy-to-follow **walking trails**. The Arendal **tourist office** (p103) can give route suggestions.

On the islets of **Store** and **Lille Torungene** rise two grand lighthouses that have guided ships into Arendal since 1844. They're visible from the coasts of both Hisøy and Tromøy.

period furnishings – ideal if you plan to spend a week here. Daily rates are cheaper outside the peak summer season, and booking for a week reduces costs significantly.

Stangholmen Fyr
Restaurant & Bar   SEAFOOD $$$
(☑37 15 24 50; www.stangholmen.no; mains 310kr; ⊙restaurant 2-10pm, bar noon-2am, both Jun-Aug only) Set in a pretty lighthouse dating from 1855, this summer restaurant makes for a gorgeous day trip from Risør and serves bouillabaisse (349kr) and lots of other fish dishes, as well as steaks and deer fillet. Boats leave from Risør (one way 50kr) from noon and run back until all guests leave.

Kast Loss   SEAFOOD $$$
(☑37 15 03 71; www.strandgata.com; Strandgata 23; mains 265-328kr; ⊙4-10pm Mon-Fri, 11am-midnight Sat, noon-10pm Sun) Seafood is, not surprisingly, a big deal here, and locals rate Kast Loss as about the best-value restaurant in town. It also happens to be endearingly dark and nautical. If you're not up for a seafood feast, the pizza is good (184kr to 214kr).

ⓘ Information

Tourist Office (☑37 15 22 70; www.risor.no; Torvet 1; ⊙10am-4pm mid-Jun–mid-Aug, 11am-3pm Mon-Fri, noon-2pm Sat rest of year) Located 50m west of the harbour.

ⓘ Getting There & Away

The nearest train station is at Gjerstad, but you'll need your own car to get there. Nettbuss (p424) buses to Oslo (332kr, 3¼ hours) connect at Vinterkjær with local buses to/from Risør (39kr, 40 minutes). It also has a direct service to Kristiansand (260kr, 1¾ hours)

Arendal

POP 41,665

Arendal, one of the larger south-coast towns, has an undeniable buzz throughout summer, with the outdoor restaurants and bars around the harbour (known as Pollen) filling up with holidaymakers, and a full calendar of festivals and open-air concerts by the water most weekends. Even in winter, some of the larger bars stay open and have live music on weekends. It's a nice place to spend a few days, with enough going on to keep you amused while retaining an intimate village-like vibe.

The matchbox-sized old district of Tyholmen, with its tightly wound core of timbered houses, adds considerable charm, while those seeking greater communion with the sea than a harbourside cafe can set off to the offshore islands of Merdø, Tromøy and Hisøy.

⊙ Sights

★ Bomuldsfabriken Kunsthall   GALLERY
(www.bomuldsfabriken.no; Oddenveien 5; ⊙noon-4pm Tue-Sun) FREE This highly regarded contemporary art gallery is a 15-minute walk from the town centre on the northern reaches of Arendal. One of the largest contemporary galleries in southern Norway, its exhibitions are housed in a stunning example of Norwegian industrial architecture, a former cotton factory from the late 19th century.

Tyholmen   AREA
Rising up behind the Gjestehavn (Guest Harbour) is the old harbour-side Tyholmen district, home to beautiful 17th- to 19th-century timber buildings featuring neoclassical, rococo and baroque influences. Tyholmen was once separated from the mainland by a canal,

which was filled in after the great sailing era. Look out for the **rådhus** (town hall), a striking wooden building dating from 1815.

🎆 Festivals & Events

Canal Street Jazz & Blues Festival   MUSIC
(www.canalstreet.no) World-class jazz and blues, with surprise acts such as Patti Smith.

🛏 Sleeping & Eating

⭐**Clarion Tyholmen Hotel**   HISTORIC HOTEL **$$$**
(☑ 37 07 68 00; www.nordicchoicehotels.no; Teaterplassen 2; s/d 1470/1710kr; ❄☎) Undoubtedly Arendal's best hotel, the Clarion combines a prime waterfront position in a restored old dockside building that emulates Tyholmen's old-world ambience. Rooms in the original wing are the most atmospheric, and have ridiculously lovely views, as do the corner suites in the new wing. The hotel restaurant is a relaxed and stylish option too.

Thon Hotel Arendal   HOTEL **$$$**
(☑ 37 05 21 50; www.thonhotels.no; Friergangen 1; s/d 1095/1395kr; ❄☎) It might not have waterfront views, but this typical Thon is just 50m from the water's edge. Bland on the exterior, the rooms are modern, large and comfortable. There's a public pay car park nearby.

Pigene på Torvet   BAKERY **$**
(☑ 465 49 136; www.facebook.com/pigenepaatorvet; Tollbodgaten 5; snacks 79-169kr; ☺10am-4pm Sat-Wed, to 5pm Thu & Fri) What you miss out on views here, you'll make up for in flavour. A brimming display of cakes and pastries – the town's best – can be taken away or wolfed at a table with coffee. Or come for a thin-crust pizza, chilli con carne or salad lunch. It also has gourmet grocery supplies to take away.

⭐**Blom Restaurant**   SEAFOOD **$$$**
(☑ 37 00 14 14; www.blomrestaurant.no; Lang-brygge 5; mains 310kr; ☺5-10pm) The most upmarket of the Pollen harbour crowd, Blom provides a respite from the overfilled plates and boozy vibe that sometimes wins out at the other waterside places. Mains are elegantly traditional (say, instead of fish soup, it's creamy seafood with a lobster stock), but the sharing menu does both aquavit-cured reindeer as well as sashimi and satays.

🍷 Drinking & Nightlife

⭐**Lille Andevinge**   BAR
(☑ 901 46 839; Nedre Tyholmsvei 10; ☺4pm-1am Wed & Thu, to 2am Fri & Sat) What looks like

traditional seaside wooden shop has been given a complete makeover inside, with a dark and urban look. Come and lounge by the fire with a bottle of wine or hang at the bar and get the friendly bartenders to customise a cocktail for you. Open year-round, there's also live music on weekends.

No.9 Kaffe & Platebar   CAFE
(☑ 958 26 041; Teaterplassen 3; ☺10am-5pm Mon-Sat) No.9 is the work of Espen Larsen, a local jazz musician who sells a range of (mostly jazz) CDs and plays them while you sip your coffee or snack on a pastry. It's occasionally open later for events.

🛍 Shopping

Tyholmen Kolonial   FOOD & DRINKS
(☑ 473 98 850; www.facebook.com/tyholmenkolonial.no/; Friergangen 5; ☺10am-4pm Mon-Sat) Just what you want in a holiday town: a produce shop that sells the best of local small producers, with everything from cheeses, preserves and flat breads to skincare and ceramics, either as picnic supplies or to take home as souvenirs. Salad and sandwich lunches, coffee and pastries are also available, eaten at a table overlooking the cobbled square.

ℹ Information

Tourist Office (☑ 37 00 55 44; www.arendal.com; Sam Eydes Plass 1; ☺10am-4pm Mon-Fri) Outside the high season hours can be erratic. Even if the office is shut, someone will be on hand to answer phone calls.

ℹ Getting There & Away

MS *Merdøy*, or one of the other ferries run by **Skilsoferga** (www.skilsoferga.no; one way adult/child 35/25kr), sails from Arendal (Pollen) to Merdø up to hourly from early July to mid-August. It also leaves hourly between 11am and 4pm on weekends year-round from Merdø and returns on the half-hour. Timetables are available from the tourist office and displayed on the dock; it costs 30kr return.

There are also ferries to Hisøy (adult/child 50/30kr).

Nor-Way Bussekspress (p420) buses to and from Kristiansand (232kr, 1½ hours, up to nine daily) and Nettbuss (p424) services to and from Oslo (364kr, four hours) call in at the Arendal Rutebilstasjon, a block west of Pollen harbour. Nettbuss' local TIMEkspressen buses connect Arendal with Grimstad (79kr, 30 minutes, half-hourly) and Risør (139kr, 1¼ hours, hourly).

Grimstad

POP 12,172

Grimstad is at its most lovely in the pedestrianised streets that lie inland from the waterfront; these are some of the most atmospheric on the Skagerrak coast. The town has a number of interesting calling cards. It was home to young playwright Henrik Ibsen and has a good museum in the pharmacy in which he once worked. And it is the sunniest spot in Norway, with an average of 266 hours of sunshine per month in June and July. The town also has an unmistakably, and welcome, young vibe, thanks to its large student population.

◉ Sights

★ Ibsenhuset Museum   MUSEUM
(www.gbm.no; Henrik Ibsens gate 14; adult/child 90/65kr; ⊙11am-4pm Mon-Sat, noon-4pm Sun Jun–mid-Sep, closed mid-Sep–May) Norway's favourite playwright, Henrik Ibsen, washed up in Grimstad in January 1844. The house where he worked as a pharmacist's apprentice, and where he lived and first cultivated his interest in writing, has been converted into the Ibsenhuset Museum. It contains a re-created pharmacy and many of the writer's belongings, and is one of southern Norway's most interesting museums. The young staff here are wonderful, their tours full of fascinating detail and the odd spot of salacious gossip.

✯✯ Festivals & Events

Sørlandet Boat Show   SPORTS
(www.baadmessen.no; ⊙May) Floating boat show held in May.

🛌 Sleeping

Bie Apartment & Feriesenter   CAMPGROUND $
(☑37 04 03 96; www.bieapart.no; off Arendalsveien; campsites 295kr, cabin/apt from 575/1460kr; 🅿🐾) The nearest camping option to Grimstad is this friendly, well-equipped site 800m northeast of the centre along Arendalsveien. As well as big, grassy pitches it has a range of huts and some seriously kitted-out apartments.

Café Ibsen B&B   B&B $$
(☑909 12 931; www.cafeibsen.no; Løkkestredet 7; s/d 600/900kr) This is a great central B&B option, run by the friendly owners of Café

Ibsen. There are six simple but character-filled rooms in a historic house, all with private bathrooms.

Scandic Grimstad   HISTORIC HOTEL $$
(☑37 25 25 25; www.scandichotels.no; Kirkegata 3; s/d 1145/1345kr; 🅿❋🐾) At the town's heart, this historic hotel spans a number of converted and conjoined timber houses, with an atmospheric breakfast room and basement restaurant. Rooms here can be absolutely delightful, if a little staid, but make sure you're not allocated one of the dark, stuffy and very noisy internal rooms overlooking the lobby.

✕ Eating

Café Ibsen   CAFE $
(☑37 27 57 63; Henrik Ibsens gate 12; sandwiches 79-99kr; ⊙10am-4pm Mon-Sat, noon-4pm Sun) Come here for homemade pastries, slabs of cake, quiches and big sandwiches. It's in a lovely rambling space opposite the Ibsenhuset Museum.

★ Apotekergården   SEAFOOD $$
(☑37 04 50 25; www.apotekergaarden.no; Skolegata 3; mains 160-260kr, pizzas 125kr; ⊙noon-midnight) The Apotekergården is a fun, busy restaurant with a cast of regulars who wouldn't eat anywhere else. It can be difficult to get a table out on the terrace in summer, especially as the night wears on. If so, head up the old wooden stairs for a beer and a game of shuffleboard.

Smag & Behag   CAFE, DELI $$
(www.smag-behag.no; Storgaten 14; mains 115-165kr; ⊙10am-10pm Mon-Sat) We concur with this upmarket deli-cafe's name: 'taste and enjoy'. Come for lunch or a casual dinner and sample the region's best produce (which is also available from the deli counter) and a carefully selected wine list. A summer salad of beets and 40-degree cured salmon is a riot of colour; an open sandwich of pulled beef and coleslaw is a revelation.

ℹ Information

Tourist Office (☑37 25 01 68; www.visitgrimstad.com; Storgaten 1a; ⊙9am-6pm Mon-Fri, 10am-4pm Sat mid-Jun–mid-Aug, 8.30am-4pm Mon-Fri mid-Aug–mid-Jun) Down on the waterfront inside the big white timber building. Staff run guided tours of the town every Wednesday and Friday in July at 1pm (adult/child 100kr/free).

ⓘ Getting There & Away

The Grimstad Rutebilstasjon is on Storgata at the harbour, though some buses only stop up at the highway, rather than coming into town. Nor-Way Bussekspress (p420) buses between Oslo (400kr, 4½ hours) and Kristiansand (240kr, one hour) call at Grimstad three to five times daily. Nettbuss (p424)' TIMEkspressen buses run to/from Arendal once or twice hourly (80kr, 30 minutes).

Lillesand

POP 9465

Lovely Lillesand has a pedestrian-only white-washed village centre full of secondhand shops and cafes, along with a stunning circular harbour. It's located between Kristiansand and Arendal.

🛏 Sleeping & Eating

Tingsaker Camping CAMPGROUND $
(☑ 37 27 04 21; www.tingsakercamping.no; campsites 230kr, cabins per week 11,000kr; P 🗢) This crowded but well-equipped campsite, on the shore 1km east of Lillesand centre, is a typical seaside holiday resort complete with camping, caravans and a range of pricey cabins.

Lillesand Hotel Norge HISTORIC HOTEL $$$
(☑ 37 27 01 44; www.hotelnorge.no; Strandgata 3; s/d 1390/1690kr; P 🗢) This boutique hotel has been thoughtfully renovated to reflect its original 1837 splendour and overflows with period touches, particularly in the public areas. The rooms, which aren't quite as ornate, include ones dedicated to King Alfonso XIII of Spain and author Knut Hamsun, both of whom stayed here.

★ Kafe Strandhaven CAFE $
(www.kafestrandhaven.com; Strandgata 10; mains 99-179kr; ☉ 10am-10pm Jul & Aug, 10.30am-5pm Mon-Thu & Sat, to 11.30pm Fri, noon-5pm Sun rest of year) In the heart of the village, with garden tables that lead down to the harbour, this is the kind of cafe that can transform a destination. Decorated in a stylish mashup of vintage and Nordic modern furniture, friendly young staff serve up wraps, salads, soups, burgers and, later, wine. And the luscious housemade cakes are as good as they look.

Information

Tourist Office (☑ 37 40 19 10; ☉ 9am-6pm Mon-Fri, 10am-4pm Sat, noon-4pm Sun mid-Jun–mid-Aug) In the town hall in summer.

ⓘ Getting There & Away

The most pleasant way to reach Lillesand in summer is by the **M/S Øya** (Map p106; www.blindleia.no; adult/child one way 335/165kr, return 510/280kr) from Kristiansand. There's also an hourly Nettbuss (p424) to Kristiansand (90kr).

Kristiansand

POP 87,400

Kristiansand is Norway's fifth-largest city and styles itself as 'Norway's No 1 Holiday Resort'. That can be a bit misleading: sun-starved Norwegians do flock to this charming big town in the summer, and there's a petite town beach and flash marina, but it tends to serve as a gateway to the villages of Norway's southern coast and the inland region of Setesdalen.

What Kristiansand offers in spades, though, is a lively cultural and shopping scene, some excellent restaurants and very healthy nightlife. In addition, anyone travelling with children will more than likely find themselves cajoled into visiting the town's outstanding children's park and zoo.

⊙ Sights

★ Sørlandets Kunstmuseum GALLERY
(SKMU; Map p106; ☑ 38 07 49 00; www.skmu.no; Skippergata 24b; adult/child 60kr/free; ☉ 11am-5pm Tue-Sat, noon-4pm Sun) This exceptional regional art museum focuses on both fine and craft-based practices, and the collection includes some particularly strong contemporary work from local, Norwegian and Nordic artists. There is also a bright, beautifully designed, pleasingly sophisticated children's wing. For anyone interested in Norwegian ceramics, the 44 works by local Kari Christensen will prove a real treat.

Odderøya PARK
This island, a rocky outcrop just by the fish market and connected by a bridge, is one of the city's wonderful green spaces. There are some delightful places for a walk, a swim or a picnic; it's also home to artists' studios and Vaktbua (p109) cafe and bar.

Kristiansand

Kristiansand Kunsthall
GALLERY

(Map p106; www.kristiansandkunsthall.no; 4th fl, Rådhusgata 11; ⊙noon-4pm Tue-Sun) **FREE** Shows change seasonally, but are usually high-concept, challenging surveys well worth a browse. It's a stunning space, with a rare elevated town outlook. It hosts key events during the annual PUNKT festival.

Kristiansand Museum
MUSEUM

(Vest-Agder Fylkesmuseet; www.vestagdermuseet. no; Vigeveien 22b; adult/child 90/40kr; ⊙10am-5pm Tue-Fri, noon-5pm Sat-Mon mid-Jun–Aug, 9am-2pm Mon-Fri rest of year; ⊡) Located 4km east of town on the E18, this open-air folk museum houses a collection of 40 farmsteads and hamlets from the Setesdalen region and Kristiansand itself. In summer there are lots of kids' activities, including some nice hands-on historical re-creations. Eastbound buses M1, M2 and M3 from Henrik Wergeland gate pass the museum.

Agder Natural History Museum & Botanic Gardens
GARDENS

(www.naturmuseum.no; Gimleveien 23; adult/child 80kr/free; ⊙11am-5pm mid-Jun–mid-Aug, 10am-3pm Tue-Fri, noon-4pm Sun rest of year) The winding paths through the established 50-hectare park at Gimle Estate lead through a botanic garden that also contains rocks, minerals, stuffed animals and greenhouses containing the largest collection of cacti in Norway. The estate house has 19th-century period interiors and extraordinary teethlike columns at the front, and there's also a historic rose garden dating from 1850. It's just over 1km from the centre, across the Oddernes bridge.

Baneheia & Ravnedalen
PARK

(Ravnedalen) Baneheia and Ravnedalen, both north of the city centre, offer greenery and a network of lakeside hiking and skiing tracks for those keen to escape the city for a while. Both parks were created between 1870 and 1880 by Kristiansand's city chairman, General

Kristiansand

Oscar Wergeland. Over a total 30-year period, the planting of 150,000 coniferous trees transformed the area into a recreational green belt.

Kristiansand Dyrepark   ZOO

(www.dyreparken.no; high season adult/child 319/299kr; ⊙10am-7pm mid-Jun–mid-Aug, to 3pm mid-Aug–mid-Jun; 🚻) Off the E18, 10km east of Kristiansand, Dyrepark is probably *the* favourite holiday destination for Norwegian kids. The former zoo is several parks rolled into one. There's a **fun fair** that includes rides such as the pirate-ship cruise, Captain Sabretooth's Treasure Trove and enchanted houses. **Cardamom Town** (Kardamomme By) is a fantasy village based on the children's stories of Thorbjørn Egner. There's a **water park** with heated pools and water slides. The biggest attraction, though, is still the **zoo** itself.

Christiansholm Fortress   FORTRESS

(Map p106; Østre Strandgate 52b; ⊙grounds 9am-9pm mid-May–mid-Sep) **FREE** Strandpromenaden's hulking centrepiece is the distinctive Christiansholm Fortress. Built by royal decree between 1662 and 1672 to keep watch over the strategic Skagerrak Straits and protect the

city from pirates and rambunctious Swedes, the construction featured walls up to 5m thick and an armoury buried within a concentric inner wall. It was connected to the mainland by a bridge over a moat (filled in during the 19th century) deep enough to accommodate tall ships.

Posebyen   AREA

(Map p106) The Kristiansand Posebyen takes in most of the 14 blocks at the northern end of the town's characteristic *kvadraturen* (square grid pattern of streets). It's worth taking a slow stroll around this pretty quarter; its name was given by French soldiers who came to *reposer* here (it's French for 'relax').

A scale model (with buildings around 1m high) of the city as it appeared when designed by Christian IV is on view at **Vest-Agder Folk Museum**. The annual Kristiansand guide, published by the tourist office, includes a good section called 'A Stroll through Posebyen' to guide your wandering. The most well-preserved buildings include **Bentsens Hus** (Map p106; Kronprinsensgate 59), which dates from 1855, the **former post office** (Map p106; Kronprinsens gate 45) dating from 1695 and **Gyldenløves gate 56** (Map p106) (1802).

🏃 Activities

Setesdalsbanen   RAIL

(www.setesdalsbanen.no; adult/child return 140/70kr; ⊙departures 11.30am, 1.20pm & 3.10pm Sun mid-Jun–Aug) The 78km-long narrow-gauge railway between Kristiansand and Byglandsfjord linked Setesdalen with the coast from 1896 to 1962. It was used to transport nickel from the Evje mines, and local timber and barrel staves that were used in the salting and export of herring. Steam- or diesel-powered locomotives still travel the last 6km between Grovane (2km north of Vennesla) and Røyknes; a 25-minute journey one way.

NSB trains run from Kristiansand to Vennesla (44kr, 12 minutes, four daily).

One Ocean Dive Center   DIVING

(📞38 09 95 55; www.oneocean.no; Årossanden 9, Søgne; 1/2 dives with equipment from 950/1300kr) A professional centre that runs dives to wrecks, including a downed plane and even a mine sweeper. It's 8km east of Kristiansand.

🎉 Festivals & Events

PUNKT   MUSIC

(www.punktfestival.no; ⊙Sep) Edgy electronic festival in September specialising in live

SOUTHERN NORWAY KRISTIANSAND

WORTH A TRIP

BRAGDØYA

In summer, Kristiansand's archipelago of offshore *skerries* (rocky islets) become a popular destination for sea-and-sun adventure. The most popular island, **Bragdøya**, lies close to the mainland and is, charmingly, home to a preservation workshop for wooden boats, which you can borrow for free. It also offers gentle forest walks and several beautiful bathing sites. In the distance you'll see the classic lighthouse **Grønningen Fyr**.

Ferries for Bragdøya leave from **Quay 6 (Map p106)**, two to four times daily in summer. Ask at the Kristiansand **tourist office** (p110) for exact schedules, as well as those for other offshore islands.

M/S Øya (p105) sails a three-hour return route to and from Lillesand every morning at 10am, except Sunday, from late June to early August. It departs Kristiansand's Quay 6.

remixes; Brian Eno, Laurie Anderson and David Sylvian were past guests.

🛏 Sleeping

Kristiansand has a large number of good chain hotels and a handful of upmarket boutique places, but can be expensive for what you get (which may be nothing unless you book early for summer, especially once the July school-holiday period begins). If you're driving, there are a number of chain hotels around the entrance to Kristiansand Dyrepark, 10km east of town.

Roligheden Camping   CAMPGROUND **$**
(📞 38 09 67 22; www.roligheden.no; Framnesveien; campsites 210kr, large cabins 2200kr; ☺ May-Sep) Tent campers are in luck at this well-run campground situated at a popular beach 3km east of the centre. Take bus 15 from the centre.

★ Sjøglott Hotell   HOTEL **$$**
(Map p106; 📞 38 70 15 66; www.sjoglott.no; Østre Strandgate 25; s/d 895/975kr; 📶) This low-key 15-room hotel in a historic building is run by a lovely young couple. The rooms are small, but have big windows and are well designed, and include extras unusual at this price, such as Nespresso machines. Breakfast, afternoon tea-time waffles and evening pizza and wine are served in an atmospheric basement, or you can relax in the sun in the cute courtyard.

★ Scandic Kristiansand Bystranda   HOTEL **$$**
(Map p106; 📞 21 61 50 00; www.scandichotels. no; Østre Strandgate 76; s/d 1290/1390kr; 🅿 @) This beachside place is big and brash, but very beautifully designed. It has a warm, textured and relaxed kind of style, and has all the facilities and extras you can expect in a hotel of this size. It's a wonderful spot for families with its beach, park and poolside position.

Hotel Q42   HOTEL **$$**
(Map p106; 📞 38 04 40 00; http://q42.no/; Elvegata 11a; s/d 1000/1300kr) This hotel is part of a church conference centre, so it certainly doesn't possess as much of a holiday vibe as some of the other hotels in town. However, the 11 junior suites and suites here are beautifully furnished, calm, spacious and stylish.

Clarion Hotel Ernst   HOTEL **$$$**
(Map p106; 📞 38 12 86 00; www.clarionernst.no; Rådhusgata 2; s/d 1480/1790kr; 🅿 @) This Clarion is in one of the town's most stately buildings. Inside it's been done out in an urban, contemporary style with huge, pearl-string lampshades, gold and silver throne-like chairs, purple lighting and massive jet-black bedheads.

🍴 Eating

In summer, everyone ends up at the small, remodelled harbour and its fish market complex for dinner, where you'll find plenty of fresh seafood, beer and ice cream. There are, however, a huge number of options in the city grid too, from modern Norwegian to sushi, pizza, burgers, cafes and bakeries, and some of them are very good indeed.

Drømmeplassen BAKERY, CAFE **$**
(Map p106; ☑38 04 71 00; www.drommeplassen. no; Skippergata 26; sandwiches, salads & soups 99-119kr; ⊘7am-6pm Mon-Sat, 10am-5pm Sun) This big, bustling bakery has lots of tables inside and on the pretty footpath. Locals flock here every morning for a great range of freshly baked *boller* (buns) and loaves of bread, or pop in later for chicken salads, tuna melts and big soups.

Snadderkiosken FAST FOOD **$**
(Map p106; Tangen 1; dishes 89-115kr; ⊘8.30am-10pm Mon-Fri, 11am-10pm Sat & Sun) We don't normally go out of our way to recommend fast-food kiosks, but Snadderkiosken is one of the best of its kind, plus it also feels apt for a seaside town. Just behind the beach, this lovely, tiled, 1920s-style kiosk serves up hearty meatballs and mashed potatoes or grilled chicken with rice and salad to beachgoers and late-night wanderers.

Pieder Ro SEAFOOD **$$**
(Map p106; ☑38 10 07 88; www.pieder-ro.no; Gravane 10; mains 285-345kr, smørrebrød & burgers 145-215kr; ⊘11am-10pm Mon-Sat, 1-9pm Sun) Kristiansand might be very good at smart-casual coastal, but it also keeps the traditionalists happy with places such as Pieder Ro, with its chandlery-chic nautical decor (How nautical? The bar *is* a boat...), chequered blinds and upholstered chairs. There's an all-day casual menu and an elegant evening one, with a focus on fresh fish but also decent steaks (including kangaroo).

 Bønder i Byen NEO NORDIC, INTERNATIONAL **$$$**
(Map p106; ☑911 47 247; www.bønderibyen.com; Rådhusgata 16; mains 295kr, 4-course menu 485kr; ⊘11am-10pm Mon-Sat, noon-8pm Sun) A beautiful extended riff on Norway's spectacular produce and on the country's rural life, Bønder i Byen's menu is both gorgeous to read, with its redolent roll call of local farmers, and to eat. This is one place on the coast where you won't get seafood; instead it's best-quality organic beef, pig and chicken (long-tailed, of course), along with vibrant tumbles of vegetables.

Gastropuben på Kick BRITISH **$$$**
(Map p106; ☑38 02 83 30; www.gastropuben.no; Dronningens gate 8; mains 230-280kr; ⊘3pm-midnight) Not to be confused with the nightclub it

secrets out the back, this is a dark, clubby pub styled on the British gastropub, with a menu of hearty local dishes and Anglophile roasts. It is, as you'd hope, serious about its beer, with 29 rotating beers on tap, including local legend Nøgne Ø.

Bølgen & Moi SEAFOOD **$$$**
(Map p106; ☑38 17 83 00; www.bolgenogmoi.no; Sjølystveien 1a; mains 225-340kr, 3-/4-/5-course set menu 545/595/645kr; ⊘3-10pm Mon-Sat, 1-6pm Sun) The fish-market harbour's upmarket choice: always-reliable chain Bølgen & Moi does a rich fish and shellfish soup, excellent *moule frites,* a tasty range of fish and steaks, as well as set menus and seafood platters. In summer the outdoor tables are packed and can get raucous once the kitchen closes (blankets provided, if required).

Drinking & Nightlife

Drinking coffee in the sun is a key Kristiansand pastime and there are a number of cafes that use local roasts and serve above-average espresso. The city is lively on weekend nights, although everything closes down at 2.30am sharp.

Vaktbua BAR
(Map p106; Odderøya; ⊘noon-3.30pm Tue, Thu & Sun, to 10pm Wed, to 2.30am Fri & Sat) This is Kristiansand's bastion of alternative culture and is where you'll find the city's most interesting locals. It's located in a beautiful island spot; head here for all-organic cake and coffee, and for a range of performances, after parties and club nights come weekend evenings.

Frk Larsen BAR
(Map p106; Markens gate 5; ⊘11am-midnight Mon-Wed, to 3am Thu-Sat, noon-midnight Sun) A great all-day drinking hole, with a mellow ambience by day and late-night music for the crowds on weekend nights. The cocktail bar opens at 8pm, but the sofas are just as attractive for a midday coffee en route to the foreshore.

ⓘ Information

DNT Sør (Map p106; ☑38 12 07 50; www.dntsor. no; Gyldenløvesgate 2b; ⊘10am-4pm Mon-Fri) Maps and information on hiking, huts and organised mountain tours in southern Norway.

Tourist Office (Map p106; ☑ 38 12 13 14; www.visitkrs.no; Rådhusgata 6; ☺ 8am-6.15pm Mon-Fri, 10am-6pm Sat, noon-6pm Sun Jul-Aug, 8am-3.30pm Mon-Fri rest of year)

❶ Getting There & Away

BOAT
Ferries to Denmark and Sweden leave from the **Colour Line Terminal** (Map p106).

BUS
There's a bus information office and left-luggage facilities inside the **bus station** (Map p106). Note, most local buses, including those to Lillesand, Grimstad and Arendal, leave from central Henrik Wergelands gate, rather than the bus station.

Buses from Kristiansand

DESTINATION	DEPARTURES (DAILY)	COST (KR)	TIME (HR)
Arendal	up to 9	220	1½
Bergen	1	640	12
Evje	7-8	160	1
Flekkefjord	2-4	250	2
Oslo	up to 9	390	5½
Stavanger	2-4	380	4½

TRAIN
There are up to four trains daily to Oslo (259kr to 687kr, 4½ hours) and up to five to Stavanger (249kr to 489kr, 3¼ hours).

Mandal
POP 15,530

Norway's southernmost official town is famous for its 800m-long beach, Sjøsanden. About 1km from the centre and backed by forests, the Copacabana it ain't, but it is one of Norway's finest stretches of sand, forest-lined and remote feeling on all but the highest summer days.

◉ Sights

Mandal Museum MUSEUM
(Vestagdermuseet; www.vestagdermuseet.no; Store Elvegata 5/6; adult/child 70kr/free; ☺ 11am-5pm Mon-Fri, noon-5pm Sat & Sun mid-Jun–mid-Aug) Displays of historical maritime and fishing artefacts and works by local artists are pleasant enough, but this museum is elevated above the mundane by impressive exhibits of works by Mandal's favourite son, Gustav Vigeland. His childhood home, **Vigeland House**, is also part of the museum.

✺ Festivals & Events

Shellfish Festival FOOD & DRINK
(www.skalldyrfestivalen.no; day pass 250kr; ☺ Aug) Fresh seafood everywhere and a range of musical performances; held in the second week of August.

☐ Sleeping & Eating

Hald Pensjonat GUESTHOUSE $
(☑ 38 26 01 00; www.haldpensjonat.no; Halseveien 37; d/q 400/500kr; 🅿 ☎) This traditional-style guesthouse has wackily ornate public spaces and a lovely garden. Basic, hostel-style rooms make it one of the few budget options on the coast besides camping. Rates do not include a 100kr per person linen charge.

Sjøsanden Feriesenter CAMPGROUND $
(☑ 38 26 10 94; www.sjosanden-feriesenter.no; Sjøsandveien 1; campsites 120kr, 2-/4-person apt 1000/1150, 2-bed cabin 1350kr; 🅿 ☎ ☀) Just a few metres away from the beach, this well-run place distinguishes itself from the other campgrounds in the vicinity. It even has its own water slide. There are motel rooms (double 750kr) as well as your usual camping huts and self-catering apartments.

Kjøbmandsgaarden Hotel HISTORIC HOTEL $$
(☑ 38 26 12 76; www.kjobmandsgaarden.no; Store Elvegate 47; s/d 899/1099kr; ☎) In the heart of the icy-white Old Town, this listed, very pretty timber hotel has rather stuffy rooms with decent bathrooms. The downstairs **restaurant** is one of the most popular places in town to eat.

★ Provianten ITALIAN $$
(☑ 482 78 888; www.provianten.no; Store Elvegate 45a; mains 199-259kr, pizza 139-185kr; ☺ 9.45am-midnight) In Norway's southernmost town it seems fitting to eat somewhere on the waterfront with a Mediterranean bent. Yes, Porvianten serves genuine wood-fired pizzas, as well as preparing tasty Norwegian dishes in the oven, but it's so much more. Possibly the most ambitious place for miles, it brews its own beer as well as distilling aquavit and schnapps on site.

❶ Information

Tourist Office (☑ 38 27 83 00; www.lindesnesregionen.com; Havnegata 2; ☺ 10am-5pm Mon-Sat, 10am-7pm Sun) On the waterfront.

ℹ️ Getting There & Away

The Mandal Rutebilstasjon lies north of the river, just a short walk from the historic district. The Nor-Way Bussekspress (p420) coastal route between Stavanger (405kr, 3½ hours) and Kristiansand (122kr, 45 minutes) passes through Mandal two to four times daily.

Lindesnes

Lindesnes – literally the 'arching land peninsula' – is the very southernmost point in Norway and provides an occasional glimpse of the power that nature can unleash between the Skagerrak and the North Sea. On calm days the series of intricate rocky coves that twist and turn their way around this snake-like coastline are incredibly enticing, either from the shore or out on a boat.

👁 Sights

Lindesnes Fyr LIGHTHOUSE
(www.lindesnesfyr.no; adult/child 60kr/free; ⊙10am-8pm late Jun-early Aug, shorter hours rest of year) Rising above the cape is the evocative Lindesnes Fyr, a classic lighthouse. In two of the buildings you'll pass as you climb to the cape, there are exhibitions on the history of the lighthouse, while the visitors centre next to the gate has an informative video. The first lighthouse on the site (and the first in Norway) was fired up in 1655 using coal and tallow candles to warn ships off the rocks. The current electrical version, built in 1915, is visible up to 19.5 nautical miles out to sea.

🛏 Sleeping & Eating

Lindesnes Camping og Hytteutleie CAMPGROUND $
(☑916 02 276; www.lindesnescamping.no; Lillehavn; campsites 220kr, cabins 280-950kr; P🐕) Set beside a tiny cove and surrounded by interesting granite outcrops, this campground, with excellent modern facilities, is on the shore 3.5km northeast of Lindesnes Fyr. There's a small kiosk and kitchen facilities, and you can also organise boat hire.

Lindesnes Havhotel HOTEL $$
(☑38 60 08 00; Bålyveien 50; s/d 1045/1295kr, 2-bed apt 1350kr; P🐕) This big, stylish resort-style place draws Norwegian families. It may be a little soulless on the outside, but it is supremely comfortable, has great facilities and can be a bargain. Views are wonderful and there are complimentary bicycles.

HERE WERE VIKINGS

From the 8th to the 11th centuries, Norway's coastline was the domain of Vikings, but the cape at Lindesnes, where the waters of the Skagerrak and the North Sea collide, proved a challenge even to these formidable seagoers. Their solution? In a spirit of creative engineering that Norway's road builders would later emulate when faced with daunting geographic forms, the Vikings carved a canal across the Lindesnes Peninsula at Spangereid (once a home port of Viking chieftains) to avoid the dangerous seas of the cape. In 2007 a replica canal was opened to re-create the Viking detour.

ℹ️ Getting There & Away

Buses from Mandal (90kr, one hour) travel to the Lindesnes lighthouse via Spangereid on Monday, Wednesday and Friday.

Flekkefjord

POP 9096

Flekkefjord is an enjoyable, serene place. The town's history dates back to 1660 when it rivalled Kristiansand, and it retains a pretty historic centre. It's 'famous' for having virtually no tidal variation, with typically less than 10cm between high and low tides.

👁 Sights

Hollenderbyen AREA
The old 'Dutch Town' district, with its narrow streets and old timber buildings, makes for a richly atmospheric walk.

Flekkefjord Church CHURCH
(Kirkegaten 10; ⊙11am-1pm Mon-Sat Jul) One building that stands out of the uniform streetscape is the unusual octagonal log-built Flekkefjord Church, which was consecrated in 1833. Designed by architect H Linstow (he of the Royal Palace (p53) in Oslo), the octagonal theme continues throughout, with the columns, steeple and baptismal font all conforming to the eight-sided shape.

Flekkefjord Museum MUSEUM
(www.vestagdermuseet.no; Dr Kraftsgata 15; adult/child 60kr/free; ⊙11am-5pm Mon-Fri, noon-5pm Sat & Sun mid-Jun–Aug) Flekkefjord Museum is housed in a home dating from 1724.

WORTH A TRIP

COASTAL ROAD TRIP FROM FLEKKEFJORD TO EGERSUND

If you have your own vehicle, forsake the E39 and take the coastal Rv44 from Flekkefjord to Egersund – it's one of southern Norway's most beautiful drives. The road swerves through barren, boulder-blotched hills with a few forested sections, lakes and moorlands, before descending to **Jøssingfjord**, around 32km west of Flekkefjord, with its breathtaking, perpendicular rock scenery and fine waterfall. Two 17th-century houses, known as **Helleren**, are nestled under an overhanging cliff and were definitely not built for the claustrophobic. Despite the danger of falling rocks, the overhang did provide protection from the harsh Norwegian climate. The houses are open year-round.

For more information on scenic lighthouses and other attractions along this route, and the entire coastal road from Kristiansand to Haugesund, visit the excellent www.nordsjovegen.no.

The 19th-century interiors, mostly the bequest of one local woman, illustrate how a high-bourgeois home of the time would have been furnished.

🛏 Sleeping & Eating

Egenes Camping — CAMPGROUND $
(☑ 38 32 01 48; www.egenescamping.no; campsites 225kr, cabins 600-1400kr) This spectacularly located campground is beside Lake Seluravatnet, 1km off the E39 and 5km east of Flekkefjord. There's boat and canoe hire, a climbing wall, minigolf, fishing and other activities on offer here, which make it a great choice for those travelling with children.

★ Grand Hotell — HISTORIC HOTEL $$
(☑ 38 32 23 55; www.grand-hotell.no; Anders Beersgt 9; s/d from 1095/1295kr; P ☎) The Grand Hotell sits perfectly in this old town. Housed in a delightful castle-like timber building, rooms have been smartly updated but retain a historic character with hand-printed wallpaper, velvet sofas and festoon drapes. It's subtly done, but if you don't fancy the period look, there's a number of straightforward modern rooms too. The restaurant and pub are charming.

Fiskebrygga — INTERNATIONAL $$
(☑ 38 32 04 90; Elvegata 9; mains 149-210kr; ⊙ 10am-4pm Mon, Tue & Sat, to 6pm Wed & Fri, to 7pm Thu) Possibly the nicest place in Flekkefjord for a light meal, this cafe-style restaurant next to the tourist office serves fish and chips, marinated spare ribs, delicious cakes and ice cream. It has a certain urban sensibility that's welcome in quiet little Flekkefjord. During the summer you might be in luck and catch one of its concerts, too.

ℹ Information

Tourist Office (☑ 38 32 69 95; www.regionlister. com; Elvegata 3; ⊙ 10am-6pm Mon-Fri, 10am-4pm Sat mid-Jun–mid-Aug, plus 11am-4pm Sun Jul, 9am-4pm Mon-Fri rest of year) Ask for the *A Tour of Flekkefjord* pamphlet.

ℹ Getting There & Away

The Nor-Way Bussekspress (p420) bus between Kristiansand (260kr, two hours) and Stavanger (260kr, two hours) passes through Flekkefjord.

Egersund

POP 11,470

One of the most picturesque towns along this western stretch of coastline, Egersund is a serene place strewn with old timber houses that are testament to the story of its long history. Its history actually goes back far further than that; intriguing rune stones found in nearby Møgedal are among the oldest written forms found in southern Norway.

⊙ Sights

Some 92 homes, nearly two-thirds of the original town, were gutted by fire in 1843, after which Egersund was reconstructed with wide streets to thwart the spread of future fires. Most buildings in the Old Town date from this period. **Strandgaten**, a street of timber houses constructed after 1843, is well worth a stroll.

Skrivergården was built in 1846 as the home of the local magistrate Christian Feyer. The small town park opposite served as his private garden. **Strandgaten 43** is arguably more beautiful and has what's known as a 'gossip mirror', which allowed the inhabitants to keep an eye on the street. The **Bilstadhuset** still has its original timberwork and includes a sailmaker's loft upstairs.

None of the houses is open to the public, but the tourist office hands out a leaflet,

Strolling in Egersund, which has a map and informative commentary.

⭐ **Egersund Fayancemuseum**   MUSEUM
(Egersund Pottery Museum; ☑51 49 26 40; www.egersundfayancemuseum.no; adult/child 50/25kr; ☺11am-5pm mid-Jun–Aug, 11am-3pm Wed-Fri & 11am-5pm Fri & Sat rest of year) A walkable 1.5km northeast of Egersund centre, this well-designed museum (squirrelled away in an unprepossessing shopping centre), houses the wares of Egersund Fayance, the ceramic and porcelain firm that sustained the district from 1847 to 1979. The collection is organised chronologically, so is a fascinating encapsulation of 19th- and 20th-century design trends, ranging from early monumental pieces to the utilitarian stoneware that has now become highly collectable. The museum sells decorative prints of original patterns and some reproductions.

Egersund Kirke   CHURCH
(Torget; ☺11am-4pm Mon-Sat, 12.30-3pm Sun mid-Jun–mid-Aug) There has been a church in Egersund since at least 1292. The cute, current manifestation dates back to the 1620s. The carved altarpiece, a depiction of the baptism and crucifixion of Christ by Stavanger carpenter Thomas Christophersen and painted by artist Peter Reimers, dates back to 1607; the baptismal font is from 1583. The cross-shaped design, intimate balconies and wonderfully decorated pew doors are all worth lingering over.

🛏️ **Sleeping & Eating**

Steinsnes Camping   CAMPGROUND $
(☑974 00 966; Tengs; campsites 180kr, cabins 325-1500kr; ℗📶) Egersund's most convenient campground is 3km north of town alongside a rushing stream; buses heading for Hellvik will get you there. As a very Norwegian touch, it sells salmon-fishing permits.

Boe Apartments   APARTMENT $$
(☑951 60 291; www.boeapartments.no; Strandgaten 72; apt 1200kr; ℗📶) Three modern, smartly furnished apartments are located in a traditional building, with the occasional original feature retained. They are very well equipped, with top-of-the-line beds, Norwegian linen and kitchens that have full-size appliances and Nespresso machines.

⭐ **Grand Hotell**   HISTORIC HOTEL $$$
(☑51 49 60 60; www.grand-egersund.no; Johan Feyersgate 3; s/d from 1350/1890kr; ℗📶) The Grand Hotell is a lovely 19th-century dame

with stylish, renovated rooms. The corner rooms have interesting streetscape views, but it's the newest rooms, some of them lofts, in the Klavita wing that are worth seeking out. These are done in a contemporary Scandinavian style – lots of pale grey and oak – softened with delicate patterns in the wallpaper and comforting textiles.

K&G House of Burger   BURGERS $$
(Kniv & Gaffel; www.knivgaffel.no/kghouseof burger; Jernbaneveien 2; burgers 189kr; ☺11am-10pm Sun-Thu, to 11pm Fri & Sat) Angus beef and brioche buns make these burgers a standout. It also offers chicken wings, onion rings and falafels.

🍸 **Drinking & Nightlife**

Mungåt Beer Bar   BEER HALL
(☑977 11 382; www.mungat.no; Torget 6; ☺6pm-1am Sat & Sun) This stylish weekend-only beer-mad basement bar focuses on the Norwegian microbreweries, though it also has speciality beers from the big national breweries. There's 14 on tap and over 100 in bottles. Ask about event and performances too.

🛍️ **Shopping**

Auduns Antikk   VINTAGE
(☑481 39 864; www.facebook.com/audunsantikk; Oluf Løwoldsgate 1; ☺10am-6pm Mon-Sat) A large treasure trove of vintage Norwegian ceramics awaits in this white wood shop. The local Eguersund mark is of course represented, along with both rare and more affordable examples of the west-coast manufacturers Figgjo and Stavanger and the southern Prorsgrun, plus Finnish and Swedish pieces too.

ℹ️ **Information**

The **tourist office** (☑51 46 82 33; www.eigersund.kommune.no; Jernbaneveien 2; ☺10am-6pm Mon-Fri, to 4pm Sat & Sun Jun-Aug) is fine for local information, but it's only open in summer. During the rest of the year the **Kulturkontonet** (Strandgaten 58; ☺8am-3pm Mon-Fri) can help with basic tourist information. The building itself is worth checking out even if you don't need any help.

ℹ️ **Getting There & Away**

Trains to/from Kristiansand (259kr to 350kr, two hours) run four times daily, and there are eight daily services to/from Stavanger (179kr, one hour). **Kolumbus** (www.kolumbus.no) buses run between Egersund and Flekkefjord and to Stavanger three to four times a day.

WORTH A TRIP

SOGNDALSTRAND

Sogndalstrand should not be missed for its picturesque timber homes and warehouses that jut out over the river. The houses, which date from the 17th and 18th centuries, feature on the covers of tourist brochures across the region and they're well worth seeking out. It's a quiet, beautiful place, some 30km southeast of Egersund and 2.5km south of the region's main town, Hauge i Dalane.

If the small village of Sogndalstrand has won your heart, consider staying at the historic **Sogndalstrand Kultur Hotell** (☑ 51 47 72 55; www.sogndal strand-kulturhotell.no; Strandgaten 22; s/d 1150/1510kr).

THE INTERIOR

Inland from Norway's southern coast, quiet mountain valleys such as Setesdalen and the magnificent peak of Gausta, close to Rjukan, are wonderful places. Another highlight is the lake-studded Telemark region, connected by a canal with pretty Seljord – home to the Nessie-esque Selma the Serpent.

Kongsberg

POP 25,090

Surrounded by dark and dense forests and with cascading rapids running through the heart of town, Kongsberg is one of the most agreeable towns in the southern interior. In addition to the pretty setting there's the fascinating and historic Royal Silver Mines, a host of low-key museums, a pretty clapboard old quarter, and one of Norway's best jazz festivals.

History

The history of Kongsberg begins and ends with silver, which was discovered by two children with an ox in 1623 in the nearby Numedal Valley. Their father attempted to sell the windfall, but the king's soldiers got wind of it and the family was arrested and forced to disclose the site of their discovery. Kongsberg was founded a year later and in the resulting silver rush it briefly became the second-largest town in Norway, with 8000 inhabitants including 4000 miners. Between 1623 and 1957, 1.35 million kilograms of pure threadlike 'wire' silver (one of the world's purest forms

of silver) was produced for the royal coffers. Kongsberg is still home to the national mint, but the last mine closed in 1957.

◉ Sights

Royal Silver Mines   MINE
(Map p90; ☑ 919 13 200; www.norsk-bergverks museum.no; Malmveien 5; adult/child 160/100kr; ⊙ hourly tours 11am-4pm Jul–mid-Aug, shorter hours mid-May–Jun, Sep & Oct) The profusion of silver mines in Kongsberg's hinterland is known collectively as Sølvgruvene. The easiest way to visit is with the tours that leave from the signposted Kongsgruvene, 700m from Saggrenda (8km south of Kongsberg along the road to Notodden), from where you'll ride a 2.3km rail along the *stoll*, a tunnel painstakingly chipped through the mountain to drain water from the mines. The main shaft of the largest mine plunges 1070m into the mountain, down to 550m below sea level.

Norwegian Mining Museum   MUSEUM
(Norsk Bergverks-museum; Map p115; http://norsk-bergverksmuseum.no; Hyttegata 3; adult/child 90/50kr; ⊙ 10am-5pm mid-May–Aug, noon-4pm Tue-Sun Sep–mid-May) Set in a smelter dating from 1844 (the old furnaces survive in the basement), this museum tells Kongsberg's story with relics, models and mineral displays. In the same building, other sections include the **Royal Mint**, which was moved from Akershus Fortress in Oslo to the source of the silver in 1686, as well as a **skiing museum** (Kongsberg is home to one of the world's oldest ski-jumping competitions) and an **arms and industry museum**. All are included in the same ticket.

⃕ Activities

Knutefjell   HIKING, SKIING
(Map p90) Kongsberg's best hiking and cross-country skiing is found in the green, forested Knutefjell, immediately west of the town. The Kongsberg tourist office sells the map *Kultur-og Turkart Knutefjell* (120kr), which details the various winter and summer tracks.

Royal Silver Mines
Rope-and-Torch Tour   MINE TOUR
(Map p90; ☑ 919 13 200; per group 10,000kr) With advance reservation you can join a rope-and-torch tour at the Royal Silver Mines, which begins with a 1km walk through Crown Prince Fredrik's tunnel. You must then abseil by torchlight 112m down into the mine (after what is hopefully not a 'crash' course in abseiling).

Kongsberg

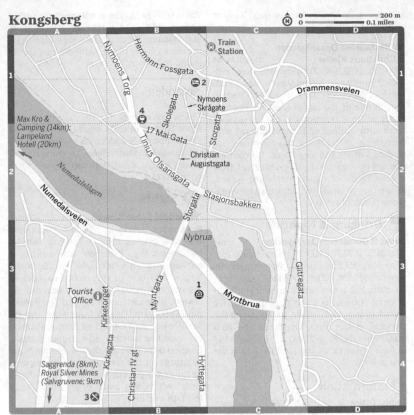

N
0 — 200 m
0 — 0.1 miles

✨ Festivals & Events

Kongsberg Jazz Festival   MUSIC
(www.kongsberg-jazzfestival.no; ⊙ Jul) Norway's second-largest jazz festival, held over four days in early July across various venues in town, draws numerous avant-garde international and Norwegian performers and often includes a pop act as well (such as Norway's A-ha in 2018). A percentage of profits goes towards humanitarian projects.

🛏 Sleeping & Eating

**Max Kro
& Camping**   CAMPGROUND $
(Map p90; ☎ 32 76 44 05; Jondalen; campsites 245kr, 4-/6-bed cabins 489/720) The nearest campground to Kongsberg is this low-key forested site, 14km northwest along the Rv37, with 10 huts and plenty of room for plenty of tents. To get here use the Kongsberg–Rjukan bus.

Kongsberg

◉ Sights
1 Norwegian Mining Museum B3

🛏 Sleeping
2 Gyldenløve Hotell B1

✖ Eating
3 Restaurant Opsahlgården &
   Christians Kjeller A4

🍸 Drinking & Nightlife
4 Jonas B Gundersen
   Jazzkjøkken B1

Gyldenløve Hotell   BUSINESS HOTEL $$$
(Map p115; ☎ 32 86 58 00; www.gyldenlove.no; Hermann Fossgata 1; s/d 1595/1885kr; 🅿@🛜) It's the giant black-and-white photographs of the town and its environs that first grab the eye on entering one of the rooms at this comfortable and well-managed hotel. There are enough other nice details to take it from being

a regular chain hotel to an appealing, if rather overpriced, option.

★**Restaurant Opsahlgården & Christians Kjeller** NORWEGIAN $$$
(Map p115; ☑ 32 76 45 00; Kirkegata 10; mains 298-348kr; ⊙ restaurant 3-10pm Mon-Fri, cafe 3-10pm Mon-Fri, 2-10pm Sat) This upmarket restaurant in one of the city's oldest houses surprises with very spot-on dishes (say smoked lamb with juniper and carrot cream), and everything is made on the premises, including sorbets and ice creams. It's complemented by a pleasant pub-cum-cafe, where a daily menu of casual meals are served, as well as a small but impressively well-stocked microbrewery.

🍷 Drinking & Nightlife

Jonas B Gundersen Jazzkjøkken BAR
(Map p115; ☑ 32 72 88 00; Nymoens Torg 10; ⊙ 3-10pm Mon, to 11pm Tue-Thu, 2pm-midnight Fri, noon-midnight Sat, 2-10pm Sun) This 'jazz kitchen' chain has a few outlets around southern Norway. This one is a cosy place to come for a drink or to see who might be playing on the weekend. It has pizza, bruschetta and club sandwiches (162kr to 214kr) so you can settle in for a while; locals say that the pizza is the best in town.

ℹ️ Information

Tourist Office (Map p115; ☑ 32 29 90 50; www.kongsberg.no; Kirketorget 4; ⊙ 9am-6pm Mon-Fri, 9am-2pm Sat late-Jun–mid-Aug, 9am-4pm Mon-Fri rest of year) This excellent tourist office has helpful staff and lots of resources.

ℹ️ Getting There & Away

Hourly trains connect Kongsberg with Oslo (204kr, 1½ hours).

Several bus companies operate near-hourly buses between Kongsberg and Oslo (235kr, 1½ hours), as well as to Notodden (120kr, 35 minutes), leaving from the train station.

If you're driving your own car and park in the town's supermarket car park, make sure you take a (free) ticket otherwise you'll get nailed with a hefty fine.

The Telemark Canal

The 105km-long Telemark Canal system, a series of lakes and canals that connect Skien and Dalen, with a minor branch from Lunde to Notodden, lifts and lowers boats a total of

72m via 18 locks. The canal was built for the timber trade between 1887 and 1892 by up to 400 workers. Today taking a slow boat along the canals is one of the highlights of a visit to southern Norway.

Notodden

POP 12,360

Unless you're here for the hugely popular Blues Festival in early August, drive straight past industrial Notodden and keep going until you reach the marvellous, imposing Heddal Stave Church, about 5km northwest of town on the E134.

👁️ Sights

★**Heddal Stave Church** CHURCH
(www.heddalstavkirke.no; Heddal; adult/child 80kr/free, grounds free; ⊙ 9am-6pm Mon-Sat mid-Jun–mid-Aug, 10am-5pm May–mid-Jun & mid-Aug–Sep) This fairy-tale church is the largest and one of the most beautiful of Norway's 28 remaining stave churches. As always, it's constructed around Norwegian pine support pillars, 12 large ones and six smaller ones, all topped by fearsome visages – and has four carved entrance portals. Of special interest are the lovely 1668 'rose' paintings on the walls, a runic inscription in the outer passageway and the 'Bishop's chair', which was made of an old pillar in the 17th century.

🎉 Festivals & Events

Notodden Blues Festival MUSIC
(www.bluesfest.no; ⊙ Aug) A long-running festival with lots of stellar headliners, along the lines of Robert Plant, ZZ Top, Little Stevie and Joss Stone.

🛏️ Sleeping

Notodden Camping CAMPGROUND $
(☑ 35 01 33 10; www.notoddencamping.com; Reshjemveien; campsites 130kr, 4-/6-bed cabins 450/550kr) Notodden Camping is an acceptable riverside site 3km west along the E134, then 200m south on Reshjemveien. You'll be lucky to find a square inch of space at festival time. Take a bus from the centre in the direction of Seljord.

ℹ️ Information

Tourist office (☑ 35 01 50 00; www.notodden.kommune.no; Teatergate 3; ⊙ 8am-3pm Mon-Fri)

ℹ️ Getting There & Away

Nettbuss (p424) TIMEkspressen buses run between the towns of Kongsberg and Notodden (98kr, 35 minutes) once or twice an hour.

Skien

POP 53,955

Industrial Skien mostly lures visitors as a setting-off point along the Telemark Canal. But if you're a fan of the great playwright Henrik Ibsen or Norwegian ceramics, there's some extra interest here for you.

◉ Sights

Henrik Ibsenmuseet   MUSEUM
(Map p90; www.telemarkmuseum.no; Venstøphøgda; adult/child 70/30kr; ⊙11am-7pm mid-May–Aug) Author, playwright and so-called 'Father of Modern Drama' Henrik Ibsen was born in Skien on 20 March 1828. In 1835 the family fell on hard times and moved out to the farm Venstøp, 5km north of Skien, where they stayed for seven years. The 1815 farmhouse has now been converted into the excellent Henrik Ibsenmuseet. There are some terrific audiovisual displays in the former barn, while guides, some of whom are Ibsen actors, show you around the family home.

Ask about Ibsen theatre performances here or at the tourist office.

Porsgrund Porselænsfabrikk   FACTORY
(Map p90; ☑35 56 21 00; www.porsgrund.com; Porselensv 12, Porsgrunn; ⊙9am-4pm Mon-Fri) In Porsgrunn, just south of Skien, is one of Norway's best-known and longest-running porcelain factories. You can book a tour to see artisans painting the famous 'straw' pattern, done with the finest of brushes, or visit the factory outlet shop.

🛏️ Sleeping

Kilden Gård   B&B $
(Map p90; Aashammeren 55; d with shared bathroom 700kr; P 🛜) In a beautiful riverside spot, 8km north of Skien, this traditional B&B in a family home offers a friendly welcome and prettily decorated rooms. It's a particularly good choice if you're here in winter for the skiing.

Thon Hotel Høyers   BUSINESS HOTEL $$
(Map p90; ☑35 90 58 00; www.thonhotels.no; Kongensgate 6; d 1340kr; P 🛜) Right next to the

AKKERHAUGEN

The attractive waterside village of Akkerhaugen sits on the northern fringes of the pretty Norsjø lake, which is itself a branch of the Telemark Canal system. The village is a popular place from which to begin or end a half-day Telemark Canal boat journey.

You can eat at Akkerhaugen's **campground** (☑35 95 84 30; www.norsjo-ferieland.no; campsites 270kr, caravan sites 340kr, cabins 1200-1900kr; P 🛜); otherwise self-cater or head to Notodden or Skien.

harbour, this family-run place is set inside a grand, very pink building and has spacious, modern, airy rooms and stately traditional public spaces. Free filter coffee is the norm for most Norwegian hotels, but they have a lobby Nespresso machine here.

ℹ️ Information

Tourist Office (Map p90; ☑35 90 55 20; www.visitgrenland.no; Nedre Hjellegate 18; ⊙9am-7pm Mon-Fri, 11am-4pm Sat & Sun mid-Jun–mid-Aug, 8.30am-4pm Mon-Fri rest of year) Has information on hiking trails and cycling routes.

ℹ️ Getting There & Away

Nor-Way Bussekspress (p420) buses run from Skien to Rjukan (289kr, 3¼ hours) once or twice daily. NSB (p420) trains run every hour or two to Larvik (97kr, 45 minutes) and Oslo (210kr to 318kr, three hours).

Dalen

POP 800

Surrounded by steep forested hills and settled comfortably beside a lazy lake busy with beavers, pretty little Dalen is a jumping-off point for ferries along the Telemark Canal system. It makes for a peaceful few days' rest.

◉ Sights

Eidsborg Stave Church   CHURCH
(guided tour adult/child 100/50kr; ⊙10am-6pm Jun-Aug, shorter hours rest of year) High above town on the Rv45 to Høydalsmo, the quaint, 13th-century Eidsborg Stave Church, dedicated to St Nicolas, has but a single nave and is

WORTH A TRIP

A SLOW BOAT THROUGH TELEMARK

Every day from June to mid-August, a variety of different boats, mostly old-fashioned steamers, chug along the canals of Telemark. Although full-day trips are available, for most people a half-day package is sufficient. One particularly good route involves catching the boat (adult/child 590/295kr, 3¾ hours, daily at 10am) from Akkerhaugen, 24km south of Notodden, from where you travel to Lunde. A bus takes you back to your starting point at Akkerhaugen. The trip can also be done in reverse by leaving your car for free at the Norsjø Hotell in Akkerhaugen and taking the bus to Lunde (it stops at the hotel), from where you catch the boat and sail serenely back to Akkerhaugen.

For a full-day trip you can make the leisurely 10-hour journey between Skien and Dalen (adult/child 995/497kr; late June to mid-August). Boats leave Skien around 8am and arrive in Dalen a little after 6pm, from where you can catch a special 'canalbus' back to Skien. It's also possible to jump off (or board) in Lunde, the halfway point, as well as various other combinations.

For seasonal departure times, boat details and to book, contact **Visit Telemark** (35 90 00 20; www.visittelemark.com).

A great way to see the canal is by canoe, kayak or bicycle. Ferries will transport your boat/bicycle for 290/180kr.

in particularly good shape. The grounds are open year-round, and a caretaker can usually open the church if it's locked.

🛏 Sleeping & Eating

Buøy Camping CAMPGROUND $
(35 07 75 87; www.buoycamping.com; campsites 250kr, cabins 650-1600kr; ⊙May-Sep; P@🛜) Surrounded on all sides by water, this attractive, well-run campground has plenty of activities for children, lots of shady pitches for tents and quaint Little Red Riding Hood–style wooden cabins that are just as cute inside as they are out. There's a restaurant here and bike rental is available for 150kr per day.

Dalen Bed & Breakfast B&B $$
(35 07 70 80; www.dalenbb.com; d 1290-1790kr; P🛜) This family-run venture is a good option: an excellent breakfast is included, and staff dole out free maps pointing you to the area's best moose- and beaver-spotting sites.

Dalen Hotel HISTORIC HOTEL $$$
(35 07 90 00; www.dalenhotel.no; s/d 1600/2600kr; P🛜) The ornate Dalen Hotel, with its faint resonance of a stave church, and a wild-west ambience inside, first opened in 1894. Although looted by the Nazis in WWII, it remains an authentic place with public areas a riot of antiques and moose heads. Room 17 is said to be haunted.

Lastein Bryggje Kafè INTERNATIONAL $
(35 07 90 00; Storvegen 42; mains 169-279kr; ⊙1-10pm Sun, Wed & Thu, to 2am Fri & Sat) This pretty riverside shed is one of the most scenic places in town, with a huge deck strewn with old-fashioned cane chairs and lap rugs. The menu offers the standards you've come to expect: burgers, fish and chips, shrimp meals and caesar salads. It turns into the town pub with late hours on a Friday and Saturday night.

ℹ Information

Tourist Office (35 07 70 65; www.visitdalen. com; Hotellvegen 5; ⊙10am-6pm Mon-Fri, to 4pm Sat & Sun May-Aug, closed Sep-Apr; 🛜) The tourist office in the village centre has free coffee.

ℹ Getting There & Away

Getting to Oslo by bus (560kr, 4½ hours) involves a change in nearby Amot on the E134.

Rjukan

POP 3385

Sitting in the shadow of what is arguably Norway's most beautiful peak, Gausta (1883m), Rjukan is a picturesque introduction to the Norwegian high country as well as southern Norway's activities centre par excellence.

The town stretches like elastic for 6km along the floor of the steep-sided Vestfjorddalen and while the centre, which consists of a couple of blocks of pastel-painted wooden buildings, is attractive, the remainder stands in utter contrast to its majestic setting.

If you're here from late September to March, you'll notice the expected winter gloom is absent, with the town's valley floor illuminated by 'concentrated solar power' – three giant remote-controlled mirrors track and reflect the much needed sunshine from the mountain above.

◉ Sights

★ Gaustabanen Cable Railway   RAILWAY
(www.gaustabanen.no; one way/return adult 250/350kr, child 125/175kr; ⊙10am-5pm late Jun–mid-Oct) Gaustabanen runs 860m deep into the core of Gausta before a different train climbs an incredible 1040m, alongside 3500 steps at a 40-degree angle, to 1800m, just below the Gaustahytte, not far from the summit. It was built by NATO in 1958 at a cost of US$1 million to ensure it could access its radio tower in any weather. Taking the railway is an incredible experience, although it's not for the claustrophobic. The base station is 10km southeast of Rjukan.

★ Norwegian Industrial Workers Museum   MUSEUM
(Norsk Industriarbeidermuseet Vemork; www.visit vemork.com; Vemork; adult/child 90/60kr; ⊙10am-6pm mid-Jun–mid-Aug, to 4pm mid-Aug–Sep & May–mid-Jun, noon-3pm rest of year) This museum, 7km west of Rjukan, is in the Vemork power station, which was the world's largest when completed in 1911. These days it honours the Socialist Workers' Party, which reached the height of its Norwegian activities here in the 1950s. There's an interesting exhibition about the race in the 1930s and '40s to make an atom bomb, plus a fabulous miniature power station in the main hall.

Krossobanen   CABLE CAR
(www.krossobanen.no; one way/return adult 65/130kr, child 30/60kr, bike 51/110kr; ⊙9am-8pm mid-Jun–Aug, 10am-4pm Sun-Thu, to 8pm Fri & Sat rest of year) The Krossobanen cable car was constructed in 1928 by Norsk Hydro to provide its employees with access to the sun. It now whisks tourists up to Gvepseborg (886m) for a view over the deep, dark recesses. The best panoramas are from the viewing platform atop the cable-car station. It also operates as the trailhead for a host of hiking and cycling trails.

Rjukanfossen   WATERFALL
Believed to be the highest waterfall in the world in the 18th century (Angel Falls in Venezuela now has that claim), the 104m-high Rjukanfossen is still a spectacular sight, even if most of the water has been diverted to drive the Vemork power station. To get the best view, take the Rv37 heading west and park just before the tunnel 9.5km west of town; a 200m walk leads to a fine viewpoint.

⚡ Activities

The tourist office can put you in touch with local tour operators running winter activities such as dog-sledding and horse-drawn sleigh rides.

Bungee Jumping   ADVENTURE SPORTS
(☎995 13 140; www.telemark-opplevelser.no; per jump 790kr; ⊙mid-May–Sep, exact times vary) Described as Norway's highest land-based bungee jump, this 84m plunge into the canyon from the bridge leading to the Norwegian Industrial Workers' Museum is Rjukan's biggest adrenaline rush. Book through the tourist office.

Gaustablikk Ski Centre   SKIING
(www.gaustablikk.no; Kvitåvatnvegen 372; 1-day pass adult/child 395/310kr) This serene ski area is overlooked by Gaustatoppen, the highest mountain in southern Norway, and has some excellent runs.

☞ Tours

Ice-Climbing   ADVENTURE SPORTS
(Kvitåvatnvegen 372) If the idea of hauling yourself up a giant vertical icicle that looks suspiciously as if it's going to crack and send you tumbling to an early grave sounds like fun, then Rjukan is fast becoming known as *the* place for ice-climbing. There are more than 150 routes in the immediate area of the town.

🛏 Sleeping

Kvitåvatn Fjellstue   HOSTEL $
(☑35 09 20 40; www.kvitaavatn.dk; Kvitåvatnvegen 398; dm/s/d 245/675/850kr, s/d with shared bathroom 450/600kr) This youth hostel offers simple accommodation in a cosy pine lodge with six bunks per room in huts. Ten 'panorama' rooms have their own balconies with great views of Gaustatoppen, a double bed and two bunk beds, a work place and private bathroom. The reception is only staffed between 8.30am to 10.30am and 4pm to 7pm.

★ Rjukan Hytteby & Kro   CABIN $$
(☑35 09 01 22; www.rjukan-hytteby.no; Brogata 9; large cabins 950-1500kr, small cabins with linen s/d 990/1195kr; 🅿) Easily the best choice in town, Rjukan Hytteby & Kro sits in a pretty spot on the river bank and has carefully decorated, very well-equipped huts that sweetly emulate

DON'T MISS

HIKING & CYCLING FROM RJUKAN

Rjukan makes a superb base from which to strike out into the surrounding wilderness on foot or by mountain bike. To get an idea of what's possible, visit the **tourist office** (p121) to pick up the free *Rjukan – og Tinn,* which has a number of route suggestions.

Gausta

The most obvious goal for peak baggers is the hike to the summit of beautiful Gausta (1883m), from where you can see a remarkable one-sixth of Norway on a clear day. The popular, and easy, two- to three-hour, 4km hiking track leads from the trailhead of Stavsro (15km southeast of Rjukan) up to Den Norske Turistforening's (DNT) **Gaustahytta** (1830m), next to the rather ugly NATO radio tower. The summit is reached by walking along the rocky ridge for a further half-hour. A 13km road link, but unfortunately no public transport, runs from the far eastern end of Rjukan to Stavsro (altitude 1173m) at Lake Heddersvann. **Taxis** (☑ 35 09 14 00) charge around 450kr one way. Allow all day for the hike, which leaves plenty of time for exploring the summit. The tourist office distributes a map of the Fv651, but the *Turkart Gausta Området* is a better option and is available for 50kr.

More-difficult, three- to four-hour routes to the summit also run from Rjukan itself and from the Norwegian Industrial Workers' Museum.

If you can't make the hike, the **Gaustabanen Cable Railway** (p119) takes you almost to Gaustahytta.

Hardangervidda

For something a little wilder, but bleaker, the Hardangervidda Plateau, the biggest mountain plateau in Europe and home to Europe's largest herd of wild reindeer, rises up to the north of Rjukan and offers a wealth of fantastic hikes that vary from easy two- to three-hour strolls to longer day hikes and multiday challenges. From Gvepseborg, the summit of the **Krossobanen cable car** (p119), the most rewarding day hike is the five-hour (without stops) return trip to the **Helberghytta DNT Hut**. The route has good waymarking and, although it can be very boggy in sections, it's easily achievable for any moderately fit walker. The first section winds up from the cable-car platform through a forest of stumpy, twisted trees before emerging onto the gently undulating plateau. The scenery, which takes in icy cold lakes, snow-streaked hills, barren moorland and views back over towards Mt Gausta, is supremely impressive.

For something more challenging, an eight- to nine-hour route, which can also be used by cyclists, leads from the cable-car platform past the Helberghytta DNT Hut (following the route described previously) and onward to **Kalhovd Turisthytte**. From there you can either catch a bus or hike nine hours down to **Mogen Turisthytte**, where you can catch the Møsvatn ferry (255kr) back to Skinnarbu, west of Rjukan on Rv37; ferry timetables are available from the Rjukan tourist office. Serious hikers can also strike out north from Kalhovd, deep into the high Hardangervidda.

Alternatively, you can follow the marked route that begins above Rjukan Fjellstue, around 10km west of Rjukan and just north of the Rv37. This historic track follows the **Sabotørruta** (Saboteurs' Route), the path taken by the members of the Norwegian Resistance during WWII. From late June until mid-August, the tourist office organises three-hour guided hikes along this route (230kr; noon Tuesday, Thursday and Sunday).

The best hiking map to use for this part of the plateau is Telemark Turistforening's *Hardangervidda Sør-Øst,* at a scale of 1:60,000. It's available from the tourist office for 105kr.

the early-20th-century hydroelectric workers' cabins. The owner is exceptionally helpful. It's a pleasant 20-minute walk along the river bank to the town centre.

Rjukan Gjestegård HOSTEL **$$**
(☑ 35 08 06 50; www.rjukangjestegard.no; Birkelandsgata 2; s/d with shared bathroom

405/610kr, d 1090kr; P @) This central guesthouse occupies the buildings of the old youth hostel and is something of a travellers' centre. Despite its bleak exterior, the rooms here are simple and fine enough; there's a guest kitchen; and the location is good if you want to be in town. Breakfast costs 80kr.

Rjukan Admini
HISTORIC HOTEL $$$

(📞908 94 909; www.rjukanadmini.com; Sølvvold-veien 3; d/ste 1690/2490kr) If you like a bit of piped-on posh, this historic hotel has large rooms with pale yellow walls, floral bedspreads and four-poster beds. Its country house setting is blissful too, with lush gardens and the mountains all around.

Gaustablikk Høyfjellshotell
LODGE $$$

(📞35 09 14 22; www.gaustablikk.no; Kvitåvatnvegen 372; d 1700kr; P🛜) With a prime location overlooking the lake and mountain, this lodge is one of Norway's better mountain hotels. Rooms have a calm modern Alpine style, with lots of raw wood, felt sofas and antlers all about, and many have lovely views of Gausta.

🍴 Eating

Kinokafeen
INTERNATIONAL $$

(📞408 56 048; Storstulgate 1; mains 139-189kr; ⊙10am-9pm Mon-Sat) Kinokafeen, at the cinema, has a pleasing airy art-deco style and its outdoor tables (summer only!) and fading interior make it the most memorable place to eat in the town centre.

Gaustablikk Høyfjellshotell
NORWEGIAN $$

(📞35 09 14 22; Kvitåvatnvegen 372; mains 129-179kr, dinner buffet 405kr; ⊙noon-5pm & 6.30-9pm) Even if you're not staying here, this mountain hotel's enormous buffet (with both seafood and meat) is worth the trip up the mountain and not just for the food – the dining room has a great rustic leather and wood interior and the views are stupendous.

ℹ Information

Tourist Office (📞35 08 05 50; www.visitrjukan.com; Torget 2; ⊙9am-6pm Mon-Fri, 10am-4pm Sat-Sun) The tourist office in Rjukan is possibly the best in Telemark, with loads of information and knowledgeable staff.

ℹ Getting There & Away

Buses connect Rjukan with Oslo (390kr, 3½ hours) via Notodden (146kr, 1¼ hours; where you need to change buses) roughly every other hour between 5.30am and 3.30pm. These buses also stop in Kongsberg (295kr, two hours).

Rjukan's linear distances will seem intimidating, but the local Bybuss runs from Vemork, 6.5km west of Rjukan, to the eastern end of the valley.

ℹ Getting Around

Bike hire from Rjukan Gjestegård (p120) costs 200kr per day.

Seljord

POP 2944

Lakeside Seljord is known mainly as the home of Selma the Serpent, the Nessie-type monster that inhabits the depths of the lake Seljordvatn. Other creatures of legend call the nearby hills home and hikers can also seek out the feuding troll women, Ljose-Signe, Glima and Tårån. Personally we haven't seen them, but locals assured us that they're there. Seljord was also the inspiration for some of Norway's best-known folk legends, including Asbjørnsen and Moe's *The Three Billy Goats Gruff*, known the world over.

👁 Sights

Seljord Church
CHURCH

(Brøløsvegen 48; ⊙11am-5pm mid-Jun–mid-Aug) This charming Romanesque church was built in the 12th century in honour of St Olav; it looks as if someone built a stave church and then changed their mind and tried to build a house around it. In the grounds, between the church and the churchyard wall, are two impressions reputedly made by two mountain trolls who were so upset by the encroachment of Christianity that they pummelled the site with boulders.

🎉 Festivals & Events

Dyrsku'n Festival
AGRICULTURAL

(www.dyrskun.no; ⊙Sep) On the second weekend of September, Seljord holds the Dyrsku'n Festival, which started in 1866 and is now Norway's largest traditional market and cattle show, attracting 60,000 visitors, almost as many cows and not all that many monsters.

> **WORTH A TRIP**
>
> ## MOOSE SAFARI
>
> **Moose Safari** (📞35 06 26 30; www.visitrauland.com; adult/child 300/150kr; ⊙book by 4pm for dusk departure, 28 Jun-23 Aug) You can get up close and personal with the largest member of the deer family in Europe on one of the moose safaris organised through the tourist office in the village of Rauland (on the Rt37 southwest of Rjukan), or head out in your own car with a downloadable map.

WORTH A TRIP

TUDDAL

Lying beside a deep blue lake surrounded by snow- and forest-dappled peaks, the handful of colourful wooden houses that make up the tiny mountain village of **Tuddal** have a setting that is hard to top. There's nothing much to do here except relish the peace and quiet and maybe embark on a gentle ramble or two. The village sits at the foot of a bleak and spectacular summer-only mountain road between Rjukan and the E134 Notodden–Seljord road.

Sleeping & Eating

Seljord Camping
og Badeplass   CAMPGROUND $

(☑ 35 05 04 71; www.seljordcamping.no; Manheimstrondi 61; tent sites 250kr, cabins 500-1400kr) There are soft grassy pitches beside the lake and cabins that range from the super-basic to the truly luxurious. The camp also serves as the dock for monster boats on Seljordvatn and has a telescope to help you spot Selma. Kayaks and canoes can also be rented here for 50kr per hour.

★ Seljord Hotell   HISTORIC HOTEL $$

(☑ 35 06 40 00; www.seljordhotel.no; Brøløsvegen 18; s/d 1090/1390kr; P @ ☎) This lovely old wooden hotel, which dates back to 1858, started life as a ladies' college, but on running out of potential 'ladies', it became a hotel. Rooms have period touches and are individually named, each with its own story. It, unusually, has the same rates all year. The restaurant is Seljord's best.

Seljord Hotell Restaurant   NORWEGIAN $$$

(☑ 35 06 40 00; www.seljordhotel.no; Brøløsvegen 18; mains 210-330kr; ☎ noon-2pm & 5-9pm) The restaurant at the Seljord Hotell is Seljord's best, with local fish and game dishes.

ⓘ Information

Tourist Office (☑ 35 05 04 00; www.seljordportalen.no; Brøløsvegen 28; ☎ 10am-6pm Mon-Fri mid-Jun–mid-Aug, shorter hours rest of year) Lots of local information, and staff revel in good troll stories.

ⓘ Getting There & Away

Nor-Way Bussekspress (p420) buses connect Seljord with Notodden (190kr, 1¼ hours) and Oslo (390kr, 3¼ hours) up to four times daily.

Setesdalen

The forested hillsides and lake-filled mountain valleys of Setesdalen, one of Norway's most traditional and conservative regions, remain little frequented by travellers, although the area now lures a new generation of outdoor enthusiasts.

Evje
POP 3585

The riverside town of Evje, surrounded by forests and rolling hills, serves as the southern gateway to Setesdalen. It's famous among geologists for the variety of rocks – a mineral park and the chance to prospect for your own rocks are among Evje's primary attractions. This town is also a first-class base for white-water rafting and other activities.

⊙ Sights & Activities

Setesdal Mineral Park   PARK
(www.mineralparken.no; Mineralvegen 1, Hornnes; adult/child 190/140kr; ☎ 10am-6pm Jul–mid-Aug, shorter hours rest of year) For displays of local and worldwide minerals, this well-run park is every rock collector's dream come true, with a wonderful world of colour and quartz, and many items for sale. It's about 10km south of Evje.

TrollActiv   ADVENTURE SPORTS
(☑ 37 93 11 77; www.trollaktiv.no; Syrtveit 4; ☎ 9am-8pm Apr-Oct) Around 6km north of Evje, this is the town's centre of high-energy thrills. White-water rafting (from 450kr per person) is its forte, but it organises all manner of activities, including overnight kayaking trips (from 1950kr), mountain-bike tours (420kr) and nightly beaver and elk safaris (adult/child 350/300kr). Other high-thrill activities include riverboarding, rock climbing, river kayaking, paintball, waterskiing and fishing safaris.

Sleeping & Eating

★ TrollActiv   HOSTEL $

(☑ 37 93 11 77; www.trollaktiv.no; Evje Vandrerhjem; d from 530kr, tents/tepees per person 80/100kr, cabins 430-650kr; P @) This energetic activities centre doubles as Evje's youth hostel, 6km north of town. It's exceptionally well run and the place to be if you're planning any one of the many activities on offer. Accommodation varies from sleeping in your own tent, kipping in a *lavvo* (tepee) or stretching out in comfort in a cabin or comfortable double room.

Revsnes Hotell
HOTEL $$

(☑37 93 46 50; www.revsneshotell.no; Byglandsfjord; s/d from 980/1240kr; ℗⊚) The good-value Revsnes is 12km north of Evje and set on the banks of lush lake Byglandsfjorden. The rooms are large and modern, and most have wonderful big windows overlooking the water. It's a family-run place and you'll be made to feel welcome.

Pernille Cafeteria
FAST FOOD $

(☑37 93 00 69; Nils Heglands veg 41; mains 115-179kr; ⊗8am-6pm Mon-Fri, to 4.30pm Sat, 10am-6pm Sun) Right in the heart of Evje, this upstairs place is popular with locals although the menu is not Norway's most inspirational. Expect burgers, and eggs and bacon alongside a few Norwegian staples.

ⓘ Information

Information Centre (☑37 93 14 00; www.setesdal.com; Verksvegen 4; ⊗11am-6pm Mon-Thu, to 7pm Fri, to 3.30pm Sat mid-Jun–mid-Aug, 10am-noon Mon-Fri rest of year) The information centre occupies the same old log building as the bus terminal. Ask here about permits for mineral prospecting.

ⓘ Getting There & Away

Nor-Way Bussekspress (p420) buses travel to Kristiansand (190kr, one hour) seven to eight times daily. Heading north from Evje, car drivers will be stung with an ever-rising toll.

Hovden

POP 405

Watching over the northern end of Setesdalen, Hovden is a winter ski resort and low-key summer hiking base.

⚡ Activities

Chairlift
CHAIRLIFT

(adult/child 110/80kr; ⊗11am-2pm Jul & Aug, 9.30am-3.30pm Dec-Apr, shorter hours rest of year) In summer, for fine views you can reach the summit of **Mt Nos** (1176m) by taking this chairlift. From the summit a number of hiking trails, ranging from an hour or two's easy ramble to an overnight slog, snake out across the high moorland plateau. The tourist office can provide more information.

🛌 Sleeping

Hovden Fjellstoge & Vandrerhjem
HOSTEL $$

(☑37 93 95 43; www.hovdenfjellstoge.no; Lundane; dm/s/d 310/690/1180kr; ℗⊚) Housed in a traditional-style wooden building with a grass roof, this jolly hostel has something to please everyone, from rooms with fairy-tale wooden bunk beds to cute cabins. There's virtually an entire zoo of stuffed local wildlife here, including a wolf and a reindeer. It's about 3.5km north of the centre.

Hovden Resort
HISTORIC HOTEL $$$

(Hovden Høyfjellshotell & Hovdestøylen; ☑37 93 88 00; www.hovdenresort.com; s/d from 1400/1620kr, apt 985kr; ℗⊚⚒) At the top end of the town, this hotel and lodge is Hovden's finest accommodation option. Rooms are tasteful and there's a host of resort amenities, including its own ski slope, an indoor pool, a sauna, a children's playroom chock-full of toys and the area's best restaurant.

ⓘ Getting There & Away

Nor-Way Bussekspress (p420) buses travel here from various towns, including Kristiansand (three hours), and Oslo (3½ hours). There is a short route from Stavanger in summer (3½ hours), but in winter you'll need to go via Tonstad (five hours).

Central Norway

Best Places to Eat

➜ Vertshuset Røros (p137)

➜ Brimi-Bue (p146)

➜ Halling-Stuene (p152)

➜ Elvesæter Hotell (p151)

Best Places to Stay

➜ Finse 1222 (p153)

➜ Erzscheidergården (p136)

➜ Elvesæter Hotell (p151)

➜ Turatgrø Hotel (p151)

➜ Kongsvold Fjeldstue (p142)

➜ Brimi-Fjellstugu (p147)

Why Go?

Bleak tundra and dramatic mountain massifs at seemingly every turn, charming villages, stave churches, fascinating wildlife and arguably Norway's best hiking and white-water rafting – with so much going for it, central Norway more than matches the fjords.

Here on the roof of Norway, trails snake their way past glaciers, waterfalls and snow-bound peaks in more than a dozen national parks. Jotunheimen National Park is one of Europe's premier hiking destinations, and is bisected by one of Norway's most beautiful drives. But Rondane, Dovrefjell-Sunndalsfjella and the desolately beautiful Hardangervidda are also superb. Within the parks' boundaries you may find wild reindeer, elk and musk ox. At the gateway to the parks, Unesco World Heritage–listed Røros, a centuries-old mining town of timber houses and turf-roofed cottages, and Lom, with its beautiful stave church, are two of inland Norway's most attractive villages.

When to Go
Roros

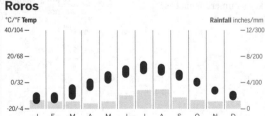

Feb Catch the Rørosmartnan (Røros Market) and skiing at Trysil. Be prepared to be *very* cold.

May & Jun Generally fine weather without the crowds of midsummer.

Jul & Aug Hiking trails are passable, rafting is in full swing and wildlife safaris are possible.

EASTERN CENTRAL NORWAY

Lillehammer

POP 27,476

Long a popular Norwegian ski resort, Lillehammer became known to the world after hosting the 1994 Winter Olympics. These Olympics, overwhelmingly considered a great success, still provide the town with some of its most interesting sights. Lying at the northern end of the lake Mjøsa and surrounded by farms, forests and small settlements, it's a laid-back place with year-round attractions, although in winter it becomes a ski town *par excellence*.

☉ Sights

★ **Olympic Park**   AREA, MUSEUM
(Map p128; ☏ 61 05 42 00; www.olympiaparken.no; Nordsetervegen 45) After Lillehammer won its bid for the 1994 Winter Olympics, the Norwegian government ploughed over two billion kroner into the town's infrastructure. In an example to other Olympic host cities, most amenities remain in use and visitors can tour the main Olympic sites over a large area called the Olympiaparken.

Lillehammer Art Museum   MUSEUM
(Lillehammer Kunstmuseum; Map p128; ☏ 61 05 44 60; www.lillehammerartmuseum.com; Stortorget 2; adult/child 100kr/free; ☉11am-5pm) Lillehammer's stunning metal-and-glass art museum looks like a spaceship that's landed in the middle of town. It explores Norwegian visual arts from the early 19th century to the present. There are a few minor works by Edvard Munch, but it's mostly devoted to less well-known names. There's a lovely cafe serving lunch.

Aulestad   MUSEUM
(☏ 61 22 41 10; www.aulestad.no; Aulestadvegen 6-14, Follebu; adult/child 130/65kr; ☉10am-5pm late May-Aug, 11am-4pm Sat & Sun Sep) Bjørnstjerne Bjørnson, winner of the Nobel Prize for Literature in 1903, lived on a farm at Aulestad, 18km northwest of Lillehammer. It has been lovingly restored and is stuffed to the rafters with antiques, furniture, books and busts reflecting the well-to-do life of the author and his wife Karoline. It's a way out of town, so you'll need your own vehicle to get here.

WORTH A TRIP

OLYMPIC SKI SLOPES

Lillehammer has two Olympic ski slopes: **Hafjell Alpine Centre** (☏61 27 47 00; www.hafjell.no), 15km north of town, hosted the downhill events, while **Kvitfjell Alpine Facility** (☏61 28 36 30; www.kvitfjell.no), 50km north of town, was used for cross-country. Both offer public skiing between late November and late April and they're connected by bus with Lillehammer Skysstasjon.

Norwegian Olympic Museum   MUSEUM
(Map p128; www.ol.museum.no; Olympiaparken; adult/child 130/65kr; ☉10am-5pm Jun-Aug, 11am-4pm Tue-Sun Sep-May) The excellent Olympic museum is at the Håkons Hall ice-hockey venue. On the ground floor there is a well-presented display covering the ancient Olympic Games, as well as all of the Olympic Games of the modern era, with a focus on the exploits of Norwegian athletes and the Lillehammer games.

Maihaugen Folk Museum   MUSEUM
(Map p128; www.maihaugen.no; Maihaugveien 1; adult/child/family Jun-Aug 170/85/425kr, Sep-May 130/65/325kr; ☉10am-5pm Jun-Aug, 11am-4pm Tue-Sun Sep-May) Step back into the past at this surprisingly fascinating folk museum, which collects together around 180 buildings from other parts of Norway, mostly from the early 1900s. They've been rebuilt to resemble a small inland village: among the buildings on show are a stave church from Garmo, traditional turf-topped houses and shops, a post office, a schoolroom, fishing cabins and farmers' barns. Costumed actors help bring the experience to life.

Bjerkebæk   MUSEUM
(Map p128; ☏ 61 28 89 00; www.bjerkebek. no; Sigrid Undsets veg 1; adult/child/family 110/55/275kr; ☉10am-5pm mid-May-Aug, 10am-5pm Sat & Sun Sep) Bjerkebæk celebrates the life of Sigrid Undset, one of Norway's most notable authors who won the Nobel Prize for Literature in 1928. Her home has been restored with memorabilia from her life.

Combination tickets with Lillehammer's other museums are available.

Central Norway Highlights

1 Sognefjellet Road (p147) Crossing lofty mountain passes and passing frozen lakes on this stunning drive.

2 Dovrefjell-Sunndalsfjella National Park (p141) Spotting your first ever musk ox or moose on a wildlife safari.

3 Jotunheimen National Park (p146) Trekking the many mountain trails of this high-altitude national park, one of Norway's best.

4 Finse (p153) Crossing the Hardangerjøkulen icecap on a guided glacier walk.

5 Røros (p133) Exploring the copper-mining heritage of this trapped-in-time town.

30 km
15 miles

N

HEDMARK

Trondheim (75km)

Berkåk

Ulsberg

E6

30

Glåmos

Olavsgruva Mine

5 Røros

31

Johan Falkberget Museum

Skårhammårdalen Gorge

Os

30

Tolga

Hummelfjellet Alpine Centre

3

Femunden

Salensjøen

28

217

Akrestrømmen

Konnang

Tynset

Alvdal

Glomma

Atna

3

Oppdal

Driva

Lake Gjevilvatnet

Gjøra

70

Store Kalken (1880m)

Sunndalsøra

62

Trollheimen

70

Eidsvåg

Andalsnes

Bjorli

Romsdal

Aursjøen

Skarstind (1883m)

Geiranger (45km); Stryn (65km)

Skjåk

Breheimen National Park

1 Sognefjellet Road

Galdhøpiggen (2469m)

Glittertind (2452m)

51

Randsverk

15

Vågåmo (Vågå)

Reinheim National Park

Dombås

E136

Fokstumyra Marshes

Snøhetta Viewpoint

2

Snøhetta (2286m)

Reinheim Hut

Dovrefjell-Sunndalsfjella National Park

Kongsvoll

Hjerkinn

Dovre National Park

E6

Grimsdalen

Bjørkhol Camping

Høgsteiga (1633m)

Folldal

Fallet

27

6 Rondane National Park

Rondslottet (2178m)

Mysuseter

Otta

Kringom

Randsverk

Kvam

Vinstra

7 Sjoa River

6 Rondane National Park (p142)
Trekking to the summit of one of the many lofty peaks.

7 Sjoa River (p143)
Braving the white water on a thrilling rafting adventure.

8 Lillehammer
(p128) Climbing to the top of Norway's most famous ski jump.

Lillehammer

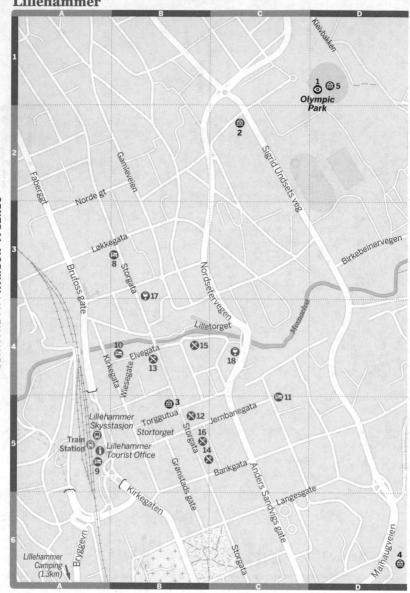

⚐ Activities

★ Lygårdsbakkene Ski Jump   SKIING

(Map p128; tower adult/child 25/15kr; ⊙9am-7pm Jun–mid-Aug, 9am-5pm May & late Aug, 11-4pm Sat & Sun Sep) The main ski jump (K120) here drops 136m with a landing-slope angle of 37.5 degrees. The opening ceremony of the Lillehammer games was held here; the tower for the **Olympic flame** (Map p128) still stands near the foot of the jump. The

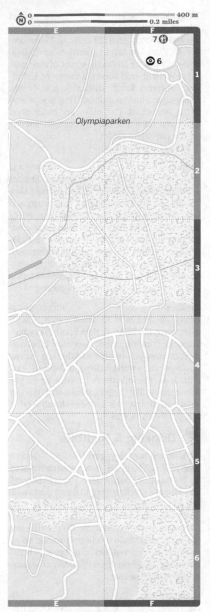

✯ Festivals & Events

Lillehammer Jazz Festival MUSIC
(☑ 81 53 31 33; www.dolajazz.no) Lillehammer Jazz Festival is held over four days in October; tickets go on sale from 1 July each year.

⛏ Sleeping

★ **HI Lillehammer Vandrerhjem** HOSTEL $
(Map p128; ☑ 61 26 00 24; www.stasjonen. no; 1st fl, Railway Station; dm/s/d/f from 395/795/895/1395kr; ℗ 🛜) If you've never stayed in a youth hostel, this one above the train station is the place to break the habit of a lifetime. The rooms are simple but come with a bathroom, bed linen and free wireless internet. There's a spick-and-span communal kitchen, but approach the downstairs cafe with caution (hot dog soup anyone?!). Free parking is a bonus.

Lillehammer Camping CAMPGROUND $
(☑ 61 25 33 33; www.lillehammer-camping.no; Dampsagveien 47; tent & 2 people 170-195kr, cabins 395-1585kr; ⊘ year-round; 🛜) Not the most attractive campsite you'll ever pitch a peg on, but the lakeside location and facilities – laundry facilities, water-sports equipment,

ski-jump chairlift ascends to a stunning panoramic view over the town, and a ticket includes entry to the viewing tower; alternatively, you can walk up the 952 steps.

children's play areas and even a mock Viking camp – make it more palatable. Note that cabins have an obligatory cleaning fee.

Øvergaard
B&B $$

(Map p128; ☑61 25 99 99; www.oevergaard. net; Jernbanegata 24; s/d with shared bathroom 445/790kr; P🖕) Just above the centre of town, this friendly B&B has simple rooms with plenty of family character in quiet surrounds. It's a well-run place and about as cheap as you'll get in Norway. It's an equally short walk to both the town centre and the Olympic sites.

★Clarion Collection Hotel Hammer
HOTEL $$$

(Map p128; ☑61 26 73 73; www.nordicchoice hotels.com; Stortorget 108b; tw/d incl breakfast & dinner from 1345/1545kr; 🖕) In an architecturally pleasing, mustard-yellow building that echoes traditional Norwegian architecture, this hotel is a solid choice. Monochrome rooms are a bit short on character, but comfortable enough – and the inclusion of both breakfast and a dinner buffet make it great value (at least for Norway).

Mølla Hotell
HOTEL $$$

(Map p128; ☑61 05 70 80; www.mollahotell.no; Elvegata 12; s/d from 1050/1760kr; P🖕) This functional hotel has been tacked on to the side of the town's old mill. The vivid yellow facade looks a bit putrid (it's supposedly inspired by a wheatsheaf), but things are a lot nicer inside: bare-brick walls, stripy carpets and plain but pleasant rooms dotted with memorabilia from the '94 Olympics. The rooftop bar has super views.

🍴 Eating

Oliven
CAFE $

(Map p128; ☑61 26 50 20; Storgata 57; salads & sandwiches 59-119kr; ⊗9am-7pm Mon-Sat, 11am-5pm Sun) A little bit of the Mediterranean has travelled north to Norway thanks to this attractive cafe, where you can tuck into spanakopita, fresh olives and hummus wraps. Olive oil, coffee and other goodies are for sale inside.

Café Opus
CAFE $

(Map p128; Stortorget 63; baguettes from 59kr; ⊗9am-6pm Mon-Fri, 9am-4pm Sat, 11am-4pm Sun) Hugely popular for its baguettes, rolls and cakes (and for its outdoor tables in summer), Café Opus gets the simple things right – tasty food, friendly service and smart-casual decor.

★Lykellige Dager
CAFE $$

(Map p128; ☑921 32 682; www.lykkeligedager.no; Storgata 49; lunch mains 129-199kr; ⊗7.30am-5pm Mon-Fri, 10am-4pm Sat) In a hard-to-miss glass-and-steel box on the main street of Storgata, this excellent cafe serves a range of tempting, on-trend lunch dishes – açai bowls, Asian-style chicken salads, Thai soups and detox smoothies. The cakes are really good too – and on a nice day, you can sit outside on the pavement tables.

'Happy Days' indeed!

Heim
GASTROPUB $$

(Map p128; ☑61 10 00 82; www.heim.no; Storgata 84; dinner mains 179-269kr; ⊗3pm-midnight Mon-Thu, 3pm-3am Fri, noon-3pm Sat) This warm and welcoming gastropub has fast become one of the town's most frequented hangouts since opening its doors in 2014. It attracts all kinds of diners, from hipsters to ale enthusiasts, and the hearty menu of fish and chips, bangers and mash and meat-and-cheese platters is just the ticket for easy, all-hours dining.

Nikkers
INTERNATIONAL $$

(Map p128; ☑61 24 74 30; www.nikkers.no; Elvegata 18; mains 159-269kr; ⊗11am-11pm) Everyone's favourite winter hangout in central Lillehammer: a brewpub-bar-bistro where a moose has apparently walked through the wall (look outside for the full effect). It's popular for big, filling mains like burgers, steaks and reindeer stew, and the riverside terrace is lovely – but it can get rowdy in season.

🍷 Drinking & Nightlife

★Lillehammer Bryggeri
BREWERY

(Map p128; ☑950 19 108; www.lillehammerbryggeri. no; Elvegata 19; ⊗5-11pm Wed & Thu, 5pm-1am Fri & Sat) This is a cracking spot to down beers with the locals – an enthusiast-run brewery with an ale-making history dating back to 1847, bar a few closures here and there. Beer bottles line the walls, and vaulted ceilings provide an atmospheric place to down some brews. There's also a no-frills, beer-friendly menu of sausages, stews and the like.

Haakons Pub
PUB

(Map p128; ☑61 26 35 50; Stortorget 93; ⊗1pm-3am Mon-Thu, noon-3am Fri & Sat) A spit-and-sawdust locals' pub, heavy on the wood and light on the luxuries. By day it's the preserve of elbow-on-the-bar drinkers; when the sun sets it kicks into action, becoming a crowded and agreeable place to drink. It can get a little raucous during the ski season.

ℹ Information

Lillehammer Tourist Office (Map p128; ☑ 61 28 98 00; www.lillehammer.com; Jernbanetorget 2, Lillehammer Skysstasjon; ☺ 8am-6pm Mon-Fri, 10am-4pm Sat & Sun mid-Jun–mid-Aug, 8am-4pm Mon-Fri, 10am-2pm Sat rest of year) Inside the train station.

ℹ Getting There & Away

Lillehammer Skysstasjon (Map p128) is the main transport terminal for buses, trains and taxis.

Lavprisekspressen (www.lavprisekspressen. no) bus services run to/from Oslo (300kr, three hours, three to four daily) via Gardermoen Airport.

Nor-Way (www.nor-way.no) runs to Bergen (646kr, nine hours, one or two daily).

Trains run to/from Oslo (414kr, 2¼ hours, around hourly) and Trondheim (from 754kr, 4¼ to seven hours, four to six daily). Some trains also stop at Hamar.

Hunderfossen

Some 15km north of Lillehammer, just off the E6, Hunderfossen has a handful of attractions worth going out of your way for.

In summer there are frequent buses from the Lillehammer Skysstasjon. In winter the service is more erratic. A considerable uphill walk is involved to reach the bobsled run.

◉ Sights & Activities

Norwegian Museum of Road History MUSEUM
(Norsk Vegmuseum; ☑ 61 28 52 50; www.vegmuseum.no; Hunderfossvegen 757; ☺ 10am-5pm mid-Jun–mid-Aug, 10am-3pm Tue-Sun rest of year) FREE The Norwegian Museum of Road History tells the story of Norway's battle to forge roads through its challenging geography. Up the hill and part of the same complex, the **Fjellsprengnings-museet** (Rock-Blasting Museum) is a 240m-long tunnel that gives you a real insight into the difficulties of building a tunnel through the Norwegian mountains.

★**Olympic Bobsled Run** ADVENTURE SPORTS
(☑ 61 05 42 00; www.olympiaparken.no; Hunderfossvegen 680, Fåberg; adult/child 250/170kr; ☺ 10am-5pm daily late Jun-late Aug, hours vary rest of year) It's not often you get the chance to hurtle down an Olympic-level bobsled run – but that's exactly what's on offer here. Wheeled 'bobrafts' take five passengers and hit a top speed of 100km/h. The real thing, **taxibobs** (990kr per person) take four passengers and reach

an exhilarating 130km/h – you're down the mountain in 70 seconds.

Hunderfossen Familiepark AMUSEMENT PARK
(☑ 61 27 55 30; www.hunderfossen.no; Fossekrovegen, Fåberg; adult/child 410/355kr; ☺ 10am-6pm late Jun–mid-Aug, hours vary early Jun & mid-Aug–early Sep, closed mid-Sep–mid-May; 🚼) The Hunderfossen Familiepark, one of Norway's best parks for children, has water rides, 3D presentations, fairy-tale palaces and wandering trolls. The latest attraction is a huge rollercoaster. If your child is under 90cm tall, he or she gets in free.

ℹ Getting There & Away

Trains from Lillehammer's Skysstasjon stop in Hunderfossen (50kr, four daily).

Hamar

POP 26,000

This medium-sized town would never win a beauty contest, but it does possess a surprising number of attractions that are worth a detour on your way between Oslo and the north.

◉ Sights

Domkirkeodden MUSEUM
(Glass Cathedral; ☑ 62 54 27 00; www.domkirkeodden.no; Strandveien 100; adult/child 110/50kr; ☺ 10am-5pm daily mid-Jun–mid-Aug, 10am-4pm

WORTH A TRIP

WORLD'S OLDEST PADDLE STEAMER

....

Skibladner (☑ 61 14 40 80; www.ski bladner.no; Hamar-Lillehammer one way/ return 250/350kr, under 12yr free; ⊙ Tue, Thu & Sat late-Jun–mid-Aug), the world's oldest paddle steamer, is a wonderfully relaxing way to explore Lake Mjøsa. First built in Sweden in 1856, the boat was re-fitted and lengthened to 165ft (50m) in 1888. From late June until mid-August, the *Skibladner* plies the lake between Hamar, Gjøvik and Lillehammer. Most travellers opt for the route between Hamar and Lillehammer (3½ hours) on Tuesday, Thursday and Saturday. The boat leaves Hamar at 11.15am, arrives in Lillehammer at 3pm and returns straight away, arriving back in Hamar at 6.45pm. If, as most people do, you only travel one way, then it's easy enough to hop on a train back to your starting point.

Tue-Sun mid-May–mid-Jun & end Aug) West of town (1.5km), this extensive open-air museum includes 18th- and 19th-century buildings, a folk history exhibit featuring the creepy Devil's Finger (a finger cast in pewter with various spooky legends attached to it), and the ruins of the castle. But the centrepiece is Hamar's tumbledown medieval cathedral, now protected inside a stunning glass enclosure.

Viking Ship Sports Arena STADIUM
(Vikingskipet; ☑ 62 51 75 00; www.hoa.no; Åkersvikaveien 1; 50kr; ⊙ 9am-8pm Mon-Fri, 9.30am-5pm Sat & Sun 1-17 Aug, 9am-3pm Mon-Fri mid-Oct–Mar, closed rest of year) Hamar's standout landmark is this sports arena, a graceful structure with the lines of an upturned Viking ship. The building, which hosted the speed skating during the 1994 Winter Olympics in Lillehammer, holds 20,000 spectators, encompasses 9600 sq metres of ice and is 94.6m long. Both in scale and aesthetics, it's an impressive place.

From late July to mid-August, it's open to the public for ice-skating (115kr per day).

Norwegian Railway Museum MUSEUM
(Norsk Jernbanemuseum; ☑ 62 51 31 60; www.jernbanemuseet.no; Strandveien 163; adult/child 90/55kr; ⊙ 10am-5pm Jul–mid-Aug, 11am-5pm Tue-Sat, 11am-4pm Sun rest of year) Train spotters will have steam blowing out of their ears at the sight of this lovely railway museum,

which brings together a fine collection of train-related ephemera – from engine sheds, rail carriages and steam locomotives to vintage station paraphernalia. Of equal interest are the displays exploring the extraordinary engineering feats required to carve the railways through Norway's rugged terrain.

It's about 2km west of Hamar's town centre.

🎊 Festivals & Events

Middle Ages Festival CULTURAL
(www.middelalderfestival.no; ⊙ 2nd weekend in Jun) Locals in period costume; Gregorian chants in the glass cathedral.

Hamar Beer Festival BEER
(Hamar Ølfestival; ⊙ early Jun) Beer, music, more beer.

🛏 Sleeping & Eating

Clarion Collection Hotel Astoria BUSINESS HOTEL $$
(☑ 62 70 70 00; www.nordicchoicehotels.no; Torggata 23; d 1090-1490kr; ☎) It might look like a gigantic cardboard box, but this reliable hotel is the most obvious place to rest up for the night in downtown Hamar. The rooms lack decorative sparkle, but they're decently sized, and breakfast and dinner is included in the rates.

Vikingskipet Hamar Vanderhjem HOTEL, HOSTEL $$
(☑ 62 52 60 60; www.vikingskipet.no; Åkersvikavegen 24; s/d 825/960kr, apt 1190-2390kr; P ☎) This excellent wood-clad modern hostel is by far the best budget option near town. There's a range of simply decorated single and double rooms of various sizes, and some terrific, spacious apartments that can sleep up to four people.

Scandic Hamar HOTEL $$
(☑ 21 61 40 00; www.scandichotels.com; Vangsvegen 121; s/d from 849/1149kr; P ☎) It's huge and unrelentingly modern from the outside, but the Scandic has a few surprises on the inside – including surprisingly attractive rooms decorated with abstract murals depicting Hamar architecture. The usual extras include a gym and decent restaurant, but it's short on charm, and a good five-minute walk to the town centre.

Kai & Mattis Café INTERNATIONAL $$
(☑ 62 53 01 45; Torggata 53; mains 150kr; ⊙ 11am-6pm) If you've ever wondered what an art-deco boudoir looked like (don't pretend you haven't!) then this place, with its burgundy red walls and over-the-top deco-

rations, will probably give you a fair idea. Boudoir or not, the meals are good – as well as the sandwich and burger staples, they do meals such as chicken curry pie.

ⓘ Information

Hamar Regional Tourist Office (☑ 400 36 036; www.visit-hedmark.no/hamarregionen; Grønnegata 52; ⊙ 9am-5pm Mon-Fri, 10am-5pm Sat & Sun mid-Jun–mid-Aug, 9am-3.30pm Mon-Fri rest of year) On the main square in the town centre.

ⓘ Getting There & Away

BUS

Lavprisekspressen (p131) buses go to Oslo (300kr) once or twice a day.

TRAIN

Trains go to Oslo (290kr, 1¼ hours, once or twice hourly), Røros (587kr, 3¼ hours, up to four daily) and Trondheim (836kr, five hours, four to six daily) via Lillehammer (143kr, 45 minutes).

Trysil

POP 6763

Surrounded by forested hillsides close to the Swedish border, and overlooked by Norway's largest collection of ski slopes, little Trysil is well worth a detour, with year-round activities taking you into the wilderness.

🏃 Activities

Although Trysil lives and breathes winter skiing, for the rest of the year you can do just about anything to keep active, from canoeing and canyoning to horse riding, as well as the more sedate pastime of fishing. The **tourist office** (☑ 62 45 10 00; www.trysil.com; Storvegen 3; ⊙ 9am-8pm Mon-Fri, to 6pm Sat & Sun mid-Jun–mid-Aug, shorter hours rest of year) can organise any of these activities for you.

Perhaps the most rewarding activity in summer is cycling. There are at least six cycle routes: the shortest 6km, the longest 38km. Route maps are available from the tourist office. Bikes can be hired from most hotels and campsites for around 200kr per day.

🛏 Sleeping

Trysil Hyttegrend   CABIN $
(☑ 901 32 761; www.trysilhytte.com; Øranset; campsites 210kr, huts 590-840kr; P 🕾) By the river's edge, 2.5km south of town, this excellent site has many drawcards, including wireless internet, a wood-fired sauna, plenty of activities, a playground for children and a perfect riverside setting. All cabins have cooking facilities.

★ Radisson Blu Resort   HOTEL $$$
(☑ 62 44 90 00; www.radissonblu.com/en/resort-trysil; Hotellveien 1; summer s/d from 990/1090kr, winter d from 1990kr; P 🕾 ⊠) One of the few Trysil hotels to open year-round, this is Trysil's most luxurious accommodation. Outside the ski season (when prices are high) it's a first-rate bargain with huge, impeccable rooms in a large wooden building surrounded by ski slopes. It also contains an impressive pool complex, a choice of two restaurants, a bowling alley and burger bar.

ⓘ Getting There & Away

The Nor-Way Bussekspress 'Trysil Ekspressen' connects Trysil with Oslo (279kr, 3¼ hours, twice daily).

Røros

POP 5576

Røros, a charming Unesco World Heritage-listed site set in a small hollow of stunted forests and bleak fells, is one of Norway's most beautiful villages. The Norwegian writer Johan Falkberget described Røros as 'a place of whispering history'. This historic copper-mining town (once called Bergstad, or mountain city) has wonderfully preserved, colourful wooden houses that climb the hillside, as well as fascinating relics of the town's mining past. It feels a little bit like a Norwegian version of the Wild West.

Røros has become something of a retreat for artists, who lend even more character to this enchanted place.

Røros is one of the coldest places in Norway – the temperature once dropped to a mighty bracing -50.4°C.

History

According to local legend, in 1644 Olsen Åsen shot a reindeer at Storvola (Storwartz), 13km from Røros. The enraged creature pawed at the ground, revealing a glint of copper ore. In the same year Røros Kobberverk (Røros Copperworks) was established, followed two years later by a royal charter that granted it exclusive rights to all minerals, forest products and waterways (and local labour) within 40km of the original discovery.

The mining company located its headquarters at Røros due to the abundant wood (fuel) and the rapids along the river Hyttelva, which provided hydroelectric power. The use of fire in breaking up the rock in the mines was a perilous business and cost Røros dearly. Røros first burnt to the ground during the Gyldenløve conflict with the Swedes between 1678 and 1679, and the smelter was damaged by fire again in 1953. In 1977, after 333 years of operation, the company went bankrupt.

👁 Sights

Røros' **historic district**, characterised by the striking log architecture of its 80 protected buildings, takes in the entire central area. The two main streets, **Bergmannsgata** and **Kjerkgata**, are lined with historical homes and buildings, all under preservation orders. The entire area is like an architectural museum of old Norway. For one of the loveliest turf-roofed homes you'll see, head up to the top of Kjerkgata to the house signposted as **Harald Sohlsbergs Plass 59** (Map p135; Kjerkgata).

If Røros looks familiar, that's because several films have been made here, including Røros author Johan Falkberget's classic *An-Magrit*, starring Jane Fonda. Flanderborg gate starred in some of Astrid Lindgren's *Pippi Longstocking* classics and Røros even stood in for Siberia in *A Day in the Life of Ivan Denisovich*.

In addition to the main museum website, www.worldheritageroros.no is an excellent resource about Røros' historical sites.

★ Smelthytta   MUSEUM
(Map p135; www.rorosmuseet.no; Malmplassen; adult/student/child incl guided tour 100/80kr/free; ⊙10am-6pm mid-Jun–mid-Aug, 10am-4pm early Jun & mid-Aug–mid-Sep, 10am-3pm mid-Sep–May) Built on the site of a former copper smelting works that burnt down in 1975, this museum brings the town's mining heritage to life. Intricate working models demonstrate the water- and horse-powered smelting processes, and if you want to watch the real thing, live copper smelting demonstrations are held daily at 3pm in July and August.

Outside the museum entrance spreads the large open area known as the **Malmplassen** (Ore Place; Map p135), where loads of ore were dumped and weighed on the large wooden scale. Just across the stream from the museum are the protected **Slegghaugen** (Slag Heaps; Map p135), from which there are lovely views over town.

Miners' Cottages (Flanderborg Gate)   AREA
(Map p135) Off the southwestern corner of the slag heaps, the historic smelting district with its tiny turf-roofed miners' cottages, particularly along Sleggveien, is one of Røros' prettiest corners.

Røros Kirke   CHURCH
(Map p135; Kjerkgata; adult/child 50kr/free; ⊙10am-4pm Mon-Sat, 12.30-2.30pm Sun mid-Jun–mid-Aug, 11am-1pm Mon-Sat early Jun & mid-Aug–mid-Sep, 11am-1pm Sat rest of year) Røros' copper industry was booming when local notables decided to finance the construction of this lovely – and large – Lutheran church in 1784, at a cost of 23,000 riksdaler (at the time, miners earned about 50 riksdaler per year). It's vast, with space for 1600 worshippers, and a fittingly grand monument to the town's mining fortunes.

Olavsgruva Mine   MUSEUM
(☑72 40 61 70; www.rorosmuseet.no/olavsgruva; adult/child/senior & student 120kr/free/100kr; ⊙tours every 2hr 11am-5pm Jun-Aug, tour times vary rest of year) For a gritty insight into Røros' mining past, head 13km north of Røros to this centuries-old mine, where ore has been extracted since the 1650s. Tours travel 50m underground down dingy tunnels to the main miners' hall. It can be slippery underfoot, so good shoes are essential, as is a warm jacket – the temperature hovers at 5°C year-round.

Johan Falkberget Museum   MUSEUM
(☑72 40 61 70; www.falkberget.no; Ratvolden; adult/child 100kr/free; ⊙guided tours by appointment) The works of Røros' favourite son, author Johan Falkberget (1879–1967), have been translated into 19 languages and cover 300 years of the region's mining history. His most famous work, *An-Magrit,* tells the story of a peasant girl who transported copper ore in the Røros mining district. Entry to the beautiful grounds surrounding the museum is free.

The museum is at Ratvolden, beside lake Rugelsjø, 20km north of Røros. To get there, take a local train to Rugeldalen station, where a small walking track leads to the museum (but call ahead first).

🏃 Activities

Canoeing, horse riding and, in winter, sleigh rides and ice fishing are possible in Røros. The tourist office (p138) has a full list of operators.

Røros Husky   DOG SLEDDING
(☑915 15 228; www.roroshusky.no; 1250kr; ⊙Nov-Apr) Owned by locals Torgeir Oren and Mary Amundsen, this husky company runs winter trips ranging from a 90-minute run to multi-day adventures. It's located about 10km north of Røros, but bookings can be made via the tourist office (p138).

Røros

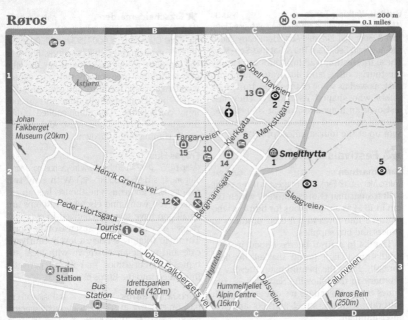

Røros

◎ **Top Sights**

◎ **Sights**

◎ **Activities, Courses & Tours**

◎ **Sleeping**

⊗ **Eating**

◎ **Drinking & Nightlife**

✪ **Entertainment**

◎ **Shopping**

Husky Point   DOG SLEDDING
(☑ 977 38 903; www.huskypoint.no; Kopparleden 9001, Os; dog-sledding winter/summer adult from 1200/1100kr, child year-round 600kr) 🐾 Based near the town of Os, about 20km south of Røros, this dogsledding company can take you on a 90-minute husky-driven ride whatever the time of year: in winter, the sleds are on skis, and in summer they're on wheels. If you feel up to it, you can even opt to take the reins.

🜲 Tours

Røros Rein   WILDLIFE
(☑ 979 74 966; www.rorosrein.no; Hagaveien 17; ☉ Nov-Apr) 🐾 If you've always wanted to learn how to steer a reindeer sleigh, then this winter-only company can help. It's run by a local Sami family, the Nordfjells, who will teach you all about the reindeer and even let you join in with the herding if you wish. Afterwards, a traditional meal is served inside a Sami *lavvo* (hut).

Guided Walking Tours
WALKING

(Map p135; adult/child 100kr/free; ☺ tours 11am, 1pm & 3pm mid-Jun–mid-Aug, 11am early Jun & mid-Aug–mid-Sep, 11am Thu & Sat mid-Sep–May) These interesting walking tours are run by the tourist office and illustrate the town's past, as well as some of the important characters who shaped its history. They last just over an hour and start at Smelthytta/Malmplassen and end at Røros church. Sign up at the tourist office (p138).

✹✹ Festivals & Events

Rørosmartnan
CULTURAL

(Røros Market; ☺ Feb) The biggest winter event is Rørosmartnan (Røros Market), which began in 1644 as a rendezvous for hunters who ventured into town to sell their products to miners and buy supplies.

Thanks to a royal decree issued in 1853 stipulating that a grand market be held annually from the penultimate Tuesday of February to the following Saturday, it continues today. Nowadays it's celebrated with cultural programs, street markets and live entertainment.

Elden
PERFORMING ARTS

(www.elden-roros.no; tickets from 290kr; ☺ late Jul-early Aug) In late July and early August, Røros stages a nightly three-hour rock opera that recounts the invasion of Trøndelag by Sweden in 1718, covering the occupation of Røros and the subsequent death of thousands of soldiers on their frozen trek homewards to Sweden. It's enacted on the slag heaps in the upper part of town.

Fermund Race
SPORTS

(www.femundlopet.no; ☺ Feb) One of Europe's longest dog-sled races starts and ends in Røros in the first week of February.

Winter Chamber Music Festival
MUSIC

(www.vinterfestspill.no; ☺ Mar) Concerts held in Røros Kirke in the first week of March.

🛏 Sleeping

Røros is overrun with day-trippers in summer and suffers heavily from coach tour overload – so if you're planning on staying overnight, reserve well ahead and expect prices to be substantially higher than elsewhere.

The tourist office (p138) keeps a list of summer cabins and guesthouses, some within walking distance of town.

★ Erzscheidergården
GUESTHOUSE $$

(Map p135; ✉ 72 41 11 94; www.erzscheidergaarden. no; Spell Olaveien 6; s 900-1150kr, d 1250-1350kr; 🅿 🛜) For our money, this cosy guesthouse is the top place to stay in Røros. It has the vibe of a traditional mountain hostelry, so expect wood, rugs, rustic furniture and old-fashioned beds – but it's all tastefully done and exceedingly comfortable. The home-cooked buffet breakfast is an absolute feast and almost worth coming for on its own.

Frøyas Hus
B&B $$

(Map p135; ✉ 72 41 10 10; www.froyashus.no; Mørkstugata 4; s/d 950/1050kr; 🛜) With only two rooms, this gorgeous guesthouse has an intimacy you won't find elsewhere. Rooms are small and have scarcely changed in over 300 years – it's rustic in the best sense of the word. Throw in friendly service, a lovely courtyard cafe and public areas strewn with local antiques and curiosities, and it's all perfectly integrated into the Røros experience.

Vertshuset Røros
HISTORIC HOTEL $$

(Map p135; ✉ 72 41 93 50; www.vertshusetroros. no; Kjerkgata 34; r 1100-1700kr; 🛜) Located in a 17th-century inn on the main pedestrian thoroughfare, the Vertshuset Røros is a wonderful choice. The wood-clad rooms are generously sized and have numerous period touches, such as original timber beams. Pricier rooms have small kitchenettes, while the two-bed apartments are perfect for families. As with all old buildings, noise can be an issue.

Do be aware that during busy periods they may book you a room at their 'sister' hotel, the **Røros Hotell** (Map p135; ✉ 72 40 80 00; www. roroshotell.no; An Magritveien 10; r 1250-1400kr; 🅿 🛜 🏊) – a very different kind of place.

Idrettsparken Hotell
HOTEL $$

(✉ 72 41 10 89; www.idrettsparken.no; Øra 25; cabins from 550kr, hotel r from 900kr; 🅿) Finding rooms on a budget is tricky in Røros, but this wallet-friendly, family-run establishment is a decent option. It has rooms of various sizes, from quad dorms and cabins to smallish doubles, and while the decor looks badly dated in places, it's all spick and span. Look out for the display of vintage pottery in the breakfast room.

🍴 Eating

Frøyas Hus
CAFE $

(Map p135; ✉ 928 83 530; Mørkstugata 4; snacks 50-100kr; ☺ 10am-5pm) A blissed-out garden courtyard cafe serving good waffles and

NATIONAL PARKS OF NORTHERN CENTRAL NORWAY

Breheimen National Park One of Norway's newest national parks, Breheimen opened in 2009 and covers 1691 sq km. It's wedged between the Jotunheimen and Jostedalsbreen national parks and has some of the best hiking in the southern half of Norway. However, walking here is not for the inexperienced. Trail markings are harder to follow than in some more trodden parks and all the DNT huts are unstaffed. This is the place for an off-the-beaten-track adventure. For more information, visit the Lom tourist office (p146).

Reinheimen National Park Founded in 2006, this 1969-sq-km park stretches from Lom in the southeast to Åndalsnes in the northwest. It's a varied and relatively unexplored park that is steep and mountainous in the west with a more gentle Alpine plateau in the east. It's home to wild reindeer, wolverines and golden eagles. For more information, visit the Lom tourist office (p146).

Dovre National Park (Map p144; www.nasjonalparkriket.no) Immediately north of Rondane National park, this 289-sq-km park was established in 2003 and is famous for having almost every Norwegian flora type within its borders. The park's highest point is Fokstuhøe (1716m).

rømmegrøt, a traditional, slightly sour porridge eaten with cured hams in the evening.

Trygstad Bakeri   BAKERY $
(Map p135; [☎]72 41 10 29; www.trygstadbakeri.no; Kjerkgata 12; snacks 30-80kr; ☺8.30am-7pm Mon-Fri, 9am-4pm Sat, noon-5pm Sun) This standout cafe and bakery will treat you to the town's most popular coffee and baked goodies.

Kaffestugu Cafeteria   NORWEGIAN $$
(Map p135; www.kaffestuggu.no; Bergmannsgata 18; mains 129-250kr; ☺10am-11pm) Set in one of Røros' classic timber buildings, with a small outdoor courtyard, this perennially popular cafe has the air of an old Norwegian tea room, and it's a good spot, indeed, for coffee, cake and pastries. Main meals tend towards the hearty and filling: *smørbrød* (open sandwich), reindeer steak, sausages and stews, often served with heaps of potato and cabbage.

★Vertshuset Røros   NORWEGIAN $$$
(Map p135; [☎]72 41 93 50; Kjerkgata 34; mains lunch 110-190kr, dinner 295-340kr, 3-/6-course menu 450/798kr; ☺10am-10pm) The town's best food is served at the Vertshuset Inn, with a strong focus on local flavours: mountain trout, Arctic char, local beef, pork and a great selection of cheeses. The highlight is the six-course evening menu, a feast of mountain flavours, served in the inn's cosy beamed dining room. Lunch mains are tasty, but less ambitious.

🍺 Drinking & Entertainment

Berkel og Bar   PUB
(Map p135; [☎]72 41 93 50; www.vertshusetroros.no/en/berkel-og-bar; Kjerkgata 34; ☺10am-11pm) This

gastropub is a welcome addition to the Vertshuset stable. It gets its name from the *berkel,* a meat slicer invented in 1898 and still used to slice up the cold meats that feature on the excellent meat and cheese platters (459kr). Otherwise, it's mainly pubby food: burgers, pulled beef brioches and the like.

The pub brews several of its own beers and also brings in a good choice from other Norwegian breweries.

Organ Recitals   CLASSICAL MUSIC
(Map p135; Kjerkgata; ☺6-6.45pm Mon-Sat early Jul–mid-Aug) For five weeks from early July to early August, the church hosts organ recitals, sometimes accompanied by orchestral musicians from across Europe.

🛍 Shopping

Potteriet Røros   CERAMICS
(Map p135; [☎]72 41 17 10; www.potteriet-roros.no; Fargarveien 4; ☺9am-4pm Mon-Fri, 10am-3pm Sat) Here you'll find pottery based on traditional designs from all over Trøndelag, along with some creative modern interpretations. The pottery workshop next door is open to the public and staff are always happy to explain the history behind each design (morning is the best time to catch them at work).

Galleri Thomasgården   CERAMICS
(Map p135; [☎]482 19 008; Kjerkgata 48; ☺11am-5pm Mon-Wed, Fri & Sat, 11am-11pm Thu, noon-5pm Sun) At the worthwhile Galleri Thomasgården, potter Torgeir Henriksen creates rustic stoneware and porcelain. You will also find the wonderful nature-inspired wood carvings

of Henry Solli. The player piano is one of only two in Norway and dates back to 1929.

Hartzgården Sølvsmie JEWELLERY
(Map p135; ☑ 72 41 05 50; Kjerkgata 35; ☺ 10am-6pm Mon-Fri, 10am-4pm Sat, noon-5pm Sun) At this silversmith's shop you'll find locally handcrafted silver jewellery with an emphasis on Viking themes, as well as a small historical-jewellery exhibit.

ℹ Information

Tourist Office (Map p135; ☑ 72 41 00 00; www.roros.no; Peder Hiortsgata 2; ☺ 9am-3.30pm Mon-Fri, 10am-4pm Sat) The first port of call for town info.

World Heritage Roros (www.worldheritageroros.no) Details Røros' historical sites.

ℹ Getting There & Away

AIR
Widerøe (www.wideroe.no) flies from Oslo a couple of times a day except Saturday. There's no airport bus; a taxi into town costs about 100kr.

BUS
There are daily buses from Røros to Trondheim (319kr, four hours, two to four daily) leaving from the **bus station** (Map p135; Johan Falkbergets vei). You can see timetables at the ATB (www.atb.no) website.

TRAIN
Røros lies on the eastern railway line between Oslo (249kr to 810kr, five hours, four or five daily) and Trondheim (from 249kr to 304kr, 2½ hours).

Femundsmarka National Park

Formed in 1971 to protect the lake, forests, marshes and mountain peaks of the area around Femunden, this 573-sq-km park is often overlooked by foreign tourists – despite the fact that it's been named one of the three best hiking areas in Norway by the Norwegian hiking association.

If you're lucky, you may see wild reindeer grazing in the heights and, in summer, a herd of around 30 musk oxen roams the area along the Røa and Mugga Rivers (in winter they migrate to the Funäsdalen area). It's thought that this group split off from an older herd in the Dovrefjell area and wandered all the way here. There are also a handful of exceedingly rare brown bears, as well as even rarer lynx and, occasionally, wolves drifting by from other areas.

✦ Activities

This is excellent hiking country and the very helpful national park information centre in Elgå can provide route suggestions and maps.

M/S Fæmund II BOATING
(☑ 963 92 017; www.femund.no; one way adult/child 255/170kr) The historic ferry M/S *Fæmund II* sails daily at 9am between mid-June and mid-August from Synnervika (also spelt Søndervika), on the northern shore of Lake Femunden, to Elgå (6½ hours return). From mid-June to late August, buses leave Røros train station for Synnervika 45 minutes before the boat's departure. Buses for Røros later meet the boat at Synnervika.

▐ Sleeping

On the western side of the lake, the two main sleeping options are **Johnsgård Turistsenter** (☑ 62 45 99 25; www.johnsgard.no; Langsjøveien 631; cabins 195-795kr, camping 200kr), 9km west of Buvika, and **Langen Gjestegård** (☑ 72 41 37 18; www.langen-gjestegaard.no; s/d from 550/900kr), a cosy, turf-roofed farmhouse near the lake.

On the eastern shore of the lake is the tiny village of **Elgå**, which is the main base for the park. It has campsites (with cabins) and a park information centre.

ℹ Getting There & Away

The M/S *Fæmund II* (p138) ferry runs a lovely, old-fashioned service on Lake Femunden between Synnervika and Elgå, with connecting buses to Røros.

Oppdal

POP 6691
Located to the north of Dovrefjell-Sunndalsfjella National Park, little Oppdal is a convenient base from which to explore the wilderness areas to the south. There's nothing much to detain you in town, but the surrounding countryside is beautiful with loads of activities on offer.

✦ Activities

★ Oppdal Safari WILDLIFE WATCHING
(☑ 986 93 200; www.moskussafari.no; Olav Skasliens veg 1; adult/child 425/300kr; ☺ May-Sep) This experienced company offers fantastic wildlife-watching safaris to spot musk ox, moose and other wild inhabitants of Dovrefjell-Sunndalsfjella. Trips last about seven hours and you'll need good footwear, warm clothes and binoculars if you have them. The

meeting point for tours is at Oppdal railway station. They also offer canoe and boat rental.

Oppdal Skisenter SKIING
(www.oppdalskisenter.no; Kjerkvegen 112; 1-day ski-pass adult/child 410/340kr) The three-part Oppdal Skisenter climbs the slopes from Hovden, Stølen and Vangslia, all within easy reach of town. The smaller Ådalen ski area nearby has two lifts. Vangslia is generally the easiest, with a couple of beginners' runs; Stølen offers intermediate skiing; and Hovden has three challenging advanced runs. The season runs from late November to late April.

Opplev Oppdal TOUR
(☑72 40 41 80; www.opplevoppdal.no; Granmo Camping, Dovre Rd 638; ⊘ rafting early Jun–mid-Aug) This multi-activity company specialises in white-water rafting on the Driva River. Their standard half-day, 14km run costs 840kr, plus a 50kr premium on Saturdays. The more sedate 4km tour, suitable for families, costs 440kr. They also offer other activities like canyoning and ziplining. Their rafting trips are based at Granmo Camping.

🛏 Sleeping & Eating

Granmo Camping CAMPGROUND $
(☑996 42 947; www.granmocamping.no; Dovre Rd 638; camping 150kr, vans 230kr, cabins 400-1050kr; ℗🛜) A well-run campsite, 6km to the south of Oppdal, offering spacious campsites and self-catering cabins, spread out over a large grassy field. There's a play area for kids and a miniature petting zoo. It's right alongside the Driva River, and rafting expeditions start nearby, run by Opplev Oppdal.

⭐ Quality Hotel Skifer BUSINESS HOTEL $$
(☑73 60 50 80; www.skiferhotel.no; Olav Skasliens vei 9; d from 1130kr; ℗🛜) A surprisingly swish hotel in the middle of Oppdal offering by far the town's best rooms, with smart grey accents, stylish furniture and a great restaurant that offers a good-value nightly buffet (310kr). Some rooms face the mountains, others the main road, but all are very comfortable.

Møllen Restaurant & Pizzeria INTERNATIONAL $$$
(☑72 42 18 00; Dovrevegen 2; pizzas from 189kr, mains from 240kr; ⊘ 1-10pm Sun-Fri, 1-11pm Sat) In the town centre alongside the E6, this jack-of-all-trades kind of place has a huge menu spanning everything from pasta to fish to steak and, just in case you haven't eaten one in a while, pizzas and burgers. It's a good choice if you feel like a sit-down meal.

ELGÅHOGNA HIKE
One especially fine, and fairly easy, hike is the 3½-hour, 10.5km-return hike up **Mt Elgåhogna** (1403m). From **Elgå**, the main village (and only real road access point into the park), head south for 4km to a small farm building on the left. A hundred metres further south is a small parking area where the trail begins. The walk is well marked with red dots painted onto rocks and trees. It starts off passing though stunted woodland before emerging onto a barren tundrascape that climbs moderately upwards. The last part to the summit is steeper and involves a little scrambling over rocks. All the time the views back down westward over the lake get steadily better, but this walk saves its best for last – a view from the summit over Sweden and across endless barren sub-Arctic moorland and tundra.

ℹ Information

Tourist Office (☑72 40 04 70; www.oppdal. com; ⊘ 9am-4pm Mon-Fri, 10am-1.30pm Sat & Sun mid-Jun–mid-Aug, 9am-4pm Mon-Fri rest of year) A small office by the train station.

ℹ Getting There & Away

BUS
Nor-Way (p131) runs services between Bergen (793kr, 12½ hours) and Trondheim (271kr, two hours) daily.

Lavprisekspressen (p131) buses also pass through once or twice daily en route between Oslo and Trondheim.

TRAIN
Trains run to Oslo (839kr, five hours, four daily), stopping at local stations including Dombås (206kr, 50 minutes) and Otta (303kr, 1½ hours). Heading north, trains run to Trondheim (236kr, 1½ hours, four daily).

Trollheimen
The small Trollheimen range, with a variety of trails through gentle mountains and lake-studded upland regions, is most readily accessed from Oppdal. From Oppdal take the west bound 70 road for 15km to the village of Albu where a toll road (50kr by car), signed Gjevilvasshytta, leads 8.8km to **Osen**, a small collection of lakeside cabins and the main entrance point to the wilderness region. You could walk the toll road, but at

weekends it's quite busy with cars and the walk wouldn't be much fun. The best map to use for the park is Statens Kartverk's *Turkart Trollheimen* (1:75,000), which is available at the tourist office in Oppdal.

Activities

Vassendsetra
HIKING

A straightforward hiking destination in Trollheimen is the hut and historic farm at Vassendsetra. From Osen (the outlet of the river Gjevilvatnet), 3km north of the main road to Sunndalsøra, you can take the boat *Trollheimen II* all the way to Vassendsetra. From July to mid-August it leaves from Osen daily at noon and from Vassendsetra at 3.30pm.

Sleeping

Vassendsetra Hut
LODGE $

(☑ Oslo 40 00 18 68; www.tt.no; dm DNT member/nonmember 255/365kr; ☺ year-round) An unstaffed but otherwise comfortable mountain lodge. Bring your own food.

Gjevilvasshytta
LODGE $$

(☑ Oslo 40 00 18 68; www.tt.no/booking-gjevilvasshytta; dm incl breakfast & dinner DNT member/nonmember 815/1630kr) One of Norway's most beautiful mountain lodges, this place's dates back to 1819 and is very well organised with beds in small dorms or twin rooms. It's open year-round but is unstaffed in the winter. It also serves evening meals.

Getting There & Away

There's no useful public transport to the Trollheimen range, so you will definitely need your own mode of travel here – whether that's car or bicycle.

Dombås

POP 1200

Dombås, a popular adventure and winter-sports centre, comprises little more than a couple of petrol stations and a shopping complex, and is far outdone in the beauty stakes by its surroundings. It does make a convenient break for travellers between the highland national parks and the western fjords, though. That said, there's more choice of activities to the north in Oppdal, while Sjoa is the region's best location for rafting.

There is one really compelling reason to pass though – and that's the chance to catch the epic Rauma Railway (p141) from Dombås to Åndalsnes, without doubt one of Norway's most beautiful train rides.

Activities

Bjorli Skisenter
SKIING

(☑ 61 24 55 77; www.bjorliskisenter.no; Bjorlivegen 84;) From early autumn until Easter, downhill skiing is possible at Bjorli Skisenter, which has 11 runs, six lifts and a dedicated children's area.

Dombås Skisenter
SKIING

(www.trolltun.no; Skitrekkvegen 18) Dombås Skisenter offers skiing from October to May, although with artificial snow for much of the season.

Sleeping & Eating

Bjørkhol Camping
CAMPGROUND $

(☑ 61 24 13 31; www.bjorkhol.no; Bjørkhol; tent/caravan sites 150/180kr, 2-/4-bed cabin with shared bathroom from 375/475kr, 2-bed cabins with bathroom 700-850kr) One of Norway's best-value, friendliest campsites is 6km south of Dombås. The facilities are in excellent condition and a bus runs several times daily from Dombås. It is, however, situated fairly close to the main road.

Trolltun Gjestegård & Dombås Vandrerhjem
HOSTEL, GUESTHOUSE $$

(☑ 61 24 09 60; www.trolltun.no; campsites 110kr, hostel dm/s/d 600/895/1150kr, cabins from 1095kr; P�) This good-value place is 1.5km northeast of town, up the hill from the E6. The setting is lovely, the rooms are tidy and the meals are reasonably priced. You're ideally located for winter skiing and summer hiking with Dovrefjell-Sunndalsfjella National Park on your doorstep. Part of the Fjordpass network.

Dombås Hotell
HOTEL $$$

(☑ 61 24 10 01; www.dombas-hotell.no; Domaasgrendi 1; s/d 1195/1475kr; P�) This middle-of-the-road hotel is about as plain and bland as they get, but it's decorated in a modern style with glass staircases, wood floors and neutral furnishings. Larger rooms have sofas and sitting areas. It's handy for the Dombås ski centre, but don't expect much character.

Moskusgrillen
DINER $$

(☑ 61 24 01 00; www.moskusgrillen.no; Kyrkjevegen 1; mains 119-189kr; ☺ 8.30am-10pm Mon-Fri, 10am-11pm Sat, 10am-10pm Sun) The pick of the limited dining options in Dombås, the Musk Ox Grill turns out decent dishes such as elk burgers, roast trout, salt lamb and potato balls, as well as umpteen types of pizza. The decor is diner-style, and it's open at all hours, so you won't go hungry.

❶ Getting There & Away

BUS

Lavprisekspressen (p131) buses pass through once a day en route between Oslo (580kr) and Trondheim (400kr).

TRAIN

Dombås lies on the railway line between Oslo (449kr to 713kr, 4¼ hours, four daily) and Trondheim (349kr to 466kr, 2½ hours). It is also the starting point for the spectacular **Rauma Railway** (Raumabanen; www.nsb.no; 230kr), which runs from Romsdalen to Åndalsnes (1½ hours, four daily).

Dovrefjell-Sunndalsfjella National Park

Bleak and dramatic, the hauntingly beautiful Dovrefjell-Sunndalsfjella National Park is a high, bitterly cold plateau of gently undulating mountains buried under a thick blanket of snow for much of the year. These mountains peak with Snøhetta (2286m), and the park provides a suitably Arctic-like habitat for Arctic foxes, reindeer, wolverines and, the park's flagship animal, musk oxen, which are easily seen during a summertime musk oxen safari.

The Knutshøene massif (1690m) section of the park, east of the E6, protects Europe's most diverse intact alpine ecosystem.

❂ Sights

★ **Snøhetta Viewpoint**   VIEWPOINT
(Norwegian Wild Reindeer Centre Pavilion) This arresting building of rippled timber and mirrored glass was commissioned by the Wild Reindeer Foundation as an educational centre and observation point. It offers astounding views over the valley to Mt Snøhetta. It's a gentle 1.5km walk along a gravel trail from the car park; the turn-off is signed off the E6 by Hjerkinn.

Fokstumyra Marshes   NATURE RESERVE
These wild marshes are home to an astonishing array of bird life. Approximately 87 species nest in the area and 162 species in total have been observed. Among the species found here are the red-breasted merganser, long-tailed duck, black-throated diver, whimbrel, wood sandpiper and short-eared owl.

Snøhetta   NATURAL FEATURE
The park's highest mountain is Snøhetta (2286m) and it was an important trading pass in previous centuries. The mountain also features in many Norwegian myths and legends. Most people view it from a distance, but it can be climbed from Snøheim (allow six hours), although it's for experienced walkers only, with equipment suitable for extreme weather.

🏃 Activities

Most non-Norwegians visit the park as part of a day-long musk ox safari or to hike: there are lots of walking trails, many of which are clearly signed. Serious hikers will fare best with the Statens Kartverk map *Dovrefjell* (1:100,000). However, it doesn't include the Knutshøene section; for that, you need Statens Kartverk's *Einunna 1519-I* and *Folldal 1519-II* topographic sheets.

Moskusopplevelse   WILDLIFE WATCHING
(www.moskusopplevelse.no; adult/child 395/195kr; ⊙May-Sep) Based at Furuhaugli Touristhytter, this guiding company offers daily wildlife spotting trips to see musk oxen (adult/child 395/195kr) and moose (295/145kr). From May to September, musk ox safaris run daily, while moose safaris run every

---

THE MUSK OX

Shaggy-haired, long-horned and weighing in at around half a tonne, musk oxen have been tramping the snowy wastes of the Arctic since the days of the woolly mammoth. Dovrefjell is one of the only places in Europe where you can see them in the wild – although they're not actually native, having been introduced here in the 20th century for their wool and meat. Around 250 of the animals now roam the park and, while generally docile, they can be bad-tempered, especially if you happen to come between a mother and a calf. The official advice is not to stray closer than 300m, and if one starts snorting and pawing the ground, then it's time to retreat: slowly move sideways and back, as musk oxen have poor eyesight and if you move directly backwards they cannot always tell that you're retreating.

The safest option is to view them on a musk ox safari: contact Oppdal Safari (p138) or Moskusopplevelse, based at Furuhaugli Touristhytter.

evening, meaning it's possible to do both in one day. Off season, private tours can also be arranged.

🛏 Sleeping

Hjerkinnhus Vanderhjem   HOSTEL $
(📞464 20 102; www.hjerkinnhus.no; N-2661 Hjerkinn; r 600-750kr; 🅿🛜) This simple mountain hostel is mainly geared towards walkers, especially long-distance trampers following St Olav's Way, which heads pretty much past the front door. Wood-clad outside, it offers basic dorms, mostly quads with shared bathrooms and kitchen facilities. The mountain views are the main selling point. Breakfast is extra at 110kr.

Furuhaugli Touristhytter   LODGE $$
(📞61 24 00 00; www.furuhaugli.no; Furuhauglie 80; 2-/3-bed cabin 1200/1300kr, 2-/4-bed cabin with shared bathroom 450/650kr) Roughly half-way between Dombås and Hjerkinn, this lodge complex makes a good Dovrefjell base. There are 28 wood-clad cabins spread out across the site, sleeping from two to eight; cheaper cabins share a toilet block, while the more expensive ones have private en suites. There's also space for camping and a simple on-site restaurant.

⭐Kongsvold Fjeldstue   LODGE $$$
(📞72 40 43 40; www.kongsvold.no; Kongsvold; s/d 1275/1850kr, with shared bathroom 1075/1450kr; 🅿🛜) This charming and historic place of intriguing early-18th-century timber buildings is 13km north of Hjerkinn on the E6. Every room is different although all are warm and cosy. Locals drive kilometres to come and enjoy the excellent evening meals (set menus 495kr to 995kr) and every other person driving past seems to stop for coffee and waffles in the cafe.

ℹ Getting There & Away

Trains run from Dombås to Hjerkinn (103kr, 30 minutes), from where you'll need your own transport.

There's no public transport inside the park.

Otta

POP 1677

Sited at the confluence of two rushing rivers, the Otta and Lågen, the town of Otta is mainly known for its white-water rafting potential. There are lots of companies, mostly based around Sjoa, that lead rafting expeditions catering for all abilities. There's not much to the town itself, but it's a useful gateway to nearby Rondane National Park.

🛏 Sleeping & Eating

Otta Camping   CAMPGROUND $
(Map p144; 📞473 67 501; www.ottacamping.no; Ottadalen; tent & car 170kr, caravan sites for 2 people 170kr, mass electricity 40kr, 4-bed cabins 350-550kr; 🌣May–mid-Oct; 🛜) The riverside Otta Camping is convenient and popular; cross the Otta bridge from the centre, turn right and continue about 1km upstream.

Thon Hotel Otta   HOTEL $$
(Map p144; 📞61 21 08 00; www.thonhotels.no/otta; Ola Dahls gate 7; d 1195kr; 🅿🛜) It's big, it's modern and it's dreadfully bland, but this chain hotel in the centre of Otta is pretty much as good as it gets in terms of hotels. The decor's studiously inoffensive – most rooms have wood floors and beige furnishings – and the restaurant serves decent meals, although for some reason it's only open from Monday to Thursday.

Pillarguri Kafé   CAFE $$
(Map p144; 📞61 23 01 04; www.pillarguricafe.no; Storgata 7A; mains 169-249kr; 🌣11am-7pm Mon-Thu, 11am-9pm Fri & Sat, 2-6pm Sun) This diner in the middle of Otta is the pick of the places to eat here, and it turns out a decent menu of elk burgers, salads, grilled chicken, pizzas and the like, along with Norwegian dishes like meatballs and reindeer stew. The small outdoor terrace is great on a sunny afternoon.

ℹ Information

Tourist Office (Map p144; 📞61 24 14 44; www.nasjonalparkriket.no/en/otta-tourist-information-centre; Ola Dahls gate 1; 🌣8am-4pm Mon-Fri mid-Jun–mid-Aug) Otta's small tourist office is located inside the train station, and is stocked with information on activities in the national park region.

ℹ Getting There & Away

Nor-Way's (p131) NW431 Fjordexpressen bus stops once daily in Otta and Sjoa en route to/from Trondheim (456kr, 4¾ hours) and Bergen (699kr, 9¼ hours).

Trains stop in Otta on the way from Oslo (633kr, 3½ hours, five daily) to Trondheim (557kr, three hours). To get to Bergen, change trains in Oslo.

Rondane National Park

Henrik Ibsen described the landscapes that now make up the 963-sq-km Rondane National Park (www.nasjonalparkriket.no) as 'palace piled upon palace'. It was created in 1962 as Norway's first national park to protect the fabulous Rondane massif, regarded by many as the finest alpine hiking country in Norway. Ancient reindeer-trapping sites and burial mounds suggest that the area has been inhabited for thousands of years. Much of the park's glaciated and lichen-coated landscape lies above 1400m, and 10 rough and stony peaks rise to over 2000m, including Rondslottet (2178m), the highest, and Storronden (2138m). Rondane's range of wildlife includes 28 mammal species and 124 bird species, and the park is now one of the last refuges of the wild reindeer.

🏃 Activities

The hiking season runs only in July and August. The most accessible route into the park is from the Spranghaugen car park, about 13km uphill along a good road from Otta and via the toll road (20kr). From there, it's a straightforward 6.2km (1½-hour) hike to **Rondvassbu**, where there's a popular, staffed DNT hut. From Rondvassbu, it's a five-hour return climb to the summit of **Storronden**. Alternatively, head for the spectacular view from the more difficult summit of **Vinjeronden** (2044m), then tackle the narrow ridge leading to the neighbouring peak, **Rondslottet** (about six hours return from Rondvassbu).

The best maps to use are Statens Kartverk *Rondane* (1:100,000; 99kr) and *Rondane Sør* (1:50,000).

★ Rondvassbu Hikes HIKING
(Map p144; ☑ Oslo DNT office 22 82 28 00; www.rondvassbu.com) This mountain hut makes a fantastic hiking base. It offers guided hiking trips three times a week to various local peaks, including Trolltinden (2018m), Storronden (2138m) and the highest peak in the Rondane range, Rondslottet (2178m).

Bicycle Hire CYCLING
(Map p144; Spranghaugen car park; adult/child bike per day 100/50kr) An automatic bicycle rental place is located inside the Spranghaugen car park. Bikes can be used only on the trail to Rondvassbu.

🛏 Sleeping

Rondvassbu DNT HOSTEL $
(Map p144; ☑ Oslo DNT office 22 82 28 00; https://rondvassbu.dnt.no; dm 250-410kr, camping 90kr; ☉ Mar-Easter & Jul-Sep) Built in 1903, this fine old mountain hostel run by the DNT is locat-

WORTH A TRIP

SJØA & WHITE-WATER RAFTING

Tucked away on the banks of the rushing Sjøa River, the small town of **Sjøa** is one of Norway's premier locations for white-water rafting. There's a trip to suit everyone here – from easy introductory runs to heart-in-the-mouth roller coasters through the rapids. There are numerous operators, all offering similar packages. Some also have campsites and hostels on site. Recommended operators include the following:

Sjøa Rafting (☑ 900 71 000; www.sjoarafting.com; Nedre Heidal; half-day 775-825kr, full-day 1050-1150kr)

Sjøa Kajakksenter (☑ 900 66 222; www.kajakksenteret.no; Nedre Heidal; day trip 140kr)

Go Rafting (☑ 61 23 50 00; www.gorafting.no; half/full day 770/1040kr)

ed 6km up a track from the Spranghaugen car park, at the southern end of Rondevatnet Lake. There are 128 beds, spread out between two-bed and four-bed rooms and a big dormitory. Duvets and pillows are supplied, but you'll need your own liner or sleeping bag.

★ Rondane Høyfjellshotell LODGE $$
(Map p144; ☑ 61 20 90 90; www.rondane.no; Mysusæter; r 795-1095kr; 🅿🛜) A comfortable upmarket option with good spa facilities, including pedicures for worn-out hikers' feet, and pine-tinged rooms that are unusually good value. The restaurant serves hearty Norwegian and international fare (set dinner menu 475kr). Needless to say, the views are a knockout. It's on the road from Otta towards the Spranghaugen car park.

Smuksjøseter Fjellstue FARMSTAY $$
(Map p144; ☑ 61 23 37 19; www.smuksjoseter.no; Høvringen; s/d 680/1320kr; 🅿🛜) Simple rooms and apartments on a traditional *seter* in Høvringen, run by the Skaugen family who've been here since the 1940s. The rooms are plainly furnished but quite modern – and there are larger apartments, which are ideal for families. Breakfast and dinner are full of traditional mountain flavours.

Rondetunet HOSTEL $$
(Map p144; ☑ 904 15 149; www.rondetunet.dk; cabins 430-1580kr, camping 125kr; 🅿) This mountain

CENTRAL NORWAY RONDANE NATIONAL PARK

Rondane National Park

0 ——————— 10 km
0 ——————— 5 miles

Rondane National Park

centre offers basic huts and fabulous camping on the southeastern edge of Rondane National Park. They also run mountain skills courses and lead guided hikes. The centre is just off Rv27, about halfway between Folldal and Ringebu.

ℹ Information

The tourist office in Otta (p142) is the best place for information on the park.

ℹ Getting There & Away

Two roads flank either side of Rondane National Park: the main E6 to the west and the more scenic Rv27 to the east; the latter has been designated as a National Tourist Route.

Most people access the park from the west along the minor road to Mysusæter; look for the turn-off a few kilometres south of Otta. Once you reach Mysusæter, there's a toll gate (20kr) and it's another 4km to the Spranghaugen car park.

There's another road that leads from the E6 into the north side of the park via Høvringen.

In summer, the 538 bus runs twice daily between Otta and Mysusæter, from where it's a further 4km to the Spranghaugen car park.

Ringebu

POP 4540

Ringebu is the southernmost small community of Gudbrandsdalen, the narrow river valley that stretches for 200km between Lake Mjøsa and Dombås. It's worth a detour for its lovely stave church.

◉ Sights

Ringebu Stave Church   CHURCH
(Ringebu Stavkyrkje; www.stavechurch.no; adult/child 60/40kr, joint ticket with Samlingene 90/50kr; ◷9am-5pm Jun-Aug) A church has existed on this site since the arrival of Christianity in the 11th century. The current version, which remains the local parish church, dates from around 1220, but was restored in the 17th century when the distinctive red tower was attached. Inside, there's a statue of St Laurence dating from around 1250, as well as some crude runic inscriptions.

ⓘ Information

Tourist Office (☑61 28 47 00; www.ringebu.com; ◷8am-6pm Mon-Thu, 8am-8pm Fri, 10am-1pm Sat, 5-8pm Sun mid-Jun–mid-Aug, 8am-3.30pm Mon-Fri rest of year) The small tourist office is inside the train station.

ⓘ Getting There & Away

Lavprisekspressen (p131) buses travel once daily to Lillehammer (300kr, 55 minutes) and Oslo (460kr; 3½ hours), and to Trondheim (520kr; five hours) in the opposite direction.

Trains go to Oslo (249kr to 428kr, 3¼ hours, four daily) and Trondheim (499kr to 653kr, 3¾ hours, four daily)

WESTERN CENTRAL NORWAY

Lom

POP 2410

If you were to set up a town as a travellers' gateway, you'd put it somewhere like Lom, in the heart of some of Norway's most spectacular mountain scenery. Rapids cascade through the village centre, houses in dark wood climb the steep hills, and roads out of town lead to Geiranger (74km) at the edge of Norway's famous fjords, via the staggering Sognefjellet Rd, which winds across the top of the Jotunheimen National Park. Aside from its location, Lom's main attraction is a lovely stave church.

◉ Sights

Lom Stavkyrkje   CHURCH
(www.lomstavechurch.no; adult/child 70/30kr; ◷9am-7pm mid-Jun–Aug, 10am-4pm May–mid-Jun & Sep) This delightful Norman-style stave church, in the centre of town on a rise by the water, is one of Norway's finest. Still the functioning local church, it was constructed in 1170, extended in 1634 and given its current cruciform shape with the addition of two naves in 1663.

Norsk Fjellmuseum   MUSEUM
(Norwegian Mountain Museum; ☑61 21 16 00; www.norskfjellsenter.no; Brubakken 2; adult/child 12-16yr 80/50kr; ◷9am-7pm Mon-Fri, 9am-5pm Sat & Sun mid-Jun–mid-Aug, 9am-4pm Mon-Fri, 10am-3pm Sat & Sun mid-Aug–mid-Jun) Acting as the visitor centre for Jotunheimen National Park, this worthwhile mountain museum contains mountaineering memorabilia and exhibits on natural history (the woolly mammoth is a highlight) and cultural and industrial activity in the Norwegian mountains. There's also a 10-minute mountain slide show and, upstairs, a scale model of the park.

Fossheim Steinsenter   MUSEUM
(Stone & Mineral Museum; ☑61 21 14 60; www.fossheimsteinsenter.no; Bergomsvegen 30; ◷10am-6pm daily Jul & Aug, 10am-4pm Mon-Sat May-Jun & Sep) **FREE** The fascinating Fossheim Steinsenter combines an impressive selection of rare and beautiful rocks, minerals, fossils, gems and jewellery for sale, and a large museum of geological specimens from all over Norway and the world; don't miss the downstairs fossil exhibition. The knowledgeable owners of the centre are especially proud of the Norwegian national stone, thulite. It was discovered in 1820 and is now quarried in Lom; the reddish colour is derived from traces of manganese.

🏃 Activities

The tourist office (p146) has details of hikes, glacier walks and ice-climbing in Jotunheimen National Park.

Lom & Skjåk Adventure   ADVENTURE SPORTS
(☑472 61 672; www.lsadventure.no; ◷May-Oct) Lom & Skjåk Adventure is a 10-minute drive northwest of Lom along the E15. It arranges white-water rafting, climbing, kayaking, caving, canyoning, hiking and river-boarding.

Hiking

Although most of the serious trekking takes place in neighbouring Jotunheimen National Park, there are several hiking trails closer to town. Many of these are passable much later into the winter than those in the high, snow-bound mountains; ask the tourist office for maps, directions and its terrific *Walks in Lom* pamphlet, which has a map and detailed route descriptions.

The three most popular hikes:

Lomseggen (1289m) Five-hour return hike past the century-old stone cottage called Smithbue, with some excellent views of Ottadalen, Bøverdalen and Norway's highest peak, Galdhøpiggen (2469m), en route.

Tronoberget Three-hour return hike up the mountain that lies west across the river from Lom, with excellent views of the peaks of Reinheimen National Park.

Soleggen & Læshø (1204m) Five-hour return hike above Lom with views of the Rondane, Dovrefjell, Reinheimen, Breheimen and Jotunheimen massifs.

White-Water Rafting

If Sjoa is too much of a scene, white-water rafting is possible from Skjåk, 18km upstream from Lom.

Sleeping

Nordal Turistsenter   HOTEL $$
(📞 61 21 93 00; www.nordalturistsenter.no; r 990-1490kr, huts 450-1170kr, campsites 250kr; ⊘ Apr–mid-Dec; 🛜) This busy accommodation complex right in the middle of town has something to cover most needs: a pleasant, motel-style main block; camping huts in the grounds; and pitches for tents and campervans. For dinner there's a no-frills pub and a casual cafeteria-style restaurant.

Fossheim Turisthotell   HOTEL $$$
(📞 61 21 95 00; www.fossheimhotel.no; Bergomsve-gen 32; hotel s 1195kr, d 1440-1795kr; P 🛜) This historic family hotel at the eastern end of town has all-wood rooms in the main hotel building (we especially like rooms 401 and 402 for the balconies and views). There are also luxurious log cabins with modern interiors and simpler, cheaper rooms (some with good views) in the adjacent annexe; although annexe rooms have dreadful sound insulation.

Eating

★ Lom Bakery   BAKERY $
(📞 61 21 18 60; www.bakerietilom.no; Sognefjellsve-gen 7; loaves from 35kr, sandwiches/pizzas 66/170kr; ⊘ 9am-5pm) Lom's other culinary star is mas-ter baker Morten Schakenda, who makes all his breads using only natural ingredients and

wood-fired ovens. You can buy freshly baked baguettes, cinnamon twists and rustic loaves by the score, of course, but there are also delicious pastries and sandwiches, and the crispiest of pizzas too. Queues often stretch out the door.

In fact, we're willing to go out on a limb and say this might just be Norway's best bakery.

★ Brimi Bue   CAFE $$
(📞 468 54 262; www.brimiland.no/brimibue; Fos-sheim Turisthotell; mains around 180kr; ⊘ 9am-9pm) This flashy establishment is home base for the town's top chef, Arne Brimi, and is where everyone wants to eat when they pass through town. It's screamingly Scandi (all big glass windows, plain wood and open plan), the perfect setting for the cafe's speciality: gourmet platters of ham, cheese and fish, plus meats flame-grilled to perfection.

Fossheim Turisthotell Restaurant   NORWEGIAN $$$
(📞 61 21 95 00; www.fossheimhotel.no; Fossheim Turisthotell; mains 295kr, 2/3 courses 395/465kr; ⊘ 1-3.30pm & 7-10pm) Specialities like wild trout, reindeer, elk and ptarmigan feature on the menu at this hotel restaurant, and while it constitutes a memorable meal for Norway, it wouldn't really stand out anywhere in southern Europe. Still, it'll fill you up – you can choose just a main dish or go for the full, belly-busting eight courses.

ⓘ Information

The main source of information is the Norsk Fjell-museum (p145), but there's also a small **tourist office** (📞 61 21 29 90; www.visitjotunheimen.com; ⊘ 9am-5pm Mon-Sat, 9am-4pm Sun Jul–mid-Aug, 9am-4pm Mon-Sat mid-Aug–early Sep; 🛜) just inside the entrance of the Co-op supermarket.

ⓘ Getting There & Away

Two daily express buses run from Oslo to Lom (477kr, 6¼ hours) and several buses a day run to/from Otta (136kr, 1½ hours, four to six daily).

The summer-only Valdresekspressen bus connects Lom with several points in Jotunheimen National Park, including the popular trailhead of Gjendesheim (126kr, 80 minutes).

Jotunheimen National Park

This is it. This is the big one. The high peaks and glaciers of the **Jotunheimen National Park** (www.jotunheimen.com; 17km SW of Lom) (1151 sq km), whose name means the 'Home

FARMS OF A MASTER CHEF

Brimi-Fjellstugu (☑61 23 98 12; www.brimiland.no/brimi-fjellstugu; r per person from 600kr) This renowned mountain lodge, owned by chef Arne Brimi, specialises in multiday mountain stays combining outdoor activities with sumptuous dinners devised by the man himself. The original building dates from 1949, and offers rustic charm blended with contemporary style, while the restaurant offers three different three-course menus (450kr to 600kr). A real treat on all fronts.

Brimi sæter (☑911 37 558; www.brimi-seter.no; dm per night 800kr; ☺Jun-Sep; [P][☎]) Arne Brimi's reinvention of a summer mountain farm is a pleasure. It offers simple accommodation spread across old farm buildings, including a hay-loft, barn and a couple of tepee-style *lavvu* in the yard. There are private rooms, as well as dorm-style 'brisk' accommodation, with bunks built in alongside one wall. Nightly meals are, unsurprisingly, rustic and delicious.

of the Giants', make for Norway's best-loved, busiest and, arguably, most spectacular wilderness destination. Seemingly hundreds of hiking routes lead through ravine-like valleys past deep lakes, waterfalls and 60 glaciers to the tops of all the peaks in Norway over 2300m; these include Galdhøpiggen (the highest peak in northern Europe at 2469m), Glittertind (2452m) and Store Skagastølstind (2403m). By one count, there are more than 275 summits above 2000m inside the park.

⊙ Sights

★**Mímisbrunnr Klimapark 2469**   TUNNEL (Map p148; ☑61 21 16 00; www.mimisbrunnr.no; adult/child 345/175kr; ☺guided tours 10.30am & 2pm late Jun-late Aug, Sat & Sun late Aug–mid-Sep) If you want to learn all about the wonders of ice, this impressive experience takes you closer than you ever thought possible. Guided tours take you 60m under the ice through a specially created ice tunnel that reveals the ice's structure and colours, and documents more than six millennia of time. It's a surprisingly moving experience, with the obvious topic of climate change looming constantly in the background.

🏃 Activities

Jotunheimen's hiking possibilities are practically endless and all are spectacular. The best maps are Statens Kartverk's *Jotunheimen Aust* and *Jotunheimen Vest* (1:50,000).

The tourist office (p146) and the Norsk Fjellmuseum (p145) in Lom can offer advice, route descriptions and guided hikes through the park.

★**Sognefjellet**   SCENIC DRIVE (Map p148) Town councillors of the world: You may have built a lot of roads in your time, and many of them are probably very useful,

but chances are none of them are as spectacular as this one. Snaking through Jotunheimen National Park (and providing access to most of the trailheads), the stunningly scenic Sognefjellet Rd (Rv55) connects Lustrafjorden with Lom, and is billed as 'the road over the roof of Norway'. With little doubt, it's one of Norway's most beautiful drives.

Constructed in 1939 by unemployed youths, the road rises to a height of 1434m, making it the highest mountain road in northern Europe. It is one of Norway's 18 National Tourist Routes.

Access from the southwest is via multiple hairpin bends climbing up beyond the treeline to Turtagrø, with a stirring view of the Skagastølstindane mountains on your right. If you're coming from Lom, the ascent is more gradual, following beautiful Bøverdalen, the valley of the Bøvra River, with its lakes, glacial rivers, grass-roofed huts and patches of pine forest. The road summit on Sognefjell offers superb views.

The snow sometimes doesn't melt until early July, although the road is usually open from May to September. The road can get very narrow and snow is often piled metres high on either side. Ample camping and other accommodation options line the road.

Although this road is mainly traversed by motorised transport, the Sognefjellet Rd has legendary status among cyclists and often appears on lists of the world's most spectacular cycle routes. It's an undertaking that requires high levels of fitness and perfect brakes.

From mid-June to late August, a daily bus runs between Lom and Sogndal (290kr, 3½ hours) via Sognefjellet Rd.

★**Besseggen**   HIKING (Map p148) No discussion of hiking in Jotunheimen would be complete without mention

Jotunheimen National Park

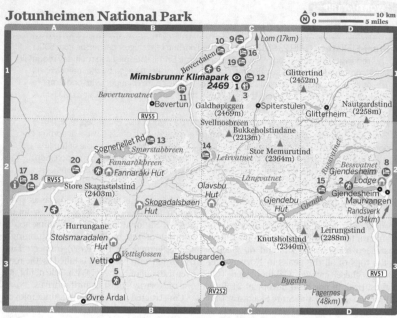

Jotunheimen National Park

of Besseggen, the most popular hike in Norway. Indeed, some travellers find it too popular, with at least 30,000 hikers walking it in the three months a year that it's passable. The day hike between Memurubu Lodge (p151) and Gjendesheim (p150) takes about six hours and climbs to a high point of 1743m. Park at Gjendesheim, hop on the M/S *Gjende* ferry and cross the lake to begin the hike.

Most people do it in this direction but there's nothing to stop you doing it in reverse, except that if you're planning on returning to the trek start point, and your car, then you need to time your walk well in order to get the last ferry back (4.30pm). Note that at busy times (which is most of the July to August period), long queues can form for the ferry and the boats operate a near continuous service.

From Memurubu, follow the signs up the steep hill. After much huffing and puffing you emerge on a flatter plateau. The trail is very obvious and it would be hard to get lost. The route winds past Bjørnbøltjørn, a small glacial lake, and offers amazing views down to the much larger, turquoise lake Gjende, which gains its extraordinary colour thanks to the 20,000 tonnes of glacial silt dumped into it each year by the Memuru river. After an undulating couple of hours, you reach the steepest part of the climb up onto the Besseggen Ridge proper. From afar this looks very narrow and precarious, but, although you do have to do quite a lot of scrambling and have a head for heights, it's actually not as hard, or narrow, as it seems from a distance. Once up onto the ridge, the route climbs gently through scree slopes to the summit of the Veslefjellet plateau before a fairly tame walk back down to Gjendesheim.

The walk is accessible to anyone of reasonable fitness. We have seen lots of families with small children doing it, although you will have to carry them up parts of it and the climb up the Besseggen Ridge becomes somewhat trickier with a young child clinging to you.

In the words of Henrik Ibsen, Besseggen 'cuts along with an edge like a scythe for miles and miles...And scars and glaciers sheer down the precipice to the glassy lakes, 1600ft below on either side.' Stirring stuff, and true as ever.

Tindevegen SCENIC DRIVE
(Map p148; www.tindevegen.no; per car 80kr; ☺May-Nov) Sometimes known as the shortcut through Jotunheimen, this is another of Norway's most epic roads. Running from Turtagrø to Ovre Årdal and beyond that all the way to Sognefjorden, it's a 32km route that offers a cinematic view of several of Norway's highest mountains, most of which stay snowcapped year-round – among them Fanaråken (2069m), Skagastølstindane (2405m) and Austabotntindane (2203m). Though it's not one of Norway's official Tourist Routes, it's an absolute stunner nonetheless. Don't miss it.

The road is usually open from May to November, though this is dependent on the snows.

Randsverk to Fagernes SCENIC DRIVE
Between Randsverk and Fagernes, the Rv51 climbs through the hilly and forested Sjodalen country onto a vast upland with far-ranging views of peaks and glaciers; it's used by hikers heading for Jotunheimen's eastern reaches. En route it passes the DNT hut at Gjendesheim (p150), the launching point for the popular day hike along the Besseggen ridge.

Jotunheimvegen SCENIC DRIVE
(www.jotunheimvegen.no; per car 100kr; ☺mid-Jun-Oct) Branching off the Rv51 at Bygdin, the 45km-long Jotunheimvegen to Skåbu is quiet and picturesque. It's usually open from mid-June until October, depending on the weather. Cars pay a 100kr toll; motorcycles travel for free. There's no public transport along the route but there are campsites at Beitostølen

and Skåbu. The route also links up with Peer Gynt Vegen (p131).

Øvre Årdal HIKING
(Map p148) From the town of Øvre Årdal, head 12km northeast up the Utladalen valley to the farm Vetti, from where hiking tracks lead to Vettisfossen, Norway's highest free-falling waterfall (275m), and to the unstaffed hut at Skølsmaradalen (p150). This is an alternative access route, via upper Utladalen, to longer hikes in Jotunheimen.

Hurrungane HIKING
(Map p148) The fabulous Hurrungane massif rises darkly above the westernmost end of the park. Although some of these prominent peaks are accessible to experienced mountaineers and, in some cases, skilled scramblers, most hikers head eastwards from Turtagrø Hotel (p151). From the hotel, a four-hour hike will take you to Norway's highest DNT hut, Fannaråki (p150), on the summit of Fannaråken (2068m).

Galdhøpiggen Summer Ski Centre SKIING
(Map p148; ☑61 21 17 50; www.gpss.no; day lift pass adult/child 405/325kr) This ski centre, at 1850m on the icy heights of Norway's highest mountain, is a stunning spot for summer skiing. From Galdesand on the Rv55, follow the Galdhøpiggen road (100kr toll) to its end at 1841m. The main season runs from June to mid-November. Apart from skiing opportunities, this road takes you to the highest point reachable by road in Norway.

It's also the starting point up Galdhøpiggen, a fairly tough, eight-hour day hike (1470m of ascent) from Spiterstulen, where the toll road begins. Although the trail is well marked, you'll need a map and compass.

🛏 Sleeping

DNT maintains staffed huts along most of the routes and there's also a choice of private lodges along the main roads. The majority of accommodation is to be found along the Sognefjellet Rd. On the Rv51, options are more limited to campsites, although there are some lodges in the vicinity of Gjendesheim, which are handy for an early start on the Besseggen Ridge. Most open from May to September.

Juvasshytta LODGE $
(Map p148; ☑61 21 15 50; www.juvasshytta.no; dm per adult/child 250/200kr) With a name that sounds like it came from *Star Wars*, and a location above 1800m close to Norway's summit, Juvasshytta is a fine base. It sits in the

shadow of Galdhøpiggen, Norway's highest peak, and can arrange guided walks, glacier hikes and climbs to the summit. The lodge-style accommodation ranges from barn-basic to quite comfortable.

Krossbu Turiststasjon   LODGE $

(Map p148; ☑ 61 21 29 22; www.krossbu.no; dm from 410kr, s 510kr, d from 610kr; P ☎) With a total of 85 beds divided between a main lodge and an annexe, this venerable overnighter offers timber-panelled rooms that, while rustic, feel authentically mountain-themed. It's mainly geared towards walkers: various routes pass by and the hotel can arrange guided walks on Smørstabbreen glacier. Breakfast is 125kr and a three-course meal is 345kr; half-board is good value.

Gjendesheim Lodge   HUT $

(Map p148; ☑ 61 23 89 10; www.gjendesheim.no; Gjendesheim; dm adult/child 210/105kr, r 1-3 beds 350/175kr, 4-6 beds 300/150kr; ☎) At the trail-head to the Besseggen trek, on the eastern side of the park, this highly organised place has good-quality accommodation and meals. It's very popular so book ahead.

Bessheim   LODGE $$

(Map p148; ☑ 61 23 89 13; www.bessheim.no; r per person 585kr, cabins 460-1420kr, camping 220-250kr; P ☎) This super-slick and or-ganised mountain lodge, just 3km east of Gjendesheim, is the best place to stay in the vicinity of the Besseggen ridge. The rustic rooms are matched by an equally down-home restaurant; three-course set dinners cost 370kr. It's extremely popular, so summer bookings are essential.

Storhaugen   HOTEL $$

(Map p148; ☑ 472 92 720; www.storhaugengard.no; Bøverdalen; cabins 775-3300kr; P ☎) At their traditional farm, the Slettede family offers an array of different accommodation op-tions in modern, fully equipped cabins and apartments with views of both the Jotunhei-men heights and Bøverdalen. Children will love the farm animals. It's all great value, but they don't provide meals so you'll need to come prepared.

Leirvassbu Lodge   LODGE $$

(Map p148; ☑ 61 21 12 10; www.ton.no/en/leirvassbu-mountain-lodge; s/d/tr with bath 755/1190/1725kr; P ☎) Run by the same family as the Elvesæter Hotel, this typical-ly Norwegian mountain lodge sits at an altitude of 1400m, hunkered down beside

Lake Leirvatnet. It's predominantly a walk-ing and skiing base, and its 100-odd rooms get full up in the height of the season. You can save some krone by opting for a shared bathroom.

Fannaråki Hut   HUT $$

(Map p148; www.ut.no; dm DNT nonmembers 970-1130kr) From the Turtagrø Hotel, a four-hour hike will take you to Norway's highest DNT hut, Fannaråki, on the summit of Fannaråken (2068m). While the hut itself is your typical DNT deal (ie clean and basic), the views are some of the best from accommodation any-where in Norway.

Stolsmaradalen Hut   HUT $$

(Map p148; ☑ 22 82 28 00; www.ut.no/hytte/3.2201; dm DNT nonmembers 970-1130kr) Hikers venturing to Hurrungane and the waterfalls at Stølsmaradalsfossen and Vet-tisfossen often make use of this small, basic DNT hut. It's about as bare bones as it gets, with simple bunk mattresses and bits of kitchenware for cooking. There's no power here, although firewood is usually on hand. Otherwise, bring everything you need in-cluding sleeping bags.

Skogadalsbøen Hut   HUT $$

(Map p148; ☑ 975 69 094, mobile 979 85 828; www.ut.no/hytte/3.2004; dm DNT nonmembers 970-1130kr) The eighth cabin to be built by the DNT, way back in 1888, this mountain hostel has heritage in spades. Accommodation is very simple, with 87 beds in doubles, quads and a couple of big dorms. It's unstaffed and mainly used by hikers exploring the area around Fannaråken.

Gjendebu Hut   HUT $$

(Map p148; ☑ 61 23 89 44; www.gjendebu.com; dm DNT nonmembers 970-1130kr; ☉ Jun-Sep) The oldest hut owned by the DNT, built in 1871, this 119-bed hostel sits at an altitude of 995m on the shores of Gjende Lake. It's an ideal hiking base, with trails to Gjendetunga, Bukkelægeret and Svartdalspiggen all on the doorstep.

Olavsbu Hut   HUT $$

(Map p148; ☑ 22 82 28 00; www.ut.no/hytte/3.1982; dm DNT nonmembers 970-1130kr) This 52-bed hut sits at the intersection of two trails: the four-hour hike from Leirvassbu and the five-hour trail between Gjendebu and Fondsbu. It's at an elevation of around 1440m; there's no permanent staff, so you'll be cooking for yourself.

Memurubu Lodge LODGE $$

(Map p148; ☑ 460 16 100, 61 23 89 99; www.ut.no/
hytte/3.2002; dm DNT nonmembers 970-1130kr)
This remote DNT hut is used by hikers on the
Besseggen Ridge. There are around 150 beds
spread across several dorms, plus space for
campers.

Jotunheimen Fjellstue LODGE $$

(Map p148; ☑ 61 21 29 18; www.jotunhei
men-fjellstue.no; s/d/tr from 996/1355/1764kr)
From the outside, this modern mountain
lodge is hugely outdone by its breathtaking surrounds, but inside are light and airy
rooms that are better than many in the
area. There's a busy in-house restaurant
and cafe.

Bøverdalen Vandrerhjem HOSTEL $$

(Map p148; ☑ 61 21 20 64; www.hihostels.no; Bøver-
dalen; s/d 600/960kr; P ☎) This riverside hos-
tel has a small cafe, tidy rooms, good cabins
and delightful surrounds to enjoy once the
day-trippers have returned home. It's popular
so be sure to book ahead in summer.

★**Elvesæter Hotell** HOTEL $$$

(Map p148; ☑ 61 21 99 00; www.ton.no/en/elve
seter-culture-and-art-hotel; Bøverdalen; s/d from
1100/1550kr; P ☎) ⚑ This extraordinary old
hostelry looks for all the world like something out of Tolkien's notebook. Accessed
through wooden gates, the hotel's timber
buildings are home to a higgledy-piggledy
collection of storybook-style rooms, complete
with painted murals, sleigh beds, antiques
and artworks. The plumbing's creaky, the
soundproofing is non-existent and it gets
busy – but it sure scores high on heritage.

It's run by the sixth generation of the
Elvesæter family and is sited next to the Sa-
gasøyla, a 32m-high carved wooden pillar
tracing Norwegian history from unification
in 872 to the 1814 constitution. Traditional
three-course dinners are 325kr.

★**Turtagrø Hotel** LODGE $$$

(Map p148; ☑ 57 68 08 00; www.turtagro.no;
Fortun; s/d/f 1610/2200/3200kr, campsites per
person per night 135kr; P ☎) An intriguing
meeting of mountain heritage old and new.
This alpine hotel has two buildings: the
original Swiss chalet dating from 1888 and
the strikingly modern main lodge, a zig-zag
structure built in 2002. Rooms reflect their
era: modern ones are clean and sleek in pine
and glass, older ones have a more trad feel.
Excellent meals are served nightly.

Røisheim Hotel HISTORIC HOTEL $$$

(Map p148; ☑ 61 21 20 31; www.roisheim.no; Bøverdalen; d from 1550kr; P ☎) ⚑ This charming
place combines architecturally stunning
buildings that date back to 1858 with modern
comforts, although there are no TVs. Some
rooms have wonderful baths made out of old
barrels. Apart from the charming accommodation, the appeal lies in the meals, which are
prepared by Ingrid Hov Lunde, one of the
country's best-loved chefs.

ℹ Information

For general information on the park, contact the
Norsk Fjellmuseum (p145) or the small tourist
office (p146), both in Lom.

ℹ Getting There & Away

Between June and September, the Valdresekspressen bus connects Lom with various areas
in the park, including Gjendesheim (126kr, one
hour 20 minutes).

HARDANGERVIDDA

The desolate and beautiful Hardangervidda plateau is part of the 3430-sq-km
Hardangervidda National Park (Norway's
largest), and ranges across an otherworldly
tundra landscape that's the southernmost
refuge of the Arctic fox (the natural population of which has increased through re-
introduction programs) and home to Norway's largest herd of wild reindeer. Long a
trade and travel route connecting eastern
and western Norway, it's now crossed by
the main railway and road routes between
Oslo and Bergen.

While reindeer numbers reached a high
of 19,000 here in 1998, due to a ban on
hunting, in more recent years a program
of resource management by the national
park's authorities has aimed to maintain a
herd size of around 10,000 reindeer during
winter.

Apart from Finse and Geilo, Hardangervidda National Park is accessible from Rjukan
and Eidfjord; there's an excellent national
park centre at the latter.

🏃 Activities

The 83km Rallarvegen (p212) bike route
crosses the Hardangervidda at Finse on its
way between Haugastøl and Flåm; the distance from Finse to Flåm is 56km. Finse
1222 (p153) rents bikes.

HIKING THE HARDANGERVIDDA

Trekking through the western Hardangervidda is possible only in July and August – for the rest of the time, snow and the possibility of sudden changes in weather conditions make setting out hazardous; new snow is a possibility at any time of year. Before exploring the park, visit the outstanding Hardangervidda Natursenter (p189), which sells maps. This centre can offer advice on hiking routes and has a wonderful exhibition on the park. Hikers and skiers will find the Turkart series (149kr to 279kr), at a scale of 1:100,000, to be the maps of choice. You should also consult Hardangerviddanett Hytteringen (www. hardangerviddanett.no), which gives a run-down on mountain huts. The Bergen Turlag DNT office (p173) is another good source of information.

There are numerous trailheads, among them the waterfalls at Vøringfoss, Finse or Geilo. Some of our favourite routes:

Finse to Vøringfoss (two days) The steepest hiking country in Hardangervidda, skirting the Hardangerjøkulen glacier and overnighting in Rembesdalsseter; you could also make the four- to five-hour (one-way) detour to Kjeåsen Farm (p180).

Vøringfoss to Kinsarvik via Harteigen (three days) To the picturesque mountain of Harteigen with its views of Hardangervidda, then down the monk's stairway to Kinsarvik.

Halne to Dyranut via Rauhelleren (two days) Trails lead south off the Rv7. There's a strong chance hikers will encounter reindeer herds.

Geilo

POP 2363

At Geilo (pronounced Yei-lo), midway between Oslo and Bergen, you can practically step off the train onto a ski lift. In summer there's plenty of fine hiking in the area. A popular nearby destination is the expansive plateau-like mountain called Hallingskarvet, frosted with several small glaciers. Apart from hiking across the Hardangervidda, it's possible to go glacier trekking on Hardangerjøkulen (1862m), horse riding, white-water rafting, riverboarding and go on elk safaris. For more information on these and other activities, contact the tourist office (p153).

🛏 Sleeping & Eating

Øen Turistsenter & Geilo Vandrerhjem
HOSTEL $

(☑ 32 08 70 60; www.oenturist.no; Lienvegen 137; dm 350kr, huts 500-950kr; P 🛜) A kilometre or so east of the town centre along the Rv7, this hostel has tidy cabins and dorms but little atmosphere. It's quite a trek from the station – 2.5km or so – and the roadside location isn't ideal either.

Ro Hotell
HOTEL $$

(☑ 32 09 08 99; www.rohotel.no; Geilovegen 55; s/d 790/1000kr; 🛜) At first glance this cheap place next door to the train station doesn't look promising, but its large and spotless rooms, good sound insulation, comfy chairs and desk, helpful staff and fast wi-fi that reaches all the rooms add up to as good value as Norway gets.

★ Dr Holms Hotel
HOTEL $$$

(☑ 32 09 57 00; www.drholms.no; Timrehaugvegen 2; s/d from 995/1490kr; P 🛜 🏊) The century-old Dr Holms has been providing a place for relaxation and recuperation amid the mountain scenery for over 100 years, and it has an air of undeniable grandeur. It's split in two halves: the historic old section, with 'English-style' rooms full of antiques and burnished furniture, and the modern annexe with more contemporary, clean-lined rooms.

There's also a traditional restaurant and, rather inexplicably, Norway's highest bowling alley.

★ Halling-Stuene
NORWEGIAN $$$

(☑ 32 09 12 50; www.hallingstuene.no; Geilovegen 56; mains 320-415kr; ☉ 1-10pm Mon-Fri & Sun, to 11pm Sat) This crimson-clad restaurant is just about as traditional as restaurants get in Norway, but it's been going strong for 25 years and seems as popular as ever. It's run by celeb chef Frode Aga, who cooks up rich, classic dishes such as *skårapølse* (lamb sausage in butter sauce), grilled grouse breast, herb-baked trout and reindeer fillet with game sauce.

The food will definitely be too rich for some palates, but there are few better places to sample the true taste of old Norway. Note that some dishes contain minke whale.

ℹ Information

Geilo Tourist Office (☎ 32 09 59 00; www.geilo. no; Vesleslåttveien 13; ⊙ 9am-6pm)

ℹ Getting There & Away

Most visitors arrive on the train between Oslo (249kr to 618kr, 3½ hours, five daily) and Bergen (249kr to 517kr, three hours).

Finse

Finse, which lies at 1222m near the Hardangerjøkulen icecap, is accessible only by train, bike or foot, and is *the* place in central Norway for a wild, Arctic-like wilderness experience. Its bleak and remote lakeside setting is addictive, whether sparkling under blue skies with a fresh coat of snow or on a cold, grey day when winds lash the tundra and glaciers.

You only need walk a few minutes away from the tiny train station to find total silence, but if you prefer your rest time to be more adrenaline-filled, then the countryside surrounding Finse offers nordic skiing in winter and hiking in summer, not to mention what could be Norway's steepest mountain-bike ride.

🏃 Activities

Finse is the starting point for some exceptional treks, including the popular four-hour trek to the Blåisen glacier tip of Hardangerjøkulen. It's a stunning walk, but no matter how tempting it looks, do not ever attempt to walk on the glacier unless on a guided glacier walk led by an expert. Adding interest to your hike is the fact that scenes set on the planet Hof in *The Empire Strikes Back* were filmed around the glacier.

It's also possible to walk around the glacier and down to Vøringfoss. The wonderful three- or four-day Finse–Aurland trek follows Aurlandsdalen down to Aurlandsfjorden and has a series of DNT and private mountain huts a day's walk apart.

Jøklagutane Glacier Walks   WALKING
(☎ 993 31 222; www.glaciertoursnorway.com; per person 650kr) Well-run, highly exhilarating glacier walks lasting roughly seven hours (with around two hours spent actually on the glacier) take you onto the edge of the ice-sheet to peer down into crevices and possibly clamber into an ice-cave, as well as climb right up onto the vast domed icecap summit. Tours leave from the train station at 11am.

Sykkel 1222   CYCLING
(☎ 919 10 140; www.finse1222.no/en/rallarvegen-the-navvy-road; per day from 695kr) The busy bike-rental office of the Finse 1222 hotel can furnish you with a machine with which to tackle the Rallarvegen trail – complete with shock absorbers to cope with the rocky, rough trail. Booking is essential in summer and bikes can be returned at Myrdal or Flåm to save you having to come all the way back (perish the thought).

🛏 Sleeping

Finsehytta   LODGE $
(☎ 56 52 67 32; www.finsehytta.dnt.no; dm 250-410kr; ⊙ mid-Mar–late Sep; ☎) Hikers, bikers and backpackers alike all congregate on this staffed DNT hut, just a short walk from the station, on a little peninsula jutting out into the lake. Dorms sleep from three to six people (the smaller ones are perfect for families) and many have super lake views. Nightly meals (395kr) and breakfast (170kr) are better value half-board.

★ Finse 1222   LODGE $$$
(☎ 56 52 71 00; www.finse1222.no; s/d/f from 1300/1400/1550kr; ☎) This high-altitude hotel is pretty much the only option this high on the Hardangervidda – and luckily, it's lovely. There's a strong mountain vibe here, and the modern, tidy, well-insulated rooms have outrageous views over the lake and glacier. Parts of the lodge are actually built out of old trains.

ℹ Getting There & Away

Five daily trains run between Oslo (706kr, 4½ hours) and Bergen (from 413kr, 2½ hours) via Finse.

Bergen & the Southwestern Fjords

Best Places to Eat

➜ Lysverket (p166)

➜ Colonialen Restaurant (p166)

➜ Renaa Matbaren (p203)

➜ Egget (p204)

➜ Tre Brør (p176)

Best Places to Stay

➜ Hotel Park (p163)

➜ Stalheim Hotel (p177)

➜ Utne Hotel (p192)

➜ Myrkdalen Hotel (p176)

➜ Energihotellet (p193)

Why Go?

If we could visit only one region of Norway and hope to grasp the essence of the country's appeal, this would be our choice.

Cool, cultured Bergen is one of the world's most beautiful cities, with its streets of whitewashed timber cottages climbing steep hillsides from busy Vågen Harbour. It's a destination in itself, but also the ideal starting point for a journey into splendid Hardangerfjord, with its gorgeous fjord-side villages, or the vast Sognefjorden network. En route to the latter, Voss is Norway's destination of choice for thrill-seekers.

Down south, boom-town Stavanger is a diverting staging post for Lysefjord, home to two of Norway's most recognisable images, impossibly high above the ice-blue waters of the fjord: Preikestolen (Pulpit Rock) and Kjeragbolten.

When to Go
Bergen

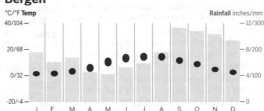

Jun Bergen International Festival and Voss' Veko for extreme sports and music.

May Hardangerfjord's fruit farms spring into a riot of blossom.

Aug & Sep Perfect for hiking to Pulpit Rock or Trolltunga.

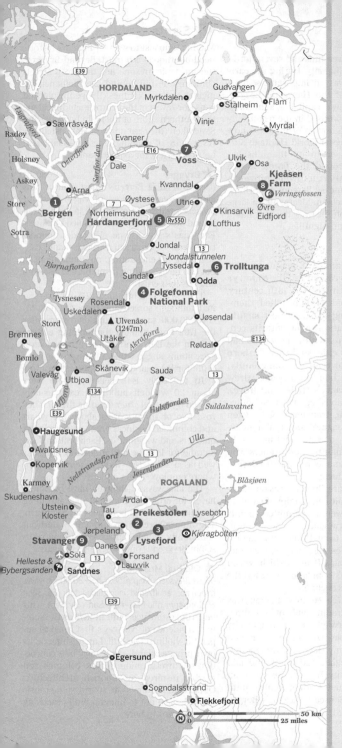

Bergen & the Southwestern Fjords Highlights

① Bergen (p156) Soaking up the Hanseatic heritage of Norway's most beautiful harbour.

② Preikestolen (p206) Trekking up to the edge of the dizzying, sky-topping cliff.

③ Lysefjord (p207) Taking a leisurely cruise along the course of this stunning waterway.

④ Folgefonna (p194) Crossing the ice – carefully – on a guided glacier walk.

⑤ Hardangerfjord (p177) Driving through the orchards and farms of this peaceful fjord.

⑥ Trolltunga (p192) Dangling your feet over the edge on this stomach-turning ledge.

⑦ Voss (p174) Kayaking, skydiving or climbing in the area's centre for adrenaline-fuelled activities.

⑧ Kjeåsen Farm (p180) Hiking up the mountain from Eidfjord to this remote, olde-worlde farm.

⑨ Stavanger (p199) Enjoying the nightlife of Norway's high-rolling oil town.

BERGEN

POP 278,121

Surrounded by seven hills and seven fjords, Bergen is a beguiling city. During the early Middle Ages, it was an important seaport and a member of the Hanseatic League, as well as Norway's capital – a heritage that can still be glimpsed in the beautifully preserved wooden houses of Bryggen, now protected as a Unesco World Heritage Site. Colourful houses creep up the hillsides, ferry-boats flit around the fjords, and a cluster of excellent art museums provide a welcome detour in case Bergen's notoriously fickle weather sets in. Meanwhile, a large student population ensures the city has a buzzy bar scene and nightlife.

History

During the 12th and 13th centuries, Bergen was Norway's capital and the country's most important city. By the 13th century, the city states of Germany allied themselves into trading leagues, most significantly the Hanseatic League with its centre in Lübeck. At its zenith, the league had over 150 member cities and was northern Europe's most powerful economic entity; the sheltered harbour of Bryggen drew the Hanseatic League's traders in droves. The League established its first office here around 1360, transforming Bryggen into one of the league's four major headquarters abroad, accommodating up to 2000 mostly German resident traders who imported grain and exported dried fish, among other products.

For over 400 years, Bryggen was dominated by this tight-knit community of German merchants, who weren't permitted to mix with or marry Norwegians. By the 15th century, competition from Dutch and English shipping companies, internal disputes and, especially, the Black Death (which wiped out 70% of Bergen's population) ensured the Hanseatic League's decline.

By the early 17th century, Bergen was nonetheless the trading hub of Scandinavia again, and Norway's most populous city with 15,000 people. During the 17th and 18th centuries, many Hanseatic traders opted to take Norwegian nationality and join the local community. Bryggen remained an important maritime trading centre until 1899, when the Hanseatic League's Bergen offices finally closed.

⊙ Sights

Making time just to wander Bergen's historic neighbourhoods is a must. Beyond Bryggen, the most picturesque are the steep streets climbing the hill behind the Fløibanen funicular station, Nordnes (the peninsula that runs northwest of the centre, including along the southern shore of the main harbour) and Sandviken (the area north of Håkonshallen). It's a maze of winding lanes and clapboard houses, perfect for a quiet wander.

★ Bryggen   HISTORIC SITE
(Map p170) FREE Bergen's oldest quarter runs along the eastern shore of Vågen Harbour (*bryggen* translates as 'wharf') in long, parallel and often leaning rows of gabled buildings. Each has stacked-stone or wooden foundations and reconstructed rough-plank construction. It's enchanting, no doubt about it, but can be exhausting if you hit a cruise-ship and bus-tour crush.

The current 58 buildings (25% of the original, although some claim there are now 61) cover 13,000 sq metres and date from after the 1702 fire, although the building pattern is from the 12th century. The archaeological excavations suggest that the quay was once 140m further inland than its present location.

In the early 14th century, there were about 30 wooden buildings, each usually shared by several *stuer* (trading firms). They rose two or three stories above the wharf and combined business premises with living quarters and warehouses. Each building had a crane for loading and unloading ships, as well as a *schøtstue* (large assembly room) where employees met and ate.

The alleyways of Bryggen have become a haven for artists and craftspeople, and there are bijou shops and boutiques at every turn. The atmosphere of an intimate waterfront community remains intact, and losing yourself in Bryggen is one of Bergen's pleasures.

★ Ole Bull Museum   MUSEUM
(Museet Lysøen; Map p158; ☑56 30 90 77; www.lysoen.no; adult/child incl guided tour 60/30kr; ⊙11am-4pm mid-May–Aug, Sun only Sep) This beautiful estate was built in 1873 as the summer residence of Norway's first musical superstar, violinist Ole Bull. Languishing on its own private island, it's a fairy-tale concoction of turrets, onion domes, columns and marble inspired by Moorish architecture. Of particular note is the soaring pine music hall: it's hard not to imagine Bull practising his concertos in here.

Outside, the grounds are criss-crossed with 13km of lovely walks, and there's a small cafe.

The best way to arrive is aboard the passenger ferry (adult/child 60/30kr, eight minutes, hourly 11am to 3pm) which runs from Buena Quay to the island.

★Edvard Grieg Museum   MUSEUM
(Troldhaugen; Map p158; ☑55 92 29 92; http://griegmuseum.no; Troldhaugvegen 65, Paradis-Bergen; adult/child 100kr/free; ⊙9am-6pm May-Sep, 10am-4pm Oct-Apr) Composer Edvard Grieg and his wife Nina Hagerup spent summers at this charming Swiss-style wooden villa from 1885 until Grieg's death in 1907. Surrounded by fragrant, tumbling gardens and occupying a semi-rural setting – on a peninsula by coastal Nordåsvatnet lake, south of Bergen – it's a truly lovely place to visit.

Apart from Grieg's original home, there is a modern exhibition centre, a 200-seat concert hall and perhaps the most compelling feature of them all, a tiny, lake-side Composer's Hut. Here the composer was always guaranteed silence, if not his muse.

From June to mid-September, there is a daily bus tour (adult/child/student and senior 250/100/200kr) departing from the tourist office (p173) at 11.30am. It includes transport, entrance and a short piano concert, and it's wise to pre-purchase tickets. Also see the website or visit the tourist office for details of summer recitals; there is a free shuttle bus for evening performances. The best public transport access is via a city-centre tram to Nesttun (two-hour ticket 36kr), alighting at the stop 'Hop'; from there it's a 2km signed walk.

★KODE   GALLERY
(Map p164; ☑53 00 97 04; www.kodebergen.no; Rasmus Meyers allé; adult/child 100kr/free, includes all 4 museums, valid 2 days)) A catch-all umbrella for Bergen's art museums, KODE showcases one of the largest art-and-design collections in Scandinavia. Each of the four buildings has its own focus: KODE 1 houses a national silver collection and the renowned Singer art collection; KODE 2 (p158) is for contemporary exhibitions; KODE 3 (p159) majors in Edvard Munch; and KODE 4 (p159) focuses on modern art.

➧ KODE 1
(Map p164; Nordahl Bruns gate 9; ⊙11am-5pm) Re-opened in 2017 after two years of renovation works, this impressive museum makes a good place to start your explorations of KODE's collection. It includes exhibitions such as one showcasing Norwegian gold and silverwork, and another exploring the eclectic arts and antiques hoard amassed by 19th-century collectors William and Anna Brugh Singer. There's also an exhibition covering the art of Queen Sonja of Norway, herself a keen amateur artist and inveterate collector.

BERGEN IN...

Two Days

Have an early morning walk around Bergen's heart, the historic harbour, until you reach the old port of **Bryggen** (p156) and its lovely wooden warehouses. Drop in to the **Bryggens Museum** (p159) to put the area in historical context, then have lunch at the **Torget fish market** (p165), where you can dine handsomely on whatever the day's catch has brought in. Spend the afternoon exploring the stellar art collection at **KODE** (p157), and finish with an equally starry dinner at **Lysverket** (p166).

On day two, begin with a coffee and pastry at **Kaffemisjonen** (p167), then take a morning **food tour** (p161) and, if you're still hungry, lunch at **Colonialen Litteraturhuset** (p166). After lunch, catch the cable car up to the top of **Mt Fløyen** (p161), and hike some of the trails nearby. For dinner, go traditional with reindeer stew or fish cakes at **Pingvinen** (p166).

Four Days

With more time, you can extend your sightseeing outside the city centre, with visits to the **Edvard Grieg Museum** (p157) on day three, and a memorable boat trip to the **Ole Bull Museum** (p156) on day four. Restaurants you won't want to miss are **Colonialen** (p166) for fine dining and the relaxed bistro of **Marg & Bein** (Map p164; ☑55 32 34 32; www.marg-bein.no; Fosswinckels gate 18; mains 255-279kr; ⊙5-9.30pm Tue-Thu, 5-10pm Fri & Sat, 5-9.30pm Sun), and perhaps for a quirky treat, the island restaurant of **Cornelius Sjømat** (p166) for seafood.

BERGEN & THE SOUTHWESTERN FJORDS BERGEN

Bergen Region

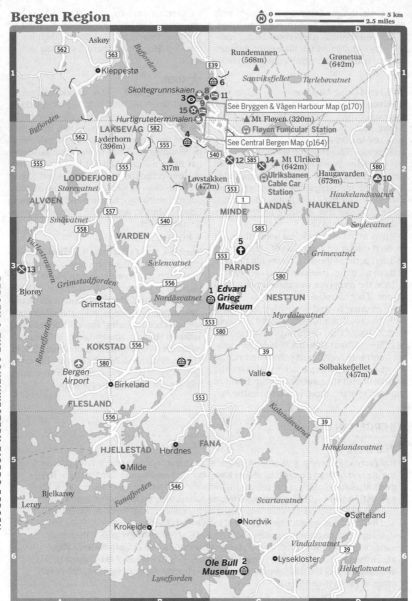

⮕ KODE 2

(Map p164; Rasmus Meyers allé 3) KODE 2 hosts several temporary exhibitions every year, as well as a contemporary art collection with a focus on Norwegian and Scandinavian artists from the 1980s onwards. Cafe **Smakverket**

(KODE 2, Rasmus Meyers allé 3; mains 179-289kr; ⊘11am-5pm) and a great gallery shop are at street level.

Note that at the time of writing, the museum was closed for redevelopment.

Bergen Region

➡ KODE 3

(Map p164; Rasmus Meyers allé 7; ⊙10am-6pm) KODE 3 is all about Edvard Munch: overall, the collection here is arguably even better than Oslo's Munch Museum. The rooms are fabulously intimate: highlights include several pieces from his Frieze of Life – a series of paintings depicting various aspects of the psyche – namely *Jealousy, Melancholy, Women in Three Stages, Evening on Karl Johan* and *By the Death Bed*.

➡ KODE 4

(Map p164; Rasmus Meyers allé 9; ⊙11am-5pm; ⊡) Modern-art aficionados will want to make a beeline to KODE 4, which is home to a large permanent collection of European Modernist works including the odd Klee, Picasso and Miró, and there is a gallery dedicated to the Norwegian landscape painter Nikoli Astrup. The arresting 1930s building was the head office of Bergen's electrical power company.

Astrup's paintings are perhaps the highlight here. His neo-romantic, almost naive, paintings, drawings and woodcuts depict the fjords, fields and mountains of his home region of Jølster, as well as traditional life there at the beginning of the 20th century. Viewing his work makes for an evocative background to your own exploration of Norway's west.

For those with little art lovers on board, **KunstLab** is Norway's first art museum especially designed for children; here kids are encouraged to explore artworks by Gauguin, Miró, Picasso and Slettemark through play and experimentation.

Restaurant and bar Lysverket (p166) is located on the ground floor.

Fisheries Museum   MUSEUM

(Norges Fiskerimuseum; Map p158; ☑53 00 61 60; http://fiskerimuseum.museumvest.no; Sandsviks-boder 23; adult/child 90kr/free; ⊙10am-6pm Jun-Aug) Housed in a series of wonky wharfside warehouses dating from the 18th century, this museum delves into the industry that sustained Bergen (along with the rest of Norway) for much of its history: fishing. The collection is wide-ranging, covering cod fishing, sealing and whaling, with vintage equipment such as antique divers' helmets and some disturbing-looking harpoons.

Bergen Kunsthall   GALLERY

(Map p164; ☑94015050; www.kunsthall.no; Rasmus Meyers allé 5; adult/child 50kr/free, from 5pm Thu free; ⊙11am-5pm Tue-Sun, to 8pm Thu) Bergen's major contemporary-art institution hosts exhibitions of international and Norwegian artists, often with a single artist's work utilising the entire space. The cleanly glamorous 1930s architecture is worth a look in itself. The attached venue and bar, Landmark (p167), also hosts video and electronic art, concerts, film, performances and lectures.

Damsgård   HISTORIC BUILDING

(Map p158; www.bymuseet.no; Alleen 29, Laksevåg; adult/child 80kr/free; ⊙noon-4pm Jun-Aug, tours at noon & 2pm) The 1770 Damsgård manor, 3km west of town, may well be Norway's (if not Europe's) finest example of 18th-century rococo timber architecture. The building's superbly over-the-top garden includes sculptures, ponds and plant specimens that were common 200 years ago. To get here, take bus 19 from Bergen's centre.

Bryggens Museum   MUSEUM

(Map p170; ☑55 30 80 30; www.bymuseet.no; Dreggsallmenning 3; adult/child 80kr/free; ⊙10am-4pm mid-May–Aug, shorter hours rest of year) This archaeological museum was built on the site of Bergen's first settlement, and the 800-year-old foundations unearthed during its construction have been incorporated into the exhibits, which include medieval tools, pottery, skulls and runes. The permanent exhibition documenting Bergen c 1300 is particularly fascinating.

Hanseatic Museum
MUSEUM

(Hanseatisk Museum & Schøtstuene; Map p170; Finnegårdsgaten 1a & Øvregaten 50; adult/child 160/60kr; ⊙ 9am-6pm Jul-Aug, 11am-2pm Tue-Sat, to 4pm Sun Sep-May) This interesting museum provides a window into the world of Hanseatic traders. Housed in a rough-timber building dating from 1704, it starkly reveals the contrast between the austere living and working conditions of the merchant sailors and apprentices, and the comfortable lifestyle of the trade partners.

Highlights include the manager's office, private liquor cabinet and summer bedroom; the apprentices' quarters, where beds were shared by two men; the fish storage room; and the *fiskeskrue* (fish press), which pressed and processed over a million pounds (450,000kg) of fish a month.

An essential complement to the Hanseatic Museum, **Schøtstuene** (Map p170; Øvregaten 50; adult/child 160/60kr incl Hanseatic Museum; ⊙ 9am-6pm Jul-Aug, 11am-2pm Tue-Sat, to 4pm Sun Sep-May) is a reconstruction of one of the original assembly halls where the fraternity of Hanseatic merchants once met for their business meetings and beer guzzling.

The admission price also includes entry to the Fisheries Museum (p159), and transport in the free shuttle bus, which runs half-hourly from Bryggen.

King Håkons Hall
HISTORIC BUILDING

(Håkonshallen; Map p170; www.bymuseet.no; Bergenhus; adult/child/student 80kr/free/40kr; ⊙ 10am-4pm mid-May–Aug, noon-3pm Sep–mid-May) Viking fans will feel right at home at this impressive ceremonial hall, built by King Håkon Håkonsson in 1247–61 and completed for his son's wedding and coronation. Spread over three floors, it's been much restored, but the highlight is the large feasting room on the top floor, where lavish banquets would have been held.

Akvariet i Bergen
AQUARIUM

(Map p158; www.akvariet.no; Nordnesbakken 4; adult/child 270/185kr; ⊙ 9am-6pm; ⚙) At the end of the Nordnes Peninsula, this aquarium makes a worthwhile trip, especially for families. There are around 60 individual aquaria here, housing lots of interesting marine species from octopi to reef fish, although kids are bound to gravitate to the shark tunnel or the seals and penguins. There's also a tropical zone housing snakes, crocodiles and other reptiles.

On foot, you can get there from Torget in 20 minutes; alternatively, take the Vågen ferry or bus 11.

Fantoft Stave Church
CHURCH

(Fantoft Stavkirke; Map p158; Paradis; adult/child/student 60/30/45kr; ⊙ 10.30am-6pm mid-May–mid-Sep) This stave church, in the leafy southern suburb of Paradis, was built in Sognefjord around 1150 and moved here in 1883. It is, in fact, a reconstruction, as the original fell victim to an early-1990s black metal/neopagan church burning. The adjacent **cross**, originally from Sola in Rogaland, dates from 1050.

SAVING BRYGGEN

So beautiful and popular is Bryggen that it seems inconceivable that conservationists spent much of the 20th century fighting plans to tear it down.

Fire has destroyed Bryggen at least seven times (notably in 1702 and again in 1955, when one-third of Bryggen was destroyed). The tilt of the structures was caused in 1944, when a Dutch munitions ship exploded in the harbour, blowing off the roofs and shifting the pilings. The explosion and 1955 fire increased the already considerable clamour to tear down Bryggen once and for all; not only was it considered a dangerous fire hazard, but its run-down state was widely seen as an embarrassment. Plans for the redevelopment of the site included modern, eight-storey buildings, a bus station, a shopping centre and a car park.

What saved Bryggen were the archaeological excavations that took 13 years to complete after the 1955 fire, and which unearthed over one million artefacts. In 1962 the **Bryggen Foundation** (http://stiftelsenbryggen.no) and Friends of Bryggen were formed; the foundation oversees its protection and restoration, although the buildings are privately owned.

One of the greatest challenges is the fact that Bryggen is actually sinking by an estimated 8mm each year. In 1979 Unesco inscribed Bryggen on its World Heritage list. For more information, visit the Bryggen Visitors Centre (p173).

From Bergen, take the tram to Fantoft (two-hour ticket 36kr).

Theta Museum
MUSEUM

(Map p170; ☑ 55 55 20 80; Enhjørningsgården; adult/child 20/10kr; ☺ 2-4pm Tue, Sat & Sun Jun–Aug) Named after the Norwegian Resistance group who occupied it between 1940 and 1945, this excellent reconstruction of a clandestine Resistance headquarters, uncovered by the Nazis in 1942, is now Bryggen's tiniest museum. It's an atmospheric experience, with vintage radios and wartime memorabilia.

Bergen Cathedral
CATHEDRAL

(Domkirke; St Olav's Church; Map p170; ☑ 55 31 58 75; Domkirkeplass 1; ☺ 11am-4pm Mon-Fri mid-Jun–mid-Aug, 11am-12.30pm Tue-Fri rest of year) **FREE** Bergen's cathedral features stonemasonry in the entrance hall carved by the same artisans who adorned Westminster Abbey's chapter house in London. From mid-June until the end of August, there are free organ recitals on Sunday and Thursday.

Rosenkrantztårnet
TOWER

(Rosenkrantz Tower; Map p170; ☑ 479 79 578; www.bymuseet.no; Bergenhus; adult/child 60kr/free; ☺ 9am-4pm mid-May–Aug, noon-3pm Sun Sep–mid-May) Built in the 1560s by Bergen governor Erik Rosenkrantz, this tower was a residence and defence post. It also incorporates parts of the keep (1273) of King Magnus the Lawmender and the 1520s fortress of Jørgen Hansson.

🏃 Activities

Ulriken643
CABLE CAR

(Map p158; ☑ 53 64 36 43; www.ulriken643.no; adult/child/family return 170/100/460kr; ☺ 9am-9pm May-Sep, 9am-5pm Tue-Sun Oct-Apr) Look up to the mountains from the harbour, and you'll spy a radio mast clad in satellite dishes. That's the top of Mt Ulriken (643m) you're spying, and on a clear day it offers a stunning panorama over city, fjords and mountains. Thankfully you don't have to climb it; a cable car speeds from bottom to top in just seven minutes.

Fløibanen Funicular
CABLE CAR

(Map p170; ☑ 55 33 68 00; www.floibanen.no; Vetrlidsalmenning 21; adult/child return 90/45kr; ☺ 7.30am-11pm Mon-Fri, 8am-11pm Sat & Sun) For an unbeatable view of the city, ride the 26-degree Fløibanen funicular to the top of Mt Fløyen (320m), with departures every 15 minutes. From the top, well-marked hiking

> ### ℹ BERGEN CARD
>
> The **Bergen Card** (www.visitbergen. com/bergencard; adult/child 24hr pass 240/90kr, 48hr 310/1120kr, 72hr 380/150kr) gives you free entrance to most of Bergen's main museums, plus discounted entry to the rest. You also get free travel on public transport, free or discounted return trips on the Fløibanen funicular (p161), depending on the time of year; free guided tours of Bergen; and discounts on city- and boat-sightseeing tours, concerts and cultural performances. It's available from the tourist office (p173), some hotels, the bus terminal and online.

tracks lead into the forest; the possibilities are mapped out on the free *Walking Map of Mount Fløyen*, available from the Bergen tourist office (p173).

👣 Tours

Bergen Guide Service (Map p170; ☑ 55 30 10 60; www.bergenguideservice.no; Holmedalsgården 4; adult/child 130kr/free; ☺ office 9am-3pm Mon-Fri) offers guided walking tours of the city year-round, and in summer **Bryggen Guiding** (Map p170; ☑ 55 30 80 30; www.bymuseet.no; Bryggens Museum, Dreggsallm 3; adult/child 150kr/free) (run by the Bryggen Museum) runs historical walking tours of the Bryggen area.

★ Bergen Food Tours
FOOD

(Map p164; ☑ 960 44 892; www.bergenfoodtours. com; adult/child 800/700kr) These 3-hour food tours are a great way to ease yourself into Nordic cuisine. The classic walk includes stops at around eight different spots around the city, where you get to sample the goods: seafood, reindeer, pastries, craft beer and *trekroneren* (hot dogs), as well as fish soup made by none other than Bergen's top chef, Christopher Håtuft of Lysverket (p166).

Tours usually leave near from near the KODE Museum.

★ Fjord Tours
TOURS

(☑ 81 56 82 22; www.fjordtours.com) Bergen is a great place for a quick one-day jaunt into the fjords – especially if you have limited time. Hardangerfjord and Sognefjord can both easily be visited in a day from Bergen, or even from Oslo thanks to the popular **Norway in a**

DON'T MISS

FJORD TOURS FROM BERGEN

There are dozens of tours of the fjords from Bergen; the tourist office (p173) has a full list and you can buy tickets there or purchase them online. Most offer discounts if you have a Bergen Card (p161). For a good overview, pick up the *Round Trips – Fjord Tours & Excursions* brochure from the tourist office, which includes tours offered by a range of private companies. Fjord Tours (p161) and Rodne Fjord Cruises are the key operators.

Nutshell tour, which packs in more than you thought possible in a single day.

The classic day-trip ticket (adult/child 1440/740kr from Bergen) combines the 6.52 morning train to Voss, a bus to the Stalheim Hotel and then on to Gudvangen, a ferry up the spectacular Nærøyfjord to Flåm, the mountain railway to Myrdal, and the train back to Bergen in time for a late dinner at 18.55. There's also an option to upgrade the cruise section onto a fancier boat for 1710/875kr.

You can also extend the standard day-trip on to Oslo as a one-way trip for 1890/980kr per adult/child, arriving around 10pm.

From May to September, Fjord Tours also runs a range of train–bus–boat return trips from Bergen, including the 10-hour **Hardangerfjord in a Nutshell** (adult/child 1430/890kr), which goes via Voss, Ulvik, Eidfjord and Norheimsund, and **Sognefjord in a Nutshell** (adult/child 1610/810kr), which explores more of Sognefjord by boat.

There are lots of other trips available, variously including Oslo, Sognefjorden, Geiranger, Ålesund and other areas – see the website for details.

If you're planning several tours and activities, it might be worth purchasing their FjordPass (150kr), which offers discounts on activities and sights across Norway, and is valid for two adults and two children.

Bergen Segway TOURS
(Map p158; ☑471 47 100; www.bergensegway.no; Bontelabo 2; standard tour 645kr, night tour 945kr) If you can't face the thought of tackling Bergen's calf-straining hills, then here's the answer: hop aboard a Segway and let the – er, motor? – do the work. The standard tour takes in Bryggen, the city centre, the fish market

and a panoramic hilltop view on Mt Fløyen. There's also a racier night-time option. Utterly bonkers, but fun.

Rodne Fjord Cruises BOATING
(Map p170; ☑55 25 90 00; www.rodne.no; Torget; adult/child/family 550/350/1250kr; ☾10am & 2.30pm daily Mar-Oct, 10am Wed-Fri, noon Sat & Sun Nov-Feb) This experienced company offers a 3½-hour fjord tour to Osterfjord and the Mostraumen strait, north of Bergen. Along the way you'll pass several waterfalls, so be prepared to get your face wet. Boats depart from the waterfront next to the fish market. Tickets can be bought onboard, at the ferry terminal before departure, or in advance at the tourist office (p173).

Fonnafly SCENIC FLIGHTS
(☑55 34 60 00; www.fonnafly.no; from 5500kr for 3 passengers) This national group will put together a custom sightseeing trip in a helicopter – the aerial views over the fjords are once-in-a-lifetime stuff, but they don't come cheap.

🎆 Festivals & Events

Bergen Beer Festival BEER
(Bergen Ølfestival; www.bergenolfestival.no; ☾Sep) Bergen's beer-drinkers get to taste brews from across the globe in this lively two-day celebration of all things ale. Well, this is a Viking nation after all.

Bergen International Festival CULTURAL
(www.fib.no; ☾late May) Held over 14 days in late May, this is the big cultural festival of the year, with dance, music, theatre and visual arts shows throughout the city.

Night Jazz Festival MUSIC
(www.nattjazz.no; ☾May) May jazz festival that is popular with Bergen's large student population.

Bergen Food Festival FOOD & DRINK
(www.matfest.no; ☾Sep) September showcase of local food producers (including whale, should you wish to avoid it).

Bergen International Film Festival FILM
(www.biff.no; ☾late Sep) Cinematic celebration held in late September.

🛏 Sleeping

Bergen has a reasonably good choice of hotels, but it's very popular and hosts regular conferences and events. It's *always* sensible to book before arriving in town, especially in summer and for festivals. The tourist office (p173) has an accommodation-booking service both online and on site.

Citybox
HOSTEL, HOTEL **$**

(Map p164; ☑ 55 31 25 00; www.citybox.no; Nygårdsgaten 31; s from 799kr, d 899-999kr, f 1545kr; 🛜) Norway's first hostel-hotel minichain began in Bergen, and it's still doing brisk business – especially since a 2017 extension has added a whole new wing. It's a long way from budget-digs territory – this is more like a smart hotel, with clean white walls, soft beds and fluffy duvets. The decor is simple, but it's a real bargain for Bergen.

Lone Camping
CAMPGROUND **$**

(Map p158; ☑ 55 39 29 60; www.lonecamping.no; Hardangerveien 697, Haukeland; campsites car with 2 people 230kr, cabins 645-1355kr) This lakeside campsite 20km from Bergen, between Espeland and Haukeland, is accessible by public transport; bus 900 runs to/from town (53kr, 30 minutes).

Marken Gjestehus
HOSTEL **$**

(Map p164; ☑ 55 31 44 04; www.marken-gjestehus.com; Kong Oscars gate 45; dm 290kr, s/d with shared bathroom 695/995kr) Midway between the harbour and the train station, this hostel-within-a-hotel has simple, modern rooms. White walls and wooden floors lend a sense of light and space, bright chairs and wall decals are cheery, and the communal areas are more stylish than you'd expect for the price. Take the lift to reception.

Bergen Vandrerhjem YMCA
HOSTEL **$**

(Map p170; ☑ 55 60 60 55; www.bergenhostel.no; Nedre Korskirkealmenning 4; dm/s/d 215/600/850kr) This wallet-friendly hostel has a lot in its favour: the dorms are great value, the decor inside is sparklingly clean, the kitchen is well equipped and there's a cracking harbour-view roof terrace. Even better – all rooms have en suite and mini-fridge. The downsides: the location can be noisy, and rates are hiked in summer.

★ Hotel Park
HISTORIC HOTEL **$$**

(Map p164; ☑ 55 54 44 00; www.hotelpark.no; Harald Hårfagresgate 35; s/d 1290/1790kr; 🛜) Two 19th-century houses combined comprise this family-run beauty, still managed by the daughters of the long-time owner. Packed with curios and antiques, it's a lovely, welcoming place to stay – all 33 rooms are slightly different, with quirky layouts and surprising design touches; corner rooms have the best views over Bergen's rooftops and Mt Fløyen.

Zander K
HOTEL **$$**

(Map p164; ☑ 55 36 20 40; www.zanderk.no; Zander Kaaesgate 8; s/d from 1050/1690kr; ❄🛜) This modern, white-fronted hotel makes a swanky addition to Bergen's rather staid sleeping scene. It offers spacious, grey-toned rooms, laid out in various configuration, from doubles to family-sized. The lobby, bar and restaurant set the stripped-back design tone, with their tall windows, swooshy sofas and globe lights, a modernistic theme that runs throughout. It's dead handy for the station, too. Bikes are available free for guests.

Klosterhagen Hotel
HOTEL **$$**

(Map p158; ☑ 53 00 22 00; www.klosterhagenhotell.no; Strangehagen 2; s/d 990/1390kr; 🛜) This little 15-room hotel in the pretty neighbourhood of Nordnes is just the ticket if you're tired of the faceless chains. Rooms are bright, colourful and modern in style, with attractive sells like slate-tiled bathrooms and smart Scandi furniture. There's a pleasant courtyard garden, and you're surrounded by classic Nordnes rowhouses and well-trimmed gardens.

Grand Hotel Terminus
HISTORIC HOTEL **$$**

(Map p164; ☑ 55 21 25 00; www.ght.no; Zander Kaaesgate 6; d 1590-1990kr, ste from 2090kr; 🛜) If it's heritage you want, then the Terminus is your place. Located directly opposite the station, this fine old hotel dating from 1928 harks back to the heyday of rail travel. The elegant lobby and the wood-panelled whisky bar make a suitably swish first impression; sadly the rooms are less starry, especially cheaper ones, so upgrades are worth it here.

Skuteviken Gjestehus
GUESTHOUSE **$$**

(Map p158; ☑ 934 67 163; www.skutevikenguesthouse.com; Skutevikens smalgang 11; 2-person apt 1100-1200kr; 🛜) This timber guesthouse, set on a small cobbled street in Sandviken, is decorated with white wicker furniture, lace cushions and a few modern touches. The rooms are sold as apartments, with separate living rooms, kitchenette and en suite bathrooms, but in truth they're just large rooms. Rates are per person; they start at 450kr in winter and 550kr in summer.

Steens Hotell
HISTORIC HOTEL **$$**

(Map p164; ☑ 55 30 88 88; www.steenshotel.no; Parkveien 22; s 890-1390kr, d 1090-1890kr; 🅿🛜) Originally built as a private house in the 1890s, this place has lashings of historical interest, from original stained-glass windows to a curving staircase that winds up

Central Bergen

to the top floor. Rooms aren't quite as impressive; they're plain in style, but top-floor ones have a pleasant view. Best of all, it has parking.

Hotel No.13

BOUTIQUE HOTEL $$$

(Map p164; ☑ 55361300; www.nordicchoicehotels. no/nordic-resort/hotel-no13; Torgalmenningen 13; d 2160-2540kr, ste 5580kr; ❄ ♠) You couldn't ask for a better location than at this smart, pale-grey building, on a pedestrianised thoroughfare just a short walk from the waterfront. Now owned by the Nordic Choice chain, it's a smart offering, with a bold (too bold?) decor choice combining black floors with puce furnishings and splashes of art. The suite has a curving glass skylight.

Det Hanseatiske Hotel

HISTORIC HOTEL $$$

(Map p170; ☑ 55 30 48 00; www.dethanseatiske hotell.no; Finnegårdsgaten 2; d from 1890kr; ♠)

This is the only hotel to be housed in one of Bryggen's original timber buildings. Spread over two buildings and connected by a glassed-in walkway, extraordinary architectural features from Bryggen's days as a Hanseatic port mix with luxe contemporary fittings. It's undeniably atmospheric, though some rooms get the mix better than others.

Clarion Hotel Admiral

HOTEL $$$

(Map p170; ☑ 55 23 64 00; www.nordicchoice hotels.no; C Sundts gate 9; s/d from 1690/1940kr; ❄ ♠) You couldn't ask for a finer view than here: most rooms look right across the harbour to Bryggen. Throw in smart rooms with a choice of wood or carpet floors, a palette of tastefully muted colours, and a decent in-house restaurant, and you have a thoroughly decent Bergen base – albeit one that's a bit short on pizzazz.

Central Bergen

✖ Eating

Bergen's culinary scene is a diverse one, taking in a small but internationally acknowledged local-food movement, lots of casual places catering to the city's student population and quite a few bastions of west-coast tradition. As might be expected, the fish and seafood are something special.

Coffee is taken seriously in Bergen, with a couple of specialist places catering for caffeine connoisseurs.

★ Torget
Fish Market
SEAFOOD $

(Map p170; Torget; lunches 99-169kr; ⊙7am-7pm Jun-Aug, 7am-4pm Mon-Sat Sep-May) For most of its history, Bergen has survived on the fruits of the sea, so there's no better place for lunch than the town's lively fish market, where you'll find everything from salmon to calamari, fish and chips, prawn baguettes and seafood salads. If you can afford it, the sides of smoked salmon are some of the best in Norway.

Royal Gourmetburger og Gin
BURGERS $

(Map p164; ☑56 90 12 33; www.royalburger. no; Neumanns gate 2a; burgers 169-219kr; ⊙3pm-midnight Sun-Thu, to 1am Fri & Sat; 🖉)

Every city needs its burger joint, and in Bergen it's Royal – a friendly corner bar with a lavish line-up of stacked burgers loaded with sauces, salads, pickles and cheeses. Vegetarians are surprisingly well catered for – try the Beirut, with falafel and spicy hummus, or the Forest King, with portobello mushroom, comté and truffle oil. The gin menu's ace, too.

Pølse
Kiosk
HOT DOGS $

(Map p170; Kong Oscars gate 1; hot dogs from 55kr; ⊙10am-2am) If you've been travelling around Norway for a while, you may be heartily sick of hot dogs bought from petrol stations. But this place has *real* sausages (including wild game, reindeer, lamb and chilli) and a better-than-average range of sauces.

Bien
BISTRO $$

(Map p158; ☑55 59 11 00; www.bienbar.no; Fjøsangerveien 30, Kronstad; lunch 109-149kr, dinner 189-285kr; ⊙noon-midnight) Easily accessible by tram to Danemarks pass, and handy if you're driving in or out of town, this restaurant and bar is a true locals' haunt. A former pharmacy, the 1930s fittings remain intact and are stunning. The menu is short and comforting: famous ragu Bolognese, fish or

Bergen

Bergen is a winning combination of colourful Scandinavian maritime architecture and a glorious setting on the cusp of Norway's glorious fjord country. Add to this a dynamic cultural life and an unmistakeable *joie de vivre* from its fish markets to traditional restaurants, and you've one of Europe's most beguiling cities.

TOMASZ WOSNIAK/SHUTTERSTOCK ©

BALIPADMA/SHUTTERSTOCK ©

1. Bryggen (p156)
Bergen's oldest quarter, World Heritage–listed and filled with boutiques and workshops.

2. KODE 4 (p159)
Designed by architects Fredrik Arnesen and Arthur Darre Kaarbø, KODE 4 is filled with European Modernist works.

3. Fløibanen Funicular (p161)
Ascending Mt Fløyen in this funicular offers breathtaking views over Bergen.

4. Torget Fish Market (p165)
A fantastic market for those wishing to try some of Norway's best and freshest seafood.

3

NOKURO/SHUTTERSTOCK ©

meat done simply, but with flair and excellent produce.

Colonialen Litteraturhuset NORWEGIAN $$
(Map p170; ☑ 55 90 16 00; www.colonialen. no/litteraturhuset; Østre skostredet 5-7; lunch 145-245kr, dinner 180-280kr; ☺ 9-11pm Tue-Fri, 11am-midnight Sat) The more laid-back, bistro sister to Colonialen Restaurant (p166), this is a favourite for Bergeners looking for a relaxed but refined lunch. It's a quietly elegant space, with neutral walls and blonde-wood tables creating that essential too-cool-for-school Nordic atmosphere, and dishes are full of flavour: leeky fish soup or meat-and-cheese platters for lunch; mountain trout or duck-leg confit for dinner.

Pingvinen NORWEGIAN $$
(Map p164; ☑ 55 60 46 46; www.pingvinen.no; Vaskerelven 14; daily specials 119kr, mains 159-269kr; ☺ noon-3am) Devoted to Norwegian home cooking, Pingvinen is the old favourite of *everyone* in Bergen. They come for meals their mothers and grandparents used to cook, and the menu always features at least one of the following: fish-cake sandwiches, reindeer, fish pie, salmon, lamb shank and *raspeballer* (sometimes called *komle*) – west-coast potato dumplings. Note that whale is served here.

★ Lysverket NORWEGIAN $$$
(Map p164; ☑ 55 60 31 00; www.lysverket.no; KODE 4, Rasmus Meyers allé 9; lunch mains 165-195kr, lunch sharing menu with/without dessert 295/395kr, 4-/7-course menu 745/995kr; ☺ 11am-1am Tue-Sat) If you're going to blow the budget on one meal in Norway, make it here. Chef Christopher Haatuft is pioneering his own brand of Nordic cuisine, which he dubs 'neo-fjordic' – in other words, combining modern techniques with the best fjord-sourced produce. His food is highly seasonal, incredibly creative and full of surprising textures, combinations and flavours. Savour every mouthful.

The restaurant is housed in the offices of the city's power company (the name means 'light works'), and there's still plenty of industrial styling – from the brass pendant lamps to the huge, deco-esque windows. If you'd rather not go the full tasting menu, bar snacks like fish soup, grain ragu and scallops with turnip emulsion are also served. In between, the lunchtime smorgasbord sharing menu is a perfect price/flavour compromise.

Colonialen Restaurant NORWEGIAN $$$
(Map p164; ☑ 55 90 16 00; www.colonialen.no/ restaurant/; Kong Oscars gate 44; 6-/8-course tasting menu 895/1195kr; ☺ Mon-Sat 6-11pm) Part of an ever-expanding culinary empire, this flagship fine-diner showcases the cream of New Nordic cuisine. It's playful and pushes boundaries, sure, but the underlying flavours are classic, and employ the very best Norwegian ingredients, especially from the west coast. Presentation is impeccable – expect edible flowers and unexpected ingredients aplenty. Strange it's on the dingy side of town.

Cornelius Sjømat Restaurant SEAFOOD $$$
(Map p158; ☑ 56 33 48 80; www.cornelius-restaurant.no; Måseskjæret 18, Holman; 3-/5-course menus incl transport 895/1095kr; ☺ 6-10.30pm) This island restaurant offers a seafood meal to remember. Their tanks are stocked with everything from scallops to sea urchins, which make it onto their 'Meteorological Menu', supplemented by foraged seaweed, home-smoked salmon and microherbs. It's in a lovely glass-fronted building on the island's shoreline; the 25-minute boat trip is included, leaving at 6pm and returning at 10.30pm.

Sky:Skraperen NORWEGIAN $$$
(Map p158; ☑ 55 32 04 04; http://ulriken643. no/; Ulrikens topp; mains 155-250kr; ☺ 9am-9pm May-Sep, 10am-4pm Oct-Apr) This is truly dining with a view. Located at the top of Mt Ulviken, this smart restaurant serves a mix of jazzed-up, down-home dishes on its 'mountain menu', from classic fish soup to mountain trout served with pickles and potatoes – but the food is only half the story here. It's the unreal view you're also coming for.

Potetkjelleren NORWEGIAN $$$
(Map p170; ☑ 55 32 00 70; Kong Oscars gate 1a; mains 315-355kr; ☺ 4-10pm Mon-Sat) The 'Potato Cellar' is one of Bergen's classic restaurants, with a monthly menu based around seasonal ingredients and Norwegian traditions. As the name suggests, it's in an atmospheric cellar dating from the 15th century. Expect rich dishes such as poached cod with artichoke cream, mussels and apple, or lamb shank with balsamic reduction.

Bryggen Tracteursted NORWEGIAN $$$
(Map p170; Bryggestredet 2, Bryggen; lunch mains 185-215kr, dinner mains 285-385kr; ☺ 11am-10pm

May-Sep) Housed in a 1708 building that ranges across the former stables, kitchen (note the stone floor, which meant that it was the only Bryggen building allowed to have a fire) and Bergen's only extant *schøtstuene* (dining hall), this restaurant serves traditional Norwegian dishes that change regularly; it's pubby and informal by day, traditionally upmarket by night.

🍷 Drinking & Nightlife

Bergen has a great bar scene and locals are enthusiastic drinking companions. Most of them favour the places in the centre or southwest of Øvre Ole Bulls plass. Big, multilevel nightclubs cluster around here, too; they are easy to spot, often fabulously trashy, and only admit those over 24.

★ Landmark
BAR, CAFE

(Map p164; ☑ 940 15 050; Bergen Kunsthalle, Rasmus Meyers allé 5; ⊙ cafe 11am-5pm Tue-Sun, bar 7pm-1am Tue-Thu, to 3.30am Fri & Sat) This large, airy room is a beautiful example of 1930s Norwegian design and is named for architect Ole Landmark. It multitasks: daytime cafe, lecture and screening hall; live-performance space, bar and venue for Bergen's best club nights. It's a favourite with the city's large creative scene. The cafe serves yummy lunches, with a choice of open-faced sandwiches and a weekly melt (995kr-1295kr).

★ Terminus Bar
BAR

(Map p164; Zander Kaaesgate 6, Grand Terminus Hotel; ⊙ 5pm-midnight) Consistently voted one of the word's best whisky bars, this grand old bar in the Grand Hotel Terminus is the perfect place for a quiet dram. It promises over 500 different tastes, and the oldest whisky dates back to 1960. The 1928 room looks gorgeous both before and after you've sampled a few.

Bryggeriet
MICROBREWERY

(Map p170; ☑ 55 55 31 55; www.bryggeriet.biz; Torget 2; ⊙ 4-10pm Tue-Thu, 6-10.30pm Fri & Sat) Bergen's brewheads and beer-nuts hold this downtown microbrewery in high esteem for its creative, interesting beers, mostly brewed in the Germanic tradition, and developed in partnership with the head chef to match the Teutonic-flavoured food. Up on the 3rd floor near the fish market, it's a rustic, cosy space with fine water views – and the beers are barnstorming.

Vågen
CAFE

(Map p170; ☑ 93 96 34 50; Kong Oscars gate 10; ⊙ 9am-7pm Sun-Thu, 9am-8pm Fri & Sat) Coffee

beans from Ethiopia, Brazil and Colombia are just a few of the selection available at this studiously shabby coffee bar, ideally placed for a caffeine fix after wandering around Bryggen or the harbour. There's a cute garden out back and plenty of pastries to munch, and there's free coffee cupping every Friday at 9am.

Apollon
BAR

(Map p164; ☑ 55 31 59 43; www.apollon.no; Nygårdsgaten 2a; ⊙ 10am-midnight Mon-Sat, noon-midnight Sun) Sink a beer while you browse for some vintage vinyl at this too-cool-for-school record store and late-night hangout, in business since the early '80s. Racks of records take up one side of the shop, with the other side occupied by a well-stocked bar serving local beers. The shop sometimes hosts in-store performances.

Blom
CAFE

(Map p164; John Lunds plass 1; ⊙ 8.30am-5pm Mon-Fri, 11am-5pm Sat & Sun; 🛜) This cafe is known for its excellent coffee (this is where off-duty baristas come for a pour-over) and attracts a fashionable, young crowd. It's a simple, warm place, with sweet service, lots of room to pull out your laptop, big sandwiches and more-ish homemade muesli slices, brownies and fruit crumbles. It's run by the people behind Kaffemisjonen.

Nobel Bopel
BAR

(Map p164; Welhavens gate 64, Møhlenpris; ⊙ 11.30am-11pm Thu & Fri, 11.30am-6pm Sat & Sun) 🍷 This cafe is a favourite weekend hangout for hipster Bergeners. It's in Møhlenpris, a studenty part of town, and is popular for its laid-back, easy-going vibe. Food is mostly organic, with bread supplied daily by Colonialen bakery (the brunch plates are particularly good), and there's a great selection of Norwegian microbrews and wines by the glass.

Una Bryggeri
BREWERY

(Map p170; ☑ 919 00 923; Bryggen 7; ⊙ noon-1am Sun-Thu, to 2.30am Fri & Sat) Craft-beer aficionados will want to reserve a good few hours to work their way through the panoply of brews available at this red-brick brewery by the harbour. The line-up represents many of Norway's top microbrews on tap, including the brewery's own; knowledgeable bar staff will happily guide you through the selection. Pub food is on offer, too.

Kaffemisjonen
CAFE

(Map p170; Øvre Korskirkealmenning 5; ⊙ 7.30am-6pm Mon-Fri, 10am-6pm Sat & Sun) Bergen's coffee

Bryggen & Vågen Harbour

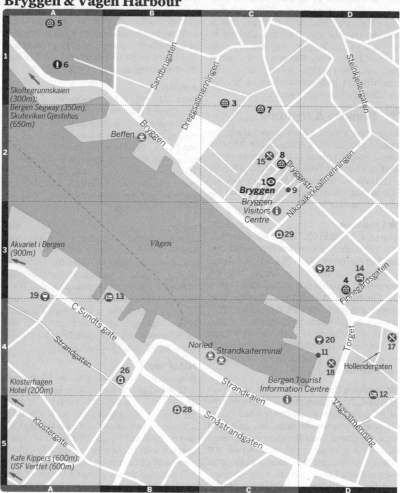

BERGEN & THE SOUTHWESTERN FJORDS BERGEN

crowd has been well served by this upmarket cafe for more than a decade now, and it's still the place to go for top-notch flat whites and pour-overs. It's a smart combo of tiles, steel and minimalism; the owners also run Blom (p167), in the more studenty quarter across town.

Det Lille Kaffekompaniet
CAFE

(Map p170; Nedre Fjellsmug 2; ⊙10am-8pm Mon-Fri, 10am-6pm Sat & Sun) This was one of Bergen's first third-wave coffee places and retains a super local feel. Everyone over-

flows onto the neighbouring stairs when the sun's out and you're not sure which table belongs to whom.

Kippers Bar & Kafe
BAR

(USF; Map p158; Georgernes Verft 12; ⊙11am-11pm Mon-Thu, noon-midnight Fri & Sat, noon-11pm Sun) For a tipple taken with a watery view, look no further than Kippers, a light and bright cafe with an unmatched outlook over the harbour, docks and far hills. Light bites are available, too, if you're feeling peckish.

Altona

Vinbar WINE BAR

(Map p170; ☎55 30 40 00; www.augustin.no/en/altona; C Sundts gate 22; ⊙6pm-12.30am Mon-Thu, to 1.30am Fri & Sat) Set in a warren of vaulted underground rooms that date from the 16th century, Altona's huge, carefully selected wine list, soft lighting and murmured conversation make it Bergen's most romantic bar (particularly when the weather's cold and wet). The bar menu tends towards tasty comfort food, such as Norwegian lamb burgers (190kr).

☆ Entertainment

Østre LIVE MUSIC

(Map p170; www.oestre.no; Østre Skostredet 3) This venue hosts cutting-edge Norwegian electronic artists, along with respected international acts. There are often three or more gigs a week; see the website for their calendar.

USF Vertfet LIVE MUSIC

(USF; Map p158; ☎55 31 00 60; www.usf.no; Georgernes Verft 12; ⊙11am-11pm) This huge arts and culture complex in a renovated warehouse space hosts a varied program of contemporary art exhibitions, theatre, dance, gigs and other cultural happenings, and also has an excellent on-site cafe, Kippers (p170).

Hulen LIVE MUSIC

(Map p164; ☎55 32 31 31; www.hulen.no; Olaf Ryes vei 48; ⊙9pm-3am Thu-Sat) Another minor legend of the Norwegian music scene, this basement club has hosted top rock and indie bands since opening its doors in 1968. *Hulen* means 'cave' and the venue is indeed underground, in a converted bomb shelter.

Fincken CLUB

(Map p164; www.fincken.no; Nygårdsgaten 2a; ⊙7pm-1.30am Wed & Thu, 8pm-3am Fri & Sat) Being pretty much the only gay club in Bergen, ensures that Fincken is nearly always completely packed out at weekends. It's a happy, upbeat place, with a varied music line-up encompassing everything from R&B to tropical reggae, Latin and pure pop. You need to be aged over 20 to be allowed entry on weekends.

Café Sanaa LIVE MUSIC

(Map p164; www.sanaa.no; Marken 31; ⊙8pm-3am Fri & Sat) This shopfront cafe just up from

Café Opera CAFE, CLUB

(Map p164; www.cafeopera.org; Engen 18; ⊙10am-12.30pm Mon-Wed, to 3pm Thu & Fri, 11am-3pm Sat, to midnight Sun) A stalwart of Bergen's cafe scene for decades, this is an attractive twin-floored space that's pleasantly set back from the harbour hustle. By day it's a place to hang over sandwiches, coffee and cake; after dark it slips into a slinkier mode for cocktails, folky gigs and DJs. The pavement tables are lovely on a sunny day.

Bryggen & Vågen Harbour

the lake spills over onto the cobblestones and draws a fun, alternative crowd with live music and, later, DJs that might be pumping out West African beats, tango, blues or jazz.

Grieghallen　　　　　　CLASSICAL MUSIC
(Map p164; ☑55 21 61 50; www.grieghallen.no; Edvard Griegs plass; ⊙Aug-Jun) Performances by the respected Bergen Philharmonic Orchestra take place inside this striking glass hall.

🛍 Shopping

★**Colonialen Strandgaten 18**　　　DELI
(Map p170; ☑55 90 16 00; www.colonialen.no; Strandgaten 18; ⊙8am-6pm Mon-Fri, 10am-6pm Sat) The latest addition to the Colonialen arsenal, this impeccably cool cafe-deli serves up lavish lunchtime sandwiches, plus an irresistible selection of cold cuts, cheeses, oils, smoked fish and so much more. It's also the best place in town to try baked goodies and breads from Colonialen's own bakery – including their to-die-for cinnamon buns.

★**Aksdal i Muren**　　　　　CLOTHING
(Map p170; ☑55 24 24 55; www.aksdalimuren.no; Østre Muralmenning 23; ⊙10am-5pm Mon-Fri, 10am-6pm Sat) This enticing shop in a historic landmark building has been ensuring

the good people of Bergen are warm and dry since 1883. The city's best selection of rainwear includes cult Swedish labels such as Didriksons, big names like Helly Hansen and Barbour, but also local gems such as Blæst by Lillebøe. We really can't think of a better Bergen souvenir than a stripey sou'wester.

Røst　　　　　　GIFTS & SOUVENIRS
(Map p170; ☑488 94 499; www.butikkenrost.no; Bryggen 15; ⊙10am-8pm Mon-Fri, 10am-7pm Sat & Sun) Short on souvenir-buying time and want something a bit more upmarket than a troll doll? You're in luck – this bright boutique right in the centre of Bryggen has a large range of well-designed Norwegian and Scandinavian objects and homewares, as well as local fashion for women, children and babies.

Pepper　　　　FASHION & ACCESSORIES
(Map p164; ☑55 32 82 60; Christies gate 9; ⊙10am-7pm Non-Fri, to 6pm Sat) If you are overcome with the urge to try for the artfully informal 'Bergen look', come to the city's best-curated fashion retailer. There's a solid selection of Swedish stars such as Filippa K and Acne, Denmark's stylish but sturdy menswear Norse Projects and haute-casual French labels A.P.C. and Maison Kitsune.

Antonio Stasi Classic Cameras PHOTOGRAPHY
(Map p170; ☑ 55 32 47 42; www.antoniostasi.com;
Lille Øvregaten 4; ☉ 10am-5pm Mon-Fri, 11am-4pm
Sat) An anti-Instagrammer's dream: Antonio Stasi's shop is a hymn to analogue photography, with a huge collection of Leica,
Contax, Rolleiflex and Polaroids. Come to
chat about classic cameras and darkroom
techniques, and you might even find yourself snapped and added to his customer
Polaroid collection.

ℹ Information

MEDICAL SERVICES
Haukeland University Hospital (☑ 05300;
Jonas Lies vei 65; ☉ 24hr) 24-hour accident &
emergency.

TOURIST INFORMATION
Bergen Turlag DNT Office (Map p164; ☑ 55
33 58 10; www.bergen-turlag.no; Tverrgaten 4;
☉ 10am-4pm Mon-Wed & Fri, to 6pm Thu, to
3pm Sat) Maps and information on hiking and hut
accommodation throughout western Norway.

Bryggen Visitors Centre (Map p170;
Jacobsfjorden, Bryggen; ☉ 9am-5pm mid-May–
mid-Sep) Maps and activities in the Bryggen
neighbourhood.

Tourist Office (Map p170; ☑ 55 55 20 00; www.
visitbergen.com; Strandkaien 3; ☉ 8.30am-
10pm Jun-Aug, 9am-8pm May & Sep, 9am-4pm
Mon-Sat Oct-Apr) One of the best and busiest in
the country, Bergen's tourist office distributes
the free, worthwhile *Bergen Guide* booklet, as
well as a huge stock of information on the region.
They also sell rail tickets. If booking or making an
enquiry, come early or be prepared to queue.

ℹ Getting There & Away

AIR
Bergen Airport (Map p158; www.avinor.no/en/
airport/bergen-airport) is at Flesland, about
18km southwest of the centre. It's served by the
following airlines:

Norwegian (www.norwegian.com) Flights to Oslo
and Tromsø.

SAS (www.sas.no) Connects with Oslo and
Stavanger.

Widerøe (www.wideroe.no) Flies to Oslo, Haugesund, Stavanger and many coastal destinations
as far north as Tromsø.

BOAT
International ferries to/from Bergen dock
at **Skoltegrunnskaien** (Map p158; Skoltegrunnskaien), northwest of the Rosenkrantz tower, while the Hurtigruten coastal ferry leaves from
the **Hurtigruteterminalen** (Map p158; Nøstegat-
en 30), southwest of the centre.

CLASSICAL MUSIC CONCERTS
Bergen has a busy program of concerts
throughout summer, many of them
focusing on Bergen's favourite son,
composer Edvard Grieg. Most take place
at evocative open-air venues such as
the Grieg Museum (p157), the **Harald
Sæverud Museum** (Siljustøl; Map p158;
☑ 55 92 29 92; www.siljustolmuseum.no;
Siljustølveien 50, Råda; adult/child 60kr/
free; ☉ noon-4pm Sun late Jun–mid-Aug),
atop Mt Fløyen and in the park adjacent
to Håkonshallen. For details, schedules
and ticket sales, see the tourist office
(p173); for some classical concert series,
the Bergen Card (p161) offers significant
discounts. Bergen Cathedral (p161) also
offers free organ recitals on Sunday and
Thursday from mid-June until the end of
August.

Several operators offer express boat, leaving
from the **Strandkaiterminal** (Map p170).

Norled (Map p170; ☑ 51 86 87 00; www.
norled.no; Kong Christian Frederiks plass
3) offers at least one daily ferry service to
Sogndal (adult/child 705/353kr, 5 hours) and
Flåm (adult/child 825/415kr, 5½ hours).

BUS
Flybussen (Map p164; www.flybussen.no; one
way/return adult 90/160kr, child 50/80kr)
Runs up to four times hourly between the
airport, the Radisson Blu Royal Hotel, the main
bus terminal and opposite the tourist office on
Vågsallmenningen.

Bergen's **bus terminal** (Map p164; Vestre
Strømkaien) is located on Vestre Strømkaien. Various companies run long-distance routes across
Norway; **Nor-Way** (www.nor-way.no) provides a
useful travel planner.

TRAIN
The spectacular train journey between Bergen
and Oslo (349-905kr, 6½ to eight hours, five
daily) runs through the heart of Norway. Other
destinations include Voss (204kr, one hour,
hourly) and Myrdal (299-322kr, 2¼ hours, up
to nine daily) for connections to the Flåmsbana
railway. Early bookings can secure you some
great discounts.

ℹ Getting Around

BICYCLE
Sykkelbutikken (www.sykkelbutikken.no; Kong
Oscars gate 81; touring bikes per day/week

BUSES FROM BERGEN

DESTINATION	COST (KR)	DURATION (HR)	FREQUENCY (PER DAY)
Lillehammer	646	8½	1
Oslo	498-577	10	4
Stavanger	475	5½	6
Voss	190	1½	1

250/850kr; ⊘10am-8pm Mon-Fri, 10am-4pm Sat) Bicycle hire near the train station.

Bergen Bike (400 04 059; www.norwayactive. no; Bontelabo 2; adult per 2hr/day 200/500kr) Rental bikes near the quay.

BOAT

The **Vågen Harbour Ferry** (Beffen; Map p170; 55 56 04 00; www.beffenfergen.no; adult/child 25/15kr; ⊘ every 10min, 7.30-4pm Mon-Fri year-round, 11am-4pm Sat May-Aug) runs between Bryggen and Tollbodhopen at Nordnes (near the Bergen Aquarium).

BUS & TRAM

Skyss (⊘177; www.skyss.no) operates buses and light-rail trams throughout Bergen. Fares are based on a zone system; one-trip tickets cost 37kr to 62kr, and can be bought from the machines at tram stops. Ten-trip tickets are also available, and you get free travel with the Bergen Card (p161).

CAR & MOTORCYCLE

Parking is a bit of an expensive headache in Bergen. Few hotels have their own car parks, which means you'll have to resort to one of the public car parks in the city centre. The largest and cheapest is the 24-hour **Bygarasjen** (150kr per 24 hours) next to the bus terminal, which also has a covered walkway leading straight to the train station. Elsewhere you'll pay upwards of 200kr per day. The tourist office (p173) has two brochures covering where to park in Bergen.

VOSS & AROUND

Though most visitors speed through the countryside around Voss, there are a few small villages that are worthy of a stop, including little Evanger, the ski-resort at Myrkdalen and the junction town of Myrdal, from where the Flåmsbana railway twists down the mountainside to Flåm on Aurlandsfjorden, an arm of Sognefjorden.

Voss

POP 14,168

Voss (also known as Vossevangen) sits on a sparkling lake not far from the fjords

and this position has earned it a world-renowned reputation as Norway's adventure capital. The town itself is far from pretty, but everyone is here for white-water rafting, bungee jumping and just about anything you can do from a parasail, most of it out in the fjords.

⊙ Sights

Voss Folkemuseum MUSEUM
(http://www.vossfolkemuseum.no/aktuelt; Mølstervegen 143; adult/child 90kr/free; ⊘10am-5pm mid-May–Aug, noon-3pm Mon-Fri Sep-Apr) This museum consists of a number of historic farms and homes, with the showpiece a hilltop farm at Mølster, high above Voss. The collection of 16 farm buildings here were once typical of the region and date from 1600 to 1870. Tours are on the hour, every hour.

Vangskyrkja CHURCH
(Uttrågata; adult/child 20kr/free; ⊘10am-4pm Tue-Sat) Voss' stone church occupies the site of an ancient pagan temple. A Gothic-style stone church was built here in the mid-13th century and although the original stone altar and unique wooden spire remain, the Lutheran Reformation of 1536 saw the removal of many original features. The 1923 stained-glass window commemorates the 900th anniversary of Christianity in Voss. Miraculously, the building escaped destruction during the intense German bombing of Voss in 1940.

Nearby is the important monument of St Olav's Cross.

St Olav's Cross MONUMENT
In a field around 150m southeast of the tourist office stands the weathered stone erected in 1023 to commemorate the local conversion to Christianity.

🏃 Activities

Voss lives for its outdoor activities, and there are loads to choose from. Bookings can be made direct or through the tourist office (p176).

Although normally done from Oslo or Bergen, the Norway in a Nutshell tour run by Fjord Tours (p161) can be done from Voss.

Voss Vind
SKYDIVING

(☑401 05 999; www.vossvind.no; Oberst Bulls veg 28; adult/child 765/565kr; ☺10am-8pm mid-June–mid-Aug, noon-8pm Wed-Sun rest of year) If you've always wanted to feel what it's like to skydive, but the thought of actually hurling yourself out of a plane fills you with mortal terror, then this amazing place can help. It has a wind tunnel that simulates the experience of freefall only without any danger of turning yourself into a cow-pat. There's a minimum age of five years.

Voss Resort
SKIING, CYCLING

(☑470 04 700; www.vossresort.no; Bavallstunet 26) The ski season in Voss usually lasts from early December until April. The winter action focuses on this resort in Bavallen, 5km north of the centre. It's used for international downhill competitions and has a snowboard park and ski school.

On the plateau and up the Raundalen Valley at Mjølfjell, you'll find excellent cross-country skiing. There are also several pistes around Mt Hangur.

In summer, the trails open up for downhill mountain-biking.

Vossafjell
HIKING

(☑991 51 500; www.vossafjell.no) This hiking company runs a number of guided walks, including to the top of Horndalsnuten and a heritage fjord walk that takes in farm villages and a cruise. There's usually a five-person minimum to run the hikes, but give them a call and see if there's a group you can join.

Voss Active
ADVENTURE SPORTS

(☑56 51 05 25; www.vossactive.no; Nedkvitnesvegen 25; ☺9am-9pm mid-May–Sep) This outdoors company specialises in organising rafting trips on local rivers including the Stranda, Raundalen and Vosso, but it also offers lots of other activities, too, from canyoning and rappelling to fishing, guided hikes and – the kids' favourites – a high-wire rope course.

Nordic Ventures
ADVENTURE SPORTS

(☑56 51 00 17; www.nordicventures.com; on the water, near Park Hotel; adult/child 1095/750kr; ☺Apr–mid-Oct) Take a guided kayak along the fjords from Voss, or book in for a multinight adventure. They have a floating office on the water near the Park Hotel, as they also run tours out of Gudvangen.

Prestegardsmoen Recreational & Nature Reserve
HIKING

The Prestegardsmoen Recreational and Nature Reserve extends south from Voss Camping in a series of hiking tracks through elm, birch and pine forests with hundreds of species of plants and birds.

★☆ Festivals & Events

Extreme Sports Festival
SPORTS

(Veko; www.ekstremsportveko.com; ☺Jun) An exhilirating week-long festival at the end of June that combines all manner of extreme sports (skydiving, paragliding and base jumping) with local and international music acts.

Vossajazz
MUSIC

(www.vossajazz.no; ☺late Mar-early Apr) An annual innovative jazz, folk and world-music festival.

⌂ Sleeping

Voss Vandrerhjem
HOSTEL $

(☑56 51 20 17; www.vosshostel.com; Evangervegen 68; dm/d/q from 375/1050/1500kr; P@☺) This modern hostel sits in a great position on the shores of Lake Vangsvatnet, with views of Mt Gråsida from many of the 40 rooms. The decor is standard-issue hostel – basic rooms and bunk beds – although twins have individual beds. You can rent bikes, canoes and stand-up paddleboards here, and there's a lakeside walkway to town.

Tvinde Camping
CAMPGROUND $

(Tvinde; ☑56 51 69 19; www.tvinde.no; off Afdalsvegen; campsites 250kr, cabins from 770kr; ☺year-round; P☺) This peaceful campsite has a glorious setting, right beside a tumbling waterfall. There's plenty of room to pitch a tent, and it all feels very sylvan. It's about 12km north of town; the Voss-Sogndal bus runs past the entrance.

Fleischer's Hotel
HISTORIC HOTEL $$

(☑56 52 05 00; www.fleischers.no; Evangervegen; d 1495-2095kr; P☺≋) This venerable old hotel was built in 1889, and looks antique, with its striking facade and turrets, supplemented by a modern extension. Unfortunately rooms seem to have got stuck in the olden days, too - expect flock carpets, heavy drapes and old furniture here. Still, it has a quaint charm, and the dining room is majestic.

★ Store Ringheim
B&B $$$

(📱 954 06 135; www.storeringheim.no; Mølstervegen 44; d/f 1590/3390kr; 🅿🛜) This old farmhouse has been impeccably renovated with style, grace and taste to provide six lovely rooms. Choices include a cosy attic room, an elegant bedroom that was once the kitchen and a romantic bolthole in the old house that has its own stone fireplace and a hand-painted box bed straight out of *Sleeping Beauty*.

🗙 Eating

★ Tre Brør
CAFE $

(📱 951 03 832; www.trebror.no; Vangsgata 28; sandwiches & light meals 85-185kr; ⊙cafe 11am-8pm Mon-Wed, 11am-2.30am Thu-Sat, 11am-8pm Sun; 🛜) The Three Brothers is the heart of Voss's social scene, and rightly so – it's everything you want from a small-town cafe. There's super coffee from Oslo's Tim Wendleboe and Ålesund's Jacu Roastery, a great range of microbrewed beers from Voss Brewery down the road, and an on-trend menu of salads, soups, burgers and Asian-tinged dishes. What's not to like?

It hosts regular gigs and DJ sets on Thursday, Friday and Saturday nights. There's also a lovely shop full of tempting treats like local jams, chocolate, chilli bites and coffee.

Ringheim Kafé
NORWEGIAN $$

(📱 56 51 13 65; www.ringheimkafe.no; Vangsgata 32; mains 160-220kr; ⊙10am-6pm Mon-Fri, 10am-5pm Sat, noon-6pm Sun) If you're just after a quick lunchtime elk burger or a bowl of *hjortekoru* (smoked sausage with potato-and-cabbage stew), this cafe on the main thoroughfare is a reasonable option, but don't go expecting any culinary fireworks. The cakes and desserts are homemade, and generally good.

🍷 Drinking & Nightlife

Voss Bryggeri
MICROBREWERY

(📱 975 40 517; www.vossbryggeri.com; Kytesvegen 396; ⊙by appointment) This much-respected brewery has made a real splash on the beer scene with standout brews such as their Oregonian pale ale, Natabjødn ('Nut Beer'), an English-style brown beer, and traditional Vossaøl, brewed with juniper tea. It's about 6km north of Voss; guided tours are available by arrangement, otherwise you can taste their beers at Tre Brør.

❶ Information

Voss Tourist Office (📱 406 17 700; www.visitvoss.no; Skulegata 14; ⊙9am-6pm Mon-Sat,

10am-5pm Sun mid-June–Aug, 9am-4pm Mon-Fri Sep–mid-June)

❶ Getting There & Away

BUS

Buses stop at the train station, west of the centre. There are frequent services to the following:

Bergen (186kr, two hours)

Flåm (121kr, 1¼ hours)

Sogndal (149kr to 229kr, three hours) via Gudvangen and Aurland.

TRAIN

Voss has fast and efficient train links. At Myrdal, you can connect with the Flåmsbåna Railway (p213). Booking ahead can get you some fantastic deals.

Bergen (204kr, one hour, hourly)

Oslo (249kr to 860kr, 5½ to six hours, five daily)

Myrkdalen

The main ski resort within reach of Voss, this winter-sports mecca is worth a visit in summer too for its hiking possibilities.

The skiing season runs from mid-November to mid-April and experiences 5m snow falls on average. During summer there's great hiking with several marked high-mountain trails starting at the hotel, a program of nature-based kids' activities, as well as easy access to Voss' roll call of outdoor pursuits.

🛏 Sleeping

★ Myrkdalen Hotel
HOTEL $$$

(📱 56 52 30 40; www.myrkdalen.no/en/myrkdalen-hotel; Myrkdalen; r/apt from 1490/1805kr) The ski resort revolves around this large, stylish, timber-clad hotel, with great rooms in a retro-modern vibe: funky lampshades, mid-century furniture, and taupes and greys accented by pops of colour. There are three restaurants serving everything from pizza to lamb shanks, salmon and fondue, plus two stylish bars, but the real selling point is outside: epic views of mountains through every window.

❶ Getting There & Away

Myrkdalen is 26km north of Voss via the E16 and Rv13. There's no public transport.

Stalheim

POP 200

High above the valley, Stalheim is a place of extraordinary natural beauty with an interesting, lively past. Between 1647 and 1909,

Stalheim was a stopping-off point for travellers on the Royal Mail route between Copenhagen, Christiania (Oslo) and Bergen. A road was built for horses and carriages in 1780. The mailmen and their weary steeds rested in Stalheim and changed to fresh horses after climbing up the valley and through the Stalheimskleiva gorge, flanked by the thundering Stalheim and Sivle waterfalls.

Although a modern road winds up through two tunnels from the valley floor, the **old mail road** (Stalheimskleiva) climbs up at an astonishing 18% gradient. As tour buses, improbably, use this road, it's one-way only: you can drive down it, but not up.

◉ Sights & Activities

Stalheim Folkemuseum   MUSEUM
(☏ 56 52 01 22; Stalheimsvegen 132; adult/child 60kr/free; ☺ on request) This folk museum, near the Stalheim Hotel, has exhibits of traditional crafts and rustic objects as well as 30 log buildings laid out as a traditional farm. It only opens if there are 10 or more visitors; ask at the hotel (p177) for details.

Husmannsplassen Nåli   HIKING
🚶 This cotter's farm, along the ledge from Stalheim high above Nærøydalen, was occupied until 1930. The route there (two hours return) is not for the faint-hearted. The path beneath the cliff wall is extremely narrow in parts and there is nothing between you and the valley floor far below; don't even think of walking here after rain.

Brekkedalen   HIKING
🚶 This three-hour return hike leads up into the valley above Stalheim. Locals claim it's the region's prettiest walk, and the views are magnificent. It's a relatively easy way to leave behind the crowds and have this stunning high country all to yourself. The tourist office in Voss (p176) has route guides, or ask at Stalheim Hotel (p177) for directions.

🛏 Sleeping

Stalheim Fjord og Fjellhytter   HUT $
(☏ 56 51 28 47; www.stalheim.no; Brekkedalen 16-24; 4–6-person cabins per week 4200-7200kr) When you really want to get away from it all, these Heidi-style timber cabins are the place to do it. Pine-clad and stocked with simple but serviceable facilities (kitchen, bathroom etc), they're wonderful to just sit and relax in. Flash Harries can upgrade to Standard Plus cabins, which come with Jacuzzi, sauna and even underfloor heating.

EVANGER

This tiny village, just off the highway around 12km west of Voss, has a delightful toy-town feel, with a tight grid of restored wooden houses and a gorgeous setting by a lake. There's absolutely zip to do here besides relax or maybe go for a languid row, but it makes a blissfully peaceful stop after a day in Voss during its high-season frenzy.

Patina (☏ 909 57 388; http://patina simpleliving.blogspot.co.uk; Knute Nelson gata 17; 2-bed apt 1200kr; ☺ cafe & shop 11am-5pm Tue-Sat Jul–mid-Aug, 11am-5pm Sat Sep-Jun) is a labour of love dreamt up by three local women – part guesthouse, part cafe and part vintage shop.

★**Stalheim Hotel**   HISTORIC HOTEL $$$
(☏ 56 52 01 22; www.stalheim.com; s/d/superior from 1160/1880/2350kr; ☺ mid-May–mid-Sep; 🅿@🛜) There's one reason to stay at this sprawling sky-high hotel, and it's not the dated decor. It's all about the view: vast, snowy mountain panoramas unfurl through the windows here, so compelling that you probably won't even notice the rather twee furnishings. The public areas are grand, filled with Norwegian design pieces and historical paintings.

Inevitably the hotel's a stop-off for coach tours, and it can feel swamped in midsummer, especially at meal times. Even if you're not staying, it's worth popping onto the terrace for the incredible outlook straight down Nærøydalen.

❶ Getting There & Away

Stalheim is about 34km north of Voss. It's reached via a steep turn-off on the E16, heading northeast towards Gudvangen.

To reach Stalheim from Voss, take any bus (110kr, one hour, hourly) towards the towns of Gudvangen and Aurland, but you may have to hike 1.3km up from the main road unless you can persuade the bus driver to make the short detour.

HARDANGERFJORD

Running from the Atlantic to the steep wall of central Norway's Hardangervidda Plateau, Hardangerfjord is classic Norwegian fjord country. There are many beautiful corners, although our picks would take in

Eidfjord, Ulvik and Utne, while Folgefonna National Park offers glacier walks and top-level hiking. It's also well known for its many fruit farms, especially apples – Hardanger is sometimes known as the orchard of Norway.

You can easily explore Hardangerfjord from Bergen; www.hardangerfjord.com is a good resource.

Norheimsund

POP 2224

Tranquil Norheimsund serves as the gateway to Hardangerfjord. There are more beautiful places further into the fjord network, but it's a pretty little town nonetheless. Ferries from here head to Eidfjord, making it a useful staging post if you're on public transport.

◉ Sights

Hardanger Maritime Museum MUSEUM
(Hardanger Fartøyvernsenter; ☑474 79 839; www.fartoyvern.no; Sandvenvegen 50; adult/child 100/60kr; ☺10am-5pm early May-early Sep; ⑭) This engaging museum keeps alive the local boat-building tradition and is home to old wooden boats, exhibitions on restoration procedures and rope-making, as well as temporary exhibitions. Children can try their hand at building a boat and other maritime skills. The museum also rents out rowboats.

Steinsdalfossen WATERFALL
Just 1km west of Norheimsund along Rv7, this 50m-high waterfall is a far cry from Norway's highest, but it does offer the chance to walk behind the water. It can get overcrowded with tour buses in summer; inexplicably, this is one of the most visited natural sites in Norway.

⌕ Sleeping & Eating

Oddland Camping CABIN $
(☑56 55 16 86; www.oddlandcamping.no; small/family cabins 700/1450kr; ☺small cabins Apr-Oct, family cabins year-round; ☞) There's no space for camping here, but the pale-green cabins are very cosy, and all have fjord views – but there's only one family-sized cabin, so book ahead if you want it. It's a relaxed place next to a fruit farm, with access to the lakeshore and pebbly beach, and a couple of rowboats for hire. It's about 4km southeast of Norheimsund.

★Sandven Hotel HISTORIC HOTEL $$
(☑56 55 20 88; www.sandvenhotel.no; Kaien 28; s/d from 1180/1440kr; ℙ☞) Located right on the waterfront in the centre of Norheimsund, the

atmospheric Sandven Hotel dates from 1857 and has loads of charm, expansive balconies and excellent views from the fjord-facing rooms. Its public spaces are lavish but unusually light, with white-painted floorboards and pale oak boiserie.

Along with the grand dining spaces, there's also a pleasant fjord-side cafe and clubby bar that offers an excellent beer selection. And, yes, it has the requisite celeb room, the Crown Prince suite, where the future king of Norway once stayed.

La Fiesta PIZZA $$
(☑56 55 10 77; Nedstegata 12; pizzas 189-279kr; ☺3-10pm Mon-Sat, 1-9pm Sun) This pizza joint is probably the best option in town for an evening meal – nothing groundbreaking, but decent pizzas with a good choice of toppings, and beer on tap.

❶ Information

Norheimsund Tourist Information (☑56 55 31 84; www.visitkvam.no; Steinsdalsfossen; ☺10am-6pm Jun-Aug, to 4pm Mon-Fri May & Sep) The visitor centre at Steinsdalsfossen also doubles as the main information point for Norheimsund and Kvam.

❶ Getting There & Away

Bergen is 78km west of Norheimsund via Fv7.

Skyss (p174) Bus 925/930 travels from Bergen to Norheimsund (124kr, 85 minutes, 10 daily). The 7.25am bus arrives in Bergen just in time to catch the 9am ferry onwards to Eidfjord.

Norled (p173) run two daily passenger-only boats from Norheimsund to Eidfjord (316kr, 2¾ hours), stopping at Utne, Lofthus, Kinsarvik and Ulvik en route.

Øystese

POP 1881

Just around the shoreline from Norheimsund, Øystese has an exceptional art museum, the kind you just don't expect to find in a small fjord-side village. Interesting detours abound, including the constant lure of Hardangerfjord's famed fruit farms.

◉ Sights

Hardanger Skyspace SCULPTURE
(www.hardangerskyspace.no; Hardangerfjordvegen; adult/child 120/40kr; ☺sunset) US light artist James Turrell is known for his fascination with light, and has created a series of 'skyspaces' around the world, which are geometrical viewing chambers with an open roof aperture letting in the light. The Hardanger

Skyspace was built in 2011 beside the fjord; it's only open at sunset, and places are limited, so bookings are required.

Kunsthuset Kabuso GALLERY
(🖉474 79 987; www.kabuso.no; Hardangerfjord-vegen 626; incl admission to Ingebrigt Vik Museum adult/child 90kr/free; ⊙10am-5pm Tue-Sun Jun-Aug, shorter hours rest of year) The Kunsthuset Kabuso runs a fascinating program that features big-name contemporary artists (Damien Hirst, Matthew Barney and James Turrell have all exhibited here in the past) during most of the year, with summer shows that focus on Norwegian identity and traditional, often local, work.

The museum also has a range of concerts right across the musical spectrum year-round; the small theatre has fantastic acoustics.

Ingebrigt Vik Museum MUSEUM
(🖉474 79 987; www.kabuso.no; Hardangerfjordve-gen 626; incl admission to Kunsthuset Kabuso adult/child 90kr/free; ⊙10am-5pm Tue-Sun Jun-Aug, shorter hours rest of year) Under the direction of the Kunsthuset Kabuso, this permanent collection of the work of Ingebrigt Vik (1867–1927), one of Norway's best-loved sculptors, is housed in a beautiful and unusual early Modernist pavilion designed by Torgeir Alvsaker. His striking pieces crafted in bronze, plaster and marble are on display here.

Steinstø Fruktgard FARM
(🖉922 52 637; www.steinsto.no; Steinstø; ⊙11am-6pm Sun-Fri, 11am-5pm Sat) 🍃 A summer pilgrimage to this farm, just east of Øystese, rewards with strawberries ripe in June and a bounty of raspberries, cherries, plums and apples in July. A cafe serves great apple juice and a rustic apple cake, as well as *lefse* (flat bread) and waffles. Come on Sunday afternoon for a homey late lunch (mains 165kr).

🛏 Sleeping

Hardangerfjord Hotel HOTEL $$$
(🖉56 55 63 00; www.hardangerfjord-hotell.no; s/d from 1500/1790kr; P🞥🞥🞥) This large modern hotel on the fjord has views across the water to mountains crowned by the Folgefonna icecap. The 87 rooms have been renovated and are comfortable, if on the bland side. It has a restaurant, heated swimming pool and minigolf, and can arrange other activities.

🛈 Getting There & Away

Øystese is 6km northeast of Norheimsund along Hardangerfjordvegen. There are at least five daily

buses between Øystese and Bergen (159kr, 1¾ hours) via Norheimsund.

Ulvik
POP 1129
Located in the innermost reaches of Hardangerfjord at the heart of Norway's apple-growing region, Ulvik is framed by mountains and affords wonderful views up the fjord. You're in the heart of stunning fjord country dotted with farmsteads and almost too many cycling and hiking opportunities in the surrounding hills. The town is bathed in silence once the tourist boats disappear.

⊙ Sights

Hardanger Saft og Suderfabrikk FARM
(Hardanger Juice & Cider Factory; 🖉901 22 835; www.hardangersider.no; Lekve Gard; ⊙10am-5pm Mon-Sat) Traditional fruit farm with apple and plum orchards, and juice and cider production facilities.

Ulvik Frukt & Cidreri FARM
(🖉911 02 215; www.hakastadsider.no; Hakastad; ⊙10am-5pm Mon-Sat) Sample homemade apple juices and ciders, plus fresh apples and cherries, at this welcoming fruit farm.

🏃 Activities

The tourist office (p180) can point you in the direction of hikes in the surrounding area, including a 5km trail that takes you past four **fruit farms** in the hills above town. Visits to the farms are possible for groups, but ask the tourist office if you can tag along on a tour that's already going.

B-Nature OUTDOORS
(🖉479 71 484; www.bnature.com; Tyssevikvegen 31; ⊙9am-8pm Jun-Aug) This fun activity company can provide endless ways to explore the surrounding landscape: kayaking, biking, hiking and boating, of course, as well as more off-the-wall pastimes like archery, birdwatching, fire-making, flint-knapping, orientation and knot-tying. They also run tours of local cider farms, and organise fabulous sea-plane trips.

Bikes/kayaks can be rented for 210/290kr per day.

🛏 Sleeping & Eating

Ulvik Fjord Hotel HOTEL, CAMPGROUND $$
(🖉56 52 61 70; www.ulvikfjord.no; Eikjeledbakkjen 2; d/tr/f 1090/1490/1790kr, camping 140-200kr, cabins 500-600kr; P🞥) For a smaller, more personal option in Ulvik if you're looking to avoid the

summer hordes, this simple hotel run by a husband-and-wife team is a good bet. Rooms with a view and balcony over the river are best, but they're all quite decent, with parquet floors, plain furniture and rather dated bathrooms. Camping is available, too.

Brakanes Hotel   HOTEL $$$

(☏ 56 52 61 05; www.brakanes-hotel.no; Promenaden 3; s 1250kr, d 2100-2500kr, f 2600kr; P 🛜 ⛲) This vast fjord-facing edifice is the favourite venue for the coach tour crowd, so don't expect to be on your own here. It's a modern structure, heavy on the balconies and glass, which make the most of the watery views – although its rooms feel a little soulless. There's a choice of buffet or à la carte for dinner.

Drøs Bakeri & Cafe   CAFE $$

(☏ 916 25 771; www.dros.no; Tyssevike 36; ⊙1-6pm Mon, 10am-6pm Tue-Wed, 11am-8pm Thu, 11am-midnight Fri, 11am-1am Sat, 1-6pm Sun) A busy, bustling cafe with an easy-going menu of wraps, tacos, sandwiches and platters, as well as good coffee and homemade cakes. At weekends, locals come here to hang out and have a drink, with a good selection of bottled beers and wines behind the bar.

❶ Information

Ulvik Tourist Office (☏ 56 52 62 80; www.visitulvik.no; Tyssevike 15; ⊙10am-6pm Mon-Fri, 10am-5pm Sat, 10am-4pm Sun Jul & Aug, shorter hours rest of year) The tourist office has walking maps and bicycle hire (half/full day 150/200kr) and can arrange fishing licences and water-skiing (from 200kr).

❶ Getting There & Away

Ulvik is on Rv572, about 43km east of Voss.

Buses run from Voss and Ulvik (139kr, 1¼ hours, four to six daily).

There's also a daily sightseeing boat, the *Tedno*, which runs from Norheimsund and stops in Lofthus, Kinsarvik, Utne and Ulvik on its way to Eidfjord.

Eidfjord

POP 950

Eidfjord is one of the most beautifully sited towns in this part of Norway, dwarfed by sheer mountains and cascading waterfalls. Eidfjord's beauty does, however, come at a price. Although it's only accessible by ferry or spiral tunnels, in summer cruise ships arrive on an almost daily basis, and the town can get overwhelmed.

Sights

Vøringsfossen   WATERFALL

At the summit after a steep 20km drive, and where Hardangervidda begins, is the stunning, 182m-high Vøringfoss Waterfall. There are actually numerous waterfalls here, which together are called Vøringsfossen. They plunge over the plateau's rim and down into the canyon, some with a vertiginous drop of 145m, and can be viewed via a series of lookouts along the road.

The best views are from the lookout next to the Fossli Hotel (parking 40kr) or from a number of lookouts reached from the **Vøringsfossen Cafeteria** back down the valley on the Rv7.

This is one of Norway's most popular natural attractions, with an endless stream of tour buses in summer (the record is 43 buses at any one time). Public buses between Geilo and Odda pass right by the falls.

Viking Burial Mounds   ARCHAEOLOGICAL SITE

(Hæreid; Troll Train 90/40kr; ⊙Troll Train hourly 10am-5.30pm Jun-Aug) The 350 Viking burial mounds found here make this the largest Iron Age site in western Norway, dating from AD 400 to 1000. The tourist office can point you in their direction and supply a basic map with a marked 90-minute walking trail.

Kjeåsen Farm   FARM

Perched 600m above Eidfjord are two farms that were, until 1974, completely inaccessible by road. Until then, residents had no choice but to lug all their goods and supplies up the mountainside – a back-breaking task (it's said that one of the buildings took 30 years to build). Nowadays it's mainly visited by tourists for the absolutely breathtaking view.

The turn-off to the farm starts in Simadal, about 8km from Eidfjord/Rv7. From here, the narrow road leads for 5km, about half of which is through a tunnel constructed in the late 1970s. Due to the narrowness of the road, traffic is only allowed to travel in each direction once an hour; going up on the hour, and coming down on the half-hour. Kjeåsen's newfound popularity with unfortunately means it's not quite as tranquil as it once was.

The farm complex is now deserted apart from one woman, Bjørg Wiik, who's lived here alone for the last four decades. Although the tunnel is open 24 hours, the latest you should drive up to the farm is 5pm, so as to respect the privacy of Kjeåsen's last inhabitant.

The other option is to climb up to the farm on foot (four hours return), but it's

MAX TOPCHII/SHUTTERSTOCK ©

Spectacular Norway

Few countries can match the sheer, jaw-dropping beauty of Norway. It begins, like so many Norwegian journeys, with the fjords, but the otherworldly rock formations of the Lofoten Islands, and the ice-bound ramparts of Svalbard are every bit as beautiful. And there's no better way to explore it all than taking to the great outdoors.

Contents
- Fjords
- Activities
- Lofoten
- Svalbard

Above The view from Trolltunga (p192), above Lake Ringedalsvatnet

1

2

ANDREW MAYOVSKYY/SHUTTERSTOCK ©

1. Norheimsund (p178), Hardangerfjord 2. Geirangerfjord (p240)
3. Preikestolen (p206), Lysefjord 4. Nærøyfjord (p216)

3

MARCO WONG/GETTY IMAGES ©

Fjords

The fjords of Norway rank among the most dramatic landforms on earth. To travel to Norway and not draw near to one of its signature fjords is to miss an essential element in Norway's enduring appeal.

If Norway's fjords were an art collection, Unesco World Heritage–listed Geirangerfjord would be its masterpiece. Yes, it gets overwhelmed by tour buses and cruise ships in summer, but they're there for a very good reason and their presence only slightly diminishes the experience. Also inscribed on the World Heritage list, Nærøyfjord is similarly popular yet unrelentingly breathtaking. It's merely one of many tributary arms of Sognefjorden, which, at 203km long and 1308m deep, is the world's second-longest and Norway's deepest fjord.

Hardangerfjord is another extensive fjord network sheltering charming villages that promise front-row seats from which to contemplate the beauty at every turn, while away to the south, Lysefjord is long and boasts some of Norway's best views. And that's just the beginning...

TOP MAINLAND FJORDS

➡ **Geirangerfjord** The king of Norwegian fjords.

➡ **Sognefjorden** A vast fjord network.

➡ **Hardangerfjord** Rolling hills and lovely villages.

➡ **Lysefjord** Plunging cliffs, cruises and death-defying lookout points.

➡ **Nærøyfjord** One of Norway's narrowest and prettiest fjords.

➡ **Eidfjord** The most spectacular branch of Hardangerfjord.

➡ **Trollfjord** An astonishingly steep fjord on Lofoten.

➡ **Vestfjorden** Sheltered bays and pretty villages separate Lofoten from the mainland.

MARIE LINNER/SHUTTERSTOCK ©

1. Skiiers in Trysil (p133) 2. Hiking outside Åndalsnes (p237)
3. Cycling the E10 near Flakstad (p301), Lofoten Islands
4. Paragliding over Aurlandsfjorden (p212)

OLGA DANYLENKO/SHUTTERSTOCK ©

Activities

Norwegians are experts at combining an appreciation of the country's wild beauty with a true sense of adventure. There's a seemingly endless list of summer activities, but winter is a wonderful time for heading out into the snow.

Hiking (Summer)

The right to wander at will in Norway has been inscribed in law for centuries and there's world-class hiking throughout the country. The best trails traverse glaciers or climb through the high country that, by some estimates, covers 90% of Norway.

Extreme Sports (Summer)

Voss, with its mountainous, fjord-strewn hinterland, is Norway's thrill-seeking capital. It's the perfect place to take to the air strapped into a parasail or hurtle towards the earth on a bungee-rope.

Snow Sports (Winter)

Slip through the snow on a sled pulled by huskies. Speed across the ice astride a snowmobile. Or join the Norwegians in their national pastime of skiing downhill or cross-country. Whichever you choose, winter is a terrific time to visit.

White-Water Rafting (Summer)

Norway's steep slopes and icy, scenic rivers create an ideal environment for veteran and beginner rafters alike. Central Norway is rafting's true Norwegian home, but the cascading waters around Sjoa offer the widest range of experiences.

Cycling (Summer)

Cyclists in search of seriously challenging but seriously beautiful routes will find their spiritual home in Norway. Longer routes abound, but there isn't a more exhilarating descent than the one from Finse down to Flåm.

LOUIELEA/SHUTTERSTOCK ©

1. Reine, Moskenesøy (p302) **2.** Værøy island (p304) as seen from Moskenesøy **3.** Ramberg, Flakstadøy (p301) **4.** Lofotr Viking Museum, Vestvågøy (p299)

2

KOCHNEVA TETYANA/SHUTTERSTOCK ©

Lofoten

It is the fjords that have forever marked Norway as a land of singular natural splendour, but the surreal beauty of the Lofoten Islands is a worthy rival. For sheer drama, this magical archipelago (which in summer is bathed in the crystal-clear light of the north) could well be Norway's most beautiful corner.

Moskenesøy

Tolkienesque landscapes and glacier-carved landforms lend Moskenesøy a supernatural beauty that is truly special. The village of Å is the island's soul, while Reinefjord is particularly scenic.

Værøy

Intimate little Værøy, occupying Lofoten's southern reaches, is Moskenesøy's rival for the title of Lofoten's most picturesque island. The combination of vast colonies of seabirds, soaring ridgelines and remote, tiny villages is glorious.

Flakstadøy

4

Isolated, wind-blown crags along the southern shore are the most eye-catching feature of Flakstadøy, but the old-world beauty of Nusfjord and the utter improbability of white-sand beaches at Ramberg and Flakstad also deserve attention.

Vestvågøy

Many travellers rush across Vestvågøy on their way deeper into the Lofoten, but the Lofotr Viking Museum captures the spirit of more epic times and the walk from Unstad to Eggum is magnificent.

Austvågøy

Most people's entry point into the Lofoten, Austvågøy is a gentle introduction to the islands' charm. The Raftsund strait and the dizzyingly narrow Trollfjord provide the backdrop, while the villages of Kabelvåg and Henningsvær offer perfect bases.

Svalbard

The Svalbard archipelago – as close to the North Pole as it is to mainland Norway, and the world's most accessible slice of the polar north – is one of the natural world's grand epics.

STAND-OUT SVALBARD

➡ **Midnight-sun hiking** Trek deep into the interior or close to Longyearbyen.

➡ **Pyramiden** Take a summer boat trip or winter snowmobile expedition past the Nordenskjöldbreen glacier to this former Russian mining settlement.

➡ **Dog-sledding** The perfect way to experience the silence of Spitsbergen.

➡ **Polar bears** Spot the Arctic's most soulful presence, but hopefully from afar.

➡ **Magdalenefjord** A serious contender for the title of Norway's most beautiful fjord.

Arguably Europe's last and most extensive great wilderness area, Svalbard has all the elements for an Arctic idyll. Here you'll find more polar bears than people, as well as a roll-call of Arctic wildlife that includes walruses, reindeer, Arctic foxes and a stunning collection of bird species. They roam a landscape that, for the most part, remains ice-bound throughout the year – an astonishing 60% of Svalbard is covered by glaciers. Splendidly uninhabited fjords, formidable peaks never traversed by a human and the echoes of the great sagas of polar exploration are all part of the mix. Whether experienced in the strange blue half-light of the Arctic night (late October to mid-February) or the midnight sun (mid-April to mid-August), Svalbard is quite simply unforgettable.

steep and quite perilous, involving at least one rope-bridge; the path begins in Sæ in Simadal with parking by Sima Power Plantask – ask the tourist office (p190) for directions. If Kjeåsen Farm has piqued your curiosity, the booklet *Kjeåsen in Eidfjord*, by Per A Holst, tells the history of the farm and its inhabitants; it's available for 20kr from the Eidfjord tourist office.

Skytjefossen
WATERFALL

Plunging almost 300m off the Hardangervidda Plateau to the valley floor below, these falls, 12km north of Eidfjord in the Simadalen valley, are among the highest in Norway. To reach the trailhead, drive as far as Tveit and park just after the last house. The hike to the falls is about 3km, and takes 1½ hours there and back including a bit of time at the waterfall.

Hardangervidda Natursenter
MUSEUM

(☑ 53 67 40 00; www.hardangerviddanatursenter. no; Øvre Eidfjord; adult/child 130/65kr; ☺ 9am-7pm mid-Jun–mid-Aug, 10am-6pm Apr–mid-Jun & mid-Aug–Oct) For an all-encompassing overview of the Hardangervidda National Park, this excellent visitor centre should be your first port of call. Interactive exhibits explore the park's flora and fauna, while staff provide copious information on the many activities you can get up to, from hiking to skiing.

🏃 Activities

★ Flat Earth
ADVENTURE SPORTS

(☑ 476 06 847; www.flatearth.no) This excellent outdoors company offers pretty much every way of exploring the fjord country that you can think of. The highlight, of course, is the chance to steer a sea kayak down the epic fjord: there's a choice of three-hour trips (adult/child 590/450kr) or full-day expeditions (1150/1000kr) that include a BBQ lunch. Climbing, rafting and mountain biking are also offered.

🛏 Sleeping & Eating

★ Eidfjord Gjestegiveri
GUESTHOUSE $

(☑ 53 66 53 46; www.ovre-eidfjord.com; Øvre Eidfjord; huts 400kr, s/d 600/890; ☺ May-Aug; ℗ 🛜) Pass through the tunnel to Øvre Eidfjord and you can't miss this handsome guesthouse, an old-fashioned, whitewashed, gabled beauty with a covered porch out front. Inside, the eight double rooms are simple but proper, stocked with vintage furniture; all share a corridor bathroom. There are also a few basic camping-style huts in the front garden, and a super pancake cafe.

Breakfasts are good (the secret's in the homemade bread) and the cafe has around 20 varieties of fantastic, filling, sweet and salty Dutch pancakes, with toppings that range from mountain trout to Hardanger apple compote – kids will absolutely love it. It also has a good range of dried meals for hikers heading out into the wilds.

Note that rates creep up by 200kr or so in summer.

Sæbø Camping
CAMPGROUND $

(☑ 53 66 59 27; www.saebocamping.com; Øvre Eidfjord; campsites for 2 people 230kr, cabins 500-1120kr; ☺ mid-May–mid-Sep; ℗ 🛜) This spacious and well-equipped lakeside campsite has a pretty location in Måbødalen, just 500m from the Hardangervidda Natursenter. The owners promise freshly baked bread in the mornings and there are canoes for hire.

Fossli Hotel
HISTORIC HOTEL $$

(☑ 53 66 57 77; www.fossli-hotel.com; Vøringfossen; s/d from 790/1050kr; ☺ May-Sep; ℗ 🛜) If you fancy falling asleep to the roar of water, then this venerable hotel occupies a prime position overlooking the Vøringfossen falls. It's a truly stunning spot, and while the rooms look pretty dated (floral curtains and bedspreads, anyone?), they're rather charming in an olde-worlde way – and you'll have the falls to yourself once the buses head for home.

The hotel is run by Erik, a quiet and engaging host with a treasure-trove of stories from the Hardangervidda region, whose great-grandfather built the hotel in the 1890s. Edvard Grieg composed his *Opus 66* in the hotel. The hotel is well signposted 1.3km off the Rv7. The hotel's restaurant (mains 190kr to 280kr) serves fine Norwegian dishes, such as lamb, baked salmon and wild deer, and there's a waffle cafe downstairs.

Fjell & Fjord Eidfjord Hotel
HOTEL $$

(☑ 53 66 52 64; www.effh.no; Lægreidsvegen 7; s/d 1195/1495kr; ℗ 🛜) If you're after a view of the fjord, then this modern hotel just uphill from Eidfjord's main road can certainly oblige. Rooms are rather bland in style, but here it's all about the scenery outside your window. Downstairs there's a pleasant lounge and restaurant with similarly fine views. Interconnecting rooms make it useful for families.

Vik Pensjonat
GUESTHOUSE $$

(☑ 53 66 51 62; www.vikpensjonat.com; Eidfjord; s/d with shared bathroom 650/1200kr, with private en suite 1200/1600kr, cabins 800-1450kr; P) An attractive option if being by the fjord is what matters. With its slate-topped gables and clapboard exterior, it looks every inch the traditional Norwegian guesthouse, but inside it's spruce and modern: uncluttered rooms, wooden floors and the essential fjord views. Rooms with balconies are the best, or you can go for the riverside cabins in the garden.

The attached cafe is a great spot for lunch or dinner, with reasonable prices (mains 165kr to 240kr) and everything from soups and sandwiches to main dishes such as mountain trout and elk steak.

ℹ Information

Eidfjord Tourist Office (53 67 34 00; www. visiteidfjord.no; Simadalsvegen 3; ⊙9am-7pm Mon-Fri, 10am-6pm Sat & Sun mid-Jun–mid-Aug, 10am-5pm Mon-Fri mid-Aug–mid-Jun)

ℹ Getting There & Away

BUS
Skyss (p174) Bus 991/990 (seven to nine daily Monday to Friday, five to seven on weekends) travels from Øvre Eidfjord to Eidfjord (19kr, 10 minutes), Kinsarvik (93kr, 50 minutes), Lofthus (115kr, one hour) and Odda (195kr, 1½ hours).

In the opposite direction, some buses run to Geilo (242kr, 80 minutes, one or two daily), where you can catch the train on to Bergen.

CAR & MOTORCYCLE
The spectacular, and often very windy, Hardanger Bridge (the longest tunnel-to-tunnel suspension bridge in the world), joins Bruravik and Brimnes, just west of Eidford along the Rv7/13.

Kinsarvik

POP 3382
The towns of Kinsarvik and nearby Lofthus rest peacefully on the shore of Sørfjorden, an offshoot of Hardangerfjord in the heart of a region known as Ullensvang, home to an estimated half a million fruit trees.

Kinsarvik wasn't always so serene – it was home to up to 300 Vikings from the 8th to 11th centuries. The small U-shaped patch of greenery opposite the Kinsarvik tourist office is all that remains of the former Viking port. Kinsarvik offers an appealing access trail past the four cooling Husedalen waterfalls, along what's known as the Monk's Stairway, and onto the network of tracks through the wild forest of Hardangervidda National Park.

If driving here from the north side of the fjord, you'll get to use the **Hardanger Bridge**, completed in 2013, and the longest tunnel-to-tunnel suspension bridge in the world. Otherwise most people arrive by cruise ship.

◉ Sights

Kinsarvik Stone Church   CHURCH
Built in around 1180, this is one of Norway's oldest stone churches. It was restored in the 1960s; the walls still bear traces of lime-and-chalk paintings depicting Michael the Archangel weighing souls while the devil tries to tip the scales. According to local legend, the church was built by Scottish invaders on the site of an earlier stave church.

🛏 Sleeping & Eating

Ringøy Camping   COTTAGE $$
(53 66 39 17; www.ringoy-camping.no; Ringøy; campsites for 2 people 200kr, cabins 800-950kr; ⊙May-Sep; P 🤶) This is a super campsite on a grassy, spacious site overlooking Hardangerfjord, 10km north of Kinsarvik. There's free wood for making campfires, and you're welcome to borrow the campsite's rowboat to explore the fjord. There's also a pretty former crofter's cabin a little way up the hill that sleeps six, with a proper kitchen, washing machine and heated bathroom.

First Hotel Kinsarvik   HOTEL $$
(53 66 74 00; www.firsthotels.com; Kinsarvik; r 1295-1845kr) This hulking hotel seems out of all proportion in little Kinsarvik, but it's a mainstay of the tour-bus circuit. There are 68 rooms in all, half overlooking the fjord, the other half overlooking the mountains. Inoffensive creams and beiges are the colour palette here; it's comfy enough for an overnight, but nothing longer.

★**Gløyp**   CAFE $$
(928 55 094; www.gloyp.no; Kinsarvik; mains 189-289kr; ⊙11.30am-10pm) This fjordside diner is a real find, offering fresh, well-executed food in a bright space, filled with colourful furniture and an open-plan kitchen. Mains change regularly, but there's a good selection of salads, fish dishes, steaks, burgers and pizzas, with delicious desserts and Italian gelato to follow.

ℹ Information

Kinsarvik Tourist Office (53 66 31 12; www. visitullensvang.no; Kinsarvik Brygge; ⊙8.30am-5.30pm Mon-Fri, 10am-4.30pm Sat, 11.30am-

4.30pm Sun Jul & Aug, shorter hours rest of year)

ℹ Getting There & Away

The Rv7 and Rv13 run directly from Eidfjord to Kinsarvik.

BOAT

Norled (p173) runs a regular car ferry between Kinsarvik and Utne (adult/child 42/21kr, car 115kr, hourly Monday to Friday, six on weekends). The crossing takes about 30 minutes.

There's also a daily passenger-only tourist boat in summer to Eidfjord, Ulvik and Norheimsund, although it's more for sightseeing than getting anywhere fast as it stops for three hours in Eidfjord.

BUS

Skyss (p174) Bus 991/990 (81kr, 35 to 50 minutes, seven to nine daily Monday to Friday, five to seven on weekends) travels from Eidfjord to Kinsarvik, before continuing on to Odda (93kr, 55 minutes to 1¼ hours).

Lofthus

POP 556

There's precious little to see in the village of Lofthus, save for a good-looking church and a surfeit of fruit farms. Still, it makes a useful base as you travel along the fjord between Eidfjord and Odda, and on a sunny day it's a rather lovely drive.

◉ Sights

Lofthus Church   CHURCH
(⊙10am-7pm late May–mid-Aug) This stone church dates back to 1250 (although the tower was added in the 1880s) and has some fine stained-glass windows. It's surrounded by an atmospheric cemetery containing some graves from the Middle Ages.

Grieg's Hut   NOTABLE BUILDING
(⊙24hr) The one-time retreat of Norwegian composer Edvard Grieg is in the garden of Hotel Ullensvang.

🛏 Sleeping & Eating

Hardanger Hostel B&B   HOSTEL $
(☑53 67 14 00; www.hardangerhostel.no; r 650-950kr) With flags flying outside, an impressive, multi-windowed frontage and a fine aerial view over Hardangerfjord, this big hostel makes a good budget base. Inside it's institutional: rooms (all twins) are sparse, but the fjordside ones have a cracking view. Only the pricier ones are en suite, however,

and the old building can be a bit noisy and draughty.

Lofthus Camping   CAMPGROUND $
(☑53 66 13 64; www.lofthuscamping.com; Lofthus; tent or caravan sites for 2 people 225kr, 2-/4-bed cabins from 495/625kr; P🔁📶⛵) A well-equipped campsite with front-row views of the fjord, and there's plenty of space for camping and caravans. Older cabins are traditional and supercute, and there are also fancier apartments that sleep up to six people. You're welcome to help yourself to cherries, plums, pears and apples from the campsite's orchards.

Ullensvang Gjesteheim   GUESTHOUSE $$
(☑53 66 12 36; www.ullensvang-gjesteheim. no; Ullensvang; s/d/f with shared bathroom from 540/1090/1490kr; ⊙May–mid-Sep; P📶) This lovingly refurbished fjordside farmhouse makes a cosy night's sleep. Clad in wood and dotted with little white windows, it's cute as a button, and while the rooms are plain, they're decent value. Five of the bedrooms are en suite, while the other six share bathrooms, and there's also a holiday house.

The downstairs **restaurant** serves a small traditional menu (mains 159kr to 240kr) as well as a large selection of Thai dishes (125kr to 165kr), either to eat in or take away.

Hotel Ullensvang   HISTORIC HOTEL $$$
(☑53 67 00 00; www.hotel-ullensvang.no; Lofthus; r 1550-2555kr, ste 3455kr; P📶📶⛵) This enormous fjord-facing establishment dates back to 1846, although it's now essentially a modern resort hotel. It has terrific views, supremely comfortable rooms and a good restaurant. There's almost nothing you can't do here: it has a sauna, swimming pool, gym, golf simulator, tennis and squash courts, and boat rental. But somehow, it all feels a bit soulless.

ℹ Information

Lofthus Tourist Office (☑457 85 822; www. visitullensvang.no; Rv13, Lofthus; ⊙11am-7pm mid-Jun–mid-Aug)

ℹ Getting There & Away

The Rv13 runs through Lofthus on its way from Eidfjord to Odda.

Skyss (p174) Bus 991/990 travels from Eidfjord to Lofthus (104kr, one hour, seven to nine daily Monday to Friday, five to seven on weekends) before continuing to Odda (69kr, 35 minutes). It's about an hour's journey in each direction, but note that at the time of writing, there were major works to the road south of Lofthus, so expect delays until the work is completed.

BERGEN & THE SOUTHWESTERN FJORDS LOFTHUS

Utne

One of the most serene, picturesque villages you'll find in Hardangerfjord, Utne is famous for its fruit-growing and its pristine traditional streets. It's also the jumping-off point for one of the region's most enchanting drives.

◉ Sights

Hardanger Folk Museum   MUSEUM
(☑474 79 884; www.hardangerogvossmuseum. no; Fergekai; adult/child 90kr/free; ◔10am-5pm May-Aug, 10am-3pm Mon-Fri Sep-Apr) This excellent open-air museum is a repository for the cultural heritage of the Hardanger region. Wander through its collection of historic homes, boats, shops, outhouses and a school, and explore exhibitions that document the exquisite local folk costume and embroidery, wedding rituals, the famed Hardanger fiddle and fiddle-making, fishing and orchard keeping. There's also a cafe with home-baked cakes.

⊨ Sleeping

Hardanger Gjestegård   GUESTHOUSE $$
(☑53 66 67 10; www.hardanger-gjestegard.no; Alsåker; s/d 895/1290kr) Dating from 1898, this chocolate-box guesthouse feels like sleeping inside a museum, with handpainted furniture, wood-panelled walls and cabin beds straight out of a Grimm Brothers fairy tale. Once a fruit-and-juice processing factory, it's a lovely, old-fashioned place to stay; some rooms are in the original house, others in an annex. It's 10km west of Utne on Fv550.

★Utne Hotel   HISTORIC HOTEL $$$
(☑53 66 64 00; www.utnehotel.no; Utne; s/d 1520/1930kr; ℗) ✦ The historic wooden Utne Hotel was built in 1722 after the Great Nordic War, giving it claim to the title of Norway's oldest hotel, and has an interesting lineage of female hoteliers. Rooms have a simple elegance that harks back to another time, although bathrooms are smart and modern. The restaurant is excellent; staying on half-board (525kr) is recommended.

❶ Getting There & Away

Utne is on the minor Rv550, 45km north of Odda and 35km northeast of Jondal.

Ferries run regularly from Utne to Kinsarvik (adult/child 42/21kr, car with driver 115kr, hourly Monday to Friday, six on weekends) and Kvanndal (38/19kr, car with driver 102kr, 20 minutes, half-hourly Sunday to Friday, hourly on Saturday).

Odda

POP 7006

After a few days gallivanting around pretty fjord towns, post-industrial Odda comes as something of a shock. Historically an important iron-smelting town, its industrial past has left Odda looking a little built-up and down-at-heel, but it makes an eminently practical base for exploring Folgefonna National Park (p194) and embarking on the trek up to Trolltunga, and there are plenty of companies that can help guide your adventures.

◉ Sights

★Trolltunga   VIEWPOINT
A slender spur of rock projecting into the void above Lake Ringedalsvatnet, Trolltunga is one of Norway's most-photographed features, and – along with Preikestolen – one of the country's most popular hiking targets. The Troll's Tongue is an epic sight, but it's a tough hike of 23km, or 10 hours return, from the trailhead at Skjeggedal, 13km northeast of Odda.

The hike is usually doable from late May to early September, depending on snowfall. The trail is well marked from the car park, with distance markers along the route outlining the distance to the summit – but the ascent is brutal in places, covering a total climb of about 1000m, so make 100% sure you're in adequate shape and have the proper gear before you decide to tackle it. En route, watch out for the **Tyssestrengene waterfall** (646m).

If you want to tackle the walk earlier in the season, or you'd just prefer to hike with a pro, Trolltunga Active (p193) offers guided hikes. You definitely won't be alone at the top – Trolltunga is one of Norway's most Instagrammed sights – but standing on the rock and staring out into thin air is worth every step to the top.

If you continue on beyond Trolltunga, you reach another fine vantage point, you reach **Preikestolen** (Pulpit Rock), a smaller version of the much more famous lookout of the same name overlooking Lysefjord, near Stavanger.

In July and August, Tide (www.tide.no) runs an express coach once a day between Tyssedal and the real Preikestolen car park near Stavanger, allowing you to summit both of Norway's most famous climbs in just a couple of days. It costs 695kr one way.

Norwegian Museum for Hydroelectric Power & Industry   MUSEUM
(Tyssedal Hydroelectric Power Station; ☑53 65 00 60; www.nvim.no; Naustbakken 7, Tyssedal; adult/

child 90kr/free; ⊙10am-5pm mid-May–Aug, 10am-3pm Tue-Fri Sep–mid-May) A tour around a hydroelectric power station might not sound that promising, but this is one industrial landmark that's worth a detour. The Tysso 1 power plant was constructed between 1906 and 1918 by Thorvald Astrup, who blended classical European architecture with austere, functionalist lines. It's a striking monument to industrial ambition, and can be explored on a guided tour.

🏃 Activities

For hikes of up to six hours around town, pick up the helpful brochure *Hikes in Odda*, or the more detailed *Hiking and Biking – Odda, Røldal, Seljestad, Tyssedal* from the tourist office.

Trolltunga Active OUTDOORS
(📞908 24 572; www.trolltunga-active.com) This excellent outdoors company offers a huge range of high-thrill activities around Odda. Their staple is a guided hike up Trolltunga (900kr), which is also available in a sunrise- or sunset-watch (2900kr). They also operate a heart-in-the-mouth zipline and, occasionally, an even more heart-in-the-mouth bungee jump.

If hiking's not your thing, they also run kayaking, mountain-biking and rafting trips, as well as speedboat rides and an overnight wilderness camp.

🛏 Sleeping

Odda Camping CAMPGROUND $
(📞413 21 610; www.oddacamping.no; Eide; tent/caravan sites 150/160kr, cabins 590-1790kr; ⊙mid-May–Aug; 🛜) A selection of campsites, rooms and huts are on offer here, in a pleasant location on the shores of Sandvinvatnet lake, a 20-minute uphill walk south of the town centre, a distance of about 1km.

Trolltunga Hotel GUESTHOUSE $$
(📞55 09 28 00; www.trolltungahotel.no; Vasstun 1; dm 450kr, s 820-1105kr, d 1045-1570kr, tr 1475kr; P🛜) You could do way worse than this simple but proper hotel, which offers a full room range: dorms, singles, doubles and triples, all attractively finished in fjord-blue tones, with touches like bedside tables made from logs and little framed pictures on the walls. It's worth upgrading to the Petite Lofts and Double Plus rooms for the stunning lake views. Note that some rooms share bathrooms.

There are good meals available from 5pm in the restaurant (mains from 189kr).

Tyssedal Hotel HOTEL $$$
(📞53 64 00 00; www.tyssedalhotel.no; Tyssedal; s 1190-1290kr, d 1690-2290kr, f 2490-3390kr; P🛜) Built in 1913, the art deco Tyssedal Hotel has terrific rooms with parquet floors and stylish fittings. Norwegian ghosts seem to have a penchant for hotels – here Eidfjord artist Nils Bergslien 'visits' the ground and 3rd floors; his earthly legacy, some fantastic fairy-tale and Hardangerfjord landscape paintings, also grace the hotel.

The restaurant is Odda's best, serving Norwegian staples (mains 199kr to 329kr).

ℹ Information

Tourist Office (📞53 65 40 05; www.visitodda. com; Torget 2; ⊙9am-7pm mid-Jun–mid-Aug, shorter hours May & Sep)

ℹ Getting There & Away

Odda is 70km south of Eidfjord on Rv13.

Skyss (p174) Bus 991/990 (seven to nine daily Monday to Friday, five to seven on weekends) travels to Eidfjord (195kr, 1½ hours) and Voss (207kr, two hours).

For travel to Oslo, take the **Nor-Way** (p173) Haukeliekspressen 930 bus (477kr, three daily, seven hours). Change at Seljestad.

Røldal

POP 359
Located 22km southeast of Odda, the small town of Røldal is worth a stop for its fine stave church, but there's not much going on outside ski season.

⊙ Sights & Activities

Røldal Stave Church CHURCH
(www.roldal.com; Røldal; ⊙9am-5pm Jul & Aug) This 13th-century stave church's wooden cross, according to local legend, sweats every midsummer's eve; the sweat is said to have healing powers. The church was an important place of pilgrimage in the Middle Ages.

Røldal Skisenter SKIING
(www.roldal.com; Rv13; ⊙Dec-Apr) This ski station offers ultra-deep snow and a long season for downhill, cross-country and backcountry skiers, and in summer there are hiking and biking trails.

🛏 Sleeping

★ Energihotellet BOUTIQUE HOTEL
(📞51 20 05 55; www.energihotellet.no; Øvre Kilen, Nesflaten; r from 1475kr; P✳🛜) Now here's something you don't get to do every day

WORTH A TRIP

JONDAL DRIVE

While there's no heart-in-mouth hairpin bends, high passes or deep, dark fjords to stir the soul, the gentle drive along the **Rv550** from Utne to Jondal is one of Norway's most delightful, especially in late spring or early summer. The road hugs the fjord the whole way, passing through orchards and by fisherman's shacks and tiny beaches. There's plenty of 'come hither' rocky outcrops for picnics, lolls in the sun or a paddle. In Hereiane, smooth rock rises straight up from the fjord to the peaks above and a small service building built entirely from natural stone sits on a brilliant yellow plinth. The ferry from Jondal takes you back to Norheimsund, but, before you depart, make time for a waffle at the boat-shed kiosk and a wander around the town's Swiss-style cottages. Or continue on to Rosendal or Odda via the Jondalstunnelen.

– sleep in a disused 1960s power station. Designed by architect Geir Grung as part of the Røldal-Suldal hydropower plant, this brutalist building has been reinvented as a boutique hotel, with clean, minimal design echoing the stark, concrete structure. Rooms are stylish and most overlook Suldalsvatnet Lake.

There's an excellent New Nordic restaurant, as well as a sauna and an outdoor heated pool in summer. The hotel is near the village of Nesflaten, about 28km south of Røldal.

Hordatun Hotel   HOTEL **$$**
(☑93 45 02 93; www.hordatun.no; s 1190-1550kr, d 1390-1890kr; P🐕) You can't possibly miss this striking hotel, a concrete curve laid out in a horseshoe shape with balconies overlooking Lake Røldalsvatnet. It's an uncompromisingly modern structure that won't be to everyone's taste, but the views are fantastic, and the rooms are smart, if slightly functional: basic furniture, wood floors, plate-glass windows. Suites and loft rooms come with cool mezzanines. There's also a decent restaurant downstairs (mains 199kr to 299kr).

ℹ Getting There & Away

Nor-Way (p173) Haukeliekspressen 930 bus (447kr, three daily, seven hours) stops in Røldal on its way south to Oslo.

Folgefonna National Park

Established in 2005, this 545-sq-km national park encompasses mainland Norway's third-largest icefield. The Folgefonn icecap covers 168 sq km and the ice is up to 400m thick in places. It's a dramatic, beautiful place, with glaciers snaking down the heights of nearby valleys.

🏃 Activities

The most popular way to explore Folgefonna is on a glacier hike. Flat Earth (p189), based in Øvre Eidfjord, and Folgefonni Breførarlag, based in Jondal, are the companies to speak to. The hikes are suitable for anyone in good physical condition with warm clothing and sturdy footwear.

For an excellent online guide to hiking on the fringes of Folgefonna, visit www.visitsunnhordland.no and look for the 'Fancy a Walk?' page, where there are links to route descriptions and downloadable maps.

★**Folgefonni Breførarlag**   HIKING
(☑55 29 89 21; www.folgefonni-breforarlag.no; Jondal; ☉mid-Jun–mid-Aug, on request at other times) The highly professional Folgefonni Breførarlag has a range of glacier hikes that set out in summer from the Fonna Glacier Ski Resort (p194) and hike onto the glaciers. The advantage of doing the walk here is the promise of exceptional views, although you do have to hike across the snow to reach the glacier.

Fonna Glacier Ski Resort   SKIING
(☑461 72 011; www.folgefonn.no; Jondal; ☉9am-4pm May-Oct) It's possible to do summer skiing, snowboarding and sledding from May until October, although the season can finish earlier. You can visit the resort by public transport from Bergen, Jondal or Norheimsund; see the resort website for details.

ℹ Information

Folgefonna National Park Centre (☑53 48 42 80; www.folgefonna.info; Skålakaien, Rosendal; ☉10am-7pm Jun-Aug)

Jondal Tourist Office (☑53 66 85 31; www.visitjondal.no; Fv550, Jondal; ☉9.30am-4pm Jun, 9.30am-6pm Jul & Aug)

ℹ Getting There & Away

The easiest access to the national park is from Jondal.

There are two direct buses from Odda to Jondal; the 980 (173kr, 2½ hours, two daily), which runs around the edge of the fjord via Utne, and the early morning 930 (104kr, 45 minutes, daily), which travels through the Jondal tunnel. To get to the national park, there's a daily, summer-only bus from Jondal to the Fonna Glacier Ski Resort, leaving Jondal at 9.45am; if you take the first 930 or 980 of the day, you'll get to Jondal in time to make it.

Rosendal

POP 944

Separated from the rest of Hardangerfjord by high mountains and the Folgefonna National Park, Rosendal sits picturesquely by the fjord with a backdrop of high hills. Access to the national park is easier from Odda and Jondal, but Rosendal has a good park centre and is a worthwhile destination in its own right.

◉ Sights

Baroniet Rosendal HISTORIC BUILDING
(☑ 53 48 29 99; www.baroniet.no; Rosendal; admission with guided tour adult/child 150/50kr, gardens only 75/25kr; ⊗ 10am-5pm Jul–mid-Aug, 11am-4pm mid-May–Jul & mid-Aug–mid-Sep) Norway's only baronial mansion dates back to 1665 and sits on a gentle rise above the town. The period interiors include a collection of tapestries, an intact library and beautiful examples of Meissen and Royal Danish porcelain. Outside there is a stunning Renaissance rose garden. Admission to the manor includes a guided tour, and in summer there are evening concerts.

To make a day of it, stop in for lunch at the delightful restored greenhouse (mains 179kr to 289kr). For something really special, you can also book for a three- or five-course feast in the manor's lavish Blue Dining Room.

The manor also offers accommodation in the farm annexe.

Steinparken PARK
🖉 Signposted off the road running to Baroniet Rosendal (p195), this intriguing little open-air gallery has rock monoliths from the Folgefonna region that have been sculpted and smoothed to stunning effect to show the region's geological diversity; some of it is the work of contemporary artist Bård Breivik. A path runs from an antique sawmill up through the park.

⌲ Tours

Rødne Fjord Cruise BOATING
(☑ 51 89 52 70; www.rodne.no; Skalafjæro; adult/child 870/440kr) This ferry company offers a daily cruise from Bergen, including a visit to Baroniet Rosendal and a two-course lunch at the greenhouse restaurant.

On weekdays, the ferry departs Bergen at 8.50am and arrives at Rosendal at 10.45am, returning at 2.25pm for arrival at 4.20pm. On weekends, it's 11am from Bergen arriving at 12.55pm, returning at 4.35pm and arriving at 6pm.

🛌 Sleeping

Sundal Camping CAMPGROUND $
(☑ 53 48 41 86; www.sundalcamping.no; Sundalsvegen 641; campsites for 2 adults 190kr, cabins 480-680kr; 🅿 🛜) Rosendal hasn't got its own campsite, so the next best thing is this pleasant site in Sundal, 28km northeast. If you've stayed on a Norwegian campsite before, you know the drill: small, medium and large huts, plus mixed tent-and-caravan camping.

Rosendal Turisthotell GUESTHOUSE $$
(☑ 53 47 36 66; www.rosendalturisthotell.no; Skålagato 17; s/d with shared bathroom from 850/990kr; 🅿 🛜) Opposite the quay, this handsome house dates from 1887, and it looks like it could be straight off a Norwegian postcard – all gables, balconies and clapboard cladding, framed against the mountains. But inside it's surprisingly modern: rooms are light and white, with careful furniture choices, antique beds and rustic textiles, although all have to share a bathroom. Corner rooms have both space and views.

Baroniet Rosendal FARMSTAY $$
(☑ 53 48 29 99; www.baroniet.no; Rosendal; s/d with shared bathroom 700/980kr; ⊗ May-Aug; 🅿) Just outside the grounds of the Baroniet Rosendal, this rambling farmhouse has attractive rooms with wrought-iron bedsteads and shared bathrooms. Dinner is available and is served in the farmhouse's large kitchen; the three-course menu (490kr) changes daily and utilises fruit, vegetables and herbs from the garden.

🍴 Eating

Martha Meidell NORWEGIAN $$
(☑ 53 47 36 66; Rosendal Touristhotel; lunch dishes 169-189kr, mains 255-325kr; ⊗ lunch 1-4pm, dinner 7-10pm) You'll struggle to find dinner in Rosendal, so be glad there's a great restaurant at the Rosendal Turisthotell. The menu changes regularly, but fish, meat and game, partnered with locally grown fruit

AROUND ROSENDAL

Sundal

At Sundal, 4km west of the tunnel, take the road up the Sundal valley (driveable for 1km), then walk 2km on a good track to lake Bondhusvatnet, where there's a wonderful view of the glacier **Bondhusbreen**. This is also a trail head for some fine hikes.

Uskedalen

In Uskedalen, 14km west of Rosendal, there's an extraordinary rock-slab mountain, Ulvenåso (1247m), offering some of the best rock climbing in Norway; contact the tourist office in Rosendal (p196) for details.

Møsevatnet

One of the prettiest (and quietest) roads in this part of Norway climbs up to the dam at Møsevatnet, from where there are good views to one of the glacier arms of the Folgefonna icecap. Take the Rv48 south of Rosendal and turn off to the southwest at Dimmelsvik; the road is signposted to Fjellhaugen, Matre and Åkra. From the road junction that signposts Matre and Åkra to the right, follow the signs left to Blådal and the winter-only Fjellhaugen Skisenter; later ignore the signs to the ski centre. From this road junction, the narrow but well-paved road climbs up through some glorious wooded, rocky hills, studded with lakes and dams.

and veg, all feature heavily. There are usually a couple of mains options for dinner, with a simpler lunch menu of meatballs, fish quenelles and the like.

Påfyll Snikkeriet   NORWEGIAN $$
(📞 414 06 991; www.snikkeriet.no; mains 150-220kr; ⊘noon-10pm Sun-Thu, noon-1am Fri & Sat Easter-Aug) Snikkeriet is known for its well-priced home-cooked Norwegian meals, including fjord trout and local sausages. It also hosts popular evening gigs.

ⓘ Information

Rosendal Tourist Office & Folgefonna National Park Centre (📞 53 48 42 80; www.visitsunn hordland.no; Skålakaien; ⊘10am-6pm Jun-Aug, 10am-3pm May & Sep)

ⓘ Getting There & Away

Rødne Fjord Cruise (p195) runs a daily return service with lunch and tour from Bergen.

Bus 770 (47kr, 1 hour, six daily) runs to Odda via Sunndal.

Rosendal can be reached via an 11km-long road tunnel (car 90kr, free midnight to 6am) under the icefield from Odda; Rosendal is 32km along the coast from the tunnel entrance/exit. There is also a tunnel connection from Jondal.

If you're heading south towards Haugesund or Stavanger, the E39 is the fastest route and includes the Rannavik–Skjersholmane ferry (car with driver 167kr). However, the route via the Utåker–Skånevik ferry (115kr) is cheaper.

HAUGALANDET

North and east of Stavanger lies a region of low-lying hills and coastal inlets and islands reminiscent of the northern Scottish isles. Happy Haugesund is the regional capital.

The region carries huge historical significance for Norwegians. It was in the nearby Hafrsfjord that the decisive battle took place in 872 and Norway was first unified. As such, the area bills itself as 'Norway's Birthplace'.

Haugesund

POP 36,538

The North Sea port of Haugesund lies beyond the well-trodden west coast routes. It was historically an important herring fishing port, and a safe harbour for ships travelling up and down the sound. These days, like many west coast towns, it's switched to the petroleum industry, but don't let that deter you – it's an attractive, lively town, with most of the interest revolving around the harbourside. There are some good bars and restaurants to investigate down by the waterfront, and lovely Karmøy island is only a short trip away.

⊙ Sights

Utsira   ISLAND
Around 18km west of Haugesund, the tiny island of Utsira barely covers 6 sq km and is home to just 235 people, but its size belies its reputation in the twitching world. It's a birdwatching hot spot, with more than

310 species observed here – twitchers travel from all across Europe, especially during the migration seasons. A ferry (www.rutebaaten utsira.no; adult/child single 79/40kr) runs daily from Haugesund harbour.

Haraldshaugen   MONUMENT
(Haraldshaugvegen) The burial site of Viking King Harald Fairhair, the first king of a unified Norway, is 1.5km north of Haugesund. The obelisk memorial, erected in 1872, commemorates the decisive 872 Battle of Hafrsfjord, which effectively led to Harald's conquest of western Norway.

Marilyn Monroe Memorial   MONUMENT
Bizarrely, Haugesund claims to be the ancestral home of Marilyn Monroe, whose father, a local baker, emigrated from here to the USA. This monument on the quay, next to the Scandic Maritim Hotel, is suitably coquettish, if not a great likeness. It commemorates the 30th anniversary of her death in 1962.

☞ Tours

The tourist office (p198) organises a comprehensive range of tours, from a guided walk around the town hall, to coastal boat trips to view historic lighthouses and visit remote island communities.

Ravnafloke RIB Island Tour   BOATING
(☑ 52 80 43 98; www.ravnafloke.no; Smedasundet 77; 540kr per person) This is a great way to explore the coastline, islands and lighthouses around Haugesund – at high speed in an inflatable rigid-hulled inflatable boat (RIB). There's a 12-person minimum to run the tours: ask at the tourist office (p197) or give them a call to see when the next tour you can join is.

✾ Festivals & Events

Silda Jazz   MUSIC
(Haugesund International Jazz Festival; www.silda jazz.no; ☉ early–mid-Aug) Well-respected music festival with international jazz, soul, folk and indie acts.

Norwegian International Film Festival   FILM
(www.filmweb.no/filmfestivalen; ☉ mid–late Aug) Norway's major film festival, considered to be the Nordic Cannes.

⌂ Sleeping

★**Clarion Collection**
Hotel Banken   DESIGN HOTEL **$$**
(☑ 52 70 00 30; www.nordicchoicehotels.com; Strandgata 161; s 960kr, d 1190-1690kr, ste 1990kr;

☎) This is, hands-down, the best place to stay in Haugesund by some margin. In a grand, turn-of-the-century stone building, rooms here are elegant, spacious and comfortable: wooden floors and super views across Smedasunden give it a boutiquey feel, even if it is largely aimed at business travellers. Aim for one of the deluxe doubles, with sloping harbour-view skylights.

Scandic Maritim Hotel   HOTEL **$$**
(☑ 52 86 30 00; www.hotelmaritim.no; Åsbygaten 3; s 875-1175kr, d 1175-1575kr, f 1325-2500kr; P ☎) This sprawling Scandic has one huge selling point: it's got the best spot of any hotel in town, right by the harbour and its haul of lively bars and restaurants. It's not the most beautiful structure, but rooms are pleasant, with maritime colours and glassed-in balconies that can be sealed in high winds.

Scandic Haugesund   HOTEL **$$**
(☑ 21 61 41 00; www.scandichotels.com; Kirkegata 166; r 1199-1699kr; ☎) A reliable, glass-fronted hotel that's largely frequented by corporate travellers, but that doesn't make it any less comfortable. Rooms are from the standard Scandic mould: sleek, uncluttered and generic, but the bathrooms are good, and upper floors have views over town.

✕ Eating

Brasserie Brakstad   GASTROPUB **$$**
(☑ 52 70 00 50; www.brasseriebrakstad.no; Kaigata 2; lunch mains 119-295kr, dinner mains 245-335kr; ☉ 11am-1.30pm Mon-Fri, noon-1.30am Sat, 1-11pm Sun) The pick of the places to eat along the harbourfront is this groovy gastropub, with an industrial, bare-brick interior and lots of tables lined up along the quay just in case the sun shines. It's a great bet for no-fuss gastropub grub: big chunky pepper steaks, bowls of mussels and baked salmon with roasted veg.

Lothes Mat & Vinhus   BURGERS **$$$**
(☑ 52 71 22 01; www.lothesmat.no; Skipperga ta 4; 3-course menu 585kr; ☉ 6-10pm Tue-Sat) Tucked up in a little space just off the waterfront, this wood-panelled restaurant is an old Haugesund favourite for solid Norwegian cuisine – not least thanks to its sweet terrace overlooking the harbour. it also has a more casual space next door, **Himla Godt**, where you get burgers, grilled meat, fish soup and the like (mains 119kr to 189kr).

BERGEN & THE SOUTHWESTERN FJORDS HAUGESUND

To Glass SCANDINAVIAN $$$
(52 70 74 00; www.toglass.no; Strandgata 169; mains 260-350kr; ☺3-11pm Mon-Fri, to midnight Sat) A popular after-work spot for hungry Hauge-sunds, this small upstairs restaurant is a little bit away from the harbour. It serves hearty food and plates of tapas to share in a swish, upscale space.

🍷 Drinking & Nightlife

Totalen CAFE
(482 48 577; www.totalen.no; Haraldsgata 173; ☺9am-6pm Mon-Sat, 10.30am-4pm Sun) This cafe has the town's best coffee, with beans from Jacu and delicious scones and biscuits. The interesting shopfront space is, in fact, an old theatre that is used by the Pionerkirken for Sunday services.

🛍 Shopping

Amundsen Spesial FOOD
(916 30 816; www.amundsenspesial.no; Skippergata 5; ☺9am-5pm Mon-Sat) This upmarket deli is filled to the brim with tempting treats: home-smoked salmon, Norwegian cheeses, cured sausages and chocolates and nuts by the tonne – as well as a range of imported products like Italian olive oil and French wine.

ⓘ Information

Haugesund Tourist Office (☑52 01 08 30; www.visithaugesund.no; Strandgata 171; ☺9am-5pm Mon-Fri, 10am-4pm Sat & Sun mid-Jun–Aug, 10am-4.30pm Mon-Fri Sep-May)

ⓘ Getting There & Away

Haugesund is 82km north of Stavanger and 18km south of Bergen. The main E39 connects all three towns, via several car ferries en route.

AIR
Haugesund Airport (☑52 85 79 00; www.avinor.no/en/airport/haugesund-airport; Helganesvegen 350, Karmøy island) is 13km southwest of the city.

SAS (p173) and **Norwegian** (p173) both fly regularly from Oslo.

Ryanair (www.ryanair.com) runs direct services to London, Bremen and other European cities.

Widerøe (p173) has flights from Bergen from Monday to Friday, and a daily direct route to Copenhagen.

Flybussen (Flybussen; www.flybussen.no/haugesund; one-way adult 100kr) runs a shuttle bus from the airport that connects with incoming flights.

BOAT
Ferries to Utsira Island run daily from Haugesund's quay.

BUS
Stavanger is serviced by an hourly express-bus service (300kr; two hours, 10 minutes) operated by **Kystbussen/Nor-Way** (www.kystbussen.no).

CAR & MOTORCYCLE
There's plenty of on-street parking around Hauge-sund, which is metered until 3pm; after that, you can park for free.

Travelling south towards Stavanger, you'll need to catch the ferry between Arsvågen and Morta-vika (www.fjord1.no; adult/child/car 6/23/185kr; half-hourly).

Karmøy Island

Low-lying Karmøy island is blessed with natu-ral beauty: besides a number of exquisite pale-sand beaches, it crams in forests, marshes, heather uplands and lakes. Culturally it's no slouch either, with a number of significant historical sites, pretty wooden villages and, in early June, a spirited Viking Festival (p199).

History

The island of Karmøy has strong links with Norway's Viking past. The settlement at Av-aldsnes was where Harald Hårfagre (Harald Fairhair) established his royal seat after win-ning an important battle at Hafrsfjord in AD 872 that effectively laid the foundations for the unified kingdom of Nordvegen. Avaldsnes remained a seat of power until 1450.

◎ Sights

St Olav's Church CHURCH
(www.olavskirken.no; Avaldsnes; adult/child 100/50kr; ☺1pm-3.30pm Sun-Tue Jun-Aug) This ancient stone church was built under the reign of King Håkon Håkonsson. Work began in 1250, although it's thought that a much earlier wooden chapel here stood here for many years before. Dedicated to St Olav, it's a fascinating relic of Viking architecture – and an important navigation aid for sailors. Guid-ed tours visit the interior in summer.

The church used to be surrounded by sev-eral stone obelisks, although now only one – an impressive 7.2m slab known as the Virgin Mary's Needle – still stands. It's leaning peri-lously towards the church wall, and legend suggests that when it actually touches the wall the Day of Judgement is at hand.

Nordvegen Historiesenter MUSEUM

(☑52 81 24 00; www.vikinggarden.no; Avaldsnes; adult/child 110/50kr, 150/50kr Jun-Aug; ☉10am-4pm Mon-Fri, 11am-4pm Sat, noon-5pm Sun Jun-Aug, shorter hours rest of year) Down a short path from the car park for St Olav's Church (p198), this history centre recreates the story of Harald Fairhair and other monarchs of the newly unified Nordvegen from the 10th century onwards. Also nearby, on a tiny forested island is a reconstructed Viking farm – it's great for kids, with staff in period dress.

Skudeneshavn HISTORIC SITE

The wonderful Skudeneshavn, 37km south of Haugesund, got very rich on the herring trade in the 19th century and is known for its 'Empire-style' wooden houses, winding main street Søragadå and pretty gardens. There's a number of year-round cafes and a tourist office next to the quay.

Avaldsnes Viking Farm FARM

(☑52 81 24 00; www.opplevavaldsnes.no; Avaldsnes; adult/child 150/50kr incl Nordvegen Historiesenter; ☉noon-4.30pm late Jun–mid-Aug; ⚙) This living history centre brings Viking culture to life, with a number of reconstructed Viking buildings, and regular displays of handicrafts, metalwork, farming and woodwork during the summer – not to mention guides dressed in full Viking regalia. It's only open in summer.

Visnes Grubeområde MUSEUM

(☑906 02 472; visnes.gruvemuseum@gmail.com; Visnes; adult/child 60kr/free; ☉noon-4pm Mon-Fri & Sun Jul-mid-Aug, Sun only late Jun & early Sep) From 1865 to 1972, the village of Visnes, 4km west of Avaldsnes, was home to the largest and most sophisticated copper mine in Norway. Over its lifetime, more than 4 million tonnes of copper, zinc and sulfur were extracted here – some of which was used to build the Statue of Liberty. This small museum explores the mine's history.

Karmoy Fishery Museum MUSEUM

(Karmøy Fiskerimuseum; ☑41334389; www.fiskerimuseum.net; Vedavågen; adult/child 30/10kr; ☉11am-4pm Mon-Fri, 2-6pm Sun Jun–mid-Aug) In Vedavågen, on the island's west coast, this striking museum explores the region's modern fishing industry and also has a saltwater aquarium. It's designed by the architectural firm Snøhetta, who also designed the Oslo Opera House and the Snøhetta

viewpoint in Dovrefjell-Sunndalsfjella National Park.

✸ Festivals & Events

Viking Festival CULTURAL

(www.vikingfestivalen.no; ☉Jun) Once a year, this Viking-themed festival brings feasting, boat races and displays of Viking craft, warfare and culture to the east coast of Avaldsnes. Events centre around the Avaldsnes Viking Farm.

⊨ Sleeping

Norneshuset B&B $$

(☑900 59 007; www.norneshuset.no; Nordnes 7, Skudeneshavn; s/d 990/1190kr) This B&B has character-filled rooms right by the harbour and very friendly service; it's located in a former warehouse that was shipped from Riga, Latvia, in the 1830s.

❶ Information

Skudeneshavn Tourist Office (☑52 85 80 00; www.visitkarmoy.no; Kaigata 5, Torget; ☉10am-4pm Mon-Sat, noon-4pm Sun Jun-Aug, open to 5pm in July & Aug)

Avaldsnes Tourist Office (☑52 81 24 00; www.opplevavaldsnes.no; Kong Augvaldsvei 101; ☉10am-4pm Mon-Fri, 11am-4pm Sat, noon-5pm Sun Jun-Aug, shorter hours rest of year)

❶ Getting There & Away

The E134 runs straight from Haugesund to the island; Avaldsnes is 9km south of town. The southernmost town of Skudeshavn is another 28km further south, and can be reached via either Rv47 on the west coast, or Rv511 on the east.

BUS

To reach Avaldsnes from central Haugesund, catch bus 209 or 210 (35kr, 22 minutes, half-hourly) from next to the post office. Bus 210 continues further south to Skudeneshavn (1¼ hours) for the same fare.

STAVANGER

POP 123,369

There's a reason this coastal town has been twinned with Houston and Aberdeen: it's sometimes known as Norway's 'Oil City' for its importance in oil exploration in the North Sea since the 1970s (Norway's largest oil company, Statoil, is based here). But while much of the outskirts are modern, you won't find too many skyscrapers – Stavanger's old centre has some of the most beautiful and best-preserved wooden buildings anywhere in Norway, many dating back to the 18th century. It's all very pretty, and in summer the waterfront comes alive in the best port-town style.

What Stavanger's oil boom has brought, however, is suburban sprawl and sky-high prices, even for Norway. It's notorious as one of the country's priciest locations, and finding a bed and a bite comes with a hefty price tag.

Nevertheless, it's a perfect launch pad for exploring nearby Lysefjorden, and for tackling the classic hike to Preikestolen (Pulpit Rock).

⊙ Sights

Several of Stavanger's museums offer joint admission: one ticket (adult/child 90/50kr) remains valid for the whole day for entry to the Stavanger Museum (p201), the Stavanger Art Museum, the Canning Museum, the Norwegian Children's Museum, **Stavanger Maritime Museum** (Sjøfartsmuseet; Map p204; ☑51 84 27 00; www.museumstavanger. no; Nedre Strandgate 17-19; adult/child 90/50kr; ☺11am-3pm Tue-Wed & Fri, 11am-7pm Thu, 11am-4pm Sat & Sun), Breidablikk (p201) and Ledaal (p201).

★ Norsk Oljemuseum   MUSEUM
(Oil Museum; Map p204; www.norskolje.museum.no; Kjeringholmen; adult/child 120/60kr; ☺10am-7pm daily Jun-Aug, 10am-4pm Mon-Sat, to 6pm Sun Sep-May; 🚼) Admittedly, the prospect of an 'oil museum' doesn't sound like the most promising prospect for an afternoon out. But this state-of-the-art place is well worth visiting – both for its striking, steel-clad architecture and its high-tech displays exploring the history of North Sea oil exploration. Highlights include the world's largest drill bit, simulated rigs, documentary films, archive testimony and a vast hall of oil-platform models. There are also exhibitions on natural history, energy use and climate change.

The museum nicely balances the technical side of oil exploration and extraction, while honouring those whose working lives have been spent in the industry. The latter is done through fascinating archival material that highlights significant moments in the history of Norwegian oil, including coverage of the *Alexander L Kielland* drilling-rig tragedy in 1980, when 123 oil workers were killed, and the 1972 decision by Norway's parliament that Statoil should be based in Stavanger.

You *will* spend longer here than you planned, especially if you have kids.

★ Gamle Stavanger   AREA
(Map p204) Gamle (Old) Stavanger, above the western shore of the harbour, is a delight. The Old Town's cobblestone walkways pass between rows of late-18th-century white-washed wooden houses, all immaculately kept and adorned with cheerful, well-tended flowerboxes. It well rewards an hour or two's ambling.

★ Canning Museum   MUSEUM
(Map p204; ☑51 84 27 00; www.museum stavanger.no; Øvre Strandgate 88a; adult/child 90/50kr incl other Stavanger museums; ☺11am-5pm Tue-Fri, 11am-4pm Sat & Sun) Don't miss this museum housed in an old cannery: it's one of Stavanger's most entertaining. Before oil, there were sardines, and Stavanger was once home to more than half of Norway's canning factories. By 1922 the city's canneries provided 50% of the town's employment. The exhibits take you through the whole 12-stage process from salting through to threading, smoking, decapitating and packing. Guides are on hand to answer your questions or crank up some of the old machines.

On the first Sunday of every month (plus Tuesday and Thursday from mid-June to mid-August), the fires are lit and you can sample smoked sardines straight from the ovens. An adjoining building houses a cafe and touchingly restored workers' cottages furnished in 1920s (downstairs) and 1960s (upstairs) styles.

Norwegian Children's Museum   MUSEUM
(Norsk Barnemuseum; Map p204; www.stavanger museum.no/en/samling/samling-norsk-barne museum; Muségata 16; adult/child 90/50kr incl other Stavanger museums; ☺10am-4pm; 🚼) Dragging kids round a museum can be a tough proposition, but this is one place that's designed specifically with them in mind. It traces the changing story of childhood through the ages, with a particular emphasis on toys: there are more than 6000 individual items on display here, from antique train sets and spinning tops through to giant dolls and Meccano sets. Many of them were made at Norway's largest toy factory, Lærdal, just outside Stavanger.

Stavanger Kunstmuseum   GALLERY
(Stavanger Art Museum; ☑51 84 27 00; www. stavangerkunstmuseum.no; Henrik Ibsensgate 55;

adult/child 90/50kr incl other Stavanger museums; ⊙10am-4pm Tue-Sun) This museum, 2.5km south of the town centre, displays Norwegian art from the 18th century to the present, including the haunting *Gamle Furutrær* and other landscape paintings by Stavanger's own Lars Hertervig (1830–1902). There's a large collection for other important Norwegian artists too, such as Frida Hansen, Kitty Kielland and Olaf Lange. There's a small sculpture garden outside.

Jernaldergarden   MUSEUM
(www.jernaldergarden.no; Ullandhaugvn 3, Ullandhaug; adult/child 100/50kr, incl entry to Archaeology Museum; ⊙11am-4pm mid-Jun–mid-Aug, 11am-4pm Sun May–mid-Jun & mid-Aug–Oct) Always wanted to experience life on an Iron Age farm c AD 350–550? Then this living exhibition 4km south of town is as close as you'll get. Staff in period dress greet you with cakes cooked over the hearth, and you can watch displays of farming, food preparation, tanning, handicrafts and so on. It's informative and fun.

Stavanger Domkirke   CHURCH
(Map p204; Håkon VIIs gate; 30kr; ⊙9am-6pm Jul & Aug, 9am-4pm May-Jun & Sep, shorter hours rest of year) This beautiful church is an impressive but understated medieval stone cathedral dating from approximately 1125; it was renovated following a fire in 1272 and contains traces of Gothic, baroque, Romanesque and Anglo-Norman influences. Despite restoration in the 1860s and in 1940, and the stripping of some features during the Reformation, the cathedral is, by some accounts, Norway's oldest medieval cathedral still in its original form.

Its interior, with wonderful stone columns, tapestries, elaborate baroque pulpit and stained-glass window depicting the main events of the Christian calendar, is moving.

Stavanger Museum   MUSEUM
(Map p204; ☑51 84 27 00; www.museumstavanger.no; Muségata 16; adult/child 90/50kr incl other Stavanger museums; ⊙10am-4pm daily) Stavanger's main museum was founded in the 19th century, and it's a wide-ranging affair, encompassing everything from Stavanger's history to Viking culture and an array of stuffed animals in the natural history section. It's in a huge, rather gloomy building on Muségata, which was renovated in 2017 to accommodate the Norwegian Children's Museum (p200).

Archaeology Museum   MUSEUM
(Arkeologisk Museum; Map p204; ☑51 84 60 00; www.am.uis.no; Peder Klows gate 30a; adult/child

---

CITY BEACHES

A 20-minute drive south of Stavanger, a number of soft-sand beaches stretch down the coast. Backed by sea-grass spiked dunes and dotted with wooden holiday shacks, they are all incredibly atmospheric, if often on the fresh side. **Sola** sits right near the airport, and has parking and a kiosk, along with the historic **Sola Strand Hotel** (p203). Further along, **Hellestø** and **Bybergsanden** form a gorgeous peaceful continuum: perfect for bracing walks whatever the weather, or a shallows frolic in summer.

50/20kr; ⊙10am-5pm Mon-Fri, 10am-4pm Sat & Sun Jun-Aug, 11am-3pm Wed-Sat, to 8pm Tue Sep-May; 🚻) This museum traces 11,000 years of human history, including the Viking Age. Exhibits include skeletons, tools, a rune stone and a description of the symbiosis between prehistoric humans and their environment. There's a program of activities for kids (eg treasure hunts and wandering Vikings) in summer.

Breidablikk   HISTORIC BUILDING
(Map p204; ☑51 84 27 00; www.breidablikkmuseum.no; Eiganesveien 40a; adult/child 90/50kr; ⊙10am-4pm Sat-Thu) This opulent manor was constructed for the merchant shipowner Lars Berentsen. Its authentic late-19th-century interiors include old farming implements, books and decorative objects.

Ledaal   HISTORIC BUILDING
(Map p204; ☑51 84 27 00; www.ledaalmuseum.no; Eiganesveien 45; adult/child 90/50kr incl other Stavanger museums; ⊙10am-4pm Sat-Thu) The empire-style Ledaal was constructed between 1799 and 1803 for wealthy merchant shipowner Gabriel Schanche Kielland. Now restored, and featuring unusual antique furniture, it serves as the local royal residence and summer home.

🏃 Activities

Stavanger is a great launch pad for adventures in Lysefjord. Boat cruises and sightseeing trips leave from the town's main Fiskespiren Quay.

NuArt Street Art Tour   TOUR
(Map p204; www.streetarttours.no; adult/child 150kr/free; ⊙1pm) These walking tours explore 15 years of the NuArt festival (p202), and explore some of the key street-art murals and more hidden works dotted around Stavanger. They

last 90 minutes, and can be booked online or through the Stavanger tourist office (p205). The meeting point is on Nedre Strandgate.

Geoparken
PLAYGROUND
(Map p204; Norsk Oljemuseum; ☉10am-7pm Jun-Aug, 10am-4pm Mon-Sat, to 6pm Sun Sep-May) FREE Children of all ages will enjoy Geoparken, a playground fashioned from oil-exploration equipment at the Norsk Oljemuseum.

☞ Tours

Guide Companiet
WALKING
(✆51 85 09 20; www.guidecompaniet.no; 2hr tour adult 450kr) Guide Companiet tours leave from outside the tourist office (p205) and cover the cathedral, old Stavanger and the listed wharf houses.

✦ Festivals & Events

International Chamber Music Festival
MUSIC
(https://www.kammermusikkfestivalen.no/; ☉early Aug) Well-respected classical-music festival, with unusual venues and interesting programming.

May Jazz Festival
MUSIC
(www.maijazz.no; ☉early May) Serious jazz acts, with at least a couple of international legends each year.

Stavanger Vinfest
WINE
(www.stavangervinfest.no; ☉mid-Apr) A week-long wine celebration takes over the city's best restaurants.

Gladmat
FOOD & DRINK
(www.gladmat.no; ☉mid-Jul) Reportedly Scandinavia's largest food festival.

🛏 Sleeping

This is an oil city and prices soar on weekdays, plus it's not uncommon for every bed in town to be occupied. That said, prices drop and availability returns on weekends and during high summer. Do, however, be sure to avoid the end of August in even-numbered years, when the Offshore Northern Seas Foundation (ONS) show entirely takes over the town.

The tourist office (p205) website has a full list of small B&Bs in and around Stavanger, though these, too, are often utilised by conference goers – book ahead when you can.

Mosvangen Camping
CAMPGROUND $
(✆51 53 29 71; www.stavangercamping.no; Tjensvoll 1b; campsites 150-250kr, huts 400-600kr;

P 🛜 🛗) About 3km south of Stavanger on the road to Ullandhaugveien, this is a fine campsite that feels a long way from the city. Grassy campsites and a selection of two- and four-bed huts (none of which are en suite) cover most bases, and it's all set among lots of greenery.

★ Thompsons B&B
B&B $
(✆51 52 13 29; www.thompsons-bed-and-breakfast.com; Muségata 79; s/d with shared bathroom 400/500kr; P) You won't find a bigger bargain in Stavanger than this homely B&B. Housed in a 1910 villa in a peaceful residential area, this four-bed B&B has a home-away-from-home vibe engendered by the warm and welcoming owner, Sissel Thompson. Rooms are cosy and comfortable, and the traditional Norwegian breakfast, taken around the downstairs dining table, is generous.

Comfort Hotel Square
HOTEL $
(Map p204; ✆51 56 80 00; www.nordicchoicehotels.no; Løkkeveien 41; s 799kr, d 999-1499kr; ❄🛜) It's part of a massive chain, yes, but this place in Gamle Stavanger offers more individuality than most. Outside, a wavy, wooden facade and a super roof terrace; inside, colourful rooms, exposed concrete and giant wall murals. Rates drop at weekends (often half-price compared to midweek), and include breakfast. You can sleep in on Sundays and check out by 6pm.

Skansen Hotel
HOTEL, GUESTHOUSE $
(Map p204; ✆51 93 85 00; www.skansenhotel.no; Skansegata 7; r Mon-Thu 995kr, Fri-Sun 770kr) This hotel is the only budget option in the city centre. Rooms are spartan but clean and there are a few pleasing extras such as tea- and coffee-making facilities and complimentary Norwegian sweets. There's also a beer garden out the back and a watering hole, locals' favourite B.broremann B.bar (p205), downstairs.

★ Darby's Inn
B&B $$
(Map p204; ✆476 25 248; www.darbysbb.com; Oscars gate 18; r 1180-1280kr; P❄🛜) The two front rooms at this understated, opulent B&B might be Stavanger's nicest, even without a sea view. Traditional interiors in this historic house combine dark wood with antique furniture, paintings, Persian rugs and a baby grand in the lounge and dining room. The large guest rooms are simpler but still have luxury linen, plump cushions and suitably heavy curtains.

Havly Hotel HOTEL $$

(Map p204; ☎51 93 90 00; www.havly-hotell.no; Valberggata 1; s/d 1030/1390kr; 📶) A little bit off the main harbour drag, this business-focused, Best Western–owned place is a cut above your usual chain hotel. Looking rather like a cruise ship seen from the side, with its uniform square windows and white-clad facade, its rooms are spacious and well appointed, if a little boring and businessy.

Stavanger B&B B&B $$

(Map p204; ☎51 56 25 00; www.stavangerbedandbreakfast.no; Vikedalsgata 1a; s 690-790kr, d 790-890kr; P📶) This reasonably priced minihotel makes a change to the generic chain hotels. It's pretty basic – decor is spartan, and some of the rooms are very small (especially the singles, which have showers and sinks squeezed in beside the beds). Rates include breakfast, and free coffee, tea and waffles are served nightly.

Sola Strand Hotel RESORT $$$

(☎51 94 30 00; www.sola-strandhotel.no; Axel Lunds veg 27, Sola; r from 1460kr; ❄📶🏊) Dating back to 1914, this family-oriented beachside hotel overlooks the sand dunes at Sola beach and offers 135 bedrooms, nearly all of which have fine sea views. Rooms are a mixed bag, but they're mostly modern with fairly generic, chain-style furniture. But extra treats like the lovely Nordsjøbadet Spa and a great restaurant make it worth a look for beach-lovers.

Unfortunately the proximity of Stavanger Airport tends to spoil the peace a bit.

Clarion Collection Hotel Skagen Brygge HOTEL $$$

(Map p204; ☎51 85 00 00; www.nordicchoicehotels.com; Skagenkaien 30; Mon-Fri r 2010-2990kr, Sat & Sun 1290-1910kr; ❄📶) Built to resemble a modern take on a row of harbour townhouses, this swish number is the preferred choice of overnighting oil execs. It's quietly luxurious, with large, water-view rooms, plush turquoise-velour chairs and tasteful tones of cappuccino and chocolate. There's a gym, free afternoon cakes and waffles, and a nice lounge. Rates almost halve at weekends.

Eating

★Renaa Xpress Sølvberget NORWEGIAN $$

(Stavanger Kulturhus; Map p204; ☎51 55 11 11; www.restaurantrenaa.no; Sølvberggata 2; panini 89-98kr, salads 170kr, pizzas 180-199kr; ⏰10am-10pm Mon-Thu, to midnight Fri & Sat, noon-10pm Sun) One of three Renaa restaurants in Stavanger, this upmarket cafe pretty much corners the lunchtime market. Go for the daily soup deal, tuck into a huge salad, enjoy a panino topped with *Parmaskinke* (Parma ham) or *røkelaks* (smoked salmon), or order a wood-fired, wild-yeasted pizza (available from 3pm). Needless to say, the cake, pastries and coffee are delicious, too. Queues can be long at lunchtime.

★Renaa Matbaren INTERNATIONAL $$

(Map p204; ☎51 55 11 11; www.restaurantrenaa.no; Breitorget 6, enter from Bakkegata; small dishes 59-125kr, mains 165-395kr; ⏰4pm-1am Mon-Fri, 11am-1am Sat, 2pm-midnight Sun) Run by top chef Sven Erik Renaa, this smart bistro offers a taste of his food at (reasonably) affordable prices. The menu is classic – mussels in beer, rib-eye with rosemary fries, squid with fennel and shallots, all with a Nordic twist. The glass and wood feels uber-Scandi, and the art collection is stellar (yes, that's an Antony Gormley statue).

Døgnvill BURGERS $$

(Map p204; ☎51 89 10 00; www.dognvillburger.no; Skagen 13; burgers 139-199kr; ⏰11am-11pm Mon-Wed, 11am-midnight Thu-Sat, noon-11pm Sun; 🖉) 🍃 The hot spot for Stavanger's hipsters (and everyone else, in fact), this slinky burger joint does everything right – from its artisan buns through to its locally sourced meats, cheeses and salads. Go for a Classic, spice things up with chipotle, add blue cheese or taleggio, or go veggie with baked beetroot or smoked aubergine and Portobello mushroom. Mmm.

NB Sørensen's Damskibsexpedition NORWEGIAN $$

(Map p204; ☎51 84 38 00; www.herlige-stavanger.no; Skagen 26; mains 149-295kr; ⏰4pm-midnight Mon-Wed, to 1am Thu & Fri, 11am-1am Sat, 1-11pm Sun) Maritime heritage comes to the fore at this fun, friendly venue, one of copious options along the waterfront. It's covered in nautical memorabilia, and the menu encompasses fish, steaks, burgers, grills and salads, plus a daily traditional Norwegian dish (169kr) served until 7pm. More sophisticated dining is available at Andre Etage on the 1st floor.

Bølgen & Moi NORWEGIAN $$

(Map p204; ☎51 93 93 51; www.bolgenogmoi.no; Kjerringholmen, Norsk Oljemuseum; lunch mains 189-239kr, dinner mains 229-369kr; ⏰11am-4pm Mon, noon-9.30pm Tue-Sat, noon-5pm Sun) Attached to the Oil Museum, this is a reliable bet for staples like pizzas, burgers, salads and mussels,

Stavanger

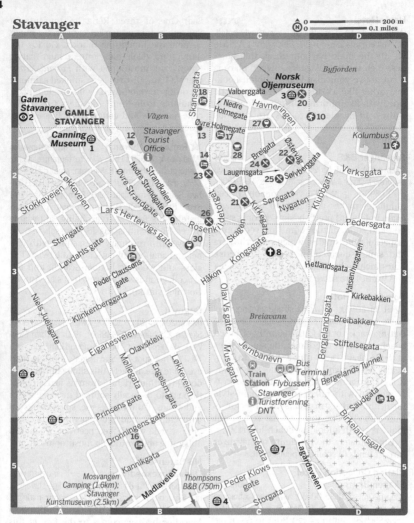

as well as a seasonally driven set menus in the evening. Glass windows over the water and swift service are all positives, even if it is part of a big national restaurant chain.

★Egget　　　　　　　　　　　　BISTRO **$$$**
(Map p204; ☑984 07 700; Steinkargata 23; dishes from 800kr; ⊗6-11pm Tue-Sat) In a clapboard building off Steinkargata, this ramshackle, rough-and-ready eatery is small in size but strong on ambition: the food is modern, creative and bang on trend, with an emphasis on freshness, seasonality and Asian-inspired flavours. There's no set menu; dishes are

chalked above the bar, from wild trout to kimchi, braised ribs or Asian slaws. The only drawback? It's pricey.

Renaa Restauranten　　　　NORWEGIAN **$$$**
(Map p204; ☑51 55 11 11; www.restaurantrenaa. no; Steinkargata 10; tasting menus 1400kr; ⊗6pm-late Tue-Sat) For a truly exclusive eating experience, head for the flagship restaurant of Michelin-lauded chef Sven Erik Renaa. With just a handful of tables and a limited number of servings, Renaa takes his cue from both place and season; fish, seafood, meat and game are combined with microherbs, foraged ingredients and edible flowers.

Stavanger

Torget Fish Market   SEAFOOD $$$

(Map p204; Rosenkildetorget; ⊙market 9am-4.30pm Mon-Sat, restaurant 11am-9pm Mon-Wed, 11am-midnight Thu-Sat) Stavanger's small fish market isn't a patch on the Bergen version. Still, you can pick up fresh fish here, and try locally harvested oysters, mussels, clams, lobsters and crabs, and the market restaurant does good fish dishes including a majestic, if eye-wateringly-priced, shellfish platter (1550kr for two people). Even if you're not eating, it's fun to look around.

Drinking & Nightlife

★ Bøker & Børst   BAR

(Map p204; ☑51 86 04 76; www.bokerogborst.webs. com; Øvre Holmegate 32; ⊙10am-2am) With all the decorative chic of a well-worn living room – complete with book-lined shelves, retro floor-lamps and old wallpaper – this lovely coffee bar is a fine spot to while away a few hours. There are plenty of beers on tap, plus pub-type snacks and pastries, and a covered courtyard at the back.

Checkpoint Charlie   CLUB

(Map p204; ☑51 53 22 45; www.checkpoint.no; Nedre Strandgate 5; ⊙8pm-2am) This venue has been around for 30-odd years, making it older than most of the current regulars. Still, everyone in Stavanger ends up here at some point and has a Checkpoint story to tell. The

website lists upcoming local and international live acts (indie to straight-out rock'n'roll) and club nights.

Cardinal   PUB

(Map p204; ☑982 04 200; www.cardinal.no; Skagen 21; ⊙3pm-1.30am Sun-Wed, from noon Thu-Sat) This trad pub is the choice for craft-beer aficionados – they serve what claims to be Norway's biggest beer selection. You can taste five at once by ordering a 'Planken' (beer flight of five half-pints).

Café Sting   CAFE

(Map p204; ☑51 89 32 84; www.cafesting.no; Valbergjet 3; ⊙noon-10pm Mon-Wed, noon-midnight Thu & Fri, 11am-midnight Sat, 1-10pm Sun) A great bet if you want to dodge the harbour hubbub, this old, whitewashed house attracts a more cultured crowd for gigs, jazz nights and exhibitions. There's a small roof terrace overlooking the nearby park.

B.broremann B.bar   BAR

(Map p204; ☑406 36 783; www.broremann.no; Skansegata 7; ⊙6pm-2am Tue-Thu & Sun, 4pm-2am Fri & Sat, closed Mon) One of Stavanger's best-loved bars, this low-key place draws a discerning over-30s crowd and, later, local hospitality staff for post-shift beers and cocktails.

ⓘ Information

Tourist Office (Map p204; ☑51 85 92 00; www.regionstavanger.com; Strandkaien 61;

⊙ 9am-8pm Jun-Aug, 9am-4pm Mon-Fri, 9am-2pm Sat Sep-May) Local information and advice on Lysefjord and Preikestolen.

Stavanger Turistforening DNT (Map p204; ☑ 51 84 02 00; www.stf.no; off Muségata; ⊙ 10am-4pm Mon, Wed, Fri & Sat, 10am-6pm Tue & Thu) Information on hiking and mountain huts.

ⓘ Getting There & Away

AIR

Stavanger Airport (☑ 51 65 80 00; https://avinor.no/en/airport/stavanger-airport/) is at Sola, 14km south of the city centre. As well as international airlines, there are a number of domestic-airline services. Seasonal flights are also available to destinations in the UK and Europe.

Norwegian (www.norwegian.com) Flights to Oslo, Bergen and Trondheim.

SAS (www.sas.no) Services Oslo and Bergen, plus international destinations like London and Aberdeen.

Widerøe (www.wideroe.no) Flies to Bergen, Kristiansand, Sandefjord, Florø and Aberdeen.

BOAT

International ferries and boat tours of **Lysefjord** (p208) from Stavanger are available.

Kolumbus (Map p204; ☑ 81 50 01 82; www.kolumbus.no; Verksgata) also runs an express ferry to Lysebotn (adult/child/car 160/80/567kr, one daily on Monday, Wednesday and Friday), as well as car ferries to several other destinations.

BUS

Most services to Oslo change at Kristiansand.

CAR & MOTORCYCLE

Stavanger is about 210km south of Bergen, and 138km south of Haugesund, both via the E39. It's an expensive route when you factor in ferries, road tolls and city tolls.

TRAIN

Most train services to Oslo change at Kristiansand. Note that you can often get much cheaper fares than those quoted by booking a week or more in advance.

ⓘ Getting Around

Between early morning and mid-to-late evening, **Flybussen** (Map p204; ☑ 51 52 26 00; www.flybussen.no/stavanger; adult single/return 120/180kr) runs three or four times an hour between the **bus terminal** (Map p204; Jernbaneven) and the airport at Sola.

LYSEFJORD

All along the 42km-long Lysefjord (Light Fjord), the granite rock glows with an ethereal light and even on dull days it's offset by almost-luminous mist. This is the favourite fjord of many visitors, and there's no doubt that it has a captivating beauty.

There are two compelling reasons to explore this wonderful place: a cruise along the fjord, or the four-hour hike to the top of Preikestolen, the plunging cliff-face that's graced a million postcards from Norway, not to mention as many Instagram posts. Daredevils might also want to brave standing on the **Kjeragbolten**, a boulder wedged between two sheer cliff faces.

The ferry ride from Stavanger takes you to the fjord head at **Lysebotn**, where a narrow and much-photographed road corkscrews spectacularly 1000m up towards Sirdal in 27 hairpin bends. From Lysebotn, the road twists up the mountain and on into the Setesdalen region and Oslo.

🏃 Activities

★ **Preikestolen**   HIKING

The sight of people perched on the edge of this extraordinary granite rock formation is one of Norway's emblematic images. Soaring 604m above the fjord, framed by cliffs on three sides, Preikestolen (Pulpit Rock) is one of the nation's most remarkable sights. It's a steep, four-hour return hike from Preikestolhytta Vandrerhjem, and is usually accessible from April to September, depending on the snows.

The two-hour, 3.8km trail begins along a steep but well-marked route, then climbs

BUSES FROM STAVANGER

DESTINATION	COST (KR)	TIME (HR)	FREQUENCY (PER DAY)
Bergen	475	5½	hourly
Haugesund	241	2	hourly
Kristiansand	406	4½	4
Oslo	742-811	9½	3

past a series of alternating steep and boggy sections to the final climb across granite slabs and along some windy and exposed cliffs to Preikestolen itself. The steepest sections are at the beginning and in the middle parts of the trail and can be challenging for the unfit. Theoretically it can be done in winter, but it's not advisable due to the likelihood of adverse weather and the more limited options for public transport.

As for many of Norway's natural attractions, there are no fences or barriers of any kind, and despite the alarming crack where it joins the mountains, it's likely to be around for a few more centuries. While the rock receives over 200,000 visitors a year, there has only been one accidental fatality, in 2013. That said, do take all due care even if other people seemingly don't. For those with vertigo, even watching other people dangling limbs over the abyss can make the heart skip a beat. Rocky trails lead up the mountains behind, offering more wonderful views.

The area also offers several other fabulous **walks** – the Vatnerindane ridge circuit (two hours), Ulvaskog (three hours), the Refsvatnet circuit (three hours), the summit of Moslifjellet (three hours) and even a two-day hike all the way to Lysebotn – all of which are accessible from the Preikestolhytta car park. For more information on possible routes and DNT huts along the trails, visit the Stavanger Turistforening DNT (p206) before setting out from Stavanger.

Fjord Expedition
KAYAKING

(🖉942 75 439; www.fjordexpedition.com; Rådhusgata 7, Jorpeland; 2950kr) What a way to explore the luminous Lysefjord – in your own kayak, with nothing but silence and nature all around. This outdoors company offers two-day guided trips to seek out some of Lysefjord's wildlife, along with hidden bays and islands that the cruise ships never reach. At night, you camp out in tents or a traditional *lavuu* (Sami tipi).

Outdoor Life
HIKING

(🖉97 65 87 04; www.outdoorlifenorway.com; ⊘day hikes per person 1290kr) Guided hikes to various spots around Lysefjord, including lots of places that are well off the standard Preikestolen trail, as well as expeditions to Kjerag and other locations. Overnight hikes are also available, along with biking and boat trips. They also run winter hiking trips, when the chances are you'll have the rock to yourself – a rare and precious experience.

Lysefjord Safari
BOATING

(Map p204; 🖉913 59 132; www.fjordevents.no; speedboat trip 900kr; ⊘May-Sep) Cruise too sedate for you? Then these seat-of-the-pants speedboat trips will probably suit you down to the ground. They race from Stavanger all the way into Lysefjord in just a couple of hours. Lifejackets are provided; seasick pills aren't. There are daily trips from Fiskespiren Quay.

Kjeragbolten
HIKING

You're bound to have seen a photo of this boulder, wedged between two sheer cliffs about 2m apart with a sickening drop below. The 10km, five-hour return hike involves a strenuous 700m ascent from the Øygardsstølen Café car park (parking 30kr), near the highest hairpin bend above Lysebotn.

From mid-May to late August, **Tide** (http://fjords.tide.no/hikingtour-kjerag) also runs 13½-hour bus–boat–hike return trips to the 'chockstone' Kjeragbolten (adult/child 590/450kr), which can otherwise be difficult to reach. It includes time for the five-hour return hike.

The route trudges up and over three ridges and in places steep muddy slopes make for tough going. Once you reach Keragbolten, actually getting down to the boulder involves some tricky manoeuvring, including traversing an exposed lodge on a 1000m-high cliff! From there you can step, or crawl, down onto the rock itself for the ultimate photo.

🛏 Sleeping

Lysefjorden Tourist Cabin
HOSTEL

(🖉948 26 602; www.lysefjordenturisthytte.dnt. no; Lysebotn; dm/q 380/1520kr; ⊘Jun-Aug) Fifty metres from the quay is the former Lyse canteen. Stavanger Hiking Association now offers rooms with shower and toilet, or cheaper accommodation in dormitories. An attached cafe and lounge is open for breakfast, lunch and dinner and is licensed for beer and wine. Bed linen and towels can be hired.

★Preikestolen Fjellstue
LODGE $

(🖉51 74 20 74; www.preikestolenfjellstue.no; Jørpeland; hostel dm/s/d/q 325/530/770/1420kr, lodge s/d 1150/1520kr) Completely overhauled not so long ago, this DNT mountain lodge and hostel at the Preikestolen trailhead means Preikestolen finally has accommodation worthy of its natural splendour. There is a range of accommodation for all budgets, including a well-kept hostel (breakfast and linen included), stylishly simple lodge rooms and family cottages. There's also a cafe for pre- and post-hike meals (mains 98kr to 288kr).

LYSEFJORD & PULPIT ROCK PLANNING

Cruises to Lysefjord

Two companies, including **Rødne Fjord Cruises** (Map p204; ☎ 51 89 52 70; www.rodne.no; Skagenkaien 35-37, Stavanger; adult/child/family 490/300/1300kr, Preikestolen boat-and-hike ticket 720kr), offer three-hour cruises from Stavanger to Lysefjord. Along the way, sights visited include the **Vagabonds' Cave** and the **Hengjane waterfall** – and look out for mountain goats on the hillsides as you go.

Lysefjord and Pulpit Rock

If you want to hike Preikestolen (Pulpit Rock) but don't have your own car, the cheapest option is to book a ticket through **Norled** (Map p204; www.norled.no; Lysefjord cruise adult/child/family 450/280/1100kr, Preikestolen boat-and-bus-ticket 320kr), or through Tide (www.tide.no). The trip costs adult/child 320/150kr, including the return fare on the Stavanger–Tau ferry, and the return bus fare between Tau and the trailhead at Preikestolhytta.

Rødne Fjord Cruises runs its own cruise-and-hike excursions (adult 780/500kr); the cruise boat fare to Tau and the bus fare between Tau and Preikestolhytta are included, but you'll need to add on the ferry fare back to Stavanger (adult/child 56/28kr).

Having your own car makes things easier. Catch the **Stavanger–Tau ferry** (p208) from Fiskespiren Quay and follow the Rv13 for 13km to the turn-off for Preikestolhytta Vandrerhjem, another 6km further on. It's a drive of about 1½ hours.

In summer you can stay in a hammock slung on a roofed dock by the lakeside at their Basecamp's 'water camp'. Canoe or walk there along Refsvatn lake – canoe rental is included in the price and they can be used throughout your stay. Hot breakfasts are prepared on the campfire. It costs 3500kr for up to 10 people, or 2500kr if you're members of the DNT.

Preikestolen Camping   CAMPGROUND $
(☎ 481 93 950; www.preikestolencamping.com; Jørpeland; tent sites for car & 2 adults 280kr; ⊙ Apr-Oct, gates open 7am-10pm) The closest campsite to Preikestolen is about 1km off the turn-off from the Rv13 on the way to Preikestolen Fjellstue. It's surrounded by forest, is well run and has good facilities, including a shop-restaurant. It's perfect for getting an early start on the crowds, although it's another 5km or so extra before you reach the trailhead.

Kjerag Restaurant   CAFE $
(Øygardsstølen; ☎ 975 11 651; Fv500, Lysebotn; snacks & light meals 79-189kr; ⊙ 7.30am-8pm mid-Jun–mid-Sep) Located at the far eastern end of Lysefjord near the settlement of Lysebotn, this sky-top cafe sits at the end of a series of punishing, veering switchbacks, but affords a mind-boggling view over the fjord through its ship's-prow–style windows. The food's basic – sandwiches, salads and snacks – but this is one place you won't regret stopping.

ℹ Information

Lysefjordsenteret (☎ 51 70 31 23; www.lysefjordsenteret.no; Oanes; salmon farm adult/child 60/30kr; ⊙ noon-5pm mid-Jun–mid-Aug, noon-5pm Sun only rest of year) In a fabulous setting north of the ferry terminal at Oanes, with tourist information, salmon farm, restaurant and geological and folk-history exhibits.

For information on the region, check out www.lysefjordeninfo.no and www.visitlysefjorden.no.

ℹ Getting There & Away

Lysefjord is about 45km from Stavanger via Rv13. There are two options to get there by car – on the direct ferry to Tau from Stavanger, or the more circuitous route via the Solvorn–Oanes ferry.

The small town of Oanes is at the western mouth of the fjord, while Lysebotn is at its eastern end – 46km direct via the fjord ferries.

BOAT

The **Stavanger–Tau Ferry** (www.tide.no; adult/child 56/28kr, car incl driver 167kr; ⊙ every 40-45min) runs at least once an hour across the fjord from Stavanger to Tau, from where you can head onwards to the Preikestolen trailhead.

The other option is to catch the quicker but more infrequent **Solvorn–Oanes Ferry** (www.lustrabaatane.no; adult/child 40/20kr, car with driver 110kr; ⊙ 4-8 times daily) on Rv13.

The Western Fjords

Best Places to Eat

➡ Maki (p247)

➡ Restaurant Arven (p214)

➡ Knutholmen (p234)

➡ Sødahl-Huset (p238)

➡ Ciderhuset (p222)

Best Places to Stay

➡ Juvet Landscape Hotel (p239)

➡ Hotel Aak (p238)

➡ Villa Norangdal (p243)

➡ Hotel Brosundet (p247)

➡ Walaker Hotell (p219)

➡ Sveggvika (p251)

Why Go?

Scoured and gouged by glaciers, ancient and modern, Western Norway's deep, sea-drowned valleys are covered by steep, rugged terrain. It's a landscape that is so utterly unique and so profoundly beautiful that it is one of the most desirable destinations in the world.

Although overshadowed by the sublime fjords, the coastline is nonetheless extraordinary, blasted by an often ferocious ocean and backed by deep green mountain peaks.

Ferries are a way of life in the west. These reliable workhorses make navigating the insane geography possible, but are also an enjoyable part of your journey as they offer staggering, otherwise inaccessible, panoramas.

This is great hiking country, whether wild walking, following one of the many signed trails or lumbering along in a guided glacier-walking group. And if, after so much fresh air, you crave some small-town sophistication, the bijou art-nouveau settlement of Ålesund has that in spades.

When to Go
Alesund

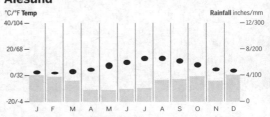

Early Jul Norsk Fjellfestival, a folk and outdoor celebration, takes place in stunning Åndalsnes.

Mid-Jul Molde parties all week long during Moldejazz.

Late Aug Savour Ålesund's seafood haul during the town's Norwegian Food Festival.

The Western Fjords Highlights

1 Geirangerfjord (p240) Taking a cruise along Norway's most famous – and frequented – fjord.

2 Trollstigen Road (p237) Braving the hairpin turns and dizzying drops on this roller-coaster road.

3 Nigardsbreen (p227) Kayaking on a glacial lake and crunching across the ancient ice.

4 Loen Skylift (p229) Zipping up the mountains for an epic fjord view.

5 Flåmsbana Railway (p213) Enjoying the journey on Norway's most scenery-packed railway.

6 Atlantic Ocean Road (p252) Crossing the many mind-

7 Stegastein
(p215) Switch-backing up the Aurlandsfjellet to snap a selfie from this striking viewpoint.

8 Ålesund (p244)
Admiring this elegant town's art-nouveau architecture and offshore islands.

9 Borgund Stave Church (p212)
Pondering Norway's medieval past at this lovely stave church, one of many around the fjords.

boggling bridges on this classic northern road trip.

Otta (70km)

RV55

15

Dalsnibba
(1496m)

Gamle
Strynefjellsvegen

Hellesylt

Styggevatnet

Sognefjellet

Turtagrø

Fortun

Øvre Årdal

E16

9 Borgund

Lærdal

Lærdalsøyri

Otternes

7 Stegastein

Gjerde

Skjolden

Lustrafjorden

Luster

Urnes

Kaupanger

Mannheller

Fodnes

Aurlandsfjellet

Tunnel
(24.5km)

Aurland

5 Flåmsbana Railway

Flåm

Myrdal

Geiterygghytta (6km)

Østerbø

Hardangervidda (30km)

Stryn

4 Loen

Olden

Jostedalsbreen National Park

Byrkjelo

Skei

Stardal River

Gaupne

Solvorn

Sogndal

Fjærland

Aurlandsfjorden

Nærøyfjord

Undredal

Gudvangen

E16

Vinje

Bergen (99km)

Nordfjordeid

E39

SOGN OG FJORDANE

Førde

Naustdal

Jølstra River

Sande

Høyanger

E39

Fjærlandsfjorden

RV13

Dragsvik

Balestrand

Vangsnes

Vik

RV13

Norddal

RV611

Florø

Kinn

Askrova

Tansøy Svanøy

Bataldon

Sognefjorden

Bremanger

Måløy

Kråkenes

RV618

Smørhamn
Frøya
Kalvåg

Froysjøen

Lighthouse

Nordfjord

50 km

25 miles

N

SOGNEFJORDEN

Sognefjorden, the world's second-longest (203km) and Norway's deepest (1308m) fjord, cuts a deep slash across the map of western Norway. In places, sheer walls rise more than 1000m above the water, while elsewhere a gentler shoreline supports farms, orchards and villages.

The broad, main waterway is impressive but it's worth detouring into its narrower arms, such as the deep and lovely Nærøyfjord, for idyllic views of abrupt cliff faces and cascading waterfalls.

There's a comprehensive guide to the area at www.sognefjord.no.

◉ Sights

★ Borgund Stave Church CHURCH
(www.stavechurch.com/en/borgund; Borgund; adult/child 90/70kr; ⊙ 8am-8pm May-Sep, 10am-5pm Oct-Apr) Some 30km southeast of Lærdalsøyri along the E16, this 12th-century stave church was raised beside one of the major trade routes between eastern and western Norway. Dedicated to St Andrew, it's one of the best known, most photographed and certainly the best preserved of Norway's stave churches. It's simple, inky interior and sublimely rustic altar are deeply moving. Beside it is the only free-standing medieval wooden bell tower remaining in Norway.

ⓘ Getting There & Away

BOAT
Norled (www.norled.no) operates a daily boat from Bergen to Flåm (adult/child 825/415kr, 5½ hours), stopping along the way at several small towns including Vik, Balestrand and Sogndal.

Fjordtours (www.fjordtours.no) also offers a 'Sognefjord in a Nutshell' tour from Bergen (1610kr, 10 hours), with an optional detour via Nærøyfjorden.

Several local ferries also cross Sognefjord, allowing passengers and cars to skip a major detour around the head of the fjord.

BUS
Various bus services serve towns around the fjord, including Flåm, Vik and Sogndal.

TRAIN
The scenic Flåmsbana Railway (p213) runs down the mountainside from Myrdal, which links up with the main Oslo–Bergen railway.

AURLANDSFJORDEN

Branching off the main thrust of Sognefjorden, the deep, narrow Aurlandsfjorden runs for about 29km, but is barely 2km across at its widest point – which means it crams an awful lot of scenery into a relatively compact space. The view is best seen from the amazing Stegastein viewpoint, which juts out from the hillside along the stunning Aurlandsfjellet road.

Aurland and Flåm both sit near the head of the fjord and are the best bases for accommodation and supplies.

Flåm

POP 450

At the head of Aurlandsfjorden, Flåm sits in a truly spectacular setting beside Sognefjord. The main attraction here is the stunning mountain railway that creeps up into the surrounding peaks and offers truly eye-popping panoramas. Unfortunately it's far from a well-kept secret, and on the busiest summer days the tiny village can find itself swamped by several thousand visitors – it's probably best left for the quieter seasons of spring and autumn, or early summer at a push. The popular 'Norway in a Nutshell' tour also stops here.

◉ Sights

Flåmsbana Museum MUSEUM
(⊙ 9am-8pm May-Sep, shorter hours rest of year) FREE This little museum is right by the Flåmsbana Railway platform. It's not, however, just about railways: there are fascinating photos of construction gangs and life in and around Flåm before cars and buses made it this far up the fjords.

🏃 Activities

The tourist office (p214) has free sheets describing local walks, varying from 45 minutes to five hours. Various places around town rent bikes, including for the Rallarvegen trail.

★ Rallarvegen CYCLING
(Navvies' Road; www.rallarvegen.com) The Rallarvegen is the service route that was once used by workers who built the Flåmsbana railway. It's now been converted into a super cycle track, running for 83km from Haugastøl (1000m) or an easier 56km from Finse. It can also be done as a very manageable day trip from Myrdal, 18km south of Flåm.

The easiest option is to hire a bike from Sykkelutleige i Flam (p213), buy a ticket for the railway to Myrdal, and then follow the route back down to Flåm for about 18km. Another option is to hire a bike from **Cafe Rallaren** (☑ 57 63 37 56; www.caferallaren.no; Myrdal; bike rental per day 350kr), based at Myrdal Station; you can leave the bikes at Flåm Station at the end of the ride.

If you want to do the whole route, the best idea is to contact one of the hotels further along the track. **Haugastøl Turistsenter** (☑ 32 08 75 64; www.haugastol.no; Haugastølvegen, Haugastøl; 2-day bike package per person from 2850kr), in Hardangervidda, who organise two-night packages on the Rallarvegen including accommodation, bike rental and transport. The more upmarket Finse 1222 (p153) offers similar bike-and-stay packages and a slightly shorter journey. Both hotels allow you to leave bikes in Flåm at the end of the route.

★ **Flåmsbana Railway**   RAIL
(www.visitflam.com/en/flåmsbana; adult/child one way 360/180kr, return 480/240kr) This 20km-long engineering wonder hauls itself up 864m of altitude gain through 20 tunnels. At a gradient of 1:18, it's the world's steepest railway that runs without cable or rack wheels. It takes a full 45 minutes to climb to Myrdal on the bleak, treeless Hardangervidda Plateau, past thundering waterfalls (there's a photo stop at awesome Kjosfossen). The railway runs year-round, with up to 10 departures daily in summer, dropping to four in winter.

Sykkelutleige i Flam   CYCLING
(Rallar Road Cycle Hire; ☑ 57 63 14 00; bike hire per day 350kr; ⊙ 9am-6pm) Bike rental company based in the yellow building between the train station and Fretheim Hotel.

Njord Sea Kayak   KAYAKING
(☑ 913 16 628; www.seakayaknorway.com; adult/child from 660/480kr) Operating from Flåm's postage stamp of a beach, this kayak company offers two daily guided trips: a three-hour paddle around the fjord (adult/child 660/480kr) or a four-hour kayak-and-hike along the old King's Path (800/580kr). Multiday wild-camping expeditions for budding Bear Grylls are also possible.

☞ Tours

Fjord Safari   ADVENTURE
(☑ 57 63 33 23; www.fjordsafari.com; adult/child 1½hr tour 640/440kr, 3hr 890/610kr) Bounce along in a Zodiac/RIB inflatable to see more fjord in less time. The team supplies full-length waterproof kit – you'll need it for this exhilarating scoot across the waters. Trips including stops last from 1½ to three hours; longer trips stop in Unredal to try local lemonade and goat's cheese.

🛏 Sleeping

★ **Flåm**
Camping & Hostel   HOSTEL, CAMPGROUND $
(☑ 940 32 681; www.flaam-camping.no; Nedre Brekkevegen 12; 1-/2-person tent 120/205kr, dm/s/tw/q with bathroom 335/550/920/1315kr, with shared bathroom 260/450/720/995kr; ⊙ Mar-Nov; P 🛜) Everyone's favourite when looking for a budget place in Flåm, this conveniently positioned hostel and campsite has accommodation options to suit all wallets: bunk-bed dorms, singles, twins, triples and quads, in simple lodge buildings with pine walls and colourful fabrics. There's also tonnes of green grassy space for caravans and campers and it's just a short walk to the marina.

Flåm Marina & Apartments   APARTMENT $$
(☑ 57 63 35 55; www.flammarina.no; s/tw 1095/1295kr, apt 1150-2450kr) This waterside establishment offers something different in Flåm: a selection of self-catering apartments sleeping one to five people, simply furnished but with the great advantage of a small lounge and proper kitchen. It's ideal for family travellers (some apartments have rooms with bunk beds). Most have a fjord view from the living room. There are also standard hotel-style rooms.

The Bryggerestaurant (p214) is on site.

Heimly Pensjonat   GUESTHOUSE $$
(☑ 57 63 23 00; www.heimly.no; s/d from 945/1295kr; ⊙ Jun–mid-Sep; 🛜) The building

THE WESTERN FJORDS FLÅM

ⓘ NORWAY IN A NUTSHELL

Although most visitors do the classic 'Norway in a Nutshell' tour from either Oslo or Bergen, you also can do a mini version (adult/child 775/400kr). This circular route from Flåm – boat to Gudvangen, bus to Voss, train to Myrdal, then train again down the spectacular Flåmsbana railway back to Flåm – is truly the kernel within the nutshell and takes in all the most dramatic elements. The Gudvangen boat leaves Flåm at 9am and the Flåmsbana train brings you home at 4.55pm.

is blocky and unpromising from the outside, but rooms at this midrange guesthouse are reasonable, if a little lacking on frills. It has a small garden out the front and is nicely set back from the harbour hubbub. Some rooms have fjord views.

Flåmsbrygga   HOTEL **$$$**
(☑ 57 63 20 50; www.flamsbrygga.no; r 1295-2590kr; ❄ ☎) Right beside the dock, this modern hotel has been made to look reassuringly rustic, with wood cladding, rugs, beams and the like. All but two of the rooms have a balcony, making for some superb fjord vistas. It's a busy location, but super handy to everything, including the attached pub and restaurant, Ægir Bryggeri.

Fretheim Hotel   HOTEL **$$$**
(☑ 57 63 63 00; www.fretheim-hotel.no; Nedre Fretheim; s 1045-1145kr, d 1400-2190kr; P ☎) A haunt of fly-fishing English aristocracy in the 19th century, the vast, 122-room Fretheim, despite its size, manages to be intimate and welcoming. In the original 1870s building, 17 rooms have been restored to their historic selves, though with full modern comfort, while the American wings are straight-up contemporary luxe.

✖ Eating & Drinking

Flåm Bakery   BAKERY **$**
(cakes & pastries 25-40kr; ⊙ 8am-5pm) This little bakery turns out muffins, Danish pastries, croissants and cakes, along with some lovely traditional Norwegian breads.

Bryggerestaurant   NORWEGIAN **$$**
(☑ 57 63 35 55; www.flammarina.no/bryggeres-taurant; mains 150-330kr; ⊙ 9am-10pm Mon-Sat, 10am-10pm Sun) A good bet for the basics – fish and chips, elk burgers, lamb stew and *klippfisk* – served in a pleasant waterfront space at the Flåm Marina & Apartments (p213).

★ Restaurant Arven   NORWEGIAN **$$$**
(☑ 57 63 63 00; www.fretheimhotel.no; Fretheim Hotel; mains 165-315kr, buffet 495kr; ⊙ 6.30-9.30pm) On the 2nd floor of the Fretheim Hotel, this reliably good restaurant offers a grandstand view over the harbour and fjord. It's not quite New Nordic, but there's a strong emphasis on seasonality and local sourcing, and an interest in reinterpreting classic Norwegian dishes with a more modern twist: smoked reindeer, halibut ceviche or brown cheese ice cream, for example.

You can dine à la carte or tuck into the evening buffet.

Ægir Bryggeri   BREWERY
(☑ 57 63 20 50; www.flamsbrygga.no/aegir-bryggeripub; Flåmsbrygga; ⊙ noon-10pm May–mid-Sep, 6-10pm mid-Sep–Apr) Looking for all the world like a stave church, Ægir Brewery, all appealing woodwork and flagstones, offers six different kinds of draught beer, all brewed on the spot. It also does a tasty creative take on Norwegian comfort food as well as burgers and pizzas (160kr to 210kr).

ⓘ Information

The seasonal **tourist office** (☑ 57 63 33 13; www.visitflam.com; Stasjonsvegen; ⊙ 8.30am-8pm Jun-Aug, to 4pm May & Sep) is located within the train station.

ⓘ Getting There & Away

BUS

The following destinations are serviced by bus from Flåm.

DESTINATION	COST (KR)	TIME	FREQUENCY (PER DAY)
Aurland	38	15min	4-8
Bergen	285-350	3hr	2-6
Gudvangen	45-56	20min	4-8
Lærdalsøyri	101	45min	2-6
Sogndal	165	1¾hr	2-6

BOAT

From Flåm, boats head out to towns around Sognefjorden.

The most scenic trip from Flåm is the passenger ferry (p216) up Nærøyfjord to Gudvangen (five daily), with a connecting bus to Voss for trains to Bergen or Oslo. The tourist office (p214) sells tickets.

From May to September, Norled (p173) runs a direct ferry to Bergen (adult/child 825/415kr, 5½ hours). There's at least one daily express boat to Balestrand (280/143kr, two hours) year-round. There are discounts if you buy in advance online.

TRAIN

Flåm is the only Sognefjorden village with a rail link, via the Flåmsbana railway (p213). There are train connections via Myrdal to Oslo (1141kr, 5½ hours) and Bergen (669kr, 2¾ hours).

Aurland

POP 1715

Peaceful Aurland is much less hectic than its neighbour, Flåm, a mere 10km south along the fjord. These days it's renowned as one end of Lærdalstunnel (24.5km), the world's longest road tunnel. This is an essential link in the E16 highway that connects Oslo and Bergen; before its completion traffic had to ferry-hop between Lærdal and Gudvangen. It's a fast alternative to the sinuous, 45km-long Aurlandsfjellet, sometimes known as the Snow Road, which crests over the mountains via one of Norway's loftiest road passes. As such, it's generally only passable from June to October.

It's your choice: speed and convenience via the Lærdalstunnel, or driving fun and massive views via the mountain road. We know which we'd choose.

◉ Sights

★ Stegastein
VIEWPOINT

Projecting out high above the fjord at an altitude of 630m, this marvel of modern engineering is one of Norway's great viewing points. Clad in pine and balancing on worryingly slender steel legs, it seems to roll down into the fjord, with nothing but a glass rail between you and a long, long drop. It's popular, so it's worth getting up early or staying late to have it to yourself.

It's about 8km up the narrow, winding road from Aurland.

★ Aurlandsfjellet
SCENIC ROAD

(SnøVegen; www.nasjonaleturistveger.no/en/rou tes/aurlandsfjellet; ⊙ Jun–mid-Oct) This 45km road is one of Norway's most fabulous, climbing from sea level to the desolate, boulder-strewn high plateau that separates Aurland and Lærdalsøyri (Lærdal). Even if you don't opt for the whole route, drive the first 8km from Aurland to the magnificent Stegastein observation point.

It's a strictly summer-only drive: the road is impassable in winter, and even in mid-summer you'll probably still see snowbanks lining the roadsides (hence it's local nick-name, Snøvegen – the Snow Road).

Otternes
HISTORIC SITE

(✍57 63 11 32; www.visitflam.com/en/se-og-gjore1/se/otternes; ⊙10am-6pm May–mid-Sep) This restored hamlet perches high above the fjord, between Flåm and Aurland. The 27 scattered buildings, the oldest dating from the early 17th century, were lived in until the 1990s. It's largely the initiative of one person, the ebullient Laila Kvellestad. Follow her 30- to 60-minute guided tour (in English, four times daily) of the houses and working farm, and then take a break for a

locally made organic ice cream, fresh apple juice or pancakes.

It can be reached via the footpath (p215) between Flåm and Aurland.

🏃 Activities

The Aurland and Lærdal tourist offices have produced six walker-friendly sheets of local walks, where the route is mapped upon an aerial photo.

Geiteryggen to Aurland Hike
HIKING

The classic trek down Aurlandsdalen from Geiteryggen to Aurland follows a stream from source to sea as you tramp one of the oldest trading routes between eastern and western Norway. From mid-July, you can start this four-day walk in Finse, on the Oslo–Bergen rail line, with overnight stops at Geiterygghytta, Steinbergdalen and Østerbø.

The final section from Østerbø (820m) to Vassbygdi (95m) is the most scenic and makes for a hugely enjoyable day hike (allow six to seven hours); it's usually open between early June and late September. Buses run twice daily between Aurland and Vassbygdi (15 minutes) and Østerbø (one hour).

Flåm to Aurland Path
HIKING

For consistently outstanding views and near-solitude, hike the 12km trail that main-ly follows the old road between Aurland and Flåm, passing by Otternes. Until 1919 and the construction of the coast road, it was the only means of land communication be-tween the two villages. Allow around three hours.

🛏 Sleeping

Lunde Gard & Camping
CAMPGROUND $

(✍997 04 701; www.lunde-camping.no; campsite for tent, car & 2 adults 210kr, cabin 650-850kr; ⊙May-Sep; 🛜) Reasonably quiet and popular with families, this campsite has a green riverside location, and all the facilities you need: decent shower block, TV room and plug-in power for campers and caravans.

Vangsgaarden Gjestegiveri
HOTEL $$

(✍57 63 35 80; www.vangsgaarden.no; s 1350kr, d 1395-1590kr, f 1890kr, 4-bed cabin from 1350kr; 🅿🛜) This whitewashed hotel is a peaceful alternative to the hectic places in nearby Flåm, and looks pretty as a picture, with its clapboard facade and 18th-century architecture. Rooms are simple but sweet, and at least most have fjord views. There are also six cabins down at water level.

The on-site Duehuset restaurant and pub is a good spot for dinner.

Aurland Fjordhotell
HOTEL **$$$**

(☑57 63 35 05; www.aurland-fjordhotel.com; s/d/f from 1190/1590/1890kr; P 🛜) With its white-wood exterior and gabled roof, this place certainly looks the ticket – unfortunately its rooms are considerably less starry, and feel more roadside motel than historic hotel. Still, it's a good fallback if everywhere in Flåm is booked out.

X Eating

Aurlandskafeen
CAFE **$**

(☑57 63 36 66; mains 110-180kr; ⊙10am-5pm Mon-Sat) This cute cafe is good for early-morning coffee, homemade pastries and cakes, and lunchtime sandwiches. It has a small terrace overlooking the river.

Duehuset
PUB, CAFE **$$**

(☑57 63 35 80; www.vangsgaarden.no; mains 140-330kr; ⊙3-11pm Jun-Aug) Part of the Vangsgaarden Gjestegiveri (p215), the Dovecot is a great spot for an early dinner or a pint while the sun sets. The menu is nothing fancy – mainly burgers, salads and fish dishes – but it's not expensive, especially by Norwegian standards, and the cracking terrace with fjord views and old-fashioned pub interior are big sells.

❶ Getting There & Away

Buses run between Aurland and Flåm (38kr, 15 minutes, up to eight times daily). The express bus to/from Bergen (350kr, three hours) stops in Aurland on the way to Flåm.

Watch out for the speed cameras in Lærdalstunnelen – along the entire stretch.

Nærøyfjord

The 17km-long sliver of Nærøyfjord lies to the west of Flåm, branching south from the main course of Sognefjorden. Its name – the Narrow Fjord – is well chosen: it's only 250m across at its narrowest point, and framed by towering 1200m-high cliffs on either side, which are often curtain of waterfalls after heavy rains and winter snow-melt. It can easily be visited as a day excursion from Flåm.

The approach by boat is wondrous, but the fjord's main town, Gudvangen, is a bit of a let-down – it's little more than a roadside service stop and is often swamped by boat and coach traffic.

◉ Sights & Activities

Kjelsfossen
WATERFALL

Kjelsfossen tumbles from the southern wall of Nærøydalen valley, above Gudvangen village. Notice, too, the avalanche protection scheme above Gudvangen. The powerful avalanches here typically provide a force of 12 tonnes per square metre, move at 50m a second and, local legend reckons, can bowl a herd of goats right across the fjord.

★Nærøyfjord Cruise
CRUISE

(www.thefjords.no; one way/return 400/870kr) Most people get their first glimpse of Nærøyfjord from the water. Regular boats shuttle along the fjord from Flåm to Gudvangen. There are five daily boats from May to September, with a choice between the older-style ferries or the flashy *Vision of the Fjords* vessel.

If you wish, when you get to Gudvangen, you can catch a connecting bus on to Voss, for trains to Bergen or Oslo. The Flåm tourist office (p214) sells tickets, plus the Flåm–Voss ferry and bus combination.

🛏 Sleeping

Vang Camping
CAMPGROUND **$$**

(☑57 63 39 26; www.vang-camping.no; campsite 190kr, cabin 500-1200kr; ⊙May–mid-Sep) On the left-hand side of the E16, around 1km out of Gudvangen, these cabins and campsites nestle between the road and the river. The older cabins are really showing their age, but the newer ones are fairly comfortable.

Gudvangen Camping
CAMPGROUND **$$**

(☑993 80 803; www.visitgudvangen.com; campsite for 2 adults 190kr, cabin 460-1345kr; ⊙mid-Apr–mid-Sep) A spacious, grassy site about 1km from the ferry port, with huts and camping pitches set under brooding, wooded cliffs. It's next door to a petrol station.

❶ Getting There & Away

In addition to the daily **passenger cruises** (p216) from Flåm, **Fjord 2** (www.fjord2.com) runs two historic car-ferries from Kaupanger (adult/child 350kr/free, car with driver 750kr, 2½ hours), the MF *Skånevik* and MF *Hardingen Sr*. Both boats are historic monuments, and the route has – rather amazingly – been running since 1875.

Scenic ferries between Gudvangen and Flåm (one-way/return 295/400kr) via Aurland run up to five times daily in summer.

Up to eight daily buses connect Gudvangen to Flåm (52kr, 20 minutes) and Aurland (65kr, 30 minutes).

Lærdal

POP 2174

The village of Lærdalsøyri, usually called Lærdal, is where the lovely green dale of the same name – whose fertile lower reaches produce the juiciest of cherries – meets the fjord. A quiet place nowadays, it was once a busy port, where produce from the surrounding area was loaded on Bergen-bound boats. A fire swept through streets in the town's southwest in early 2014, and while devastating for those who lost homes and were injured, it has not affected the town's charm for visitors.

◉ Sights

The historic centre (Gamle Lærdalsøyri) makes for pleasant strolling through its well-preserved 18th- and 19th-century heart. There's well over a hundred lovingly maintained homes, warehouses and fishermen's shacks to explore here. The tourist office has a free town map that describes the best of them and sets out a walking route.

Norwegian
Wild Salmon Centre   WILDLIFE RESERVE
(Norsk Villaks Senter; ☑915 51 043; www.norsk-villakssenter.no; adult/child 90/60kr; ⊙10am-6pm Jul-Aug, noon-6pm May & Sep) The River Lærdalselvi is one of the top spots for wild salmon fishing in Norway. Salmon fishing has been part of the culture here since time immemorial, but English aristocrats were the first to spot the area's tourist potential in the 1850s. This museum explores the area's salmon history, and it's an engaging tale – using archive film and photographs, as well as a 20m aquarium stocked with salmon and sea trout.

🏃 Activities

There's free fishing in the fjord, and the upper reaches of the Lærdal river are good for trout (day permits are available from the tourist office or nearest campsite).

For hiking, pick up the free leaflet of walks in the area from the **tourist office** (☑57 66 67 71; www.sognefjord.no; Øyraplassen 7; ⊙11am-6pm Jul & Aug, shorter hours rest of year). It also sells a much more detailed local map (139kr) at a scale of 1:50,000.

🛏 Sleeping & Eating

★**Sanden Pensjonat**   GUESTHOUSE $
(☑57 66 64 04; www.sandenpensjonat.no; Øyragata 9; s/d with shared bathroom from 475/550kr, with bathroom 850/975kr; ☎) Used as a guesthouse for almost 100 years, this charming historic house was restored and returned to its original use by owners Jon and Hallvard in 1994. It retains the simplicity and cosy scale of its era, but is furnished with care and a clever eye for detail. The vintage furniture, period details, such as old-fashioned sinks, and slightly retro decor are great fun.

Lærdal Ferie og
Fritidspark   CAMPGROUND, MOTEL $
(☑57 66 66 95; www.laerdalferiepark.com; campsite 180-330kr, cabin 800-1020kr, motel s/d 550/750kr; ☎) This campsite, almost at the water's edge, has sweeping views of the fjord. Its motel has communal self-catering facilities, plus a common room with a terrace and broad picture window that give a magnificent panorama of the fjord.

Lindstrøm Hotell   HOTEL $$
(☑57 66 69 00; www.lindstroemhotel.no; s/d 1100/1450kr; ⊙Apr-Oct; P ☎) This central fifth-generation family-run hotel is divided between a beautiful Swiss-style gabled building in a garden and the main '60s block across the road. The latter – a charming warren of lounges and libraries, filled with splendid original mid-century Scandinavian design and some Norwegian baroque for good measure – has neat rooms that follow suit. The 19th-century ones are stylish, too.

Laksen Pub & Restaurant   PUB FOOD $$
(☑57 66 86 20; lunch dishes 190kr, dinner mains 210-290kr; ⊙10am-6pm Jul & Aug, same hours as museum rest of year) The informal Laksen at the Wild Salmon Centre (p217) offers substantial meals, and sells a small range of snacks, salads, cakes and sandwiches during the daytime.

ℹ Information

Lærdal Tourist Office This small tourist office in a clapboard building, which was once the village bank, books accommodation and activities.

ℹ Getting There & Away

If you're driving south, you have the choice between the world's longest road tunnel, linking Aurland and Lærdal (mercifully, it's toll free) or, in summer, climbing up and over the mountain, following the Aurlandsfjellet road. Express buses run to/from Bergen (328kr, 3¾ hours, two or three daily) via the tunnel.

The **Fjord 2** (www.fjord2.com) car ferry from Kaupanger to Gudvangen (adult/child 350kr/free, car with driver 750kr) stops in Lærdal en route.

Lustrafjorden

Branching northeast from the main branch of Sognefjorden for around 40km, from the town of Solvorn to Skjolden, Lustrafjorden is a quiet and tranquil fjord. It's also a useful gateway to other areas: along the Rv55 road that runs along its western shore, you'll pass the turn-off to Nigardsbreen Glacier and the southern side of Jotunheimen National Park. If you follow the road past Skjolden, it leads up onto epic Sognefjellet Road, which crosses the lofty mountain plateau into the wilds of Hardangervidda National Park.

Undredal

POP 112

Undredal is a truly lovely little village, traditional and quiet, at least until the first boats of the day arrive. Its locally renowned for its cheeses, produced from the milk of around 500 goats roaming free over the fjord-side slopes around the village. There are two types: the firm yellow Undredal cheese and its brown, slightly sweet variant, made from the boiled and concentrated whey. You can pick up a hunk of each at one of the village cheese shops.

◎ Sights

Undredal Church   CHURCH
(adult/child 40kr/free; ⊙noon-5pm mid-May–mid-Sep) Originally built as a stave church in 1147 and seating 40, this barrel-vaulted village church is the smallest still-operational house of worship in mainland Scandinavia. Look up at the roof with its charmingly naive roof paintings of angels, Christ on the cross and other biblical figures, surrounded by stylised stars.

⌁ Sleeping

Undredal Camping   CAMPGROUND $
(☑57 63 30 80; www.visitundredal.no; campsites for car, tent & 2 people 230kr) Undredal's small campsite in the village centre makes a tranquil place to pitch a tent. There aren't many facilities – a shower and toilet block are about all that's on offer – but it's perfect if you're after peace and quiet.

❶ Getting There & Away

Undredal is 6.5km north of the E16 down a narrow, steeply threading road (until its construction in 1988, the only access was by sea). If travelling by bus, get off at the eastern end of the 11km tunnel that leads to Gudvangen. Best of all, take the bus out, walk down the spectacular valley along the lightly trafficked road and return by boat (press the switch beside the yellow blinking lamp on the cafe wall beside the jetty to alert the next passing ferry).

Urnes

◎ Sights

★**Urnes Stave Church**   CHURCH
(www.stavechurch.com/en/urnes; adult/child 90/70kr; ⊙10.30am-5.45pm May-Sep) If you only have time on your itinerary to visit one stave church, the one at Urnes has to figure at the top of the list (along with Borgund). Dating from the 12th century, it's Norway's oldest place of worship and a Unesco World Heritage Site. Serenely placed on the shores of Lustrafjorden, backed by lofty mountains, and covered in elaborate wood carvings of intertwining vines and battling beasts, it looks like a forgotten set from *Lord of the Rings*.

The present church was mostly built around 1170 on the site of the original chapel, built around 100 years before.

Ticket prices include an interesting 45-minute tour in English.

✗ Eating

Gamlefjøsen Cafe   CAFE $
(www.urnes.no; ⊙11am-5.30pm Jun-Sep) This little farmhouse cafe is a wonderful spot to sit and watch the fjord slide by. Treats on offer include homemade fruit juices, raspberry lemonade and honey from the farm, plus a snacky menu of sandwiches, cakes and possibly the best waffles this side of Sognefjord, slathered with the farm's own blueberry jam.

❶ Getting There & Away

The **Lustrabaatene ferry** (www.lustrabaatane.no; adult/child/car 40/20/110kr) runs to Urnes from Solvorn from 7.45am in summer; the last ferry back is at 6pm. It can carry cars, but if you're just visiting the church, you might as well just park you car on the Solvorn side and save some cash.

Solvorn

Diminutive Solvorn is everything you'd want a fjord-side village to be: spectacularly sited, fetchingly pretty, quiet as a mouse but with warmly welcoming locals. It's all that *and* in striking distance of some of the region's best hiking, biking and paddling.

There are two very different, but equally appealing, accommodation options here, making it a wonderful place to base yourself for at least a few days.

🏃 Activities

Mollandsmorki Circuit   MOUNTAIN BIKING
This 25km circuit from Solvern travels a combination of sealed, gravel and finally dirt roads, with stunning views for much of the distance. It's not easy going, with some sections of dirt rugged enough to require you to get off and push, but it's incredibly rewarding – some say, despite its modest distance, even more so than Rallarvegen (p212) cycle route.

FjordSeal   KAYAKING
(Map p225; ☑ 957 74 196; www.fjordseal.com; Marifjøra; adult/child 700/550kr; ☉ tours 9.30am May-Sep) For a delightful four hours of peaceful paddling on smooth-as-silk Lustrafjord, and the chance to cruise among a colony of seals, sign on with one of the daily guided kayak tours of FjordSeal, based at Marifjøra, just off the Rv55, 17km north of Svolvorn.

🛏 Sleeping

★ Eplet   HOSTEL $
(☑ 416 49 469; www.eplet.net; camping per person 110kr, dm/s/d 220/640/740kr; ☉ May-Sep; @ 🛜) Set in the middle of an apple orchard and circled by raspberry canes and blueberry bushes, this special hostel has rooms in two rustic wooden buildings, along with some garden campsites. From its windows there are magnificent views of Lustrafjord (which are even nicer from a hammock in the garden). Rooms are sweetly furnished with local touches. Breakfast isn't included.

Everything you'd expect in terms of self-catering facilities are provided, as well a small organic juice factory, croquet course, lambs to pet and free bikes to borrow.

Bestebakken   B&B $$$
(☑ 901 68 449; www.bestebakken.no; Hafslo; s/d/tr 1300/1900/2850kr; 🅿) In the lakeside hamlet of Hafslo, about 7km northwest of Solvorn, this swooningly pretty farmhouse stands in splendid isolation, clad in yellow timber and ringed by a white picket fence. Its 16 rooms are pretty, cosy and chock-full of charm: some have handmade beds, others antique

furniture, all squeezed into the house's higgledy-piggledy architecture. A slap-up supper is served nightly.

You can also chill in the outside Jacuzzi and organise a spa treatment or massage.

★ Walaker Hotell   HOTEL $$$
(☑ 57 68 20 80; www.walaker.com; historic house d 2400-2900kr, annexe d 1900kr; ☉ May-Sep; @🛜) This wonderful lemon-yellow hotel is the oldest family-run hotel in Norway. Dating from 1640, it's a historical treasure, packed with period detailing, lovely antiques, old-fashioned beds and clawfoot baths. There are three buildings: two historic, plus a deeply incongruous 1960s motel-style extension. The oldest part is the Tingstova wing, with four rooms furnished with hand-painted furniture.

Outside there's a lovely lawn and a garden of lilac, roses, apple and cherry trees. A formal four-course dinner is served nightly in the dining room and is available on a half-board basis.

ℹ Getting There & Away

Bus 153 travels between Sogndal and Solvorn (48kr, 15 minutes, four or five times daily).

Skjolden

POP 500
Skjolden sits in a fine spot at the northern limit of Lustrafjord, framed by a funnel of mountains. It's a quiet village, mainly of interest as a stop along the epic Sognefjellet road. Most of the interest is located under one roof: at the Fjordstova, you'll find the tourist office, a cafe, a swimming pool, climbing wall and even a shooting gallery. The bit of industrial-looking junk on display outside is a turbine from the Norsk hydropower station.

The village was home to Austrian philosopher Ludwig Wittgenstein between 1913 and 1914. The fjords obviously worked their magic, as it was one of the most productive years of his life.

About halfway between Solvorn and Skjolden is the small village of **Luster**, worth a stop for its pretty church (built of stone, not wood, for once!) and a great bakery.

◉ Sights & Activities

East of Skjolden, the Rv55 runs beside the lovely turquoise glacial lake **Eidsvatnet**. **Mørkridsdalen**, the valley that runs north of the village, makes for some excellent hiking.

Dale Kyrkje
CHURCH

(Map p225; Luster; ⊙10am-8pm) Spectacular wooden stave churches get all the attention around here, but this little gem of a medieval parish church built of stone shouldn't be overlooked. Constructed around 1250, it's mainly Gothic in style with a wooden tower and elaborately painted western entrance (the work of a typically near-anonymous ecclesiastical artist known simply as 'Nils the Painter') that were added in the early 1600s. The crucifix above the chancel arch and fine multicoloured pulpit are from the church's earliest days.

The naive 16th-century paintings in the chancel were revealed only in the 1950s, when the whitewash was removed.

🛏 Sleeping & Eating

Skjolden Vandrerhjem
HOSTEL

(Map p148; ☑57 68 61 88; www.hihostels.no/skjolden; dm/s/d/f 280/790/990/1290kr, all incl breakfast; P ≋) This compact hostel shares facilities and the same beautiful site as the surrounding campsite (p220); its private rooms are modern, if a bit institutional. Wi-fi can be patchy outside the main building.

Vassbakken Kro & Camping
CAMPGROUND $

(Map p148; ☑57 68 61 88; www.vassbakken.com; campsite for car, tent & 2 adults 200kr, cabin 690-990kr; ⊙May-mid-Sep) Along the Rv55, 3km from Skjolden, this smallish campsite is set beneath a surging waterfall. There's a popular cafe-restaurant here called The Tavern, which does a brisk trade in Norwegian dishes.

The HI-affiliated Skjolden Vandrerhjem (p220) is located here too.

★ Skjolden Hotel
HOTEL $$

(Map p148; ☑57 68 23 80; www.skjoldenhotel.no; Skjolden; s 800kr, d 1150-1350kr, tr 1550kr; P ❋ ≋) The bones of this hotel might be 1970s, but its skin is contemporary – a revamp has filled the main lounge with swooshy furniture, designer lamps, trendy fabrics and coffee table books. The rooms can't entirely hide their retro origins (bathrooms are dated), but the cracking Lustrafjord views make up for shortcomings. The fjord-facing terrace and manicured lawn are stunning.

Good food is served here too: burgers, steaks and grilled chicken on the bar menu, and more upmarket, creative dishes in the restaurant downstairs.

Lustrabui
BAKERY

(Map p225; ☑469 48 845; www.lustrabui.no; Luster; ⊙7am-5pm Mon-Fri, to 3pm Sat) The two local women behind this traditional bakery trained with Bakeriet i Lom's Morten Schakenda, who is considered Norway's best baker. All natural sourdough is made by hand, with minimal ingredients, but it's the sweet goods that people drive miles for. There are tables to enjoy your *skillingsbollar* (sweet buns), cinnamon swirls and espresso on the spot.

ℹ Information

Tourist Office (Map p148; ☑992 31 500; www.skjolden.com; ⊙11am-7pm mid-Jun-mid-Aug; ≋) Inside the Fjordstova building, this efficient tourist office rents out bikes and kayaks and has lots of info on local hikes.

ℹ Getting There & Away

Bus 153 connects Skjolden with Sogndal (150kr, 1½ hours, three to five daily).

If you're heading north on Rv55 to the Sognefjellet (p147) road, check your fuel gauge; Skjolden's petrol stations are the last for 77km.

Vik

POP 2731

Vik has two small but stunning churches dating from the early Middle Ages, both sensitively restored by the 19th-century architect Peter Blix (who designed, among much else, many of the stations on the Oslo–Bergen railway line). The restoration of these two churches were a lifelong passion for Blix, and he poured many years into bringing them back to their former glory.

◎ Sights

Hove Stone Church
CHURCH

(www.stavechurch.com/en/hove-2; adult/child 50/40kr; ⊙11am-4pm end Jun-mid-Aug) The region's oldest stone building, dating from the late 12th century, this church retains its original form beneath Peter Blix's elaborate makeover. This includes the abstract wall painting of nave and chancel, the wooden figures from Norse legend in the roof beams and the external gables.

Hopperstad Stave Church
CHURCH

(www.stavechurch.com/en/hopperstad-2; adult/child 70/50kr; ⊙10am-5pm late May-late Sep) On the southern outskirts of the village stands this splendid stave church, Built in 1130, and Norway's second oldest, it escaped demolition by a whisker in the late 19th century. It's thought that the church consists of around 2000 individual parts, which would have been created by itinerant craftsmen and assembled with the help of local villagers. Common motifs such as vines, foliage and mythical beasts adorn the exterior, enhanced by colourful canopy paintings inside.

ℹ Getting There & Away

BOAT
A passenger ferry runs across to/from Balestrand (86kr, 15 minutes, twice daily).

BUS
Skyss Bus 970 runs to Voss (124kr, one hour, twice daily).

CAR & MOTORCYCLE
There's a useful Norled car ferry from Dragsvik across the fjord to Vangsnes (123kr, several times hourly), about 11km north of Vik. If you're travelling south to Voss or Bergen, this is a serious time-saver.

Balestrand

POP 1337

Yet another beautiful fjord-side village in a country that's full of them, Balestrand is still well worth a detour for its period 19th-century architecture, which is particularly lovely despite the addition of some pretty dreadful modern buildings. In addition to a cute-as-a-button church, the town also has a travel museum to trumpet about, and while it's a popular stop-off for cruise ships, on quiet days in the off-season it's as peaceful as can be.

⊙ Sights

Norwegian Museum of Travel & Tourism   MUSEUM
(Norsk Reiselivsmuseum; ☑ 57 69 14 57; www.reise livsmuseum.no; adult/child 80/30kr; ⊙10am-6pm Jun-Aug, to 4pm Tue-Sun May & Sep, to 3pm Mon-Fri Oct-Apr) A museum examining the history of tourism might not immediately sound like the biggest must-see, but bear with us: the story of how people travelled around the fjords, and how the landscape and culture has been changed in the process, is actually an important part of the

Norwegian story. So this impressive museum, constructed from uncompromising concrete and glass beside Balestrand's quay, is well worth a stop.

Church of St Olav   CHURCH
Often known locally as 'the English Church', this charming wooden chapel was built in 1897 in the style of a traditional stave church. It gets its nickname from the lady who built it: English expat Margaret Green, who married a local hotel-owner. Should you find it closed, the owner of Midtnes Hotel has the key. There are occasional guided tours.

Viking Age Barrows   ARCHAEOLOGICAL SITE
Less than 1km south along the fjord, excavation of this pair of barrows revealed remnants of a boat, two skeletons, jewellery and several weapons. One mound is topped by a statue of legendary King Bele, erected by Germany's Kaiser Wilhelm II. Obsessed with Nordic mythology, he regularly spent his holidays here prior to WWI (a similar monument, also funded by the Kaiser and honouring Fridtjof, the lover of King Bele's daughter, peers across the fjord from Vangsnes).

Sognefjord Aquarium   AQUARIUM
(www.kringsja.no/eakvainfo.html; adult/child 70/35kr; ⊙10am-7pm May-Sep) This modest, rather old-fashioned aquarium focuses on the saltwater inhabitants of the Sognefjord, with some 24 aquariums stocked with crustaceans, fish and plankton. It's interesting enough to while away a couple of hours on a wet day.

The entry price includes an hour of canoe or rowing-boat hire.

🛏 Sleeping

Vandrerhjem Kringsjå   HOSTEL $
(☑ 57 69 13 03; www.kringsja.no; Laerargata 9; dm 290kr, s/d/f with bathroom 800/990/1200kr, all incl breakfast; ⊙mid-Jun–mid-Aug; 🖥) Uphill from the dock, Balestrand's family-run, HI-affiliated hostel is nowadays an outdoor activities centre during the school year. It started life as a hotel, and this shows; it's a fine lodge-style place with comfortable rooms and decent self-catering facilities.

★ Midtnes Hotel   HOTEL $$
(☑ 57 69 42 40; www.midtnes.no; s 890-1100kr, d 950-1390kr; 🅿🖥) This old family house

near St Olav's Church is pretty as a picture, with its whitewashed frontage and double-gabled roof overlooking a neatly trimmed lawn. Compared to most places in Norway, the rooms are very good value, especially when you factor in the heritage architecture. The terrace makes a sweet setting for the lavish breakfast or three-course dinner (325kr).

Balestrand Hotell   HOTEL **$$**

(✒ 57 69 11 38; www.balestrand.com; s 950-110kr, d & tw 1290-1640kr; ⊙ mid-May–mid-Sep; 🛜) From the outside, this modern concrete hotel has about as much charm as a multistorey office block, but don't be put off: the rooms inside are jolly and colourful, if a bit on the basic side, and the best ones have knockout fjord views.

Kviknes Hotel   HOTEL **$$$**

(✒ 57 69 42 00; www.kviknes.no; d 1420-1750kr; ⊙ May-Sep; P ❄ 🛜) It's hard to believe all the rooms at this gargantuan hotel could ever be filled, so vast is it. It's a hotel of two parts: the original lovely, pale-yellow timber building and an entirely unlovely 1960s annexe, which unfortunately has the best views. The old lounge is a highlight, full of paintings and period furniture.

✖ Eating

★ Ciderhuset   NORWEGIAN **$$**

(✒ 984 77 765; www.ciderhuset.no; Sjøtunsvegen 32; tapas 65-100kr, lunch menu 250kr, dinner menu 295kr; ⊙ noon-10pm late Jun-mid Aug) 🌱 On a fruit farm that produces its own ciders, jams and juices, the Cider House offers tours and tasting sessions in its distillery, after which you can head into the greenhouse restaurant for a pie-and-salad lunch, mix-and-match tapas or whatever the dish of the day is for dinner. Desserts feature fruit from the orchard and come with local organic cream.

Pilgrim   CAFE **$$**

(✒ 915 62 842; www.detgylnehus.no; meals 140-190kr; ⊙ 4-9pm) This homey restaurant is located inside a landmark building near the harbour known as Det Gylne Hus (The Golden House), which is now occupied by an art gallery and studio. The food is classic home cooking: reindeer sausage, grandma's meatballs, poached salmon and troll soup (mushroom soup with veggies), served either in the eclectic interior or the outside terrace.

Gekkens   CAFE **$$**

(✒ 57 69 14 14; Holmen 15; mains 120-190kr) In business for 25 years, this little yellow clapboard cafe is fine for a no-nonsense Norwegian lunch: fish soup, grilled salmon, meatballs with lingonberry jam and other such dishes. The frilly interior is cute and there's a tiny streetside terrace.

ⓘ Information

Tourist Office (✒ 992 31 500; www.visitbal estrand.no; ⊙ 9am-4pm Mon-Fri, 10am-4pm Sat & Sun Jul & Aug, shorter hours rest of year) Not far from the quayside, Balestrand's small tourist office can help with cruise bookings and local activities.

ⓘ Getting There & Away

BUS

Buses link Balestrand and Sogndal (145kr, one hour, three daily).

BOAT

Express boats run to/from Bergen (600kr, 3¾ hours, twice daily) and Sogndal (190kr, 45 minutes, once daily).

A Norled passenger ferry runs across to/from Vik (86kr, 15 minutes, twice daily).

From June to August, a daily ferry (single/return 480/950kr, 1¾ hours) follows the narrow Fjærlandsfjorden to Fjærland, gateway to the glacial wonderlands of Jostedalsbreen.

CAR & MOTORCYCLE

To get to Balestrand, you need to cross on the car ferry from Hella to Dragsvik (94kr, several times hourly). There's also a car ferry service from Dragsvik across the fjord to Vangsnes (123kr, several times hourly), which provides a handy shortcut to Vik, Myrkdalen and Voss.

The scenic Gaularfjellsvegen (Rv13) is an exciting drive north across the mountains to Førde, on Førdefjord, negotiating hairpin bends and skirting Norway's greatest concentration of roadside waterfalls.

Sogndal

POP 7477

Mostly built from functional concrete, Sogndal certainly isn't the area's prettiest town, but it has a nice community feel and it's good as an overnight stopover or as a base for outdoor activities. It's also close enough for a day trip up to the southern side of Jotunheimen National Park, which is about 60km away along the shores of Lustrafjord.

THE SOGNEFJELLET CIRCUIT
....

A spectacular circular, day-long drive, this route runs beside one of Norway's loveliest fjords, climbs a sizeable chunk of the magnificent **Sognefjellet road** (p147), meanders along a lonely, lightly travelled single-lane road that threads across the heights, then plunges in a knuckle-clenching descent, once more to fjord level. The trip can't be done by public transport and cyclists will need to be very fit, and attempt it over a few days.

From Sogndal, head out on the Rv55 to the northeast as it hugs, for the most part, lovely Lustrafjord all the way to Skjolden at the head of the waters. About 5km beyond this tiny settlement, the road starts to seriously twist and climb. You're following an ancient highway where for centuries, when it was no more than a rough track, fish and salt would be hauled up from the coast to be exchanged for iron, butter and hides from communities deep inland.

At wind-battered Turtagrø you can continue along the Rv55, which runs through Jotunheimen National Park, up and over northern Europe's highest road pass (1434m) and on to Lom.

To return to Sogndal, turn right to leave the Rv55 and head for Årdal. The narrow road, known as **Tindevegen** (p149), the Route of the Peaks, keeps climbing, just above the treeline, until the pass (1315m) and a tollbooth. Then it's a plunge down through woods of spindly birch to the emerald-green waters of Årdalsvatnet and the undistinguished village of Øvre Årdal. From here, the Rv53 takes you, via the ferry between Fodnes and Mannheller, back to Sogndal.

◉ Sights & Activities

Kaupanger Stave Church
CHURCH
(www.stavechurch.com/en/kaupanger; Kaupanger; adult/child 70/50kr; ⊙ 10am-5pm Jun-Aug) The area's most impressive sight is this stave church, raised in 1184. It impresses from within by its sheer height, although much of what you see dates from a fundamental renovation in the 17th century. Wall paintings in the nave feature musical annotation, while vine and flower motifs entwine around the chancel. The Celtic-style chancel arch is unique.

Sogn Folkmuseum
MUSEUM
(☑ 57 67 82 06; www.dhs.museum.no; adult/child 80/30kr; ⊙ 10am-3pm May & Sep, to 5pm Jun-Aug, 10am-3pm Mon-Fri Oct-Apr; ◉) This extensive open-air folk museum is between Sogndal and Kaupanger, beside the Rv5. More than 30 buildings, including farms, a schoolhouse and a mill, have been brought from their original sites and embedded in the surrounding woods. Each is well documented in Norwegian and English. There are three short, themed walking trails with informative panels (reception has English translation sheets).

There's also a collection of fishing memorabilia and freight boats in one of the buildings.

Children can pet the animals, build their own log cabin and indulge in other backwoods activities, plus there are gorgeous picnic spots.

Sogndal Guiding
OUTDOORS
(☑ 57 62 99 88; www.sogndallodge.no; Almenningen 10) Pretty much every outdoor pursuit you could wish for is on offer here: hiking, kayaking, climbing, glacier walks and skiing, or longer trips involving all of the above. Sea kayaks, mountain bikes and stand-up paddleboards can be rented here.

It's based in the middle of town at Sogndal Lodge (p224), where there's hostel accommodation.

🛏 Sleeping

Sogndal Vandrerhjem
HOSTEL $
(☑ 57 62 75 75; www.hihostels.no/sogndal; Helgheimsvegen 9-10; s/d from 510/850kr; ⊙ mid-Jun–mid-Aug) It's located beside a busy road junction near the bridge that carries the Rv5, but this large hostel makes a handy place to crash. Accommodation is in single and double rooms, and breakfast is served in the big dinner hall. It's only open during school holidays, as it doubles as a boarding school the rest of the time.

Kjørnes Camping
CAMPGROUND $
(☑ 57 67 45 80; www.kjornes.no; campsite 270kr, cabin 500-1625kr; 🐾) Space is at a premium at this fjord-side campsite, especially when the caravans roll in, so it's worth booking into one of the cabins by the water's edge, which have heated floors, mini-kitchens and

a private terrace on the fjord. It's 3km from Sogndal off the Rv5, direction Lærdal.

★ Sogndal Lodge
HOSTEL $$

(☑57 62 99 88; www.sogndallodge.no; Almenningen 10; d/tr/q 850/1260/1600kr, entire lodge from 3500kr) This excellent hostel has four funky rooms that are Scandi-simple in style but have been jazzed up with vintage finds to lend character. There's a great lounge stocked with sofas, hiking books and blackboard, and a total of 12 beds spread across the quartet of rooms.

Quality Hotel Sogndal
HOTEL $$$

(☑57 62 77 00; www.nordicchoicehotels.com; Gravensteinsgata 5; s/tw 1550/1850kr; P🖭) A reliable outpost of the Quality chain, with a striking curved glass frontage, modern decor and well-appointed rooms, all with wood floors, big windows and good bathrooms, even if the furnishings feel a little sparse. There's a choice of restaurants, one offering Italian dishes, the other serving mainly Norwegian standards.

Hofslund Fjord Hotel
HOTEL $$$

(☑57 62 76 00; www.hofslund-hotel.no; Fjørevegen 37; s/d 1195/1495kr; P@🖭🏊) For full-blown hotel accommodation, this vast edifice is the premier place in town. Dating from 1912, it's a trad place with trad decor to match, but it makes the most of its location, with fjordview balconies, a good restaurant and lawns leading down to the water's edge. The outdoor heated pool is a bonus.

✖ Eating

Kafe Krydder
CAFE $

(☑908 43 828; www.gallerikrydder.no; Parkvegen 6; salads 80-140kr, sandwiches 70-95kr; ⊙11am-5pm Mon-Sat, 10am-4pm Sun) The town's most frequented lunch spot is great for gourmet salads, well-stuffed sandwiches and paninis, morning muffins and afternoon cakes. There's a large terrace outside and a small play area for kids. The building itself is one of the few period structures left in Solvorn.

❶ Getting There & Away

AIR

Sogndal has Sognefjord's only airport, which has a couple of daily flights to/from Bergen and Oslo.

BUS

Local destinations from Sogndal:

Bergen (400kr to 460kr, 4½ to five hours, five daily) Netbuss NX450.

Flåm (220kr to 300kr, two hours, four daily)

Kaupanger (35kr, 10 minutes, eight to 10 daily)

Balestrand (105kr, 1¼ hours, three daily)

BOAT

Express boats run to/from Bergen (600kr, 3¾ hours, twice daily) and Balestrand (190kr, 45 minutes, once daily).

JOSTEDALSBREEN NATIONAL PARK

For years mighty Jostedalsbreen, mainland Europe's largest icecap, crept countercurrent, slowly advancing while most glaciers elsewhere in the world were retreating. Now Jostedalsbreen itself has succumbed and is also withdrawing.

It's still a powerful player, though, eroding an estimated 400,000 tonnes of rock each year. With an area of 487 sq km and in places 600m thick, Jostedalsbreen rules over the highlands of Sogn og Fjordane county. The main icecap and several outliers are protected as the Jostedalsbreen National Park.

The northern and southern sides of the national park are some distance apart, so they need to be visited separately – and you'll have a tough time without your own car. For accessing the southern side of the park, the towns of Solvorn, Sogndal and Fjærland are the most useful gateways, while on the northern side, Stryn, Loen and Olden are within easy driving distance and have plenty of accommodation.

Fjærland

POP 310

If you're still looking for that perfect fjord-side village, then here's another strong contender. Beautifully sited at the end of Fjærlandsfjorden, it's a sleepy one-street town lined with clapboard buildings and surrounded on all sides by huge cliffs. Most people come to experience its pair of particularly accessible glacial tongues, Supphellebreen and Bøyabreen, but Fjærland is also known as the Book Town of Norway (www.bokbyen.no) – 10 shops in town sell second-hand books, mostly in Norwegian, but some in English and other languages too.

The village virtually hibernates from October onwards, then leaps to life in early May, when the ferry runs again.

Jostedalsbreen National Park

N 0 ——— 10 km
  0 ——— 5 miles

◉ Sights

★ **Norwegian Glacier Museum**   MUSEUM
(Norsk Bremuseum; Map p225; ☎ 57 69 32 88; www.
bre.museum.no; adult/child 125/65kr; ⊙ 9am-7pm
Jun-Aug, 10am-4pm Apr-May, Sep & Oct) You can't

miss this striking museum: it's a concrete wedge marooned among a sea of grass on the way into Fjærland, and even has a couple of model woolly mammoths outside. It provides a great overview of general glacier geology, as well as process of fjord formation, and the ecology and wildlife of Jostedalsbreen itself. Highlights are the simulated ice tunnel and the tusk of a Siberian woolly mammoth who met an icy demise 30,000 years ago.

Bøyabreen
GLACIER

(Map p225) The more spectacular of the two glacial tongues accessible from Fjærland, Bøyabreen looms majestically at the end of the wooded valley. There's a car park next to the visitors centre and cafe, from where it's a short walk down to the glacial lake and an un-interrupted panorama over the glacier itself. It's a mighty hunk of ice indeed.

Supphellebreen
GLACIER

(Map p225) Reached via a turn-off from the main road north from Fjærland, this small glacier creeps down the mountainside into an isolated valley. Trails lead from the small car park right up to a rushing stream fed by the glacier's meltwater. Depending on the time of year and how the ground underfoot is, it might even be possible to get close to the ice itself – but take care.

Ice blocks from here were used as podiums at the 1994 Winter Olympics in Lillehammer.

🏃 Activities

Fjærland Guiding offer guided hikes and glacier walks on request.

The tourist office (p227) provides a free *Escape the Asphalt* guide listing 12 marked walking routes, varying from 30 minutes to three hours. For greater detail, supplement this with *Turkart Fjærland* (80kr) at 1:50,000, which comes complete with route descriptions and trails indicated. Pull on your boots and you're away. Most walks follow routes the local shepherds would have used until quite recently to lead their flocks to higher summer pastures.

Fjærland Guiding
KAYAKING

(🏃 tourist office 57 69 32 33; www.fjaerland.org/fjaerland-guiding; Sandaneset; guided hikes from 500kr, glacier hikes from 800kr) Hikes and glacier tours led by adventure guides take place on a by-request basis. Options include a walk over Haugabreen Glacier, a hike up Mt Skeidsnipa and a high-trail hike for a view over Supphellebreen. Bookings can be made through the tourist office (p227).

🛏 Sleeping & Eating

Bøyum Camping
CAMPGROUND $

(Map p225; 🏃 57 69 32 52; www.boyumcamping. no; dm 225kr, campsites 230kr, r 390-590kr, cabins

810-1490kr; ⊗ May-Sep; 🅿 🛜) Three kilometres from the Fjærland ferry landing, Bøyum Camping has something for all pockets and sleeping preferences, not to mention a great view of the Bøyabreen glacier at the head of the valley. Pitches are grassy and spacious, and there's a small shop and cafe.

★ Hotel Mundal
HOTEL $$$

(🏃 57 69 31 01; www.hotelmundal.no; s/d from 1045/1650kr; ⊗ May-Sep; 🅿 🛜) What a sight this historic hotel is. Gabled and slate-topped, it's been in the same family since 1891, and is a classic slice of late-19th-century grandeur, with a wonderful period interior filled with oil paintings, rugs, leather armchairs and burnished furniture. Rooms feel endearingly old-fashioned, with wooden floors, metal bedsteads and antiques aplenty. Fjord views are essential.

For 500kr extra, you can sleep the night in the tower's one suite, complete with wraparound views of fjord and glacier – as did US ex-vice president Walter Mondale, whose family came from Mundal, and the present Queen of Norway (not, as the charming receptionist explains, on the same occasion). There's a choice for food: the relaxed Kafe Mikkel, or the more upmarket hotel restaurant that serves traditional four-course Norwegian dinners (380kr). Non-guests need to book by 6pm.

Fjærland Fjordstove Hotel
HISTORIC HOTEL $$$

(🏃 410 00 200; www.fjaerlandhotel.com; s/d/f/ste 1050/1490/1990/2390kr; 🅿 🛜) This lovely old guesthouse is so quaint it almost looks like a museum exhibit. Clad in white wood, and with a glorious spot right beside the fjord, it's a rickety old place that's packed with history. Rooms are antique in feel, with floral furnishings and kitsch watercolour pictures. Downstairs the book-lined lounge has a grandstand view over the water.

Food is excellent – and surprisingly up to date – for such an olde-worlde location. Lunch is à la carte, but the three-course dinner (550kr, or 650kr for non-guests) is a feast of seasonal, creative flavours.

Brævasshytta
CAFE $

(Map p225; 🏃 57 69 32 96; www.facebook.com/brevasshytta; mains 1400-2100kr; ⊗ 8am-8pm May-Sep) Do visit the Brævasshytta, built into the moraine of Bøyabreen glacier's latest major advance, even if it's only for a cup of coffee. With the glacier right there and in your face, it's like you're in an IMAX cinema – only it's real. Simple meals such as meatballs, grilled chicken, sandwiches and burgers are on offer throughout the day and evening.

 Shopping

Various spots around town sell books, ranging from just a few shelves to the large selection at Bøk & Bilde, where the town's tourist office is located. Most titles tend to be in Norwegian, although you can occasionally find an English title or two.

ℹ️ **Information**

Tourist Office (📞 57 69 32 33; www.fjaerland. org; ⏰ 10am-6pm Jun-Aug, to 4pm Sep-May) Inside the Bok & Bilde bookshop, this small tourist office handles accommodation bookings and rents out bikes.

ℹ️ **Getting There & Away**

BUS

Buses bypass the village and stop on the Rv5 near the Norwegian Glacier Museum. Four to six services run daily to/from Sogndal (90kr, 30 minutes) and Stryn (230kr, two hours). Timetables are available from Kringom (www.kringom.no).

BOAT

In the summer only, from June to August, a ferry (single/return 480/950kr, 1¾ hours, twice daily) runs from Balestrand to Fjærland via Hella.

Jostedalsbreen & Nigardsbreen

The narrow valley of Jostedalen meanders north from the shores of Lustrafjord all the way to another impressive glacier, Nigardsbreen – perhaps the easiest of all to access and definitely the best if you want to do a glacier walk. Remote and beautiful, the valley actually sits between the borders of two national parks, Jostedalsbreen and Breheimen.

🏃 **Activities**

If you're an experienced hiker and prefer to go it solo, continue further up the road past the braided glacial streams at Fåbergstølsgrandane to the dam that creates the big glacial lake, Styggevatnet. Along the way you'll find several scenic glacial tongues and valleys offering excellent wild hiking.

Otherwise, guided hikes can easily be arranged at the Breheimsenteret (p228) visitors centre.

★ **Ice Troll** GLACIER TOURS

(Map p225; 📞 970 14 370; www.icetroll.com; glacier hikes adult/child 800/650kr) This company offers arguably the best choice of glacier trips around Nigardsbreen. It's run by Andy, a Kiwi, and offers memorable excursions involving kayaking across the lake followed by a full-blown ice-walk. There's also an option to take a dinghy tour across the lake if you prefer. For the more adventurous, ice-climbs, snowshoeing and river-rafting are also offered.

There's even an option to sleep out on the glacier if you're feeling really hard-core, or go white-water rafting on the glacial river (from 450kr).

You can reserve a spot online, or ask about availability at the Breheimsenteret (p228) tourist office.

Jostedalen Breførarlag GLACIER TOURS

(Map p225; 📞 57 68 31 11; www.bfl.no; glacier hikes per person 660kr) Jostedalen Breførarlag leads several guided glacier walks on Nigardsbreen, ranging from one to five hours. The easiest is the family walk to the glacier snout and briefly along its tongue (around one hour on the ice; adult/child 300/150kr); more challenging is the full-day Blue Ice Hike (660kr per person). Bookings can be made online or through the visitors centre (p228).

🛏️ **Sleeping**

★ **Jostedal Camping** CAMPGROUND $

(📞 57 68 39 14; www.jostedalcamping.no; campsite for car & 2 adults 220kr, cabin 460-1650kr; 🅿️ 🛜) We're willing to stick our necks out and say this might just be one of the most spectacularly located campsites anywhere in Norway. It's in a gloriously isolated spot, in a riverside meadow just south of the Breheimsenteret. It's impeccably run by owner Astrid, with great facilities including a communal terrace, kitchen, lounge and dining space.

Jostedal Hotel HOTEL $$

(📞 57 68 31 19; www.jostedalhotel.no; s/d/f 920/1190/1440kr; 🅿️ 🛜) 🍴 Pretty much the only hotel option in the valley, this friendly place has been in the same hands for three generations and is currently under Laila's care. Rooms are light, comfortable and have very pretty views down the valley. The restaurant is a great bet for dinner, serving Norwegian staples with produce from the nearby family farm.

ⓘ Information

Breheimsenteret (Map p225; ☏ 57 68 32 50; www.jostedal.com/en/breheimsenteret; ◷ 9am-6pm mid-Jun–Aug, 10am-5pm May–mid-Jun & Sep), Jostedal's striking, pyramid-like visitors centre, has a small museum of geological displays, a shop and a cafe with spectacular views down the valley to the winding blue glacial tongue. The website has information on all the various tour and activities operators in Jostedalen and Breheimen.

ⓘ Getting There & Away

BUS

During the summer only, **Jostedalsbrebussen** (No 160; Glacier Bus; www.jostedal.com/brebussen; adult/child 158/79kr) runs from Sogndal via Solvorn to the foot of the Nigardsbreen glacier, leaving at 8.35am and 1.35pm, and returning from Nigardsbreen at 4.55pm and the Breheimsenteret at 5pm. The trip takes between two-and-a-half and three hours.

BOAT

From mid-June to early September, the *Jostedalsrypa* ferry (70kr return, around 10am to 6pm) shuttles over Nigardsvatnet, the glacial lagoon, from a jetty near the car park. From the landing, it's a sturdy walk over rocks to the glacier face itself.

Should you be unfortunate enough to miss the last ferry back, there's always a rowing boat left at the landing point for the use of the tardy.

CAR & MOTORCYCLE

The easiest way to reach Jostedalsbreen is to follow Rv55 west along Lustrafjord from Sogndal, and then take the turn-off onto Rv604 when you reach the small village of Gaupne.

From the Breheimsenteret visitors centre, the Brevegen toll road (60kr per vehicle) runs for 3.5km to the Nigardvatnet car park next to the lake. It's usually open from April to October.

If you want to dodge the toll, you can walk instead; there are interpretative panels to read along the way.

Briksdalsbreen & Kjenndalsbreen

The northern side of the national park is best explored via its two main valleys, Oldendalen and Lodalen, which run roughly parallel to each other, and both lead up to a different offshoot of the Jotunheimen Glacier: Oldendalen leads up to Briksdalsbreen, while Lodalen leads to Kjenndalsbreen.

Of the two, Briksdalbreen receives the vast majority of visitors (and the coach

tours); Kjenndalsbreen is generally a good deal quieter.

◉ Sights

Kjenndalsbreen   GLACIER
(Map p225) It's a picturesque run of 21km or so up the Lodalen valley to reach this offshoot of the glacier, perhaps the least visited of the four main tongues. The road leads past the brilliant turquoise glacial lake of Lovatnet, then reaches a toll gate (40kr), where you can stop at a lovely picnic spot and hire a bike, canoe or rowing boat, before undertaking the final 5km to the glacier viewing point.

Briksdalsbreen   GLACIER
(Map p225) The main target for most visitors on the northern side of the park is this impressive glacier, which can be reached along a scenic 23km road from Olden. Once you reach the car park, it's a 5km return walk up a steepish path to the glacial face; alternatively, there's a longer, gentler cart track. There are currently no guided walks on the ice itself due to dangerous crevasses, but there are dinghy tours (p229) on the lake.

For the last century or so, the traditional way to get up to the glacier was in a pony-cart, but these have now been replaced by troll cars operated by Oldedalen Skyss (p229), which look rather like giant golfing carts (195kr per person). From their turnaround point, there's still a 15-minute hike on a rough path to see the ice. You can book transport at the Briksdalsbreen visitors centre (p229), but it's worth reserving ahead, as demand often outstrips supply.

Bødalsbreen   GLACIER
(Map p225) Near to Kjenndalsbreen is this minor glacial tongue providing a couple of good hiking possibilities.

🛏 Sleeping

Briksdalsbre Fjellstove   LODGE $$
(Map p225; ☏ 57 87 68 00; www.briksdalsbre.no; s/d 990/1290kr, 4-bed cabin 1390kr) Not far from the Briksdalsbreen visitors centre, this simple hut and lodge complex is the nearest place to stay to the glacier. It's not the most tranquil place by day, but once the tour buses leave, the valley is yours. There's a pleasant restaurant serving mountain trout, elk burgers and the like (mains 180kr to 300kr).

Melkevoll Bretun   CAMPGROUND $$
(Map p225; ☏ 57 87 38 64; www.melkevoll.com; campsite for tent & 2 adults 220kr, cabin 400-850kr,

plus per person 70kr; ⊘May-Sep) There's no bad positions here: depending on your pitch, you've got a grandstand view of the Melkevollbreen glacier, Volefossen, Oldevatnet Lake and Briksdalsbreen glacier. Pitches are spacious, and there's a choice of cabin style: basic and retro or more well-equipped and modern.

ℹ Information

Jostedalsbreen National Park Centre (Jostedalsbreen Nasjonalparksenter; Map p225; www.jostedalsbre.no; Oppstryn; adult/child 80/40kr; ⊘10am-4pm or 6pm May–mid-Sep) You'll find this excellent visitors centre in the village of Oppstryn. There's a worthwhile and informative 10-minute film about the glacier, plus exhibits illustrating avalanches and rock falls and a variety of stuffed wildlife. Outside, enjoy its unique garden with more than 300 species of endemic vegetation, each labelled in Norwegian, English and French. A cluster of picnic tables offers a spectacular vista over the lake.

ℹ Getting There & Away

Between June and August, **Oldedalen Skyss** (☑57 87 68 05; www.oldedalenskysslag.com) runs a Glacier Bus from Stryn to Briksdal (101kr, one hour, daily), calling by Loen and Olden.

NORDFJORD

For most visitors the 100km-long Nordfjord is but a stepping stone between the much better-known fjords of Sognefjorden and Geirangerfjord. At the eastern end of the fjord, the small towns of Loen Olden and Stryn make useful overnight stops, especially if you're headed to the southern side of Jotunheimen National Park.

Olden

POP 498

There's really not much going on in the small village of Olden, but it is useful as a transit town for people heading north from Nordfjord or west towards Briksdalsbreen Glacier. Most people who linger here are arriving on a cruise ship: Olden is one of the 10 most visited stop-offs in Norway, so it can be absolutely swamped if you time your arrival badly.

🏃 Activities

Briksdal Adventure   HIKING
(☑918 44 474, 901 38 308; www.briksdaladventure.com; Olden; glacier hike per person 500kr; ⊘May-Sep) This guiding service based in Olden

leads hikes up to Brikdalsbreen followed by a dinghy ride around the glacial lake. If you actually want to get onto the ice, hikes over the Tystigbreen Glacier at Strynefjellet, near Stryn ski resort (800kr), are also possible.

🛏 Sleeping

Olden Fjordhotel   HOTEL $$$
(☑57 87 04 00; www.olden-hotel.no; s/d from 1390/1690kr; ⊘May–mid-Sep; P🛜) Near the tiny settlement of Olden, this huge fjord hotel lurks on the water's edge like a battle tanker. It's a deeply ugly building, but the rooms are passable, with cheery floral fabrics and balconies for practically every room.

ℹ Information

Tourist Office (☑57 87 40 54; www.nordfjord.no; ⊘10am-4pm mid-Jun–mid-Aug) This small tourist office dispenses information on the Nordfjord area, including a free map with suggested walks.

ℹ Getting There & Away

Nor-Way Fjordexpressen (www.nor-way.no) NW431 travels to Bergen (533kr, 6¾ hours, twice daily).

Loen

POP 398

The fjord-side village of Loen is mainly of use as a gateway to the glaciers. From this tiny village, a road leads up the Lodalen valley to the spectacular Bødalen and Kjenndalen glacial tongues.

🏃 Activities

Loen makes a good base for hikers. Arm yourself with *Walking in Loen & Lodalen* (50kr; 1:50,000), which describes 20 day walks.

One great, though strenuous, hike leads to the Skålatårnet tower, atop the 1848m-high summit of Skåla. The route begins at a signed car park 2.5km east of Loen. Allow seven to eight hours – considerably more than the course record of under 70 minutes for La Sportiva Skaala annual uphill race.

Local activity-focused hotels and tourist offices, such as the one in Olden, usually stock copies.

★**Loen Skylift**   CABLE CAR
(☑57 87 59 00; www.loenskylift.com; Mt Høven; adult/child return 485/240kr; ⊘9am-10pm Jul–mid-Aug, 9am-7pm Sun-Thu & 9am-9pm Fri & Sat May-Jun & mid-Aug–Oct, noon-4pm Fri &

10am-4pm Sat & Sun Nov-Apr) Loen's swishest attraction is this sleek cable car, one of the steepest in the world, which whisks you from the edge of the fjord to the top of Mt Høven – 1011m in about five minutes. Obviously the views at the top are epic, but there are also lots of trails to hike and, in winter, great skiing. There's also a fine restaurant (mains 140kr to 365kr) with what has to be one of the best dinner views anywhere in Norway.

★ **Loen Active**   OUTDOORS
(🖰 57 87 58 00; www.loenactive.no) The highlight activity offered by this Loen-based provider is a vertiginous climb along various *via ferrata* (1270kr including the Loen Skylift), a system of ropes and ladders bolted into the sheer rock face of Mt Høven. It's not a pastime to consider if you're even vaguely afflicted with vertigo. Guided hiking, biking and pedalboat rental are offered here too.

🛏 Sleeping

Sande Camping   CAMPGROUND $
(Map p225; 🖰 57 87 45 90; www.sande-camping.no; campsite for car, tent & 2 adults 250kr, 4-person hut from 1050kr) You could spend an active day or two in the lovely environs of Sande Camping, a few kilometres southeast of town. It offers lakeside camping and traditional huts, and you can hire bikes, kayaks and fishing rods. There's a small supply store next to reception and a pleasant cafe (try the local trout), and the toilet block has been upgraded.

Hotel Alexandra   HOTEL $$$
(🖰 57 87 50 00; www.alexandra.no; s/d incl breakfast from 2000/3000kr; 🅿 ✳ 🛜 ﹦) This huge,

pricey, fjord-side resort caters for pretty much everything you might need, with a brace of restaurants, two cafes, a luxurious spa, indoor and outdoor pools and even its own nightclub. The rooms themselves are fairly standard: comfy enough, if unexciting. There are no fewer than eight categories: fjord views and floor space command premiums.

❶ Getting There & Away

The Nor-Way Fjordexpressen (www.nor-way.no) NW431 bus stops in Loen on its way from Bergen (533kr, 6¾ hours, twice daily).

Stryn
POP 2300

The small town of Stryn, which is the de facto capital of upper Nordfjord, is a modern regional hub. It does sprawl, but retains some of its original wooden houses along the river and, in any case, its 'real' vibe is nicely energising if you've been in the wild for a while.

🏃 Activities

Stryn Summer Ski Centre   SKIING
(Stryn Sommerskisenter; www.stryn.no/sommerski; adult/child 370/300kr) Some 9km along the Gamle Strynefjellsvegen, you reach the Stryn Summer Ski Centre. From late May until some time in July, it offers Norway's most extensive summer skiing; most of those photos of bikini-clad skiers you see around were snapped right here. It's a bleak place outside the short season.

THE LOVATNET DISASTERS

Ascending Lodalen, you'll see what appear to be islands that nearly split the lake into two. These are in fact giant rocks that were dislodged from Ramnefjell and crashed down into the lake in three separate calamities. In 1905, when the resulting giant wave swept away 63 people – only nine of whom were ever found – *Lodalen,* the lake steamer, was deposited 400m inland. In 1936, an estimated 1 million cubic metres of rock crashed down, its wave killing 72 and lifting the steamer even higher. The third, in 1950, left a bigger scar on the mountain, but fortunately claimed no lives.

A path signed Pilgrimssti (Pilgrim's Path; indicated by blue markers), descends steeply through birchwood to a simple wooden cross that marks the site of a memorial to the victims of the 1905 disaster – itself swept away in the 1936 cataclysm. It can be found 100m before the toll road signs to Kjenndalsbreen. On the way, besides a series of edifying biblical tracts, you can spot the rusting remains of *Lodalen,* the lake steamer beached this far inland after being carried on the waves of disasters one and two. Allow 35 to 45 minutes for this out-and-back walk.

GAMLE STRYNEFJELLSVEGEN

This spectacular 130km route takes a comfortable four hours. Head eastwards from Stryn along the **Rv15** as it runs alongside the river that descends from Lake Strynevatnet, then follows the lake shore itself. It's an inspirational ride with mountain views as impressive as anywhere in the country.

After 20km, make your first stop at the **Jostedalsbreen National Park Centre** (p229) in the village of **Oppstryn** for glacier information, stuffed wildlife, a unique garden and stellar views over the lake.

At an interpretive panel and sign 17km beyond the National Park Centre, turn right to take the **Rv258**. It took a team of local and immigrant Swedish navvies more than 10 years to lay the **Gamle Strynefjellsvegen** (old Stryn mountain road) over the mountain. The road, considered a masterpiece of civil engineering at the time, opened to traffic in 1894. For more than 80 years, it was the principal east-to-west route in this part of the country. Until well into the 1950s, a team of some 200 workers, armed only with spades, would keep it clear in winter, digging through several miles of metres-high snow.

The climb to the high plateau is spectacular, enhanced by thin threads of water tumbling from the heights and a trio of roaring roadside torrents carrying glacial melt. There are several stopping points as you ascend this narrow strip. Savour, in particular, the viewing platform above Videfossen, where the water churns beneath you.

Some 9km along the Gamle Strynefjellsvegen, you reach **Stryn Summer Ski Centre** (p230), a bleak place outside the short season. But from late May until some time in July, it offers Norway's most extensive summer skiing; most of those photos of bikini-clad skiers you see around were snapped right here.

The steep ascent behind you, continue along a good-quality unsurfaced single-track road that runs above a necklace of milky turquoise tarns overlooked by bare, boulder-strewn rock. Here on this upland plateau, the sparse vegetation hugs the ground close.

After crossing the watershed 10km beyond the ski centre, there begins a much more gentle descent to rejoin the Rv15. Turn left for a fast, smooth, two-lane run beside **Lake Breidalsvatn** before diving into the first of three long tunnels that will bring you back to the National Park Centre and onward, retracing your steps back to Stryn.

After the completion of these three linked tunnels in 1978, the old road was over-shadowed by its younger alternative: 12 speedy kilometres along a wide road against 27km of winding single track – there was no comparison. But the Gamle Strynefjellsvegen always drew travellers with time on their hands and lovers of wild scenery. Now, freshly designated a National Tourist Route, it again enjoys a share of a new, if softer, limelight.

The Gamle Strynefjellsvegen is normally free of snow from June to October. Electronic signs along the Rv15 indicate if the 'Strynfjellet' (its official name) is indeed open.

🛏 Sleeping

Stryn Camping
CAMPGROUND $

(☑57 87 11 36; www.stryn-camping.no; Bøavegen 6; campsite for car, tent & 2 adults 260kr, cabin 400-1700kr; ⊙year-round) There's a holiday camp vibe to this pleasant, if busy, campsite, just a couple of blocks away from Stryn's main drag. It's dominated by caravans and cabins, so campers tend to feel a bit squeezed out here when it's busy.

Still, the facilities are good – there's a playground, minigolf and trampolines for the kids, and a washing machine and tumble-dryer for guests – and it's close enough to town to easily stock up on supplies.

Stryn Vertshus B&B
B&B $$

(☑57 87 05 30; www.strynvertshus.no; s/d 800/1300kr; 🐾) Tucked up in the eaves of this century-old house, above the town's top cafe, you'll find five sweet, cosy rooms that are a good deal more charming than many of the behemoth hotels around this end of Nordfjord. Little touches like brass lights and B&W prints add character and there are fjord glimpses – plus a super breakfast.

★ Visnes Hotel
HOTEL $$$

(☑57 87 10 87; www.visneshotel.no; Prestestegen 1; s/d/f 1295/1495/1950kr; ⊙mid-May–Sep; 🅿🐾) The Visnes, run by the same family for six generations, occupies two magnificent listed properties, each with its own character. Most rooms are in the larger building, constructed in 1850, which is furnished in period style but with a rustic restraint. The more expensive rooms have stunning fjord views and there are also a couple of large family rooms.

To feel like royalty, request a room in the smaller 1890 'dragon style' building that was occupied by King Rama V of Siam during his 1908 tour, or the one where King Oscar of Sweden and Norway rested his head in 1913. The restaurant, in the hotel's larger building, serves traditional dishes made with local produce.

✖️ Eating

★ Stryn Vertshus   CAFE $$
(✆ 57 87 05 30; www.strynvertshus.no; Tonningsgata 19; mains 100-195kr; ☺ 9am-11pm Mon-Sat, 11am-8pm Sun) Now this is what a fjord-side village cafe should be like: run by friendly staff and comfy as an old pair of slippers. The menu is simple – mainly burgers, pasta, sandwiches and pizza – but it's well done, and will fill you up nicely. The coffee and cake are great.

ℹ️ Getting There & Away

The Nor-Way Fjordexpressen NW431 bus connects Stryn with Bergen (533kr, 6¾ hours, twice daily), stopping in Loen and Olden. Nettbuss Express NX146 heads to Oslo (349kr to 609kr, seven to eight hours, twice daily), and Nettbuss Express NX146 to Ålesund (319kr, 2¾ hours, twice daily), with a change at Ørsta.

THE FJORD COAST

Precious few travellers make the pilgrimage out to the far western coastline, preferring to stick around the well-known fjords further inland. But this fractured, fissured coastline has many charms – especially if you're a fan of wild and windswept scenery. Lonely lighthouses and wind farms dot the coastline, and numerous remote islands lie just offshore – including the haunting medieval monastery on Selja Island.

Florø

POP 8450

Florø, Norway's westernmost town, is a pleasant if sleepy settlement whose coat of arms features, appropriately, three herrings rampant – like most of Norway's coast, it once relied almost entirely on fishing for its livelihood.

Fishing has largely been supplanted by oil these days: the large Fjord Base, just northeast of town, serves the giant Snorreankeret offshore oilfield.

A group of several offshore islands is easily accessible by local ferry and make for an atmospheric day trip to a number of significant historical sites and to take in their incredible natural beauty.

◉ Sights

On and around Strandgata, Florø's main street, the most significant 19th-century timbered houses are well signed and documented in both Norwegian and English.

For a scenic overlook on the town, it's an easy 10-minute climb up the **Storåsen hill** from the Florø Ungdomsskule on Havrenesveien.

★ Kinn Island   ISLAND
If you're on limited time, a visit to this little island is a great way of getting a flavour of the coastline around Florø. After a quick boat ride from the quay, you're met by a guide on the island who takes you on a 40-minute, 1km walk up to see the island's famous stone church, telling tales of the island and Florø's fishing heritage on the way. The stout stone church, dating from the 12th century, is stunning.

Coast Museum   MUSEUM
(Sogn og Fjordane Kystmuseet; ✆ 57 74 22 33; www.kyst.museum.no; Brendøyvegen; adult/child 70kr/free; ☺ 11am-6pm Mon-Fri, noon-4pm Sat & Sun Jun-Aug, 10am-3pm Mon-Fri, noon-3pm Sat & Sun Sep-May) A catch-all museum covering the whole of Sogn og Fjordane county, this museum explores the coast in all its varied forms. It's spread over several buildings: one is dedicated to fishing, including a model 1900 fishing family's home; and exhibits on the foundation of the island as a small herring trading post barely 150 years ago. A second houses a collection of coastal boats. The Snorreankeret display illustrates the exploration and exploitation of the North Sea oil and gas fields.

It's about 2km south of the town centre.

Offshore Islands
Local ferries leaving from Florø's Fugleskjærskaia Quay connect the mainland to several

small islands, each making for a stimulating off-the-beaten-track day trip. The tourist office (p234) can reserve ferries and also advise on island accommodation.

Askrova has a prehistoric Troll Cave, whose deepest depths have never been explored. On the island of **Batalden**, check out the gallery and small museum at Batalden Havbu. You can overnight in their sensitively restored cottage B&B.

Kinn has a beautifully restored 12th-century church, believed to have been built by British Celts sheltering from religious persecution.

On **Svanøy**, enjoy the hiking and pass by the small deer centre.

At 233m, the highest point on **Tansøy** offers great panoramic views over the surrounding archipelago.

Activities

Boating
For coastal explorations, Florø Rorbu and Efinor Camping Krokane rent out rowing and motor boats.

Hiking & Cycling
The tourist office (p234) sells the useful *Cycling in Flora* (10kr) booklet and has maps of local hikes.

🛏 Sleeping

★ **Efinor Camping Krokane**   CAMPGROUND **$**
(📲57 75 22 50; www.efinor.no/camping; campsite 150kr, cabin 450-1100kr; 🛜) This campsite on a secluded peninsula about 2.5km east of town really offers a chance to get away from the crowds. Cabins are spread out under the trees and the shoreside meadow is a camper's delight. Rowing boats (200kr per day) and motor boats (from 390kr per four hours) can be rented here, too.

★ **Quality Hotel Florø**   HOTEL **$$**
(📲57 75 75 75; www.nordicchoicehotels.no; Hamnegata 11; r 1295-1695kr; 🅿@🛜) The waterfront location sells this place before you even step inside. It's right by the marina and most rooms have lovely views of bobbing boats. The older part of the building was once a herring store, since extended with a modern annexe. It's worth upgrading here: the more expensive rooms have much more space and some have balconies and original beams.

Florø Rorbu   APARTMENT **$$**
(📲913 92 888; www.florbu.com; Krokane Kai; apt 950-1250kr; 🛜) These excellent, family-owned, fully furnished flats are right beside a tiny inlet and have their own moorings. They're really well appointed, and prices drop for stays of more than one night. Motor boats (400kr per day) and sea kayaks (200kr per day) are available for hire, and they'll happily lend you crab traps and fishing gear.

Comfort Hotel Florø   HOTEL **$$**
(📲57 75 25 52; www.nordicchoicehotels.com; s 1050kr, d 1150-1650kr; 🛜) A decent option right in the heart of town, with a little bit more character than you'd expect from a big chain hotel. It has a fresh, modern design, with murals and designer furniture livening up the lobby, a theme that runs through into the upstairs rooms. The in-house pub-restaurant, **Kysten**, is only open on Friday and Saturday.

🍴 Eating & Drinking

Bistro
To Kokker   CAFE **$**
(📲57 75 22 33; http://bistro.bistrotokokker.no; Strandgata 33; dishes 140-175kr; ⏲9am-10pm) This canteen-style place is a bit short on charm, but it's great for fill-you-up, cheap-as-chips food. Crispy cod, fried salmon, steaks, pork chops and fish skewers are all served with a generous helping of mash and

---

THE WORLD'S LONGEST HERRING TABLE

OK, so the competition may not be all that extensive but a herring table 400m long is an impressive achievement in its own right. Each year, Florø and Haugesund, further down the coast, used to vie with each other for the year's largest and longest spread but, now that Haugesund has retired, there's no longer the same north–south rivalry and Florø has the field to itself.

On the third Friday in June, the table is erected in the heart of Florø. Just imagine a standard 400m running track, straightened out and laden with plates of herring, potatoes, bread and drinks, all free of charge, and you've got the scene. Then, once the table's cleared away, the festivities continue all weekend.

veg and there's always a dish of the day on offer.

Hjørnevikbua PUB FOOD $$
(☑ 57 74 01 22; www.hjornevikbua.bistrotokokker. no; Strandgata 23; dinner mains 280-320kr, 3-course menu 475kr; ⊙ 5-10pm Mon-Sat) In an attractive clapboard building, this place has two settings: a salty downstairs pub and an upstairs restaurant that turns out some decent fish dishes, plus hearty mains like reindeer fillet and steaks. Standards are pubby rather than sophisticated, but they'll fill you up and the views are pleasant.

Vesle Kinn PUB
(☑ brewery 473 39 047; www.kinn.no; Strandgata 58; ⊙ 4-11pm Wed-Thu, to midnight Fri & Sat) This fantastic microbrewery started brewing in 2009, and its creative beers have proved a big hit across Norway and Europe. Its taproom in the town centre has around 12 of their beers to try, plus several gins and a white stout.

Tours of the brewery are available: ask at the bar or contact the tourist office (p234).

ℹ Information

Tourist Office (☑ 57 74 30 00; www.fjordkysten. no; Strandgata 30; ⊙ 9am-6pm Mon-Fri, 10am-4pm Sat, 11am-3pm Sun Jun-Aug) This well-run tourist office handles activity bookings, including for trips to Kinn Island and visits to the Kinn Brewery, and provides information on hiking and guided tours.

ℹ Getting There & Away

AIR
Florø airport is located 2km south of the town centre. Widerøe (www.wideroe.no) flies direct to Florø from Oslo, Bergen and Stavanger.

BOAT
Florø is the first stop on the Hurtigruten coastal ferry as it heads north from Bergen.

Norled express boats call in twice daily on the run between Bergen (718kr, 3½ hours) and Måløy (253kr, one hour).

CAR
If you're driving, the most scenic way north to Måløy by road is via Bremanger island.

Kalvåg

POP 453

If you're travelling between Florø and Måløy via Bremanger island, do make the 5km detour from the ferry landing point at Smørhamn to the small, sensitively pre-

served fishing village of Kalvåg. Nowadays there's just one giant fish-processing factory on the village outskirts that operates when the herring and mackerel shoals come near, but at its peak Kalvåg had over 50 herring salt houses that employed a seasonal workforce of around 10,000.

✕ Eating

★ Knutholmen SEAFOOD $$$
(☑ 57 79 69 00; www.knutholmen.no; mains 298-350kr, seafood platters 695kr; ⊙ 8am-midnight) One of the best addresses for fresh fish on the west coast. Scoff a plate of the freshest shrimps, split some crab or lobster claws, or tuck into a lavish seafood platter, served on the dockside terrace with the fishing boats right before you. It's a wonderful place to while away the time between ferries.

There's attractive accommodation upstairs (double 1390kr to 1890kr), with wooden floors and a vaguely maritime theme.

ℹ Information

Tourist Office (☑ 481 40 488; www.fjordkysten. no; ⊙ 10am-6pm Mon-Fri, to 4pm Sat, noon-4pm Sun Jul-mid-Aug, 10am-4pm Mon-Fri rest of year) The quayside tourist office can arrange visits to herring salt houses.

ℹ Getting There & Away

Kalvåg is inconvenient to get to – and to explore – unless you have your own car.

Måløy

POP 3500

On a blasting winter's day in the teeth of an Atlantic gale, the isolated fishing port of Måløy feels like the end of the earth – but catch it on a rare sunny, windless day and it's as peaceful and pleasant a small town as you could hope for. Like most of this corner of Norway, it's a town with a long fishing heritage that's now been upstaged by oil.

It sits at the mouth of Nordfjord, and is actually on a separate island, Vågsøy, linked to the mainland by the graceful S-curve of Måløybrua bridge. Commercial boats ply up and down and it's a refreshingly real, working town.

⊙ Sights

Refviksanden BEACH
Running for more than 1.5km, this wonderful white-sand beach is one of the best

THE ROLLING ROAD TO KRÅKENES LIGHTHOUSE

The 42km return trip can be comfortably driven in a couple of hours, including stops. Take the Rv617 from Måløy, then follow signs for Kråkenes Fyr (Kråkenes Lighthouse). On the way there or back, it's worth the short, signed detour to visit **Refviksanden** (p234), a 1.5km reach of white sand, voted Norway's finest beach in a 2010 online poll.

The road rolls over treeless, windswept grassland, runs past a long line of twirling windmills (step outside your car and you'll understand why they're sited right here) and offers staggering views of steep cliffs.

Kråkenes Lighthouse (p235), at the very end of the road, perches precariously on a rock shoulder. Sunny or stormy, it's a romantic spot with stunning views of the cliffs and pounding ocean; it's also possible to stay in its B&B or bridal suite.

A bridal suite, complete with circular bed, occupies the main house or there are five double rooms in the former stormhouse.

places for a wild sea swim on the west coast – assuming you can handle the perennially chilly temperatures, that is. On a sunny day, it's a glorious spot, but it's a rare day indeed that there's no wind. It's about 10km drive from Måløy; there's a simple campsite near the beach with toilets and showers.

Kannesteinen　　　　NATURAL FEATURE
A short drive about 10km west of town brings you to the bizarre – and much Instagrammed – rock formation, rising from the sea like the tail of a whale. It's completely natural, but it looks for all the world like a piece of abstract sculpture.

🛏 Sleeping

Steinvik Camping　　　　CAMPGROUND $
(☑ 57 85 10 70; www.steinvik-camping.no; campsites 250kr, cabins 400-1200kr, apts 550-800kr; ☺ year-round) The nearest campsite to Måløy has spectacular views over the busy sea lane and a particularly cosy common room with sofas and armchairs. To get there, cross the bridge to the east bank, turn right after 2km beside a school and follow the track downhill for 1.2km. No credit cards.

Torget Hotell　　　　HOTEL $$
(☑ 953 33 133; www.torgethotell.no; Gate 1 49; s/d 1090/1290kr; P 🛜) By far the best place to stay in Måløy, this stylish hotel occupies what was once an old canning factory. Rooms are sleek and smart, with wood floors and neutral tones, and around half have a water-view balcony. There's a great loft space on the top floor with sloping mansard windows, through which you can watch boats dock in the harbour.

Kråkenes Lighthouse　　　　GUESTHOUSE $$$
(www.krakenesfyr.com; d with bathroom 3150kr, with shared bathroom 2000kr, ste 3950kr, 3-night minimum stay; P 🛜) This remote lighthouse lies at the end of a spectacular 42km drive from Måløy, and it's a place which takes getting away from it all to another level. Inside is a fancy bridal suite (complete with circular bed), plus five cosy rooms in a stormhouse nearby. The suite has private facilities; rooms share a kitchen and only two have an en suite.

🍴 Eating

Snorre Sjømat　　　　CAFE $
(Havfruen; ☑ 57 85 23 36; ☺ 10am-4.30pm Mon-Fri, to 2pm Sat) This no-nonsense, no-frills seafood bar is the place in town to come if you just want to enjoy the fruits of the sea with nary a starched napkin in sight. Think fish cakes and mash, cod and chips, crab-stuffed sandwiches, pints of prawns and umpteen varieties of *klippfisk*. If you're self-catering, they also offer fresh fish to take away.

Kraftstasjonen　　　　SEAFOOD $$
(☑ 57 85 12 60; Gate 1; dinner mains 250-350kr; ☺ 11am-10pm Mon-Thu, to 1am Fri & Sat) For brunch, lunch or dinner, this funky mainstreet bistro serves up something that fits the bill. There's usually a choice of fish, tapas-y dishes, quinoa salads, burgers and the like, as well as the house special fish soup that has a loyal local following.

ℹ Information

Tourist Office (☑ 57 84 50 77; www.nordfjord. no; ☺ 8am-4pm or 5pm Mon-Fri, 10am-4pm Sat Jul & Aug, hours vary rest of year) This small tourist office can help with boat bookings, birdwatching tours and other activities.

ⓘ Getting There & Away

BOAT
Norled's express boat to/from Bergen (865kr, 4½ hours, twice daily) stops in at Måløy on its way to Selje. The Hurtigruten coastal ferry also calls in.

BUS
Nettbuss express NX146 runs to/from Oslo (719kr, 11 hours, twice daily) via Stryn.

Selje & Selja Island

POP 700

Few visitors make it as far west as **Selje**, and therein lies the charm of this village on the western edge of Norway, with its strand of pristine, white beach. **Vestkapp**, 32km by road from Selje, isn't Norway's westernmost point, despite the name, but it still provides superb sea views – and several spots nearby have become popular with Norway's hard-core, cold-water surfers. But the main reason to visit is the chance to visit the 12th-century Selja Monastery, which sits on a rocky island just offshore.

◉ Sights

★**Selja Monastery**   HISTORIC SITE
(www.seljekloster.no) The haunting ruins of Selja monastery and the church of St Sunniva on Selja Island date from the 11th and 12th centuries respectively: this has been a place of pilgrimage for over 1000 years. A 40m-high tower is still intact and can be climbed for a splendid panorama. It's about a 15-minute boat rode from Selje; regular boat trips (adult/child 275/120kr) run from the town quay.

🛏 Sleeping & Eating

Doktorgarden   B&B $$
(📱 909 29 771; www.doktorgarden-selje.no; s 750kr, d with shared bathroom 1090kr; ☺ Easter-Oct; 🅿🛜) Up the hill from the port, you can wake in this lovely old house to sea views and the aroma of freshly baked cakes. On the 2nd floor, four big, carefully decorated rooms share a large, spotless bathroom and a guest kitchen. Downstairs there's a basement gallery, bookshop and bright cafe (p236).

Doktorgarden Cafe   CAFE $
(📱 909 29 771; cakes 35-50kr; ☺ 9am-6pm Jun-Aug, 10am-3pm Sat & Sun rest of year) A light, homey space at the Doktorgarden B&B where cakes are the thing: plum cake, cheesecake, carrot cake and classic Norwegian jam and cream-filled sponge.

ⓘ Information

Tourist Office (📱 57 85 66 06; www.nordfjord. no; ☺ 9am-4.45pm Mon-Fri mid-Jun–mid-Aug) Selje's tourist office, at the harbour, keeps a list of cabins and apartments in the area and can give you directions to local artisans and food producers, as well as suggesting walking trails and beaches. Staff are also incredibly knowledgeable about the region's rich cultural heritage, from its pilgrim routes to its WWII tunnels and fortifications.

ⓘ Getting There & Away

From Måløy, you have two stunningly attractive ways of reaching Selje – the splendid fjord-side drive along the Rv618, or aboard the Nordfjord express boat (91kr, 25 minutes, twice daily).

THE NORTHERN FJORDS

As you travel north from Nordfjord, a web of deep, craggy fjords bites into the coastline, creating a myriad of islets and inlets along the coastline, and etching out some truly breathtaking scenery.

The main draw here is undoubtedly the epic Geirangerfjord, a Unesco World Heritage Site, and near the top of most visitors' must-see lists. There's no doubt that it's a glorious sight, but its charm is sadly marred by the sheer number of people who want to see it – there's a seemingly never-ending stream of sightseeing boats and cruise ships chugging up and down the channel.

Away from this fjord, however, you'll soon find yourself well off the beaten track with the scenery to yourself. Further north, the elegant towns of Ålesund and Kristiansund are well worth a visit, while two epic roads – the Trollstigen and the Atlantiksvegen – are the stuff of driving dreams.

Åndalsnes

POP 2244

There are two equally dramatic ways to approach Åndalsnes: by road through the Trollstigen Pass or along Romsdalen as you ride the spectacularly scenic Rauma Railway. The rail route down from Dombås ploughs through a deeply cut glacial valley flanked by sheer walls and plummeting waterfalls. Badly bombed during WWII, the modern town, nestled beside Romsdalfjord, might be nondescript, but the locals are delightful and the surrounding landscapes are absolutely magnificent.

◉ Sights

★ Trollstigen   MOUNTAIN ROAD

(www.trollstigen.net; ⊘ May-Oct) This twist-
ing, sky-topping corkscrew of a road is the
most famous stretch of tarmac in Norway.
Completed in 1936 after eight years of labour, the Troll's Ladder is a stunning feat
of road-building, spiralling up the mountainside through 11 hairpin bends and a 1:12
gradient, and after heavy rain, waterfalls
cascade down the mountainside, drenching
cars as they pass. To add to the thrill, much
of it is effectively single-lane, meaning traffic jams and vehicle-passing are part of the
hair-raising experience.

At the crest of the pass, a gravity-defying
platform and a series of viewpoints have
been built out of rusting steel and concrete,
a striking artificial counterpoint to the bare
rock and natural scenery all around. Tee-
tering precipitously over the plunging cliff
and allowing stomach-churning views right
down the mountain, the site was designed
by top architect Reiulf Ramstad and has become one of the most famous locations on
the National Tourist Route network: don't
miss it.

The road can be done in either direction,
from Valldal or Andalsnes, a distance of about
38km. The road passes through Reinheimen
National Park, established in 2006 and Norway's third largest, where wild reindeer still
crop the mosses and soft grass.

The pass is usually cleared and open from
late May to mid-October, although it's entirely
dependent on the seasonal snowfall.

★ Rauma Railway   SCENIC RAILWAY

(s 297kr, 1 child free per adult; ⊘ 4 daily) A classic
Norwegian train ride that railway buffs definitely won't want to miss, the 114km-long
Rauma Railway clatters from Åndalsnes
and Dombås, high in the mountains of
central Norway. It's a super trip, taking in
fjords, forests, valleys, lakes and mountains
en route, and passing through six tunnels and 32 bridges. There's also a shorter
summer-only tourist train with onboard
commentary that runs twice daily from
June to August from Åndalsnes' lakeside
station up to Bjorli, at 600m.

Trollveggen   NATURAL FEATURE

(Troll Wall) From Dombås, the E136 and
rail line drop in parallel northwest down
to Romsdalen (you might have a sense of
déjà vu if you've seen *Harry Potter and
the Half-Blood Prince,* in which the valley

features). Near Åndalsnes, the dramatic
Trollveggen, first conquered in 1958 by a
joint Norwegian and English team, rears
skywards. The highest vertical mountain wall in Europe, its ragged and often
cloud-shrouded summit, 1800m from the
valley floor, is considered the ultimate
challenge among mountaineers.

🏃 Activities

Fishing

John Kofoed Fishing Trips   FISHING

(☑ 971 79 442; www.rauma-jakt-fiskesafari.no; adult/
child 380/180kr, plus per rod 120kr) John Kofoed
runs three-hour fishing tours on Romsdalsfjorden three times daily in summer.
There are 68 different fish in the fjord, with
the most common catches being coalfish, pol-
lack, cod, haddock, turbot, halibut, whiting,
herring and mackerel. Reserve directly or
through the tourist office (p238).

Hiking

The *Geiranger Trollstigen* (30kr) pamphlet describes seven signed hiking trails in
the Trollstigen area. You'll need to supplement this with the *Romsdals-Fjella* map at
1:80,000. The tourist office (p238) carries both
and can also arrange mountain walks of four
to six hours with a qualified guide.

★ Aksla/Nesaksla   HIKING

(www.romsdal.com) An excellent half-day day
hike begins in town, along Romsdalsvegen,
50m north of the roundabout before the
Esso petrol station. It takes around one to
1½ hours to reach the summit of Nesaksla
(715m), the peak that rises above Åndalsnes.
The ascent rewards with the most astonishing views of the Romsdal Alps, the River
Rauma and the Romsdal fjord.

Climbing

The best local climbs are the less extreme
sections of the 1500m-high rock route on
Trollveggen and the 1550m-high Romsdalshorn, but there are a wealth of options.
Serious climbers should buy *Klatring i
Romsdal* (300kr), which includes rock- and
ice-climbing information in both Norwegian
and English.

Skiing

Romsdalen is considered among the best skiing areas in the country, with the rewards of
untouched powder and continuous views of
fjords and wild peaks awaiting those who are
up to its ski up, ski down challenges.

Kirketaket (1439m) is one of the Romsdalen 'classics' and takes three to five hours to ascend, but delivers over 1000 vertical metres of steep downhill slopes, from where you can ski right down to the fjord. Spring and early summer skiing is possible once the Trollstigen road opens as well.

See www.romsdal.com and www.kirketaket.com for more information. For ski guiding see www.skiromsdal.no or contact Hotel Aak, which also organises ski guides.

Festivals & Events

Rauma Rock   MUSIC
(www.raumarock.com; ☉Aug) Central Norway's largest outdoor rock gathering held over two days in early August.

Norsk Fjellfestival   SPORTS
(Norway Mountain Festival; www.norsk-fjellfestival.no; ☉Jul) A weeklong get together in early July for lovers of the great outdoors, with plenty of folk events thrown in.

Sleeping

Åndalsnes Camping   CAMPGROUND $
(✎71 22 16 29; www.andalsnes-camping.com; campsite for tent, car & 2 adults 190kr, cabin 400-975kr; 🛜) Less than 2km from Åndalsnes, this friendly campsite enjoys a dramatic setting beside the River Rauma and nestled below the peaks. There's a good cafe, cosy TV/recreation room and you can order fresh bread to be picked up each morning. Bikes, canoes and stand-up paddleboards can be hired at reception.

Trollstigen Resort   CAMPGROUND $
(✎71 22 68 99; www.trollstigenresort.com; campsite 210kr, cabin 980-1040kr; 🛜) Recognisable by the strapping wooden troll at its entrance, this well-kept campsite is 2km along the Rv63 highway from Åndalsnes, direction Geiranger. The welcome's warm and the location, overlooking the River Rauma and embraced by mountains, is scenic and peaceful. All but one of the cabins have bathrooms and the two-bedders are smartly renovated. Open year-round, it's popular with skiers in winter.

Åndalsnes Vandrerhjem   HOSTEL $
(✎71 22 13 82; www.hihostels.no/hostels/andalsnes; dm/s/d/f 365/760/860/1160kr; ☉Mar-Nov; 🅿🛜) This is a great hostel, spread across several buildings and surrounded by lawns, greenery and nature, 1.5km from Åndalsnes. As you'd expect, the rooms are nothing to write home about, but they're fine for a couple of nights. There's a nice lounge area if you want to

mingle with other guests and the breakfast spread is particularly generous.

★**Hotel Aak**   HOTEL $$$
(✎71 22 17 00; www.hotelaak.no; s/d 1300/1600kr; ☉mid-May–Sep; 🅿🛜) 🍃 What a beauty: a historic mountain hotel that's been given a thoughtful, charming overhaul by the young Rønning family. The decor in the rooms is sparse but tasteful, and the best rooms have lots of space and knockout mountain views. The building's rustic past still shines through, though. Breakfast is a real mountain feast, and you can arrange dinners too.

Grand Hotel Bellevue   HOTEL $$$
(✎71 22 75 00; www.grandhotel.no; Åndalgata 5; s/d 1195/1650kr; 🅿🛜) Looming over town, this large hotel dates back to the 1800s but renovation has brought it nicely up to date. Mountain murals adorn the walls in the light, white rooms, and while they're not huge, nearly all 86 have views. The restaurant serves a rather starchy dinner (mains 275kr to 345kr) Monday to Saturday.

Eating

★**Sødahl-Huset**   CAFE $$
(✎400 66 401; Romsdalsvegen 8; mains 120-200kr; ☉11am-7pm Sun-Fri, to 2am Sat, shorter hours in winter) 🍃 This place is the model of what every small-town cafe should be like. Mix-and-match furniture, regular beer tastings and gigs, and a blackboard menu chock-a-block with delicious, homemade, local-produce food, from sinful chocolate cake and *kraftkar* (blue cheese) burgers to more healthy options like Asian salmon salad. As the sign says, it's run by three lovely ladies, and the welcome is warm.

ℹ Information

Tourist Office (✎71 22 16 22; www.visitandalsnes.com; ☉9am-8pm Jun-Aug, to 3pm Mon-Fri Sep-May) Located next to the train station, this tourist office has tonnes of info on ways to explore the area, and can hook you up for guided hikes, climbing lessons, stand-up paddleboarding and more. Bikes (hour/day 100/400kr), both standard and electric, can be rented here.

ℹ Getting There & Away

BUS
Åndalsnes is on the Golden Route to the stunning Trollstigen Pass. Buses run across the route to Geiranger (one way/return 239/478kr, three hours, twice daily) from mid-June to August.

There are also buses to Molde (169kr, 1½ hours, up to eight daily) and Ålesund (345kr, 2¼ hours, four daily).

TRAIN

Trains to/from Dombås (249kr to 297kr, 1½ hours, up to four daily) link up with the Oslo–Trondheim route.

Valldal

Most people pass through the small village of Valldal on their way to or from the famous Trollstigen Pass, or after the blissful ferry journey from Geiranger. Perched in a nick of Norddalsfjord, it's a dramatic spot, with rushing rivers framed by lofty, cloud-shrouded peaks. Several waterfalls tumble through the valley, including Holsfossen, Gudbrandsjuvet and Skjerdsura, all of which can be viewed along the Rv63 road.

Valldal is also home to some of Europe's northernmost orchards. Here apples, pears and even cherries thrive and you'll find strawberries in profusion, commemorated in an annual **Strawberry Festival**, usually on the last weekend in July.

◉ Sights & Activities

Gudbrandsjuvet   NATURAL FEATURE
Fifteen kilometres up the valley from Valldal, this popular viewpoint overlooks a maelstrom of foaming, crashing water, where the river sluices and thunders through a 5m-wide, 20m-deep canyon. It's an impressive sight, enhanced by a rusting steel viewing walkway built as part of the National Tourist Routes project. There's a cafe nearby.

Stordal Old Church   CHURCH
(Rosekyrka; Stordal; adult/child 30/15kr; ☉11am-4pm mid-Jun–mid-Aug) Twenty-five kilometres northwest of Valldal on the Rv650 towards Ålesund, this stave church was built in 1789 on the site of an earlier chapel, elements of which were retained. Inside, the roof, walls and every last pillar are sumptuously painted with scenes from the Bible and portraits of saints – a riot of colour that accounts for its local nickname: the Rose Church.

Valldal Naturopplevingar   ADVENTURE SPORTS
(🖉900 14 035; www.valldal.no) This outdoors company is based along the fjord's edge, near the ferry dock and the tourist office. It specialises in water-based pursuits – especially river-rafting (adult 950kr per day) and kayaking (1050kr) – but it also runs canyoning trips, climbing and overnight camps.

🛏 Sleeping

Fjellro Turisthotell   HOTEL $$
(🖉70 25 75 13; www.fjellro.no; Syltegata; s/d 1140/1820kr; ☺cafe-restaurant noon-10pm May-Sep; 🅿🛜) This pretty, red-roofed hotel has been in business for decades, and it makes a pleasant, if undeniably old-fashioned, place to break your journey – plus it's the only real place to stay. Rooms are serviceable, if dated. On the ground floor there's a restaurant that specialises in fish, and out back there's a tranquil garden with a small playground.

★ Juvet Landscape Hotel   DESIGN HOTEL $$$
(🖉950 32 010; www.juvet.com; Alstad; birdhouse s/d 1650/2100kr, cabin 3300kr; ☺Mar-Sep; 🛜)
🌿 This amazing complex of futuristic cabins spread along a forested river is probably one of the boldest architectural hotels anywhere in Norway. It's the brainchild of owner Knut Slinning, who bought the adjoining farm and commissioned these striking, timber-clad, steel-framed pods with cinematic plate-glass windows that seem to invite nature in. They were used in the sci-fi film *Ex Machina*.

The main cabins have been supplemented by two basic 'birdhouses' slightly uphill, which are considerably less flash (they only have basic bathrooms and a hand-held shower), but are considerably cheaper.

Breakfasts and evening meals (550kr per person) take place around a long communal table in the rustic barn, and there's a riverside spa where you can sit in a hot tub or sauna and watch the clouds race overhead.

Note that to retain privacy, casual visits are not allowed.

Jordbærstova   CAFE $$
(🖉70 25 76 58; mains 140-210kr; ☺noon-5pm May-Sep) This roadside cafe is where most people stop to eat for lunch in Valldal. It's a homey place, with a long wood-panelled dining room where Norwegian staples like meatballs and reindeer stew are on offer. There's a huge Sunday lunch buffet, and the strawberry desserts are legendary. It's about 5km northwest of the village on Rv63.

🔒 Shopping

Valldal Safteri   FOOD
(Syltetøysbutikken; www.baer.no; ☺10am-5pm Wed-Fri, 11am-4pm Sat) This artisanal jam producer on the road behind and east of Valldal's

church has a huge selection of jams and juices, pressed and simmered in the small factory behind the shop and sourced in the main from local farmers.

❶ Information

Tourist Office (📞917 80 746; www.visit alesund-geiranger.com; ⊙10am-6pm mid-Jun–mid-Aug, to 5pm Mon-Fri rest of year) In a hut by the fjord, not far from the ferry dock. Bikes (25/100kr per hour/day) are available for hire here.

❶ Getting There & Away

BUS

Valldal is a stop on the 'Golden Route' bus service (adult/child 956/478kr, twice daily) that runs between Åndalsnes and Geiranger via the Trollstigen Pass.

BOAT

The ferry cruise (adult/child one way 240/130kr, return 370/190kr, 2¼ hours, twice daily) that runs between Valldal and Geiranger from mid-June to mid-August is spectacular.

CAR & MOTORCYCLE

Rv63 leads up the mountainside directly to the Trollstigen Pass, which is usually open from May to October depending on snowfall. The highest point of the pass is about 37km from Valldal.

Geirangerfjord

POP 250

Well, this is the big one: the world-famous, Unesco-listed, oft-photographed fjord that every visitor to Norway simply has to tick off their bucket list. And in purely scenic terms, it's impossible to argue against the case for its inclusion: it is, quite simply, one of the world's great natural features, a majestic combination of huge cliffs, tumbling waterfalls and deep blue water that's guaranteed to make a lasting imprint on your memory.

Unfortunately with prestige comes popularity. Some 600,000 visitors come here to see the sights every year and scores of cruise ships dock at the port every day in summer. You're unlikely to enjoy much peace and quiet, especially around the main port of Geiranger.

Thankfully, out on the fjord itself, peace and tranquillity remains and a ride on the Geiranger–Hellesylt ferry is an essential part of your Norwegian adventure.

◉ Sights

Flydalsjuvet   VIEWPOINT
Somewhere you've seen that classic photo, beloved of brochures, of the overhanging rock Flydalsjuvet, usually with a figure gazing down at a cruise ship in Geirangerfjord. The car park, signposted Flydalsjuvet, about 5km uphill from Geiranger on the Stryn road, offers a great view of the fjord and the green river valley, but doesn't provide the postcard view down to the last detail.

For that, you'll have to drop about 150m down the hill, then descend a slippery and rather indistinct track to the edge. Your intrepid photo subject will have to scramble down gingerly and with the utmost care to the overhang about 50m further along. If it's a selfie, we advise care when walking backwards.

Dalsnibba   VIEWPOINT
(www.dalsnibba.no) For the highest and perhaps most stunning of the many stunning views of the Geiranger valley and fjord, take the 5km toll road (130kr per car) that climbs from the Rv63 to the Dalsnibba lookout (1500m). Since August 2016, the view has been enhanced by a new viewing platform, the Geiranger Skywalk, with a see-through floor and glass rail making it seem as though you're walking on air.

Several buses run up to the viewpoint, including the Nibbebus (adult/child 310/200kr return, three daily mid-June to August).

Alternatively, you can catch a public bus, the 211 (adult/child return 335/273kr, twice daily mid-June to August), but it only stops for around 20 minutes to enjoy the view at the top.

A more luxurious and leisurely option is the Panorama Bus (adult/child 450/300kr return, three daily mid-June to August), which allows around three hours for the return trip to Geiranger.

Norsk Fjordsenter   MUSEUM
(📞70 26 38 10; www.verdsarvfjord.no; adult/child 120/60kr; ⊙10am-6pm) The Norwegian Fjord Centre puts the Geiranger area into context, with exhibitions covering avalanches, floods, the building of early roads and the rise of tourism. Its located up the hill along the Rv63. Even if you don't go inside, the structure itself is worth a visit.

➶ Activities

Get away from the seething ferry terminal and life is altogether quieter. All around Geiranger there are great signed hiking routes to abandoned farmsteads, waterfalls and vista points. The tourist office's aerial-photographed *Hiking Routes* map (10kr) gives ideas for 18 signed walks of between 1.5km and 5km.

A popular longer trek begins with a ride on the Geiranger Fjordservice sightseeing boat. A steep 45-minute ascent from the landing at Skagehola brings you to Skageflå, a precariously perched hillside farm. You can retrace your steps to the landing, where the boat stops (on request; tell the crew on the way out or just wave). To stretch your legs more, continue over the mountain and return to Geiranger via Preikestolen and Homlung.

☞ Tours

★ Geiranger Fjordservice   BOATING
(☑70 26 30 07; www.geirangerfjord.no; Homlong; 1½hr tours adult/child 250/135kr) This long-running company runs sightseeing boat trips up and down the fjord from Geiranger. The standard 1½-hour trip runs up to five times daily in midsummer, just once daily in April and October, and not at all from November to March.

From mid-June to August, they also operate a smaller, 15-seater RIB boat (adult/child 695/395kr) and run kayaking tours (525/469kr), all from their base at Homlong, 2km from Geiranger.

🛏 Sleeping

Grande Hytteutleige & Camping   CAMPGROUND $
(☑70 26 30 68; www.grande-hytteutleige.no; Rv63; campsite for car, tent & 2 adults 200kr, cabin 550-1290kr; ⊘Apr-Oct; P🐾🛜) If camping, take the smaller, northernmost of its two fields for the best views up the fjord. Camping perks are good: laundry block, showers, a small hotplate kitchen and free wi-fi in all fields. Sea kayaks and fishing gear are available for hire and a boat taxi to the fjord farms, accessible only by sea or on foot, can be arranged.

Geirangerfjorden Feriesenter   CAMPGROUND $
(☑951 07 527; www.geirangerfjorden.net; Grande; lakefront campsite for car, tent & 2 adults 255kr, cabin from 990kr; ⊘late Apr–mid-Sep; P🛜) A more tranquil option than camping in town is to head along the northern shore to this lovely spot, with spacious pitches, well-maintained facilities and particularly pretty, well-decorated cabins. If you don't mind not being right beside the water, you can save 300kr.

Geiranger Camping   CAMPGROUND $
(☑70 26 31 20; www.geirangercamping.no; campsite for car, tent & 2 adults 185kr; ⊘mid-May–end Sep; P@🐾🛜) A short walk from the ferry terminal, Geiranger Camping is sliced through by a fast-flowing torrent. Though short on shade it's pleasant and handy for an early morning ferry getaway, but it can be a noisy spot to camp by day.

★ Westerås Farm   CABIN $$
(☑932 64 497; 2-bed cabin 870-1040kr, apt 1250kr; ⊘May-Sep) This beautiful old working farm, 4km along the Rv63 towards Grotli, sits at the end of a narrow road dizzyingly high above the bustle. Stay in one of the two farmhouse apartments or five pine-clad cabins. The barn, dating from 1603, is home to a restaurant, where Arnfinn and Iris serve dishes made with their own produce.

Hotel Utsikten   HOTEL $$$
(☑70 26 96 60; www.classicnorway.no/hotell/hotell-utsikten-geiranger; s/d 1290/1590kr; ⊘May-Sep; P🐾) 'A temple to lift your spirits' – so observed King Rama V of Siam when he stayed during his grand tour. High on the hill above Geiranger (take Rv63, direction Grotli), the family-owned Utsikten, constructed in 1893, still has stunning views over town and fjord over a century later. Rooms, however, are small and a little more prosaic.

Hotel Union   HOTEL $$$
(☑70 26 83 00; www.hotelunion.no; d 1495-2690kr; ⊘Feb–mid-Dec; P❄🐾🏊) The sprawling, spectacularly situated Union is high on the hill above town. It's got a long history, but today takes the form of a large modern complex that includes a spa with a couple of pools and sauna. Public areas have the air of luxury you'd expect at the town's best, but rooms are nothing special.

Eating

Olebuda & Cafe Olé   INTERNATIONAL $
(☑70 26 32 30; www.olebuda.no; Maråkvegen 19, Geiranger; restaurant mains lunch 155-255kr, dinner 310-355kr; ⊘cafe 9am-7pm, restaurant 6-10pm) Occupying Geiranger's old general store, the pretty upstairs restaurant does a range of international-style dishes and good local standards like poached salmon roulade and house-smoked goat; all fish and meat are local. Downstairs is a colourful, casual cafe with cakes, all-day snacks and good coffee.

Brasserie Posten   BRASSERIE $$

(☎70 26 13 06; www.brasserieposten.no; lunch mains 140-250kr, dinner mains 195-290kr; ⊗noon-11pm Apr-Sep, shorter hours rest of year) 🍴 A simple menu of salads, burgers, steaks, fish and pizza is elevated above the norm by a passionate local chef who sources organic dairy from Røros and makes the most of fresh herbs and vegetables. The modern Scando interior is bright and atmospheric, but the fjord-side terrace wins.

🛍 Shopping

★Geiranger Sjokolade   CHOCOLATE

(☎967 25 205; www.geirangersjokolade.no; ⊗10am-8.30pm May-Sep, Nov & Dec) Bengt Dahlberg's scented trail can reach as far as the dock as he handcrafts his wares in the basement of an old boathouse. Follow your nose and pick up a selection of his inspired work, including truffles flavoured with brown cheese or cloudberry, or go for instant gratification in the form of ice cream or hot chocolate.

Out of season, if the shop's closed, pop downstairs and knock.

ⓘ Information

Tourist Office (☎70 26 30 99; www.geiranger. no; ⊗9am-6pm mid-May–mid-Sep, shorter hours rest of year) This efficient, if occasionally overwhelmed, tourist office books boat and cruise tickets, hands out hiking leaflets, and generally aims to make your stay as pleasurable as possible. It's located right beside the pier.

ⓘ Getting There & Away

BOAT

The car ferry between Geiranger and Hellysylt is a stunner. There are four to eight sailings a day between May and early October (adult/child one way 260/130kr, return 360/180kr, 1½ hours). With a car, the one-way fare is 530kr for one passenger or 1040kr with up to five people. Tickets can be booked online through the Visit Flåm (www. visitflam.com) website.

From mid-April to mid-October, the Hurtigruten coastal ferry makes a detour from Ålesund (departs 9.30am) to Geiranger (departs 1.30pm) on its northbound run.

BUS

From mid-June to mid-August, sightseeing buses make the spectacular run from Geiranger to Ån-dalsnes (one way 478/239kr, three hours, twice daily), known as the 'Golden Route'.

Hellesylt

POP 250

The old Viking port of Hellesylt, through which a roaring waterfall cascades, is altogether calmer, if far less breathtaking, than nearby Geiranger. There's not much to see, but it makes a tranquil overnight base.

◉ Sights & Activities

The **tourist office** (☎948 11 332; ⊗10am-5pm mid-Jun–Aug) carries the *Tafjardfjella*, a walking map at 1:50,000, and the *Hellesylt Mountain Biking Map*.

Peer Gynt Galleriet   CULTURAL CENTRE

(Peer Gynt Gallery; ☎950 13 170; www.peergynt galleriet.no; adult/child 120/60kr; ⊗10am-6pm Jun-Aug) An only-in-the-fjords extravaganza, bas-relief wood carvings fashioned by local carpenter Oddvin Parr illustrate the Peer Gynt legend, along with a 35-minute audiovisual show (three daily in English). There's an attached cafeteria with lovely big windows overlooking the fjord.

🛌 Sleeping

Hellesylt Camping   CAMPGROUND $

(☎902 06 885; Hellesyltvegen 64; campsite for tent, car & 2 adults 230kr; 🛜) Caravans tend to take up most of the space at this fjord-side site, but there are usually at least a few pitches for campers. It's a bit exposed, especially when it's windy, but it's very handy for the ferry pier. Facilities are basic but serviceable.

Hellesylt Hostel   HOSTEL $$

(☎70 26 51 28; www.hihostels.no/hellesylt; dm 265kr, s 430-550kr, d 690-790kr, tr 750-930kr, q 990-1140kr; ⊗year-round; @🛜) This HI-affiliated hostel perches on the hillside overlooking Hellesylt. It's not flash but the location is beautiful. Dorms are in four- or six-bed coeds, and there are lots of private rooms sleeping, although not all are en suite. If you're arriving by bus, ask the driver to drop you off to save a long slog back up the hill.

ⓘ Getting There & Away

The car ferry from Geiranger (one way adult/child/car with driver 260/130/530kr, 1½ hours, four to eight daily) runs from May to early October. Tickets can be booked at www. visitflam.com.

Norangsdalen

Norangsdalen is one of the most inspiring yet little-visited crannies of the northern fjords. This glorious hidden valley connects Hellesylt with the Leknes–Sæbø ferry on the scenic Hjørundfjorden, via the village of Øye.

The boulder-strewn scenery unfolds among towering snowy peaks, ruined farmsteads and haunting mountain lakes. In the upper part of the valley at **Urasætra**, beside a dark mountain lake, are the ruins of several stone crofters' huts. Further on, you can still see the foundations of one-time farmhouses beneath the surface of the pea-green lake **Langstøylvatnet**, created in 1908 when a rock slide crashed down the slopes of Keipen.

Hikers and climbers will find plenty of scope in the dramatic peaks of the adjacent **Sunnmørsalpane**, including the lung-searingly steep scrambling ascent of Slogen (1564m) from Øye and the superb Råna (1586m), a long, tough haul from Urke.

🛏 Sleeping

★**Villa Norangdal**   HISTORIC HOTEL $$$
(📞70 26 10 84; www.norangdal.com; s/d 1450/1950kr; P🔊) This enchanting 'mountainpolitan style' hotel began welcoming guests in 1885. The current owner, a descendant of the hotel's founder, began restoration in 2007, after it lay abandoned for decades. Six rooms are each an homage to a different 20th-century decade, utilising iconic Scandinavian design pieces, including Norwegian gems by Nora Gulbrandsen and Grete Prytz Kittelsen.

Hotel Union Øye   HISTORIC HOTEL $$$
(📞70 06 21 00; www.unionoye.no; r 1790-2290kr; ⊙May-Sep; P🔊) Constructed in 1891, the Union has attracted mountaineers, writers, artists and royalty for over a century. Looking rather like an Austrian country house that's been transported to the fjords, with period artwork, frilly furnishings, wood panelling and old-world charm galore, it's an over-the-top delight. The restaurant serves lavish, multicourse lunches and dinners in the elegant dining room.

ℹ Getting There & Away

There's no useful public transport here. Rv665 runs through the valley, via a turn-off on Rv60 just west of Hellesylt. Several car ferries run across the fjord from Leknes.

Runde

POP 100

The squat island of Runde, 67km southwest of Ålesund and connected to the mainland by a bridge, plays host to half a million sea birds of around 230 species, including 100,000 pairs of migrating puffins that arrive in April to breed and stay around until late July. There are also colonies of kittiwakes, gannets, fulmars, storm petrels, razor-billed auks, shags and guillemots, plus about 70 other species that nest here. Boat trips to see the bird and seal colonies leave from the island's quay several times a day in summer.

👁 Sights

Runde Miljøsenter   SCIENCE CENTRE
(Runde Environmental Centre; 📞70 08 08 00; www.rundecentre.no; exhibition adult/child 85/35kr; ⊙10am-6pm Jun-Aug, to 4pm May; P) 📍 This international research station is dedicated to studying Runde's birdlife, a testament to the island's importance in the ornithological arena. There's a small exhibition on the centre's work and you can take a birdwatching trip (3400kr for up to 12 people) in the company of one of the centre's biologists.

Accommodation is available here if you want to make an extended birdwatching stay (single/double 900/1500kr, five-bed apartment 2000kr).

🛏 Sleeping

Goksöyr Camping   CAMPGROUND $
(📞70 08 59 05; www.goksoyr.no; campsite 190kr, cabin 310-570kr; ⊙May-Sep) Before the road north peters out, waterside Goksöyr Camping has a range of basic cabins and rooms along with a campsite. The owners, long-term residents on the island, are welcoming and readily dispense information on birdwatching and walking trails.

ℹ Information

Tourist Office (📞901 83 455; www.runde centre.no; Runde Miljøsenter; ⊙10am-6pm Jun-Aug, to 4pm May) Located in the international research station.

ℹ Getting There & Away

Boats to Runde leave from Ålesund's Skateflukaia quay (adult/child 494/253kr) daily in summer. The crossing takes about two hours.

It's also possible to drive to the island, a distance of about 82km via the Sulesund–Hareid ferry (adult/with car 42/115kr).

Ålesund

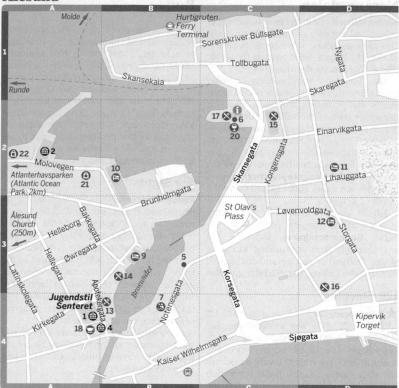

Molde
Hurtigruten
Ferry Terminal
Sorenskriver Bullsgate
Skansekaia
Tollbugata
Nygata
Runde
Skaregata
17 6
15
Einarvikgata
20
22 2
Molovegen
10
11
Atlanterhavsparken
(Atlantic Ocean
Park; 2km)
21
Lihauggata
Brunholmgata
St Olav's
Plass
Løvenvoldgata
Ålesund
Church
(250m)
Helleborg
Øwregata
Bakkegata
9
5
12
Storgata
Korsegata
Hellegata
14
Latinskolegata
Brosundet
16
Jugendstil
Senteret
Apotekergata
13
7
Notenesgata
Kipervik
Torget
18
1
4
Kirkegata
Sjøgata
Kaiser Wilhelmsgata

Ålesund

POP 42,317

The far northern port of Ålesund might be far from the bright lights of metropolitan Norway, but it's rich with some of the country's finest examples of Jugendstil (art nouveau) architecture – a legacy of a huge rebuilding project that took place after a devastating fire in 1904. Set out over a hook-shaped peninsula, the town is now the home base for Norway's largest cod-fishing fleet, and it's an attractive, lively town and unsurprisingly has some superb seafood to try.

◉ Sights

★ Jugendstil Senteret   MUSEUM

(Art Nouveau Centre; Map p244; 70 10 49 70; www.jugendstilsenteret.no; Apotekergata 16; adult/child incl KUBE 80kr/free; ⊙10am-5pm Jun-Aug, 11am-4pm Tue-Sun Sep-May, to 8pm Thu year-round) The city's unique architectural heritage is documented in a former pharmacy, the first listed Jugendstil monument in Ålesund. Apart from the building's own exquisite and almost entirely original interior, including a sinuous staircase and florid dining room, displays include textiles, ceramics, furniture, posters and other ephemera. Even if you're not a keen aesthete, a 'Time Machine' capsule is great fun, presenting 'From Ashes to Art Nouveau', a 14-minute multi-media story of the rebuilding of Ålesund after the great fire.

Kniven Viewpoint   VIEWPOINT

(Map p244) For the best view over Ålesund and its fishhook-shaped peninsula, as well as the mountains and islands beyond, head up the 418 steps to the summit of Aksla Hill and this panoramic viewing point. On a sunny day it's a cracking scene indeed, and it looks pretty special when the town lights start to twinkle at twilight, too.

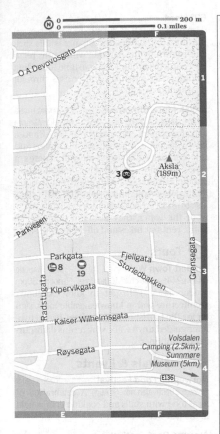

Godøy
ISLAND

The furthest offshore island from Ålesund, Godøy has a real off-the-map feeling, especially in the depths of winter. There are some great walks here, and the island's lighthouse (p246) at Alnes has served as an important sailors' mark for centuries. You can climb to the top for wonderful views across the island's coast.

KUBE
MUSEUM

(Møre & Romsdal County Museum of Art; Map p244; Apotekergata 16; adult/child incl Jugendstil Senteret 80kr/free; ⊙10am-5pm Jun-Aug, 11am-4pm Tue-Sun Sep-May, to 8pm Thu year-round) Ålesund's primary contemporary art space highlights Norwegian artists, as well as hosting the occasional design- and architecture-focused show. The old Bank of Norway building's upstairs gallery has a wonderful view of the harbour. Ticket price also covers entry to Jugendstil Senteret, next door.

Fishing Museum
MUSEUM

(Fiskerimuseet; Map p244; ☑70 16 48 42; www.sunnmoremuseum.no/english/fisheries-museum; Molovegen 10; adult/child incl Aalesunds Museum 60/30kr; ⊙9am-4pm Mon-Fri, noon-4pm Sat & Sun mid-May–mid-Sep, by appointment Feb-May) The 1861 Holmbua warehouse (one of the very few buildings to survive the 1904 fire) has exhibits on the development of fishing across the centuries and special sections on *klippfisk* (salted cod) production and the processing of cod-liver oil. Its entrance area recreates an old grocery shop, a delight in itself. Admission includes entry to the Aalesunds Museum, which illustrates the history of sealing, fishing, shipping and industry in the Sunnmøre region, the fire of 1904 and the town's Jugendstil rebirth, and the German occupation during WWII.

Alnes Lighthouse
HISTORIC BUILDING

(☑70 18 50 90; www.alnesfyr.no; adult/child 25/10kr; ⊘noon-6pm May-Oct) This picturesque 1853 lighthouse is in the fishing station of Alnes. For that end-of-the-world feeling, climb to the circular balcony via the five floors of this all-wood structure. Each displays the canvases of Norwegian artist and Godøy resident Ørnulf Opdahl.

Atlanterhavsparken
AQUARIUM

(Atlantic Ocean Park; www.atlanterhavsparken. no; Tueneset; adult/child 180/80kr; ⊘10am-6pm Sun-Fri, to 4pm Sat Jun-Aug, 11am-4pm Tue-Sun Sep-May; 🖼) At the peninsula's western extreme, 3km from the town centre, this aquarium can consume a whole day. Be introduced to the North Atlantic's teeming undersea world and the astonishing richness of coastal and fjord life. Children can dangle a line for crabs or feed the fish in the touch pool, while the enormous 4-million-litre aquarium appeals to everyone. The grounds offer superb coastal scenery and walking trails (look out for WWII bunkers and gun batteries).

Sunnmøre Museum
MUSEUM

(☑70 16 48 70; www.sunnmore.museum.no; Borgundgavlen; adult/child 80/40kr; ⊘10am-4pm Mon-Fri, noon-4pm Sun May-Sep, 10am-3pm Tue-Fri, noon-4pm Sun Oct-Apr) Ålesund's celebrated Sunnmøre Museum is 4km east of the centre. Here, at the site of the old Borgundkaupangen trading centre, active from the 11th to 16th centuries, over 50 traditional buildings have been relocated. Ship-lovers will savour the collection of around 40 historic boats, including replicas of Viking-era ships and a commercial trading vessel from around AD 1000.

Ålesund Church
CHURCH

(Aspegata; ⊘10am-4pm Tue-Sun) Built of solid stone in 1909, Ålesund's parish church has a strikingly wide chancel, every square inch covered in frescoes over the wide sweep of its tunnel arch. Notable, too, are the stained-glass windows, especially those in the northern aisle with their appropriately nautical theme.

🏃 Activities

The four offshore islands of Valderøy, Vigra, Giske and Godøy, which are all linked to the mainland by bridges, make a pleasant day trip from Ålesund – provided you have your own car, that is.

62° Nord
TOUR

(Map p244; ☑70 11 44 30; www.62.no; Skansekaia) Ålesund's top outdoors company is this slick outfit down by the harbour, which runs regular boat trips around the coastline, including wildlife safaris (950kr) and cruises through Hjørundfjord (950kr).

Kayak More Tomorrow
KAYAKING, HIKING

(Map p244; ☑911 18 062; www.kayakmoretomorrow.com/en; Notenesgata 3) 🏄 Choose how you want to get out on the water, and this company will cater for you. There's a range of daily sea kayaking and stand-up paddleboarding expeditions (from around 515kr per person) and kayaks and SUPs rentals (from 185kr per hour) are available. Away from the water, they also run guided bike tours, rent out bikes and offer city walks.

👉 Tours

Guided Town Walk
WALKING

(Map p244; adult/child 100kr/free; ⊘noon-1.30pm mid-Jun–mid-Aug) To get to know Ålesund's architecture with a knowledgeable local, sign on for the tourist office's excellent 1½- to two-hour guided town walk, which runs daily during the summer.

🎭 Festivals & Events

Norwegian Food Festival
FOOD & DRINK

(www.matfestivalen.no; ⊘Aug) A celebration of local food with stalls and cooking demos held in the last week of August.

Ålesund Boat Festival
SAILING

(www.batfestivalen.no; ⊘Jul) A week of watery pleasures in the first half of July.

Jugendfest
MUSIC

(www.jugendfest.no; ⊘Aug) Norwegian and international bands all over town on one weekend in the second half of August.

🛌 Sleeping

Ålesund Vandrerhjem
HOSTEL $

(Map p244; ☑70 11 58 30; www.hihostels. no; Parkgata 14; dm 295-345kr, s/d/tr/q 690/890/990/1290kr; ⊘year-round; @🛜) In a pretty residential area a few minutes' walk from the port, this attractive Jugendstil building has big, pristine rooms. There's a large self-catering kitchen and breakfast is included. Most doubles come with a bathroom and there are apartments with their own kitchen and sea views.

Volsdalen Camping
CAMPGROUND $

(☑70 12 58 90; www.volsdalencamping.no; Volsdalsberga; campsite 120-180kr, cabin 550-2450kr; ☺year-round) Above the shore about 2km east of the centre, this particularly friendly campsite is the nearest to town. Mainly for caravans and motor homes, or for those wanting a cabin, it does have a secluded grassy area for campers at its far end.

Scandic Scandinavie Hotel
HOTEL $$

(Map p244; ☑70 15 78 00; www.scandichotels.com; Løvenvoldgata 8; r 1190-1490kr; P❋☎) Ålesund's oldest hotel, which was the first constructed after the 1904 fire, has beautiful Jugendstil bones indeed, and since being taken over by the Scandic chain, it's been given a much-needed refresh. Through the lovely art-nouveau doorway, there's a bright lobby filled with modern art and, upstairs, lots of clean-lined rooms in whites, beiges and greys. There's private parking underground.

★Hotel Brosundet
HOTEL $$$

(Map p244; ☑70 11 45 00; www.brosundet.no; Apotekergata 5; s/d 1330/1530kr, d with view 1730kr; P❋☎) Right on the waterfront and designed by superstar architects Snøhetta, this former warehouse is one of Norway's most charming hotels. Wonderful old beams and exposed brick walls are combined with contemporary comfort and style. Bedroom furnishings are of white oak, bathrooms are set behind smoky glass walls and beds are draped with brown velvet and sheepskins.

Scandic Parken
BUSINESS HOTEL $$$

(Map p244; ☑70 13 23 00; www.scandichotels.com; Storgata 16; r 1295-2250kr; ❋☎) One of a trio of Scandics around Ålesund, this is an undeniably corporate place: a blocky, modern structure faced in glass, with a huge downstairs lobby that blends into the breakfast space. So far, so chainy – but there's one reason to book here, and that's the brilliant views over the old town you get from the upper floors.

Ask for a room on the highest floor possible. Rack rates are heavily discounted on booking sites.

Scandic Hotel Ålesund
HOTEL $$$

(Map p244; ☑21 61 45 00; www.scandichotels.com; Molovegen 6; s 1500kr, d 1600-1900kr, ste 2400kr; ❋@☎) Wood floors, plenty of space and a prime harbour position all provide big ticks for this efficient hotel. The standard doubles are fine, but at the top end in the superior extra and suites, you get round lookout windows, perfect for harbour-watching. Downstairs there's a decent restaurant and a lobby-lounge filled with purple furniture.

✖ Eating

Invit
CAFE $$

(Map p244; ☑70 15 66 44; www.invit.no; Apotekergata 9; sandwiches 35-55kr, mains 85-165kr, seafood buffet 300-450kr; ☺8.15am-4.30pm Mon-Fri, 6pm-midnight Thu, 10am-4.30pm Sat) Invit does central Ålesund's best coffee and is its most stylish lunch spot. Daily changing sandwiches and salads are super-fresh and inventive, healthy soups are warming and the nutty, fragrant cakes are homemade. If the streetside bar is full, spread out downstairs at one of the beautiful big wooden tables.

If you're in town on a Thursday evening, you're in luck – book in for their weekly seafood buffet and well-chosen glasses of wine. They also run barista training courses.

Lyspunktet
CAFE $$

(Map p244; ☑70 12 53 00; www.lyspunktet.as; Kipervikgata 1; mains 130-170kr; ☺noon-5pm Sat-Mon, 10am-1pm Tue-Fri, open late summer weekends) Premium coffee, local craft beers and a comforting menu of foccacias, pulled-pork rolls, home-style fish soup, pies, burgers and tacos make this shabby-chic hangout a favourite for the town's grooviest ers. There are deep sofas to lounge in, art on the walls and a bare-brick hearth that provides warmth in winter. All in all, the Spotlight is spot on.

★Maki
SEAFOOD $$$

(Map p244; ☑70 11 45 00; Apotekergata 5; mains 150-360kr, 4-/6-course menu 600/780kr; ☺6-10pm) In a nautical cellar space of the hip Hotel Brosundet, this first-rate seafooderie is Ålesund's most creative and interesting place for a fine-dining dinner. Fish, crustaceans and seafood from along the Sunnmore and Runde coastline form the core of the menu, from delicate cured pollack fillets to crispy halibut and a sublimely creamy fish soup. Expensive, but justified.

Anno
NORWEGIAN, PIZZA $$$

(Map p244; ☑71 70 70 77; Apotekergata 9b; mains 235-335kr, pizza 145-200kr; ☺11am-11pm Mon-Thu, to 3am Fri & Sat) A stylish, waterfront venue for super wood-fired pizzas or upmarket à la carte dishes like poached salmon, *klippfisk*, steaks and so on. Local provenance is strong.

Kabb
GASTROPUB **$$$**

(Map p244; ☑70 12 80 08; www.xlgruppen.no; Kongensgate 19; mains 230-345kr; ☺5pm-midnight Tue-Fri, 3pm-1am Sat) If you don't fancy a sit-down dinner, this gastropub might be just the thing. It serves hearty dishes like brisket burgers, fish and chips, mussels and lamb shank, and has a trendy vibe with its rough brick and industrial decor.

XL Diner
SEAFOOD **$$$**

(Map p244; ☑70 12 42 53; www.xlgruppen.no; Skaregata 1; mains 250-340kr; ☺5-11pm Mon-Sat) Adventurous seafood is the staple at this attractive, modern diner, one of a cluster of eating places owned by the same team. Local specialities like salt cod, pan-fried cod tongues and the self-proclaimed 'best fish soup in town' are all on the menu. The 1st-floor harbour-view space is a lovely place to dine.

🍷 Drinking & Nightlife

★ Jacu Coffee Roastery
COFFEE

(Map p244; ☑997 28 802; www.jacu.no; Parkgata 18; ☺9am-3pm Mon-Fri, 10am-2pm Sat) The west coast's most highly respected coffee roastery is headquartered in this sensitively remodelled industrial space. Drop in for an espresso or a made-to-order filter, breakfast pastries and lunch sandwiches. If you're keen to discover more about the Norwegian coffee scene, they offer tastings and classes, too. Apart from roasting the best beans, they also host art exhibitions.

Milk
BAR

(Map p244; ☑70 12 42 53; www.xlgruppen.no; Skateflua 1b; ☺3pm-1am Tue-Thu, to 2.30am Fri & Sat) A very stylish big-windowed bar that is right on the water and open late. While grown Norwegians are indeed known to neck a glass of the white stuff, it's the good wines, beer on tap and cocktails that draw the locals here; the name comes from the building's former role as a milk delivery depot.

Apoteker'n
CAFE

(Map p244; ☑70 10 49 70; Apotekergata 16; sandwiches around 50kr; ☺10am-5pm Jun-Aug, 11am-4pm Tue-Sun Sep-May) Within Jugendstil Senteret (p244), this stylish, friendly little place offers excellent coffee and cake. There's also a good lunch menu of sandwiches and salads, made from top-quality local produce sourced from Matbuda, a Stranda providore.

🛍 Shopping

★ Trankokeriet Antikk
ANTIQUES

(Map p244; ☑70 12 01 00; www.trankokeriet.no; Molovegen 6b; ☺10am-5pm Mon-Sat) A delver's dream, this place: a chaotic antiques shop stacked floor to ceiling with curiosities and collectibles, from nautical pieces like old diver's helmets and barometers to traditional Norwegian craft pieces, ceramics, vintage dolls and design pieces. It's not cheap, but it's huge fun just to wander round and see what's for sale. There's a quirky **cafe** (Map p244; ☑971 58 985; Apotekergata 10; sandwiches 79kr; ☺11am-5pm Wed-Sun) here, too.

★ Ingrids Glassverksted
GLASS

(Map p244; www.ingridsglassverksted.no; Molovegen 15; ☺10am-5pm Mon-Fri, to 3pm Sat) In the old harbour district near the fishing museum, this quirky glassworks turns out all manner of curious creations – from technicolour chicken jugs to delicate bowls, glasses and miniature houses. You can watch the process in action at the studio here. They also have a shop in the town centre on Løvenvoldgata.

Invit Interior
HOMEWARES

(Map p244; ☑70 15 66 44; Apotekergata 9; ☺11am-4.25pm Tue-Sat) Appropriately for such a design-forward town, this shop displays the very best of creative modern furniture and Scandinavian kitchenware and home appliances.

ℹ️ Information

Tourist Office (Map p244; ☑70 15 76 00; www.visitalesund.com; Skaregata 1; ☺8.30am-6pm Jun-Aug, 9am-4pm Mon-Fri Sep-May) This efficient, modern office is full of fun ideas on things to do in the Sunnmøre region. Its booklet *Along the Streets of Ålesund* (30kr) details the town's architectural highlights in a walking tour.

ℹ️ Getting There & Away

AIR
Ålesund has great air links to the rest of Norway, with frequent flights to Bergen, Oslo, Trondheim and Stavanger. European destinations include Amsterdam, Copenhagen and London.

BOAT
On its northbound run, the Hurtigruten makes a popular detour, mid-April to mid-October, to Geiranger, departing from the **Hurtigruten ferry terminal** (Map p244).

Sightseeing boats, including one to Runde Island (adult/child 494/253kr), leave from ÅndasInes' Skateflukaia quay in summer.

BUS

To get to Oslo and Trondheim, it works out cheaper (and obviously much quicker) to fly than to take the bus, but the bus to Bergen (700kr, 9¼ hours, one to two daily) is competitive, if excruciatingly slow.

There are also buses to Molde (69kr, 1½ hours, up to eight daily) and Åndalsnes (345kr, 2¼ hours, four daily).

Getting Around

Ålesund's airport is on Vigra island, which is connected to the town by an undersea tunnel.

The **airport bus** (www.frammr.no; 113/57kr) (about 25 minutes) stops at the Skateflukaia ferry terminal and the **bus station** (Map p244).

Molde

POP 25,936

Molde, hugging the shoreline at the wide mouth of Romsdalsfjorden, is known as the 'Town of Roses' for its fertile soil, rich vegetation and mild climate. But the town's chief claim to fame is its annual jazz festival, held in July.

Modern Molde, though architecturally unexciting, is a pleasantly compact place whose coastal landscapes recall New Zealand or Seattle's Puget Sound. To test the comparison, drive or take the one-hour signed walking trail up to the **Varden overlook**, 400m above the town.

Sights

Ona ISLAND

The beautiful islet of Ona, with its bare rocky landscapes and picturesque lighthouse, is still home to an offshore fishing community of about 25 people. It makes a popular day trip from Molde: Fram buses (adult/child 318/161kr) leave Molde early in the morning and take you (with a quick ferry ride) to Aukra and the Småge ferry harbour, from where the boats to Ona leave.

Romsdalmuseet MUSEUM

(www.romsdalsmuseet.no; Per Amdamsveg 4; adult/child 100/80kr; ⌚park 8am-10pm) There are nearly 50 old buildings within this open-air museum, shifted here from around the Romsdal region. Among the barns, farms and storehouses, there's a short street of typical townhouses and a small reconstructed chapel with adornments rescued from abandoned churches. After rambling around the ample grounds, take a break in **Bygata**, a townhouse that functions as a summertime cafe. In summer, there are very worthwhile guided tours from the town centre (150kr).

Festivals & Events

Moldejazz MUSIC

(www.moldejazz.no; ⌚Jul) Every July Moldejazz pulls in up to 100,000 fans and a host of jazz greats. The line-up is primarily Scandinavian, though every few years it includes international top liners.

Sleeping

Kviltorp Camping CAMPGROUND $

(☎71 21 17 42; www.kviltorpcamping.no; Fannestrandveien 142; campsite 275kr, cabin 450-1000kr) This fjord-side campsite occupies a potentially noisy spot at the end of the airport runway, but fortunately there are only a few flights a day. Cabins are bright and sweetly furnished and available year-round. The Flybussen airport bus passes right by.

Molde Fjordstuer BOUTIQUE HOTEL $$$

(☎71 20 10 60; www.classicnorway.com; Julsundvegen 6; s/d 1115/1440kr; P 📶) This smart hotel makes a great Molde base. Built to resemble a modern take on a terrace of wharfside warehouses, it's a stylish option: rooms are unexciting, although if you can secure a harbour view, there's plenty of entertaining boat-watching along the harbour outside. The restaurant (mains 285kr to 360kr) is really good, with local fish and seafood featuring heavily.

Scandic Seilet Hotel HOTEL $$$

(☎71 11 40 00; www.rica.no; Gideonvegen 2; r 1050-1350kr, ste 2059-3050kr; P 📶) One thing's for sure – you'd have a hard time missing this hotel, which thrusts skywards like a glass sail. The decor is beige and bland, but most rooms have picture windows opening onto magnificent views over the sound. It's undeniably corporate, but comfy enough. The 15th-floor Masta Skybar makes a definite photo op.

Quality Hotel Alexandra HOTEL $$$

(☎71 20 37 50; www.choice.no; Storgata 1-7; r 1240-1840kr; P @ 📶) The exterior of this place is pretty devoid of interest, but give it a chance: rooms are surprising, with wooden floors, comfy beds, big TVs and minimal clutter, although you'll have to upgrade to a deluxe for the nicest. It's on the main street, too, so it's handy for dinner.

✗ Eating

Kneippen
CAFE $

(☑71 21 94 00; Storgata 28; cakes 350-500kr, sandwiches 660-900kr; ☺9-6pm Mon, 8am-8pm Tue-Sat) We dare you to walk into this lovely cake shop and cafe and not succumb to something sweet and sticky: a classic *skolebrød* (custard tart), a sweet almond fancy, a lavish slice of strawberry tart, and endless other yummy treats besides. To assuage your guilty conscience, order a gourmet sandwich, too – they're equally delicious.

Fole Godt
CAFE, BAKERY $

(☑930 91 333; Storgata 61; sandwiches & salads 120-180kr; ☺7.45am-5pm Mon-Sat) You'll struggle to get a table in the main room come lunchtime at this ever-popular cafe, but luckily there's a second space out the back next to the kitchen. It's worth hunting for a spot, as the sandwiches, salads and cakes served here are the best lunch option in town.

Rød
CAFE $$

(☑71 20 30 00; Storgata 19; mains 140-190kr; ☺11am-11pm Mon-Thu, to 2am Fri & Sat, 1-9pm Sun) Basic fill-your-tummy-up grub is what's on offer at this pubby venue, which majors in burgers, steaks and pasta standards. It's budget-friendly, but don't expect any culinary fireworks.

★ Glass
ITALIAN $$$

(☑90 41 30 89; www.glassmolde.no; Torget 1; pizzas 150-230kr, mains 180-340kr; ☺4-10pm Mon-Fri, 2-10pm Sat, 3-9pm Sun) This popular bistro near the waterfront is everyone's favourite place to eat in Molde, so it's well worth making reservations. It's a swish space that looks more big city than coastal town: big glass windows, chrome furniture, trendy music and a good menu of antipasti, pasta, steaks and delicious thin-and-crispy pizzas.

♟ Drinking & Nightlife

Syd Vin & Matbar
WINE BAR

(☑415 66 028; Fjordgata 3; ☺11.30am-11.30pm Tue, to midnight Wed & Thu, to 1am Fri, noon-1am Sat) No, it's not the name of your host for the night but Norwegian for 'south': the way this wine bar faces. Looking out over the fjord, its terrace offers an inspirational panorama. A good selection of French and Italian wines are available by the glass, perfectly matched by charcuterie and cheese platters (145kr to 165kr). Bruschetta, fish soup and burgers are also on the menu.

ℹ Information

Tourist Office
(☑71 20 10 00; www.visitmolde.com; Torget 4; ☺9am-6pm Mon-Fri, to 4pm Sat, noon-5pm Sun mid-Jun–mid-Aug, 8.30am-4pm Mon-Fri rest of year) Located on Torget, the main square near the express ferry terminal.

ℹ Getting There & Away

AIR
Molde's shore-side **Årø airport** (☑67 03 23 10; www.avinor.no/en/airport/molde-airport) is located 5km out of the city centre. Widerøe flies daily to Bergen and Kristiansund, while Norwegian and SAS both have daily flights to Oslo.

The airport bus (adult/child 35/18kr) meets flights.

BOAT
Some seasonal tourist boats stop here, eg from Andalsnes and Kristiansund, but the main boat service that's of interest is the Molde–Vastnes car ferry (adult/child/car with driver 50/25/146kr, 35 minutes, every 15 minutes).

The Hurtigruten ferry stops at Molde daily.

BUS
The hourly Fram 101/100 Express Bus stops in Molde on its way from Kristiansund (219kr, 1½ hours) to Ålesund (232kr, 2¼ hours).

CAR & MOTORCYCLE
Travelling northwards on the Rv64, the Tussentunnelen shortcut avoids a dogleg and lops off a good 15 minutes off travel time.

Bud

The Rv664 coastal route between Molde and Kristiansund is a scenic alternative to the faster E89. En route lies the little fishing village of Bud, huddled around its compact harbour. It's difficult to believe, but in the 16th and 17th centuries Bud was the greatest trading centre between Bergen and Trondheim.

⦿ Sights

Drågen Smokehouse
FACTORY

(☑958 64 425; www.draagensmokehouse.com; ☺8am-4pm) Petter Aune set up this operation, where freshly caught Aukra salmon are smoked with pure local wood and herbs, after tiring of the poor quality industrial product. It's one of only a few left in Norway and the resulting salmon does indeed have the elusive 'smakupplevelse' – a melt-in-your-mouth quality. Come here to see the process, sample and buy.

Ergan Coastal Fort
FORT

(Ergan Kystfort; www.romsdalsmuseet.no; adult/child 90/50kr; ⊘10am-5pm mid-Jun–late Aug, 11am-3pm Tue-Sun late Aug–mid-Sep & mid-May–mid-Jun) Serving as a WWII museum and memorial, this defensive fortification was erected by Nazi forces in 1940. Various armaments and a network of bunkers and soldiers' quarters are dispersed around the hill with the sickbay and store sunk deep inside the mountain.

✖ Eating

Bryggjen i Bud
SEAFOOD $$

(⌨71 26 11 11; www.bryggjen.no; mains 150-220kr; ⊘noon-9pm Mon-Sat, to 6pm Sun Jul-Aug, noon-6pm Mon-Thu, to 8pm Fri & Sat rest of year) This unpretentious place attracts people from miles around for coastal comfort food: fish soup, two varieties of fish ball, salted coalfish and, of course, *klippfisk* (Norway's largest *klippfisk*-drying sheds are just up the road).

❶ Getting There & Away

There's no useful public transport to Bud. The town is about 40km north of Molde via the Rv64 and Rv664.

Averøy

Averøy has all the silence and wild beauty of one of Norway's offshore islands, but the definite advantage of a tunnel connection to Kristiansund along with direct access to the excellent Atlantic Ocean Road. For those road tripping along the coast, or here to experience the Atlantic Ocean Road, its rocky sea-swept villages make a far more atmospheric base than Kristiansund.

🛏 Sleeping

Skjerneset Bryggecamping
CABIN $

(⌨71 51 18 94; www.skjerneset.com; Ekkilsøy; campsite for 2 adults 230kr, cabin 430-880kr, 4-bed cottage 640-980kr) These converted *rorbuer* (fishermen's cabins) on the island of Ekkilsøy make an atmospheric spot to sleep. They're rustic, wood-panelled and endearingly old-fashioned; if you want something a bit more recent, there are also cottages to rent. The owners are fishermen themselves, and will gladly arrange fishing trips or supply some fresh for you to cook in your cabin. There's also space to pitch a tent.

★Håholmen Havstuer
HISTORIC HOTEL $$$

(⌨71 51 72 50; www.haholmen.no; Håholmen; s/d/f 1090/1690/3290kr; ⊘late Jun–mid-Aug; 🛜) This enchanting 'hotel' is in fact a small former fishing village on its own islet just off Averøy. Rooms here are 18th- and 19th-century cottages, mostly for doubles though there are a couple with multiple bedrooms, too. Some are more rustic than others, with exposed timber, but all are charming. **Ytterbrugga**, its restaurant, serves the freshest of fish.

Parking is on the island of Geitøya, on the Atlanterhavsveien, from where a motor boat makes the five-minute sea journey. It leaves the roadside car park on the hour, between 11am and 9pm, or by appointment.

★Sveggvika
GUESTHOUSE, CABIN $$$

(⌨400 18 192; www.sveggvika.no; Seivågneset; d 950-1600kr; 🅿🛜) Lie in bed and watch the reflection of tiny pink clouds track their way across the still water of the bay or experience a ferocious North Sea storm sweep in – the stylish, if simple, rooms in this converted 1920s *klippfisk* (salted cod) warehouse make you feel part of the coastal landscape whatever the weather. Breakfast and dinners are excellent too.

Boats and bikes are available for guests to rent.

❶ Getting There & Away

The coastal Rv64 runs to Kristiansund, about 31km west of Averøy. Public transport is patchy out to the islands; ask at the tourist office (p254) in Kristiansund for details of local buses.

Kristiansund

POP 24,131

The historic cod-fishing and drying town of Kristiansund still looks below the sea for its wealth. Even though the waters are no longer so bountiful, cod-processing remains important. A significant amount of the world's *klippfisk* (salted cod) is cured around the town, while Mellemværftet, unkempt and chaotic, hangs on as a working boatyard. Kristiansund also plays a significant role in servicing Norway's North Sea oilfields, with its hotels, bars and restaurants catering to off-duty oil workers (with oil worker wages to spend).

The town ranges over three islands; its port and centre was bombed heavily during WWII and rebuilt in uncompromising concrete, although the soul of the old town survives on the island of Innlandet, a quick boat ride over from the harbourfront.

Most people passing through Kristiansund are on their way to or from the wonderful

Atlanterhavsveien, the epic road that links together several islands between Kristiansund and Bud.

◎ Sights

★ Atlanterhavsveien   SCENIC ROAD
(Atlantic Ocean Road; www.nasjonaleturistveger. no/en/routes/atlanterhavsvegen) The eight storm-lashed bridges of the Atlantic Ocean Road buck and twist like sea serpents, connecting 17 islets between Vevang and the island of Averøya. The UK's *Guardian* newspaper once crowned it the world's best road trip. For a highway that is barely 8km long, the weight of expectation may be too great, but it's certainly hugely scenic. During the autumn storms you'll experience nature's wrath at its most dramatic. In season, look out for whales and seals offshore.

You can do the road in either direction: from Molde, hit the coast at Bud; from Kristiansund and the north, take the undersea road tunnel that connects with Bremsnes. Whichever your direction, rather than driving the Rv64, which cuts across inland Averøya, choose the quieter, prettier road, signed for Kvernes, which loops around the island's southern coast and takes no longer.

Several scenic overlooks are stationed along the route, with striking structures built as part of the Nasjonaleturistvegen project, which aims to promote 18 of Norway's scenic roads and enhance them with cutting-edge architecture. Key stops include the rest area and walking path at **Eldhusøya**, an island off the southwest of Averøya, and the glass-fronted viewing platform at **Askevågen**, which is a little over 10km north of Bud and gives you a 360-degree panoramic view of the archipelago, the ocean and the shore. The most impressive – and longest – bridge is **Storseisund**, a gravity-defying marvel that seems to curl and twist on its way from Eide to Averøy island. It's starred in umpteen car advertisements.

You don't necessarily need your own car to follow the road, although it does make it a lot more fun.

Grip   ISLAND
(www.gripruta.no) Fourteen kilometres out to sea from Kristiansund, the island of Grip has a long tradition of cod-fishing stretching back centuries, but was abandoned by the last permanent inhabitants in 1974.

Much of its architecture survives, however, and its huddle of pastel-painted houses dotted across the island's rocky shoreline is enormously picturesque. From late May to late August, a boat (adult/child 350/150kr return, 40 minutes) leaves for the island from Kristiansund's Piren pier once or twice daily.

The return trip takes about 3½ hours (with 1½ hours on the island) and includes a guided tour – but you're free to wander about as you wish. Landmarks to look out for include the 15th-century stave church and the 47m-tall Bratthårskollen lighthouse, built in 1888 on a rocky *skerry* (islet). Wandering round the silent island, it's hard to imagine that more than 1000 fisherfolk once called this place home.

Gamle Byen   HISTORIC SITE
Kristiansund's old town lives on in a part of the island of Innlandet, with clapboard buildings that date back to the 17th century. The grandiose **Lossiusgården**, at its eastern end, was the distinguished home of an 18th-century merchant. The venerable 300-year-old Dødeladen Café (p253) still makes a lovely place for a drink or a bite to eat.

The most enjoyable way of getting here is on the Sundbåten Ferry (p254) from Piren pier; otherwise it's a 15-minute walk over Heinsgata bridge.

Mellemværftet   HISTORIC SITE
FREE Something of a nautical junkyard, Mellemværftet, free and accessible any time, is best approached on foot along the quayside from the Smia Fiskerestaurant (p254). It's difficult to make out what's amid the clutter, but it includes the remnants of Kristiansund's 19th-century shipyard, a forge, workshop and workers' quarters.

Norsk Klippfiskmuseum   MUSEUM
(⌨ 71 58 70 00; www.nordmore.museum.no; Gomalandet; adult/child incl guided tour 70kr/free; ☺ noon-5pm late Jun–early Aug) This museum, situated in an 18th-century warehouse, tells you all that you could ever wish to know (and probably a lot more than that) about Kristiansund's cod-drying heritage. There are various bits of equipment, vintage photos and other fishy memorabilia, and you can sometimes watch the cod-drying process in action. From the town centre, take the Sundbåt ferry and ask to be dropped off.

Kirkelandet Church CHURCH
(Langveien 41; ⊙ 9am-3pm Sun-Fri) Architect Odd Østby's inspirational church was built in 1964 to replace the one destroyed by Nazi bombs. The angular exterior, where copper and concrete alternate, is sober and measured. Inside, all lines direct the eye to the 320 panes of stained glass at the rear of the chancel. Moving upward from the earthy colours at the base, they become more pale and, at the top, replicate the 'celestial light of heaven'.

Kvernes Stave Church CHURCH
(www.stavechurch.com/en/kvernes-2; Fv247, Kvernes; adult/child 60kr/free; ⊙ 11am-5pm late Jun–mid-Aug) This beautifully sited stave church about 26km south of Kristiansund dates from 1300, but has been repaired since. The interior is richly decorated: look out for the amazing 300-year-old model ship and unusual 15th-century altarpiece, with the Virgin Mary figuring prominently: Catholic to the core. While many such altarpieces were destroyed at the time of the Reformation, this one luckily survived, although a stylised Lutheran surround was added in 1695.

🎎 Festivals & Events

Operafestukene MUSIC
(www.oik.no; ⊙ Feb) A two-week opera festival in early February.

Nordic Light Photo Festival ART
(www.nle.no; ⊙ Sep) This large fine art photography festival that attracts big names and up to 70,000 visitors to its exhibitions and workshops in September.

Tahiti Festivalen MUSIC
(www.tahiti-festivalen.no; ⊙ Jun) A weeklong music festival in late June held on Innlandet. Norwegian pop and rock acts dominate the bill.

🛏 Sleeping

Dala Bergan CABIN $
(☏ 71 67 30 25; www.havfiske-kristiansund.no; Dalabergan 1; r 600kr, cabin 800-2100kr; P 🛜) Out along Dalaveien, these fishermen's-shack-style cabins have a rustic seaside location. All have bathrooms, TVs and sunbathing platforms. There are also a couple of simple rooms for rent and boat hire available. It's about a 10-minute walk to the centre.

Atlanten Camping & Motell CAMPGROUND, MOTEL $
(☏ 71 67 11 04; www.atlanten.no; Dalaveien 22; campsite 150-190kr, cabin 495-1295kr, motel s/d

595/795kr; P 🛜) This hostel and campground is 3km north from the centre. It's a friendly place and the motel has a well-equipped kitchen, TVs in the rooms and a big screen in the lounge for sporting events. Camping facilities have been fully renovated and the furnished apartments are a great deal for small groups.

Thon Hotel Storgata HOTEL $$
(☏ 71 57 03 00; www.thonhotel.com; Storgata 17; s/d from 890/790kr; P 🛜) The main selling point at this hotel in the modern part of town is the prospect of bagging a view over the harbour to Innlandet: it's worth insisting on, as its otherwise a fairly nondescript chain hotel. Still, the decor is light and clean, there's covered parking (100kr per night), and **Christian's Bar** (☏ 71 57 03 00; Storgata 17) makes a fun place for a nightcap.

Thon Hotel Kristiansund HOTEL $$
(☏ 71 57 30 00; www.thonhotels.com; Fiskergaten 12; s/d from 1195/1495kr; P ✳ 🛜) Thon Hotel has two locations in Kristiansund – one on Storkaia and this one on Innlandet. It's a good 20-minute walk to the centre, but that usually means cheaper rates and more available rooms. The setting in a converted 1915 warehouse adds character, with modern lines matched by old beams, big windows and a harbour-view terrace.

Scandic Hotel Kristiansund HOTEL $$$
(☏ 71 57 12 00; www.rica.no; Storgata 41; ⊙ r 1300-1700kr; P @ 🛜) Towering over the harbour like a grey-clad office block, this big business hotel does a brisk trade with the oil industry crowd, but it's a perfectly passable option for visitors, too. It's functional, not pretty, but rooms are pleasant enough and get more spacious the further up the price scale you go. A sauna, gym and on-site parking are bonuses.

🍴 Eating

Plan A CAFE $$
(☏ 475 12 949; Nedre Enggate 9; lunch mains 140-180kr; ⊙ 9am-6pm Mon, Tue & Thu, to 10pm Wed, Fri & Sat) This popular cafe in the centre of town is busy at lunchtime with a mix of ladies who lunch, shop-workers and assorted other locals, who come for the generous sandwiches, good pizzas and tempting cakes. It's a bright, modern space and is very laid-back – just the place to hang out with your laptop over an afternoon coffee.

Dødeladen Café NORWEGIAN $$
(☏ 71 67 50 30; www.dodeladen.no; Innlandet; mains 160-290kr; ⊙ 2-11pm Tue-Thu, to 2am Fri

& Sat) There's a little slice of history to go with your cake here. This timber-clad cafe dates back to the early 1700s and fits right in alongside the other antique buildings of the old town. Fittingly it serves old-timey dishes to match its yesteryear architecture: classic cream fish soup, salt cod in tomato sauce, *svele* (pancakes), waffles and *smørrebrød*-style sandwiches.

You can get here on the Sundbåten ferry.

★**Bryggekanten**   RESTAURANT, BAR $$$

(☑71 67 61 60; www.fireb.no; Storkaia 1; lunch 150-200kr, dinner mains 290-340kr; ⊙11.30am-10pm or midnight Mon-Sat) This waterside brasserie is just the ticket for brunch, lunch or dinner, with a great terrace wrapped in glass and a good varied lunch menu of pasta dishes, burgers, salads, mussels and bruschetta. Things turn a bit more sophisticated after dark, with creative fish and meat dishes on offer.

Smia Fiskerestaurant   SEAFOOD $$$

(☑71 67 11 70; www.smia.no; Fosnagata 30b; mains lunch 145-195kr, dinner 285-345kr; ⊙11am-10pm Mon-Sat, 2-8pm Sun) Located in an old smithy on the cobbled street of Fosnagata (it's still covered with blacksmiths' tools), this well-respected fish restaurant is a good place to try *klippfisk* (salted cod), if you haven't already, along with fish soup, salmon and a catch of the day. Minke whale is served here, which may influence your decision on whether to dine.

Sjøstjerna   SEAFOOD $$$

(☑71 67 87 78; www.sjostjerna.no; Skolegata 8; mains 245-295kr; ⊙noon-midnight Mon-Sat) *Klippfisk* served several ways, along with other fishy dinners, are the order of the day at this fun, if rather kitschy, maritime-themed restaurant. The scallops and mussels are particularly good. It's not in the prettiest part of town, sadly, overlooking a rather bleak concrete plaza.

ℹ Information

Tourist office (☑71 58 54 54; www.visitkristiansund.com; Kongens plass 1; ⊙9am-6pm Mon-Fri, 10am-4pm Sat & Sun mid-Jun–mid-Aug, 9am-4pm Mon-Fri rest of year; ☎) In the centre, back up the hill from the waterfront. Offers free internet access.

ℹ Getting There & Away

AIR

The town's **Kvernberget airport** (☑71 68 30 50; Nordlandet) is on Nordlandet island. There are frequent daily flights to/from both Oslo and Bergen.

Buses travel regularly to/from the airport (80kr, 15 minutes, up to eight daily) to meet incoming flights.

BOAT

Express boats connect Kristiansund with Trondheim (3½ hours, up to three daily from Nordmørskaia). The Hurtigruten coastal ferry also calls in daily at Holmakaia.

BUS

Inland buses run hourly to Molde (67kr, 1½ hours) and on to Ålesund (159kr, 3¾ hours).

Northwards, there are services to Trondheim (510kr, 4¾ hours, three daily).

ℹ Getting Around

The **Sundbåten Ferry** (www.sundbaten.no; adult/child day ticket 100/35kr) has supposedly been in business since 1876, which would make it the world's oldest public transport system in uninterrupted use. Whatever the history, it's well worth the ride for its own sake and for the special perspective it gives of the harbour. Boats leave from Piren pier at the foot of Kaibakken hill, linking the town centre and the islands of Innlandet, Nordlandet and Gomelandet. Services run every half-hour, Monday to Saturday; the full circuit takes 20 minutes.

THE WESTERN FJORDS KRISTIANSUND

Trøndelag

Best Places to Eat

➡ Baklandet Skydsstasjon (p264)

➡ Restaurant Norveg (p271)

➡ Ravnkloa Fish Market (p263)

➡ Brod & Cirkus (p269)

➡ Vertshuset Tavern (p264)

Best Places to Stay

➡ Scandic Nidelven Hotel (p263)

➡ Radisson Blu Royal Garden Hotel (p263)

➡ Pensjonat Jarlen (p262)

➡ Scandic Stiklestad Hotell (p268)

➡ Scandic Rock City (p270)

Why Go?

Trøndelag, where Norway begins to narrow and head for the Arctic, may be small but it sure packs a lot in. Trondheim is the centrepiece, a beguiling city brimful of historic architecture, including Nidaros Cathedral, Scandinavia's largest medieval structure. But Trondheim's present is as appealing as its past, with buzzing student life and pretty waterfront restaurants and bars. Not far away to the northeast, and an easy detour from the Arctic Highway, atmospheric Stiklestad is famous as the site of the martyrdom of King Olav (St Olav) and lies at the heart of every Norwegian's sense of national identity. Elsewhere, Trøndelag is quintessential Norway, a region of rumpled hills, stippled with oxblood-coloured farmsteads and ruffled green with wheat and barley. Here, there's always water near at hand, whether sea, lake or incised fjord with fascinating coastal settlements worth lingering over.

When to Go
Trondheim

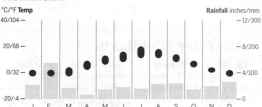

Mid–late Jun Winter has retreated, and visitors are relatively few.

Late Jul Festivities in honour of St Olav in Trondheim and Stiklestad.

Sep Trondheim has a fresh buzz as its student population returns.

TRONDHEIM

POP 190,464

With its colourful warehouses, waterways and wooded hills, Trondheim is without doubt one of Norway's most photogenic towns. Norway's third-largest city and its historic capital is a pleasure to explore, with wide streets and a partly pedestrianised heart, some great cafes, restaurants and museums to visit – plus Europe's northernmost Gothic cathedral. Fishing boats putter around the harbour, gulls wheel and screech overhead, and beyond the city's outskirts there's a wealth of wilderness to explore.

Trøndelag Highlights

① Nidaros Cathedral (p257) Exploring Norway's most sacred building and one of its most handsome.

② Stiklestad (p267) Stepping back to the dawning of Norway at the place where St Olav was martyred.

③ Baklandet Skydsstasjon (p264) Crossing Trondheim's Gamle Bybro to eat at this marvellous eatery, then down to Solsiden for a drink.

④ Bymarka (p262) Hiking in the wilderness right in Trondheim's backyard.

⑤ Norveg (p271) Learning about coastal life at this stunning multimedia museum in Rørvik.

⑥ Leka (p271) Leaving behind well-tramelled byways and heading offshore to this beautiful island with an intriguing story.

⑦ Hell (p267) Snapping a selfie at the 'Welcome to Hell' sign, which will win gasps back home.

History

In AD 997 King Olav Tryggvason moored his longboat alongside a broad sandbank at Nidaros (meaning 'mouth of the River Nid') and established his farm. One plausible theory has it that Leifur Eiríksson (or Leif Ericson as he's usually transcribed in English) visited the king there before setting sail for Iceland and Greenland and possibly becoming the first European to set foot in North America. If you're from the USA, the **Viking** (Map p258; Hurtigrutenkai, Havnegata) staring out to sea near the Hurtigruten quay may seem familiar. That's because he's an exact replica of the Ericson statue in Seattle that commemorates the tens of thousands of Norwegian emigrants to the New World.

In 1030 another, subsequently more famous, King Olav (Haraldsson) was martyred in battle at Stiklestad, about 90km to the northeast, and later canonised. As the site of Olav's grave, Nidaros became a centre for pilgrims from all over Europe, its bishopric embracing Norway, Orkney, the Isle of Man, the Faroe Islands, Iceland and Greenland. It served as the capital of Norway until 1217, ruling an empire that extended from what is now western Russia to, possibly, the shores of Newfoundland. The cult of St Olav continued until the Reformation in 1537, when Norway was placed under the Lutheran bishopric of Denmark.

After a fire razed most of the city in 1681, Trondheim was redesigned with wide streets. It enjoyed its golden age in the 18th century, when merchants outdid each other in the grandeur of their dwellings. The city's location became key once again in WWII, when German naval forces made it their base for northern Norway, although fortunately the city avoided major damage. Nowadays, Trondheim, with its Norwegian University of Science & Technology and a research institute that employs more than 2000 staff, is the recognised tech capital of Norway.

◉ Sights

★ Nidaros Domkirke
CATHEDRAL

(Map p258; ☑73 89 08 00; www.nidarosdomen.no; Kongsgårdsgata; adult/child/family 90/40/220kr, tower 40kr, with Archbishop's Palace & crown jewels 180/90/440kr; ⊙9am-6pm Mon-Fri, to 2pm Sat, to 5pm Sun mid-Jun–mid-Aug, shorter hours rest of year) Nidaros Cathedral is Scandinavia's largest medieval building, and the northernmost Gothic structure in Europe. Outside, the ornately embellished, altar-like west wall has top-to-bottom statues of biblical characters and Norwegian bishops and kings, sculpted in the early 20th century. Several are copies of medieval originals, nowadays housed in the museum. Note the glowing, vibrant colours of the modern stained-glass in the rose window at the west end, a striking contrast to the interior gloom.

The altar sits over the original grave of St Olav, the Viking king who replaced the pagan Nordic religion with Christianity. The original stone cathedral was built in 1153, when Norway became a separate archbishopric. The current transept and chapter house were constructed in 1130–80 and reveal Anglo-Norman influences (many of the craftspeople were brought in from England), while the Gothic choir and ambulatory were completed in the early 14th century. The nave, repeatedly ravaged by fire across the centuries, is mostly a faithful 19th-century reconstruction.

Down in the crypt is a display of medieval carved tombstones (the majority restored from fragments since many headstones were broken up and carted away to be recycled in domestic buildings). Look for one inscribed in English and dedicated to William Miller, Shipmaster, of Dundee, Scotland, who met his end near Trondheim in the 18th century.

You can wander around freely but, between early June and early August, it's worth joining a **tour** (a 15-minute canter or a more detailed 45-minute visit). Times vary but there are up to four daily in English. Music-lovers may want to time their visit to take in a **recital** on the church's magnificent organ.

From mid-June to mid-August, you can climb the 172 steps up the cathedral's **tower** (40kr) for a great view over the city. There are guided ascents every half-hour from its base in the south transept, with a limit of 20 people per ascent. Black metal fans: this is the church on the cover of Mayhem's *De Mysteriis Dom Sathanas* album.

★ Archbishop's Palace
MUSEUM, HISTORIC BUILDING

(Map p258; Kongsgårdsgata; adult/child/family 90/40/220kr, crown jewels 90/40/220kr, with cathedral & crown jewels 180/80/440kr; ⊙10am-5pm Mon-Fri, 10am-3pm Sat, noon-4pm Sun mid-Jun–mid-Aug, shorter hours rest of year) The 12th-century archbishop's residence (Erkebispegården), commissioned around 1160 and Scandinavia's oldest secular building, is beside the cathedral. In its west wing, you'll find Norway's shimmering **crown jewels** and its **museum**.

Trondheim

10 Havnegata

18

Rockheim 🏛 **3**

Pirterminalen

Brattørkaia

Trondheimfjord

Trondheim Sentralstasjon

Østre Kanalhavn

24

Intercity Bus Terminal

Fjordgata

20 🏛 **39**

Ferries to Munkholmen **17**

Brattørgata

34

41

48 **36**

53 **50**

51

Olav Tryggvasonsgate

Vestre Kanalhavn

49

Thomas Angells gate

19

21

Dronningens gate

Stiftsgården 🏛 **4**

Søndre gate

Nordre gate

6

44

13

Prinsens gate

St Olavsgata

Kjøpmannsgata

Sandgata

23

Torvet

Tordenskiolds gate

47

8 Munkegata

7 Kongens gate

Kongens gate

16

Ila Brainnstasjon (350m); Sverresborg Trøndelag Folkemuseum (1.6km); Vertshuset Tavern (1.7km)

31

37

Erling Skakkes gate

32

5

33

🏛 **12**

KALVSKINNET

30 **15**

Bispegata

Prinsens gate

Gangbrua

🏛 **Nidaros 2 Domkirke**

Nideleva

11

🏛 **Archbishop's 1 Palace**

Kongsgårdsgata

Arkitekt Christies gate

14

Elgeseter Bru

Klostergata

Øvre Bakklandet

Elgesetergate

Mauritz Hansens gate

Klostergata

Christian Frederiks gate

43

After visiting the well-displayed statues, gargoyles and carvings from the cathedral, drop to the lower level with a selection of the myriad artefacts revealed during the museum's late-1990s construction.

The palace also has an enjoyable 15-minute audiovisual program. If you're visiting Trondheim's cathedral, it's cheaper to buy the combination ticket, which covers admission to all three attractions (archbishop's palace, crown jewels and cathedral).

★ Stiftsgården   PALACE
(Map p258; www.nkim.no/stiftsgarden; Munkegata 23; adult/child 90/50kr; ⊙10am-4pm Mon-Sat, noon-4pm Sun Jun-late Aug) Scandinavia's largest wooden palace, the 140-room late-baroque Stiftsgården, was constructed as a private residence in the late 18th century, at the height of Trondheim's golden age. It is now the official royal residence in Trondheim. Admission is by tour only, every hour on the hour. The publicly accessible garden around the east side (enter via Dronningens gate) is one of Trondheim's loveliest corners.

★ Rockheim   MUSEUM
(Map p258; www.rockheim.no; Brattørkaia 14; adult/concession/child 130/100/free; ⊙11am-6pm Tue-Sun) This terrific museum is devoted to pop and rock music, mainly Norwegian, from the 1950s until yesterday. It's a dockside temple to R&B, where a huge projecting roof featuring Norwegian record covers extends above an equally vast converted warehouse. Within, there's plenty of action and interaction (mix your own hip-hop tape, for example). Home of Rock is on the quayside, very near Pirbadet and the fast-ferry landing stage.

From mid-June to mid-August, there's a free, English-language tour of the museum.

National Military Museum   MUSEUM
(Ruskammeret; Map p258; ☑73 99 52 80; Kongsgårdsgata; ⊙10am-4pm Mon-Sat, noon-4pm Sun mid-May–early Sep) FREE In the same courtyard as the Archbishop's Palace, the National Military Museum is full of antique swords, armour and cannons, and recounts the days from 1700 to 1900, when the palace served as a Danish military installation. On the top floor is the **Hjemmefront** (Home Front) museum, devoted to Trondheim's role in the WWII resistance.

Gamle Bybro   BRIDGE
(Old Town Bridge; Map p258) There's been a bridge here since 1681, connecting the city

Trondheim

with the Kristiansten Fort (p261) and guarded at each end by a watch-house (although only one now remains, currently occupied by a kindergarten). The present bridge dates from 1861, and it's a beauty – pedestrianised and clad in planks, it's the best place in town to get that essential shot of Trondheim's riverside warehouses. It's also the quickest way to get over to Bakklandet from the city centre.

Trondheim Kunstmuseum GALLERY
(Map p258; ☑73 53 81 80; www.trondheim kunstmuseum.no; Bispegata 7b; adult/child 100/50kr; ☉10am-4pm Jun-Aug, noon-4pm Tue-Sun Sep-May) Trondheim's Art Museum, a stone's throw from the cathedral, houses a permanent collection of modern Norwegian and Danish art from 1800 onwards, including a hallway of Munch lithographs. It also runs temporary exhibitions.

Synagogue SYNAGOGUE
(Jødisk Museum; Map p258; ☑401 69 801; www. jodiskemuseum.no/english; Arkitekt Christies gate 1b; museum guided tour adult/child 60/30kr; ☉tours 10.30am, 12.30pm & 2.30pm Mon-Fri, 1pm Sun mid-Jun–mid-Aug, by appointment rest of year) Trondheim's synagogue claims to be the world's northernmost. It has a small **museum** dedicated to the history of the local Jewish community, which was decimated by the Holocaust. Admission is by guided tour. For those with a deeper interest, an information board and map outside shows sites around town with historic links to Trondheim's Jewish community.

Nordenfjeldske
Kunstindustrimuseum GALLERY
(Museum of Decorative Arts; Map p258; ☑73 80 89 50; www.nkim.no; Munkegata 5; adult/child 100kr/free; ☉10am-4pm Mon-Sat, noon-4pm Sun Jun-late

Aug, 10am-3pm Tue, Wed, Fri & Sat, noon-8pm Thu, noon-4pm Sun late Aug-May) The permanent collection of this splendid museum exhibits the best of Scandinavian design, including a couple of bijou art-nouveau rooms. A whole floor is devoted to the pioneering works of three acclaimed female artists: the tapestry creations of Hannah Ryggen and Synnøve Anker Aurdal, and the innovative glasswork of Benny Motzfeldt.

Vitensenteret
MUSEUM

(Map p258; www.vitensenteret.com; Kongens gate 1; adult/child/family 95/50/330kr; ⊙10am-5pm Mon-Fri, 11am-5pm Sat & Sun late Jun–mid-Aug, 10am-4pm Mon-Fri, 11am-5pm Sat & Sun rest of year; ⓐ) Children especially will enjoy the hands-on experiments at this practical, active centre with over 150 models to choose from.

Ringve Music Museum
MUSEUM

(📞73 87 02 80; www.ringve.no; Lade Allé 60; adult/child 120kr/free; ⊙10am-5pm May-Aug, 11am-4pm Tue-Sun Sep-Apr; 🚌3, 🚌4) The Ringve Museum is Norway's national museum for music and musical instruments. The Russian-born owner was a devoted collector of rare and antique musical instruments, which students demonstrate. You can also browse the old barn with its rich collection of instruments from around the world. The botanic gardens, set within the surrounding 18th-century estate, are a quiet green setting for a stroll. Take bus 3 or 4 and walk up the hill.

King Olav Tryggvason Statue
STATUE

(Map p258; Torvet) The epicentre of town is Torvet, the central square (also spelt 'Torget') with its statue of King Olav Tryggvason atop a column that acts as a huge sundial. The slightly scruffy square is slated for a much-needed overhaul from late 2017.

Olavskirken Ruins
RUINS

(Map p258; Kongens gate; ⊙10am-7pm Mon-Thu, 10am-6pm Fri, 11am-4pm Sat) FREE During excavations for the library on Kongens gate, archaeologists found the ruins of a 12th-century church, thought to be Olavskirken, now visible beneath the courtyard, together with the skeletons of two adults and a child.

Gregorius Kirke Ruins (Sparebanken)
RUINS

(Map p258; Søndre gate 4; ⊙8.15am-3pm Mon-Wed & Fri, to 5pm Thu) FREE In the basement of Søndre gate 4 are the ruins of the medieval Gregorius Kirke (Sparebanken), discovered during earlier excavations.

Kristiansten Fort
FORTRESS

(Map p258; Festningsgata; ⊙guided tours noon & 2pm daily Jun-Aug) FREE For a bird's-eye view of the city, climb 10 minutes from the Gamle Bybro (p259) to Kristiansten Fort, built after Trondheim's great fire of 1681. During WWII the Nazis used it as a prison and execution ground for members of the Norwegian Resistance. The grounds are open year-round at no cost, whenever the flag is raised.

Munkholmen
ISLAND

(Monks' Island) During Trondheim's early years, the islet of Munkholmen, 2km offshore, was the town execution ground. Over the centuries it has been the site of a Benedictine monastery, a prison, a fort and, finally, a customs house. Today it's a popular picnic venue and has the city's best beach. From mid-May to September, **ferries** (Map p258; www.trippsbatservice.no; return trip adult/child 90/40kr; ⊙10am-6pm Jun–mid-Aug, shorter hours mid-end May & mid-Aug–Sep) leave at least hourly between 10am and 4pm or 6pm from beside the Ravnkloa Fish Market (p263).

Hospitalkirken
CHURCH

(Map p258; Hospitalsløkka 2-4; ⊙for church services) The cobblestone streets immediately west of the centre are lined with mid-19th-century wooden buildings, notably the octagonal 1705 timber church, Hospitalkirken, in the hospital grounds.

Sverresborg Trøndelag Folkemuseum
MUSEUM, ARCHITECTURE

(📞73 89 01 00; www.sverresborg.no; Sverresborg Allé 13; adult/5-15yr/child incl guided tour 155/115kr/free mid-Jun–Aug, 115/95kr/free Sep–mid-Jun; ⊙10am-5pm Jun-Aug, 10am-3pm Tue-Fri, noon-4pm Sat & Sun Sep-May; 🚌18, 🚌8) Three kilometres west of the centre, this folk museum is one of the best of its kind in Norway. The indoor exhibition, Livsbilder (Images of Life), displays artefacts in use over the last 150 years – from clothing to school supplies to bicycles. The rest of the museum is open-air, comprising over 60 period buildings, adjoining the ruins of King Sverre's castle and giving fine views of the city.

🏄 Activities

Harbour Sightseeing
BOATING

(Tripps; Map p258; 📞950 82 144; www.trippsbatservice.no; adult/child 170/60kr; ⊙cruises 11am,

12.30pm & 3pm Tue-Sun mid-Jun–mid-Aug, noon Thu-Sun mid-May–Jun & mid-Aug–Sep) Tripps runs a one-hour cruise (at 11am) along the estuary of the River Nidelva, with two longer 90-minute versions (at 12.30pm and 3pm) out into the fjord. Departures are from beside the Ravnkloa Fish Market (p263) and you buy your ticket at the small kiosk next to the wharf.

Pirbadet SWIMMING
(Map p258; ☑73 83 18 00; www.pirbadet.no; Havnegata 12; adult/child 175/150kr; ⊙6.30am-8pm Mon, Wed & Fri, 10am-8pm Tue & Thu, 10am-6pm Sat & Sun late Jun–mid-Aug, shorter hours rest of year) On the Pirterminalen quay, Pirbadet is Norway's largest indoor water park. It has a wealth of liquid pleasures, including a wave pool, sauna and 100m water slide.

⊂〒 Tours

Walking Tours WALKING
(Map p258; ☑73 80 76 60; www.visittrondheim. no; tours 130-2540kr; ⊙2pm daily late Jun–mid-Aug, 2pm Sat rest of year) In addition to their standard two-hour guided city walk (185kr per person), the tourist office organises a fascinating portfolio of walks, some guided, some self-guided, with themes that range from coffee or music to gourmet-food experiences.

TRONDHEIM HIKING

Two easy strolls within town are the steep, but short, ascent through the traffic-free lanes of Bakklandet to Kristiansten Fort and the riverbank footpaths beside the Nidelva between Bakke Bru and Gangbrua bridges.

West of town spreads the **Bymarka**, a gorgeous green woodland area laced with wilderness footpaths and ski trails. Take the Gråkallbanen tram, in itself a lovely scenic ride through the leafy suburbs, from the St Olavsgata stop to **Lian**. There you can enjoy excellent views over the city and a good swimming lake, **Liannvannet**.

To the east of Trondheim, **Ladestien** (the Lade Trail) follows the shoreline of the Lade peninsula, beginning only 1km from the town centre.

🎊 Festivals & Events

★UKA CULTURAL
(www.uka.no; ⊙Oct/Nov) Trondheim's 25,000 university students stage this three-week celebration, Norway's largest cultural festival. Every other year (in odd-numbered years) in October and November, it's a continuous party with concerts, plays and other festivities based at the round, red Studentersamfundet (p266) (student centre).

★Olavsfestdagene CULTURAL
(www.olavsfestdagene.no; ⊙Jul-Aug) In honour of St Olav and held during the week around his saint's day, 29 July. There's a medieval market and a rich program of classical music, folk, pop and jazz.

★Nidaros Blues Festival MUSIC
(www.nidarosbluesfestival.com; ⊙Apr) A who's who of the international blues scene with local acts as well.

Pstereo MUSIC
(www.pstereo.net; ⊙late Aug) Major pop and rock festival over a weekend in late August, with up to 300 performers descending on Trondheim.

Kosmorama FILM
(www.kosmorama.no; ⊙Mar-early May) Trondheim's international film festival occupies an intensive week in spring, anytime between March and early May.

🛏 Sleeping

★Pensjonat Jarlen GUESTHOUSE $
(Map p258; ☑73 51 32 18; www.jarlen.no; Kongens gate 40; s/d/tr 540/690/960kr, cat or dog 100kr; 🖙) Price, convenience and value for money are a winning combination here. After a 2010 overhaul, the rooms at this central spot have a contemporary look and are outstanding, although some bathrooms could do with a spruce-up. Some rooms have polished floorboards, others carpet, and most have a hot plate and fridge thrown in.

Flakk Camping CAMPGROUND $
(☑940 54 685; www.flakk-camping.no; car/caravan site 240/330kr, cabins 525-695kr; ⊙May-Aug; 🅿) Sitting right beside Trondheimfjord (there's minimal disturbance from the nearby ferry point), this welcoming campground is about 10km from the city centre. Take Rv715 from Trondheim. It also has tents for rent if you don't have your own and don't fancy a cabin.

Singsaker Sommerhotel HOTEL $
(Map p258; ☎73 89 31 00; www.sommerhotell.sing saker.no; Rogertsgata 1; dm/s/d 300/880/950kr, s/d with shared bathroom 535/745kr; ⊙mid-Jun–mid-Aug; P 🛜) On a grassy knoll in a quiet residential neighbourhood, this imposing building was originally built as a club for occupying German officers. It represents great value. Bus 63 from the train station passes by. If driving, take Klostergata eastwards from the Studentersamfundet and follow the signs. The free parking is a winner and the rooms are tidy.

★**Radisson Blu**
Royal Garden Hotel HOTEL $$
(Map p258; ☎73 80 30 00; www.radissonblu.com; Kjøpmannsgata 73; s/d from 895/1245kr; P ✳ @ 🛜 🛋) This first-class, contemporary riverside hotel (you can fish from your window in some rooms, although most overlook a leafy internal patio) is open and airy from the moment you step into the atrium, where the light streams in through the all-glass walls. Rooms are supremely comfortable.

City Living
Hotel & Apartments HOTEL, APARTMENTS $$
(Schøllers Hotel; Map p258; ☎73 87 08 00; www.citylliving.no; Dronningens gate 26; r/apt from 637/922kr) Slick modern rooms in the heart of the city, just across from the town's loveliest little garden, and with just the right mix of style and comfort. Most rooms have parquetry floors and modern furnishings, but some have carpets. The prices, too, are brilliant value for what you get and where you get it.

Clarion Collection
Hotel Grand Olav HOTEL $$
(Map p258; ☎73 80 80 80; www.nordicchoice hotels.no; Kjøpmannsgata 48; r from 1245kr; @🛜) The Clarion offers sleek luxurious living above an airy shopping complex and the Olavshallen concert hall. It has 27 different styles among more than 100 rooms, so no guest can complain of a lack of choice. The location is handy for everything in Trondheim, with the Solsiden waterfront area to Nidaros Cathedral all within walking distance.

P-Hotel HOTEL $$
(Map p258; ☎73 80 23 50; www.p-hotels.no; Nordre gate 24; s/d from 695/895kr; @🛜) This efficient hotel is a short walk from the train station and the main shopping street. It's part of the Norwegian P-Hotels chain, so it's short on imagination – but rooms are comfortable and simply appointed. Upper floors are preferable to avoid noise from the restaurant underneath. Breakfast-in-a-bag (a bottle of juice and a sandwich) is delivered to your door.

Chesterfield Hotel HOTEL $$
(Map p258; ☎73 50 37 50; www.cht.no; Søndre gate 26; s/d from 715/895kr; @🛜) All 43 rooms at this venerable hotel are spacious and represent terrific value by Norwegian standards. The rooms have a fresh look with modern furnishings to go with the older style in public areas. Those on the 7th (top) floor have huge skylights with broad city views.

★**Scandic Nidelven Hotel** HOTEL $$$
(Map p258; ☎73 56 80 00; www.scandichotels.com; Havnegata 1-3; r 1449-2149kr, ste from 3995kr; P @🛜) A big business hotel with over 340 rooms and the full suite of facilities (conference rooms, gym, meeting spaces etc). It's split into several box-shaped wings projecting over the water, so many rooms have river views. Rooms are smallish but attractive, and the breakfast is a corker – Twinings awarded it 'Norway's best hotel breakfast' for 10 years running from 2006 to 2015.

In 2016 it came third, but it still wins our vote. Why? A fresh juice bar, a real-life barista and astonishing choice of every possible breakfast food imaginable...

Scandic Bakklandet HOTEL $$$
(Map p258; ☎72 90 20 00; www.scandichotels.no; Nedre Bakklandet 60; r/ste from 1349/1799kr; P🛜) At the northern end of Bakklandet, this upmarket choice has plenty in its favour: a great waterside location overlooking the river, an excellent Norwegian restaurant and a very decent bar. The rooms aren't terribly exciting – expect generic furniture and neutral colour schemes, partnered with occasionally adventurous wallpaper. River-view rooms are the best here.

🍴 Eating

★**Ravnkloa Fish Market** SEAFOOD $
(Map p258; ☎73 52 55 21; www.ravnkloa.no; Munkegata; snacks from 50kr, mains 140-215kr; ⊙10am-5pm Mon-Fri, to 4pm Sat) Everything looks good at this fish market that doubles as a cafe with quayside tables. The fish cakes are fabulous and it also does shrimp sandwiches, mussels and a fine fish soup.

TRØNDELAG TRONDHEIM

In addition to seafood, it sells an impressive range of cheeses and other gourmet goods.

Bror
DINER $

(Map p258; ☑ 458 31 526; www.brorbar.no; Olav Tryggvasons gate 29; burgers 98-119kr, tacos 139-149kr; ⊙ 11am-12.30am Mon-Thu, 11am-2.30am Fri & Sat, noon-2.30am Sun) There are two choices at this trendy brewpub – charcoal-grilled burgers or tacos – but the variety of flavours is impressive, taking in everything from chicken with mango chutney and smoked-paprika mayo, to smoked-cod tacos with radish, lemon and cayenne-spiced nuts. You get a digi-beeper that tells you when your order's ready to be collected from the hatch.

Café ni Muser
CAFE $

(Galleriet Cafe; Map p258; ☑ 73 53 63 11; www.ni muser.no; Bispegata 9; mains 119-175kr; ⊙ 11am-10pm Sun-Thu, to 1am Fri & Sat) For inexpensive light meals and an arty crowd, go to the cafe at the Trondheim Kunstmuseum (p260). Food ranges from pulled-turkey burgers and the soup of the day to salads and baguettes. On sunny afternoons, the outdoor terrace turns into a beer garden.

Persilleriet
VEGETARIAN $

(Map p258; ☑ 73 60 60 14; www.persilleriet.no; Erling Skakkes gate 39; lunch from 119kr; ⊙ 2-6pm Mon-Fri & noon-6pm Sat Jul, 11am-7pm Mon-Fri, 2-6pm Sat Aug-Jun; ☑) This tiny, lunchtime-only box of a place does tasty vegetarian fare, to eat in or take away. The menu changes regularly and the cuisine is eclectic. On any day it may include, for example, elements of Thai, Middle Eastern or Mexican dishes.

Jordbær Pikene
CAFE $

(Map p258; ☑ 73 92 91 80; www.jordbarpikene.no; cnr Erling Skakkes gate & Prinsens gate; mains 135-185kr; ⊙ 9am-8pm Mon-Fri, to 6pm Sat) 'Strawberry Girls' serves pasta, salads and sandwiches in an informal, congenial setting. It's good for juices too. You won't find anything particularly original, but you will enjoy decent, reliable, well-priced cooking.

★ Baklandet Skydsstasjon
NORWEGIAN $$

(Map p258; ☑ 73 92 10 44; www.skydsstation.no; Øvre Bakklandet 33; mains 158-275kr; ⊙ 11am-1am Mon-Fri, noon-1am Sat & Sun) If you're still searching for that quintessentially Norwegian meal, then you won't get much more traditional than this. Originally an 18th-century coaching inn, it's now everyone's favourite homely hang-out in Trondheim, with rambling rooms crammed with old furniture and clad in flock wallpaper, and a menu stuffed with comforting classics such as fish or reindeer soup, baked salmon and liver paste.

It also does a fine herring buffet (188kr to 239kr) and wild-reindeer casserole, and has a truly epic list of aquavits.

The food is more about heartwarming home-cooked meals than presentation, and we like it all the more for that.

Søstrene Karlsen
NORWEGIAN, INTERNATIONAL $$

(Map p258; ☑ 73 60 00 25; www.sostrenekarlsen. no; Tmv-kaia 25; lunch mains 145-275kr, dinner mains 195-365kr; ⊙ 11am-midnight Mon-Thu, 11am-2am Fri & Sat, noon-10pm Sun) Despite the irresistible energy of the Solsiden waterfront area, most of the restaurants are, surprisingly, of the chain variety – most people come here for the atmosphere rather than the quality. Søstrene Karlsen is a slight cut above the rest, serving everything from sandwiches to more substantial mains of the usual fish and meat variety.

★ Vertshuset Tavern
NORWEGIAN $$$

(☑ 73 87 80 70; www.tavern.no; Sverresborg Allé 11; mains 175-315kr; ⊙ 4-9pm Mon, to 10pm Tue-Fri, 2-10pm Sat, to 9pm Sun) Once located in the heart of Trondheim, this historic (1739) tavern was later lifted and transported, every last plank, to the Sverresborg Trøndelag Folkemuseum (p261) on the outskirts of town. Tuck into rotating specials of traditional Norwegian fare or just graze on waffles with coffee in one of its 16 tiny rooms, each low-beamed, with sloping floors, candlesticks, cast-iron stoves and lacy tablecloths.

Havfruen
SEAFOOD $$$

(Map p258; ☑ 73 87 40 70; www.havfruen.no; Kjøpmannsgata 7; mains 189-315kr; ⊙ 4-10pm Mon-Sat) Fish, fish and more fish – that's what you'll find at this upmarket restaurant, housed inside a fine old beamed warehouse, overlooking the river and the old-town bridge. The standards are high, reflected in the prices, but you won't get fresher or finer fish anywhere in town. Dishes, which include whale, are traditional and sauce-heavy, but the next-door bar is more relaxed.

If you'd like to catch your own, fishing rods are available from 3pm.

To Rom og Kjøkken
NORWEGIAN $$$

(Two Rooms & a Kitchen; Map p258; ☑ 73 56 89 00; www.toromogkjokken.no; Carl Johans gate 5; mains 255-395kr; ⊙4pm-1am Mon-Thu, to 2am Fri & Sat) The service is friendly here, and the ambience – with original, changing artwork on the walls – is bright and brisk. Dishes range from baked monkfish to Trøndelag beef sirloin, with ingredients sourced locally, wherever feasible. For a sample of its subtle cuisine with a less formidable price tag, savour its daily bar special (179kr).

🍷 Drinking & Nightlife

⭐ Ila Brainnstasjon
BAR, LIVE MUSIC

(☑ 489 55 036; www.ilabrainnstasjon.no; Ilevollen 32b; ⊙ 4-11pm Tue-Thu, to 1am Fri, noon-1am Sat, to 9pm Sun) This Trondheim institution is the best place in the city to see live music (most nights around 9pm; on Thursdays at 6pm), but it's a fine little bar-cafe even when nothing's on the bill. We especially love its 2pm Sunday jazz jam session when local musicians turn up to play – when it works, it's one of our favourite places to be in Trondheim.

Check the website (click on 'Hvar Skjer') to see what's coming up.

⭐ Jacobsen og Svart
CAFE

(Map p258; ☑ 902 44 226; www.jacobsenswart. no; Ferjemannsveien 8; ⊙ 7am-6pm Mon-Fri, 9am-6pm Sat, 11am-6pm Sun) One of Trondheim's trendiest coffee cafes, Jacobsen og Svart does what many claim to be the city's best coffee. Throw in a very cool soundtrack and near-perfect, freshly baked cinnamon rolls and you're somewhere close to cafe heaven.

⭐ Antikvariatet
CAFE, BAR

(Map p258; ☑ 942 20 557; Nedre Bakklandet 4; drinks from 79kr; ⊙ 2pm-1.30am Tue-Fri, noon-1.30am Sat & Sun) Now this is our kind of place – it has craft beers on tap, shelves lined with books, lovely views over the water and regular live gigs to boot. Unsurprisingly it's popular with students and trendy types, and it's in a delightful location among the wooden houses of the Bakklandet. You'll have to be lucky to snaffle a balcony table.

⭐ Trondheim Microbryggeri
MICROBREWERY

(Map p258; ☑ 73 51 75 15; www.tmb.no; Prinsens gate 39; ⊙ 3pm-midnight Mon, 3pm-2am Tue-Fri, noon-2am Sat) This splendid home-brew pub deserves a pilgrimage as reverential as anything accorded to St Olav from all committed øl (beer) quaffers. After a 2014 renovation and with up to eight of its own brews on tap and good light meals available, it's a place to linger, nibble and tipple. It's down a short lane, just off Prinsens gate.

⭐ Cafe Løkka
BAR

(Map p258; ☑ 400 00 974; www.cafelokka.no; Dokkgata 8; ⊙ 11am-midnight Sun-Tue, to 2am Wed-Sat) Long before its latest makeover, mustard-yellow Cafe Løkka was a boat-repair workshop. It now carries a good range of beers, on draught and in bottle, and also does milkshakes. It's more an early-evening venue than a serious late-night drinking den. It also does a good range of meals.

Café Le Frère
CAFE

(Map p258; ☑ 900 90 989; Søndre gate 27; ⊙ 8am-5pm Mon-Fri, 10.30am-4.30pm Sat, 11.30am-4pm Sun) This agreeable little corner cafe is strewn with flowerpots outside and inside its story is told in two mottos: 'probably the best espresso in the world' and 'all shots double unless requested'. It also serves pastries and light snacks, but here it's all about the coffee.

Habitat
BAR

(Map p258; ☑ 955 22 669; www.facebook.com/habitattrondheim; Olav Tryggvasons gate 30; ⊙ 11am-11pm Mon-Thu, to 2am Fri & Sat) This fine little craft-brewery pub serves an intriguing range of sour beers (or what they call 'experimental beers') and 'hand-crafted pizzas' to an appreciative crowd that's a slight cut above the student crowd. Try the Berliner Weisse.

Bare Blåbær
BAR

(Map p258; ☑ 73 53 30 32; www.barebb.no; Innherredsveien 16; ⊙ 11am-1am Sun-Thu, to 2am Fri & Sat) Join the throng that packs both the interior and dockside terrace of this popular place over near the Solsiden waterfront area. It's renowned for its cocktails – and for preparing what many believe to be some of the finest pizzas in town, including the intriguing *chilli bollocks* (presumably a winter special).

Studentersamfundet
BAR
(Student Centre; Map p258; www.samfundet.no; Elgesetergate 1) During the academic year, this place has 10 lively bars, a cinema and frequent live music, while in summer it's mostly a travellers' crash pad. It shuts down in summer, which is one of Trondheim's great shames.

☆ Entertainment

★ Dokkhuset
CULTURAL CENTRE
(Map p258; ☎911 59 045; www.dokkhuset.no; Dokkparken 4; ☺3-10.30pm Mon-Thu, noon-2am Fri & Sat) In an artistically converted former pumping station (look through the glass beneath your feet at the old engines), the Dock House is at once auditorium (on some nights you'll hear experimental jazz or chamber music), restaurant and cafebar. Sip a drink on the jetty or survey the Trondheim scene from its roof terrace. Things are quiet to the point of closure in summer.

Olavshallen
CONCERT VENUE
(Map p258; ☎73 99 40 50; www.olavshallen.no; Kjøpmannsgata 44) Trondheim's main concert hall is within the Olavskvartalet cultural centre. The home base of the Trondheim Symphony Orchestra, it also features international rock and jazz concerts, mostly between September and May.

🛍 Shopping

★ Bryggerekka Bruktmarked
MARKET
(Map p258; www.midtbeyn.no/bruktmarked; Kjøpmannsgata; ☺10am-4pm Sun mid-May–early Sep) Along the waterfront close to where Kongens gate hits the water, the colourful wharf-side warehouses provide a lovely backdrop for this summer-only Sunday flea market. It's mostly antiques, second-hand and the occasional vintage, with coffee and waffles at regular intervals.

★ Ting
HOMEWARES
(Map p258; ☎452 00 700; www.ting.no; Olav Tryggvasonsgate 10; ☺10am-6pm Mon-Sat) Modern designer homewares dominate this funky shop – it's all about Scandinavian cool without an outrageous price tag. A couple of doors up, **Småting** (Map p258; ☎47 48 92 88; www.ting.no; Olav Tryggvasonsgate 6; ☺10am-6pm Mon-Sat), run by the same

people, brings the same creative eye to children's toys.

Sukker
DESIGN
(Map p258; ☎476 53 637; www.sukkerdesign.no; Nedre Bakklandet 9; ☺2-5pm Fri, 11-4pm Sat & Sun) Designer just about anything is what this gorgeous little boutique is all about – jewellery and other accessories, clothing, artworks, ceramics, homewares…the designers actually run the shop and you'll want to spend both serious time and money here. It's just a pity (or perhaps just as well) it doesn't open longer hours.

Elin Aune
CERAMICS
(Trønderkeramikk; Map p258; ☎73 51 74 10; www.elinaune.no; Prinsens gate 21; ☺10am-5pm Mon-Fri, to 3pm Sat) This family has been making local ceramics since 1797 and it shows – this handmade pottery using hand-drawn designs has the charm of local industry and design that mass-produced ceramics will never match. There are pots, bowls, cups and more. Although there's an entrance on Prinsens gate, you can also enter through the Trondheim Torg Shopping Centre from Torvet.

Søstrene Grene
STATIONERY, HOMEWARES
(Map p258; ☎73 51 02 00; www.sostrenegrene.com; Olav Tryggvasons gate 14; ☺10am-6pm Mon-Wed, Fri & Sat, to 7pm Thu) Very cool stationery items and a few homewares in pastel hues – most things on sale here capture that Scandinavian flair for design in a trendy but understated way.

Moods of Norway
FASHION & ACCESSORIES
(Map p258; ☎924 25 722; www.moodsofnorway.com; Olav Tryggvasonsgate 29; ☺10am-6pm Mon-Sat) The quirky fashions of this stunning Norwegian success story recognise the virtue in eccentricity. Bright colours and harmless fun are recurring themes.

Husfliden
ARTS & CRAFTS, CLOTHING
(Map p258; ☎73 83 32 30; www.norskflid.no; Olav Tryggvasonsgate 18; ☺9am-6pm Mon-Fri, to 4pm Sat) Need a bunda for Norwegian national day? Or simply on the lookout for a traditional Norwegian gift? Husfliden is your place.

ℹ Information

INTERNET
There's free internet access at the tourist office (p267) and the **library** (☎72 54 75 00; Kongens gate; ☺10am-6pm Mon, 10am-4pm Tue-Fri, 11am-4pm Sat).

POST

Main Post Office (Map p258; Dronningens gate 10) Undergoing major renovations in 2017. If your postal needs are urgent, ask at the tourist office for your nearest branch office.

TOURIST INFORMATION

Tourist Office (Map p258; ☑ 73 80 76 60; www. visittrondheim.no; 1st fl, Nordre gate 11; ☺ 9am-6pm mid-Jun–mid-Aug, to 6pm Mon-Sat rest of year) In the heart of the city, with an accommodation booking service.

❶ Getting There & Away

AIR

Værnes airport is 32km east of Trondheim, with flights operated by SAS (www.sas.no), Norwegian (www.norwegian.no) and Widerøe (www.wideroe. no). There are flights to all major Norwegian cities, as well as Copenhagen and Stockholm. Norwegian flies to/from London (Gatwick) and Berlin, and KLM covers Amsterdam.

To/From the Airport

Flybussen (www.flybussen.no; adult one way/ return 130/220kr) runs every hourly (less frequently at weekends), stopping at major landmarks such as the train station. The journey time is about 35 minutes to/from the train station.

Værnes Ekspressen (☑ 905 74 475; www. vaernesekspressen.no; adult/child one way 120/60kr, return 210/105kr) also connects the airport with, among other downtown stops, Solsiden and the Radisson Blu Hotel.

It's actually cheaper to catch the train, which connects the Værnes airport station (82kr, 30 to 40 minutes, hourly) with Trondheim Sentralstasjon. Not all trains terminate at Trondheim, however, so watch departure boards carefully.

BOAT

Trondheim is a major stop on the Hurtigruten coastal-ferry route. Express passenger boats between Trondheim and Kristiansund (3½ hours) depart from the **Pirterminalen quay** (Map p258; Havne) up to three times daily.

Ferries to Munkholmen (p261) From mid-May to September, ferries leave at least hourly between 10am and 4pm or 6pm from beside the Ravnkloa Fish Market (p263).

BUS

The **intercity bus terminal (Rutebilstasjon)** (Map p258; Fosenkaia) adjoins Trondheim Sentralstasjon (train station, also known as Trondheim S).

As the main link between southern and northern Norway, Trondheim is a bus-transport crossroads. Nor-Way Bussekspress (p87) services run to/from destinations including the following:

GO TO HELL

It may be a cliché, but who hasn't been tempted to pull over and snap a photo of themselves under the sign at Hell train station? If you give in to the temptation – and, hell, we have – you'll have the perfect riposte whenever someone tells you to go to hell. I've already been, you can reply, to Hell *and* back... Trondheim's Værnes airport is next door, but clearly naming Trondheim's main portal Hell International Airport was a road too far for the Norwegian authorities. For the record, the town's name means 'prosperity' in Norwegian.

Bergen (808kr, 14 hours) One overnight bus.
Namsos (413kr, 3¾ hours) Four daily via Steinkjer (273kr, 2¼ hours).

If you're travelling by public transport to Narvik and points north, it's quicker – all is relative – to take the train to Fauske or Bodø (the end of the line), then continue by bus.

TRAIN

There are two to four trains daily to/from Oslo (937kr, 6½ hours). Two head north to Bodø (1088kr, 9¾ hours) via the following:
Fauske (1052kr, nine hours)
Mo i Rana (908kr, 6½ hours)
Mosjøen (817kr, 5½ hours)

As always, a *minipris* ticket will considerably undercut these standard prices.

You can also train it to Steinkjer (241kr, two hours, hourly).

THE ROUTE NORTH

Stiklestad

It's difficult to overstate the importance of Stiklestad in Norwegian history – thanks to the 11th-century Battle of Stiklestad that still resonates for Norwegians today, many historians place this as the site where modern Norway became possible.

The site, around most of which you can wander for free, is laid out rather like a sprawling theme park, with exhibits on the battle, an outdoor folk museum and, predating all, the 12th-century Stiklestad church.

◉ Sights

Stiklestad Church   CHURCH
(⊙11am-6pm Mon-Sat, 12.30-6pm Sun mid-Jun–mid-Aug) The lovely Stiklestad Church was built in 1150–80 above the stone on which the dying St Olav reputedly leaned. The original stone was believed to have healing powers, but it was removed during the Reformation and hasn't been seen since.

Stiklestad National Cultural Centre   MUSEUM
(Stiklestad Nasjonale Kultursenter; ☑74 04 42 00; www.stiklestad.no; adult/child/family 180/90/450kr; ⊙9am-6pm Sep-Jun, to 8pm Jul & Aug) This grandiose wooden structure includes **Stiklestad 1030**, an evocative exhibition about the Battle of Stiklestad, with dioramas and plenty of shrieks on the soundtrack; a 15-minute film on St Olav; a guided tour including a visit to the church; and a small WWII resistance museum. In the grounds there are over 30 historical buildings (admission free), from humble artisans workshops to the **Molåna**, a much grander farmhouse. In summer, actors in period costume bring the buildings to life.

✦ Festivals & Events

St Olav Festival   CULTURAL
(www.stiklestad.no/english/the-saint-olav-festival; ⊙Jul) Every year during the week leading up to St Olav's Day (29 July) Stiklestad hosts the St Olav Festival with a medieval market, wannabe Vikings in costume and a host of other activities. The high point of the festival is an outdoor pageant (held over the last five days nightly at 7pm) dramatising the conflicts between the king and locals.

Some of Norway's top actors and actresses traditionally take the major roles, while locals play minor parts and swell the crowd scenes. Tickets to the drama cost 500/450kr per adult/child.

⬓ Sleeping & Eating

Although most travellers visit on a day trip or while passing between Trondheim and the north, there is one excellent option for those who want to sleep among the ghosts of battles past.

The Stiklestad Hotell has a decent restaurant. Otherwise, there's more choice in Steinkjer or Namsos.

Scandic Stiklestad Hotell   HOTEL $$
(☑74 04 42 00; www.stiklestad.no/hotell; s/d from 950/1250kr; P❋☎) Inside the Stiklestad National Cultural Centre, this fine hotel is overseen by the Scandic chain but retains its own way of doing things. Rooms combine a contemporary look (think dark tones and parquetry floors) with symbolism from the Stiklestad story.

ⓘ Getting There & Away

The site of Stiklestad lies 5km east of the E6 on Rv757. There is no public transport to the site.

Steinkjer
POP 21,151

Medieval sagas speak of Steinkjer as a major trading centre. Little remains of such a

---

THE BATTLE OF STIKLESTAD

What we know about the Battle of Stiklestad we owe to the great Norse saga, *Heimskringla*, written by Snorri Sturluson some two centuries after the event. According to Sturluson, in 1030 Olav Haraldsson, back in Norway after a period of exile, marched over the mountains that separate Norway and Sweden with around 3600 soldiers. On 29 July 1030, around 80km north of Trondheim and at a farm known as Stiklestad, Olav's army ran up against a peasant army nearly 15,000 strong and led by pagan, feudal chiefs. Olav's army was routed and Olav was killed. His supporters carried the body to Trondheim, where he was buried.

According to Sturluson, a year later Olav's coffin was opened and his body had not decayed at all – his hair and fingernails had even grown in the intervening years. Wherever the truth lay, such was the power of Olav's story that his martyrdom became a defining pillar of Norway's historical story.

The Battle of Stiklestad marks Norway's passage between the Viking and medieval eras. Although Olav was killed, the battle is generally lauded as a victory for Christianity in Norway and the slain hero is recalled as a martyr and saint. He was canonised in Trondheim in 1031 and Pope Alexander III confirmed Olav's sainthood in 1164. St Olav developed a following all over northern Europe and his grave in Trondheim's Nidaros Cathedral became a destination for pilgrims from across the continent.

significant past, although it does serve as a crossroads of the two major routes to the north. Even so, you may not even realise you've passed through town, not least because there's little here to hold your attention, aside from the town's Egge Museum, an open-air farm complex 2.5km north of town. On the same hilltop site are several Viking burial mounds and stone circles.

◉ Sights

Egge Museum   MUSEUM
(☑ 74 13 44 90; www.eggemuseum.no; Fylkesmanns-gården; adult/child 70kr/free; ⊙ 10am-4pm mid-Jun–mid-Aug, shorter hours rest of year) This open-air farm complex lies 2.5km north of town. If you've visited this kind of museum (ie traditional farm buildings, wandering animals and volunteers in traditional dress), you won't find much new here, but the kids should enjoy it. On the same hilltop site are several Viking burial mounds and stone circles.

🛏 Sleeping & Eating

There are a couple of sleeping options in Steinkjer, but most visitors pass through en route between Trondheim and the north.

Føllingstua   CAMPGROUND $
(☑ 74 14 71 90; www.follingstua.com; E6, Følling; car or caravan sites 240kr, cabins 590-1500kr, d with shared/private bathroom 700/750kr) Beside the E6, 14km north of Steinkjer near the Snåsa-vatnet lake's southwestern end, this lovely, welcoming campground may tempt you to linger for a day or two, fish in the lake or rent one of its boats and canoes (200kr per day).

Tingvold Park Hotel   HOTEL $$
(☑ 74 14 11 00; www.tingvoldhotel.no; Gamle Kongeveien 47; s/d from 1100/1300kr; P @ 🛜) Beside an old Viking burial site, this secluded, well-run option is a member of the Best Western group. Overlooking Steinkjer, it has a pleasant lawn and garden, and the rooms are tidy if unexciting.

Brod & Cirkus   NORWEGIAN $$$
(☑ 74 16 21 00; www.brodogcirkus.no; Kongens gate 33; mains from 285kr, 3-course meals 495kr; ⊙ 11am-4pm Tue, 11am-4pm & 6-9pm Wed-Fri, 6-10pm Wed-Sat) 🍴 Meat, fish and shellfish are all sourced locally at this fine restaurant, and bread and desserts are all created on the premises.

❶ Information

Tourist Office (☑ 74 40 17 16; www.visitinn herred.com; Sjøfartsgata 2a; ⊙ 9am-6pm

❶ TRAVELLING NORTH FROM STEINKJER

Leaving Steinkjer, the E6 follows the north shore of the 45km-long, needle-thin lake **Snåsavatnet**, bordered by majestic evergreen forests. You may prefer to take the Rv763 along the quieter southern shore to see the **Bølarein**, a 5000- to 6000-year-old rock carving of a reindeer and several other incised carvings.

Mon-Fri, 10am-4pm Sat & Sun mid-Jun–mid-Aug, 9am-4pm Mon-Fri rest of year) Beside the E6, opposite the Amfi shopping centre. From the train station take the foot tunnel. Doubling as the Kystriksveien Info-Center, it can book accommodation in town and along the coastal route. It also rents bikes (per hour/day 75/200kr).

❶ Getting There & Away

Buses connect Steinkjer with Trondheim (273kr, 2½ hours, four daily), but the train is faster with more frequent departures to Trondheim (241kr, two hours), Trondheim's Vaernes Airport (183kr, 1½ hours) and Mosjøen (602kr, 3½ hours).

If driving and heading north, at Steinkjer, the road branches – take the E6 Arctic Highway (follow the signs to Narvik) or the prettier Rv17, the Kystriksveien towards Namsos.

Namsos

POP 12,906

Namsos is the first port town of consequence on the northbound coastal route between Trondheim and Bodø; it makes a pleasant overnight stop and has a few interesting diversions, but like with most Norwegian coastal towns, it's the setting and the scenery en route that will live longest in the memory.

◉ Sights

Rock City   MUSEUM
(☑ 950 84 939; adult/child 120/60kr; ⊙ 5-9pm Sun-Fri, 4.30-6pm Sat) The large white cube is a temple to rock and roll – and homage to the disproportionately large numbers of artists from Namsos who have made it big on the Scandinavian popular-music scene. Music fans will love it. Everyone else should enjoy the soundtrack.

⚡ Activities

Bjørumsklumpen   WALKING

An easy scenic 20-minute walk up Kirkegata from the centre will take you to the lookout atop the prominent loaf-shaped rock (114m) with views over Namsfjorden, Namsos and its environs. About a third of the way up, a sign identifies a track leading to some impressive WWII Nazi bunkers hewn from solid rock.

Oasen   SWIMMING

(www.oasen-namsos.no; Jarle Hildrums veg; adult/child 120/70kr; ⊙ 9am-8pm Mon, Tue & Thu, 10am-8pm Wed & Fri, 10am-4pm Sat & Sun Sep-Jun, 10am-6pm Mon-Fri, to 4pm Sat & Sun Jul & Aug) About 1km east of town and built deep inside the mountain, this swimming hall has three heated pools and a 37m water slide – ample reward for the kids who've endured long Norwegian road trips.

🛏 Sleeping & Eating

Namsos Camping   CAMPGROUND $

(📳 74 27 53 44; www.namsos-camping.no; Fly-plassvegen 10; tents/caravans 150/300kr, 4-bed cabins with outdoor bathroom from 525kr, with private bathroom 850-1150kr) This superior campground has a large kitchen and dining room, playground and minigolf. Basic cabins are a bargain and the more expensive ones are well equipped. Alongside is a shallow lake that's ideal for children, who'll also enjoy the go-karts and communing with the squirrels. From Namsos, take Rv17, direction Grong, then follow the airport signs.

★ Scandic Rock City   HOTEL $$

(📳 74 22 40 00; www.scandichotels.no; Sverres gate 35; r from 1149kr; 🔊) Right next door to Rock City (p269) and stylish and contemporary in the way of most Scandic hotels, this is one of the best places to stay in town. Rooms have daring modern art, strong colour schemes and high levels of comfort. Excellent breakfasts are another highlight.

Tino's Hotell   HOTEL $$

(📳 74 21 80 00; www.tinoshotell.no; Verftsgata 5; s/d from 1095/1300kr; 🔊) Rooms are large and comfortable at this hotel, just a stone's throw from the waterside. A terrific restaurant and warm service round out a fine package.

★ Tino's Restaurant   ITALIAN $$$

(Verftsgata 5; pasta/pizza from 155/140kr, mains 275-305kr; ⊙ noon-11pm) Tino, the owner, who is as Italian as they come despite many years in Norway, runs a great restaurant that serves both international food and fine Italian cuisine (such as 24 varieties of pizza), a continent away from Norway's usual pizza and pasta joints.

🛍 Shopping

Aakervik   FOOD

(📳 74 27 20 90; www.facebook.com/maakervik; cnr Havnegata & Herlaugs gate 16; ⊙ 9am-4.30pm Mon-Wed, to 5pm Thu & Fri, to 4.30pm Sat) This gourmet food shop is a great place to buy wild salmon and other fish, reindeer, roe deer and elk. The interior is a mini-menagerie of stuffed animals and birds eyeing you glassily from all angles; pay your respects to the amiable brown bear.

ℹ Information

The seasonal **tourist office** (📳 74 22 66 04; www.visitnamdalen.com; Havnegata 9; ⊙ 9am-5pm Mon-Fri, 10am-4pm Sat mid-Jun–mid-Aug, shorter hours rest of year) rents out cycles (60/150kr per hour/day) and also provides information about the Kystriksveien.

ℹ Getting There & Away

Nor-Way Bussekspress runs four times daily between Namsos and Trondheim (413kr, 3½ hours) via Steinkjer (186kr, 1½ hours).

Rørvik

POP 2949

Tiny Rørvik buzzes whenever the northbound and southbound Hurtigruten coastal ferries meet each other here every day around 9.30pm. What gets passengers up early from the dinner table is the splendid Norveg.

HERLAUGSHAUGEN

Within easy walking distance of Leka's port area lies Herlaugshaugen, the second-largest Viking burial mound in Norway. Its origins date to the 10th century when, according to the Icelandic sagas, Harald Håfagre (known as Harald Fair Hair in English), Norway's first king, marched along the coast. As he neared Leka, the island's King Herlaug chose to be buried alive along with 11 of his men, rather than face Harald's all-conquering armies. Excavations in the 18th century revealed human and animal skeletons, weapons and even the remains of a boat.

⊙ Sights

★ Norveg
MUSEUM

(☑74 36 07 70; www.kystmuseetnorveg.no; Strandgata 7; adult/child incl audio guide 80/40kr; ⊙10am-10pm mid-Jun–Aug, 11am-3pm rest of year & when Hurtigruten is in port) Architecturally exciting and resembling a sailing ship, Norveg recounts 10,000 years of coastal history through a variety of media, including an accompanying audio guide, available in English. It also runs a well-regarded gourmet restaurant.

🛏 Sleeping & Eating

There's nowhere to stay in Rørvik – most visitors visit from the passing Hurtigruten or en route elsewhere.

★ Restaurant Norveg
NORWEGIAN $$$

(☑488 80 025; www.kystmuseetnorveg.no/restaurant-norveg; Strandgata 7, Kystmuseet; mains from 295kr; ⊙10am-10pm) The restaurant at the Norveg museum is one of the finest in Trøndelag, with visiting Michelin-starred chefs and a high-class menu that changes with the seasons. Dress nicely and book ahead.

❶ Getting There & Away

Aside from being a stop of the Hurtigruten coastal ferry, the swiftest way to travel between Rørvik and Namsos is by express passenger boat (adult/child 245/124kr, 1½ hours, one to three times daily).

By road, Rørvik is 320km north of Trondheim.

Leka

POP 589

You won't regret taking a short side trip to the wild and beautiful island of Leka; for hikers, the desert-like windswept landscape is enchanting. Aside from the fascinating geological story – the wind-eroded rocks once formed part of the seabed, now uplifted, and they turn wonderful shades of red and yellow – Leka is home to Viking burial mounds, sea eagles and Stone Age rock paintings. For more information visit www.visitleka.no.

🏃 Activities

There are a remarkable 34 marked hiking trails on Leka, ranging from 500m to 9km in

length. Various cycling routes also circumnavigate the island, covering 28km – rent bikes from Lekamøya Spiseri.

For brief hiking and cycling route descriptions, pick up the brochure *Leka Tourist Guide – Cycling & Hiking*, which is available from regional tourist offices.

Lekamøya Spiseri
CYCLING

(☑417 68 615; Skeismyrveien 29; child/adult/tandem bicycle per day 125/225/350kr) Conveniently close to where the ferries arrive and depart from Gutvik, Lekamøya Spiseri rents out bicycles for exploring the island.

🛏 Sleeping

Leka Motell og Camping
CAMPGROUND $

(☑74 39 98 23; www.leka-camp.no; tent/caravan sites 140/240kr, r 400-850kr, huts or apt 1100-1900kr) You can camp at Leka Motell og Camping, but for more comfort reserve one of its well-equipped, reasonably priced motel rooms. For something different and more spartan, hire a sod-roofed stone hut (400kr), sleeping up to four in bunk beds.

Leka Brygge
APARTMENT $$

(☑957 93 318; www.lekabrygge.no; apt from 1375kr; 🅿🛜) Attractive modern apartments in a white-wood building on Leka's east coast make this the island's best choice. Each of the 13 apartments has parquetry floors, a kitchen, sea views and access to a common laundry.

❶ Getting There & Away

Leka is accessed by hourly ferry from Gutvik (adult/child/car 37/18/94kr), a 20-minute drive from the Rv17 coastal road. The first ferry leaves Gutvik at 7.30am, the last at 10.55pm.

SCARY SEA EAGLES

Birdwatchers love Leka for the chance to see the majestic white-tailed sea eagle, but historically parents have been less happy to see them. It was here, in 1932, that a particularly cheeky specimen snatched a three-year-old local girl called Svanhild and carried her off. She was, locals assure us, deposited by the eagle high on a mountain ledge, from where she was rescued…

Nordland

Best Places to Eat

➡ Fiskekrogen (p298)

➡ Børsen (p295)

➡ Anitas Sjømat (p304)

➡ Krambua (p304)

➡ Umami (p313)

Best Places to Stay

➡ Svinøya Rorbuer (p295)

➡ Henningsvær Bryggehotel (p297)

➡ Lofoten Suite Hotel (p294)

➡ Lovund RorbuHotell (p286)

➡ Fru Haugans Hotel (p274)

➡ Hotell Marena (p310)

Why Go?

For those with a love of all things Arctic, this is where Norway really starts to get interesting. Heading northwards through long, slim Nordland, lush fields give way to lakes and forests, vistas open up, summits sharpen and the treeline descends ever lower on the mountainsides. Above the imaginary curve of the Arctic Circle, travellers get their first taste of the midnight sun in summer, while in winter, the northern lights dance across the night sky.

Linger along the spectacular Kystriksveien Coastal Route. Or travel the inland Arctic Highway: more direct, yet almost as lovely. And then there's Lofoten, where razor-sharp peaks stab at the sky and timeless fishing villages survive. Connected by bridges, the islands are easy to hop around, cycling is possible and hiking is as gentle or as tough as you care to make it.

When to Go
Bodø

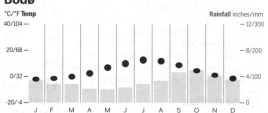

Late Mar Take in Lofoten and then Svolvær's World Cod Fishing Championship.

Late May–mid-Jul Midnight sun on Lofoten and elsewhere and good weather for activities.

Nov–Jan Long nights and good chances to see the northern lights.

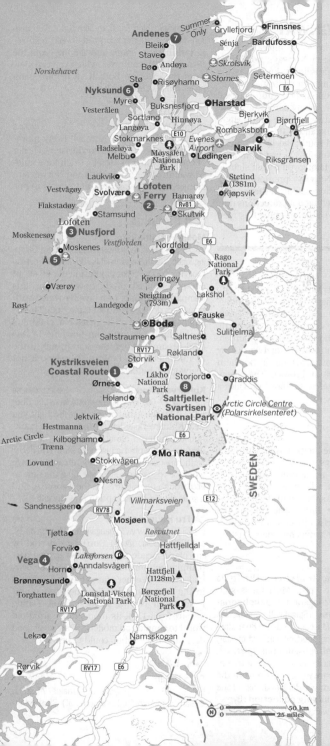

Andenes **7** Summer Only Gryllefjord •Finnsnes
Bleik• Senja Bardufosso
Stave•
Bø• Andøya •Skrolsvik
Norskehavet Stø• •Risøyhamn •Stornes Setermoen
Nyksund 6 Myre• E6
Vesterålen Sortland Buksnesfjord •Harstad
Langøya Hinnøya Bjerkvik Bjørnfjell
Stokmarknes E10 Rombaksbotn
Hadseløya Møysalen •Narvik
Melbu• National Lødingen
Park Riksgränsen
Laukvik• Evenes Airport
Stetind
Vestvågøy Svolvær •Lofoten (1381m)
Ferry Hamarøy •Kjøpsvik
Flakstadøy 2 •Skutvik
Stamsund RV81
Lofoten
Moskenesøy **3 Nusfjord** Nordfold E6
Moskenes• Vestfjorden Rago
Å **5** National Park
•Værøy Kjerringøy
Steigtind •Lakshol
Røst Landegode (793m)
•Fauske
Bodø •
Saltstraumen• Saltnes•
Sulitjelma
RV17
Kystriksveien Storvik Røkland
Coastal Route 1 Lákho
Ørnes• National Storjord •Graddis
Park 8
Holand• Saltfjellet-
Svartisen Arctic Circle Centre
Jektvik• **National Park** (Polarsirkelsenteret)
Hestmanna
Arctic Circle Kilboghamn• E6
Træna
Lovund •Stokkvågen •Mo i Rana
•Nesna SWEDEN
Sandnessjøen• RV78 Villmarksveien E12
Mosjøen
Tjøtta• Røsvatnet
Forvik• Hattfjelldal
Vega 4 Laksforsen
Horn• •Anndalsvågen Hattfjell
Brønnøysund• (1128m)
Torghatten Lomsdal-Visten Børgefjell
National Park National Park
Leka• RV17
Namsskogan
Rørvik• RV17 E6

0 — 50 km
N 0 — 25 miles

Nordland Highlights

1 Kystriksveien Coastal Route (p285) Driving along one of the most beautiful coastlines in the world from Sandnessjøen to Storvik.

2 Lofoten ferry (p296) Taking the ferry from Skutvik to Svolvær, one of the world's great ferry journeys.

3 Nusfjord (p302) Returning to the postcard-perfect fishing past of Lofoten in this lovely village.

4 Vega (p283) Experiencing the eider-duck economy and leaving the clamour of the modern world behind in Unesco-recognised Vega.

5 Å (p302) Lingering in the tiny, preserved fishing village that lies in Lofoten's deep south.

6 Nyksund (p307) Discovering the blissful isolation of this reborn village, then hiking the coastal Queen's Route to Stø in Vesterålen.

7 Andenes (p308) Taking to the seas to look for whales and puffins then driving west-coast Andøya.

8 Saltfjellet-Svartisen National Park (p277) Getting cold feet on one of the glaciers in this spectacular park.

ARCTIC HIGHWAY

The Arctic Highway – the interior's main thoroughfare between Norway's north and south, and more prosaically known as the E6 – cops something of a bad rap. Comparing it to the jaw-droppingly beautiful coastal Kystriksveien, it invariably comes up short. And yet it's all relative. Yes, the Arctic Highway has more traffic and is the faster route between north and south. But by any measure this passage from one Norway to another is a beautiful road, taking you within sight of some of northern Norway's prettiest scenery and crossing the Arctic Circle in the process. If you plan on travelling both directions during your visit, make sure you take this road on one of them.

Mosjøen

POP 9820

When arriving in Mosjøen (moo-sher-en), along the E6, you may be put off by the industrial face of this aluminium-producing town, especially if you're coming from the north. Don't be. Along the shore of Vefsnfjorden, historic Sjøgata and a street or two nearby are among the most charming in northern Norway and merit a browse. The steep-walled mountain across the fjord provides a stunning backdrop.

◉ Sights

★ Sjøgata   HISTORIC SITE

A stroll around the Sjøgata area, with over 100 listed buildings, takes you past galleries, coffee shops, restaurants and private homes in attractively renovated former warehouses, workshops and boat sheds. *The History of a Town,* available at the museum and tourist office, is an excellent small booklet that brings Mosjøen's history to life.

Vefsn Museum   MUSEUM

(adult/child 50kr/free; ⊙10am-6pm Mon-Fri, to 3pm Sat & Sun) The Vefsn Museum is split over two sites. In Sjøgata, the **Jakobsensbrygga Warehouse** (Sjøgata 31b; admission with ticket for Vefsn Museum; ⊙10am-8pm Mon-Fri, to 3pm Sat Jun-Aug, shorter hours rest of year) is an excellent small museum that portrays, via some particularly evocative photo enlargements, the history of Mosjøen from the early 19th century onwards. Northeast of the centre, the **rural building collection** (Bygdesamlinga; admission with ticket for Vefsn Museum;

⊙10am-3pm Mon-Fri, 11am-3pm Sat & Sun mid-Jun–mid-Aug, shorter hours rest of year) features 12 farmhouses, shops and the like from the 18th and 19th centuries, which you can view from the exterior. Both have helpful pamphlet guides in English.

⛳ Tours

Guided Walking Tours   WALKING

(adult/child 50kr/free; ⊙10am Jul) Every morning in July, head for the northeastern corner of the Fru Haugans Hotel garden for a guided walking tour (in English and Norwegian) along Sjøgata. It lasts for 45 minutes to one hour.

🛏 Sleeping

Mosjøen Camping   CAMPGROUND $

(✆75 17 79 00; www.mosjoencamping.no; Campingvegen 1; tent/caravan sites 180/255kr, 4-person cabin from 650-1350kr; ⛱) Beside the E6 about 500m southeast of the town centre, this campground tends to be overcrowded with travellers doing the North Cape rush. There's a pool with water slide, snack bar, children's playground – even tenpin bowling. In this land of superlatives, the sole urinal in the men's toilet must rank as Norway's, if not the world's, highest.

Kulturverkstedet   GUESTHOUSE $$

(✆75 17 27 60; www.kulturverkstedet.net; r 1100-1600kr) By the same people who brought you Café Kulturverkstedet (p275), these five guesthouses scattered along Sjøgata can be wonderfully atmospheric places to stay. The decor is, in most cases, delightfully retro and hence won't be to everyone's taste – take the time to go through the pictures on the website to find a style that suits. Reception is at the cafe.

★ Fru Haugans Hotel   HOTEL $$$

(✆75 11 41 00; www.fruhaugans.no; Strandgata 39; s/d 1250/1650kr; @🛜) Don't be deterred by the bland facade that somehow slipped past planning authorities. Fru Haugans (the original owner; see her stare from her portrait in the lounge above the Ellenstuen restaurant) is northern Norway's oldest hotel. Dating in part from 1794, its rooms range from old world to simple and modern. They're all good deals and the location couldn't be better.

🍴 Eating

Cafe Umami   CAFE $

(✆461 89 840; Sjøgata 35; mains 74-183kr; ⊙9am-5pm Mon-Fri, 11am-5pm Sat) Sandwiches, open and otherwise, a mean hot chicken soup and some creative salads make up the menu here. This fine choice has smooth contemporary decor within the antique shell of an old Sjøgata building – an alternative to the prevailing wooden tables and frilly curtains elsewhere along this street. In summer it sometimes opens 11am to 3pm on Sundays.

★Gilles Cafe & Musikk
CAFE, NORWEGIAN $$

(☑75 17 54 54; www.gilles.no; Sjøgata 6; mains 145-245kr; ◎8am-11pm Mon-Fri, 10am-11pm Sat) This excellent place near the northern end of Sjøgata serves up snacks such as scampi tempura, pizzas and more traditional mains – it does a great fish soup. This is also the liveliest place in town, with live music at 9pm most nights in summer, less often the rest of the year. It even organises occasional mountaintop concerts just outside town.

Café Kulturverkstedet
CAFE $$

(☑75 17 27 60; www.kulturverkstedet.net; Sjøgata 22-24; mains from 125kr; ◎8am-4pm Mon-Sat) Run by the local heritage society, this delightful cafe enjoys, appropriately, one of Sjøgata's largest renovated buildings. There are books to leaf through and you can sip and nibble in its interconnecting art gallery.

★Ellenstuen
NORWEGIAN $$$

(☑75 11 41 00; Strandgata 39; mains 255-365kr; ◎6-11pm) Ellenstuen, in Fru Haugans Hotel (p274), is an intimate place that preserves many of the hotel's original fittings. It has a particularly creative menu (if you're in luck, you'll find roasted stag fillet and lightly smoked grouse breast in a raspberry sauce on offer).

ⓘ Information

Tourist office (☑75 01 80 00; www.visithelge land.com; ◎9am-7pm Mon-Fri, 11am-5pm Sat & Sun mid-Jun–early Aug, 10am-4pm Mon-Fri rest of Aug, 10am-3pm Mon-Fri rest of year) At the northern end of Sjøgata.

ⓘ Getting There & Away

Widerøe (www.wideroe.no) has flights to Bodø (via Mo i Rana) and Trondheim.

Buses run from Mosjøen to Brønnøysund (325kr, three hours, once or twice daily except Saturday) and Sandnessjøen (215kr, 1¾ hours, three to five daily except Saturday). There are also services to/from Mo i Rana (190kr, 1¾

WORTH A TRIP

A DETOUR VIA HATTEN

For drivers, a lovely detour that bypasses Mosjøen follows the wild, scenic Villmarksveien route, which runs parallel to the E6 east of the town and approaches the bizarre 1128m peak of Hatten (or Hattfjell). From the end of the nearest road, the hike to the top takes about two hours.

hours, two to four daily), but the train takes less time.

Mosjøen lies on the rail line between Trondheim (817kr, 5½ hours, two to three daily), Fauske (577kr, 3½ hours, three daily) and Bodø (675kr; 4¼ hours, three daily).

Mo i Rana
POP 26,314

Mo i Rana (or just plain Mo to those who know it well) is the third-largest city in the north and the gateway to the spruce forests, caves and glaciers of the Arctic Circle region. Its friendly reputation is often attributed to its rapid expansion due to the construction of the now-closed steel plant, which in its time employed more than 1000 workers; nearly everyone here once knew how it felt to be a stranger in town. It's certainly not Norway's prettiest town, but there are a few reasons to break up the journey here.

⊙ Sights

Havmannen Statue
STATUE

(Map p276) *Havmannen* (Man of the Sea), a sculpture forever up to his knees in water, turns his back on the town and gazes resolutely out over the fjord. His clean lines and rounded profile are the work of iconic British sculptor Antony Gormley.

⊨ Sleeping

★Fjordgaarden Mo
HOTEL $$

(Map p276; ☑75 12 10 50; www.fjordgaarden.no; Søndre gate 5; ◎s/d from 790/940kr) Handy for the train station, close to the water and really rather stylish as well, Fjordgaarden Mo has simple rooms and the newer ones have nice photo walls. The prices are surprisingly good, making it a good all-round package.

Mo i Rana

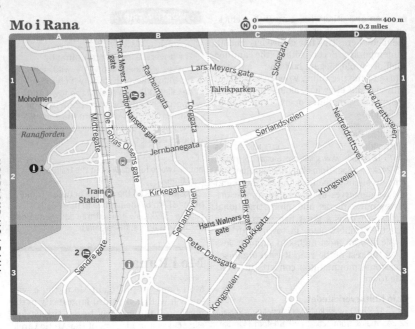

Mo i Rana

⊙ Sights
1 Havmannen Statue A2

🛏 Sleeping
2 Fjordgaarden Mo A3
3 Meyergården Hotell...........................B1

⊗ Eating
Søilen...(see 3)

Meyergården Hotell   HOTEL **$$**
(Map p276; ☑ 75 13 40 00; www.meyergarden.no;
Fridtjof Nansens gate 28; r 915-1595kr; P @ 🖥) An
affiliate of the Scandic chain, Mo's longest-
established hotel is full of character, with
fine rooms, most of them with a slick, con-
temporary look.

✗ Eating

Søilen   BISTRO **$$$**
(Map p276; ☑ 75 13 40 00; Fridtjof Nansens gate 28;
mains lunch 145-165kr, dinner 145-365kr; ⊙1-11pm
Mon-Sat, to 10pm Sun) The highly regarded
Arctic Menu restaurant of Meyergården Hotell gets its meat, dairy products and even
honey from local sources. Save a corner for
its signature caramel pudding with whipped
cream.

❶ Information

Tourist office (Map p276; ☑ 75 01 80 00; www.
arctic-circle.no; Ole Tobias Olsens gate 3; ⊙9am-
7pm Mon-Fri, 11am-5pm Sat & Sun late Jun-early
Aug, shorter hours rest of year) Has free internet
access.

❶ Getting There & Away

Mo i Rana's Røssvoll airport is 14km northeast
of town, and has flights to/from Bodø and
Trondheim. You'll enjoy an excellent panorama
of the Svartisen icecaps unless it's misty down
below.

By **bus** (Map p276), your options are fairly
limited. There are one to three daily services
to/from both Sandnessjøen (340kr, 2¾ hours,
one to three services daily) and Mosjøen
(190kr, 1¾ hours, two to four daily). At least
one Länstrafiken (www.tabussen.nu) bus runs
daily between Mo i Rana's bus station and
Umeå (eight hours) and other destinations in
Sweden.

Most visitors arrive at Mo i Rana's attractive
octagonal **train station** (☑ 75 15 01 77; www.
nsb.no), from where trains run to the following
destinations:

TRAINS FROM MO I RANA

DESTINATION	COST (KR)	TIME (HR)	FREQUENCY (PER DAY)
Bodø	507	3	3
Fauske	395	2¼	3
Mosjøen	218	1½	4
Trondheim	908	7½	3

Saltfjellet-Svartisen National Park

The 2102-sq-km **Saltfjellet-Svartisen National Park** is one of mainland Norway's most dramatic landforms. In the west, it embraces the rugged peaks of the Svartisen icecap, Norway's second-largest glacier, and glacier tongues are visible from the Kystriksveien Coastal Route, north of the ferry crossing of Forøy. To the east, the bleak, high moorlands of the Saltfjellet massif roll to the Swedish border. Charismatic wildlife also inhabit the park, including wolverine, Eurasian lynx, elk and a breeding population of Arctic fox, although most are elusive.

Northbound travellers on the Hurtigruten coastal ferry can visit the Svartisen glacier as an optional add-on to their journey.

◎ Sights

Polarsirkelsenteret   LANDMARK
(⌖75 12 96 96; www.polarsirkelsenteret.no; optional film adult/child 80/40kr; ◎10am-8pm Jun-Aug, to 6pm May) Latitude 66°33' N marks the southernmost extent of the midnight sun on the summer solstice and the ragged edge of the polar night on the winter solstice. Where the Arctic Highway between Mo i Rana and Fauske cuts across this imaginary line, in a high, broad valley that remains snowbound for much of the year, the Polarsirkelsenteret (Arctic Circle Centre) occupies a lovely natural setting.

⚡ Activities

Svartisen
The two Svartisen icecaps, separated by the valley Vesterdalen, straddle the Arctic Circle between Mo i Rana and the Meløy peninsula. At its thickest, the ice is around 600m deep. The average height is about 1500m but some tongues lick down into the valleys and are the lowest-lying glaciers

in mainland Europe. You can experience Svartisen from either its eastern or more spectacular western side. Most visitors to either side just make a quick hop by boat, but hikers will find more joy approaching from the east.

Østisen, the eastern glacier, is more accessible from Mo. From the end of the Svartisdalen road, 20km up the valley from Mo i Rana's airport, **ferries** (adult/child return 170/60kr; ◎mid-Jun–Aug) cross Svartisen lake (Svartisvatnet) four times daily. From the ferry landing, it's a 3km hike to the beginning of the Austerdalsisen glacier tongue. There's a kiosk and campground at the lake.

From the end of the road you can also trek up to the hut on the shore of the mountain lake Pikhaugsvatnet, which is surrounded by peaks and ice. This is an excellent base for day hikes up the Glomdal valley or to the Flatisen glacier.

Saltfjellet
The broad upland plateaus of the Saltfjellet massif transcend the Arctic Circle, connecting the peaks surrounding the Svartisen icecap and the Swedish border. Within this relatively inhospitable wilderness are traces of several ancient Sami fences and sacrificial sites, some dating from as early as the 9th century.

A 15km walk to the east leads to Graddis, near the Swedish border, and the venerable Graddis Fjellstue og Camping (p278).

By car, access to Saltfjellet is either along the E6 or the Rv77, which follows the southern slope of the Junkerdalen valley. Rail travellers can disembark at Lønsdal en route between Fauske and Trondheim. Check whether you need to request a stop.

⌂ Tours

Svartisen Moose   WILDLIFE
(⌖465 13 892; www.svartisenmoose.no; moose-watching adult/child 90/50kr, guided tour adult/child 175/90kr; ◎10am-3pm Jun–mid-Aug, guided tours 10.45am & 2.45pm) Captive, tame moose (known as elg, or elk in these parts) like it if you get up close and personal here. Wander around the enclosures or take a guided tour to get close enough for selfies and, yes, kisses. Kissing a moose is said to make you irresistible, or at least that's what they tell you here. Each to their own, we guess.

WORTH A TRIP

CHEESE FARM

This working dairy farm of **Strandli Gård** (☑ 472 37 246; www.strandligard. no; Fv273; ⊙ by appointment) is a charming excursion off the E6. In addition to selling lovely cheeses and yoghurts produced on the farm, it also has accommodation and the warmest of welcomes.

🛏 Sleeping

Graddis Fjellstue og Camping   CAMPGROUND, GUESTHOUSE $
(☑ 75 69 43 41; graddis@c2i.net; s/d from 550/750kr; ⊙ mid-Jun–mid-Aug) This cosy little guesthouse has been run by the same family since its establishment in 1867. It makes an excellent base to launch yourself into one of Norway's least-tramped hiking areas. Camping is also available, and Methuselah, a 1000-year-old pine tree, is a nearby attraction.

❶ Information

MAPS

The best map for trekking is Statens Kartverk's *Saltfjellet* at 1:100,000.

TOURIST INFORMATION

Svartisen Tourist Information (☑ 416 30 365; www.visitmeloy.no; Rv 17, Holand; ⊙10am-5pm Mon-Fri Jun–mid-Aug) Seasonal tourist office with good information on the national park. It's in the hamlet of Holand, 14km east of the ferry dock at Forøy and 25km southwest of Glomfjord.

❶ Getting There & Away

For the most part, you'll need your own vehicle to get really close to the park boundaries. On the west side, any transport along the Rv17 can drop you at the boat port, north of the vehicle crossing at Forøy.

Fauske

POP 9508

Most travellers on the way north end up passing through Fauske – it's the Arctic Highway gateway for Bodø (for Lofoten), Sulitjelma and Rago National Park – although it has few charms of its own beyond that of a crossroads. Few linger longer than it takes to fill up on petrol or change buses or trains.

◉ Sights

Fauske is known for its fine marble. Its Norwegian Rose stone features in many a monumental building, including the Oslo Rådhus, the UN headquarters in New York and the Emperor's palace in Tokyo. Suitably, its main attraction is the marble-themed **town square**.

Check out the park-like collection of historic buildings of the Fauske branch of the **Salten Museum** (☑ 75 50 33 00; Sjøgata; adult/child 60/10kr; ⊙11am-5pm mid-Jun–mid-Aug, to 3pm Mon-Fri rest of year), whose grounds are a lovely spot for a picnic.

🛏 Sleeping

Lundhøgda Camping og Motell CAMPGROUND $
(☑ 97 53 98 94; www.lundhogdacamping.no; Lundveien 62; car/caravan sites 100/200kr, d/q cabin 600/800kr, s/d 500/600kr; ⊙May-Sep) This complex, 3km west of town, has superb views of the fjord and surrounding peaks. Accommodation is nothing special, but it's all about the location here.

★**Fauske Hotell**   HOTEL $$
(☑ 75 60 20 00; www.fauskehotell.no; Storgaten 82; d 890-1140kr; 🛜) Fauske's only year-round upmarket choice has nice rooms with splashes of colour and contemporary art. There's a good restaurant, occasional live music and a bar that's surprisingly lively for a hotel bar.

❶ Information

Tourist Office (☑ 75 50 35 15; www.visit bodo.com; Sjøgata; ⊙11am-6pm Mon-Fri, 11am-5pm Sat, noon-6pm Sun mid-Jun–mid-Aug) This seasonal office shares its premises with the Salten Museum in the heart of town.

❶ Getting There & Away

BUS

Buses run to/from Bodø (105kr; 1½ hours, three to six daily) and Narvik (315kr, 5½ hours, two daily).

TRAIN

Trains ply the Nordlandsbanen between Trondheim (1052kr, 9½ hours) and Bodø (138kr, 45 minutes), via Fauske, twice daily and there are additional trains (up to four daily) between Fauske and Bodø. As always booking online may reap huge savings on the ticket price. To continue further northwards, you've no option but to hop on a bus.

Narvik

POP 18,787

Narvik has a double personality. On the one hand, its location is spectacular, pincered by islands to the west and mountains in every other direction, while spectacular fjords stretch north and south. At the same time, heavy industry casts a pall of ugliness over the rather scruffy downtown area – the town was founded in 1902 as the port for the coal-mining town of Kiruna in Swedish Lapland and the trans-shipment facility bisecting the city still loads several million tonnes of ore annually from train wagons on to ships.

But Narvik's appeal lies elsewhere, with unique sporting and sightseeing activities offered by its majestic surroundings and the spectacular Ofotbanen Railway to Sweden.

◉ Sights

Red Cross War Museum   MUSEUM
(Krigsminnemuseum; ☑76 94 44 26; www.warmuseum.no; Kongens gate; adult/child 100/50kr; ☉10am-7pm Mon-Fri, 10am-6pm Sat, noon-6pm Sun mid-Jun–mid-Aug, 10am-4pm Mon-Sat & noon-4pm Sun rest of year) This small but revealing museum illustrates the military campaigns fought hereabouts in the early years of WWII. The presentation may not be flash but it will still move you. Pick up a folder that explains each of the museum's sections.

🏃 Activities

★Narvikfjellet   CABLE CAR
(☑905 40 888; www.narvikfjellet.no; Mårveien; adult one way/return 120/180kr, child under 7yr free; ☉1pm-1am Jun–mid-Jul, 1-8pm mid-Jul–mid-Aug, shorter hours rest of year) Climbing 656m above town, this cable car offers breathtaking views over surrounding peaks and fjords – even as far as Lofoten on a clear day. Several marked walking trails radiate from its top station or you can bounce down a signed mountain-bike route. From February to April, it will whisk you up high for trail, off-piste and cross-country skiing with outstanding views.

It's a popular place to watch the midnight sun.

If you're keen to go even higher, ask about its guided hikes that climb above the top station (adult 645kr, under 15 years 445kr). There's also a climbing park (adult/child 250/200kr) that's loads of fun.

Ofotbanen Railway   RAIL
(☑76 92 31 21; www.nsb.no/en/our-destinations/our-regional-railway-lines/ofotenrailway; one way adult/child 160kr/free) The spectacular mountain-hugging Ofotbanen Railway trundles beside fjord-side cliffs, birch forests and rocky plateaus as it climbs to the Swedish border. The route from Narvik to Riksgränsen, the ski resort just inside Sweden, features some 50 tunnels and snow sheds. Towards the Narvik end, you might make out the wreck of the German ship *Georg Thiele* at the edge of the fjord.

You can run the line as a day or half-day trip, leaving Narvik at 10.26am. The 11.39pm return train from Riksgränsen allows time for coffee and a quick browse or you can walk a trail in this stunning alpine country and catch the 4.02pm back to Narvik. For the best views, sit on the left side heading from Narvik.

The railway, which opened in 1903, was constructed by migrant labourers at the end of the 19th century to connect Narvik with the iron-ore mines at Kiruna, in Sweden's far north. Currently it transports around 15 million tonnes of iron ore annually and is a major magnet for visitors.

In Sweden, several long-distance trails radiate out from the railway, including the world-renowned Kungsleden, which heads south from Abisko into the heart of Sweden.

The Narvik tourist office (p281) organises guided trips (per person 900kr).

> **WORTH A TRIP**
>
> ## HAMSUNSENTERET
>
> Around halfway between the E6 and the ferry crossing to/from the Lofoten Islands at Skutvik, along the Rv81, the **Hamsunsenteret** (☑75 50 34 50; www.hamsunsenteret.no; Presteid, Hamarøy; adult/child 100/50kr; ☉10am-6pm Jun–mid-Aug, 10am-3.30pm Tue-Fri, 11am-5pm Sat & Sun rest of year, closed Jan)is a must for anyone with a vaguely literary bent. The daring architecture is one of northern Norway's most striking examples of contemporary design, while the museum commemorates the life of Knut Hamsun, who won the Nobel Prize for Literature in 1920. The museum covers his life and work with well-presented displays and helpful staff keen to promote Hamsun's works.

Narvik Golfklubb GOLF

(☑971 46 082; www.narvikgolf.no; all-day/9-hole pass 400/250kr) The fjord-side journey to this unique golf course at Skjomendalen is wondrous (follow the signs to Skjomdal just before the Skjomen bridge on the E6, about 18km south of town). Sheer, treacherous faces will leave you guessing how there could possibly be a golf course here. Yet nature works wonders, and there's a valley hidden amid the peaks. Worthwhile hiking is nearby.

Narvik og Omegns Turistforening HIKING

(NOT; Narvik Trekking Association; ☑915 52 908, 402 40 987; www.turistforeningen.no/narvik) Narvik og Omegns Turistforening is an excellent source of information about hiking. It maintains more than 15 cabins, mostly between Narvik and the Swedish border. Collect keys from the tourist office (p281) against a deposit of 150kr.

✯✯ Festivals & Events

Vinterfestuka MUSIC, FESTIVAL

(☑76 95 03 50; www.vinterfestuka.no; ☺Mar) Each year during March, Narvik holds its Vinterfestuka, an action-packed winter week of events, partly in commemoration of the navvies who built the railway.

🛏 Sleeping

Narvik Camping CAMPGROUND $

(☑76 94 58 10; www.narvikcamping.com; Rombaksveien 75; tent/caravan sites 150/250kr, 2-bed cabin 450kr, 4-/6-bed cabin with bathroom 800/1000kr) Sound sleep is not guaranteed for those under canvas at what's otherwise an perfectly adequate campground, overlooking the fjord and E6, 2km northeast of the centre and Narvik's only choice. Trucks rumble along the highway and long wagon trains clank by on the railway, just above.

★ Breidablikk Gjestehus GUESTHOUSE $$

(☑76 94 14 18; www.breidablikk.no; Tore Hunds gate 41; dm 350kr, s 600-1150kr, d 1195-1750kr;) It's a steep but worthwhile walk from the centre to this pleasant hillside guesthouse with rooms for all budgets and sweeping views over the town and fjord. There's a cosy communal lounge and dorms have six beds.

Scandic Hotel Narvik HOTEL $$

(☑76 96 14 00; www.scandichotels.no/hotell/norge/narvik; Kongens gate 33; d 895-1495kr; ☎) Towering over the downtown area, this striking glass edifice houses Narvik's most stylish hotel. Rooms are slick and contemporary and those on the upper floors have fabulous views. There's also a fine restaurant and 16th-floor bar (p281).

🍴 Eating

Arild's Grillbar FAST FOOD $

(☑76 94 56 00; Torgsvingen 9; mains 60-180kr; ☺11am-11pm Mon-Fri, noon-11pm Fri & Sat) Fast food is ubiquitous in Norway, but if you're on a tight budget and can't face another petrol-station hot dog, this place does simple things well. Pizza, burgers, salads and sit-down tables make this a good solid option. It's at the bottom of the steps, next to the fish market.

Fiskekroken CAFE $

(☑76 94 36 60; Kongens gate 42; mains 80-190kr; ☺noon-6pm Tue-Thu, 1-9pm Fri & Sat) This tiny cafe, offshoot of the adjacent fish shop, offers tasty ready-to-eat dishes, such as fish cakes and fish and chips to eat in or take away. The fish couldn't be fresher.

NARVIK, ORE & WAR

During WWII control of this strategic port was essential to the Nazi war machine, intent upon halting iron supplies to the Allies and usurping the bounty. In April 1940, 10 German destroyers ploughed through a blizzard to enter the port and sink two Norwegian battleships. The next day five British destroyers arrived and a fierce naval battle resulted in the loss of two ships on each side. In May, British, Norwegian, French and Polish troops disembarked and took back the town.

The Nazis, however, didn't retreat and the town was decimated, as evidenced by the remains of soldiers in the cemeteries and 34 ships of five nations (Norway, Britain, France, the Netherlands and Germany) in the harbour. On 8 June 1940 the Allies surrendered Narvik, which remained under German control until 8 May 1945.

All along the E6 in both directions from Narvik, signs to 'Narvik 1940' indicate roadside memorials and information boards on key moments in the battle for Narvik and the march of Norwegian General Carl Gustav Fleischer in a bid to recapture the town.

Kafferiet   INTERNATIONAL **$$**

(📞 76 96 00 55; Dronningensgate 47; light meals 109-179kr, mains 159-309kr; ⊙10.30am-1.30am Tue-Thu, to 3am Fri & Sat) Narvik's slickest venue is a stylish, modern place with outdoor tables that tumble down the steps. Pasta, fish and grilled meats dominate an extensive if largely unimaginative menu, while it turns into a bar/nightclub once the kitchen closes.

🍷 **Drinking & Nightlife**

Tøtta Bar   COCKTAIL BAR

(16th fl, Kongens gate 33, Scandic Hotel Narvik; ⊙11am-1am Mon-Fri, 11am-2am Sat, 6pm-1am Sun) Encased in glass on the 16th floor of the Scandic Hotel Narvik (p280), this classy cocktail bar has fabulous views and is not just for those staying at the hotel.

ℹ️ **Information**

In the centre of town, the **tourist office** (📞 76 96 56 00; www.destinationnarvik.com; Kongens gate 41-43; ⊙10am-7pm Mon-Fri, to 6pm Sat & Sun mid-Jun–mid-Aug, 10am-4pm Mon-Sat & noon-4pm Sun rest of year) holds Narvik og Omegns Turistforening cabin keys (150kr deposit), has free wi-fi and rents out bikes (250kr per day).

ℹ️ **Getting There & Away**

AIR

Nearly all flights leave from Harstad-Narvik Evenes airport, 1¼ hours away by road. Narvik's tiny Framneslia airport, about 3km west of the centre, serves only Bodø, Tromsø and Andenes.

BUS

Express buses run from the **bus station** northwards to Tromsø (280kr, 4¼ hours, three daily) and south to Bodø (325kr, 6½ hours, two daily) via Fauske (315kr, 5½ hours, two daily). For Lofoten, two Lofotekspressen buses run daily between Narvik and Svolvær (from 280kr, 4¼ hours) and continue to Å.

Between late June and early September, bus 91 runs twice a day up the E10 to Riksgränsen (45 minutes) in Sweden and on to Abisko and Kiruna (three hours).

TRAIN

Heading for Sweden, there are two daily services between Narvik and Riksgränsen (one hour) on the border, and Kiruna (three hours). Trains continue to Lulea (7¼ hours) via Boden, from where you can pick up connections to Stockholm. The route takes you up the spectacular Ofotbanen Railway and, in Sweden, past Abisko National Park, which offers excellent hiking and lovely Arctic scenery.

DON'T MISS

RALLAVEIEN

The Rallarveien is a popular hike that parallels the **Ofotbanen Railway** (p279), following an old navvy (railway worker) trail. Few walkers attempt the entire way between Abisko National Park and the sea, opting instead to begin at Riksgränsen or Bjørnfell, the next station west. It's an undemanding descent as far as Katterat, from where you can take the evening train to Narvik.

For more exertion, drop down to Rombaksbotn at the head of the fjord and site of the main camp when the railway was being built (it's since returned to nature). From here, a boat (adult/child 345/140kr) runs erratically to Narvik in summer. Check with the **tourist office** (p281) to avoid an unwelcome supplementary 10km trek at the end of the day.

KYSTRIKSVEIEN – THE COASTAL ROUTE

Welcome to one of Europe's most spectacular drives. Longer, yes, more expensive, yes (gosh, those ferry tolls mount up). But if you've even a day or two to spare, divert from the Arctic Highway and enjoy the empty roads and solitary splendours of Kystriksveien, the coastal alternative that follows the coast for 650km. If the whole route seems daunting, it's quite possible to cut in or out from Steinkjer, Bodø or, midway, Mosjøen and Mo i Rana. It's one to drive; don't even attempt it by bus or you'll still be waiting when the first snows fall.

Off the coast are around 14,000 islands, some little more than rocks with a few tufts of grass; others, such as Vega, supporting whole communities that for centuries have survived on coastal fishing and subsistence agriculture – they're wonderfully rewarding detours in their own right.

Brønnøysund

POP 5037

The small coastal settlement of Brønnøysund is flanked on one side by an archipelago of islets and on the other by rolling farm country. It's one of the prettier settings for a town of this size along the southern end of the Kystriksveien, and worth visiting for the views alone.

⊙ Sights

★ Torghatten   MOUNTAIN
A dramatic local landmark rears up from Torget island, some 15km south of Brønnøysund. The peak, pierced by a hole 160m long, 35m high and 20m wide, is accessed from its base by a good 20-minute walking track. The best perspective of the gap is from the southbound Hurtigruten coastal ferry as it rounds the island.

Hildurs Urterarium   GARDENS
(www.urterariet.com; Tilrem; adult/child 60kr/free; ⊙noon-5pm mid-Jun–mid-Aug) Around 400 types of herb, 100 varieties of rose and 1000 species of cactus flourish at Hilde's Herb Garden, about 6km north of Brønnøysund; the team also produces their own wine. There are some rustic old farm buildings, a small art gallery and a shop that carries locally grown products. The garden also makes a lovely stop for lunch.

⌖ Tours

This one's a real winner. The tourist office (p282) sells tickets for a spectacular **mini-cruise** on the Hurtigruten. Leaving at 5pm, the coastal ferry passes Torghatten on its way south to Rørvik in Trøndelag – allowing an hour to explore the town and visit its splen-

<table>
<tr><td>

ⓘ KYSTRIKSVEIEN PLANNING RESOURCES

The splendid free *Kystriksveien* (Coastal Route) booklet, which is distributed by tourist offices and many lodgings along the way, is a mini-Bible. Its website (www.visitnorway.no/reisemal/trondelag/kystriksveien) gives even more detail. For greater depth, invest in *The Coastal Road: A Travel Guide to Kystriksveien* (298kr) by Olav Breen.

Click on the website's links to Cycle Touring for a recommended 12-day bike-and-ferry journey along the full length of the Kystriksveien. The free brochures *Cycling from Steinkjer to Leka* or *Exploring the Islands by Bicycle* have detailed maps, and list highlights and the best bicycle-friendly accommodation.

For a budget approach to the notoriously expensive route, visit www.backpacker17.com.

</td></tr>
</table>

did **Norveg Centre for Coastal Culture** and Industries before you hop aboard the northbound ferry to reach Brønnøysund again at 1am. Prices vary with the seasons and availability.

⋿ Sleeping

Torghatten Camping   CAMPGROUND $
(⌕75 02 54 95; www.visittorghatten.no; tent/caravan sites 250/280kr, cabins 1500-1950kr) This lovely option with its small beach beside a constructed lake is great for children. Around 10km southwest of Brønnøysund, it's handy for an ascent of the Torghatten (p282) peak.

Thon Hotel Brønnøysund   HOTEL $$
(⌕75 00 89 00; www.thonhotels.no/bronnoysund; Sømnaveien 98; r from 1245kr; P🅿🛜) Modern rooms, good breakfasts and sweeping views from the upper floors make this local outpost of the reliable Thon chain the best place to stay in town.

✕ Eating

★ Restaurant Sagastua   NORWEGIAN $$$
(Hildurs Urterarium; ⌕75 02 52 12; www.hildurs.no/restaurant; Tilrem; lunch main without/with dessert 195/295kr, 2-/3-course meal from 375/495kr; ⊙1-5pm) Exquisite tastes, professional service and artful presentation make this one of the best places to eat in this part of the country. The fish dishes are particularly memorable but the steaks, too, are perfectly cooked. The menu changes with the seasons.

ⓘ Information

Tourist Office (⌕75 01 80 00; www.visithelgeland.com; Sømnaveien 92; ⊙9am-7pm Mon-Fri, 11am-5pm Sat & Sun mid-Jun–mid-Aug, shorter hours Mon-Fri & closed Sat & Sun rest of year) One block from the Hurtigruten quay. It rents bicycles (200kr per day).

ⓘ Getting There & Away

Widerøe (www.wideroe.no) flies to Brønnøysund from Trondheim, Oslo and Bergen; the most common approach route passes right over Torghatten and the azure seas that lap around it.

Up to three buses run between Brønnøysund and Sandnessjøen (340kr, three hours, daily except Sunday) and to/from Mosjøen (325kr, three hours, once or twice daily except for Saturday).

Brønnøysund is also a port for the Hurtigruten coastal ferry.

Vega

POP 900

The island of Vega remains a very Norwegian destination (we have been the only non-nationals on our numerous ferry journeys to and from the islands). This and the more than 6500 *skerries* (islets) and simply large rocks that form the Vega archipelago are a Unesco World Heritage Site. This distinction comes not for any grand building or monument, nor for the scenery (which is stunning, nevertheless). It's for human endeavour – recognising that the archipelago reflects the way generations of fisherfolk and farmers have, over the past 1500 years, maintained a sustainable living in an inhospitable seascape. This lifestyle is based on the now unique practice of eiderdown harvesting, which is undertaken mostly by women. For more on these very special ducks and their down, visit the splendid little E-huset museum or visit www.verdensarvvega.no.

🏃 Activities

Birdwatchers have special reason to make the journey through the Vega Archipelago. The archipelago is home to 228 recorded species, and it is an extremely important winter area for sea birds. The barnacle geese for which Svalbard is famous spend a period resting here on their way north for the summer, while the largest breeding colony of cormorants breeds on one of the westernmost *skerries*.

🛏 Sleeping

Vega Camping   CAMPGROUND $
(☑ 943 50 080; www.vegacamping.no; Floa; car/caravan sites 175/210kr, cabins 600-850kr; ☺ year-round) The close-cropped green grass extending to the still water's edge make this simple campground one of the prettiest in Norway. You can rent a boat or bike (350/175kr per day) or go for a trot at the adjacent horse-riding school.

★Vega Havhotell   HOTEL $$
(☑ 75 03 64 00; www.havhotellene.no; Viksås; s/d/ste 1290/1390/1790kr; ☺ closed Oct & Mon Nov-Mar) This isolated getaway at Vega's secluded northern limit is tranquillity itself (you won't find a radio or TV in any of its 21 impeccably turned-out rooms). It's a place to unwind, go for breezy coastal strolls or simply watch the mother eider

duck and her chicks pottering. It also has an excellent restaurant and Anna and Jon are lovely hosts.

🛍 Shopping

★Utvær et Lånen   HOMEWARES, ACCESSORIES
(☑ 452 72 654; www.lanen.no; Lånen) In the Vega Archipelago, on the island of Lånen around 30km northwest of the main Vega island, Utvær et Lånen sells mittens, pillows, duvets and other products filled with eiderdown – both exceptionally warm and smooth as silk. If you can't make it out to the islands themselves, it is also possible to shop online.

ℹ Information

Tourist Office (☑ 75 03 53 88; www.visitvega. no; ☺ 9am-7pm Mon-Fri, 9.30am-3.30pm Sat & Sun mid-Jun–mid-Aug, 8.30am-3.30pm rest of year) In Gladstad, the island's largest hamlet.

ℹ Getting There & Away

Express boats make the trip to/from both Brønnøysund and Sandnessjøen, while car ferries cross to Vega from the mainland at Horn and Tjøtta.

Sandnessjøen

POP 5930

Quiet little Sandnessjøen is a boom town in waiting – oil has been discovered offshore and big changes are expected here. Until this change comes, this is a slightly scruffy little coastal settlement where life revolves around the fishing port and the pedestrianised Torolv Kveldulvsons gate, one block from the harbour.

The main attractions are the imposing **Syv Søstre** (Seven Sisters) range, south of town.

👁 Sights

★Petter Dass Museum   MUSEUM
(☑ 75 11 01 50; www.petterdass.no; off Fv17, Alstahaug; adult/child 85kr/free; ☺ 10am-6pm daily mid-Jun–mid-Aug, 10am-3.30pm Tue-Fri & 11am-5pm Sat & Sun rest of year) Even if you've never heard of the medieval Norwegian poet Petter Dass (1647–1707), don't miss this stunning museum at Alstahaug south of Sandnessjøen. Dass lived here for the last 18 years of his life and the museum is at once an avant-garde architectural showpiece and a fascinating insight into Dass's life and work.

🏃 Activities

The tourist office can suggest walks in the **Syv Søstre (Seven Sisters)** range, reached most conveniently via the Rv17 at Breimo or Sørra, about 4km south of town. From there you'll need to walk a couple of kilometres to the trailhead at the mountains' base. Alternatively, you can also get a **taxi** (☑ 75 04 02 12) to the base. Trails are blazed with red dots and the tourist office (p286) can provide simple maps and basic route descriptions, but pack *Alstahaug*, a reliable map at 1:50,000. As a security precaution (the weather can dramatically change with little warning in these parts), let the tourist office know when and where you're going.

Hardy hikers can reach all seven summits (ranging from 910m to 1072m) in a day. Every several years there's a competition that takes in all the peaks – the record is three hours, 54 minutes, although most mortals should count on 15 to 20 hours as a minimum. The climb to Botnkrona (1072m), the highest of the peaks, takes most hikers of reasonable fitness three to four hours one way, while count on two to three hours to climb each of the other peaks (also one way).

ℹ️ FERRIES FROM SANDNESSJØEN TO STORVIK

The long day's drive from Sandnessjøen to Bodø is slowed down considerably by the three ferry crossings you'll need to make. Timetables are available from most tourist offices along the way, including at both Sandnessjøen and Bodø. Remember that, even in the height of summer, most ferry crossings happen no more frequently than once an hour, all of which can mean a lot of waiting time if you don't plan carefully. A good resource for many ferry crossings is www.torghatten-nord.no. The three crossings are as follows:

Levang–Nesna (passenger/car 42/85kr, 20 minutes).

Jetvik–Kilboghamn (passenger/car 65/206kr, 70 minutes to two hours).

Forøy–Ågskardet (passenger/car 33/79kr, 15 minutes).

Sign your name in the book at each summit, fill in a control card and leave it at the tourist office – in return, you'll receive a diploma in the mail.

Another possibility is the ascent of **Dønnmannen** (858m), an 8km-return hike that is rated as challenging and is for serious hikers only. The trails start at Hagen, on the island across the water from Sandnessjøen to the west. The tourist office in Sandnessjøen has route descriptions and can provide ferry timetables.

🛏️ Sleeping

Sandnessjøen Camping CAMPGROUND **$**
(☑ 975 62 050; www.ssj.no; Fv17; tents/caravans 150/250kr, cabins 600-1200kr) Some 10km south of Sandnessjøen is a well-run place with fabulous views, as well as the usual campsites and simple cabins.

★ Scandic Syv Søstre HOTEL **$$**
(☑ 75 06 50 00; www.scandichotels.no; Torolv Kveldulvsons gate 16; d from 1350kr; 🛜) This large hotel close to the Hurtigruten ferry terminal offers all the comfort you'd expect from a member of the Scandic chain, with splashes of style in the rooms, excellent breakfasts and fine views from most rooms.

Leinesodden Cabins CABIN **$$**
(www.sandnessjoenovernatting.no; off Fv17; cabin per night/week 1200/6000kr) Run by Sandnessjøen but a far more imaginative choice, especially for families or groups, are its Leinesodden Cabins, across the water and a 10-minute drive from town. They sleep five to 10 people, are tastefully furnished and have a wonderful sense of isolation.

Clarion Collection Hotel Kysten HOTEL **$$**
(☑ 465 06 935; www.nordicchoicehotels.no; Havnegata 4; d from 1295kr; 🛜) This fabulous hotel overlooks the waterfront with stylish rooms with contemporary decor (think bold wallpaper, big mirrors and creative lighting). The breakfast is a cut above average and a light but excellent evening buffet meal is included in the rate.

🍴 Eating & Drinking

Restaurante Soprano ITALIAN **$$**
(☑ 407 00 006; www.restaurant-soprano.no; Torolv Kveldulvsons gate 33; mains 149-289kr; ⊘ noon-10pm Mon-Thu, noon-11pm Fri & Sat, 2-10pm Sun)

WORTH A TRIP

KYSTRIKSVEIEN FROM SANDNESSJØEN TO STORVIK

Superlatives come thick and fast along this stretch of coastline, and if you do only one segment of the coastal highway, make it the length between Sandnessjøen and the improbable sandy beach at Storvik, 100km south of Bodø. Much of this is a National Tourist Route, a designation awarded only to the most scenic of Norway's scenic roads. With three ferry crossings and ample reasons to stop and stare, it's a long day (especially if you're keen to reach Bodø by dinner time), but one you'll never forget as the road bucks and weaves between the ocean and mountains whose summits remain flecked with snow even into summer.

The pick of the views from the southern end comes as the road climbs after the Låvong–Nesna ferry crossing. Further on, as the road nears Mo i Rana, it's a dramatic run in its own right alongside pretty **Ranafjord** to Stokkvågen, soon after which you can roam around the Nazi coastal fort of **Grønsvik**, one of more than 350 defences built along Norway's coastline. Around 1km beyond the fort, a lookout offers more stunning views.

The route crosses the **Arctic Circle** somewhere along the hour-long Kilboghamn–Jektvik ferry crossing (the ferry captain usually makes an announcement – watch for the silver globe on the eastern shore). The further north you go, the more spectacular the views, from the snowbound mountains of the Svartisen ice sheet to islands, islets and *skerries* too numerous to count. Along the way, sea eagles circle above you and spring wildflowers show off their best in the relatively mild climate, warmed by the very last of the Gulf Stream's flow. For long stretches the highway rolls right beside the water.

The best views of Svartisen come after the Ågskardet–Forøy ferry, with dramatic views of the glacier tongues dropping down off the icefields towards the water from the road alongside Holandsfjorden.

To get even closer, a **ferry** (📞 95 92 03 27; www.engenbreenskyss.no; adult/child return 170/60kr) makes the 10-minute trip across Holandsfjorden from the small settlement of Holand roughly hourly. You can hire a bike (three/six hours 75/100kr) to travel the 3km gravel track between the jetty and the tip of the Engebreen glacial tongue.

A 15-minute walk from the ferry landing takes you to a seasonal information centre with cafe, shop and restaurant. It does guided one- to two-hour glacier walks (600kr) and longer four- to five-hour treks (1100kr) from the end of Engabrevatnet lake. Reserve in advance. You can also slog independently up the steep route along the glacier's edge to the Tåkeheimen hut (1171m), near the summit of Helgelandsbukken (1454m). Follow the 'T' markers and allow eight hours out and back. The Turistsenter can also advise on cabin accommodation in the area.

If you've time to spare, consider breaking the journey at **Furøy Camping** (📞 75 75 05 25; www.furoycamp.no; Forøy; tent/caravan site 180/220kr, cabin 500-950kr). Aside from the magnificent views of the Svartisen glacier across the fjord, this place has a five-star kids' playground (with trampoline and minicabins). It's barely 1km from the Ågskardet–Førøy ferry terminal, but do reserve your cabin in advance; a trail of vehicles heads from the ferry towards reception in summer.

A good alternative to the hotel restaurants, the Soprano is nothing special but it does serve authentic Italian pasta and pizza dishes. It's a slight cut above most other restaurants of its kind in Norway. For lunch try the manicotti – pieces of crêpes filled with meat sauce and topped with baked cheese.

Onkel Oskar BAR
(📞 75 04 18 88; www.onkeloskar.no; Torolv Kveldulvsons gate 40; ⏰ 8pm-1am Mon-Thu, to 3am Fri & Sat)

With a wonderful old fireplace and an antique air, this place has semi-regular pub quizzes and is a surprisingly cool place for provincial little Sandnessjøen. And we love its motto: 'Alcohol may be man's worst enemy, but the Bible says love your enemy.' Says it all really.

❶ Information

Tourist Office (📞 75 01 80 00; www.visit helgeland.com; Torolv Kveldulvsons gate 10;

⊙ 9am-7pm Mon-Fri, 11am-5pm Sat & Sun mid-Jun–mid-Aug, 10am-3pm Mon-Fri rest of year) In the heart of town; an excellent resource for the entire Helgeland region.

ⓘ Getting There & Away

Widerøe (www.wideroe.no) has direct flights to Oslo, Bodø, Trondheim, Mo i Rana and Mosjøen.

Bus destinations from Sandnessjøen include Brønnøysund (340kr, three hours, daily except Sunday), Mosjøen (215kr, 1¾ hours, three to five daily except Saturday) and Mo i Rana (340kr, 2¾ hours, one to three services daily).

The Hurtigruten coastal ferry pulls in twice a day, while ferries also go from here to Brønnøysund, Træna and Vega – the **tourist office** (p286) has the latest timetables.

Træna

Træna is an archipelago of more than 1000 small, flat *skerries,* only five of which are inhabited. Of these, head for **Husøy**, which has most of Træna's population and lodgings, and the adjacent island of **Sanna**. This drop in the ocean is just over 1km long with a miniature mountain range running the length of its spine and culminating at the northern end in the 318m spire, Trænstaven. The recurring feeling out here is that of standing on Norway's quiet outer reaches, with your back to Europe and having stumbled on a place that time forgot.

✪ Festivals & Events

Trænafestivalen   MUSIC
(www.trena.net; ⊙ Jul) Every year Træna hosts what must be one of Europe's more remote music festivals. That notwithstanding, Norwegian and international acts turn up and the festival is a wonderful way to spend four days.

⌸ Sleeping

Træna Gjestegård   GUESTHOUSE $
(☑75 09 52 28; www.trænagjestegård.com; Burmaveien; r per person 500kr) Rooms are as simple as they come but they're the cheapest in the archipelago and the owners cook up some terrific food for lunch and dinner.

Træna Rorbuferie   GUESTHOUSE $$$
(☑979 83 276; www.rorbuferien.no; r 1050-1300kr) These lovely, ochre-hued *rorbuer* (fisher's cabins) have fine views, simple furnishings and a blissful sense of isolation. Each

one has a kitchen but meals can also be arranged.

ⓘ Getting There & Away

Express passenger boats connecting Træna with Bodø, Sandnessjøen and Mo i Rana run one or two times daily. Ferries from the mainland dock on Husøy.

Lovund

Lovund is a dramatic, starkly beautiful island covering just 47 hectares, with a handful of red wooden houses huddled against the Atlantic elements beneath a towering rocky outcrop that rises 623m above the sea. Prolific bird colonies roost here, and every 14 April the island (home to barely 250 people) celebrates Lundkommardag, the day 200,000 puffins return to nest until mid-August.

⌸ Sleeping

★**Lovund RorbuHotell**   HOTEL $$$
(☑75 09 20 30; www.lovund.no; Fv406; s/d from 1345/1645kr) You don't expect to find a place like this out here. Contemporary (nay, ultra-modern) rooms, some in a sleek modern building, others in more traditional, refurbished old fishing buildings, make this one of the best places to stay along the coast. The food here is just as good as the accommodation.

ⓘ Getting There & Away

Ferries connect Lovund to Stokkvågen (two hours) on the mainland up to a couple of times daily. Fares vary depending on whether it's an express or stopping-all-stations service.

Bodø

POP 50,000

Bodø, the northernmost point of the staggeringly beautiful Kystriksveien Coastal Route and 63km west of Fauske on the Arctic Highway, is the gateway to Norway's true north. It is also the northern terminus of Norway's railway system and a jumping-off point for the spectacular Lofoten Islands.

The town centre, which had to be rebuilt after being almost completely levelled by WWII bombing, is unexciting architecturally. The city's main charm lies in its backdrop of distant rugged peaks and vast

KJERRINGØY

It's easy to see why this sleepy peninsula, some 40km north of Bodø, washed by turquoise seas and with a backdrop of soaring granite peaks, is a regular location for Norwegian filmmakers.

Here, the entrepreneurial Zahl family established, back in the 19th century, an important trading station. The **trading post** (Kjerringøy Handelssted; ☑75 50 35 05; www.nordlandsmuseet.no/kjerringoy_handelssted; Rv 834; adult/child 100/50kr; ⊙11am-5pm late May-late Aug) provided local fishing families with supplies in exchange for their catch. Most of the timber-built structures of this self-contained community have been preserved. The spartan quarters and kitchens of the fishing families contrast with the sumptuous decor of the merchants' housing. There's a 20-minute audiovisual presentation included in the entry price. Admission to the main building is by guided tour.

Bus 10 connects Bodø and Kjerringøy twice daily. In summer it's possible to squeeze in on the same day a return trip that allows a good 2½ hours of browsing time. Check the current timetable at Bodø's tourist office.

Whether by bus or car, the trip includes the 10-minute ferry crossing between Festvåg and Misten. Along the way, you pass the distinctive profile of **Landegode Island**, the white sandy beaches at **Mjelle** (whose car park is a 20-minute walk away) and the dramatic peak **Steigtind**, which rises a few kilometres south of Festvåg.

skies. Dramatic islands that support the world's densest concentration of white-tailed sea eagles – not for nothing is Bodø known as the Sea Eagle Capital – dot the seas to the north.

⊙ Sights

Norsk Luftfartsmuseum MUSEUM
(Norwegian Aviation Museum; www.luftfartsmuseum.no; Olav V gate; adult/child/family 160/80/450kr; ⊙10am-7pm) Norway's 10,000-sq-metre aviation museum is huge fun to ramble around if you have a passing interest in flight and aviation history – allow at least half a day. If you're flying into Bodø for real, you'll see that from above the striking modern grey and smoked-glass main museum building has the shape of an aeroplane propeller. Exhibits include a complete control tower and hands-on demonstrations. In 2016, it opened the excellent, interactive Civil Gallery on the dream of flying.

Bodin Kirke CHURCH
(Gamle riksvei 68; ⊙10am-3pm late Jun–mid-Aug) **FREE** The charming little onion-domed stone church, around 3km from downtown, dates from around 1240. The Lutheran Reformation brought about substantial changes to the exterior, including the addition of a tower. A host of lively baroque elements – especially the elaborately carved altar – grace the interior.

Nordlandmuseet MUSEUM
(Map p288; ☑75 50 35 00; www.nordlandsmuseet.no; Prinsens gate 116; adult/child 60/10kr; ⊙11am-5pm mid-Jun–Aug, 9am-3pm Mon-Fri Sep–mid-Jun) Recounting the short history of Bodø, this little gem of a museum has a cheerily entertaining and informative 25-minute film with English subtitles on the town's development. Museum highlights include a mock-up of a fisher's *rorbu*, a section on Sami culture complete with sod hut and ritual drum, regalia relating to the town's fishing heritage and a small hoard of 9th-century Viking treasure that was discovered nearby in 1919.

🎉 Festivals & Events

Nordland Music Festival MUSIC
(www.musikkfestuka.no; ⊙Aug) Ten days of classical music, jazz and opera in the first half of August. Ask at the tourist office (p290) for its 'Musical Views' app, a cool tool whereby you can listen to specially chosen music at some of the city's best viewpoints.

Parken Festival MUSIC
(www.parkenfestivalen.no; ⊙Aug) An action-packed, twin-staged fiesta of rock, R&B and pop held over a weekend in late August. It gets an eclectic mix of big international and internationally known Norwegian names, such as Franz Ferdinand in 2017 and a-ha in 2018.

Bodø

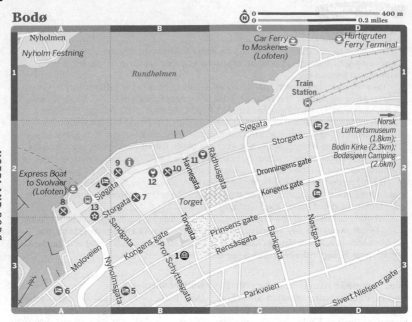

Bodø

◉ Sights
1 Nordlandmuseet B3

🛏 Sleeping
2 City Hotell.. D2
3 Opsahl Gjestegård D2
4 Scandic Havet....................................... A2
5 Skagen Hotel B3
6 Thon Hotel Nordlys............................. A3

✖ Eating
7 Bjørk B2
8 Bryggeri Kaia A2
9 Løvolds B2
10 Paviljongen... B2
Roast..(see 4)

🍷 Drinking & Nightlife
11 Dama Di – Kunst, Kaos & Bar............. B2
12 Public B2

✪ Entertainment
13 Stormen Konserthuset........................ A2

🛏 Sleeping

Bodøsjøen Camping   CAMPGROUND **$**
(☑75 56 36 80; www.bodocamp.no; Kvernhusveien 1; tent/caravan sites 180/250kr, plus per person 50kr, cabins 300-950kr) At this waterside campground, 3km from the centre, cabins are par-

ticularly well equipped. There's a nice grassy area with picnic tables exclusively for tent campers. Buses 12 and 23 stop 250m away.

City Hotell   HOTEL **$**
(Map p288; ☑75 52 04 02; www.cityhotellbodo.no; Storgata 39; dm 250kr, s/d from 650/750kr, tw with shared bathroom 695kr; @🛜) This hotel has 19 smallish but well-priced standard rooms and plenty of flexibility. Three dorms sleeping three to six cater for backpackers. Beneath the eaves are a couple of very large family rooms and two rooms have a kitchenette.

★Skagen Hotel   HOTEL **$$**
(Map p288; ☑75 51 91 00; www.skagen-hotel.no; Nyholmsgata 11; s/d from 915/1135kr; @🛜) Skagen occupies two buildings (one originally a butcher's, though you'd never guess it). Facing each other, they're connected by a passage that burrows beneath the street. Rooms are attractively decorated and a continent away from chain-hotel clones. There's a bar and free afternoon waffles and coffee, and excellent breakfasts. Staff can give advice on a raft of vigorous outdoor activities.

★Thon Hotel Nordlys   HOTEL **$$**
(Map p288; ☑75 53 19 00; www.thonhotels.no; Moloveien 14; s/d from 995/1205kr; 🛜) Arguably Bodø's most stylish hotel, with touches of

subtle Scandinavian design throughout, it overlooks the marina and runs a reasonable restaurant. We love the wall-sized photos of the northern lights in some rooms.

Opsahl Gjestegård B&B $$
(Map p288; ☑75 52 07 04; post@opsahl-gjesteg aard.no; Prinsens gate 131; s/d 1094/1300kr) On a quiet residential street, this guesthouse has 18 comfortable rooms with decor ranging from flowery to the less florid, and a small bar for guests. It's no cheaper than the larger hotels, but still remains an attractive alternative to hotel life. There are also four apartments with minikitchen.

Scandic Havet HOTEL $$$
(Map p288; ☑75 50 38 00; www.scandichotels.no/ hotell/norge/bodo/scandic-havet; Tollbugata 5; s/d 1449/1649kr; 🛜) The Scandic chain's pitch for Bodø's best designer hotel, this place has terrific views over the town and/or water (you can see the Lofoten Islands on a clear day from the western-side rooms). But inadequate plugs near the desk, the absence of minibars and other small but significant failings suggest a slight triumph of style over substance.

🍴 Eating

Paviljongen CAFE $
(Map p288; ☑75 52 01 11; Torget; mains 149-194kr; ⊙10am-11pm Mon-Fri, 1-11pm Sat, noon-11pm Sun) This great outdoor spot in the main square is the place to down a coffee or one of its three choices of draught beer, and perhaps nibble on an inexpensive lunch while watching the world pass. It serves pasta, fried salmon with couscous and even a hangover burger – very considerate.

★ Roast INTERNATIONAL $$
(Map p288; ☑75 50 38 35; www.roastfood.no/ bodo; Tollbugata 5, 17th fl; mains 189-350kr; ⊙11am-1am Mon-Thu, to 2.30am Fri & Sat, to 5pm Sun) High above the city on a 17th-floor perch in the Scandic Havet hotel, Roast is true to its name – you could play around with different tastes but you really must order the roast board, with its different meats (ribs, steak...) all beautifully presented. And the views from up here are simply wonderful.

Bryggeri Kaia NORWEGIAN $$
(Map p288; ☑75 52 58 08; www.bryggerikaia.no; Sjøgata 1; snacks from 150kr; mains 215-335kr; ⊙11am-3.30am Mon-Sat, noon-3.30am Sun) Bryggeri Kaia is a firm favourite. You can dine well, snack, enjoy its weekday lunch buffet

(195kr), its Saturday herring buffet (195kr) or quaff one of its several beers. Enjoy your choice in its large pub-decor interior, on the street-side terrace or, best of all should you find a seat spare, on the verandah overlooking the harbour.

Bjørk CAFE $$
(Map p288; ☑75 52 40 40; www.restaurant bjork.no; Storgata 8, 1st fl, Glasshuset; lunch specials 149-179kr, pizzas from 160kr, mains 295-329kr; ⊙10am-10pm Mon-Sat, 3-10pm Sun) This pleasant place has quickly become a popular haunt, especially of Bodø's younger movers and shakers. It serves a variety of creative snacks, wood-fired pizzas, tapas and sushi, and partly occupies the sealed bridge above the shopping mall's main alley. Its speciality is grilled stockfish served with pea puree, poached egg, bacon butter and aioli potatoes.

Løvolds CAFE $$
(Map p288; www.lovold.no; Tollbugata 9; mains 150-180kr; ⊙9am-6pm Mon-Fri, to 3pm Sat) This popular historic quayside cafeteria, Bodø's oldest eating choice, offers sandwiches, grills and hearty Norwegian fare with quality quayside views at no extra charge.

🍸 Drinking & Nightlife

Dama Di – Kunst, Kaos & Bar BAR
(Map p288; Sjøgata 18; ⊙10pm-3.30am) With a motto that translates roughly as 'art and chaos bar', Dama Di combines sophistication with an edgy, contemporary feel and eclectic decor. Art exhibitions and a pool table keep the strange juxtapositions going, and its motto – 'ugly coffee and nice people' – is fine as long as you're not here for hot drinks.

Public BAR
(Map p288; Sjøgata 12; ⊙8pm-3.30am) Supersized stills from punk-rock shows line the walls and a life-sized Elvis props up the bar of this minimalist place with its black leather stools. It claims to open every night of the year, but we didn't stop by on 25 December or Good Friday to check.

☆ Entertainment

Stormen Konserthuset CONCERT VENUE
(Map p288; ☑75 54 90 00; www.stormen.no/ konserthuset; Storgata 1b; ⊙box office 9am-4pm Mon-Fri, noon-3pm Sat) Bodø's showpiece concert hall is one to watch for big-name classical concerts – this is where the Northern

NORDLAND BODØ

Norway Opera & Orchestra (www.noso.no) performs. Guided tours are available on request.

ℹ️ Information

Tourist Office (Map p288; ☎ 75 54 80 00; www.visitbodo.com; Sjøgata 15-17; ☺9am-8pm Mon-Fri, 10am-6pm Sat & Sun mid-Jun–Aug, 9am-3.30pm Mon-Fri Sep–mid-Jun) Publishes the excellent free *Bodø* brochure and offers free wi-fi.

ℹ️ Getting There & Away

AIR

From Bodø's airport (www.avinor.no), southwest of the city centre, there are at least 10 daily flights to Oslo, Trondheim and Tromsø. Other destinations in northern Norway include Leknes, Narvik, Harstad and Mo i Rana.

BOAT

Bodø is a stop on the **Hurtigruten coastal ferry** (Map p288; ☎ 97 05 70 30).

Car ferries (Map p288; www.torghatten-nord. no) sail five to six times daily in summer (less frequently during the rest of the year) between Bodø and Moskenes on Lofoten (car including driver/adult/child 702/196/98kr, three to 3½ hours). If you're taking a car in summer avoid a potential long wait in line by booking in advance (an additional 100kr; online reservation at www. torghatten-nord.no).

Most days, at least one ferry calls in at the southern Lofoten Islands of Røst and Værøy.

There's also an **express passenger ferry** (Map p288; www.torghatten-nord.no) between Bodø and Svolvær (adult/child 385/198kr, 3¾ hours) once daily.

BUS

From the **bus station** (Map p288; ☎177), buses run to/from Narvik (325kr, 6½ hours) via Fauske (105kr, 1½ hours) twice daily, with extra services to/from Fauske.

TRAIN

DESTINATION	COST (KR)	TIME (HR)	FREQUENCY (PER DAY)
Fauske	138	¾	5
Mo i Rana	507	3	3
Mosjøen	675	4¼	3
Trondheim	1088	9¾	2

ℹ️ Getting Around

Local buses cost 50kr per ride. The **tourist office** (p290) rents out bikes for 230kr per day.

Saltstraumen

Welcome to one of Norway's most unusual natural phenomenon. The Saltstraumen Maelstrom is quite the spectacle and worth planning your day around if you're anywhere in the area.

◉ Sights

Saltstraumen Maelstrom   NATURAL FEATURE
The Saltstraumen Maelstrom is one of Norway's more unusual natural occurrences, which is guaranteed to occur four times every 24 hours. At the 3km-long, 150m-wide Saltstraumen Strait, the tides cause one fjord to drain into another, creating the equivalent of a maelstrom at sea. The result is a churning, 20-knot watery chaos that shifts over 400 million cu metres of water one way, then the other, every six hours. Being there at the right time involves careful planning.

This maelstrom, claimed to be the world's largest, is actually a kinetic series of smaller whirlpools that form, surge, coalesce, then disperse, and it's an ideal environment for plankton, which in turn attract an abundance of fish and therefore anglers. In spring, you can also see the squawking colonies of gulls that nest on the midstream island of Storholmen.

At its best – which is most of the time – it's an exhilarating spectacle. Should you be unlucky enough to hit an off day, it may recall little more than the water swirling around your bath plug. The experience is more immediate from the shoreline, but for the best views, stand on the arching Saltstraumbrua bridge, overlooking the strait, and watch as the waters swirl like nebulae.

As a general rule, when the tide is coming in from the west, the best views are on the east side of the bridge. When the tide's going out, they're on the west side. Arrive early enough to visit the visitor centre and check which way things are going.

Pick up a tide table in advance from the tourist office in Bodø or elsewhere, or your hotel; none are on display at the site itself.

🛏️ Sleeping & Eating

Pluscamp Saltstraumen   CAMPGROUND $
(☎75 58 75 60; Knaplund; tent/caravan site 250/250kr, huts 500-1100kr; ℗) A fairly standard and rural Norwegian campground sits just north of the visitor centre and short walk uphill from the water's edge.

Saltstraumen Hotel HOTEL **$$**
(☑75 50 65 60; www.saltstraumenhotell.no; Fv17; r/
cabins from 1295/1500kr; ℗🛜) Right next to the
visitor centre and a two-minute walk from the
maelstrom viewpoints, this hotel is a decent
choice if you don't want to miss the main
event or even want to see it twice. Rooms are
tidy if unspectacular, but it has a gym and out-
door hot tubs. It also has some self-catering
cabins.

★**Kafe Kjelen** CAFE **$$**
(☑936 86 963; www.kafekjelen.no; Ripnesveien
40; mains 115-225kr; ⊙10am-10pm Mon-Sat, noon-
8pm Sun) On a promontory overlooking the
maelstrom, this warm and wonderful little
cafe is gorgeous. Run by the same family
since 1955, it does a simple menu that includes local fish, pastries and real specialities worth trying, such as *møsbrømetse* (flat-
bread served with brown cheese, sugar and
melted butter). We could spend a whole afternoon here just watching the waters swirl.

🛈 Getting There & Away

Saltstraumen is 30km south of Bodø by road
(and much nearer by boat). Ask at Bodø's **tourist
office** (p290) for details of the privately run boat
excursions/tours that head down here.

There are seven buses daily (two on Saturday and Sunday; one hour) between Bodø and
Saltstraumen bridge. If you're driving, allow *at
least* 45 minutes to get here.

LOFOTEN

You'll never forget your first approach to the
Lofoten Islands. The islands spread their tall,
craggy physique against the sky like some
spiky sea dragon. The beauty of this place is
simply staggering.

The main islands, Austvågøy, Vestvågøy,
Flakstadøy and Moskenesøy, are separated
from the mainland by Vestfjorden, but all are
connected by road bridges and tunnels. On
each are sheltered bays, sheep pastures and
picturesque villages. The vistas and the special
quality of the Arctic light have long attracted
artists, represented in galleries throughout
the islands. One of the best ways to appreciate
the view is to follow the E10 road, which runs
along the islands from tip to toe, taking just
about every detour you have time for en route.

Austvågøy

POP 9150
Many visitors make their acquaintance with
Lofoten on Austvågøy, the northernmost island in the archipelago. It's a pretty enough
place with some fascinating attractions, but

NORDLAND AUSTVÅGØY

Lofoten

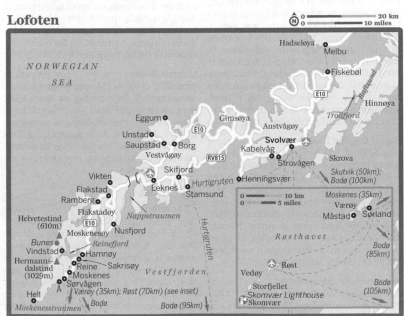

it's more appealing as a gateway to the archipelago than as a destination in its own right.

Svolvær

POP 4598

The port town of Svolvær is as busy as it gets in Lofoten. The town once sprawled across a series of *skerries*, but the in-between spaces are being filled in to create a reclaimed peninsula. Although the setting is beautiful with a backdrop of high mountains, the hotchpotch of modern buildings clutters things somewhat. It's a good place to eat and refuel, but the magic of Lofoten lies elsewhere.

◎ Sights

★ **Foto Galleri**   GALLERY

(Map p293; ☑ 954 98 150; www.lofotfotografen. no; cnr Vestfjordgata & Kirkegata; ◎ 10am-4pm & 6.30-8pm Mon-Fri, 10am-3pm & 6.30-8pm Sat mid-Jun–mid-Aug, closed evenings rest of year) **FREE** Stunning photos of the Lofoten Islands in all their brooding glory, most of them for sale, are the work of photographer Anders Finsland. It's worth stopping by even if you don't plan to buy.

★ **Magic Ice**   SCULPTURE

(Map p293; ☑ 76 07 40 11; www.magicice.no; Fiskergata 36; adult/child 175/95kr; ◎ 11am-11pm Sun-Thu, to midnight Fri & Sat mid-May–mid-Sep, 4-11pm Sun-Thu, to midnight Fri & Sat rest of year) Housed appropriately in what was once a fish-freezing plant, this is the ultimate place to chill out (perhaps with something to warm the spirit). The 500-sq-metre space is filled with huge ice sculptures, illustrating Lofoten life. If you can't return to northern Norway in winter, this is a great, if brief, approximation. Admission includes warm clothing and a drink in an ice glass.

Galleri Dagfinn Bakke   GALLERY

(Map p293; ☑ 76 07 19 98; www.dagfinnbakke.no; Richard Withs gate 4; ◎ 11am-3pm Mon-Wed & Fri, to 7pm Thu, to 2pm Sat) **FREE** One of Svolvær's more interesting little private galleries, this place showcases works by local artist Dagfinn Bakke, in which the distinctive light and natural formations of Arctic Norway take centre stage, with a range of other painters also on display. As always, many of the pieces are for sale.

Nordnorsk Kunstnersenter   GALLERY

(North Norwegian Artist's Centre; Map p293; ☑ 400 89 595; www.nnks.no; Torget 20; ◎ 10am-6pm mid-Jun–mid-Aug, to 4pm Tue-Sun rest of year) **FREE** On the main square and beside the tourist office, the North Norwegian Artist's Centre hosts changing exhibitions of paintings, sculpture, ceramics and more by artists from northern Norway. Its shop is a good source for a tasteful souvenir of Norway's north.

Lofoten Krigsminnemuseum   MUSEUM

(Map p293; ☑ 917 30 328; www.lofotenkrigmus. no; Fiskergata 12; adult/child 100/30kr; ◎ 10am-4pm Mon-Sat, noon-3pm & 6-10pm Sun mid-Jun–mid-Aug, upon request rest of year) Housed in the town's old post office, Lofoten's little war-memorial museum recounts the islands' role in the drama of WWII, when the islands were occupied by the Nazis. The collection includes lots of fascinating period photos, plus original uniforms, ordnance and even a couple of (decommissioned) mines.

术 Activities

★ **Svolværgeita**   HIKING, CLIMBING

You'll see it on postcards all over Lofoten – some daring soul leaping between two fingers of rock high above Svolvær. To hike up to a point just behind the two pinnacles (355m), walk northeast along the E10 towards Narvik, past the marina, then turn left on Nyveien and right on Blatind veg. The steep climb begins just behind the children's playground.

The climb takes around half an hour, or an hour if you continue up to the summit of Floya. To actually climb Svolværgeita and take the leap, you'll need to go with a climbing guide – ask the tourist office for recommendations or try Northern Alpine Guides (p298).

Lofoten Diving   DIVING, SNORKELLING

(Map p293; ☑ 400 48 554; www.lofoten-diving.com; Sjømannsgata 5; 3hr snorkelling per person 850kr, diving per person 690-990kr) For those willing to brave the Arctic waters, diving or snorkelling in the Lofotens is high on novelty value. This professional outfit has an office in Svolvær and another in Ballstad, way down in the south of Vestvagøy.

⌒ Tours

XX Lofoten   KAYAKING

(Map p293; ☑ 916 55 500; www.xxlofoten. no; JE Paulsens gate 12; from 690kr; ◎ mid-May–Aug) Kayaking around the Svolvær waters is a fabulous way to explore, and this well-organised company offers regular, three-hour guided excursions using two-seater kayaks. It also rents out bikes and organises fishing trips, and sometimes seafood-cooking courses as well.

Svolvær

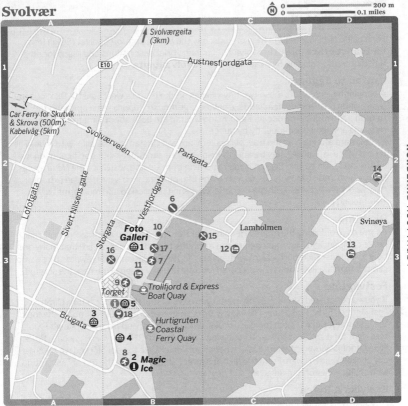

Svolvær

Lofoten Photo Tours   TOURS
(☑ 951 38 505; www.lofotenphototours.no; 1395kr;
☺10am Mon-Thu Sep-Apr by appointment) Four-hour photo tours outside high season (the best time for photographing the Arctic light) run by local photographer Geir Nøtnes.

✪ Festivals & Events

World Cod Fishing Championship   CULTURAL
(☺Mar) The town's annual World Cod Fishing Championship, a celebration of all things piscatorial, takes place over the

DON'T MISS

HIKING LOFOTEN

For a guide to hiking trails in the Lofotens, buy the *Hiking Lofoton* booklet (80kr) from the **tourist office** (p296) in Svolvær. It contains brief descriptions and maps for nine different trails, including Svolvær's very own **Svolværgeita** (p292).

Unstad to Eggum

A popular hike connects these two tiny villages on the island's west coast. A 9km coastal track winds past several headlands, a solitary lighthouse, superb seascapes and the ruins of a fortress by the ocean. Eggum and Unstad are both about 9km from the main road and are served infrequently by buses.

Take care after rain as the trail, particularly around Unstad, can be slick with mud. The tourist office in Svolvær may be able to help with bus timetables, but don't count on it.

Around 1.5km beyond Eggum if you're coming from Unstad, watch for the *Head* sculpture by Swiss artist, Markus Raetz. Part of the Skulpturlandskap series, it is an extraordinary work of art, changing shape in subtle ways and taking on 16 different forms as you walk around it.

Glomtind

As you drive out along the road to Henningsvær from the E10, you'll come across all manner of campers and hikers just before you reach the town. The chances are that many are here to conquer Glomtind (419m), a steep one- to 1½-hour ascent that rewards those who climb with marvellous views. Be prepared for a particularly steep climb near the summit.

Festvågtind

If you've conquered Glomtind, and even if you haven't, the three-hour return climb to Festvågtind (541m), also near Henningsvær, is an even more popular climb. At the top of the first steep slope (watch for loose rocks, both underfoot and from hikers higher up), turn right for a smaller climb and good views from Nipen (211m). Where the path forks, Heiavatnet is a lovely sheltered lake where some hikers like to cool off (and we mean really cool off) with a swim. From the lake, it's a very steep climb to the top of Festvågtind, with stellar views of Henningsvær and beyond.

Kvalvika & Ryten

As you travel beyond Ramberg in the direction of Å, follow the signs to Fredvang and keep going as far as Torsfjorden. From the car park, the trail climbs to 170m above sea level. It then follows the clear trail down to Kvalvika, from where another trail climbs steeply northeast, then northwest to Ryten (543m). It's a tough, three-hour climb from the car park, but the views are some of the best in Lofoten.

---

last weekend of March with hundreds of participants.

🛏 Sleeping

Scandic Hotel Svolvær HOTEL **$$**
(Map p293; 📞 76 07 22 22; www.scandichotels.no; Lamholmen; r from 995kr; 🅿 🛜) The Rica here is built on a tiny island, above the water and supported by piles. Room 121 has a hole in the floor so guests can drop a fishing line directly into the water below. Such novelties aside, the rooms are functional rather than memorable – make sure you get one with a balcony.

★ Thon Hotel Lofoten HOTEL **$$$**
(Map p293; 📞 76 04 90 00; www.thonhotels.no; Torget; d 1545-2695kr; 🛜) This stylish, central hotel has a high-rise profile and sheets of mirror glass from the outside. The main selling point is the fabulous views – ask for a room on the upper floors (avoid the 2nd and 3rd floors). The binoculars in each room are a nice touch. The breakfast won the Twinings prize for the best in Norway in 2016.

★ Lofoten Suite Hotel BOUTIQUE HOTEL **$$$**
(Map p293; 📞 476 70 100; www.lofoten-suite hotel.com; Havnepromenaden; ste 1450-3300kr; 🛜) This striking wood-and-glass structure seems to hover above the harbour-front of Svolvær, so it's perhaps unsurprising that practically all its swanky suites have an ocean view with floor-to-ceiling windows. Stripped wood and colourful fabrics conjure

a contemporary feel, and some rooms have little kitchenettes for preparing snacks.

★ Svinøya Rorbuer   CABIN $$$

(Map p293; ☑76 06 99 30; www.svinoya.no; Gunnar Bergs vei 2; cabins & ste 1600-3500kr) Across a bridge on the islet of Svinøya, site of Svolvær's first settlement, are several cabins, some historic, most contemporary, and all cosy and comfortable. Reception is a veritable museum – a restored and restocked *krambua* (general store), constructed in 1828, which was Svolvær's first shop. It has properties all over the area and some of the best *rorbuer* (fisher's cabins) in Lofoten.

SH Rorbu Anlegget   RORBUER $$$

(Map p293; ☑948 94 806; www.svolvaerhavn.no; Vesterøyveien 23; r from 2500kr; [P][🛜]) A modern take on the *rorbuer* idea, these luxury, dazzlingly white wooden homes on one of Svolvær's peninsula's have three bedrooms and a whole lot of style. This is high-end *rorbuer* living with modern furnishings and impeccable style. It's wonderfully quiet too.

✕ Eating

Hjerterommet Kafe   CAFE $

(Map p293; Vestfjordgata; snacks from 80kr; ⊙10am-4pm Mon-Fri, 11am-4pm Sat) More a coffee and cake kind of place, this eclectic little cafe is a fine little pit stop. The decor ranges from a bed mattress to cutesy and colourful wood, and the whole place is brimful of personality and warmth.

Ni Hao   ASIAN $$

(Map p293; ☑76 07 79 00; www.ni-hao.no; Havnepromenaden; mains 155-275kr; ⊙noon-11pm Mon-Sat, 1-11pm Sun) One of northern Norway's better Asian restaurants, Ni Hao has a lovely waterfront setting with a few outdoor tables, a stylish interior dining room and assured cooking. The beef dishes, using tender sirloin, are a real highlight.

★ Børsen   NORWEGIAN $$$

(Map p293; ☑76 06 99 30; www.svinoya.no; Gunnar Bergs vei 2; mains lunch 195-235kr, dinner 295-345kr; ⊙11.30am-3.30pm & 6-10pm mid-Jun–mid-Aug, 6-10pm rest of year) Located at the Svinøya complex, this is one of the town's top tables. A former fish house, it was called the 'stock exchange' after the bench outside, where the town's old geezers would gather to debate. In its dining room, with its beams and wooden floors, stockfish and Lofoten lamb are the specialities.

Anker Brygge   NORWEGIAN $$$

(Kjøkkenet; Map p293; ☑76 06 64 80; www.anker-brygge.no; Lamholmen; pub mains 159-300kr; restaurant mains 300-450kr; ⊙4-11pm) Anker Brygge, originally a shack for salting fish and nowadays furnished like an old-time kitchen, is a wonderfully cosy place to dine. The cuisine is just as traditional and the recommended menu choice is (of course) fish – try the halibut with Jerusalem-artichoke puree and champagne sauce. Outside, the pub terrace is far more casual with pizzas, burgers and steaks.

🍷 Drinking & Nightlife

Bryggabaren   PUB

(Map p293; Lamholmen; ⊙10am-late) In the same complex as Anker Brygge, this low-beamed, cosy watering hole is bedecked with tools of all kinds. The bar is a lifeboat from a WWII Polish troop ship that washed up in Svolvær in 1946. There's a regular bill of live music from May to September and sometimes at other times.

Styrhuset   PUB

(Map p293; ☑76 04 90 00; OJ Kaarsbøs gate 5; ⊙7pm-1am Sun-Thu, 6pm-2.30am Fri & Sat) Svolvær's oldest pub is all dark crannies that speak of sailors long gone. There's football on the telly whenever there's a big game.

DON'T MISS

TROLLFJORD BOAT TRIPS

From the port, several competing companies offer sailings into the constricted confines of nearby Trollfjord, spectacularly steep and narrowing to only 100m. Take the two-hour sea-eagle trip, the three-hour cruise or sign on for a four-hour trip that includes the chance to dangle a line and bring home supper. Buy your ticket at the **quayside** (Map p293; Vestfjordgata) or at operators such as **Lofoten Explorer** (Map p293; ☑971 52 248; www.lofoten-explorer.no; adult/child 795/600kr; ⊙9am, 11.30am & 2pm Jul, 11.30am & 2pm Jun & Aug, 11.30am rest of year), **RiB Lofoten** (Map p293; ☑904 16 440; www.rib-lofoten.com; adult/child 750/600kr; ⊙11am & 1pm May-Aug) or **Trollfjord Cruise** (Map p293; ☑451 57 587; www.trollfjordcruise.com; adult/child 700/350kr).

ℹ️ Information

Tourist Office (Map p293; ☑️ 76 07 05 75; www. lofoten.info; Torget; ⊘ 9am-9pm Mon-Fri, to 7pm Sat & Sun mid-Jun–mid-Aug, shorter hours rest of year) Provides information on the entire archipelago.

ℹ️ Getting There & Away

AIR

From Svolvær's small airport there are up to six flights daily to Bodø, and at least one daily Wideroe flight direct to Oslo.

There's no airport shuttle, so you'll have to catch a taxi.

BOAT

Svolvær is a stop on the **Hurtigruten coastal ferry** (Map p293; Torget). Two other sea routes connect Svolvær to the mainland. For timetables and reservations, visit www.torghatten-nord.no.

Skutvik (car/passenger 383/112kr, 1¾ to 2¼ hours, up to 10 daily) The most regular and popular crossing.

Bodø (adult/child 385/198kr, 3¾ hours) Daily **express** (p295) passenger-only boat.

BUS

Leknes (143kr, 1½ hours, four to six times daily) With connections to Å (230kr, 3½ hours).

Narvik (from 280kr, 4¼ hours, two direct daily).

Sortland (202kr, 2¼ hours, three to five times daily) On Vesterålen via Stokmarknes (1¾ hours).

Henningsvær

POP 444

A delightful (and rather narrow) 8km shoreside drive southwards from the E10 brings you to the still-active fishing village of Henningsvær, perched at the end of a thin promontory. Its nickname, 'the Venice of Lofoten', may be a tad overblown, but it's certainly the lightest, brightest and trendiest place in the archipelago.

It's also been an important fishing centre for many centuries. There's even a local saying dedicated to the town's piscatorial heritage: 'A real Lofoten cod am I, for I was born in Henningsvær.'

⊙ Sights

Kaviar Factory   GALLERY
(☑️ 907 34 743; www.kaviarfactory.com; Henningsværveien; adult/child 100/80kr; ⊘ 10am-7pm Sun-Thu, 2.30-7pm Fri & Sat) This fabulous art gallery inhabits an arresting, restored 1950s factory with a changing cast of cutting-edge temporary art exhibitions.

The design shop at the entrance is also very cool and worth a look.

Engelskmannsbrygga   GALLERY
(☑️ 481 29 870; www.engelskmannsbrygga.no; Dreyersgate 1; ⊘ 10am-9pm mid-Jun–mid-Aug, shorter hours rest of year) **FREE** Here at 'Englishman's Wharf' is the open studio and gallery of three talented local artists: potter Cecilie Haaland, wildlife photographer and guide John Stenersen and glass-blower Mette Paalgard, with whom you can sometimes try your hand at blowing your own glass.

🏃 Activities

Kayak Lofoten   KAYAKING
(☑️ 468 05 648; www.kayaklofoten.com; Gammelveien 6; kayak rental per day 450kr, 3hr guided tour 650kr) Take a three-hour tour out on the water or go it alone – whichever you choose, the waters around Henningsvær are magnificent for a paddle.

🐋 Courses & Tours

North Norwegian Climbing School   CLIMBING
(Nord Norsk Klatreskole; ☑️ 905 74 208; www.nordnorskklatreskole.no; Misværveien 10; ⊘ Mar-Oct) This outfit offers a wide range of technical climbing and skiing courses all around northern Norway. Climbing the peaks with an experienced guide costs around 2200kr per day, including equipment, for one to four people.

Lofoten Oppleveiser   OUTDOORS
(Lofoten Adventure; ☑️ 905 81 475; www.lofotenoppleveiser.no; Misværveien) Based in Henningsvær, this adventure company offers a wealth of maritime activities. In summer, try sea-eagle safaris (adult/child 650/500kr, 1½ hours), midnight-sun safaris (900/750kr, 2½ hours) and snorkelling sorties (850/700kr, two hours). In winter, chase the northern lights (700kr, two hours) as well as orca safaris (including snorkelling with them!) in Andenes, a four-hour drive north of Henningsvær.

⭐ Festivals & Events

Codstock   FOOD & DRINK
(www.codstock.com; ⊘ mid-May) This marvellously named festival celebrates Henningsvær's fishy heritage, with three days of cooking, fishing and sea shanties. Visiting musicians liven things up considerably.

LOFOTEN CYCLING & OTHER ACTIVITIES

Lofoten is perfect cycling terrain, thanks to its combination of generally flat roads, stunning scenery and enticing detours at frequent intervals.

For 83km of breathtaking cycling, head to Holandshamn and make your way back to Svolvær along the **Kaiser Route**. Lonely shoreline, jagged mountains and abandoned farms will be your constant companion. Unlike the west of Lofoten, this trip takes in parts of the island largely undiscovered by tourists. A long stretch runs parallel to Trollfjord. Ask at the tourist office for information about hiring bikes and getting to Holandshamn.

Another possibility is the 63km from Henningsvær to Stamsund, a lightly trafficked route that takes in some fabulous scenery and quiet beaches en route.

The **tourist office** (p296) in Svolvær can give further cycling suggestions. Grab the *Hjulgleder* handbook to cycling in Lofoten.

Lofoten Links (☑ 76 07 20 02; www.lofotenlinks.no; Hov, Gimsøysand; 9-/18-hole/24hr green fees 550/850/1400kr; ⊙ May–mid-Oct) Surely one of Europe's most beautiful golf courses, Lofoten Links faces out into the ocean and offers that once-in-a-lifetime opportunity to play golf under the midnight sun. A true links course, it's a challenging round and the par-three 2nd hole was voted Norway's best in 2016. There's on-site luxury accommodation for those keen to make a package out of it.

Lofothest (☑ 905 90 309; www.lofothest.no; Valbergsveien 966-981, Rolvsfjord; 3/5hr trips per person from 1550/2150kr; ⊙ May-Nov) From 90-minute to two-day excursions across Vestvågøy, from Rolvsfjord, along the Rv815 north of Stamsund.

Hov Hestegård (☑ 76 07 20 02, 917 69 809; www.hovhestegard.no; Tore Hjortsvei 471, Gimsøysand; 1½hr/2hr/half-day/full-day trail ride per person from 690/950/1350/1950kr; ⊙ May-Jul) Fine trail rides on the small island of Gimsøya, which lies between Vestvågøy and Austvågøy and is accessible off the E10.

🛏 Sleeping

Johs H Giæver Sjøhus og Rorbuer
GUESTHOUSE $

(☑ 76 07 47 19; www.giaever-rorbuer.no; Hellandsgata 79; rorbuer 650-1200kr, sea house 500-750kr) From mid-June to mid-August workers' accommodation in a modern sea house belonging to the local fish plant is hired out to visitors. Spruce rooms (some with space for four) have shared facilities, including a large kitchen and dining area, and are good value. The company also has 10 *rorbuer* with bathrooms in the heart of town.

Lofoten Arctic Hotel
HOTEL $$

(☑ 76 07 07 77; www.lofotenarctichotel.no; Sauøya 2; r 1353kr) Simple motel-style rooms at the entrance to the village make this a decent if uninspiring choice – some rooms are better than others so ask to see a few. Views are stunning from many parts of the property.

★ Henningsvær Bryggehotel
HOTEL $$$

(☑ 76 07 47 19; www.henningsvaer.no; Hjellskjæret; d from 1395-1895kr; ☏) In a beautiful wood-clad building by the harbour, this heritage hotel is hands down the best place to stay in Henningsvær. The rooms are styled in cool greys and creams; most have watery views, and some have fun loft-space beds for kids. Its restaurant, the **Bluefish**, is excellent – the menu prides itself on serving fish species 'you've probably never heard of'.

🍴 Eating

★ Kafé Lysstoperiet
CAFE $

(☑ 905 51 877; www.henningsvarlys.no; Gammelveien 2; mains 98-149kr; ⊙ 10am-8pm) This casual place in the heart of town is wildly (and deservedly) popular. The organic food ranges from Lofoten's best cakes and sweet treats to light meals such as soup, open sandwiches, pies, pasta salad and home-made pizzas. There are a couple of small outside tables, but the interior is warmly eclectic and filled with personality. Great coffee, too.

Klatre Kafeen
CAFE $$

(☑ 909 54 619; www.nordnorskklatreskole.no/klatrekafeen; Misværveien; mains 140-210kr; ⊙ 11am-1am Sun-Thu, 11am-2.30am Fri & Sat mid-Jun–mid-Aug, 6pm-1am Wed & 6pm-2am Fri & Sat mid-Aug–mid-Jun) With a few tables out over the water and an inviting interior dining area, this relaxed place is run by the neighbouring North Norwegian Climbing School (p296). The food ranges from open shrimp sandwiches and couscous salad to codfish soup. Watch for live music on Friday and Saturday nights in summer. It also has some simple rooms (dorm/single/double 300/500/600kr).

★ Fiskekrogen   SEAFOOD $$$

(☑76 07 46 52; www.fiskekrogen.no; Dreyersgate 29; mains lunch 185-265kr, dinner 245-325kr; ⊙12.30-10pm Jun-Aug, shorter hours rest of year) This dockside restaurant – a favourite of the Norwegian royal family – is Henningsvær's culinary claim to fame. Try, in particular, the outstanding fish soup (198kr), but there's everything else on the menu from fish and chips to fried cod tongues. Between 4pm and 5pm in summer it serves fish soup and seafood stew only. Quite right, too.

Next door, **Bar Nord** (open from 7pm) is a more casual affair, with lovely waterside views. And it's not too far to go for your post-dinner drink.

🛍 Shopping

Drops   HOMEWARES

(☑948 60 514; www.drops-henningsvaer.no; ⊙10am-8pm mid-Jun–mid-Aug, shorter hours rest of year) An eclectic collection of casual and, in some case, stylish homewares make for a fun browse along the town's main thoroughfare. As the sign outside says, 'We are not a souvenir shop, but we sell nice things that Norwegians really like'.

ℹ Getting There & Away

There's a regular bus to Henningsvær from Svolvær (50kr, 40 minutes, at least six daily) via Kabelvåg (35 minutes).

Kabelvåg

POP 1733

Kabelvåg, 5km southwest of Svolvær, is an intimate and cosy place. At its heart is a small square and tiny harbour, while its **Storvågen** district, 2km off the E10 to the south, has an enticing trio of museums and galleries.

⊙ Sights

A combination ticket (adult/child 220/110kr) gives entry to Lofotmuseet, Lofoten Aquarium and Galleri Espolin, all in Storvågan. They're an easy walk from each other.

Galleri Espolin   GALLERY

(☑76 07 84 05; www.museumnord.no/galleri-espolin; adult/child 90/40kr; ⊙10am-6pm Jun–mid-Aug, shorter hours rest of year) This gallery features

the haunting etchings and lithographs of one of Norway's great artists, Kaare Espolin-Johnson (1907–94). Espolin – his work all the more astounding as he was nearly blind for much of his life – loved Lofoten and often featured its fisherfolk, together with other Arctic themes.

Vågan Kirke   CHURCH

(Lofotkatedralen; ☑76 06 71 90; www.lofotkatedralen.no; Villaveien 9; 40kr; ⊙10am-6pm Mon-Sat, noon-6pm Sun late Jun–mid-Aug) Built in 1898 and Norway's second-largest wooden church, Vågan rises above the E10 just north of Kabelvåg. Built to minister to the influx of seasonal fisherfolk, its seating capacity of 1200 far surpasses Kabelvåg's current population. Watch for organ concerts in summer.

Lofoten Aquarium   AQUARIUM

(Lofotakvariet; www.museumnord.no/lofotakvariet; Storvågaveien 28; adult/child 130/70kr; ⊙10am-6pm Jun-Aug, shorter hours Feb-May & Sep-Nov) If you want to learn all about the deep, cold waters that surround Lofoten, then this aquarium is a good place to start. There are various exhibits relating to the *skrei* – the species of east Atlantic cod that migrates from the Barents Sea to Lofoten every winter to spawn – as well as tanks filled with king crab, salmon and other species, plus playful troupes of seals and sea otters (feeding times are noon, 3pm and 6pm).

Lofotmuseet   MUSEUM

(☑76 15 40 00; www.museumnord.no/lofotmuseet; Storvågaveien; adult/child 90/40kr; ⊙10am-6pm Jun-Aug, shorter hours rest of year) The islands' major folk museum is on the site of what can be considered the first town in the polar region, where traces of the original *rorbuer* (fisher's cabins) have been excavated. The museum's main gallery was once the merchant's mansion. An easy, undulating, scenic 2km heritage path leads from the museum to the centre of Kabelvåg.

🏃 Activities & Tours

Northern Alpine Guides   ADVENTURE SPORTS

(☑942 49 110; www.alpineguides.no; Kalleveien 21) Offers climbing and sailing expeditions in the Lofoten Islands in summer; ski adventures in winter. A very professional group that comes highly recommended.

Lofoten Kajakk   ADVENTURE

(☑76 07 30 00; www.lofoten-aktiv.no; Kabelvåg) A reliably good adventure company that offers a range of seasonal activities. In summer you can kayak or sail in the fjords, or take a guided mountain-bike tour, while in winter you can go aurora-hunting, experience cross-country skiing or try out your snowshoeing skills. It also rents out kayaks, mountain bikes and other outdoor gear.

🛏 Sleeping

Kabelvåg Feriehus og Camping   CAMPGROUND **$**
(☑ 76 07 86 20; www.kabelvag.com; Mølnosveien 19; tent/caravan/car 200/260/300kr, r 800-1500kr) Described by one traveller as having 'the best facilities in a camping ground in Norway', this is an immaculate, well-run place in a pretty setting.

Kabelvåg Vandrerhjem & Sommerhotell   HOSTEL **$**
(☑ 76 06 98 80; www.lofotensommerhotell.no/nb/hjem; Finnesveien 24; dm/s/d with shared bathroom 335/650/850kr, d with bathroom 995kr; ⊙ Jun-early Aug; 🛜) Less than 1km from the centre of Kabelvåg, the Lofoten Folkehøgskole school becomes a hostel and hotel outside the teaching year. There's a kitchen for guest use. Hostel rooms have one, two or four beds.

Nyvågar Rorbuhotell   CABIN **$$$**
(☑ 76 06 97 00; www.classicnorway.no/hotell/nyvagar-rorbuhotell; Storvåganveien 22; 4-bed sea-facing/land-facing rorbu incl breakfast 2450/2050kr) At Storvågan, this snazzy complex of seafront cottages is almost entirely modern, but its contemporary *rorbuer* are attractive and fully equipped. They're available in various configurations and sizes, and the hotel can organise activities from cycling to sea-fishing. Rates drop outside the high summer season.

🍴 Eating

Præstengbrygga   PUB, CAFE **$$**
(☑ 76 07 80 60; www.prestengbrygga.no; Torget 9; mains 130-175kr; ⊙10.30am-1am Mon-Thu, 10.30am-2.30am Fri & Sat, noon-1am Sun) This is a general-purpose hang-out, as popular for laid-back pub lunches as for late-night drinking. It's a cosy space, with lashings of wood and a lovely dockside terrace. The food is hearty and filling, with dishes such as reindeer stew, seafood platters (sometimes including whale) and big, generous pizzas. Occasional live music in summer make this a great place to chill.

★ Lorchstua Restaurant   NORWEGIAN **$$$**
(☑ 76 06 97 00; www.classicnorway.com/hotels/nyvagar-rorbuhotell/restaurant; Storvåganveien 26; mains lunch 105-205kr, dinner 219-325kr;

KING ØYSTEIN STATUE

Behind the old prison in Storvågen, a trail climbs to the statue honouring King Øystein. In 1120 he ordered the first *rorbuer* to be built to house fishers, who previously had been sleeping beneath their overturned rowing boats. His Majesty needed to keep his fisherfolk warm, dry and content since the tax on exported dried fish was the main source of his revenue.

⊙6-10.30pm Jun-mid-Aug) ✐ The acclaimed Lorchstua restaurant, run by Nyvågar Rorbuhotell, serves primarily local specialities with a subtle twist, such as baked fillet of halibut in a cod brandade. The atmosphere is formal and the food excellent.

ℹ Getting There & Away

The regular bus between Henningsvær and Svolvær stops in Kabelvåg (50kr, at least six daily).

Vestvågøy

POP 11,000
The general rule when exploring this central Lofoten island is that the most appealing areas lie away from the main E10. The Viking Museum is an exception. You can cross Vestvågøy in an hour if you drive straight through, but you could easily spend the best part of the day exploring.

Stamsund, a Hurtigruten port, is the pick of the traditional fishing villages, while there are fine views if you detour to Eggum and continue on past the town.

⊙ Sights

★ Lofotr Viking Museum   MUSEUM
(☑ 76 15 40 00; www.lofotr.no; adult/child incl guided tour mid-Jun–mid-Aug 200/150kr, rest of year 140/100kr; ⊙10am-7pm Jun–mid-Aug, shorter hours rest of year; ♿) In 1981 at Borg, near the centre of Vestvågøy, a farmer's plough hit the ruins of the 83m-long dwelling of a powerful Viking chieftain, the largest building of its era ever discovered in Scandinavia. The resulting museum, 14km north of Leknes, offers a glimpse of life in Viking times. You can walk 1.5km of trails over open hilltops from the replica of the chieftain's longhouse (the main building, shaped like an upside-down boat) to the Viking-ship replica on the water.

NORDLAND VESTVÅGØY

BREAKING FREE FROM THE E10

Instead of continuing to roll along the E10 as it snakes its way through the heart of Vestvågøy island, take the even more attractive, much less travelled and only slightly longer Rv815. It starts just beyond the bridge that links Austvågøy, runs southwestwards for 28km and rejoins the E10 at Leknes. For the most part it hugs the shoreline with sheer mountains rearing to landward.

Costumed guides conduct multilingual tours and, inside the chieftain's hall, artisans explain their trades. It's all great fun and quite educational, especially for kids.

The museum also hosts a **Viking Festival** in early August, and in summer at 6.30pm until 9pm (including time to visit the museum) you can join a Viking feast (adult/child 820/595kr) where you'll be served Lofoten lamb and honey wine, and be entertained by Vikings – advance reservations are essential and can be made through the museum or the tourist office (p296) in Svolvær.

The Svolvær–Leknes bus passes the museum's entrance.

Lofoten Gårdsysteri　　　　　　FARM
(📞76 08 96 31; www.lofoten-gardsysteri.no; Saupstadveien 235, Bøstad; ⊙10am-9pm Mon-Sat mid-Jun–mid-Aug, shorter hours rest of year) On the road to Saupstad, this lovely little farm has goats, pigs and chickens that the kids will enjoy. But we like it because it's a working organic farm and cheese factory. It sell its produce, including cheese, handmade sausages and honey – ideal if you're planning a picnic, such as just around the corner, past Eggum.

Galleri 2　　　　　　GALLERY
(📞909 56 546; www.galleri2.no; JM Johansens vei 18, Stamsund; adult/child 40kr/free; ⊙noon-6pm Tue-Sun Jun-Aug, by appointment rest of year) The gallery of Lofoten painter Scott Thoe is barely 175m from the Hurtigruten quay in Stamsund, a short detour from the Rv185. It displays the works of a number of contemporary Norwegian artists, including scale models of his own grand open-air projects.

🏃 Activities

Unstad Arctic Surf　　　　WATER SPORTS
(📞970 61 201; www.unstadarcticsurf.com; Unstadveien 105; 4hr SUP tour 1295kr) Keen to learn how to surf in Lofoten? Taken by the idea of a coastal tour by stand-up paddleboard? Both are possible and more at this very cool place at Unstad. It has a range of packages to get you inspired, can arrange accommodation at its campground and can pick you up from Leknes or Svolvær.

🛏 Sleeping & Eating

Brustranda Sjøcamping　　　CAMPGROUND $
(📞76 08 71 44, 916 28 682; www.brustranda.no; Rolvsfjord; car/caravan sites 200/220kr, 4-bed cabins 500-1600kr; ⊙mid-May–Aug) This well-tended, beautifully situated seaside campground stretches around a lovely inlet. It's beside the Rv815, 14km northeast of Stamsund, and it's the sort of place you'll want to stay and just sit for a week.

Justad Rorbuer og Vandrerhjem　　HOSTEL $
(📞76 08 93 34; dm/s/d with shared bathroom 200/380/550kr, 4-bed cabins from 700kr; ⊙Mar–mid-Oct) The island's HI-affiliated youth hostel is a 1.2km walk from the Hurtigruten quay in Stamsund and has its regular clientele who come back year after year – one particularly loyal guest has stayed here over 50 times – so be sure to reserve. It's right beside the water in an old fishing complex.

Skjærbrygga Sjøhus　　　　CAFE $$$
(📞76 05 46 00; www.skjaerbrygga.no; Skjæret 2, Stamsund; dinner mains 195-345kr; ⊙pub food from 11am, dinner 5-10pm) Low-beamed, large yet cosy, this place is right at the water's edge in Stamsund. It has a limited dinner menu (three starters, three fish dishes and two meat mains) that includes all the local favourites such as tender Lofoten lamb. Opening hours were in a state of flux at the time of writing.

ℹ Information

Tourist Office (📞76 08 75 53; vti@online. no; Storgata 31, Leknes; ⊙9am-5pm Mon & Fri, 9am-6pm Tue & Wed, 9am-7pm Thu, 9am-4pm Sat & noon-4pm Sun mid-Jun–mid-Aug, 10am-4pm Mon-Wed & Fri, 9am-6pm Thu, 10am-2pm Sat rest of year) It's tucked into the ground floor of Lofotsenteret, a large shopping centre in the lacklustre town of Leknes.

⊕ Getting There & Away

AIR
There are up to eight Widerøe flights daily connecting Leknes airport with Bodø.

BOAT
Stamsund is the island's port for the Hurtigruten coastal ferry. You can catch a bus from the quayside direct to Leknes.

BUS
Destinations from Leknes include the following.

Å (145kr, 1¾ hours, four to five daily).

Stamsund (55kr, 25 minutes, four to seven daily).

Svolvær (145kr, 1½ hours, four to six daily).

Flakstadøy

POP 1600

Most of Flakstadøy's residents live along its flat north shore, around the town of Ramberg, but, as with Vestvågøy, it's the craggy south side that has the most dramatic scenery. Many visitors just zip through, but it's worth stopping to sun yourself on Ramberg's beach (sandy beaches are the exception in Lofoten), visit the glass-blowers of Vikten and build in a detour to the gorgeous, arty village of Nusfjord.

Ramberg

POP 350

Imagine an arc of white sand fronting a sparkling blue-green bay against a backdrop of snowcapped Arctic peaks. That's pretty much Ramberg and Flakstad **beaches**, on the north coast of Flakstadøy, when the sun shines kindly on them. Should you hit such a day, no one back home will believe that your holiday snaps of this place were taken north of the Arctic Circle, but you'll certainly know it if you stick a toe in the water.

🛏 Sleeping & Eating

Ramberg Gjestegård   CAMPGROUND $
(☑76 09 35 00; www.ramberg-gjestegard.no; E10; car/caravan site 190/240kr, cabin 1050-1600kr) At this welcoming campground right on the beach, you can rent a bike, kayak, rowing boat or even a motorboat to explore the island. There's an excellent on-site restaurant, the cabins are well cared for and staying here gives a whole new perspective on Ramberg once the day trippers have moved on.

⭐**Kafe Friisgården**   CAFE $
(☑415 62 281; E10; mains from 120kr; ⊗noon-9pm mid-Jun–mid-Aug) Divine cakes, tasty home-cooked meals such as chicken casserole with an ice cream dessert and great coffee make this a fine roadside stop. The stunning building, back terrace and warm welcome make it a real find.

⭐**Ramberg Gjestegård**
Restaurant   NORWEGIAN $$
(mains 220-295kr; ⊗noon-9pm Tue-Sun) Ramberg Gjestegård's justifiably popular Arctic Menu restaurant does mainly fish dishes and, if you're lucky, its own splendid Flakstad Menu (cod, cured roast lamb and rhubarb compote for dessert). It also offers cheaper but still very tasty lunch specials and it also does a Sunday lunch buffet (200kr).

⊕ Information

The island's seasonal **tourist office** (☑76 09 31 10; henkirk@online.no; ⊗10am-3pm Wed-Sat mid-Jun–Aug) is in Ramberg's Galleri Steinbiten.

⊕ Getting There & Away

Buses between Svolvær or Leknes and Å pass along the main street.

Flakstad

POP 1383

Just off the E10, Flakstad is a quiet little hamlet, home to one of Lofoten's most beautiful churches and close to a popular beach for water sports. Otherwise, Flakstad is a quiet, unobtrusive sort of place, which is just the way locals like it. Nearby, 4km around the coast from the E10 at Vareid is the stunningly sited village of Vikten, home to the famous Glasshytta. Even if you've no interest in glass-blowing, the village is worth the detour just for the scenery.

⊙ Sights

⭐**Glasshytta**   GALLERY
(☑76 09 44 42; www.glasshyttavikten.no; Vikten; ⊗10am-7pm May-Aug) A 4km side trip signposted from the E10 at Vareid, north of Flakstad, brings you to Vikten and the showpiece gallery of the glass-blowing Tangrand family.

Watch the glass-blowing as it happens and browse the stunning glassware in the showroom and shop. Across the road from the striking main building is a small cafe, as well as an exhibition of ceramics by the same talented family.

Flakstad Kirke
CHURCH

(guided tours adult/child 50kr/free; ⊙ 11am-3pm late Jun-late Jul) Set back from Flakstad beach and bypassed by the E10, the red onion-domed Flakstad Kirke was built in 1780 but has been extensively restored over the years. Most of the original wood was ripped out of the ground by the Arctic-bound rivers of Siberia and washed up here as driftwood.

🛈 Getting There & Away

Flakstad is around 1km off the E10 – buses between Svolvær and Å can drop you at the either of the two turnoffs.

Nusfjord
POP 50

If you take one detour off the E10 between Svolvær and Å, make it Nusfjord, one of the loveliest villages in Norway's north. The road in here, just 6km long, is a stunning byway, hemmed in by towering bare crags. The ox-blood-red wooden buildings of Nusfjord, which feels like a hidden treasure, hug its tiny, tucked-away harbour. Many artists consider it to be the essence of Lofoten but be warned: so do tour operators and in summer it gets so crowded that parking attendants manoeuvre vehicles this way and that. But don't let this put you off – even with all this, it's worth every second you spend here.

It costs 50kr for adults (children under 12 free) just to walk around plus a further 50kr to see *The People & The Fish,* a 12-minute video about Nusfjord, past and present.

👁 Sights

To snap the postcard-perfect shot of Nusfjord that you'll see everywhere around the island, you'll need to climb the rocky slope above the closed end of the little harbour. The path can be slippery after rain.

🛏 Sleeping & Eating

Nusfjord Rorbuer
CABIN $$

(📞 76 09 30 20; www.classicnorway.no/hotell/nusfjord/rorbuene; rorbuer 1395-2795kr) Many of the *rorbuer* (fisher's huts) here are quite

simple on the inside (most have photos on the website), but they're faithful representations of the traditional fishing cabin and they're all extremely comfortable. Apart from anything else, it's the wonderful silence that descends on the village in the evening that's the real draw. Reception is at the village entrance.

Karoline Restaurant
CAFE $$

(📞 76 09 30 20; mains from 149kr; ⊙ 11am-4pm & 5-10pm mid-Jun–mid-Aug, shorter hours rest of year) Wonderful views from the terrace, local dishes with fish in abundance and a casual atmosphere add up to a fine place for a meal – if you can snaffle a table, which can be a challenge.

🛈 Getting There & Away

There's no public transport in Nusfjord. Parking is on a hill at the entrance to the village.

Moskenesøy
POP 1225

The 34km-long island of Moskenesøy is the southernmost of the Lofoten Islands. Its spiky, pinnacled igneous ridge, rising directly from the sea and split by deep lakes and fjords, could almost have been conceived by Tolkien. A paradise for mountaineers, some of the tight gullies and fretted peaks of this tortured island – including its highest point, Hermannsdalstind (1029m) – are accessible to ordinary mortals as well. It's also home to one of the Lofoten's most glorious viewpoints at Reine and one of its loveliest villages, Å.

Å
POP 1162

At the southern tip of Moskenesøy and the Lofoten Islands, the bijou village of Å (appropriately, the last letter of the Norwegian alphabet), sometimes referred to (and signposted across Lofoten) as Å i Lofoten, is something of a living museum – a preserved fishing village with a shoreline of red *rorbuer,* cod-drying racks and picture-postcard scenes at almost every turn. It's an almost feudal place, carved up between two families, now living very much from tourism but in its time a significant fishing port (more than 700,000 cod would be hung out to dry here every season until as recently as WWII).

Do the village a favour and leave your vehicle at the car park and walk in through the short tunnel.

⊙ Sights

★Norsk Fiskeværsmuseum   MUSEUM
(Norwegian Fishing Village Museum; ☑ 76 09 14 88; www.museumnord.no/fiskevarsmuseum; adult/child 80/40kr; ⊙9am-7pm mid-Jun–Aug, 10am-5pm Sep-May) This museum takes in 14 of Å's 19th-century boathouses, storehouses, fishing cottages, farmhouses and commercial buildings. Highlights (pick up a pamphlet in English at reception) include Europe's oldest cod-liver-oil factory, where you'll be treated to a taste of the wares and can pick up a bottle to stave off those winter sniffles; the smithy, who still makes cod-liver-oil lamps; the still-functioning bakery, established in 1844; the old *rorbu* with period furnishings; and a couple of Lofoten fishing boats.

Lofoten Tørrfiskmuseum   MUSEUM
(adult/child 70/35kr; ⊙11am-4pm Jun-Aug) The Lofoten Stockfish Museum is housed in a former fish warehouse. You'll be bowled over by Steinar Larsen, its enthusiastic, polyglot owner, who meets and greets every visitor. This personal collection, a passionate hobby of his, illustrates Lofoten's traditional mainstay: the catching and drying of cod for export, particularly to Italy. Displays, artefacts and a DVD take you through the process, from hauling the fish out of the sea through drying, grading and sorting to dispatch.

🛏 Sleeping

Å-Hamna Rorbuer & Vandrerhjem   HOSTEL $
(☑76 09 12 11; www.lofotenferie.com; dm 280kr, 2-4 bed cabins 1200-1700kr, 6-bed cabin 2150kr) Most of the *rorbuer* (fisher's huts) in Å have been turned into holiday cabins, offering the chance for an atmospheric night's sleep. Wood-clad inside and out, the cabins are simple but cosy, and some are furnished with antiques and fishing ephemera.

Moskenesstraumen Camping   CAMPGROUND $
(☑76 09 11 48; camping for 1/2/3 people 150/200/240kr, caravans 250kr, 2-/4-bed cabins from 550/850kr, 2-/4-bed cabins with bathroom 900/1000kr; ⊙Jun-Aug) This wonderful clifftop campground, just south of the village, has flat, grassy pitches between the rocks, just big enough for your bivouac. Cabins too have great views, as far as the mainland on clear days.

DON'T MISS

MOSKENESSTRAUMEN STRAIT

Beyond the campground at the southern limit of Å, there's an excellent hillside view of Værøy island, across the waters. The mighty maelstroms created by tidal flows between the two islands were first described 2000 years ago by Pytheas and later appeared as fearsome adversaries on fanciful early sea charts. They also inspired tales of maritime peril by Jules Verne and Edgar Allan Poe. They're still considered to be among the world's most dangerous waters. Strain your eyes as you might, your chances of seeing the maelstroms from land are extremely small. Your best bet is to book an excursion through **Aqua Lofoten** (p304).

Å Feskarbrygga Rorbuer   RORBUER $$
(☑911 61 999; www.lofoten-info.no/aa-fb; cabins 1000-1400kr, 4-bed apt 900kr) Open year-round this collection of self-catering *rorbuers* and apartments lie scattered around the harbour area; furnishings are simple rather than luxurious. They're at their best after day trippers have headed home.

🍴 Eating

★Bakeri   BAKERY $
(☑76 09 14 88; ⊙9am-3pm daily mid-May–Aug, shorter hours rest of year) In a building that dates from 1844 and whose stone oven dates from the same year, this atmospheric bakery is the essence of Å. It turns out fresh bread every day, plus a small number of other pastries, among which is the utterly divine *kanelsnurr* (cinnamon roll; 35kr) that tastes every bit as good as its rather lovely name sounds.

Brygga Restaurant   SEAFOOD $$$
(☑76 09 11 21; mains 195-329kr, lunch specials 185-205kr; ⊙11am-10pm Jun-Sep) Hovering above the water, this is Å's one decent sit-down dining choice. The menu, as is right and proper in a village with such a strong fishing tradition, includes mainly things with fins.

ℹ Getting There & Away

Å is pretty much as far south as you can go in Lofoten.

There are between three and six buses a day to Moskenes (52kr, 10 minutes), where you can catch the car ferry back to Bodø on the mainland.

Most buses continue onwards to Reine, Marka, Hamnøy and Leknes.

Sakrisøy

In the heart of some stunning country on an arm of Reinefjord, Sakrisøy is a small, pretty island with services far out of proportion to its size – two places to eat, a place to stay and plenty to do.

◎ Sights & Activities

Museum of Dolls & Toys   MUSEUM
(Dagmars Dukke og Leketøy Museum; ☑76 09 21 43; adult/child 80/40kr; ⊙10am-6pm May & Sep, to 8pm Jun-Aug, by appointment rest of year) In Sakrisøy, Dagmar Gylseth has collected more than 2500 dolls, antique teddy bears and historic toys over 20 years for her Museum of Dolls & Toys. There's also an affiliated antiques shop upstairs.

Aqua Lofoten Coast Adventure AS   BOATING
(☑990 19 042; www.aqualofoten.no; E10) From June to mid-August, three-hour boat trips are run by Aqua Lofoten to the bird- and fish-rich Moskenesstraumen maelstrom, as well as other nearby attractions, with snorkelling and fishing also possible.

🛏 Sleeping & Eating

Sakrisøy Rorbuer   CABIN $$
(☑76 09 21 43; www.sakrisoyrorbuer.no; cabin 1100-2150kr; P 🐾) Sakrisøy Rorbuer is a relatively authentic complex of ochre-coloured cottages hovering above the water. They're postcard-perfect from the outside and the supremely comfortable interiors have an authentic wood-panelled aesthetic. Views are splendid in this area – you don't have to walk far to see what we mean.

★ Anitas Sjømat   CAFE $
(☑900 61 566; www.sakrisoy.no/sjomat; E10; ⊙10am-8pm mid-Jun-mid-Aug, shorter hours rest of year) Part delicatessen and part waterside cafe, this fab place sells all sorts of stockfish snacks, Kong Oskar sardines and dishes such as uncommonly good fish soup, fish cakes, fresh shrimp and fish burgers – our favourite is the pulled-salmon burger. Go on, be adventurous, try the seagulls' eggs... and don't be put off by the fearsome dried-cod heads outside.

Underhuset Restaurant   NORWEGIAN, SEAFOOD $$
(☑900 35 419; www.sakrisoyrorbuer.no/restaurant; mains lunch from 149kr, dinner 242-315kr;

⊙noon-11pm mid-Jun–mid-Aug, 4-11pm rest of year) The Sakrisøy Rorbuer's more formal (though only just...) restaurant doesn't mess around with a wide variety of dishes – it's cod/bacalo, sirloin of ox or a bucket of shrimp. And they're all exceptionally good. A terrific range of local beers and a wickedly good homemade chocolate mousse round things out nicely.

ℹ Getting There & Away

Sakrisøy lies along the E10 – buses between Leknes and Å pass through here.

Hamnøy

POP 1000

Blink and you might miss Hamnøy, on its own small island northwest of Reine and Sariskøy. But it's still a picturesque corner of the Lofotens with a backdrop of the waters of dramatic Reinefjord and craggy peaks.

🛏 Sleeping & Eating

★ Eliassen Rorbuer   RORBUER $$
(☑458 14 845; www.rorbuer.no; off E10; rorbuer 890-1990kr; P 🐾) Terrific collection of 26 *rorbuer* close to Reine, with refurbished interiors; some have great views. Take your time choosing the right one for you – the website is slow but it's worth persisting.

★ Krambua   NORWEGIAN $$$
(☑486 36 772; www.krambuarestaurant.no; off E10; mains 265-315kr; ⊙7am-11pm Mon-Sat, 8-10am & 6-10pm Sun late May–early Sep) This fabulous restaurant inhabits an 1882 building and Noemi and Mikael Björkman serve up a seasonal menu with the freshest fish imaginable. Try the smoked shrimp or cod tongues for starters. The menu usually includes expertly prepared tomato-based fish stew, lightly smoked Lofoten lamb and smoked Lofoten cod.

ℹ Getting There & Away

Buses between Svolvær or Leknes and Å pass through Hamnøy.

Southern Islands

Værøy

POP 600

Craggy Værøy, its handful of residents hugely outnumbered by over 100,000 nesting sea birds – fulmars, gannets,

Arctic terns, guillemots, gulls, sea eagles, puffins, kittiwakes, cormorants, eiders, petrels and a host of others – is a mere 8km long with white-sand beaches, soaring ridges, tiny, isolated villages, granite-gneiss cliffs and sparkling seas. It's a glorious place to spend a few days if you value raw natural beauty and blissful isolation.

Activities

Hiking is the most popular activity on Værøy, but boat excursions (adult/child 590/450kr) to the sea cliffs and bird rookeries can be organised through the tourist office (p305) or your accommodation.

Hiking

Walking routes approach some of the major **sea-bird rookeries**. The most scenic and popular trail begins at the end of the road around the north of the island, about 6km from **Sørland** and 300m beyond the former airstrip. It heads southward along the west coast, over the Eidet isthmus to the mostly abandoned fishing village of **Måstad**, on the east coast, where meat and eggs from the puffin colonies once supported 150 people; Måstad is the origin of the Norwegian Lundehund dog breed.

Fit hikers who relish a challenge may also want to attempt the steep climb from Måstad to the peak of **Måhornet** (431m), which takes about an hour each way. Alternatively, from the quay at Sørland you can follow the road (or perhaps the more interesting ridge scramble) up to the NATO installation at **Håen** (438m).

Sleeping

Gamle Prestegård   GUESTHOUSE $$
(Old Vicarage; ☑76 09 54 11; www.varoyrhs.com/prestegaarden; s/d with shared bathroom 495/830kr, with private bathroom 595/930kr) Værøy's smartest lodging and dining is on the island's north side. It's the large house with wood-lined rooms and a flagpole in the garden beside the church, just where you'd expect the vicar to have lived. Food is nicely prepared with fish at every turn. It's a simple but lovely place to stay.

Information

Tourist Office (☑75 42 06 00; Fv 791; ☉9.30am-3pm Mon-Fri mid-Jun–mid-Aug, 9am-2pm Mon-Fri rest of year) In the town hall at Sørland, the main village.

Getting There & Away

The car ferry runs most days to/from Bodø (passenger/car 196/702kr), directly or via Moskenes (94/317kr). The ferry also links Værøy with Røst (110/377kr).

Lufttransport (☑75 43 18 00; www.lufttransport.no; one way 8926kr) runs helicopter flights between Bodø and Værøy once or twice daily, February to October.

Røst

POP 605

The 365 islands and *skerries* of Røst (one for each day of the year) form Lofoten's ragged southern edge. Røst stands in sharp contrast to its rugged neighbours to the north, and were it not for a small pimple in the middle, the main pond-studded island of Røstlandet would be dead flat. Thanks to its location in the heart of the Gulf Stream, this cluster of islets basks in one of the mildest climates in Norway and attracts 2.5 million nesting sea birds to some serious rookeries on the cliffs of the outer islands.

Sleeping & Eating

Kårøy Rorbucamping   CAMPGROUND $
(☑76 09 62 38; www.karoy.no; r per person 250kr; ☉May–mid-Sep; @☞) Rooms sleep two, four or six at this authentic *rorbu* on the minuscule island of Kårøy. Bathrooms are communal and there are self-catering facilities. You can borrow a rowing boat for free or rent a motorboat. Phone from the ferry on arrival and a boat will be sent to collect you.

Røst Bryggehotel   HOTEL $$
(☑76 05 08 00; www.rostbryggehotell.no; s/d 9900/1220kr; ☞) This modern development in traditional style is right on the quayside. It has 16 comfortable doubles, and hires out bikes, boats and fishing tackle. It also has a restaurant. Easily the best place to stay on Røst.

Querini Pub
og Restaurant   PUB FOOD $$
(☑930 07 458, 76 09 64 80; Klakkenveien 1; mains from 149kr; ☉1pm-2am Wed & Fri-Sun Jun-Aug) Named after the shipwrecked merchant from Venice, this is a reliable choice among Røst's few eating options and the only place that kicks into life in the evening.

ⓘ Information

Tourist Office (☑ 76 05 05 00; ⊘ 9am-2pm mid-Jun–mid-Aug) Røst's tourist office is a short walk from the ferry dock. It's staffed by volunteers – don't expect to find it open at the designated times, although it does generally open for ferry arrivals and departures.

ⓘ Getting There & Away

There are flights to/from both Bodø and Leknes.

Røst, like Værøy, is served by the car ferry that runs between Bodø (passenger/car 238/865kr) and Moskenes (167/596kr).

VESTERÅLEN

Although the landscapes here aren't as dramatic as those in Lofoten, they tend to be much wilder and the forested mountainous regions of the island of Hinnøya are a unique corner of Norway's largely treeless northern coast. There are many reasons to visit, but our top three would be whale-watching from Andenes or Stø, a drive along Andøya's lovely west coast and a visit to the reborn hamlet of Nyksund.

Langøya

Stø

POP 250

The small fishing village of Stø clings to Langøya's northernmost tip. It's the sort of place that's so quiet sea birds nest in the low cliffs that abut the main street through town.

People come here for two reasons: whale-watching expeditions, which resumed in 2017, and the chance to hike one of Vesterålen's prettiest walks.

🏃 Activities

Stø used to be a whale-watching centre to rival Andenes, but the last operator closed its doors a few years back. Thankfully another excellent company has taken up the mantle and whale-watching is again possible from Stø. As a general rule, reaching the whale-feeding grounds – sperm whales and pilot whales in summer, orcas and humpbacks in winter – takes a good deal longer from here than from Andenes. While this means a whale-watching expedition from Stø is a full-day expedition, they've adapted this nicely to include other elements,

such as birdwatching and the chance to see seals.

★ **Arctic Whale Tours** WHALE WATCHING
(☑ 76 13 43 00; www.arcticwhaletours.com; adult/child 1100/600kr; ⊘ 10am late May–Aug) Summer whale safaris have returned to Stø with the excellent Arctic Whale Tours. Its all-day safaris offer a whale guarantee – if you don't see at least one whale or dolphin, you get a free second trip. Sperm whales are most commonly sighted. The boat trip also visits sea-bird and seal colonies, making for a wonderful day's outing.

★ **Queen's Route** HIKING
The walk over the headland between Nyksund and Stø, waymarked with red letter Ts, merits a short day of your life. Most hikers sweat a little on the outward leg of this three- to five-hour circular trek via the 448m Finngamheia, then breathe easy, returning via the simpler sea-level route.

🛌 Sleeping

★ **Gunnartangen Rorbuferie** RORBUER
(☑ 416 96 223; www.gunnartangen.no; Fv935; s/d from 850/950kr; ℗ 🛜) These five self-catering cabins, or traditional *rorbuer,* overlook the quiet harbour at Stø. Built over the years by Gunnar himself, these *rorbuer* have warmth and personality and represent a lovely retreat from the crowds of Norway in summer (though they're open year-round).

Stø Bobilcamp CAMPGROUND $
(☑ 76 13 25 30; www.stobobilcamp.no; car/caravan campsite 150/180kr; ⊘ mid-May–mid-Aug) Small, waterside Stø Bobilcamp is stark indeed and a windy spot to pitch your tent, but it does run an unpretentious little restaurant, serving primarily fish. There are no cabins.

ⓘ Getting There & Away

Two weekday buses run between Sortland and Stø (1¼ hours). Otherwise, you'll need your own wheels to reach here.

Sortland

POP 9983

Sortland, Vesterålen's commercial centre and transit hub, occupies a nick in the island's east coast. Its mostly chunky, rectangular buildings are painted a soothing sea-blue, the project of local artist Bjørn Elvenes who wanted to turn the town into a three-dimensional painting. Or perhaps it was to distract you from the fact that there's very little to detain you as you turn north towards Stø or south towards Lofoten.

✯ Festivals & Events

Sortland Jazz MUSIC
(www.sortlandjazz.no; ⊙ Sep) Sortland Jazz takes place over a couple of weeks and is a worthy member of Norway's fine jazz-festival circuit.

🛏 Sleeping & Eating

Sortland Camping og Motell CAMPGROUND $
(📞 76 11 03 00; www.sortland-camping.no; Vesterveien 51; car/caravan site 280/280kr, cabin 400-2800kr) Around 1.3km from the centre and signposted off the road to Stokmarknes, this place is a fairly standard Norwegian campground, but the cafe offers home cooking, strong on northern Norway cuisine. It occupies an extensive, semi-wooded area, and produces a useful information sheet about the area too.

Information

Tourist Office (📞 76 11 14 80; www.visitvest eralen.com; Kjøpmannsgata 2; ⊙ 9am-5.30pm Mon-Fri, 10am-3.45pm Sat, noon-3.45pm Sun mid-Jun–mid-Aug, 8.30am-3pm Mon-Fri rest of year) Covers the whole Vesterålen region.

ℹ Getting There & Away

Sortland is a stop on the Hurtigruten coastal ferry.
The following are the available bus services.
Andenes two hours, two to four daily, via Risøyhamn (one hour)
Harstad 2¼ hours, one to three daily
Narvik 3½ hours, three to five daily
Svolvær 2¼ hours, two to four daily

Nyksund

POP 5 (WINTER), 35 (SUMMER)
Nyksund is the essence of Norway's wild northern coast, an abandoned village reborn and a beautiful spot thrown in. Visiting here is to participate in a heart-warming story of renewal and is one of the main reasons to come to Vesterålen.

NYKSUND'S STORY

The population of the small fishing village of Nyksund was already dwindling when, in the 1960s, the bakery and post office, the heart of any community, closed down. Then, after a storm wrought havoc in 1975, nearly everyone else left. Finally, in 1975, the last inhabitant, blacksmith Olav Larsen, packed

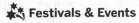
WORTH A TRIP

HURTIGRUTEN MUSEUM

The **Hurtigrutemuseet** (www.hurtigrutemuseet.no; Markedsgata 1, Stokmarknes; adult/child 90/35kr; ⊙ 10am-6pm mid-Jun–mid-Aug, shorter hours rest of year) portrays the history of the coastal-ferry line in text and image. Hitched to the quayside is the retired ship MS *Finnmarken*, claimed to be the world's largest museum piece, which plied the coastal route between 1956 and 1993.

his bags. The village fell silent. Sheep and vandals moved in.

For many rural communities across Europe, that's where the story ends. But for Nyksund, it was only the beginning of a remarkable story of renewal. Slowly over the decades life has been breathed back into this charming, remote settlement, reborn as an artists' colony. The crumbling old structures and commercial buildings have been faithfully restored, and nowadays modern Nyksund boasts a summer population of around 40, and some half-dozen hardy souls endure throughout the harsh winters.

One of those is Ssemjon Gerlitz, the German owner of Holmvik Brygge, who has lived year-round in Nyksund for a decade and more. Over the years, he and his team of helpers have gleaned, picked and scavenged what could be salvaged from Nyksund's crumbling buildings and incorporated them into the higgledy-piggledy guesthouse, where every room has its own personality.

Two things in particular keep him here, at road's end. He speaks of the lure of silence, nothing but the rhythm of wind and waves for most of the year and of his sense of communion with long-gone fisherfolk ('Every rusty nail I pull out was hammered in by someone who lived and worked here').

◉ Sights

Nyksund Museum MUSEUM
(www.nyksund.com; ⊙ 11am-5pm mid-Jun–mid-Aug) FREE Nyksund's small museum contains a number of local artefacts and before-and-after photos that chart the village's transformation. Then again, the whole town is something of a museum piece, one that's anything but static.

🛏 Sleeping

★ Holmvik Brygge   GUESTHOUSE $$

(📞 958 63 866, 76 13 47 96; www.nyksund.com; s/d with shared bathroom 850/910kr, r/apt with private bathroom 990/1150kr) 🍴 This cosy, hugely welcoming guesthouse and cafe in itself justifies the detour to Nyksund. You can either cater for yourself or eat at its Holmvik Stua, where the food's locally sourced and the fish smoked on the premises. Rooms are warm and cosy, constructed from local wooden materials, while apartments have a little more space but the same charm.

Expedisjonen   B&B $$

(📞 481 18 068; www.ekspedisjonen.wordpress.com; s/d with shared bathroom 790/1190kr, with private bathroom 990/1450kr) Predominantly a restaurant and coffee bar, Expedisjonen has a handful of prim wooden rooms that suit Nyksund's eclectic style perfectly. It's an inviting place with white-wood walls, splashes of colour and fine views from some rooms. Some rooms have shared bathrooms, others private. It also has some other rooms elsewhere in the village.

ℹ Getting There & Away

The route to Nyksund is along a narrow (and rather pretty) ribbon of road that hugs the shoreline (the last 10km of which is unpaved). Alternatively, walk the **Queen's Route** (p306), a fine trek over the headland from Nyksund to Stø (three hours return).

There is no public transport to Nyksund.

Andøya

Andenes

POP 2718

The straggling village of Andenes, with its rich fishing history, is northern Norway's main base for whale-watching and there are a host of other nature-based activities possible in the vicinity. The town has a lonely, end-of-the-road feel – stand on the windswept harbourside quay and stare out into the North Atlantic and you'll see what we mean. That changes somewhat in summer when the seasonal ferry connects Andenes to Senja and the town bustles with uncharacteristic activity.

◉ Sights

★ Spaceship Aurora   MUSEUM

(📞 76 14 46 00; www.spaceshipaurora.no; Bleiksveien 46; 3D film adult/child 75/50kr, virtual missions 350/175kr; ⊙ 10.30am-5.30pm mid-Jun–mid-Aug, 9am-3pm Mon-Fri rest of year) Around 1km south of the town entrance along the road to Bleik, this innovative space centre has a widescreen 16-minute movie and other exhibits about the aurora borealis (rockets sent up from here aid in the study of this phenomenon) and Norway's role in space research. To really get into the spirit, join a virtual mission (one hour to 1¾ hours) aboard the Spaceship Aurora and even send up a virtual rocket – what fun! Ring ahead or book online.

Andenes Fyr   LIGHTHOUSE

(📞 76 11 56 00; off Richard Withs gate; adult/child 90/45kr; ⊙ by appointment late Jun-Aug) The town's landmark red lighthouse, automated for many years, opened in 1859 and still shines on. To climb its 40m and 148 steps, arrange a guided tour through the reception at the whale-safari centre (p309). The views from the summit are extraordinary.

Museum Nord   MUSEUM

(Andøymuseet; 📞 76 11 54 32; www.museumnord.no/andoymuseet; Hamnegata; adult/child 50/25kr; ⊙ 10am-5pm mid-Jun–mid-Aug, shorter hours rest of year) The quaint, Arctic- and polar-themed Museum Nord has displays on local hunting and fishing traditions. There's extensive coverage of the 38 winter hunting expeditions in Svalbard undertaken by local explorer Hilmar Nøis, who also collected most of the exhibits.

Hvalsenteret   MUSEUM

(Havnegate 1; adult/child 110/55kr; ⊙ 8.30am-7pm mid-Jun–mid-Aug) The whale centre provides a perspective for whale-watchers, with displays on whale research, hunting and the life cycle of these gentle giants. Most people visit in conjunction with a whale safari (a museum visit is included). Whale skeletons and a host of fascinating information panels make this a fine complement to a safari to see the real thing. There's also an on-site restaurant. It sometimes stays open as late as 10pm in July and August.

FARGEKLATTEN

Fargeklatten, meaning the 'splash of colour', is a very special place, the creation of Grethe Kvalvik. For years, Grethe was the receptionist at Andrikken Hotell until she lost her sight. After two long years of blindness, partial vision returned and she could again perceive shapes and, above all, colours.

DON'T MISS

ANDØYA ACTIVITIES

Husky-Andøy (📞 954 50 632; www.husky-andoy.com; Fv973, Risøyhamn; adult/child 850/450kr) Winter dog-sledding trips lasting two to three hours are a wonderful way to explore the region; in summer, the sleds have wheels. In summer it can also arrange hiking, fishing and climbing expeditions.

Andøy Friluftssenter (📞 76 14 88 04; www.andoy-friluftssenter.no; 610kr; ⏱ 8.30pm Tue-Fri late Jun–mid-Aug) Offers summer moose (elk) safaris, and is one of few places outside central Norway to do so. The safaris leave from its base at Buksnesfjord, 63km south of Andenes – bookings can be made at the **tourist office** (p310) in Andenes. It also offers wilderness walks, as well as fishing, cycling and winter activities such as ice fishing and northern-lights trips.

Determined to live a full life anew, she rescued Fargeklatten in the centre of town – at the time it was earmarked for demolition to make way for a car park. This complex of historical buildings now includes a couple of small **galleries** (📞 97 76 00 20; www.fargeklatten.no; ⏱ 11am-4pm) **FREE** displaying the art and crafts of northern Norway and a small **turf museum** (www.fargeklatteneng.weebly.com/peat-turf-museum.html; Sjøgata 38a; adult/child 50kr/free) – plus some attractive accommodation options.

🏃 Activities

In addition to the activities based in Andenes, with whale-watching the main attraction, ask the tourist office (p310) about moose safaris in Buksnesfjord, birdwatching in Bleik, as well as sea-kayaking.

⭐ **Sea Safari Andenes**   WILDLIFE WATCHING
(📞 916 74 960; www.seasafariandenes.no; Hamnegata; whale-watching adult/child 995/850kr, birdwatching adult/child 495/400kr; ⏱ May-Sep) The smaller of Andenes' whale-watching outfits, with its base on the docks just off the road to the lighthouse, runs 1½- to three-hour whale-watching trips in smaller boats with up to two daily departures in season. Also offers seal- and birdwatching trips (1½ hours, adult/child 450/400kr), plus winter outings to look for orcas, humpbacks and fin whales.

It even arranges snorkelling with orcas (that's killer whales to the rest of us...) in winter and with puffins in summer.

⭐ **Whale Safari**   WILDLIFE WATCHING
(📞 76 11 56 00; www.whalesafari.no; Hamnegata; adult/concession/child 975/850/690kr; ⏱ late May-early Sep) Far and away Andøya's biggest outfit, Whale Safari runs popular whale-watching cruises between late May

and mid-September. It also operates the Whale Centre (p309). Tours begin with a guided visit to the centre, followed by a two- to four- or five-hour boat trip. There's a good chance of spotting (and getting really close to) sperm whales in summer.

Trips depart at least once daily with up to three sailings (11am, noon and 4pm) in high summer. Bad weather and/or high seas only rarely prevent a sailing. All the same, try to build in an extra day on the island just in case you're unlucky. If you fail to spot at least one whale, your money is refunded or you can take another trip for free. Your fee includes coffee, tea and soup and seasickness bags...

Contact them in advance if you're coming in winter as they only have two sailings a week.

Wild Ocean   WHALE WATCHING
(📞 469 32 899; www.wildocean.no) Whale-watching (including from November to March) is only a part of what it does here – it also runs coastal sightseeing, fishing and birdwatching trips. It doesn't have an office – make your booking through the tourist office.

🛏 Sleeping

Andenes Camping   CAMPGROUND $
(📞 76 11 56 00; www.whalesafari.no; Bleiksveien 31; car/caravan sites 120/150kr; ⏱ Jun-Aug) This basic roadside campground, 3.5km from town, is on a gorgeous seaside meadow, as green and smooth as a golf course. It has a well-equipped kitchen and large common room. It's quite exposed to the elements, which does, of course, mean great views.

⭐ **Hotell Marena**   BOUTIQUE HOTEL $$
(📞 900 84 600, 915 83 517; www.hotellmarena.no; Storgata 15; s/d incl breakfast from 1090/1190kr; 📶) This is an exciting and particularly

tasteful addition to Andenes' accommodation choices. Public areas feature nature photographs by local photographer Espen Tollefsen, as do each of the 12 bedrooms, individually designed with colours matching the tones of the blown-up images. There's free coffee around the clock and homemade cakes.

Fargeklatten
APARTMENT $$

(☑977 60 020; www.fargeklatten.no; Sjøgata 38a; r from 950kr, 5-bed apt from 1600kr) Rooms in 'Veita', a restored 18th-century home, are attractively furnished in antique style, while apartments are spacious and well equipped at these renovated properties at the eastern end of the village.

Hotel Andrikken
HOTEL $$$

(☑76 14 12 22; www.andrikkenhotell.no; Storgata 53; s/d 1220/1520kr; P🖨) Although dull and boxy from the outside, Andrikken has comfortable and well-equipped rooms and friendly staff. With far more personality, its *rorbuer* down by the harbour are excellent value.

✕ Eating & Drinking

★ Lysthuset
NORWEGIAN $$

(☑76 14 14 99; Storgata 51; mains 175-325kr; ⊙noon-3pm & 6-10pm Tue-Sat) This is the best of Andenes' limited dining options. Ignore the casual cafe out the front – the restaurant proper serves Arctic specialities such as salted local lamb, monkfish with shellfish sauce and salmon in various forms. For dessert, indulge in a little 'Sex on the Mountain' – an orgasmic confection of ice cream, cream, blackberries and cloudberries, all doused in eggnog.

Orion Cafe & Restaurant
NORWEGIAN $$

(☑968 64 106; Havnegate; mains 199-269kr; ⊙noon-10pm) Down by the water, the Orion has the best setting of any restaurant in Andenes. It serves reindeer stew, grilled stockfish and some lighter international options in an agreeable setting.

Mea Pub & Cafe
CAFE, BAR

(☑473 25 392; Sjøgata 20-22; ⊙6pm-1am Wed & Thu, 3pm-2.30am Fri & Sat, 3pm-1am Sun) A cosy, lantern-lit drinking den is just the spot for a night-time tipple in the Arctic. It also serves food but it's more about nursing your drink of choice in an intimate setting while the wind blows outside.

❶ Information

Tourist office (☑76 14 12 03; www.visitandoy.info; Kong Hans gate 8; ⊙9am-5.30pm Mon-Fri, 10am-5.30pm Sat, noon-4.30pm Sun mid-Jun–mid-Aug, 9am-4pm 1st half Jun & 2nd half Aug, shorter hours rest of year) Covers the whole island. Its *Vesterålen* brochure is excellent.

❶ Getting There & Away

AIR
The flight between Andenes and Tromsø, via Narvik or Bodø, is a contender for the world's most scenic flight, with spectacular aerial views of the landscapes, seas and agricultural patterns.

BOAT
From late May or early June to the end of August, a car ferry (www.senjafergene.no) connects Andenes with the port of Gryllefjord (1¾ hours, two to three daily) on the island of Senja, passing magnificent coastal scenery. It's just a pity it doesn't operate year-round.

BUS
Two to four daily buses run south to Sortland (two hours) via Risøyhamn, where a bus to/from Andenes meets and greets the Hurtigruten.

Bleik
POP 460

It is difficult to imagine a more idyllic setting for a seaside hamlet. Bleik nestles in a sheltered stretch along the glorious arc of west-coast Andøya, overlooking a long, ash-white beach, one of several claimants to be Norway's longest – it extends for almost 3km. Puffin safaris are the main reason people come here, but we could happily spend a week here just staring at the view.

☞ Tours

★ Puffin Safari
BIRDWATCHING, FISHING

(☑908 38 594; www.puffinsafari.no; puffin safari adult/child 450/250kr, deep-sea fishing safari

---

WHICH WHALES?

In summer, you're most likely to see the majestic sperm whales, and possibly pilot whales. In winter, when herrings migrate to the seas off Andenes, orcas (killer whales), humpback and fin whales are all possible.

800/300kr; ⊘puffin safaris 1pm & 3pm daily mid-Jun–mid-Aug, 3pm daily 1st half Jun) Puffin Safari, based in Bleik, does warmly recommended, well-presented and informative daily 1½-hour birdwatching boat trips off the island of Bleiksøya, with sightings of puffins and sea eagles guaranteed; more than 80,000 puffins breed around here. Other birds to watch for include cormorants, black guillemots, razorbills and gannets. You can also bring home dinner from the four-hour deep-sea fishing trips.

🛏 Sleeping

★Stave Camping CAMPGROUND $
(☑926 01 257; www.stavecamping.no; Fv974; tent/caravan site 75/180kr, cabins 500kr, apt 600-850kr, hot tub/sauna per person 250/250kr; ⊘late May-Aug) This excellent campground has an array of sites right near the beach, a handful of cute cabins and some apartments, all strung out along the coast with fine views of west-coast Andøya never far away. Perhaps best of all, it has a beach sauna and a series of outdoor 38°C hot tubs. It's hugely popular so advance reservations are required.

Midnattsol Camping CAMPGROUND $
(☑478 43 219; www.midnattsolcamping.com; Gårdsveien 8; small/large tent site 100/150kr, caravan 150kr, cabins 800-1200kr) A good campground at the northern entry to the village with fine views from most sites.

❶ Getting There & Away

Bleik lies 10km south of Andenes along the spectacular Fv974. Public transport is nonexistent along Andøya's west coast.

Hinnøya

Harstad

POP 24,676

On a hillside close to the northern end of Hinnøya, Harstad, the area's largest town, is a small industrial and defence-oriented place, full of docks, tanks and warehouses. Contrasting with so many tourism and fishing towns to the south, it has a certain purposeful bustle. We wouldn't go out of our way to make it here, but if you're on an extended tour of Vesterålen it's worth an overnight stop.

◉ Sights

Trondenes Kirke CHURCH
(off Trondenesveien; ⊘10am-4pm Mon-Fri late Jun–mid-Aug, hours vary rest of year) FREE Trondenes Church was built by King Øystein around 1150. For ages it was the northernmost church in Christendom, and still lays claim to being Norway's northernmost medieval *stone* church. Originally of wood, the current stone structure replaced it around 1250 and quickly came to double as a fortification against Russian aggression. Absurdly for one of northern Norway's major cultural sights, it's often locked so do check with the tourist office.

★ Festivals & Events

Arctic Arts Festival PERFORMING ARTS
(Festspillene i Nord-Norge; ☑77 04 12 30; www.festspillnn.no; ⊘Jun) Harstad's Arctic Arts Festival, formerly the Festival of North Norway and approaching its 50th incarnation, is a full week of music, theatre and dance in the second half of June.

🛏 Sleeping

Harstad Camping CAMPGROUND $
(☑77 07 36 62; www.harstad-camping.no; Nesseveien 55; car/caravan site 225/290kr, cabin 460-1230kr) Follow the Rv83 towards Narvik for 4km, then take a side road to reach this small waterside site, where you can rent all manner of boats. You're a fair way from the centre of town, but the reward is a grassy (if slightly crowded) stretch of land easing down the hill to the water's edge.

Clarion Collection Hotel Arcticus HOTEL $$
(Map p312; ☑77 04 08 00; www.nordicchoice hotels.no; Havnegata 3; s/d incl breakfast & light evening meal from 900/1150kr; @🛜) This hotel shares a harmonious modern building with Harstad's cultural centre. A short, pleasant jetty walk from the centre, it has 75 particularly large rooms. It's extra for the superior standard – a waterside room with splendid views over the fjord to the mountains beyond.

Scandic Hotell Harstad HOTEL $$
(Grand Nordic Hotel; Map p312; ☑77 00 30 00; www.scandichotels.no; Strandgata 9; r 950-1690kr; 🅿@🛜) This is the grand dame of the Harstad hotels. Make sure to request one of the larger, more pleasantly decorated rooms in the newer section. Many locals still know it by its old name, the Grand Nordic Hotel.

Harstad

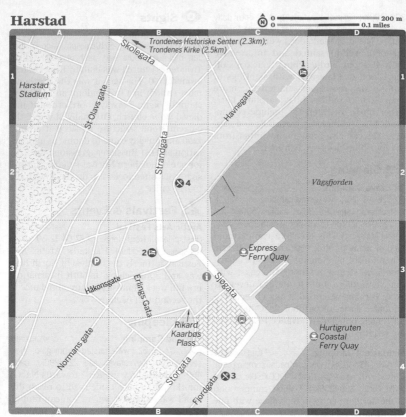

Trondenes Historiske Senter (2.3km);
Trondenes Kirke (2.5km)

0 — 200 m
0 — 0.1 miles

Vågsfjorden

Harstad

Sleeping
1 Clarion Collection Hotel
   Arcticus... C1
2 Scandic Hotell Harstad B3

Eating
3 Café & Restaurant De 4 Roser C4
4 Umami B2

Eating

Café & Restaurant De 4 Roser
CAFE, NORWEGIAN $$

(Map p312; ☑ 77 01 27 50; www.de4roser.no;
Torvat 7; mains 149-355kr, 3-/4-course set menu
545/655kr; ☺ cafe 10am-10pm, restaurant
6-10pm Mon-Sat) On one floor, the Four Ros-
es is a buzzing cafe that offers sandwiches,
pasta, burgers and salads and a trio of dai-
ly lunch specials, in large prtions.

Above the cafe, in more intimate surround-
ings, the restaurant offers fine gourmet Nor-
wegian cuisine. The restaurant entrance is at
street level at the other end of the building.

★ Umami
NORWEGIAN $$$

(Map p312; ☑ 950 90 911; www.umamiharstad.no;
Havnegata 23a; 3-/5-course set menu 595/745kr;
☺ 6-11pm) Umami is the work of Kim-Havard
Larsen and Sigrid Rafaelsem, both of whom
have worked in some of Norway's best restaurants. *Umami* means 'pleasant and savoury'
in Japanese and the cooking here is creative,
assured and changes with the seasons. Their
cakes are divine.

Information

Tourist Office (Map p312; ☑ 77 01 89 89; www.
destinationharstad.no; Sjøgata 1b; ☺ 10am-6pm
mid-Jun–mid-Aug, 8am-3.30pm Mon-Fri rest
of year) Faces the waterfront, just around the
corner from the bus station.

ℹ Getting There & Away

AIR

From the Harstad-Narvik airport at Evenes there are direct flights to Oslo, Bodø, Tromsø and Trondheim.

BOAT

The easiest, most scenic option to Tromsø is by boat. There are two to four express passenger ferries daily between Harstad and Tromsø (three hours), via Finnsnes (1¾ hours).

There's also a seasonal **express passenger ferry** (Map p312; www.tromskortet.no) between Stornes, just north of Harstad and Skrolsvik (1¼ hours; two to three daily mid-May to August), at the southern end of Senja island. Here you'll find bus connections to Finnsnes and on to Tromsø. Harstad is also a stop on the **Hurtigruten coastal ferry** (Map p312).

BUS

From the **bus station** (Map p312; ☑ 78 40 70 00; Torvet 8), buses to Sortland (2½ hours) run one to three times daily. There's one bus to/from Narvik via Harstad-Narvik Evenes airport (2½ hours, daily except Saturday) and a daily service between Harstad and Fauske (5¾ hours).

ℹ Getting Around

Flybussen (225, kr50 minutes) shuttles between the town centre and Harstad-Narvik Evenes airport several times daily.

Buses connect Trondenes with the central bus station approximately hourly, Monday to Saturday.

Call if you need a taxi (☑ 77 04 10 00).

The Far North

Includes →

Best Places to Eat

Best Places to Stay

Why Go?

Norway's northernmost counties of Troms and Finnmark arc across the very top of Europe, where broad horizons share the land with dense forest. Although winter tourism is on the rise, most travellers come in summer to enjoy Tromsø, the region's only town of any size. The museums of this sparky, self-confident place will orient you for the Arctic lands beyond. You'll probably respond to the call of Nordkapp (North Cape), the European mainland's self-declared most northerly point. But to really feel the pull of the north, you need to venture further to explore the sparsely populated plateaus of Inner Finnmark and its wild northeastern coast, the Norwegian heartland of the Sami people. For alternative adventure (say, scudding aboard a snowmobile or behind a team of yapping huskies), plan to return in winter, when soft blue light envelops the snowy lands, outsiders are few and the northern lights streak the sky.

When to Go

Tromsø

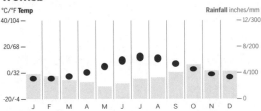

Early Feb Lots of snowy activities and, with luck, the northern lights on tap.

Easter Week The Sami party in Kautokeino before dispersing to their summer pastures.

Mid- to late Jun Hotels and sights reopen, and the crowds have yet to come.

TROMS

Troms, where the Gulf Stream peters out, mitigating the harshness of winter, boasts a couple of near-superlative places: Tromsø, the only place large enough to merit the name 'city' in northern Norway, and Senja, Norway's second-largest island, a less trodden rival to the Lofotens for spectacular scenery. Deep in the interior, Øvre Dividal and Reisa national parks are wilderness gems.

Tromsø

POP 72,681

Located 400km north of the Arctic Circle at 69°N, the small town of Tromsø bills itself as Norway's gateway to the Arctic, and there's definitely more than a hint of polar atmosphere around town. Surrounded by chilly fjords and craggy peaks that remain snow-capped for much of the year, Tromsø sits on the eastern edge of Tromsøya, and is linked to the mainland by a gracefully arched bridge.

In previous centuries, the town was a centre for seal hunting, trapping and fishing, and was later a launch pad for several important Arctic expeditions, including some led by Roald Amundsen. These days it's best known as one of the better places in the north of the country to spot the northern lights.

It's also a notoriously lively city, with a large university, a happening cultural calendar and an animated nightlife (Tromsø prides itself on having more pubs per capita than any other Norwegian town).

◉ Sights

Tromsø's northerly location means that it's subject to the polar night and the midnight sun. Due to the inclination of the earth, from the end of November to mid-January the sun never quite makes it above the horizon, while from mid-May to mid-July, the sun never quite sets.

Around town you'll find a number of interesting churches. **Domkirke** (Map p320; www.kirken.tromso.no; Storgata; ⊙1-3pm Mon-Fri Jun & Jul, 1-4pm Mon-Fri Aug, 1-5pm Mon-Fri rest of the year) FREE is one of Norway's largest wooden churches. Up the hill is the town's **Tromsø Catholic Church** (Map p320; Storgata 94; ⊙9am-7.30pm) FREE. Both were built in 1861 and each lays claim to be 'the world's northernmost bishopric' of its sect.

You'll find more early-19th-century timber buildings around the town centre, including a stretch of 1830s shops and merchants' homes along Sjøgata.

★**Arctic Cathedral** CHURCH
(Ishavskatedralen; ☑476 80 668; Hans Nilsens veg 41; adult/child 50kr/free, organ recitals 70-170kr; ⊙9am-7pm Mon-Sat, 1-7pm Sun Jun–mid-Aug, 3-6pm mid-Aug–mid-May, opens at 2pm Feb) The 11 triangles of the Arctic Cathedral (1965), aka Tromsdalen Church, suggest glacial crevasses and auroral curtains. The glowing stained-glass window that occupies the east end depicts Christ descending to earth. The west end is filled by a futuristic organ and icicle-like lamps of Czech crystal. Unfortunately, its position beside one of Tromsø's main thoroughfares somewhat spoils the serenity outside. It's on the southern side of the Bruvegen bridge, about 1km from town. Take bus 20 or 24.

★**Fjellheisen** CABLE CAR
(☑77 63 87 37; www.fjellheisen.no; Solliveien 12; adult/child 170/60kr; ⊙10am-1am late May–mid-Aug, shorter hours rest of the year) For a fine view of the city and the midnight sun, take the cable car to the top of Mt Storsteinen (421m). There's a restaurant at the top, from where a network of hiking routes radiates. Take bus 26 to get here.

★**Mack Brewery** BREWERY
(Mack Ølbryggeri; Map p320; ☑77 62 45 80; www.mack.no; Storgata 5) This venerable institution merits a pilgrimage. Established in 1877, it produces 18 kinds of beer, including the very quaffable Macks Pilsner, Isbjørn, Haakon and several dark beers. At 3.30pm Monday to Friday year-round (plus 2pm June to August) tours (170kr, including two tastings) leave from the brewery's own Ølhallen Pub (p323). It's wise to reserve in advance.

★**Polar Museum** MUSEUM
(Polarmuseet; Map p320; ☑77 62 33 60; www.uit.no/tmu/polarmuseet; Søndre Tollbodgate 11; adult/child 60/30kr; ⊙9am-6pm mid-Jun–mid-Aug, 11am-5pm rest of the year) Fittingly for a town that was the launch pad for many pioneering expeditions to the Pole, Tromsø's fascinating Polar Museum is a rollicking romp through life in the Arctic, taking in everything from the history of trapping to the groundbreaking expeditions of Nansen and Amundsen. There are some fascinating artefacts and black-and-white archive

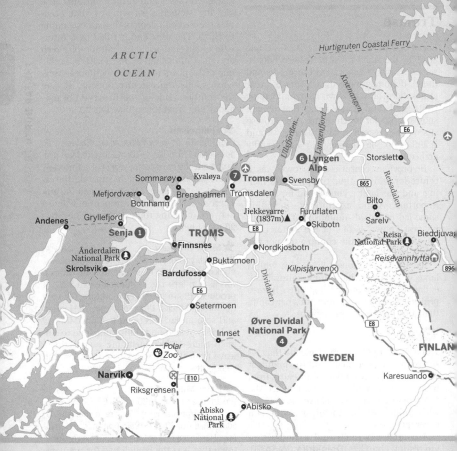

The Far North Highlights

1 Senja (p325) Cycling or driving the spectacular, lightly trafficked northern coast of this beautiful island.

2 Karasjok (p347) Visiting the museums, parliament and knifemakers to learn about the unique culture of the Sami.

3 Stone Age rock carvings (p327) Exploring Alta's fabulous open-air museum, a Unesco World Heritage Site.

4 Øvre Dividal National Park (p325) Dog-mushing through the snow and bruise-blue winter light.

5 Knivskjelodden (p335) Leaving the crowds behind to

hike to continental Europe's
northernmost point.

6 **Lyngen Alps** (p324)
Hiking out into the wilderness
of Norway's far north.

7 **Tromsø** (p315) Taking

in an organ recital as the
midnight sun streams into the
Arctic Cathedral, then dancing
till dawn.

8 **Hamningberg** (p342)
Exploring mainland Europe's

outer reaches along lonely
roads beloved by birders.

9 **Lakselv** (p337) Going
salmon fishing and riding
Icelandic horses.

photos; the stuffed remains of various formerly fuzzy, once blubbery polar creatures are rather less fun. It's in a harbourside building that served as Tromsø's customs house from 1833 to 1970.

Note the exploding harpoons outside; the whale didn't stand much of a chance.

★ Polaria   MUSEUM, AQUARIUM
(Map p320; ☑ 77 75 01 11; www.polaria.no; Hjalmar Johansens gate 12; adult/child 130/65kr; ☉ 10am-7pm mid-May–Aug, 10am-5pm Sep–mid-May) This Arctic-themed attraction provides a multimedia introduction to northern Norway and Svalbard. Kick things off by watching the two films *In the Land of the Northern Lights* and *Spitsbergen – Arctic Wilderness,* then follow the Arctic walkway past exhibits on shrinking sea ice, the aurora borealis, aquariums of cold-water fish and – the big draw – some yapping, playful bearded seals (feeding time is at 12.30pm year-round, plus 3pm in summer or 3.30pm in winter).

Blåst   FACTORY
(Map p320; ☑ 77 68 34 60; www.blaast.no; Peder Hansens gate 4; ☉ 10am-5pm Mon-Fri, 10am-4pm Sat) FREE Pass by the world's most northerly glass-blowing workshop to see the young team puffing their cheeks and perhaps to pick up an item or two.

Tromsø University Museum   MUSEUM
(☑ 77 64 50 00; www.uit.no/tmu; Lars Thøringsveg 10; adult/child 60/30kr; ☉ 9am-6pm Jun-Aug, 10am-4.30pm Mon-Fri, noon-3pm Sat, 11am-4pm Sun Sep-May) Near the southern end of Tromsøya, this museum has well presented and documented displays on traditional and modern Sami life, as well as on ecclesiastical art and accoutrements, and a small section on the Vikings. Downstairs, you can learn about rocks of the north and ponder a number of thought-provoking themes (such as the role of fire, the consequences of global warming and loss of wilderness).

Roald Amundsen Statue   STATUE
(Map p320) This statue to Norway's most famous polar explorer sits just uphill from the tourist office.

Tromsø War Museum   MUSEUM
(Tromsø Forsvarsmuseum; ☑ 77 65 54 40; www. tromsoforsvarsmuseum.no; Solstrandveien; adult/child 50/25kr; ☉ noon-5pm Wed-Sun Jun-Aug, Sun only May & Sep) The cannons of a Nazi coastal artillery battery and a restored command bunker form the basis of the Tromsø Forsvarsmuseum. It also tells of the giant German battleship *Tirpitz,* sunk near the town on 12 November 1944, and the Nazi army's retreat from Leningrad, when many of its 120,000 troops were evacuated by ship from Tromsø. The museum is on the mainland, beside the E6, 4.5km south of Tromsø bridge. Take bus 12 or 28.

Activities & Tours

For many people, the main reason to visit Tromsø is the chance to hunt for the northern lights. There are lots of companies around town offering aurora-spotting safaris. Go with a small, independent operator, otherwise you might end up with a coach party from one of the city's big hotels.

The tourist office's *Summer Activities in Tromsø* and its winter equivalent provide comprehensive checklists of tours and activities.

Wandering Owl Tours   ADVENTURE
(☑ 484 60 081; www.wanderingowl.com; Sommerlystvegen 7a) One of the more creative operators around town, Wandering Owl Tours has excellent summer guided hikes, a trip to a wilderness sauna and scenic driving tours from mid-May to mid-August, with a host of winter activities that include northern-lights photography workshops.

Active Tromsø   ADVENTURE
(☑ 481 37 133; www.activetromso.no) An excellent company offering the full range of summer and winter activities, with dog-sledding expeditions a particular speciality – including overnight husky trips with the chance to spot the aurora en route. Bookings can be made online or at the tourist office (p324).

Arctic Adventure Tours   ADVENTURE
(☑ 456 35 288; www.arcticadventuretours.no; Straumsvegen 993) A range of activities from dog-sledding and skiing in winter, to fishing and hiking expeditions in summer. You can book ahead via their website or at Tromsø's tourist office (p324).

Tromsø Friluftsenter   ADVENTURE SPORTS
(☑ 907 51 583; www.tromso-friluftsenter.no; Kvaløyvågvegen 669) Tromsø Friluftsenter runs summer sightseeing, boat trips and

a full range of winter activities (including trips to Sami camps). One intriguing possibility is their five-hour humpback-whale and orca safari from late November to mid-January. Book online or at Tromsø's tourist office (p324).

Tromsø Villmarkssenter OUTDOORS
(Map p320; ☑77 69 60 02; www.villmarks-senter.no; Stortorget 1, Kystens Hus) Tromsø Villmarkssenter offers dog-sled excursions ranging from a one-day spin to a four-day trek with overnight camping. This booking office is in town; the centre, 24km south of Tromsø on Kvaløya, also offers a range of summer activities such as trekking, glacier hiking and sea kayaking, as well as seal and seabird safaris.

Guide Gunnar ADVENTURE SPORTS
(Map p320; ☑934 43 443; www.guide-gunnar.no; Sjøgata 29, 1st fl) Gunnar Hildonen gets rave reviews for his summer and winter excursions, but travellers particularly enjoy learning from his impressive survival skills, nature immersion and 'Theatre of Food' add-ons that can include a midnight sun dinner. His downtown office is signed as 'Guides Central'.

Tromsø Safari OUTDOORS
(Map p320; ☑953 03 888; www.tromsosafari.no; Radisson Blu Hotel Tromsø) Zodiac excursions, Sami cultural visits, midnight-sun and northern-lights trips, sea fishing, hiking and whale-watching (late October to February) are all part of the portfolio at Tromsø Safari. This booking desk is at the Radisson Blu Hotel Tromsø.

Tromsø Outdoor OUTDOORS
(Map p320; ☑975 75 875; www.tromsooutdoor.no; Sjøgata 14; ☺9am-6pm Mon-Fri, 10am-6pm Sat & Sun Jun-Aug, shorter hours rest of the year) Tromsø Outdoor is for those who prefer a DIY approach to summer or winter activities, with equipment rental for everything from snowshoes and skis to bicycles (from 250kr per day).

Winter Activities
In and around Tromsø (operators will normally collect you from your hotel), winter activities outnumber those in summer, and include chasing the northern lights, cross-country skiing, Sami cultural visits, reindeer herding, reindeer- and dog-sledding, snowshoe safaris, ice fishing and snowmobil-

WORTH A TRIP

KVALØYA & SOMMARØY

From Tromsø, this half-day trip is more for the drive than the destination. It's an extraordinarily pretty, lightly trafficked run across Kvaløya, much of it down at wet-your-feet shore level as far as the small island of Sommarøy. If you decide to stay the night, there's the **Sommarøy Kurs & Feriesenter** (☑77 66 40 00; www.sommaroy.no; Skipsholmsveien 22, Sommarøy; r 1090-1490kr, apt from 2300kr, sea house from 3400kr; ℗@☎).

If you're arriving from Senja by the **Botnhamn–Brensholmen ferry** (p327), the vistas as you cross Kvaløya, heading westwards for Tromsø, are equally stunning.

ing. Whale-watching in a variety of boats (including kayaks!) is also an exciting possibility, with the season running from late October to mid-January or into February.

Arctic Guide Service SCENIC DRIVE
(Map p320; ☑922 07 901; www.arcticguideservice.com; Bankgata 1; adult/student/child 975/800/465kr) This guide company runs a nightly aurora-hunting trip at 6.15pm between mid-September and March. Minibus trips last six hours and visit several locations around Tromsø, using the latest weather forecasts to maximise your chances of seeing the show. Obviously there are no guarantees, but if there's solar activity and clear skies, there's a chance. The office is located underneath the Radisson Blu Hotel.

Natur i Nord SNOW SPORTS
(☑975 17 583; www.naturinord.no; Sommerlystvegen 23) Natur i Nord runs northern-lights trips in winter, with a midnight-sun version in summer.

Arctic Trip OUTDOORS
(☑476 63 447; www.arctictrip.no) Roy Saetre, a qualified ski instructor, runs this small but professional outfit that organises summer excursions as well as ice fishing, cross-country skiing, northern-lights excursions and wilderness expeditions. Bookings can be made through the tourist office (p324).

Tromsø

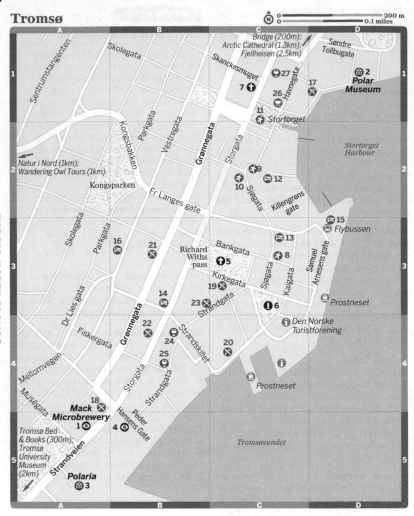

Summer Activities

Summer activities in the Tromsø hinterland include hiking, fishing, visits to Sami camps, food-centric excursions, boat sightseeing and sea kayaking. Trips to scenic locations to see the midnight sun and general sightseeing trips are widely available. Wildlife enthusiasts can also go looking for seabirds and seals.

Nordre Hestnes Gård   HORSE RIDING
(☑ 909 82 640; www.nordre-hestnes-gaard.no; Selnesveien 1007) Midnight-sun horseback excursions, hikes and other summer (and also winter) activities.

✨ Festivals & Events

In summer at the Arctic Cathedral, there are Midnight Sun Concerts (adult/child 170/50kr; 11pm June to mid-August) and organ recitals (70kr; 2pm June and July). Experiencing the swelling organ and the light of the midnight sun streaming through the huge west window could be one of the great sensory moments of your trip.

The Domkirke (p315) holds half-hour organ recitals (70kr; 5pm June, 3pm July) of classical music and folk tunes.

Tromsø

Otherwise Tromsø's two biggest annual bashes take place in deepest winter.

Tromsø International
Film Festival FILM
(☎77 75 30 90; www.tiff.no; ☉mid-Jan) One of the world's most northerly film festivals kicks off for a week in mid-January, with film screenings and talks at various locations around town (there are even a few outdoor screenings for hardcore film-goers). As you'd expect, there's a strong Arctic theme to many of the films.

Sami Week CULTURAL
(www.msm.no/sami-week-in-tromsoe.242995. en.html; ☉early Feb) Includes the national reindeer-sledge championship, where skilled Sami whoop and crack the whip along the main street in Tromsø. It centres on the week surrounding Sami National Day (6 February).

Midnight Sun Marathon SPORTS
(www.msm.no; ☉Jun) The world's most northerly marathon is held one Saturday in June. In January there's also the Polar Night Half Marathon.

Northern Lights Festival MUSIC
(☎77 68 90 70; www.nordlysfestivalen.no; ☉Jan) Six days of music of all genres. If it coincides with a northern-lights spectacular, you've hit the jackpot.

🛏 Sleeping

Bookings are advisable for the peak summer months from June to August, and for the main winter season from January to March.

Check out the home-stay section of the tourist office website (www.visittromso.no) for apartments and rooms in private homes.

Smart Hotel Tromsø HOTEL $
(Map p320; ☎415 36 500; www.smarthotel.no/en/tromso; Vestregata 12; d from 695kr; 🛜) The northernmost outpost of this budget minichain offers some of the best rates in town, and it's a fine base – as long as you don't mind the boxy rooms, basic facilities and institutional decor (battleship-grey is the colour of choice, combined with graffiti-style slogans like 'You Are Smart'). It's deservedly popular, so book ahead. The buffet breakfast costs 110kr.

Tromsø Camping CAMPGROUND $
(☎77 63 80 37; www.tromsocamping.no; Tromsdalen; tent/caravan sites 180/400kr, cabins 695-2095kr; 🅿@🛜) Tent campers can enjoy leafy green campsites beside a slow-moving stream, and there are some excellent modern cabins here, though the better ones don't come cheap. Public bathroom and cooking facilities at this veritable village are stretched to the limit in July and August. Take bus 20 or 24.

★ **Tromsø Bed & Books**   GUESTHOUSE **$$**
(☑77 02 98 00; www.bedandbooks.no; Strandvegen 45; s/d 850/950kr; 🕾) Run by a pair of seasoned globetrotters, this lovely guesthouse has two 'homes' – a Fisherman's and a Writer's – all stuffed with books, retro furniture, old maps and curios, and thoughtfully designed for budget travellers. The rooms can feel cramped when full, and are noisy, but that's part of the budget trade-off. There's no breakfast, but both houses have shared kitchens.

Scandic Grand Hotel   HOTEL **$$**
(Map p320; ☑77 75 37 77; www.scandichotels.no; Storgata 44; r 950-1790kr; 🅿@🕾) The Grand is Tromsø's oldest hotel, but there's little that's antique inside as the place has twice burnt to the ground. Ask for a room on one of the newer top two floors. Rates include a particularly ample breakfast with fresh fruit and hot dishes.

Clarion Hotel Aurora   HOTEL **$$**
(Map p320; ☑77 78 11 00; www.nordicchoice hotels.no; Sjøgata 19/21; s/d from 990/1090kr; @🕾) This stylish 121-room waterside hotel, which pokes towards the sea like the prow of a ship, is architecturally stunning with its odd angles, aluminium trim, pictures on bedroom ceilings, sauna, and a top-floor hot tub where you can savour the picturesque harbour and mountain views as you bubble and boil. Room rates include breakfast and a light but ample evening meal.

Radisson Blu Hotel Tromsø   HOTEL **$$**
(Map p320; ☑77 60 00 00; www.radisson blu.com/hotel-tromso; Sjøgata 7; s/d from 995/1295kr; 🅿@🕾) The bedrooms here were comprehensively renovated when the attractive newer wing was grafted onto the solid, rectangular block of the original building. Of its 269 rooms (it's worth the 200kr extra for one in the newer wing), around half have harbour views. It runs a decent pub, the **Rorbua**, and a fine **Arctic Menu** restaurant.

★ **Scandic Ishavshotel**   HOTEL **$$$**
(Map p320; ☑77 66 64 00; www.scandicho tels.no; Fredrik Langes gate 2; d/ste from 1699/2499kr; 🅿🕾) This is the prime spot in Tromsø if you want a waterside view – the Scandic Ishavshotel's architecture evokes an ocean-going vessel, complete with a flag-topped mast and crow's nest. The

rooms are sleek, smart and business-like, dressed in cappuccino-browns and slate-greys. Breakfast is included; rooms are 20% cheaper on weekends.

Eating

★ **Risø**   CAFE **$**
(Map p320; ☑416 64 516; www.risoe-mk.no; Strandgata 32; mains 95-179kr; ⊙7.30am-5pm Mon-Fri, 9am-5pm Sat) You'll find this popular coffee and lunch bar packed throughout most of the day: young trendies come in for their hand-brewed Chemex coffee, while local workers pop in for the daily specials, tasty open-faced sandwiches and delicious cakes. It's small, and the tables are packed in tight, so you might have to queue.

Dragøy   FISH & CHIPS **$**
(Map p320; ☑77 67 32 30; www.dragoy.no; off Havnegata; mains 89-149kr; ⊙8am-4pm Mon-Sat) This wharfside fishmonger sells Tromsø's best fish and chips, as well as a mean fish burger, homemade ravioli and fish soup. The setting is fast food in atmosphere, but the pricing is a winner and the fish couldn't be fresher.

★ **Emma's Under**   NORWEGIAN **$$**
(Map p320; ☑77 63 77 30; www.emmasdrom mekjokken.no; Kirkegata; lunch mains 165-335kr; ⊙11am-10pm Mon-Fri, noon-10pm Sat) Homely and down-to-earth Norwegian cuisine is the dish of the day here. You'll find hearty dishes like fish gratin, king crab and baked *klippfisk* on the lunch menu, served in a cosy space designed to echo a traditional kitchen à la grandma. Upstairs is the more formal Emma's Drømmekjøkken (p323), which shares its menu with Emma's Under after 5.30pm.

Presis   TAPAS **$$**
(Map p320; ☑77 68 10 20; www.presistapas.no; Storgata 36; tapas 68-136kr; ⊙4-10pm Tue-Thu, 4-11pm Fri, 6-11pm Sat) You might be in the far north, but that doesn't mean you can't find a bit of Mediterranean atmosphere, even in Tromsø. This refined place offers a creative take on tapas, blending Spanish and Nordic flavours into a rather convincing package. The king crab in garlic and ginger butter is particularly delicious.

Driv   CAFE **$$**
(Map p320; ☑77 60 07 76; www.driv.no; Storgata 6; mains 175-195kr; ⊙noon-1.30am Mon-Thu,

THE FAR NORTH TROMSØ

to 3am Fri & Sat, kitchen shuts 9pm) This student-run diner in the Mack Brewery (p315) serves meaty burgers (try its renowned Driv burger), sandwiches and great salads. It organises musical and cultural events and has a disco every Saturday.

★ Kitchen
& Table   NORWEGIAN, INTERNATIONAL $$$

(Map p320; ☑ 77 66 84 84; www.kitchenandtable. no/tromso; Kaigata 6; mains 235-375kr; ⊗ 5-10pm Mon-Sat, to 9pm Sun) Combining a touch of Manhattan style with Arctic ingredients, chef Marcus Samuelsson serves up some of the freshest and most original tastes in Tromsø – there's reindeer fillet with mango chutney, reindeer ratatouille, burgers with quinoa or kimchi, and even slow-cooked Moroccan lamb.

★ Mathallen   BISTRO $$$

(Map p320; ☑ 77 68 01 00; www.mathallentromso.no; Grønnegata 60; lunch mains 100-210kr, dinner mains from 310kr, 4-course tasting menu 685kr; ⊗ bistro 11am-11pm Tue-Sat, deli 10am-6pm Mon-Fri, 10am-4pm Sat) With its industrial styling, exposed pipes and open-fronted kitchen, this elegant place wouldn't look out of place in Oslo or Stockholm. It serves some of the best modern Norwegian food in town, majoring in fish and local meats; the lunchtime special is a steal at 100kr. There's a deli next door selling tapenades, cheeses, smoked salmon and *lutefisk* (stockfish).

★ Emma's
Drømmekjøkken   NORWEGIAN $$$

(Map p320; ☑ 77 63 77 30; www.emmasdrommekjokken.no; Kirkegata; mains 285-365kr, 3-/5-course menu 390/630kr; ⊗ 6pm-midnight Mon-Sat) Upstairs from Emma's Under (p322), this stylish and highly regarded place pulls in discriminating diners with its imaginative cuisine, providing traditional Norwegian dishes married with top-quality local ingredients such as *lutefisk* (stockfish), blueberry-marinated halibut, ox tenderloin and gratinated king crab. Advance booking is essential.

● Drinking & Nightlife

Ølhallen Pub   PUB

(Map p320; ☑ 77 62 45 80; www.olhallen.no; Storgata 4; ⊗ 10am-7.30pm Mon-Wed, 10am-12.30am Thu-Sat) Reputedly the oldest pub in town, and once the hangout for salty fishermen

HARD DRINKING, TROMSØ STYLE

It takes real stamina to stay the course of a proper Tromsø night out . With work over, friends will meet for *Fredagspils* – Friday drinks to plan the campaign ahead. Then it's time for *Vorspiel*, or foreplay, a preliminary oiling at a friend's house before setting off around midnight to hit a club or bar. At the statutory throwing-out time of 3.30am, it's *Fyllemat,* fill-up time, when you pick up a burger, kebab or hot dog from one of the street stalls that lurk outside major venues, before heading once more to a friend's pad for a few hours' *Nachspiel*, or afterplay.

By now it's bed for middle-distance runners, while the marathon crowd stamps its feet outside Ølhallen's, waiting for the sliding of bolts that marks its 10am opening. 'If you can stand, we'll serve you', is the bar staff's rule of thumb.

and Arctic sailors, Ølhallen is now the brewpub for the excellent Mack Brewery (p315). There are 67 ales to try, including eight on tap – so it might take you a while (and a few livers) to work your way through them all.

Kaffebønna   CAFE

(Map p320; ☑ 77 63 94 00; www.kaffebonna.no; Stortorget 3; ⊗ 8am-6pm Mon-Fri, 9am-6pm Sat, 10am-6pm Sun) One of our favourite Tromsø cafes, this cool little spot right in the town centre does the city's best coffee, accompanied by tasty pastries.

Bastard   BAR, CLUB

(Map p320; ☑ 922 00 519; www.facebook.com/bastardbar; Strandgata 22; ⊗ 6pm-2am Mon-Thu, 6pm-3am Fri-Sun) Bastard (with the stress on the second syllable; let's not get unwittingly confrontational) is a cool basement hangout with low beams and white, furry walls (no polar bears killed during construction). It engages art-house and underground DJs (Friday and Saturday) and bands (up to three times weekly). Showing UK and Norwegian football, it also has a faithful following of armchair-sporting regulars.

Verdensteatret
BAR, CAFE

(Map p320; ☑ 77 75 30 90; www.verdensteatret.no; Storgata 93b; ⊗ 11am-2am Mon-Thu, 11am-3.30am Fri & Sat, 1pm-2am Sun; ⊛) Norway's oldest film house will satisfy both cinephiles and those in search of a great cafe. The bar is a hip place with free wi-fi and weekend DJs. At other times, the bartender spins from the huge collection of vinyl records, so expect anything from classical music to deepest underground.

Ask staff to let you peek into the magnificent cinema with its early-20th-century murals.

Blå Rock Café
BAR

(Map p320; ☑ 77 61 00 20; www.facebook.com/Blaarock; Strandgata 14/16; ⊗ 11.30am-2am Mon-Thu, 11.30am-3am Fri & Sat, 1pm-2am Sun) The loudest, most raving place in town has theme evenings, almost 50 brands of beer, occasional live bands and weekend DJs. The music is rock, naturally. Every Monday hour is a happy hour.

ℹ Information

Tourist Office (Map p320; ☑ 77 61 00 00; www.visittromso.no; Kirkegata 2; ⊗ 9am-5pm Mon-Fri, 10am-5pm Sat & Sun Jan-Mar & mid-May–Aug, shorter hours rest of year; ⊛) In a wooden building by the harbour, Tromsø's busy tourist office books accommodation and activities, and has free wi-fi. It also publishes the comprehensive *Tromsø Guide*.

ℹ Getting There & Away

AIR

Tromsø Airport (☑ 77 64 84 00; www.avinor.no/flyplass/tromso) is about 5km from the town centre, on the western side of Tromsøya and is the main airport for the far north. Destinations with direct Scandinavian Airlines flights to/from the airport include Oslo, Narvik/

Harstad, Bodø, Trondheim, Alta, Hammerfest, Kirkenes and Longyearbyen.

Norwegian (www.norwegian.no) flies to and from most major cities in Norway, plus UK destinations including London (Gatwick), Edinburgh and Dublin.

Widerøe (www.wideroe.no) has several flights a day to Svolvær and Leknes in the Lofoten Islands. All flights are via Bodø.

BOAT

Tromsø is a major stop on the Hurtigruten coastal-ferry route.

Express boats connect Tromsø and Harstad (2½ hours), via Finnsnes (1¼ hours), two to four times daily and leave from the **Express Ferry Terminal** (Map p320) on Strandskillet.

BUS

The **main bus terminal** (Map p320; Samuel Arnesens gate) (also known as Prostneset) is on Kaigata, beside the Hurtigruten ferry quay. There are up to three daily express buses to/from Narvik (280kr, 4¼ hours) and one to/from Bodø (410kr, 6½ hours). To get further south, you need to catch the daily bus to Fauske, then the night train to Trondheim and Oslo – but it's a long and pricey journey, so it's much more practical to fly.

Heading north, there's a daily bus to Alta (620kr, 6½ hours). The fare includes the two Lyngen ferries.

Tromskortet (www.tromskortet.no) has a daily bus on weekdays to Narvik, where there's a connecting bus to Svolvær (eight hours) in the Lofoten Islands.

ℹ Getting Around

Tromsø has ample paid parking in the centre. There's also the huge Trygg underground car park tunnelled into the hill; its entrance is on Vestregata (closed to trailers and caravans).

Lyngen Alps

Some of the most rugged alpine heights in all Norway unfold along the spine of the heavily glaciated Lyngen Peninsula, east of Tromsø; you'll get the best views of them from the eastern shore of 150km-long Lyngenfjord. The peaks, the highest of which is Jiekkevarre (1837m), offer plenty of opportunities for climbers, but this challenging glacial terrain is strictly for the experienced.

The Lyngsdalen valley, above the industrial village of Furuflaten, is an altogether more accessible and popular hiking area. The usual route begins at the football pitch south of the bridge over the Lyngdalselva and climbs up the valley to the tip of the glacier Sydbreen, 500m above sea level.

Contact **Den Norske Turistforening** (DNT; Map p320; ☑77 68 51 75; www.troms.dnt. no; Kirkegata 2; ⊙noon-4pm Wed, noon-6pm Thu, noon-2pm Fri) in Tromsø for hiking advice. The best map for hiking is Statens Kartverk's *Lyngenhalvøya* (1:50,000).

ⓘ Getting There & Away

Buses (route 460) connect Furuflaten, the gateway to the Lyngen Alps, with Nordkjosbotn (45 minutes, two to three daily) along the E6, which can be reached from Tromsø.

Øvre Dividal National Park

Between Setermoen and the Swedish and Finnish borders lies the wild, roadless, lake-studded Øvre Dividal National Park. It's a remote, semi-forested, 750-sq-km upland wilderness with plenty of alpine peaks and views. The park is also rich in wildlife, with brown bear, wolf, Arctic fox, Eurasian lynx and one of the densest populations of wolverine anywhere in Europe.

🏃 Activities

Hiking

The most popular hike is the eight-day **Troms Border Trail**, which connects with Abisko National Park, in northern Sweden, where you'll find the start of Sweden's renowned Kungsleden hiking route. The map to use for the Troms Border Trail and the Abisko Link is Statens Kartverk's *Turkart Indre Troms* (1:100,000 scale). In summer the mosquitoes will drive you to distraction; use a head net, smear yourself liberally with repellent and swat every single last buzzing bastard you can, in the interests of those who follow in your footsteps.

Dog-Sledding

Winter visitors can join a dog-sled trip through Arctic Norway led by renowned and resourceful musher, **Bjørn Klauer** (☑77 18 45 03; www.huskyfarm.de). In addition to tours through Øvre Dividal National Park, he runs expeditions deeper into Finnmark. In summer, he and his team organise cycle and canoe tours or you can do your own thing and hike the several signed trails that pass nearby. His farm is also a delightful place to stay.

WORTH A TRIP

POLAR PARK

The large, open-air zoo **Polar Park** (☑77 18 66 30; www.polarpark.no; Industriveien 10, Bardu; adult/child/family 260/160/750kr; ⊙10am-6pm mid-Jun–Aug, 10am-4pm Mon-Fri, noon-4pm Sat & Sun Sep–mid-Jun) is 23km south of Setermoen and 3.3km east of the E6. It features wildlife of the boreal *taiga* (marshy forest) in spacious enclosures that, but for the metal fencing, are scarcely distinguishable from the surrounding birch forests. Here you can observe animals such as brown bears, deer, musk oxen, reindeer, wolves, Eurasian lynx, wolverines, badgers and both red and polar fox. There are also zip-lines of varying lengths, which cost extra.

Follow the keeper around at predator feeding time (normally 1pm; check at reception); there's a host of other up-close encounters possible.

🛏 Sleeping

Other than wild camping, for which you'll need to bring your own equipment, Bjørn Klauer Huskyfarm (p325) provides an excellent place to stay. If it's full, there's another, affiliated husky farm nearby that was yet to get off the ground at the time of research.

ⓘ Information

Contact **Den Norske Turistforening** (p325) in Tromsø for hiking advice and maps.

ⓘ Getting There & Away

You'll need your own wheels to reach Øvre Dividal National Park.

Senja
POP 7808
Senja, Norway's second-largest island, rivals Lofoten and Vesterålen for natural beauty yet attracts a fraction of the visitors (we meandered the length of its northern coastline in the height of summer and saw very few vehicles). It's an island that warrants patient exploration, and at least two full days to fully appreciate its quiet beauty.

◉ Sights

A broad agricultural plain laps at Innersida, the island's eastern coast facing the mainland. By contrast, birchwoods, moorland and sweetwater lakes extend beneath the bare craggy uplands of the interior. Along the northwestern coast, called Yttersida, knife-ridged peaks rise directly from the Arctic Ocean. Here, the Rv86 and Rv862, declared a National Tourist Route, link isolated, still-active fishing villages such as Hamn and Mefjordvær and traffic is minimal. The now flat, mildly bucking road, almost always within sight of the shore, is a cyclist's dream. On the way, pause at the strikingly designed **Bergsbotn viewpoint**, and at the **Tungeneset viewpoint** and scramble over broad slabs of weathered rock to savour the spiky peaks to the west and, eastwards, more gently sculpted crests. Off the northern coast and connected to the main island by a causeway, **Husøy** is a particularly beautiful village.

Senjatrollet   AMUSEMENT PARK
(☑77 85 88 64; www.senjatrollet.no; adult/child/family 130/90/380kr; ◎9am-8pm late May-early Sep) It's true, there can't be much competition outside Scandinavia. But the Senja Troll, 18m high and weighing in at 125,000kg, is the world's biggest troll, attested by the *Guinness World Records*. There's a tractor and railway carriage for kids to clamber on and a cafe with shelf upon shelf of warty, bucktoothed trolls (and some fine pewterwork on display for mum and dad to look at). You can even enter the bowels of the grinning giant and explore his intestines.

ⓘ MIND THAT REINDEER

Do keep an eye out for reindeer on the road. They're not dangerous and they're decidedly more charming than annoying. But they might slow your progress and bring you to a very abrupt halt if you hit one at speed. Sometimes wandering alone, now and again in herds, they might not be fazed by your inanimate car. If they refuse to budge, just get out, walk towards them and they'll amble away.

There's also a wall for kids to hang their pacifiers or dummies, as a sign that they're ready to move on in life.

🏃 Activities

Various places to stay also arrange activities, including Hamn i Senja (p327), Camp Steinfjord (p327) and Fjordbotn Camping (p326). **Basecamp Senja** (☑917 09 618; www.basecampsenja.no; Hamnaveien 24) arranges fjord sightseeing, whale-watching and themed special dinners.

The list of possible summer activities is long but includes hiking, body rafting, midnight-sun kayaking, cycling and boat sightseeing trips, fishing, and beach drop-offs that allow you to spend a day on a remote beach.

In winter you can go whale-watching, as well as taking the usual boat trips in search of the northern lights.

🐾 Courses

★ Senja Mat Studio   COOKING
(Senja Food Studio; ☑922 23 882; www.senjamatstudio.no; Hamnveien 749) This brilliant place offers up experiences based around food. A typical day involves breakfast, a packed lunch and time spent fishing for your dinner (all the while keeping an eye out for seals, sea eagles and whales), followed by an evening cooking class. It's a wonderful idea, with plenty of time built in for long beach walks.

🛏 Sleeping

Fjordbotn Camping   CAMPGROUND $
(☑77 84 93 10; www.fjordbotn.no; Stønnesbotn, Botnhamn; tent/caravan sites 200/250kr, cabins 450-1090kr; ☞) This professionally run campground sits in the heart of northern Senja's spectacular fjord and mountain country, and it can arrange all manner of activities.

Mefjord Brygge   CABIN, APARTMENT $$
(☑77 85 89 80; www.mefjordbrygge.no; Mefjordvær; s/d 1050/1200kr, cabins 1295-1995kr, houses 1495-3495kr, apt from 1695kr; ☞) Everything from simple wharfside hostel rooms, cabins and converted houses, to lovely apartments opened in 2016 – this fine collection of accommodation seems to take up an entire village. They have a good restaurant as well.

★ **Camp Steinfjord**   HOTEL $$$
(The Fat Cod; ☑908 98 235; www.thefatcod.
com; Steinfjorden 13, Skaland; d for 4/7 days
5600/9800kr) Opened in April 2017, the reno-
vated rooms here in a lovely wooden former
fishing factory combine Scandinavian mini-
malist style with high levels of comfort. The
fjordside setting is lovely, there is a terrific
on-site restaurant, and they also rent out
fishing gear. Highly recommended.

★ **Hamn i Senja**   RESORT $$$
(☑400 20 005, 77 85 98 80; www.hamnisenja.no;
s/d mini r 1035/1320kr, s/d studio 1472/1788kr,
s/d ste 2064/2382kr, d apt 2600kr; P ⊙) On
the site of a former fishing hamlet, Hamn
i Senja is a delightful, self-contained, get-
away-from-it-all place that sits in its own
little cove. Nearby is the small dam that
held back the waters for what is claimed
to be the world's first hydroelectric plant,
established in 1882.

✕ **Eating**

Segla Grill og Pub   NORWEGIAN $$
(☑928 19 619; www.facebook.com/seglagrill;
Arnakkveien 1, Fjordgard; mains from 129kr; ⊙2-
9pm Sun-Thu, noon-2am Fri & Sat) All manner
of creative things go on here, from season-
al soups to a rather yummy pizza buffet
on some nights. It's a pretty casual place
that has a great mix of fine food and fun
atmosphere.

❶ **Getting There & Away**

Our favourite way to arrive is the spectacular,
summer-only Andenes–Gryllefjord car ferry
(adult/child/car 168/120/431kr, 1¾ hours,
three to four daily). Other transport options:
➡ Two to three daily buses run from Finnsnes
to Tromsø (2¾ hours) and Narvik (three hours)
with a connection in Buktamoen.
➡ Express ferries connect Finnsnes with
Tromsø (1¼ hours) and Harstad (1¾ hours) two
to three times a day.
➡ It's possible to drive the whole of the north-
west coast from Gryllefjord to Botnhamn,
with its **car-ferry link** (www.tromskortet.no)
to Brensholmen on Kvaløya, then onwards to
Tromsø.
➡ Westbound, a summertime car ferry con-
nects Skrolsvik, on Senja's south coast, to
Harstad (1½ hours, two to four daily).
➡ Finnsnes is also a stop for the Hurtigruten
coastal ferry.

WESTERN FINNMARK

Finnmark's wild northern coast is dotted
with fishing villages and riven with grand
fjords, while the vast interior is dominat-
ed by the broad Finnmarksvidda plateau,
which is a stark wilderness. This is the
home of Nordkapp, but also so much more,
with Alta, Hammerfest and Honningsvåg
providing gateways to some really stun-
ning country.

History

Finnmark has been inhabited for around
12,000 years, first by the Komsa hunters of
the coastal region and later by Sami fish-
ing cultures and reindeer pastoralists, who
settled on the coast and in the vast interior,
respectively.

More recently, virtually every Finnmark
town was decimated at the end of WWII
by retreating Nazi troops, whose scorched-
earth policy aimed to delay the advancing
Soviets. Towns were soon reconstructed in
the most efficient, yet boxy, building style,
which is why, in contrast to the spectacu-
lar natural surroundings, present-day Fin-
nmark towns are, for the most part, archi-
tecturally uninspiring.

Alta

POP 14,472

Alta has a number of big-ticket attractions
– the Unesco-listed Alta Museum with its
ancient petroglyphs, the Northern Lights
Cathedral and the lush green Sautso-Alta
canyon. The town, strung out along the
coast, is largely unattractive, although it
stands in the heart of some pretty spectac-
ular country. And to cap it all off, although
this fishing and slate-quarrying town lies
at latitude 70°N, it enjoys a relatively mild
climate.

◉ **Sights**

★ **Alta Museum**   MUSEUM
(☑417 56 330; www.alta.museum.no; Altaveien
19; adult/child 110/35kr May-Sep, 75/20kr Oct-Apr;
⊙8am-8pm mid-Jun–Aug, shorter hours rest of year)
This superb museum is in Hjemmeluft, at the
western end of town. It features exhibits and
displays on Sami culture, Finnmark military
history, the Alta hydro-electric project and
the aurora borealis (northern lights). The

ⓘ ALTA MUSEUM: WHICH LOOP?

Alta Museum's short walking loop (1.2km; allow around 45 minutes, including viewing time) is the most visited. A longer one (2.1km, taking around 1¼ hours) begins with a steepish descent, followed by a pleasant seaside walk that takes in more sites.

---

cliffs around it, a Unesco World Heritage Site, are incised with around 6000 late–Stone Age carvings, dating from 6000 to 2000 years ago and it's these petroglyphs that will live longest in the memory.

★**Northern Lights Cathedral** CHURCH
(Løkkeveien; adult/child 50/25kr, incl Borealis Alta show 150/75kr; ☉11am-9pm Mon-Sat & 4-9pm Sun mid-Jun–mid-Aug, 11am-3pm Mon-Sat rest of year) Opened in 2013, the daringly designed Northern Lights Cathedral, next to the Scandic Hotel Alta, is one of the architectural icons of the north, with its swirling pyramid structure clad in rippling titanium sheets. The interior is similarly eye-catching, with an utterly modern 4.3m-high bronze *Christ* by Danish artist Peter Brandes – note how the figure gets lighter as your eyes move up the body.

Sautso-Alta Canyon CANYON
The Altaelva hydroelectric project has had very little effect on the most scenic stretch of river, which slides through 400m-deep Sautso, northern Europe's grandest canyon.

🏃 Activities

Sorrisniva BOATING
(☑78 43 33 78; www.sorrisniva.no; Sorrisniva 20; 1/2hr riverboat tours per person 895/1495kr) Sorrisniva, at the Sorrisniva Igloo Hotel (p329), runs several riverboat rides along the Altaelva. Boats set out at noon daily from June to mid-September. They also offer winter snowmobiling. To reach Sorrisniva, head 16km south of Alta along the Rv93, then a further 6.5km along a marked road.

Glød ADVENTURE SPORTS
(☑997 94 256; www.glodexplorer.no) Both a summer and winter player (its name means 'Glow'), Glød can lay on ice fishing, dog-sledding, snowshoe trekking and other icy fun.

Holmen Husky DOG SLEDDING
(☑78 43 66 45; www.holmenhusky.no; Holmen 48; 3hr dog-sledding per adult/child 1450/625kr) Specialises in dog-sledding (mid-December to April, dog-carting in summer), with outings ranging from three hours to five days.

Alta Adventure ADVENTURE SPORTS
(☑78 43 40 50; www.alta-adventure.no) Trekking, canoeing and salmon fishing. Also, on request and not something you'll do around home: ptarmigan hunting.

Winter Activities

Sorrisniva has 80 snowmobiles, the largest such fleet in northern Norway. It offers guided outings (one-/two-person snowmobile 1450/1700kr), and, after your exertions, you can relax in its steaming hot tub. Gargia Fjellstue (p329) also offers a range of summer and winter outdoor activities.

Sarves Alta Alpinsenter SKIING
(☑906 99 741; www.altaski.no; Nordelvdalen 170; ☉Dec-Apr) Alta's ski centre at Rafsbotn, 10km northeast of Alta along the E6, has five downhill runs and plenty of snowboarding possibilities. Equipment rental is easy to arrange at the centre and a semi-regular bus connects Rafsbotn to Alta during the season – ask at the tourist office (p329).

🎓 Courses

★**Trasti i Trine** DOG SLEDDING, COOKING
(Northern Lights Husky; ☑458 53 144; www.trasti ogtrine.no; Gargiaveien 29; 2hr dog-sledding adult/child 1450/750kr) Dog-sledding trips from 2½ hours to multiday expeditions. They also run cooking courses, have special meals with commentary and offer accommodation (p329). Located about 10km outside Alta.

🎉 Festivals & Events

Finnmarksløpet SPORTS
(www.finnmarkslopet.no; ☉Mar) The 1000km-long Finnmarksløpet, Europe's longest dog-sled race, starts and ends in Alta in March and traverses the length of the far north. It coincides with Alta's Borealis Alta (p329).

Alta Blues & Soul Festival MUSIC
(www.altasoulogblues.no; ☉May/Jun) Brings in top Norwegian bands and starts in late May or early June.

Borealis Alta   CULTURAL
(www.facebook.com/borealis.alta; ☺ Mar) Five days of concerts and culture in March, designed to dispel winter's gloom.

🛏 Sleeping

⭐ Wisløff Camping   CAMPGROUND $
(☑ 78 43 43 03; www.wisloeff.no; per person/site 50/220kr, cabins 500-1450kr) One of three excellent riverside campsites in Ovre Alta, 3.5km south of the E6 along the Rv93 to Kautokeino, Wisløff Camping was declared Campground of the Year in 2000, and it still deserves the accolade. Travellers too sing its praises.

⭐ Trasti i Trine   LODGE $$
(☑ 78 40 30 40; www.trastiogtrine.no/accommo dation; s/d from 750/1300kr) Some 10km outside Alta and in a forest down by the river, this wonderful wooden lodge is classy, sophisticated and warmly inviting all at once. The on-site husky farm adds loads of personality, the rooms are impeccably turned out and the food outstanding. The communal living area has a fireplace and overall it's the kind of place you'll never want to leave.

Gargia Fjellstue   LODGE $$
(☑ 78 43 33 51; www.gargia-fjellstue.no; Gargi aveien 96; r from 1100kr) Around 25km south of Alta, in the direction of Kautokeino, this mountain lodge offers a forest getaway, plenty of activities year-round, and the best foot access to the Sautso-Alta canyon (p328).

Thon Hotel Vica   HOTEL $$
(☑ 78 48 22 22; www.thonhotels.no; Fogdebakken 6; s/d from 950/1200kr; P @ 🛜) Right from the stuffed brown bear that greets you at the door, the Vica beckons you in. In a timber-built former farmhouse, it used to be a family-run concern and still retains a more personal feel than many other hotels in this chain. There's a sauna (100kr), steaming outdoor hot tub (wonderful in winter when all around is snowcapped) and a good restaurant (p329).

Sorrisniva Igloo Hotel   ICE HOTEL $$$
(☑ 78 43 33 78; www.sorrisniva.no; B&B s/d 3000/5000kr; ☺ mid-Dec–mid-Apr; P) The 30 bedrooms – and beds too – are made entirely of ice, as are the chapel, bridal suite (no complaints of wedding night frigidity so far) and the stunning ice bar with its weird and wonderful sculptures lit by fibre optics. Sorrisni-

va is south of Alta – drive 16km along the Rv93, then 6.5km along a signposted road.

Scandic Hotel Alta   HOTEL $$$
(☑ 78 48 27 00; www.scandichotels.no; Løkkeveien 61; s/d from 1450/1690kr; @ 🛜) Alta's classiest hotel has attractive rooms (some have large photos of the northern lights) and excellent service, although some rooms are on the small side. Try for one of the west-facing rooms with views over the Northern Lights Cathedral. The **Alta restaurant** (mains from 265kr, dinner buffet per person 295kr; ☺ 5-11pm) is also also excellent and there's a bar (closed Sundays).

🍴 Eating

Du Verden Matbar   NORWEGIAN, INTERNATIONAL $$
(☑ 459 08 213; www.duverden.no/alta; Markedsga ta 21; mains 185-365kr; ☺ 10am-midnight Mon-Sat, 1-10.20pm Sun) A cool brasserie-style place, Du Verden does fish soup, king crab, stockfish, shellfish platters, reindeer fillet and tapas, as well as salads and a wide range of drinks.

⭐ Restaurant Haldde   NORWEGIAN $$$
(☑ 78 48 22 22; Fogdebakken 6; mains 249-349kr; ☺ 4-11pm Mon-Sat, 2-10pm Sun) 🍴 This quality restaurant within Thon Hotel Vica relies almost entirely upon local ingredients in the preparation of choice dishes such as reindeer steak, grilled stockfish and its *Flavour of Finnmark* dessert of cloudberries and cowberry-blueberry sorbet.

🍷 Drinking & Nightlife

Barila   BAR
(☑ 970 23 454; Parksentret Bldg, Sentrum; ☺ 11am-1am Sun-Thu, to 3am Fri & Sat) There may not be many places to drink in Alta, but this sassy little spot takes up the slack through sheer variety – they serve great coffee, good beer and exotic cocktails, have live music from time to time and there's even a dance floor.

ℹ Information

Tourist Office (☑ 991 00 022; www.visitalta. no; Bjørn Wirkolasvei 11; ☺ 9am-8pm daily mid-Jun–mid-Aug, shorter hours rest of year) This should be your first stop for organising summer and winter activities.

ℹ Getting There & Away

Alta's **airport** (☑ 78 44 95 55; www.avinor.no) is 4km northeast of Sentrum at Elvebakken. SAS has direct flights to/from Oslo, Tromsø,

Hammerfest, Lakselv and Vadsø. Norwegian connects Alta with Oslo.

Buses leave from the **terminal** in Sentrum:
Hammerfest (335kr, 2¼ hours, two daily)
Honningsvåg (496kr, four hours, one daily)
Karasjok (525kr, 4¾ hours, two daily except Saturday)
Kautokeino (298kr, 2¼ hours, one daily except Saturday)
Tromsø (620kr, 6½ hours, one daily)

❶ Getting Around

Fortunately, this sprawling town has a local bus to connect its dispersed ends. On weekdays buses run more or less hourly between the major districts and to the airport. Services are less frequent on Saturday and don't run at all on Sunday.

Taxis (☑78 43 53 53) cost about 180kr from the airport into town.

Hammerfest

POP 7938

Welcome to Norway's, and perhaps even the world's, northernmost town – other Norwegian communities, while further north, are, Hammerfest vigorously argues, too small to qualify as towns!

If you're arriving on the Hurtigruten coastal ferry, you'll have only 1½ hours to pace around, pick up an Arctic souvenir or two and visit the Royal & Ancient Polar Bear Society. For most visitors that will be ample, Hurtigruten or not.

History

Because of its strategic location and excellent harbour, Hammerfest has long been an important way station for shipping, fishing and Arctic hunting. In its heyday, ladies wore the finest Paris fashions and in 1890 Europe's first electric street lighting was installed.

Neither man nor nature has been kind to the town: it was set alight by the British in 1809, decimated by a gale in 1856, burnt severely in 1890, then torched again by the Nazis in 1944. Its parish church has gone up in flames five times over the centuries. All the same, fortune may at last be smiling on the town in a way that is having a huge impact.

A 143km-long undersea pipeline starts beneath the Barents Sea, fed from the huge natural gas fields of Snøhvit (Snowhite: an evocative name for such a giant industrial project). It runs to the small island of Melkøya out in the bay, where the gas is liquefied and transported by tanker to Europe and the USA. With estimated reserves of 193 billion (yes, billion) cu metres, the pumps, which came on tap in 2007, are expected to pound for at least 25 years.

◉ Sights

★**Hammerfest Kirke** CHURCH
(Map p331; Kirkegata 33; ⊙9am-2pm mid-Jun–mid-Aug) The design of Hammerfest's contemporary church, consecrated in 1961, was inspired by the racks used for drying fish in the salty sea air all across northern Norway. Behind the altar, the glorious stained-glass window positively glows in the summer sun, while the wooden frieze along the organ gallery depicts highlights of the town's history. The chapel in the cemetery across the street is the only building in town to have survived WWII.

★**Royal & Ancient Polar Bear Society** MUSEUM
(Isbjørklubben; Map p331; ☑78 41 21 85; www.isbjornklubben.no; Hamnegata 3; ⊙8am-6pm Jun & Jul, 9am-4pm Mon-Fri, 10am-2pm Sat & Sun Aug–May) FREE Dedicated to preserving Hammerfest culture, the Royal & Ancient Polar Bear Society (founded in 1963) features exhibits on Arctic hunting and local history and shares premises with the tourist office. For 200kr you can become a life member and get a certificate, ID card, sticker and pin. At times, the link to polar bears here can feel a little tenuous. But if you think of the place in terms of the Norwegian name (Isbjørklubben, simply Polar Bear Club), you're less likely to be disappointed.

Membership (there are around 250,000 members worldwide) entitles you to attend the annual general meeting of the society in January. And not everyone can join, it seems. In 1973, one Elvis Presley wrote to the society asking to join, but his application was refused – to become a member, one must be physically present in Hammerfest.

If simple membership is not enough and you're part of a group, for 300kr you also receive a schnapps glass and get dubbed with the large bone from a walrus's penis. Honestly. It's well worth the extra for the conversation this unique honour will generate down the pub once you're home. Advance reservations for this ceremony are necessary.

Hammerfest

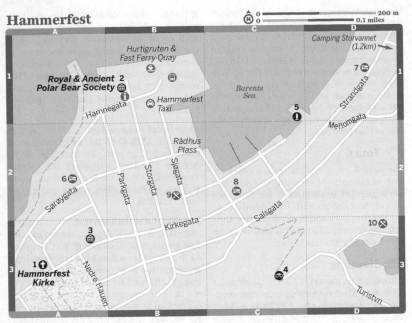

Hammerfest

One of the exhibits covers Adolf Henrik Lindstrøm, a Hammerfest-born cook who accompanied Roald Amundsen and Fridtjof Nansen (among others) and ended up travelling on more polar expeditions that any other person on earth, great explorers included. The town erected a **statue of Lindstrøm** (Map p331) in time for the 150th anniversary of his birth in 2016.

Gjenreisningsmuseet
MUSEUM
(Map p331; ☎ 78 40 29 40; www.kystmuseene.no; Kirkegata 21; adult/child 80kr/free; ⊙ 10am-4pm Jun–mid-Aug, 9am-3pm Mon-Fri, 11am-2pm Sat & Sun rest of year) Hammerfest's Reconstruction Museum is a great little museum, with particularly thoughtful and sensitive pan-els and captions (each section has a synopsis in English). It recounts the forced evacuation and decimation of the town during the Nazi retreat in 1944; the hardships that its citizens endured through the following winter; and Hammerfest's postwar reconstruction and regeneration.

Salen Hill
VIEWPOINT
(Map p331) For panoramic views over the town, coast and mountains (there's a free pair of binoculars for you to sweep the bay), climb Salen Hill (86m), topped by the Turistua restaurant (p332), a couple of Sami turf huts and a lookout point. The 15-minute uphill walking trail begins at the small park behind the Rådhus.

Meridian Monument HISTORIC SITE
(Meridianstøtta) **FREE** Situated on the Fuglenes peninsula, just across the harbour, is the Meridianstøtta, a marble column commemorating the first survey (1816–52) by Russian scientist Friedrich Georg Wilhelm Struve to determine the arc of the global meridian and thereby calculate the size and shape of the earth. It forms part of a Unesco World Heritage Site known as the Struve Geodetic Arc.

☞ Tours

The tourist office (p333) runs a one-hour tour of the city (in English, German and Norwegian) at 10.45am daily for 285kr per person. It coincides with the arrival of the Hurtigruten ferry and its exact starting time depends on when the boat docks. Book no later than 3pm the day before.

🛏 Sleeping

Camping Storvannet CAMPGROUND $
(☑78 41 10 10; storvannet@yahoo.no; Storvannsveien 103; car/caravan sites 200/230kr, 2-/4-bed cabins 500/600kr; ☺Jun-Sep) Beside a lake and overlooked by a giant apartment complex, this pleasant site, Hammerfest's only decent camping option, is small so book your cabin in advance.

★ Smarthotel Hammerfest HOTEL $$
(Map p331; ☑415 36 500; www.smarthotel.no/hammerfest; Strandgata 32; s/d 950/1050kr;

WHAT'S WITH THE POLAR BEARS?

A wild polar bear hasn't been seen in Hammerfest for thousands of years, and yet polar bears adorn the city's coat of arms, statues of polar bears guard various public buildings and there's even the **Royal & Ancient Polar Bear Society** (p330). Cashing in without cause? Well, not quite. In the 19th and 20th centuries, Hammerfest was a major base for Arctic hunting expeditions to the Norwegian territory of Svalbard (or Spitsbergen as it was better known). Returning expeditions brought back numerous captive polar bears (particularly cubs) and from Hammerfest they were shipped to zoos around the world.

🛜) From the outside, Smarthotel Hammerfest looks like a stylish designer hotel, so it comes as a pleasant surprise to find simple but stylish contemporary rooms at excellent prices within; prices also drop considerably when things are quiet. The rooms with harbour views are best, and there's a decent buffet breakfast included in the price.

Thon Hotel Hammerfest HOTEL $$
(Map p331; ☑78 42 96 00; www.thonhotels.no/hammerfest; Strandgata 2-4; r from 935kr; @🛜) A fairly standard outpost of the reliable Thon chain, this place is right by the water and has bright modern rooms and a good buffet breakfast.

Scandic Hotel Hammerfest HOTEL $$
(Map p331; ☑78 42 57 00; www.scandichotels.no; Sørøygata 15; d 950-1799kr; P@🛜) Constructed in agreeable mellow brick, this hotel has an attractive if somewhat dated bar and lounge, and well-furnished rooms – they're worth it if you get a harbour view, but overpriced if not. Some of the bathrooms are so small that they require a contortionist's flexibility. Its Arctic Menu restaurant, **Skansen Mat og Vinstue** (Map p331; mains 185-355kr; ☺6-11pm), serves excellent local fare.

✕ Eating

Kaikanten PIZZA, PUB FOOD $$
(Map p331; ☑78 41 04 70; www.kaikanten.no; Sjøgata 19; pizza 170-240kr; ☺3pm-1am Sun-Thu, 3pm-3am Fri & Sat) The 'Quayside' is a popular pub that serves pizzas and other snacks. Nautically themed (the backdrop to the bar represents old Hammerfest's dockside, and sail canvases billow beneath the ceiling), it has comfy sofas into which you sink deep. It's the sort of place that works well if you want to have a meal and then not have to move on for drinks.

Turistua CAFE $$
(Map p331; ☑94 15 46 25; Salen Hill; mains 155-275kr; ☺3.30-10pm) From atop Salen Hill (p331), Turistua offers great views over the town and sound. The off-putting name is for a lady named Turi, though *turist* buses often stop here too.

Du Verden Matbar NORWEGIAN, TAPAS $$$
(Map p331; ☑452 50 700; www.duverden.no; Strandgata 32; mains 185-365kr; ☺11am-mid-

night Mon-Sat, 3-9pm Sun) Part of a stylish chain that we've enjoyed across Norway, this brasserie-style place does Norwegian classics, sometimes with a contemporary twist to suit the modern surrounds, as well as tapas. It's inside the Smarthotel Hammerfest (p332).

ⓘ Information

Tourist Office (Map p331; ☑78 41 21 85; www.visithammerfest.no; Hamnegata 3; ⊙8am-6pm Jun & Jul, 9am-4pm Mon-Fri & 10am-2pm Sat & Sun Aug-May; 🛜) Has free wi-fi and rents out electric bikes for 159/399kr per hour/day.

ⓘ Getting There & Away

Buses (Map p331; Hamnegata) run to/from Alta (335kr, 2¼ hours, two daily), Honningsvåg (468kr, 3½ hours, one to two daily) and Karasjok (450kr, 4¼ hours, twice daily except Saturday), with one service extending on to Kirkenes (1155kr, 10¼ hours) via Tana Bru (810kr, eight hours) four times weekly.

The **Hurtigruten coastal ferry** (Map p331; Hurtigrutenkai, Hamnegata) stops in Hammerfest for 1½ hours in each direction. A Hurigruten hop to Tromsø (11 hours) or Honningsvåg (five hours) makes a comfortable alternative to a long bus journey.

There's a **taxi office** (Map p331; ☑78 41 12 34; www.hammerfesttaxi.no) opposite the tourist office.

Nordkapp & Magerøya

POP 3300

Magerøya is a large island, and has the honour of being the furthest point north that you can travel by land in Norway. At its northernmost tip sits Nordkapp, which is a place of pilgrimage for hundreds of thousands of tourists every year. Despite Magerøya lying so far north, its waters remain ice-free year-round, thanks to the Gulf Stream, meaning that cruise ships (and the Hurtigruten ferry) make regular stops here.

🏃 Activities

North Cape Experience ADVENTURE SPORTS (☑913 11 557; www.thenorthcape-experience.com; Oterveien 1, Skarsvåg) Based in Skarsvåg, this operator runs king-crab safaris, wildlife-watching boat trips and trips to Knivskjelodden (p335).

🛏 Sleeping

Kirkeporten Camping CAMPGROUND $ (☑78 47 52 33; www.kirkeporten.no; Storvannsveien 2, Skarsvåg; per person/campsite 50/155kr, cabins 460-970kr; ⊙May-Oct) Just outside the hamlet of Skarsvåg, this welcoming campsite is a favourite of British adventure tour groups. Its claim to be the world's northernmost camping stands up; there is a rival on Svalbard but it doesn't have cabins. The cosy cafe does reindeer and a fresh-fish daily special, as well as soup and pizzas.

Nordkapp Camping CAMPGROUND $ (☑78 47 33 77; www.nordkappcamping.no; E69, Skipsfjorden; per adult/child/site 50/25/160kr, d 710kr, cabins 610-1495kr; ⊙May–mid-Sep; 🛜) The well-equipped communal kitchen, friendly service and variety of lodging options more than compensate for the stark location of this campground, the nearest to Honningsvåg.

Scandic Nordkapp HOTEL $$ (☑78 47 72 60; www.scandichotels.no; Skipsfjorden; r from 1099kr; 🅿🛜) Out along the road to Nordkapp, this full-service wilderness hotel has the feel of a ski lodge and is wonderfully silent in the evening. Rooms are simpler than others in the Scandic chain, but they're comfortable and there's an on-site restaurant.

ⓘ Getting There & Away

Getting to Magerøya means getting to Honningsvåg, which is reached via the Hurtigruten coastal ferry, buses (to/from Alta and Hammerfest) and the pretty E6 road (beware reindeer if driving).

❶ Getting Around

BUS

Between mid-May and late August, a local bus (adult/child 545/295kr, 45 minutes) runs daily at 11am and 9.30pm between Honningsvåg and Nordkapp. It sets off back from the cape at 1.15pm and 12.45am (so that you can take in the midnight sun at precisely midnight). From 1 June to 15 August, there's a supplementary run at 5pm, though this returns at 6.15pm, giving you barely half an hour at Nordkapp unless you want to hang around for the service that returns at 12.45am. Check precise departure times with the **tourist office** (p336). Ticket prices include the Nordkapp entry fee.

If you're on a budget, carefully read the terms of any inclusive tours, which probably charge considerably more for similar services.

CAR & MOTORCYCLE

Until the blacktop road to Nordkapp was constructed in the mid-1950s, all access was by boat. Nowadays the route winds across a rocky (and often snowbound) plateau past herds of grazing reindeer. Depending upon snow conditions, it's open to private traffic from April to mid-October. In other months, ring the tourist office if the weather looks dicey.

A taxi to/from Nordkapp from Honningsvåg costs at least 1500kr, including an hour of waiting at the cape – plus the Nordkapp admission charge per passenger.

Nordkapp

Nordkapp is the one attraction in northern Norway that everybody seems to visit. It is a tourist trap, however – billing itself as the northernmost point in continental Europe, it sucks in visitors by the busload – some 200,000 every year.

Nearer to the North Pole than to Oslo, Nordkapp sits at latitude 71°10'21" N, where the sun never drops below the horizon from mid-May to the end of July. Long before other Europeans took an interest, it was a sacrificial site for the Sami, who believed it had special powers.

---

❶ NORDKAPP ENTRY

To reach the 'tip of the continent' – by car, by bike, on a bus or by walking in – you have to pay a toll (adult/child/family 270/95/635kr) at the final entrance to Nordkapp. This allows unlimited entry over two days.

Yes, it's a rip-off, but Nordkapp is a stunning, hauntingly beautiful place. Even after the novelty wears off, it's the view that thrills the most. In reasonable weather you can gaze down at the wild surf more than 300m below, watch the mists roll in and simply enjoy the moment.

History

Richard Chancellor, the English explorer who drifted here in 1553 in search of the Northeast Passage, first gave it the name North Cape. Much later, after a highly publicised visit by King Oscar II in 1873, Nordkapp became a pilgrimage spot for Norwegians. It's also, bizarrely, one for Thais, thanks to a visit by King Chulalongkorn in 1907.

◉ Sights

Nordkapp Visitor Centre   VISITOR CENTRE
(☏78 47 68 60; www.visitnordkapp.net; ⊙11am-1am mid-May–mid-Aug, 11am-10pm mid-end Aug, 11am-3pm Sep–mid-May) Presiding over a scene of considerable natural beauty is this visitor centre, a vast bunker of a place, topped by a giant, intrusive golf ball. Within you'll find a detailed account of WWII naval actions off the cape; a cafeteria and restaurant; the Grotten bar, with views of Europe's end through its vast glass wall; a one-room Thai museum; the St Johannes chapel ('the world's northernmost ecumenical chapel'); a post office (for that all-important Nordkapp postmark); and an appropriately vast souvenir shop.

A 120-degree five-screen theatre shows an enjoyable 17-minute panoramic film.

🛏 Sleeping

Astoundingly, you can spend the night in your motor home or caravan at Nordkapp itself (fill up on water and make sure your back-up electricity is all charged though, because you won't find these resources here). Otherwise, you'll need to find accommodation elsewhere on Magerøya.

❶ Getting There & Away

A good road, the 36km-long E69, connects Honningsvåg with Nordkapp. In winter you may need to travel in a convoy behind a snowplough.

Buses, both tour and the public variety, connect the two – ask **Honningsvåg's tourist office** (p336) for advice on what's leaving next.

HIKING TO KNIVSKJELODDEN

The continent's real northernmost point, Knivskjelodden, is mercifully inaccessible to vehicles and devoid of tat. Lying about 3km west of Nordkapp, it sticks its finger a full 1457m further northwards. You can hike to the tip of this promontory from a marked car park 6km south of the Nordkapp toll booth – the trails are likely to be snowbound (and hence impassable) deep into May and possibly as early as September.

The 9km track, waymarked with giant cairns, isn't difficult despite some ups and downs, but it's best to wear hiking boots since it can be squelchy. When you get to the tall beehive-shaped obelisk at latitude 71°11'08" N, down at sea level, sign the guest book. Should you wish, note down your reference number from the book and you can buy – nothing but the hike comes free on this island – a certificate (50kr) authenticating your achievement from **Nordkapp Camping** (p333) at Skipsfjorden or Honningsvåg's **tourist office** (p336). Allow five to six hours for the return-trip hike.

Honningsvåg

POP 2415

Deep in Norway's Arctic North, tiny Honningsvåg is the gateway to Nordkapp. For much of the time, it's a quiet place strung out around a harbour with some cod-drying racks along the shoreline. But it gets overwhelmed by visitors stocking up on supplies and souvenirs whenever a cruise ship (or the Hurtigruten ferry) docks, which happens especially often in summer. At such times, it's a chaotic, unappealing place brimful of jostling hordes.

◉ Sights

Nordkapp Museum   MUSEUM
(📞78 47 72 00; www.nordkappmuseet.no; Fiskeriveien 4; adult/child 50/10kr; ⊙10am-7pm mid-Jun–mid-Aug, 11am-3pm Mon-Fri rest of year) Honningsvåg's Nordkapp Museum, next to the Hurtigruten dock, illustrates the impact of early visitors to the cape, the hard days in the immediate aftermath of WWII and the daily life of a town that, until the advent of tourism, lived primarily from the sea.

🏃 Activities & Tours

Ask at Honningsvåg's tourist office for a list of possible activities, many of which are run by **71° Nord** (📞472 89 320; www.71-nord.no; Holmen 6c) or North Cape Experience (p333) – these include year-round king-crab safaris, winter activities such as snowmobile expeditions, and summer ocean rafting, quad-biking and deep-sea fishing.

The tourist office (p336) organises 1½-hour guided walking tours of the town (adult/child 99/50kr) at noon from June to late August; no reservations are required.

They also offer guided bus transfers to/from Nordkapp (650kr). Ask also about the guided walks (475kr per person) led by a local fisherman in Skarsvåg.

🛏 Sleeping

Scandic Hotel Bryggen   HOTEL $$$
(📞78 47 72 50; www.scandichotels.no; Vågen 1; r from 1649kr; 🅿🛜) There are two Scandic hotel options in Honningsvåg, and the Bryggen is the newer. It has tidy, contemporary rooms that could be a little larger, but they're at the quieter end of town and have superior views.

Scandic Hotel Honningsvåg   HOTEL $$$
(📞78 47 72 20; www.scandichotels.no; Nordkappgata 4; r from 1390kr; 🛜) The big plus of this hotel, reliable as all others in this Norway-wide chain, is its position, right beside the docks. **Grillen**, its à-la-carte restaurant, is well worth a visit, whether you're staying at the hotel or elsewhere.

🍴 Eating

Arctic Sans   CAFE $$
(📞415 11 351; Storgata 22; mains 125-285kr; ⊙10am-8pm Mon-Thu, 10am-10pm Fri, 11am-10pm Sat, 1-7pm Sun) Great coffee is where you suspect its passion lies, but Arctic Sans also serves up crispy cod tongues, creamy fish soup and chicken wings. It's far enough away from the ferry docks for it to be a little more relaxed than other places further around the harbour.

Corner   CAFE $$
(📞78 47 63 40; www.corner.no; Fiskerveien 2a; mains 195-275kr; ⊙10am-11pm) Corner serves the usual pizzas and snacks, but also offers great seafood such as crispy cod tongues or,

GUARANTEEING A BUS SEAT

Should you see a cruise ship (or the Hurtigruten ferry) heading for port, rush to the **tourist office** (p336) to reserve your bus journey to Nordkapp. Travellers tell horror tales of scrimmages, arguments and bus drivers simply driving on by once these monsters of the waves disgorge their masses.

more conventionally, fried fillet of cod. It also has plenty of meaty mains and a bar with an inviting outdoor terrace overlooking the water.

King Crab House SEAFOOD $$$
(☎458 75 330; www.kingcrabhouse.no; Sjøgata 6; mains 280-320kr; ⊙noon-10pm daily mid-Jun–mid-Aug, shorter hours rest of year) King crabs are the centrepiece here, but they also do other local seafood and a range of tapas. We enjoyed the pan-fried cod with king-crab risotto and white-wine sauce. They also have smaller servings for those with lesser appetites.

Drinking & Nightlife

★Artico BAR
(☎78 47 15 00; www.articoicebar.com; Sjøgata 1a; ⊙11am-4pm Apr–mid-May, 10am-7pm late May, 10am-9pm Jun–mid-Aug, 10am-7.30pm late Aug, 11am-3pm Sep) For a shiver in summer and a sense of how Nordkapp must hit the senses in winter, visit Artico (adult/child 139/40kr), one of Norway's original ice bars. Owner, Spaniard José Milares, a polar photographer and adventurer, talks with passion about the shapes, bubbles and inadvertent abstract art in the pure ice that he garners afresh each season.

The kids can crawl into an igloo that he constructs each year.

Information

Honningsvåg's **tourist office** (☎78 47 70 30; www.nordkapp.no; Fiskeriveien 4; ⊙10am-10pm Mon-Fri, noon-8pm Sat & Sun mid-Jun–mid-Aug, 11am-2pm Mon-Fri rest of the yr; 📶), beside the harbour, has free wi-fi that tends to crash when the cruises arrive, as well as information on visiting Nordkapp.

Getting There & Away

There are a few options for getting to and from Nordkapp and Magerøya:

- The Hurtigruten coastal ferry calls by Honningsvåg, and its 3½-hour northbound stop allows passengers a quick buzz up to Nordkapp.
- From mid-May to late August, a local bus (adult/child 545/295kr, 45 minutes) runs daily at 11am and 9.30pm between Honningsvåg and Nordkapp.
- An express bus connects Honningsvåg with Alta (520kr, four hours, one to two daily) and there's also a run to/from Hammerfest (468kr, 3½ hours, one to two daily).
- If you're driving, the road approach from the E6 is via Olderfjord, where the E69 branches north.

Kamøyvær

POP 70

A short detour from the E69 between Honningsvåg and Nordkapp brings you to this tiny, sheltered fishing hamlet, its pastel-shaded cottages and cabins encircling the small harbour. It's a place to escape the crowds, with a fine hotel and even an art gallery.

Sights

Gallery East of the Sun GALLERY
(☎78 47 51 37; www.evart.no; Risfjordveien 5, Arran; ⊙noon-9pm mid-May–mid-Aug) FREE Call by the Gallery East of the Sun, which features the sinuous shapes, bright canvases and intriguing collages of German artist Eva Schmutterer.

Sleeping

Nordkapp Arran Hotell HOTEL $$
(☎75 40 20 85; www.arran.as; s 750-980kr, d 1000-1250kr; ⊙mid-May–Aug; P📶) Nordkapp Arran Hotell has 44 rooms spread over three quayside buildings. The Sami family who run it bake their own bread and the menu here is always the freshest of fish, hauled from the seas off Magerøya. To vary the cuisine it also offers a reindeer special.

Getting There & Away

The only way to get to Kamøyvær is with your own wheels.

Gjesvær

POP 160

It's a stunning drive to the remote fishing village of Gjesvær, 34km northwest of Honningsvåg and 21km off the Honningsvåg–Nordkapp road, where you'll find two excellent birdwatching outfits. Rolling tundra, punctuated by dark pools and cropped by reindeer, gives way to a stark, rocky landscape, and then a sudden view of low *skerries* (rocky islets) and the Gjesværstappan islands.

🏃 Activities

★ Stappan Sjøprodukter
BIRDWATCHING, FISHING

(☑ 950 37 722; www.stappan.com; Gjesvær; ☺ Jun-Aug, rest of year by reservation) Fisherman Roald Berg, who built the Stappan Sjøprodukter complex with his own hands, will take you birdwatching (adult/child 650/475kr) in *Aurora,* his small boat (two departures daily). Or join him for a 2½-hour fishing expedition (3000kr, maximum four passengers). He also organises northern-lights safaris in winter and king-crab safaris year-round.

He also has a restaurant and two well-furnished apartments (1000kr for two people, plus 100kr per person for bedding and towels).

★ Bird Safari
BIRDWATCHING, FISHING

(☑ 416 13 983; www.birdsafari.com; Gjesvær; adult/youth/child 675/350kr/free; ☺ early Apr-late Sep) Bird Safari sails two to three times daily between June and late August to the bird colony on the Gjesværstappan islands. There are an estimated three *million* nesting birds, including colonies of puffins, skuas, razorbills, kittiwakes, gannets and white-tailed eagles. Bird Safari also has simple seafront accommodation and can also arrange fishing.

ℹ️ Getting There & Away

Apart from one daily bus from Honningsvåg, the only way to reach Gjesvær is with your own vehicle – the village is 34km northwest of Honningsvåg, signposted off the Nordkapp road.

Lakselv

POP 2258

The name of the plain fishing village of Lakselv, at the head of long, slim Porsangerfjord, means 'salmon stream', which reflects its main appeal for Norwegian holidaymakers. Most travellers fill up with petrol, then drive right on by, but if you've always wanted to try your hand at salmon fishing or would like to ride an Icelandic horse, you might want to plan to stay a little longer.

🏃 Activities

★ Saarela Gård - Ridesenter
HORSE RIDING, FISHING

(☑ 958 42 071; www.saarela.no; Saarelaveien 1; 1hr group/private riding per person 200/300kr) This horse-riding centre is reason enough to come to Lakselv. These are horse rides with a certain cachet, using Icelandic horses, the so-called 'horses of the Vikings', for rides into the scenic country south of Lakselv or along the fjord beaches. Trips last an hour or days, depending on your level of interest and expertise. They also organise salmon fishing.

🛏️ Sleeping & Eating

Lakselv Vandrerhjem
HOSTEL $

(☑ 907 45 342; www.hihostels.no/no/hostels/lakselv; dm 400kr, s/d with bathroom 500/600kr, cabins with bathroom & kitchen 750kr; ☺ mid-Jun–mid-Aug) This HI-affiliated hostel is in a secluded site amid trees and surrounded by small lakes. It makes a great base for gentle strolls and has self-catering facilities. Follow the E6 southwards from Lakselv for 6km, then take a dirt road to the left for 2km.

Lakselv Hotell
HOTEL $$$

(☑ 78 46 54 00; www.lakselvhotell.no; Karasjokveien; s/d 1195/1495kr; P 🛜) Just 2km south of town beside the E6, this hotel has cosy rooms, hilltop fjord views, a sauna that's free for guests and a restaurant that does a good summertime dinner buffet (325kr). Guests can also rent bikes (120kr per day).

Åstedet Café & Bistro
CAFE $$

(☑ 78 46 13 77; Georg Bjørklis vei 1; mains around 150kr; ☺ noon-10pm) Both pub and cafe-restaurant, Åstedet Café & Bistro serves a range of meaty mains plus the usual burgers, pizzas and salads.

ℹ️ Information

Tourist Office (☑ 406 33 386; www.visitporsanger.no; off E6; ☺ 10am-6pm mid-Jun–mid-Aug) Friendly office with a few brochures.

ℹ️ Getting There & Away

Lakselv's **North Cape Airport**, an important link for central Finnmark, has up to three daily flights to/from Tromsø.

In summer, a daily bus running between Nordkapp and Rovaniemi via Ivalo (both in Finland) passes by.

Within Finnmark, services running Sunday to Friday include the following:

Alta (399kr, 3¼ hours, four daily)

Honningsvåg (390kr, three hours, three daily)

Karasjok (195kr, 1¼ hours, three daily)

Stabbursnes

At Stabbursnes, 16km north of Lakselv and beside one of the most attractive sectors of Porsangerfjord, there are a couple of important protected areas. The Stabbursnes Naturhus og Museum and visitor centre serves both the Stabbursdalen National Park and the Stabbursnes Nature Reserve.

Sights

Stabbursdalen National Park NATIONAL PARK

No roads cross through the 747 sq km of Stabbursdalen National Park, which offers a spectacular glacial canyon and excellent hiking in the world's most northerly pine forest. The park is a haven for elk (moose), wolverine and the Eurasian lynx, although you'll be lucky to spot the last two species.

Stabbursnes Naturhus og Museum MUSEUM

(☎78 46 47 65; www.stabbursnes.no; adult/concession/child 80/60kr/free; ⏲9am-8pm mid-Jun–mid-Aug, shorter hours rest of yr) The Stabbursnes Naturhus og Museum serves both the Stabbursdalen National Park and Stabbursnes Nature Reserve. It sells field guides, maps and fishing permits and has a well-mounted exhibition about the birds, animals and geology of the interior high plateau, river valleys and coast. It also serves as a visitor centre for the park and reserve – entry to that section is free.

Stabbursnes Nature Reserve NATURE RESERVE

The Stabbursnes Nature Reserve extends over the wetlands and mudflats at the estuary of the Stabburselva. Birdwatchers come to observe the many species of duck, geese, divers and sandpipers that rest in the area while migrating between the Arctic and more temperate zones. Ask the nature centre for a full list of birds recorded in the reserve and their seasons.

Sleeping

Stabbursdalen Resort CAMPGROUND $

(☎78 46 47 60; www.stabbursdalen.no; car/caravan sites 200/300kr, cabins 500-3500kr, apt 1100kr; ⏲mid-May–Sep) Beside the salmon-rich Stabburselva and packed with gumbooted fisherfolk in quest of 'The Big One' (the cafe's TV relays real-time images from the riverbed), this extensive campsite enjoys a beautiful position. Facilities, however, are stretched in high season.

Stabbursdalen Lodge LODGE $$

(☎909 16 485; www.stabbursdalenlodge.no; off E6; cabins from 1600kr; P Wi-Fi) Appealing, self-catering log cabins that each have two bathrooms and sleep eight people – this could just be the perfect base for those in a group who are planning to stay a few days.

Getting There & Away

Buses along the E6 between Alta and Lakselv drop you at the gateway to Stabbursnes, but it's a lot easier if you have your own vehicle as most of the access points and the visitor centre are some distance apart.

WORTH A TRIP

KONGSFJORD GJESTEHUS

Gorgeous, deliciously remote guesthouse **Kongsfjord Gjestehus** (☎78 98 10 00; www.kongsfjord-gjestehus.no; Veines; s 770-1370kr, d 990-1560kr; P Wi-Fi) has 18 beautifully restored rooms, with lovely wooden walls and tastefully chosen furnishings, many with a marine-blue hue. It's a wonderful place, 100km beyond Tana Bru, to spend a week away from the world. There's excellent birdwatching around here, too. Ase and Margherita are fine hosts.

EASTERN FINNMARK

Welcome to one of the most remote corners of Europe. For those who make it out here, Eastern Finnmark, heartland of the Eastern Sami culture, has some charming coastal villages and a unique frontier history that encompasses Finns, explorers and wartime destruction. Terrific birdwatching, deliciously empty coastlines and villages where you might just be the only visitor – get ready to explore. Kirkenes has few sights, but plenty of activities to enjoy in both summer and winter.

SAMI MUSEUMS

Ceavccageadge (⊙11am-4pm mid-Jun–late Aug) At Mortensnes, on the E75, about 15km east of Varangerbotn, you can stroll towards the shore amid traces of early Sami culture. At the western end, past burial sites, the remains of homesteads and a reconstructed turf hut, is the namesake *ceavccageadge*, a pillar standing near the water, which was smeared with cod-liver oil to ensure luck while fishing. On a hill to the east the Bjørnstein, a rock resembling a bear, was revered by early Sami inhabitants.

Varanger Sami Museum (Várjjat Sámi Musea; ☑ 952 62 155; www.varjjat.org; adult/child 80kr/free; ⊙10am-6pm mid-Jun–mid-Aug, 10am-3pm Mon-Fri rest of year) In Varangerbotn, close to where the E6 meets the E75 17km east of Tana Bru, this is a fun, informative and hi-tech display about Sami life and culture, with Sami-related temporary exhibitions and artwork by contemporary Sami artists. Outside is a small, permanent, open-air display of Sami turf huts, fishing equipment and domestic life.

Tana Bru

POP 668

Tiny Tana Bru takes its name from the bridge over the great Tana River, the only one for miles up- and downstream. It's all about salmon fishing here, but the pleasant setting, a couple of decent places to eat and an excellent silversmith shop make it worth a stopover on your way through.

🏃 Activities

Here, on one of Europe's best salmon reaches, locals use the technique of constructing barrages to obstruct the upstream progress of the fish; the natural barrage at Storfossen falls, about 30km upstream, is one of Norway's finest fishing spots. You'll need good luck to pull out anything to compare with the record 36kg specimen once played ashore here. Elva Hotel can get you kitted out and provide advice.

🛏 Sleeping & Eating

Elva Hotel   HOTEL $$$
(☑78 92 82 22; www.elvahotel.no; Silbageaidnu 10; campsites 250kr, s/d 1400/1850kr; ⊙mid-Jun–mid-Aug; P🐾) You'll find a campground, comfortable – though overpriced – rooms, a restaurant and bar at Elva Hotel, a convenient staging post in a classic wooden building at the junction of the Rv98 and E6/E75. Hotel rates include a light evening meal. It's also the best place in town for organising salmon-fishing outings.

Elvekanten Spiseri   NORWEGIAN $$
(☑78 92 82 22; Silbageaidnu 10; mains from 155kr; ⊙noon-10pm) Attached to the Elva Hotel, this simple place has one very clear and appealing calling card – most days, they serve local salmon (from 175kr), usually oven-baked, fresh from the river.

🛍 Shopping

Tana Gull og Sølvsmie   JEWELLERY
(☑78 92 80 06; www.tanagullogsolv.com; off Rådhusveien; ⊙9am-6pm Mon-Fri, 10am-4pm Sat, noon-4pm Sun late Jun–early Aug, shorter hours rest of year) Tana Gull og Sølvsmie was established in 1976 as eastern Finnmark's first gold- and silversmith. Andreas Lautz now creates some very fine gold, silver and bronze jewellery, inspired by traditional Sami designs. The shop also displays items such as quality textiles, ceramics and glassware, as well as traditional Sami knives and a few fossils.

ℹ Getting There & Away

There are daily buses to/from Kirkenes (2½ hours) and Vadsø (1¼ hours). Westbound, the Kirkenes–Alta bus passes through four times weekly.

Vadsø

POP 5116

If the sun's out, there's much to recommend this remote town. The birdwatching here is first rate, the surrounding country is rather beautiful and there are some good places to stay and eat. Come to Vadsø when it's grey and overcast and the wind is howling, however, and you'll wonder if you've stumbled across the border into Siberia. It's not up to you, of course, which Vadsø you encounter, but trust us, it's worth

NESSEBY CHURCH

Along one of the prettiest stretches of the E75 (which is a designated National Scenic Route; see www.nasjonale turistveger.no), the lovely white church of Nesseby sits far out on the shoreline against the dramatic backdrop of distant mountains. The church itself was built in 1858 and was one of the few in Finnmark to survive the ravages of WWII. The church is signposted off the main road, 0.8km along a quiet road. Alongside the church is the small **Nesseby Nature Reserve**, beloved by birders.

hanging around until the sun comes out if you can.

Sights

Luftskipsmasta   HISTORIC SITE

This oil-rig-shaped airship mast on Vadsø island was built in the mid-1920s as an anchor and launch site for airborne expeditions to the polar regions. The expedition of Roald Amundsen, Umberto Nobile and Lincoln Ellsworth, which floated via the North Pole to Alaska in the airship *Norge N-1,* first used it in April 1926.

Two years later it was the launch site for Nobile's airship, *Italia,* which attempted to repeat the journey but crashed on Svalbard. Amundsen – together with 12 steamships, 13 planes and 1500 men – joined the rescue expedition and disappeared in the attempt, becoming a national martyr as well as a hero. It's well worth the breezy 600m stroll across the grass flats to savour the rich variety of aquatic birds in the small lake just beyond.

Activities

Vadsø is a big draw for birdwatchers, especially in early summer when they come to see Steller's eider; one even stayed for the 2017 summer. Vadsø Fjordhotell (p340) is the place to start for birders – the knowledgeable staff are all over recent sightings and have plenty of useful brochures. **Arntzen Arctic Adventures** (☑907 60 412; www.varanger.info; Fossesvingen 25) is also excellent, and has its own hides and bird park.

Festivals & Events

Varangerfestivalen   MUSIC

(☑982 55 600; www.varangerfestivalen.no; ☺Aug) One of northern Norway's oldest music festivals, Varangerfestivalen sees jazz, rock and world music come to Vadsø.

Sleeping

Vestre Jakobselv Camping   CAMPGROUND $

(☑78 95 60 64; www2.vj-camping.no; Lilledalsveien; per tent/site 100/200kr, cabins 550-2000kr, r 500-1000kr; ☺May-Sep) Rooms and cabins are very reasonably priced at Vadsø's nearest campsite, 17km west of town. Only 200m from a fast-flowing salmon river, it's a popular venue for fisherfolk.

★Vadsø Fjordhotell   HOTEL $$

(☑450 60 345; www.vadsoefjordhotell.no; Brugata 2; s/d from 995/1195kr; 🅿🛜) With staff who are extremely knowledgeable about local birding (it's also known as Base Camp for Birders) and located close to the trailhead for the Luftskipsmasta, this friendly place has simple but comfy rooms, most of which look out over the water. Breakfast is ample and prices drop the longer you stay. Campervans are also allowed to overnight here.

Scandic Hotel Vadsø   HOTEL $$

(☑78 95 25 50; www.scandichotels.no; Oscarsgate 4; r 1049-1455kr; 🅿@🛜) Plumb in the town centre, the friendly Scandic Hotel Vadsø has spruce rooms with parquet flooring. Complete with free sauna and minigym, it represents Vadsø's most upmarket choice.

★Ekkerøy Holiday House   APARTMENT $$$

(☑908 91 558; post@ekkeroy.net; Fv321, Ekkerøy; apt from 1490kr) Beloved by birders and those looking for the warmth of a converted wooden Varanger home, this fine place is 15km east of Vadsø and well worth considering as a base for the area, whether you're here for the birdwatching or not.

Eating

Hildonen   CAFE $

(☑78 95 15 06; Centrum 8; snacks & light mains 34-77kr; ☺7am-4pm Mon-Fri, 9am-3pm Sat) The aroma of warm bread and sweet cakes draws you into this bakery and cafe, hugely popular with locals for its pastries, focaccia, baguettes and paninis.

Opticom Kaffebar
INTERNATIONAL $$

(78 95 33 00; Tollbugata 9; mains 149-215kr; ⊙11am-midnight Mon-Thu, 11am-2am Fri & Sat, 3-11pm Sun) Vadsø's coolest venue serves great coffee, has a long list of alcoholic drinks and serves up open sandwiches, burgers and wraps to well-dressed locals who like the slick decor and smooth music.

Oscar Mat og Vinhus
NORWEGIAN $$$

(78 95 25 50; www.scandichotels.no; Oscarsgate 4, Scandic Hotel Vadsø; mains 185-395kr; ⊙6-10.30pm) Oscar Mat og Vinhus, the Scandic Hotel Vadsø restaurant, is the town's finest, offering king crab in all its varieties (natural, marinated in garlic...) to go with its regular cast of reliable Norwegian specialities, including reindeer. There are simpler burgers for those counting their kroner.

❶ Information

Vadsø Tourist Office (📞 450 01 875; www. varanger.com; Tollbugata 9-11, Frivillighets-sentralen; ⊙10am-6pm Mon-Fri, 10am-4pm Sat & Sun mid-Jun–mid-Aug) Open in summer only but handy for maps and moderately useful info on museums and the wider Varanger area.

❶ Getting There & Away

Vadsø is a stop only on the northbound Hurti-gruten coastal ferry, which heads for Kirkenes at 8am. There are at least two buses daily to/from Tana Bru (1¼ hours) and Vardø (1½ hours).

Vardø

POP 1893

Vardø qualifies as Norway's easternmost town and is well off the beaten track for all but the most diehard travellers. Although this butterfly-shaped island is connected to the mainland by the 2.9km-long Ishavstun-nelen (Arctic Ocean tunnel), locals maintain that theirs is the only 'mainland' Norwegian town lying within the Arctic climatic zone (its average temperature is below 10°C). Once a stronghold of trade with the Russian Pomors, it's now a major fishing port and home to many Russian and, strangely, Sri Lankan immigrants. It's not Norway's pret-tiest town, but it does have a certain wind-swept Siberia-esque appeal.

And getting here is half the fun: it's a pancake-flat 75km drive between Vadsø and Vardø, along a designated National Tourist Route, but the ribbon of road has a lonely charm as it threads its way between shoreline, hardy grasses and tough, low shrubs.

◉ Sights

★Steilneset Memorial
MONUMENT

(⊙24hr, guided visits 11am mid-Jun–mid-Aug) This stunning monument, a collaboration between French artist Louis Bourgeois and Swiss architect Peter Zumthor, is dedicated to the 91 people executed for witchcraft and sorcery in 17th-century Vardø. Zumthor's beautiful 125m-long memorial hall has one illuminated window for each of the victims, while Bourgeois' installation is a chair sur-rounded by five gas flames and seven oval mirrors. The site is carefully chosen – it is believed that many of the executions took place near here.

Vardøhus Festning
FORT

(916 88 558; Festningsgate 20; 50kr; ⊙8am-9pm mid-May–Aug, 10am-6pm rest of year) The star-shaped Vardøhus Fortress – yes, of course, it's the world's most northerly – was constructed in 1737 by King Christian VI. For a fortress, it's painted in unusually gentle fairy-tale colours. Stroll around the flower-festooned bastions, past turf-roofed buildings and Russian cannons after you've paid the admission fee, either at the guard office or by dropping it into the WWII sea mine that guards the entrance.

🏃 Activities

Hornøya
BIRDWATCHING

(return 200kr) In summer there are regular boat trips from the port to the island of Hornøya, to see its picturesque lighthouse and teeming bird cliffs. To be all alone after the last shuttle pulls out, reserve one of only three beds at the lighthouse (p342).

WITCHCRAFT IN VARDØ

Between 1621 and 1692, around 91 Vardø women were accused of witchcraft and burned; a sign and flag at Kristian IV gate 24 commemorates the site, and the exceptional **Steilneset Memorial** pays tribute to their memory. On **Domen**, a hill about 2km south of town on the mainland, is the cave where they were supposed to have held their satanic rites and secret rendezvous with the devil.

Wild Varanger WILDLIFE WATCHING, SNORKELLING
(☑ 992 49 515; www.wildvaranger.com; Havnestien 12, Kiberg) This experienced operator can arrange snorkelling with guillemots, deep-sea fishing, birdwatching, excursions to the bird cliffs of Hornøya, sea rafting and king-crab safaris out of Vardø.

🛏 Sleeping & Eating

Kiberg Bed & Boat GUESTHOUSE $
(☑ 413 28 679; Havnegata 37, Kiberg; s/d with shared bathroom 420/575kr) In Kiberg, 13km south of Vardø, genial owner Ronny Larsen runs these renovated fisherfolk's sleeping quarters, with lounge and well-equipped guest kitchen. Rooms are trim and tidy and there's no better place in Norway to suck on the limbs of a giant king crab (around 375kr). Ronny can organise four-hour fishing trips and birdwatching walks. Reception is open between 6pm and midnight.

Hornøya Lighthouse BOUTIQUE HOTEL $$
(☑ 78 98 72 75; per person 550kr) To be all alone overnight out on the island of Hornøya, reserve one of only three beds at the lighthouse. It's no frills but wonderfully evocative and listening to the wind howl all night (while staying warm) is true immersion.

ABC Thai THAI $$
(☑ 78 94 46 00; Kristian IV gate 3; mains from 150kr; ☺ noon-11pm Feb-Nov) This place might look simple but it punches above its weight. Order a dish of tasty, authentic Thai cooking in – you've guessed it – mainland Europe's most northerly Thai restaurant. Accompany this with one of the 36 kinds of bottled beer

on offer, including equally authentic Thai Singha beer.

🍷 Drinking & Nightlife

Nordpol Kro PUB
(www.nordpolkro.no; Kaigata 21; ☺ 10am-3pm Mon, 10am-3pm & 8pm-midnight Tue & Thu, 10am-3pm & 8pm-3am Fri, 8.30pm-3am Sat, 8pm-midnight Sun) Dating from 1858, with wooden boards and antique bric-a-brac, Nordpol Kro lays good claim to being northern Norway's oldest eatery. Your friendly landlord, Bjørn Bredesen, has what must be just about anywhere's most comprehensive collection of beer mats. Pick the right night and you can enjoy live music too.

ℹ Information

Vardø has a seasonal **tourist office** (☑ 78 98 69 07; www.varanger.com; Havnepromenaden; ☺ 9am-5pm Mon-Fri, 2-5pm Sat & Sun Jun-Aug).

ℹ Getting There & Away

Vardø is a stop on the Hurtigruten coastal ferry route. Buses follow the scenic seaside route between Vadsø and Vardø (1½ hours) at least twice daily and two services run to Kirkenes (3½ hours) daily except Saturday.

Kirkenes

POP 3498
This is it: you're as far east as Cairo, further east than most of Finland, a mere 15km from the border with Russia – and at the end of the line for the Hurtigruten coastal ferry. It's also road's end for the E6, the highway that runs all the way down to Oslo.

WORTH A TRIP

HAMNINGBERG

A warmly recommended 88km return trip northwards along the coast from Vardø brings you to the tiny, semi-abandoned, timber-built settlement of Hamningberg.

The single-lane road runs through some of northern Norway's most fascinating geology: inky tarns, copses of scrubby bushes clinging to the meagre topsoil for dear life, flecks of snow even in late July and looming, lichen-covered eroded stone pillars, the remnants of sedimentary layers turned on end. En route, you'll pass reindeer herds and several sandy beaches. Save the bucket-and-spading, though, until the return journey when, 7.3km south of Hamningberg, you can walk to the broadest beach through the small nature reserve of **Sandfjordneset**, with its protected sand dunes set back from the shoreline.

What makes the village special is that, being so remote, it was saved from the general destruction of the Nazi retreat in WWII. Only one house was destroyed – and that by a Russian bomber. The rest, abandoned in the 1960s except for summer visitors, still stand as living reminders of what was once one of eastern Finnmark's largest fishing villages. Here where the road ends, there's a small summertime cafe.

Kirkenes

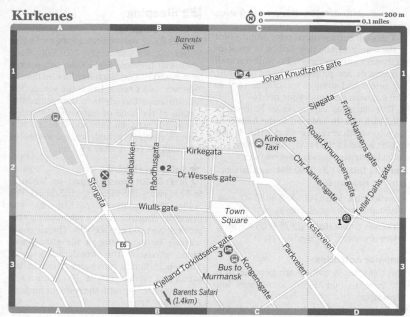

THE FAR NORTH KIRKENES

This tiny, nondescript place, anticlimactic for many, has a distinct frontier feel. You'll see street signs in Norwegian and Cyrillic script and hear Russian spoken by trans-border visitors and fishermen, who enjoy better prices for their catch here than in their home ports further to the east.

The town reels with around 100,000 visitors every year, most stepping off the Hurtigruten to spend a couple of hours in the town before travelling onward. But you should linger a while here, not primarily for the town's sake but to take one of the many excursions and activities on offer.

⦿ Sights

Andersgrotta   HISTORIC BUILDING
(Map p343; ☑ 78 97 05 40; www.kirkenessnow hotel.com; Tellef Dahls gate; adult/child 200/100kr; ⊙ visits 12.30pm Jun-Aug) Drop down the steep stairs of Andersgrotta into this cave that once served as an air-raid shelter and bunker as wave upon wave of Russian bombers sought to knock out the Nazi ore-shipping facility. There's a multilingual presentation, and a nine-minute video also tells the tale. Wrap up warmly as the temperature here is 3°C, even in summer.

Gabba Reindeer & Husky Park   ZOO
(☑ 78 97 05 40; www.kirkenessnowhotel.com; Sandnesdalen 14; adult/child 250/125kr; ⊙ noon-4pm Jun-Sep) This may not be so much of a treat for the children if you've been driving in Eastern Finnmark and have stopped to relate to communing roadside reindeer. But it's worth the visit if you've just rolled in on the Hurtigruten; they'll enjoy petting the huskies too.

☞ Tours & Activities

Kirkenes offers a wealth of tours and activities. For an overview according to season, get one of the comprehensive brochures,

Summer Activities or *Winter Activities*, from your hotel.

There's a summertime reservation point in the Scandic Arctic Hotel lobby, or book directly with tour operators. Do your research – operators are professional and well-run, but prices and timings sometimes vary so find out what best suits your needs.

Tour agencies can arrange in-town or hotel pick-ups. In addition to the following, it's also worth checking what BIRK Husky (p346), based in the Pasvik River Valley, and Sollia Gjestegård (p344) have on offer.

Barents Safari (📞901 90 594; www.barents safari.no; Fjellveien 28)

Pasvikturist (Map p343; 📞78 99 50 80; www. pasvikturist.no; Dr Wessels gate 9)

Kirkenes Snow Hotel (📞78 97 05 40; www. kirkenessnowhotel; Sandnesdalen 14)

Summer Activities

The following activities are popular from late June to mid-August, sometimes into September:

King-crab safari (adult/child 1650/825kr)

Quad-bike safari (per person from 1490kr)

Half-day tours of the Pasvik River Valley (adult/child 1000/500kr)

Visiting the Russian border and iron-ore mines (adult/child 700/350kr)

Boat trips along the Pasvik River (adult/child 990/500kr)

Winter Activities

Activities to try between December and mid-April:

Snowmobile safaris (per person from 1890kr)

Ice fishing (from 1800kr)

Snowshoe rental (half-/full day from 250/400kr)

Dog-sledding (adult/child from 2100/1050kr)

King-crab safari (adult/child 1500/750kr)

RUSSIAN MARKET

On the last Thursday of most months, Russian merchants set up shop around the town centre of Kirkenes, selling everything from craftwork to binoculars. Prices aren't as cheap as in Russia, but they're still a bargain for Norway.

🛏 Sleeping

Kirkenes Camping CAMPGROUND **$**
(📞78 99 80 28; www.kirkenescamping.no; Ekveien 19, Hesseng; tent/caravan sites 200/250kr, 4-bed cabins with bathroom 1100-1900kr, with outdoor bathroom 500-700kr; ☺ Jun-Aug) Beside the E6, 8km west of Kirkenes, this is the sole option for campers, although its future seemed uncertain at the time of our visit. Reception opens only between 9am and 7pm (no way to run a campsite in high season) so reserve in advance if you're after a cabin.

★**Sollia Gjestegård** HOTEL **$$**
(📞78 99 08 20; www.storskog.no; apt 1420kr, 2- to 4-bed cabins 1215-1825kr, s/d 665/815kr) The Sollia, 13km southeast of Kirkenes, was originally constructed as a tuberculosis sanatorium and you can see why. The air could scarcely be more pure or the atmosphere more relaxed at this wonderful getaway. The whole family can sweat it out in the sauna and outdoor tub, while children will enjoy communing with the resident huskies. Rooms are simple.

Thon Hotel Kirkenes HOTEL **$$**
(Map p343; 📞78 97 10 50; www.thonhotels.no/ kirkenes; Johan Knudtzens gate 11; r from 1016kr; 📶) This newish waterside hotel is Thon-boxy from the exterior. Within, though, it's open, vast and exciting, offering great views of the sound and a cluster of laid-up Russian trawlers. The restaurant is just as architecturally stimulating, and you could easily dangle a line from the open-air terrace.

Scandic Arctic Hotel HOTEL **$$**
(Map p343; 📞78 99 11 59; www.scandichotels. no; Kongensgate 1-3; d from 1050kr; 🅿@🏊) The Scandic Arctic, a pleasing modern block in the town centre, boasts Norway's most easterly swimming pool, heated and open year-round. The other special attribute, its **Arctic Menu** restaurant (summer buffet 395kr), is the best of the town's limited hotel dining options.

★**Kirkenes Snow Hotel** HOTEL **$$$**
(📞78 97 05 40; www.kirkenessnowhotel.com; Sandnesdalen 14; adult/child half-board from 3100/1550kr; ☺20 Dec–mid-Apr) Yes, the prices are steep but you'll remember the occasion for life. And bear in mind that 25 tonnes of ice and 15,000 cu metres of snow are shifted each winter to build this ephemeral structure. For dinner, guests cook reindeer sausages over an open fire, then enjoy a warming main course of baked salmon.

And what's the experience like? Well, it's high on novelty value and something we'd definitely recommend trying once, but once is enough.

If it's all just too cold for you, try their beautifully designed (and much warmer) Gamme cabins (double, half-board from 2700kr).

✖ Eating

Surf & Turf INTERNATIONAL, NORWEGIAN **$$**
(Map p343; ☑ 464 45 245; Dr Wessels gate 2; mains from 189kr; ⊙ 11am-10pm Mon-Sat) One of the better in-town options in a place of few, Surf & Turf does a decent fish soup and serves up everything from steaks to pasta and even whale. The setting, too, is much nicer than others in town and the thoughtful presentation of dishes is rare in Kirkenes.

★ Gapahuken NORWEGIAN **$$$**
(☑ 78 99 08 20; www.storskog.no/en/restaurant gapahuken; Storskog; mains 290-395kr, buffet 450kr; ⊙ 4-10pm Mon-Sat, 3-7pm Sun mid-Jun–Aug, on demand rest of year) The restaurant of the Sollia Gjestegård hotel (p344) is clad in wood and glass, and from its broad picture windows there's a grand panorama of the lake at its feet and the Russian frontier post just beyond. Discriminating diners drive out from Kirkenes to enjoy gourmet Norwegian cuisine made with fresh local ingredients such as reindeer, king crab, salmon and halibut. Sunday is buffet only.

ⓘ Information

Kirkenes has no functioning tourist office. Your best bet for information and brochures are hotels or tour operators. A collection of local tour operators and hotels have set up the generally excellent website www.visitkirkenes.no.

ⓘ Getting There & Away

From **Kirkenes Airport** (☑ 67 03 53 00; www. avinor.no), 13km southwest of town, there are direct flights to Oslo (SAS and Norwegian) and Tromsø (Widerøe).

Kirkenes is the terminus of the Hurtigruten coastal ferry, which heads southwards at 12.45pm daily. A bus (120kr) meets the boat and runs into town and on to the airport.

From the **bus stop** (Map p343), buses run four times weekly to Karasjok (five hours), Hammerfest (10¼ hours), Alta (10½ hours) and many points in between.

Independent travellers armed with a Russian visa (which you'll need to get in your home country) can hop aboard one of the two daily **buses**

ⓘ A FORBIDDING FRONTIER

Don't even think about stepping across the Russian border for a photo. Nowadays, in addition to vestiges of old Cold War neuroses on both sides, Norway, as a Schengen Agreement country, is vigilant about preventing illegal immigrants from entering. Both Norwegian and Russian sentries have surveillance equipment and the fine for illegal crossing, even momentarily, starts at a whopping 5000kr. Using telephoto or zoom lenses or even a tripod also qualify as violations. As the guidance document sternly warns: 'It is prohibited to intentionally make contact with, or act in an insulting manner towards persons on the other side of the border and to throw items across the borderline. Any attempts at violations will be punished as if they had been carried out.' You have been warned!

---

to Murmansk (Map p343) (one way/return 510/780kr, five hours).

ⓘ Getting Around

The airport is served by the Flybuss (85kr, 20 minutes), which connects the bus terminal and the Scandic Arctic Hotel with all arriving and departing flights.

Kirkenes Taxi (Map p343; ☑ 78 99 13 97; www.kirkenestaxi.no; Presteveien 1) charges 350/425kr for a day/evening run between town and the airport.

There are car-rental agencies at the airport, or ask at your hotel.

Pasvik River Valley

Even when diabolical mosquito swarms make life hell for warm-blooded creatures, the remote lakes, wet tundra bogs and, to their south, Norway's largest stand of virgin *taiga* forest lend appeal to little **Øvre Pasvik National Park**, in the far reaches of the Pasvik River Valley.

Some 100km south of Kirkenes and 200 sq km in area, this last corner of Norway seems more like Finland, Siberia or even Alaska. Here, wolves, wolverines and brown bears still roam freely. The park is also home to some of the most northerly elk in Europe, Eurasian lynx and a host of relatively rare birds such as the Siberian jay, pine grosbeak,

WORTH A TRIP

GRENSE JAKOBSELV

Grense Jakobselv is the place to come for a haunting sense of history on the border between Europe and Russia. The first settlement here, 60km northeast of Kirkenes, probably appeared around 8000 years ago, when the sea level was 60m lower than it is today. Only a small stream separates Norway and Russia here, and along the road you can see the **border obelisks** on both sides.

The only real attraction – apart from the chance to gaze over the magic line – is the isolated 1869 **stone church**. It was constructed within sight of the sea to cement Norway's territorial claims after local people complained to the authorities that Russian fishing boats were illegally trespassing into Norwegian waters; it was thought that the intruders would respect a church and change their ways. Whether it worked or not isn't recorded.

During school holidays, you can make a day trip between Kirkenes and Grense Jakobselv (1½ hours) on Monday, Wednesday and Friday. The bus leaves at 9am and departs Grense Jakobselv at 11.30am, allowing an hour to explore. Some Kirkenes tour operators also arrange outings here.

redpoll and smew. Sightings of all of these are rare, but you never know...

History

The Stone Age Komsa hunting culture left its mark here in the form of hunters' pitfall traps around lake Ødevann and elsewhere in the region; some date from as early as 4000 BC. Nearer to our own times, in the mid-19th century farmers from southern Norway established homesteads here with government support, opening up these near-virgin lands and helping to assert this ill-defined frontier territory as Norwegian.

⊙ Sights

Sør-Varanger Museum   MUSEUM
(📞78 99 48 80; www.varangermuseum.no/no/sor-varanger; adult/child 80kr/free; ⊙9.30am-5pm late Jun-Aug, shorter hours rest of year) It's worth a stop at the Strand branch of the Sør-Varanger Museum, which preserves Norway's oldest public boarding school and illustrates the region's ethnic mix. Visit, too, the timber-built **Svanvik chapel** dating from 1934, and a couple of 19th-century farms, **Bjørklund** and **Nordre Namdalen**.

Høyde 96   VIEWPOINT
The Cold War lookout tower Høyde 96 offers a view eastward to the bleak Russian mining town of Nikel.

🏃 Activities

Numerous Kirkenes operators run boat and snowmobile safaris down the Pasvik River Valley. Independent hiking is also possible.

BIRK Husky   DOG SLEDDING
(📞909 78 248; www.birkhusky.no) From its base down in the Pasvik River Valley, BIRK Husky offers a range of dog-sledding excursions of varying duration in winter, as well as hiking, boat trips and birdwatching in summer.

Hiking

Douse yourself liberally in mosquito repellent before heading off into the wilds. The most accessible route is the poor road that turns southwest 1.5km south of Vaggatem and ends 9km later at a car park near the northeastern end of Lake Sortbrysttjørna. There, a marked track leads southwestward for 5km, passing several scenic lakes, marshes and bogs to end at the **Ellenvann-skoia hikers' hut**, beside the large lake, Ellenvatn.

Also from the Ødevasskoia car park, it's about an 8km walk due south to **Krokfjell** (145m) and the **Treriksrøysa**, the monument marking the spot where Norway, Finland and Russia meet. Although you can approach it and take photos, you may not walk around the monument, which would amount to an illicit border crossing!

The topographic sheet to use is Statens Kartverk's *Krokfjellet,* which conveniently covers the entire park at 1:25,000.

🛏 Sleeping

Øvre Pasvik Café & Camping   CAMPGROUND **$**
(📞959 11 305; www.pasvikcamping.no; Vaggetem; tent/caravan sites from 100/200kr, cabins 600-700kr) This place deep in the forest rents out canoes and bicycles, and provides information on local wilderness and attractions.

Cabins are simple and the sites close to the water's edge.

ℹ Information

The **Øvre Pasvik National Park Centre** (🖉 46 41 36 00; ⊘ 8am-8pm mid-Jun–mid-Sep, 9am-3pm Mon-Fri rest of yr) is set in lovely gardens near Svanvik, about 40km south of Kirkenes.

ℹ Getting There & Away

Two weekday buses leave Kirkenes for Skogfoss (1½ hours) via Svanvik and one continues to Vaggatem (2¼ hours).

INNER FINNMARK

Nestled against the Finnish border, Norway's 'big sky country' is a place of lush greenery in summer and deep ice-blues in winter. It's also the epicentre of the Sápmi, the 'land of the Sami'. Kautokeino, a one-street town if ever there was one, is the traditional heart of the region, although Karasjok is altogether livelier and has more Sami institutions.

Karasjok

POP 2668

Kautokeino may have more Sami residents, but Karasjok (Kárásjohka in Sami) is Sami Norway's indisputable capital. It's home to the Sami Parliament and library, NRK Sami Radio, a wonderful Sami museum and a Sami theme park. This is also one of the best places in Norway to go dog-sledding in winter.

It's a lovely forested drive between Karasjok and Kautokeino, following, for the most spectacular stretch, the River Jiešjokka.

◎ Sights

Sápmi Park   AMUSEMENT PARK, MUSEUM
(🖉 78 46 88 00; www.visitsapmi.no; Leavnnjageaidnu 1, off Porsangerveien; adult/child/family 160/80/400kr; ⊘ 9am-7pm mid-Jun–mid-Aug, 9am-4pm late Aug, 9am-4pm Mon-Fri, 11am-3pm Sat Sep–mid-Dec, 10am-2pm Mon-Fri Jan-May) Sami culture is big business here, and this impressive theme park includes a wistful, hi-tech multimedia introduction to the Sami in the 'Magic Theatre', plus Sami winter and summer camps and other dwellings to explore on the grounds. There's also, of course, a gift shop and cafe – and **Boble Glasshytte**, Finnmark's only glass-blowing

workshop and gallery. Reindeer are also often around.

Sami Parliament   NOTABLE BUILDING
(Sámediggi; 🖉 78 47 40 00; www.samediggi.no; Kautokeinoveien 50; ⊘ hourly tours 8.30am-2.30pm Mon-Fri except 11.30am late Jun–mid-Aug, 1pm Mon-Fri rest of year) **FREE** The Sami Parliament was established in 1989 and meets four times annually. In 2000 it moved into this glorious building, encased in mellow Siberian wood, with a birch, pine and oak interior. The main assembly hall is shaped like a Sami tent, and the **Sami library**, lit with tiny lights like stars, houses over 35,000 volumes, plus other media. Tours last 30 minutes. There are similar Sami parliaments in Finland and Sweden.

Sami National Museum   MUSEUM
(Sámiid Vuorká Dávvirat, De Samiske Samlinger; 🖉 78 46 99 50; www.rdm.no; Museumsgata 17; adult/concession/child 90/60kr/free; ⊘ 9am-6pm mid-Jun–mid-Aug, shorter hours rest of year) Exhibits at the Sami National Museum, also called the Sami Collection, include displays of colourful, traditional Sami clothing, tools and artefacts, and works by contemporary Sami artists. Outdoors, you can roam among a cluster of traditional Sami constructions and follow a short trail, signed in English, that leads past and explains ancient Sami reindeer trapping pits and hunting techniques. In summer a guided walk is included in the ticket price.

🏃 Activities

★**Engholm's Husky**   ADVENTURE SPORTS
(www.engholm.no; 1hr dog-sledding 1000kr, 1-/4-/5-/8-day winter husky safari 2000/8700/11,600/19,900kr) Engholm's Husky, in the lodge (p348) bearing the same name, offers winter dog-sled tours. These are sometimes run by Sven Engholm, one of dog-sledding's most celebrated names. They can also arrange summer walking tours with a dog to carry at least some of your gear. Consult the website for the full range of activities.

Ravdol Reindeer Herding   OUTDOORS
(🖉 995 48 376; www.ravdolreindeerherding.com; Ravdojok 24; day/evening trip 1300/1100kr; ⊘ mid-Jan–mid-Apr) This Sami-run venture is an excellent way to get up close to Sami herding culture in winter – they take you out among the herds, teach you about Samis' existence with the reindeer and initiate you into other areas of Sami traditional life.

Sami Path
BOATING, FISHING

(📞78 60 06 11; www.samipath.com; Niitosjogas 27) This group of local Sami run a range of activities from boat trips on the river and canoeing to salmon fishing and reindeer-herding experiences.

🧭 Tours

Turgleder
OUTDOORS

(📞911 67 303; www.turgleder.com) Run by Sven Engholm's daughter Liv, this fine outfit offers a year-round range of activities, from cross-country-skiing excursions to 24-hour 'Scout-for-a-day' experiences.

🛏 Sleeping

Karasjok Camping
CAMPGROUND $

(📞970 72 225; www.karacamp.no; Avjovargeaidnu 88; per person/site 20/140kr, dm 210kr, cabins 410-1200kr; 🛜) Friendly Karasjok Camping occupies a hillside site with river views and a range of cabins. Campers can pitch their tents on its particularly lush, springy grass. Everyone can lie back on reindeer skins to the crackle of the nightly birch-wood fire in the cosy *lavvo* (Sami tent).

★Engholm Husky Design Lodge
CABIN $$

(📞915 86 625; www.engholm.no; s/d full board from 1500/2500kr, s/d hut only from 750/1100kr; P🛜) 🍽 About 6km from Karasjok along the Rv92, Sven Engholm has built this wonderful haven in the forest with his own hands. Each rustic cabin is individually furnished with great flair, with every item (from reindeer-horn toilet brushes to creative lampshades) hand-carved by Sven. All have kitchen facilities; two have bathrooms. You sink into sleep to the odd bark and yelp from the sled dogs.

A plentiful dinner costs 300kr. Signed trails lead through the forest and barely a five-minute stroll away there's a salmon stream with a fine beach, where you can rent canoes. You can also join the team on their daily puppy walk or take a boat ride on a nearby lake as the adult huskies run, yap and swim alongside. There's also a sauna and a wood-heated outdoor hot tub.

Scandic Hotel Karasjok
HOTEL $$

(📞78 46 88 60; www.scandichotels.no; Porsangerveien; d 850-1600kr; P@🛜) Adjacent to Sápmi Park, this is Karasjok's premier hotel lodging, with handsome rooms and Sami motifs throughout, plus, outside in summertime, **Gammen**, an impressive Arctic Menu

restaurant. They also have a range of budget rooms.

🍴 Eating

Biepmu Kafeà
CAFE $$

(Biepmu Cafe; 📞78 46 61 51; Finlandsveien; mains 140-240kr; ⏰1-8pm) This simple cafeteria in the centre of town serves up hearty local dishes and snacks, with daily specials (starting at 175kr) including a fish buffet on Wednesday. Other dishes include shredded reindeer meat. The heavy wooden benches resemble church pews and it's very much only locals in attendance.

★Gammen
NORWEGIAN $$$

(📞78 46 88 60; off Porsangerveien; mains 265-395kr; ⏰11am-10pm mid-Jun–mid-Aug) It's reindeer or reindeer plus a couple of fish options at this summer-only rustic complex of four large interconnected Sami huts, run by the Scandic Hotel. Although it may be busy with bus-tour groups, it's an atmospheric place to sample traditional Sami dishes, from reindeer stew to reindeer fillet, or simply to drop in for coffee or beer around the fire.

🛍 Shopping

★Knivsmed Strømeng
ARTS & CRAFTS

(📞78 46 71 05; www.samekniv.no; Markangeaidnu 10; ⏰8.30am-6pm Mon-Fri, 10am-4pm Sat mid-Jun–mid-Aug, shorter hours rest of year) This shop calls on five generations of local experience to create original handmade Sami knives for everything from outdoor to kitchen use. They're real works of art, but stay true to the Sami need for durability, made with birch-and-brass handles and varying steel quality. Prices start at around 1000kr for a Sami kid's knife up to 2000kr for the real deal.

ⓘ Information

The **tourist office** (📞78 46 89 81; Leavnnjageaidnu 1, off Porsangerveien; ⏰9am-7pm mid-Jun–mid-Aug) is in Sápmi Park, near the junction of the E6 and the Rv92. It will change money if you're stuck with euros after crossing the border from Finland.

ⓘ Getting There & Away

Twice-daily buses (except Saturday) connect Karasjok with Alta (525kr, 4¾ hours) and Hammerfest (450kr, 4¼ hours). There's a service to Kirkenes (580kr, five hours) four times weekly.

A daily Finnish Lapin Linjat bus runs to Rovaniemi (785kr, eight hours) via Ivalo (315kr, 3½ hours), in Finland.

Kautokeino

POP 2931

Kautokeino, the traditional winter base of the reindeer Sami (as opposed to their coastal kin), remains more emphatically Sami than Karasjok, which has made concessions to Norwegian culture. Some 85% of the townspeople have Sami as their first language and you may see a few non-tourist-industry locals in traditional national dress.

The town is, frankly, dull in summer, since so many of its people are up and away with the reindeer in their warm-weather pastures (in winter, by contrast, around 100,000 reindeer live hereabouts). What makes a visit well worthwhile is Juhls' Sølvsmie (Juhls' Silver Gallery), just out of town and housing a magnificent example of the best of Scandinavian jewellery design. It's also a rather pretty place when seen from the surrounding hills.

History

From as early as 1553, during the gradual transition between nomadic and sedentary lifestyles, records reveal evidence of permanent settlement in the Kautokeino area. Christianity took hold early and the first church was built in 1641.

The first road to Kautokeino didn't arrive here until the 1960s.

☉ Sights

★ Juhls' Sølvsmie   GALLERY

(Juhls' Silver Gallery; ☎78 48 43 30; www.juhls.no; Galaniitoluodda; ☉9am-8pm mid-Jun–mid-Aug, 9am-6pm rest of year) This wonderful building, all slopes and soft angles, was designed and built by owners Regine and Frank Juhls, who first began working with the Sami over half a century ago. Their acclaimed gallery creates traditional-style and modern silver jewellery and handicrafts. One wing of the gallery has a fine collection of Asian carpets and artefacts, reminders of their work supporting Afghan refugees during that blighted country's Soviet occupation. Staff happily show you around and most items are for sale.

Kautokeino Museum   MUSEUM

(☎481 17 266; www.rdm.no/english/kautokeino_bygdetun; Boaronjárga 23; adult/child 50kr/free; ☉9am-6pm Mon-Sat, noon-6pm Sun mid-Jun–mid-

WORTH A TRIP

REISA NATIONAL PARK

Although technically in Troms county, 803-sq-km **Reisa National Park** (www.reisa-nasjonalpark.no) is equally accessible by road from Kautokeino. For hikers, the 50km route through this remote Finnmarksvidda country is one of Norway's wildest and most physically demanding challenges. The northern trailhead at Sarelv is accessible on the Rv865, 47km south of Storslett, and the southern end is reached on the gravel route to Reisevannhytta, 4km west of Bieddjuvaggi on the Rv896, heading northwest from Kautokeino.

Aug, shorter hours rest of year) Outside, this little museum has a fully fledged traditional Sami settlement, complete with an early home, temporary dwellings, and outbuildings such as the kitchen, sauna, and huts for storing fish, potatoes and lichen (also called 'reindeer moss' – prime reindeer fodder). Nothing's signed, so pick up a sheet with a site plan and description on the reverse at reception. Inside is a fascinating, if cluttered, display of Sami handicrafts, farming and reindeer-herding implements, religious icons and winter transport gear.

⚡ Festivals & Events

★ Sami Easter   RELIGIOUS

Easter week is a time for weddings and an excuse for a big gathering marking the end of the dark season, before folk and flocks disperse to the summer grazing. It's celebrated with panache, with the reindeer-racing world championships, the Sami Grand Prix – not a souped-up snowmobile race but the premier *yoik* (rhythmic poetry) and Sami pop contest – and other traditional Sami and religious events.

🛏 Sleeping & Eating

Arctic Motell & Camping   CAMPGROUND $

(☎78 48 54 00; www.arcticmotel.com; Suomaluodda 16; car/caravan sites 220/280kr, cabins 400-1400kr, motel r from 650kr; ☉Jun-Aug) At the southern end of town, this is a hyperfriendly place where campers and cabin dwellers have access to a communal kitchen. Its *lavvo* (Sami tent) is a warm and cosy spot to relax by a wood fire and sip steaming coffee, laid on nightly at 8pm. If you ask, the small cafe will also rustle up *bidos,* a traditional reindeer-meat stew.

★ Thon Hotel Kautokeino   HOTEL $$$

(☎78 48 70 00; www.thonhotels.no; Biedjovagge-luodda 2; s/d from 1250/1450kr; P@🛜) This lovely contemporary hotel inhabits a shell of mellow wood, built low to blend in with its surroundings. Rooms are cheerful and cosy. Make sure you get a 2nd-floor room with views over the town; those on the backside overlook the scruffy car park. Duoattar, its gourmet restaurant, serves fine cuisine, and breakfast is one of the best in Norway's far north.

The hotel organises a number of winter excursions (including snowmobile safaris and trips to local Sami camps) and fishing in summer.

Duoattar   NORWEGIAN $$$

(☎78 48 70 00; Biedjovaggeluodda 2, Thon Hotel Kautokeino; dinner mains 195-395kr; ⊙5-10pm Mon-Thu, 6-10pm Fri-Sun) At Kautokeino's best restaurant, the main item on the menu, as you'd expect in such a town, is reindeer, served in several guises, with Sami tapas a small but imaginative starter. Some travellers have left disappointed, but we've always enjoyed eating here, quite apart from the fact that you're not exactly spoilt for choice in this town.

Kautokeino Villmarksenter   CAFE $$

(☎78 48 76 02; Hannoluohkka 2; mains 155-215kr; ⊙noon-10pm Mon-Sat) Set above the main road in Kautokeino is this functional, scruffy sort of hostel whose main asset is its cafe-restaurant, with an attractive open-air deck.

🛍 Shopping

Avzi Design   ARTS & CRAFTS

(☎958 08 839; www.avzidesign.com; ⊙10am-5pm Mon-Fri, 10am-3pm Sat) Around 8km east of Kautokeino in the tiny hamlet of Avzi (ask at the tourist office for directions), this friendly little showroom sells Sami mittens, shawls and other textiles.

Kautokeino Sølvsmie   JEWELLERY

(☎78 48 63 11; www.kautokeinosolvsmie.no; Boaronjárga 15; ⊙9am-4pm Mon-Fri, 10am-2pm Sat) Next to the Kautokeino Museum, this place offers finely crafted silver jewellery and other pieces inspired by Sami culture and the local environment.

Information

The **tourist office** (☎481 17 266; Boaronjárga 23; ⊙9am-6pm Mon-Sat, noon-6pm Sun mid-Jun–mid-Aug) has occupied five different venues on our last five visits. At the time of research it was in the Kautokeino Museum.

ℹ Getting There & Away

Public transport to Kautokeino is slim. Buses run between Kautokeino and Alta (298kr, 2¼ hours) daily except Saturday. From July to mid-August, the Finnish Lapin Linjat bus connects Kautokeino with Alta (1¾ hours) and Rovaniemi (eight hours), in Finland once daily.

Svalbard

POP 2573

Best Places to Eat

➜ Huset (p359)

➜ Fruene Kaffe og Vinbar (p359)

➜ Coal Miners' Bar & Grill (p359)

➜ Gruvelageret (p360)

➜ Kroa (p360)

Best Places to Stay

➜ Basecamp Spitsbergen (p358)

➜ Svalbard Hotell & Lodge (p358)

➜ Coal Miners' Cabins (p358)

➜ Radisson Blu Polar Hotel (p359)

Why Go?

Svalbard is the Arctic North as you always dreamed it existed. This wondrous archipelago is a land of dramatic snow-drowned peaks and glaciers, of vast icefields and forbidding icebergs, an elemental place where the seemingly endless Arctic night and the perpetual sunlight of summer carry a deeper kind of magic. One of Europe's last great wildernesses, this is also the domain of more polar bears than people, a terrain rich in epic legends of polar exploration.

Svalbard's main settlement and entry point, scruffy Longyearbyen, is merely a taste of what lies beyond and the possibilities for exploring further are many: boat trips, glacier hikes, and expeditions by snowmobile or led by a team of huskies. Whichever you choose, coming here is like crossing some remote frontier of the mind: Svalbard is as close as most mortals can get to the North Pole and still capture its spirit.

When to Go
Longyearbyen

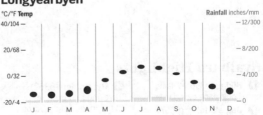

Dec–Feb Deep immersion in the polar night and a winter jazz festival.

Feb–Apr The light returns with week-long festivities; from late February there's a blue tinge to the light.

Jun–Aug Days without end and an array of activities in the summer light.

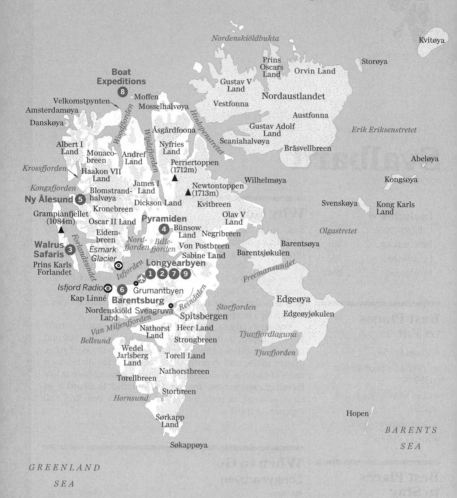

Svalbard Highlights

1 Hiking (p356) Walking onto Longyearbreen glacier.

2 Dog-sledding (p357) Experiencing the polar silence like explorers of old.

3 Walrus safaris (p356) Taking a summer day trip to see walruses on Prins Karls Forlandet.

4 Pyramiden (p362) Travelling to this eerie abandoned Soviet outpost.

5 Ny Ålesund (p364) Taking a day trip to this remote settlement.

6 Barentsburg (p361) Drinking vodka in this intriguing Russian village.

7 Longyearbyen museums (p354) Immersing yourself in Svalbard's history.

8 Boat expeditions (p359) Circumnavigating Svalbard in search of polar bears.

9 Longyearbyen dining (p359) Sampling Arctic cuisine at Gruvelageret, Coal Miners' Bar & Grill and Huset.

History

The first mention of Svalbard occurs in an Icelandic saga from 1194. Officially, however, the Dutch voyager Willem Barents, while in search of a northeast passage to China, is regarded as the first visitor from the European mainland (1596). He named the islands Spitsbergen, which means 'sharp mountains'. The Norwegian name, Svalbard, comes from the Old Norse for 'cold coast'. Today Spitsbergen is the name of only Svalbard's largest island. In 1920 the Svalbard Treaty granted Norway sovereignty over the islands and restricted military activities. Initially signed by nine nations, it now has over 40 adherents, whose citizens enjoy the same rights and obligations on the islands as Norwegians themselves.

Wildlife

In addition to polar bears, Svalbard is home to other emblematic Arctic species. The species you're most likely to see are the Arctic fox (also known as the polar fox) and Svalbard's unusually squat reindeer.

Svalbard's reindeer are genetically akin to their distant Canadian cousins and some have been found bearing Russian tags, proving that they walked in over the ice. Unlike their cousins on the mainland, they don't live in herds but in family groups of two to six animals. As they have no predators other than humans, they thrive and the estimated population of around 10,000 is kept constant by an annual cull. Most Svalbard reindeer starve slowly to death when they're about eight years old, their teeth having been ground to stumps by the stones and pebbles they mouth along with sprigs of edible matter.

Despite having been hunted to the brink of extinction in centuries past, whales can still be seen on occasion in Svalbard's waters, while seals are also common. Walruses, too, suffered from relentless hunting, although a population of between 500 and 2000 still inhabits Svalbard.

ⓘ Getting There & Away

Unless you're travelling on a boat cruise from the Norwegian mainland, the only way to reach Svalbard is by air, with either SAS or Norwegian, from Tromsø or Oslo.

Longyearbyen

POP 2100

Longyearbyen is like a portal to a magical sub-polar world. Just about every Svalbard experience begins here, but if you came to Svalbard and spent the whole time in Longyearbyen (Svalbard's only town of any size), you'd leave disappointed. That's because although Longyearbyen enjoys a superb backdrop including two glacier tongues, Longyearbreen and Lars Hjertabreen, the town itself is fringed by abandoned mining detritus and the waterfront is anything but beautiful, with shipping containers and industrial buildings. The further you head up the valley towards the glaciers, the more you'll appreciate being here. Even so, Longyearbyen is a place to base yourself for trips out into the wilderness rather than somewhere to linger for its own sake.

History

Although whalers had been present here in previous centuries, the town of Longyearbyen was founded in the early 20th century as a base for Svalbard's coal-mining activities; the town was named after the American John Munro Longyear, who first set up the coal-mining operations here in 1906. For decades, Store Norsk, the owner of the coal pits, possessed the communal mess, company shop, all transport in and out, and almost the miners' souls. Then in 1976 the Norwegian state stepped in to bail the company out from bankruptcy. Today most of the few people who live here year-round enjoy one-year tax-free contracts. There are at least seven mines dotted around Longyearbyen and the surrounding area, although only one, Mine No 7, 15km east of town, is still operational. The town's gritty coal-mining roots still show through, commemorated in the statue of a grizzled miner and his pick near the Lompensenteret.

◉ Sights

★ Wild Photo Gallery   GALLERY
(✎ 405 17 775; www.wildphoto.com; ⊙ 10am-4pm Jun-Aug, shorter hours Mar-May, Sep & Oct) FREE
This gallery of stunning Svalbard photos by Ole Jørgen Liodden and Roy Mangersnes is small but filled with utterly unforgettable

images. A book that contains most of the displayed images, *Svalbard Exposed,* is sold here, and the two photographers run photo expeditions in Svalbard and elsewhere.

Svalbard Global Seed Vault   LANDMARK
(www.seedvault.no) Deep inside a mountain, down beneath the permafrost, a vast artificial cavern, already dubbed the Doomsday Vault or a vegetarian Noah's Ark, was opened in 2008. It's a repository with a capacity for up to four million different seed types (and up to 2.25 billion seeds in all), representing the botanical diversity of the planet. Note that casual visitors are not welcome.

Svalbard Bryggeri   BREWERY
(☑ 902 86 205; www.svalbardbryggeri.no; guided tour 350kr; ⊘ guided tours 6pm Mon, Wed & Sat) Having opened for business in 2015, Svalbard's very own brewery makes the very quaffable Spitsbergen IPA, Spitsbergen Pilsener and Spitsbergen Pale Ale – 16% of the water used in making their beers comes from the Bogerbreen glacier. They also offer 90-minute guided tours of their operations with free tastings thrown in. Advance reservations are essential and can be made through the tourist office (p361).

North Pole Expedition Museum   MUSEUM
(Spitsbergen Airship Museum; ☑ 957 35 742; www.spitsbergenairshipmuseum.com; adult/child 90/40kr; ⊘ 10am-5pm) This fascinating private museum houses a stunning collection of artefacts, original newspapers and other documents relating to the history of polar exploration. There's intriguing archive footage and labels are in English – you could easily spend a couple of hours here reliving some of the Arctic's most stirring tales. It's across the road from the back side of Svalbard Museum, down near the waterfront.

Svalbard Museum   MUSEUM
(☑ 79 02 64 92; www.svalbardmuseum.no; adult/student/child 90/50/15kr; ⊘ 10am-5pm Mar-Sep, noon-5pm Oct-Feb) Museum is the wrong word for this impressive exhibition space. Themes on display include life on the edge formerly led by whalers, trappers, seal and walrus hunters and, more recently, miners. It's an attractive mix of text, artefacts, and birds and mammals, stuffed and staring. There's a cosy book-browsing area for lounging, too, with sealskin cushions and rugs.

Galleri Svalbard   GALLERY
(☑ 79 02 23 40; www.gallerisvalbard.no; adult/concession/child 70/40/20kr; ⊘ 11am-5pm Mar-Sep, 1-5pm Tue-Sat & 11am-3pm Sun Oct-Feb) Galleri Svalbard features the Svalbard-themed works of renowned Norwegian artist Kåre Tveter (1922–2012), so pure and cold they make you shiver, as well as works by other artists, such as Olav Storø (www.storoe.no). It also has fascinating reproductions of antique maps of Svalbard, historical drawings with a Svalbard focus and temporary exhibitions. The gallery has a small cafe and an excellent shop.

Activities

Restrict yourself to Longyearbyen and you'll leave with little sense of the sheer majesty of Svalbard's wilderness. Fortunately, there's a dizzying array of short trips and day tours. The tourist office (p361) has an extensive weekly activities list. All outings can be booked through individual operators (directly or via their websites; see also www.svalbard.net).

Also possible are half-day summer excursions with wheeled sleds pulled by pack dogs, horse riding and fat bike excursions.

Summer

Birdwatching
More than 160 bird species have been reported in Svalbard, with the overwhelming number of these present during the summer months; the only species to overwinter in the archipelago is the Svalbard ptarmigan. If you're in Longyearbyen in summer, among the common species you're likely to see are the barnacle goose, king eider, common eider, Arctic tern, purple sandpiper, glaucous gull and snow bunting; the best chance for sighting these species is in the Adventdalen delta southeast of the centre on the road to Mine No 7; the Arctic tern and snow bunting are easily seen on the Longyearbyen outskirts. A little further afield, especially on the boat trips to Barentsburg or Pyramiden, the little auk, black guillemot, puffin and fulmar are among the most commonly sighted species. Some tour operators run short boat trips to the 'bird cliffs' close to Longyearbyen, while birders should buy the booklet *Bird Life in Longyearbyen and Surrounding Area* (50kr), which is available from the tourist office.

Boat Trips

The range of boat day trips you can undertake to get out into the further reaches of Svalbard is growing with each passing year. Barentsburg and Pyramiden are the most popular with daily departures, but Ny Ålesund is also now within reach.

To Ny Ålesund

At the time of research, two companies were offering day trips to Ny Ålesund, one of the Arctic's best day trips and bringing one of the world's northernmost settlements within reach of the day tripper. Note that they don't operate every day and hence require careful planning.

Better Moments (☏ 400 95 965; www.better moments.no) runs Friday expeditions (11 hours, 3990kr).

Spitsbergen Guide Service (☏ 941 70 070; www.spitsbergenguideservice.no) offers two to five weekly trips (10 hours, 4150kr).

To Barentsburg & Pyramiden

The most popular boat excursions are to the Russian settlements of Barentsburg and Pyramiden; some stop at glacier tongues along the way (Esmarkbreen for Barentsburg, Nordenskjöldbreen for Pyramiden).

Arctic Explorer (☏ 954 78 500; www.arctic explorer.no) uses fast boats to enable you to visit both Barentsburg and Pyramiden in a single day (2900kr, 11 hours). You'll only get 1½ hours in Barentsburg and 2½ hours in Pyramiden, but you'll see some glorious scenery en route and it's an ideal taste for those with little time.

Henningsen Transport & Guiding (☏ 918 53 756, 79 02 13 11; www.htg.svalbard.no)

POLAR BEARS UNDER THREAT

Polar bears are one of the most enduring symbols of the Arctic wilderness – loners, immensely strong and survivors in one of the world's most extreme environments. But for all the bears' raw power, some scientists predict that they could be extinct by the end of this century if the world continues to heat up.

Polar bear numbers had been in decline since the late 19th century, when intensive hunting began. But ever since the 1973 treaty for the Conservation of Polar Bears and their Habitat, signed by all the countries whose lands impinge upon the Arctic, polar bear numbers have been gradually increasing again and latest estimates by the World Wildlife Fund (WWF) suggest that there are between 22,000 and 31,000 left in the wild; Svalbard has a population of around 3500.

But as is the case throughout the Arctic, Svalbard's glaciers are retreating and the ice sheet, their natural habitat and prime hunting ground for seals, the mainstay of their diet (an adult bear needs to eat between 50 and 75 seals every year), is shrinking. In 2017, a particularly bad year, even most of Svalbard's north coast remained ice-free throughout the winter – one polar bear that was being tracked by the WWF remained stranded on the island of Storøya, off the archipelago's far northeastern coast, after sea ice that usually connects the island to the rest of Svalbard failed to form.

Shrinking sea ice matters because although polar bears are classified as marine mammals and are powerful swimmers, many risk drowning as they attempt to reach fresh ice floes that are ever more separated by open water. Less sea ice also means that some populations will become isolated and inbred, weakening their genetic stock. The birth rate may also fall since females need plenty of deep snow to dig the dens in which they whelp. And hungry bears, on the prowl and desperate for food, could lead to increasing confrontations with humans.

Your chances of seeing one, unless you're on a cruise and observing from the safety of a ship, are minimal, especially in summer. In any event, contact is actively discouraged, both for your and the bear's sake (if a snowmobiler gives chase, for example, he or she will be in for a stiff fine). Bears under pressure quickly become stressed and overheat under their shaggy coats and may even die of heat exhaustion if pursued.

Should you come within sight of one on land, don't even think about approaching it. An altogether safer way to track polar bears is to log onto www.panda.org/polarbears, managed by the WWF. Here, you can track the movements of bears that scientists have equipped with a collar and satellite transmitter.

does excellent 10-hour summer-only trips to Barentsburg and Pyramiden (1950kr). En route, they tend to sail closer to shore than other companies, rather than sailing down the middle of the fjord.

Polar Charter (📞480 55 700; www.polarcharter.no) sends out the MS *Polargirl* to Barentsburg and the Esmark glacier (1700kr, eight to 10 hours, three weekly), and to Pyramiden and Nordenskjöldbreen (1700kr, eight to 10 hours, four weekly); prices include a lunch cooked on board.

Svalbard Booking (📞79 02 50 00; www.svalbardbooking.com) runs fjord trips to Pyramiden (1550kr, eight hours) six times a week.

Shorter Boat Excursions

Basecamp Spitsbergen (📞79 02 46 00; www.basecampexplorer.com/spitsbergen) offers boat safaris to Isfjord Radio (seven hours, 1990kr) from Wednesday to Saturday. They can also arrange three-day expeditions with two nights at this remote spot.

Henningsen Transport & Guiding (p355) does six-hour Friday-evening trips to Yoldiabukta and Wahlenberg glacier for 1550kr.

Polar Charter has five-hour Friday trips to the Borebreen glacier (1200kr).

Spitsbergen Travel (p358) runs daily Isfjord boat trips to Fuglefjella and Hiorthhamn (three hours, 890kr).

Hiking & Fossil Hunting

Summer hiking possibilities are endless and any Svalbard tour company worth its salt can organise half-, full- and multi-day hikes. The easiest options are three-hour fossil-hunting hikes (from 400kr), some of which take you up onto the moraine at the base of the Longyearbreen glacier.

Some popular destinations for other hikes, many of which include glacier hikes, are Platåberget (three hours, 500kr); up onto the Longyearbreen glacier itself (five hours, 750kr); Sarkofagen (525m above sea level; six hours, 690kr); Trollsteinen via Lars glacier (six hours, 795kr); Fuglefjella (seven hours, 990kr); and Nordenskiöldtoppen (eight hours, 990kr).

Poli Arctici (📞913 83 467, 79 02 17 05; www.poliartici.com) is among the better smaller operators, with numerous options, but all companies can get you out and walking.

Kayaking

Kayaking on Adventfjorden is a popular summer outing. Five-/seven-hour trips start from 850/1050kr, with evening and midnight-sun excursions also possible. **Svalbard Wildlife Expeditions** (📞79 02 22 22; www.wildlife.no), which offers numerous weekly departures, also offers a 10-hour combined kayak and mountain-summit hike four times a week for 1499kr. Spitsbergen Outdoor Activities (p356) is the other major kayaking operator, with at least one daily departure.

Walrus Safaris

One of the most exciting new types of tours to hit Svalbard in years, walrus safaris now run to Prins Karls Forlandet (with

---

POLAR BEAR DANGER

Don't let your desire to see Svalbard's symbol, the polar bear, blind you to the fact that a close encounter with this iconic creature rarely ends well. As the signs on the outskirts of Longyearbyen attest, polar bears are a real danger almost everywhere in Svalbard. If you're straying beyond Longyearbyen's confines, you're strongly advised to go with an organised tour. Walk leaders carry guns and know how to use them. Standard equipment too, especially if you're camping, are trip wires with flares and distress flares – to fire at the ground in front of the bear, not to summon help, which could be hours away.

With patterns of polar bear behaviour changing as sea ice levels shrink and tourist numbers increase, close encounters with polar bears are becoming more common. In 2015 a tourist was injured when a bear attacked his tent, while four polar bears were shot in self-defence in 2016 (double the annual average). In one incident, four tourists shot and killed a bear that attacked them while they were skiing in the far north of the archipelago. An investigation found that the tourists had correctly followed all procedures. In another incident, a three-year-old polar bear was sedated and relocated to another part of Svalbard after it was sighted in Longyearbyen.

The last bear fatality was in 2011 in the vicinity of the Von Post glacier, 40km from Longyearbyen. The previous fatality, in 1995, happened only 2km from Longyearbyen.

a glacier stop en route) from mid- or late May to August or mid-September. You can get to within 30m (either on land or at sea) of the great blubbery things lounging on the beach. A warming soup is included in tours prices and both of these companies are excellent:

Better Moments (p355) has four departures weekly (seven hours, 2190kr), as does Svalbard Booking (seven hours, 1990kr to 2390kr).

🎿 Winter

Basecamp Spitsbergen and Spitsbergen Travel (p358) in particular offer some truly epic, multiday cross-country ski expeditions, but it's worth spending time looking at what all of the tour companies have to offer.

Dog-Sledding

The environmentally friendly rival to snowmobiling, dog-sledding is in many ways the iconic Svalbard winter activity – the soundtrack of huskies barking and the scrape of the sled across the ice are a far more agreeable accompaniment in the wilderness than the drone of a snowmobile engine. Expect to pay around 1590kr for a four-hour excursion, although longer expeditions are possible.

Dedicated dog-sledding operators include the following:

Green Dog Svalbard (☏79 02 61 00; www.greendog.no)

Polardogs Svalbard (☏966 59 126; www.polardogssvalbard.com)

Svalbard Husky (☏78 40 30 78; www.svalbardhusky.no)

Svalbard Villmarkssenter (☏79 02 17 00; www.svalbardvillmarkssenter.no)

Snowmobiling

Riding or driving a snowmobile is the main way of getting around Svalbard in winter and it certainly enables you to cover a greater distance and see more than is otherwise possible.

Before setting out, pick up a copy of *Driving a Snowmobile in Svalbard* from the tourist office (p361). To drive a snowmobile scoot, you'll need to flash your home driving licence. Check with the tourist office; many areas are off-limits for snowmobiles. Daily rates start from 1200kr to 1500kr for the basic model.

Most companies will offer snowmobile safaris. Spitsbergen Travel (p358) has a particularly wide range of excursions, while Svalbard Booking offers snowmobile rental.

Sample expeditions (prices may vary between companies) include the following:

➡ Barentsburg (eight hours, 2400kr)
➡ Coles Bay (four hours, 1900kr)
➡ East coast Spitsbergen (10 hours, 2500kr)
➡ Elveneset (four hours, 1900kr)
➡ Northern-lights safari (three hours, 1750kr)
➡ Pyramiden (11 hours, 2500kr)
➡ Von Post glacier (eight hours, 2400kr)

🧭 Tours

City Sightseeing & Mine Tours

Gruve-3 Svalbard (☏911 65 929; gruve3@snsk.no; adult/child 590/295kr; ⊙9am & 1pm) Coal mining has always been central to the Longyearbyen story. Three-hour tours to Mine No 3 are a sobering experience, heading underground as countless miners have done in the past, and guides will take you through the mining story and give you a feel for what it must have been like to work underground.

Rana Itinerans (walking tour without/with lunch 450/600kr; ⊙9am, 12.15pm, 3pm & 6pm Sun-Thu, 9am, 12.15pm & 3pm Fri & Sat Jun-Aug) runs 2½-hour guided Longyearbyen city walks.

Svalbard Maxi Taxi (☏79 02 13 05; www.taxiguiden.no; per person 345kr; ⊙10am & 4pm Jun-Aug) offers two-hour minibus tours that take you further than you might think possible around Longyearbyen. When the weather's fine there are stunning views from a number of the places visited, and you can cover more distance than you would on foot, without needing a gun and guide.

Food & Drink Sightseeing

There are tours and tastings at Longyearbyen's brewery, Svalbard Bryggeri (p354), three times a week, while Karlsberger Pub (p360) also offers whisky tastings thrice weekly.

Arctic Tapas (📋 46 27 60 00; www.arctictapas.com; per person 895kr; ☺ 6.30-9pm Tue, Thu, Fri & Sun), a tour bus with a difference, offers a sightseeing tour of Longyearbyen accompanied by an on-board four-course meal with a focus on northern Norwegian produce and specialities – think cheese, trout, salmon, reindeer, herring... There's one free drink included in the cost of the tour.

Spitsbergen Travel (Hurtigruten Svalbard; 📋 79 02 61 00; www.spitsbergentravel.com) offers an Arctic Wilderness Evening at 7pm four nights a week, which includes dinner out in the wilds of Adventdalen, with an informative lecture on polar bears and Spitsbergen history thrown in (1045/500kr per adult/child).

🎉 Festivals & Events

Dark Season Blues MUSIC
(www.svalbardblues.com; ☺ Oct) A five-day jam session to warm you up before the onset of winter and the long months of darkness.

Polar Jazz MUSIC
(www.polarjazz.no; ☺ Feb) A long winter weekend of jazz in the bruise-blue half-light of February.

Sunfest CULTURAL
(www.solfest.no; ☺ early Mar) Week-long celebrations beginning on 8 March to dispel the polar night.

🛏 Sleeping

Longyearbyen has some excellent accommodation, from the world's northernmost full-service hotel right down to a campground or simpler rooms once used for miners' accommodation. To sleep in a hammock strung out above one of the husky kennels (per person 400kr), contact Svalbard Villmarkssenter (p357).

Longyearbyen Camping CAMPGROUND $
(📋 79 02 10 68; www.longyearbyen-camping.com; campsites per adult/child under 13yr 120kr/free; ☺ Apr & Jun-Aug) Near the airport on a flat stretch of turf, this particularly friendly campground with kitchen and showers overlooks Isfjorden and the glaciers beyond. It's about an hour's walk from town. You can also hire a tent (150kr), mattress (10kr) and sleeping bag (50kr). There are no cabins, but it does issue certificates for those who bathe naked in the fjord...

Coal Miners' Cabins GUESTHOUSE $
(Spitsbergen Guesthouse; 📋 79 02 63 00; www.spitsbergentravel.no; dm 400kr, s 590-1050kr, d 875-1400kr; ☺ mid-Mar–mid-Sep; ☎) This guesthouse is a subsidiary of Spitsbergen Travel (p358) and can accommodate up to 136 people. Spread over four buildings (the terrific Coal Miners' Bar & Grill is housed in one), the renovated rooms are simple and generally great value for money, albeit at Norway prices.

Mary-Ann's Polarrigg HOTEL, GUESTHOUSE $$
(📋 79 02 37 02; www.polarriggen.com; Skjæringa; s 790-1350kr, d 1050-1600kr; ☎) Run by the ebullient Mary-Ann and adorned with mining and hunting memorabilia, the Polarrigg brims with character, although most of this is in the public areas; rooms are quite simple. In the main wing, rooms have corridor bathrooms and doubles come with bunk beds. There are two large, comfortably furnished lounges, while in the smart, if somewhat overpriced, annexe, rooms have every comfort.

★ **Svalbard Hotell & Lodge** HOTEL $$$
(📋 79 02 50 00; www.svalbardbooking.com/Accommodation/Svalbard-Hotell; s/d/apt from 1790/1990/2250kr; ☎) Svalbard Hotell & Lodge offers stylish rooms with dark Scandinavian wood tones offset by stunning large photos above the beds and splashes of colour in the linens. There are flat-screen TVs, and you couldn't be more centrally located for the main shops and restaurants of Longyearbyen. The two- and three-bedroom apartments, known as Svalbard Lodge, are similarly outstanding.

★ **Basecamp Spitsbergen** LODGE $$$
(📋 79 02 46 00; www.basecampexplorer.com; s 1150-2600kr, d 1600-3000kr; ☎) Imagine a recreated sealing hut, built in part from recycled driftwood and local slate. Add artefacts and decorations culled from the local refuse dump and mining cast-offs. Graft on 21st-century plumbing and design flair and you've got this fabulous place, also known as Trapper's Lodge. The 16 cabin-like rooms are

MULTIDAY BOAT CRUISES AROUND SVALBARD

To really get a taste for the inner and outer reaches of Svalbard in a short space of time, there's no better alternative than a multiday coastal boat cruise. They don't come cheap, but these are once-in-a-lifetime journeys. Any of the following run such cruises:

Arctic Wildlife Tours (☑958 97 730; www.arcticwildlifetours.com) Wildlife and photography tours to Svalbard aboard specially chartered vessels.

Discover the World (☑UK 01737 214 250; www.discovertheworld.co.uk) UK company with cruises that include Iceland, mainland Norway and Spitsbergen.

G Adventures (www.gadventures.com) Eight-day cruises along the Spitsbergen shore.

Hurtigruten (www.hurtigruten.com) A range of cruises including a complete and utterly unforgettable circumnavigation of Svalbard.

Naturetrek (☑UK 01962 733051; www.naturetrek.co.uk) Has 10-day Svalbard cruises with a wildlife focus.

Wildfoot Travel (☑UK 0800 195 3385; www.wildfoottravel.com) Wildlife-themed five- to 15-night cruises including one that takes in Franz Josef Land and Jan Mayen.

the definition of cosiness and comfort, and the breakfasts are splendid.

Radisson Blu Polar Hotel   HOTEL **$$$**
(☑79 02 34 50; www.radissonblu.com/en/hotel-spitsbergen; s 1390-3100kr, d 1690-3400kr, ste from 2800kr; ⑨) This 95-room chain hotel ('the world's northernmost full-service hotel') is the town's premier address, although the rooms are functional and extremely comfortable rather than luxurious; the suites in the neighbouring annexe are nicer. It costs 200kr extra for a 'superior room' with partial views of the fjord and Hiorthfjellet mountain beyond, and a coffee machine.

Spitsbergen Hotel   HOTEL **$$$**
(☑79 02 62 00; www.spitsbergentravel.com/start/accommodation/spitsbergen-hotel; r from 1611kr; ⊙Feb-Oct; ⑨) This comfortable place (sink yourself low into the leather armchairs of its salon) is where the mine bosses once lived. Rooms are comfortable, with a vaguely old-world air, while public areas are adorned with memorabilia from Longyearbyen's past.

🍴 Eating

Longyearbyen's eating scene gets better with each passing year, ranging from agreeable and informal pub restaurants to temples of high gastronomy. In addition to the stand-alone establishments, there are good restaurants in the Spitsbergen Hotel and Svalbard Hotell & Lodge. The excellent guided tour with Arctic Tapas will also appeal to foodies looking for a different dining experience.

★**Fruene Kaffe og Vinbar**   CAFE **$**
(The Missus; ☑79 02 76 40; Lompensenteret; lunch mains 45-89kr; ⊙10am-6pm Mon-Fri, 10am-5pm Sat, 11am-5pm Sun; ⑨) 'The Missus' is a welcoming and popular cafe, serving decent coffee, baguettes, pizza, snacks and other light meals. There's free wi-fi, the walls are adorned with stunning photography and the food's good – lunch specials usually include a soup or a salad. The soups are particularly outstanding.

★**Coal Miners'**
Bar & Grill   NORWEGIAN, INTERNATIONAL **$$**
(☑79 02 63 00; www.spitsbergentravel.com/start/food/coal-miners-bar-grill; mains from 199kr; ⊙kitchen 3-10pm) A renovation of this former mining mess hall has transformed it into one of Longyearbyen's coolest venues. There's warming decor, fabulous charcoal-grilled meals (the spare ribs and burgers are excellent) and the humming backdrop of a happy crowd that often hangs around to drink long after the kitchen closes; they throw people out at midnight (1am on Friday and Saturday).

★**Huset**   NORWEGIAN **$$**
(☑79 02 50 02; www.huset.com; bistro mains 150-220kr, restaurant mains 295-369kr, Nordic Tasting Menu 900-1100kr; ⊙bistro 4-10pm Sun-Fri, 2-10pm Sat, restaurant 7-10pm Tue-Sun) It's something of a walk up here but it's worth it. Dining in the bistro is casual, with well-priced dishes such as reindeer burger or reindeer stew with lingonberries on the menu. Its signature dish is the coal-grilled hamburger (160kr) – a meaty

ICEBERG WATER

Relatively new to the list of Svalbard souvenirs, Svalbarði (www.svalbardi.com) is such a quintessentially Svalbard product that we wonder why no one thought of it until now – premium drinking water from Svalbard glaciers. It all began back in 2013 when Norwegian-American Jamal Qureshi took some glacier meltwater to his wife as a gift, and the idea was born of marketing Svalbard's purest commodity – pure water that has spent thousands of years inside the pristine glaciers of Kongsfjorden. Packaged in designer bottles, Svalbarði can be bought for around 400kr at a number of shops around Svalbard, or online with worldwide shipping.

burger with all the trimmings, so juicy, we're told, that lonely scientists in their tents dream of it.

In the same building, the highly regarded restaurant serves up dishes such as terrine of Svalbard reindeer, fillet of reindeer and quail. Its wine cellar has over 20,000 bottles. The Nordic Tasting Menu takes in everything from Isfjord cod and bearded seal to Svalbard reindeer sausage and common eider egg.

Mary-Ann's Polarrigg   THAI, NORWEGIAN $$
(☑ 79 02 37 02; www.polarriggen.com; Skjæringa; mains 175-345kr; ⊙ 4-10pm) This excellent restaurant offers up spicy Asian rice dishes in a wonderful glasshouse setting, festooned with living plants that, unlike their native Svalbard counterparts, entwine and climb much more than 2cm high. Also served are some local Norwegian specialities, including Svalbard reindeer or seal steak.

Kroa   NORWEGIAN $$
(☑ 79 02 13 00; www.kroa-svalbard.no; mains lunch 106-161kr, dinner 159-269kr; ⊙ 11.30am-2am) This pub restaurant was reconstructed from the elements of a building brought in from Russian Barentsburg (the giant white bust of Lenin peeking from behind the bar gives a clue), and it feels like a supremely comfortable and spacious trapper's cabin. Service is friendly and mains verge on the gargantuan. Dishes range from pepper steak and butter chicken to Arctic char carpaccio.

★**Gruvelageret**   NEW NORDIC, INTERNATIONAL $$$
(☑ 79 02 20 00; www.gruvelageret.no/en; 4-course set menu 895kr; ⊙ 6-10pm) Opened in the winter of 2015, Gruvelageret occupies a stunningly converted wooden mining warehouse and serves up an exceptional set menu that begins with Atlantic salmon, moves on to borscht soup and reindeer fillet before climaxing with the gorgeous 'crushed cheesecake'. The location, high on a hill deep in the valley, is as splendid as the food.

Advance reservations are essential and payment is by credit card only.

 ## Drinking & Nightlife

Although alcohol is duty-free in Svalbard, it's rationed for locals and visitors must present an onward airline ticket to buy beer and spirits (not wine). The booze outlet **Nordpolet** (☑ 79 02 25 34; www.svalbardbutikken.no/no/vareutvalg/nordpolet; ⊙ 10am-6pm Mon-Fri, 10am-3pm Sat) is at the back of the Coop Supermarket; 'XO Svalbard Cognac' makes an original gift.

Longyearbyen has its own brewery, Svalbard Bryggeri (p354), while Basecamp Spitsbergen (p358) has a stunning, glass-roofed 'Cognac Loft', perfect for watching the winter northern lights (guests only, but this may be relaxed when things are quiet).

Karlsberger Pub   BAR
(☑ 79 02 20 00; www.karlsbergerpub.no; Lompensenteret; ⊙ 5pm-2am Sun-Fri, 3pm-2am Sat) Enter this place, put on your shades and be dazzled at the sight of over 1000 bottles of whisky, brandy and sundry spirits shimmering behind the bar at this snug pub. They also serve pub meals. Ask about their whisky tastings (595kr per person), which happen at the dangerous time of 5pm (where do you go from there?) on Monday, Wednesday and Friday.

Huset   BAR, CLUB
(The House; ☑ 79 02 50 02; www.huset.com; ⊙ bar 4-11pm Mon-Sat, 2-11pm Sun, nightclub 10pm-4am Fri & Sat) Huset is your all-purpose night spot, with a bar and nightclub (cover charge 100kr) where live acts take to the stage on weekends. The wine cellar here has a staggering 20,000 bottles and is one of Scandinavia's best – tastings can be arranged with advance reservations.

Kroa   BAR
(The Pub; ☑ 79 02 13 00; www.kroa-svalbard.no; ⊙ 11.30am-2am) Bustling Kroa, with metal

bar stools fashioned from old mine stanchions and sealskin rugs, is enduringly popular and blurs the line between restaurant and bar in a most agreeable way.

Svalbar BAR
(☑ 79 02 50 03; www.svalbar.no; ⊙ 11am-2am Mon-Thu, noon-2am Fri-Sun) Svalbar is your fairly standard Norwegian bar with a dartboard, billiard table, and small menu of food until 11pm. It's popular with a younger crowd.

🛍 Shopping

Gullgruva JEWELLERY, CLOTHING
(☑ 79 02 18 16; ⊙ 10am-6pm Mon-Fri, 10am-4pm Sat) A cut above many other souvenir outlets in town, Gullgruva puts Arctic designs at the heart of everything they do, from the tasteful polar-bear-themed jewellery to Svalbard-themed clothing.

Svalbardbutikken DEPARTMENT STORE
(☑ 79 02 25 20; www.svalbardbutikken.no; ⊙ 10am-8pm Mon-Fri, 10am-6pm Sat, 3-6pm Sun) Part supermarket, part department store and with a small but decent selection of local souvenirs, Svalbardbutikken is Longyearbyen's catch-all shopping experience.

Skinnboden CLOTHING, ARTS & CRAFTS
(☑ 79 02 10 88; www.skinnboden.no; ⊙ 10am-6pm Mon-Fri, 10am-3pm Sat, noon-3pm Sun) The range of 'Arctic Products' at this place is something of a catch-all and includes all manner of rather unusual products – reindeer-skin boots, sealskin gloves, hats and vests, and even rugs made from the pelts of musk ox and other Arctic creatures. It also has a small range of jewellery. It won't be everyone's cup of tea, but at least it's different.

ℹ Information

MEDICAL SERVICES
Apotek 1 Spitsbergen (☑ 79 02 12 12; ⊙ 10am-5pm Mon-Fri, 10am-2pm Sat) Pharmacy.
Longyearbyen Sykehus (☑ 79 02 42 00) The town's hospital.

TOURIST INFORMATION
Sysselmannen På Svalbard (☑ 79 02 43 00; www.sysselmannen.no; ⊙ 8.30am-3.30pm Mon-Fri) For independent hiking and gun permits.
Tourist Office (☑ 79 02 55 50; www.visitsvalbard.com; ⊙ 10am-5pm May-Sep, noon-5pm Oct-Apr) Produces a helpful weekly activities list and has other information about the Svalbard archipelago.

ℹ Getting There & Away

SAS (www.flysas.com) flies from Longyearbyen to/from Oslo directly in summer (three flights weekly) or via Tromsø (three to five times weekly) year-round.
Norwegian (www.norwegian.com) also flies three times a week between Oslo Gardermoen and Longyearbyen.

TO/FROM THE AIRPORT
The airport bus **Svalbard Busservice** (☑ 79 02 10 52; www.svalbardbuss.no/flybussen; adult/student/child 75/50/25kr) meets arriving and departing planes and takes passengers to hotels around town. Otherwise, **Svalbard Maxi Taxi** (☑ 79 02 13 05) and **Longyearbyen Taxi** (☑ 79 02 13 75) charge 120kr to 150kr for the journey between town and airport.

ℹ Getting Around

BICYCLE
Bicycles can be rented for between 150kr and 350kr from **Poli Arctici** (p356) or **Basecamp Spitsbergen** (p356) and various other, well-signposted outlets around town. Street bikes (no off-roading) are available for those staying at **Longyearbyen Camping** (p358).

CAR & MOTORCYCLE
You can't go that far by car, but **Arctic Autorent** (☑ 917 02 258; www.autorent.no; per day 890-1050kr), with an office in the airport arrivals hall, can get you your own set of wheels.

Barentsburg
POP 471

Visiting the Russian mining settlement of Barentsburg is like stumbling upon a forgotten outpost of the Soviet Union somewhere close to the end of the earth. Although efforts are being made to spruce it up, the bleakness of its Soviet-era architecture in the icy north still seems like a grim evocation of Arctic Siberia.

The first thing you see upon arrival is its power-station chimney, belching dark black smoke into the blue sky. This isolated village continues to mine coal against all odds and still produces up to 350,000 tonnes per year – the seam is predicted to last until around 2030. With its signing in Cyrillic script, still-standing bust of Lenin, murals of muscled workers in heroic pose and a rundown and dishevelled air, Barentsburg is a wonderfully retro Soviet time warp.

History

Barentsburg, on Grønfjorden, was first identified as a coal-producing area around 1900, when the Kullkompaniet Isefjord Spitsbergen started operations. Several other companies also sank shafts and in 1920 the town was founded by the Dutch company Nespico; 12 years later it passed to the Soviet Trust Arktikugol.

Barentsburg, like Longyearbyen, was partially destroyed by the British Royal Navy in 1941 to prevent it falling into Nazi hands (ironically, the German navy itself finished the job later). In 1948 it was rebuilt by Trust Arktikugol and embarked on a period of growth, development and scientific research that lasted until the fall of the Soviet Union.

Barentsburg, like every other pit on Svalbard, has known tragedy. In 1996 many of those who perished in a plane crash during a blizzard near Adventdalen were miners' families from Ukraine. A year later 23 miners died in a mine explosion and fire.

🛏 Sleeping

Pomor Hostel   HOSTEL $
(📞 941 30 128; www.goarctica.com; s/d/tr 500/600/800kr; 📶) This simple place was renovated in 2015 and has unadorned but tidy rooms that have a slightly institutional feel but are well priced. Some have fine views of the surrounding mountains. The hostel is a cheaper alternative to the Barentsburg Hotel. The Red Bear Pub & Brewery across the road is good for meals and drinks.

BLOMSTRANDHALVØYA

Gravelly Blomstrandhalvøya was once a peninsula, but in the early 1990s it was released from the icy grip on its northern end and it's now an island. In summer the name Blomstrand, or 'flower beach', would be appropriate, but it was in fact named for a Norwegian geologist. Ny London, at the southern end of the island, recalls one Ernest Mansfield of the Northern Exploration Company who attempted to quarry marble in 1911 only to discover that the stone had been rendered worthless by aeons of freezing and thawing. A couple of buildings and some forlorn machinery remain.

Barentsburg Hotel   HOTEL $$
(📞 941 30 128; www.goarctica.com; s/d/ste 800/1000/1200kr; 📶) The Barentsburg Hotel has reasonable rooms that are, like Barentsburg itself, a fine evocation of former Soviet times. Despite the old-fashioned decor, the rooms were renovated in 2013 and make for a comfortable and atmospheric stay.

The restaurant serves traditional Russian meals, featuring such specialities as boiled pork with potatoes and Arctic sorrel, parsley and sour cream. Breakfast/lunch/dinner costs 150/250/300kr.

Bookings in advance for both rooms and meals are essential. In the bar you can enjoy a deliciously affordable and generous slug of vodka or a Russian beer, as well as live music on Friday and Saturday evenings. It also sells large tins of the Real McCoy caviar at prices you'll never find elsewhere in the West, let alone Norway.

🍷 Drinking & Nightlife

Red Bear Pub & Brewery   BREWERY, PUB
(🕗 8am-10pm Jun-Aug, shorter hours rest of year) The locally brewed beer (using pure glacier water) is the big attraction here, but they also serve meals (breakfast/lunch/dinner 150/250/200kr), and they do a rather quaint 'Sweet Saturday' with homemade ice cream, milkshakes and baked goodies.

ⓘ Getting There & Away

Three companies offer summertime boat excursions (p355) to Barentsburg from Longyearbyen – **Arctic Explorer** (p355), **Henningsen Transport & Guiding** (p355) and **Polar Charter** (p356). The Henningsen Transport & Guiding and Polar Charter boats head across the fjord to the vast Esmark glacier on the homeward journey, while Arctic Explorer offers a faster boat and enables you to visit Pyramiden on the same day. The price includes a couple of hours in Barentsburg, mostly occupied by a guided tour.

In winter, it's possible to travel between Longyearbyen and Barentsburg as part of a snowmobile safari. **Spitsbergen Travel** (p358) is one of many operators offering this excursion.

Pyramiden

POP 4–15

Formerly Russia's second settlement in Svalbard, Pyramiden, named for the pyramid-shaped mountain that rises nearby, is a rewarding day trip from Longyearbyen, although you can now stay overnight for the full isolation experience.

AROUND SVALBARD

Magdalenefjord The lovely blue-green bay of Magdalenefjord in Nordvest Spitsbergen, flanked by towering peaks and intimidating tidewater glaciers, is the most popular anchorage along Spitsbergen's western coast and is one of Svalbard's prettiest corners. If you catch it on a sunny day (or a moody one with atmospheric storm clouds lurking), you'll think you've wandered into some Arctic paradise. Most visitors come as part of a multiday cruise.

Krossfjorden This 30km-long fjord north of Ny Ålesund is a popular detour for cruise ships, partly for the scenic beauty of Lillehöökbreen (its grand tidewater glacier), but also for the abundance of cultural relics scattered around the shores – the first whaling station on Spitsbergen was established here in 1611. Despite being so far north, as with Ny Ålesund, much of the fjord's shore is free of snow in summer.

Virgohamna One of the most intriguing sites in northwest Spitsbergen is Virgohamna, on the bleak, gravelly island of Danskøya, where the remains of several broken dreams now lie scattered across the lonely beach. Among them are the ruins of three blubber stoves from a 17th-century whaling station and eight stone-covered graves from the same era. You'll also find the remains of a cottage built by English adventurer Arnold Pike, who sailed north and spent a winter subsisting on polar bears and reindeer.

Prins Karls Forlandet On the west coast of Spitsbergen, the oddly shaped, 86km-long, 11km-wide island of Prins Karls Forlandet is a national park set aside to protect breeding walruses, seals and sea lions. The alpine northern reaches, which rise to Grampianfjellet (1084m), are connected to Saltfjellet (430m), at the southern end, by a long, pancake-flat plain called Forlandsletta.

A skeleton staff of Russians still lives at Pyramiden to keep the flag flying, and the reopening of a couple of places to stay has breathed a little life into the settlement, although it remains a largely empty and poignant Arctic outpost. The combination of astonishing beauty (Nordenskjöldbreen, one of Svalbard's most dramatic glaciers, is just across the water), the busts of Lenin, towering Soviet exhortations to defend the motherland and the relics of coal-mining operations tumbling down hillsides is a very Svalbard scene. Staggering beauty scarred by a one-time industrial wasteland make for a jarring juxtaposition of the pristine with the post-apocalyptic.

History

In the mid-1910s coal was discovered here and operations were set up by the same Swedish concern that exploited Sveagruva. In 1926 it was taken over by a Soviet firm, Russkiy Grumant, which sold out to the Soviet Trust Arktikugol, exploiters of Barentsburg, in 1931. In the 1950s there were as many as 2500 Russian residents, exceeding the population of Longyearbyen today. During its productive heyday in the early 1990s it had 60km of shafts, 130 homes, agricultural enterprises similar to those in Barentsburg and the world's most northerly hotel and

swimming pool. But with the mine no longer yielding enough coal to be profitable and with Russia not willing or able to subsidise the mine, Pyramiden was abandoned in 1998.

⊙ Sights

Focal points for your walk around town are the 1970s-era **Soviet architecture**, a prominent **bust of Lenin** and the **sports hall**. There's a small hotel shop selling a small selection of Soviet memorabilia and a bar serving vodka shots.

Across Billefjorden to the east, **Nordenskjöldbreen** is a stunning glacier running as a broad front from the Svalbard interior to the fjord shoreline; most boat excursions from Longyearbyen draw near for photos. The boat journey itself from Longyearbyen is a splendid trip, passing striated cliffs and accompanied by puffins and fulmar.

🛏 Sleeping

Pier Hostel HOSTEL $
(Pyramiden Container; ☑941 30 128; www.go arctica.com; dm 300kr; ⊘Mar-Oct) Sleeping in a shipping container somehow captures the industrial spirit of Pyramiden. Indeed, it doesn't come much simpler than the 12 bunk beds in these three converted containers down by the port – as their own

publicity states, the place isn't really romantic, but the views across the fjord more than compensate.

Tulpan Hotel   HOTEL $$
(☑941 30 128; www.goarctica.com; s 800-1000kr, tw 1000-1200kr, ste 1500kr) The Tulpan Hotel is a wonderful throwback to another age. Modern rooms are comfortable but unremarkable, though waking up in the cheaper and faithfully preserved 'Soviet-style' rooms will have you wondering if the Iron Curtain ever really lifted. And the sense of silence right outside your window once the day trippers return to Longyearbyen is so pure as to be unnerving.

There's an on-site restaurant (advance reservations required) serving Russian specialities – both set menus (meals 150kr to 250kr) and à la carte choices are available.

Note that payment is in cash only and there's no wi-fi.

ⓘ Getting There & Away

In summer, four Longyearbyen-based tour agencies offer a range of day cruises (p355) to Pyramiden – **Arctic Explorer** (p355), **Henningsen Transport & Guiding** (p355), **Polar Charter** (p356) and **Svalbard Booking** (p356).

In winter, snowmobile safaris between Longyearbyen and Pyramiden are possible.

Ny Ålesund

POP 30–130

Despite its inhospitable latitude (79°N), you'd be hard pressed to find a more awesome backdrop anywhere on earth than the scientific post of Ny Ålesund, 107km northwest of Longyearbyen. Ny Ålesund likes to claim that it's the world's northernmost permanently inhabited civilian community (although you could make a case for three other equally minuscule spots in Russia and Canada). There's a hardy year-round population of around 30 scientists, rising to 130 in summer (never more as that's the number of beds available) as researchers from about 15 countries fly in.

With day visits from Longyearbyen now possible in summer, a visit to Ny Ålesund is no longer the sole preserve of cruiseship passengers, and a visit here somehow captures Svalbard's otherworldliness, most notably its remoteness, its resilient human footholds and its natural power and beauty.

◉ Sights

Mine Museum   MUSEUM
(Gruvemuseum; donation suggested; ⊘24hr) Ny Ålesund's neat little Mine Museum is in the old Tiedemann's Tabak (tobacco) shop. It recounts the coal-mining history of the area – it's a simple but pleasing affair with a good mix of artefacts and information panels.

ⓘ Getting There & Away

Although there is a small airstrip here, it's solely for visiting scientists, and the only way to reach Ny Ålesund is on a summer cruise ship or day-trip boat excursion from Longyearbyen.

Understand Norway

History

Norway may have become the epitome of a modern, peaceful country, but its history is soaked in blood. It is a story peopled with picaresque characters that revolves around recurring grand themes, from the Vikings to the battle for supremacy in Scandinavia, from the struggles of the Sami to the dark days of World War II, from extreme poverty to previously unimaginable riches. How it all happened is one of world history's great epics.

Darkness & Ice

Some of the most lasting impressions travellers carry with them after visiting Norway – a land of snow and ice, a bountiful coast, extreme climatic conditions and a thinly populated land – have been present here since the dawn of Scandinavian civilisation. Indeed, the human presence in Norway was for thousands of years overshadowed by Norway's geography and climate, which have strong claims to being the most enduring personalities of Norwegian history.

The History of Norway – From the Ice Age to Today (2003), by Oivind Stenersen and Ivar Libæk, provides more than enough historical detail for most travellers and is available at larger bookshops in Norway.

During the last ice age, Norway was barely habitable. But if Norway was less than hospitable, it was a paradise compared to northern Russia at the time and, as the ice began to melt, it was from the east that the first major, lasting migration to Norway took place when, around 11,000 years ago, the Komsa, who would later become the Sami, arrived in Norway's Arctic North.

As the climate warmed and Norway became increasingly habitable, migrations of the Nøstvet-Økser people of central Europe began arriving along the southern Norwegian coast, drawn by relatively plentiful fishing, sealing and hunting. Wild reindeer also followed the retreating ice, moving north into the still ice-bound interior, and the hunters that followed them were the first humans to traverse the Norwegian high country. Their presence was, however, restricted to itinerant, seasonal camps and there remained few human footholds in an otherwise empty land dominated by glaciers and frozen wastes.

Over the millennia that followed, settled cultures began to take root, to the extent that during the later years of the Roman Empire, Rome provided Norway with fabric, iron implements and pottery. The iron tools allowed

TIMELINE	12,000 BCE	9000 BCE	4000 BCE
	The last ice age thaws and Norway takes on its present physical form with a new body of water separating Norway from northern Europe.	The hunting culture of the Komsa, the forerunner of the Sami, arrives in northern Scandinavia; the Komsa establish the first permanent settlements in Norway's Arctic North.	The earliest example of the Unesco World Heritage–listed rock art is painted by Stone Age peoples close to modern Alta in Norway's far north, charting the region's human and natural history.

farmland to be cleared of trees, larger boats were built with the aid of iron axes, and a cooling climate saw the establishment of more permanent structures built from stone and turf. By the 5th century Norwegians had learned how to smelt their own iron from ore found in the southern Norwegian bogs. Norway's endless struggle to tame its wild landscape had begun.

Here Come the Vikings

Few historical people have captured the imagination quite like the Vikings. Immortalised in modern cartoons (*Asterix* and *Hägar the Horrible*, to name just two) and considered to be the most feared predators of ancient Europe, the Vikings may have disappeared from history, but as a seafaring nation with its face turned towards distant lands, they remain

THE KEYS TO WORLD DOMINATION

The main god who provided strength to the Viking cause was Odin (Oðinn), the 'All-Father' who was married to Frigg. Together they gave birth to a son, Thor (Þór), the God of Thunder. The Vikings believed that if they died on the battlefield, the all-powerful Odin would take them to a paradise by the name of Valhalla, where Viking men could fight all day and then be served by beautiful women.

Not surprisingly, it was considered far better for a Viking to die on the battlefield than in bed of old age and Vikings brought a reckless abandon to their battles that was extremely difficult for enemies to overcome – to die or to come away with loot, the Vikings seemed to say, was more or less the same. Equally unsurprising was the fact that the essential Viking values that emerged from their unique world view embodied strength, skill in weapons, heroic courage, personal sacrifice and a disregard for death.

But the Vikings were as much the sophisticates of the ancient world as they were its fearless warriors. Viking ships were revolutionary, fast, manoeuvrable vessels capable of withstanding torrid and often long ocean journeys. Longboats were over 30m long, had a solid keel, a flexible hull and large, square sails, and could travel up to 12 knots (22km) per hour; they enabled the Vikings to launch and maintain a conquest that would go largely unchallenged for 200 years.

Perhaps the most curious aspect of Viking voyages, however, was the navigational tool they employed to travel through uncharted territory. Norse sagas mention a mysterious device known as a *solarsteinn* (sunstone), which allowed navigation even when the sky was overcast or the sun was below the horizon and celestial navigation was impossible.

It is now generally agreed that the *solarsteinn* was a crystal of cordierite, which is found around Scandinavia and has natural polarising qualities. When observed from below and rotated, light passing through the crystal is polarised blue when the long axis is pointed towards the source of the sunlight. Even today, jet planes flying over polar regions, where magnetic compasses are unsuitable, use a sky compass that determines the position of the sun by filtering sunlight through an artificial polarising lens.

2500 BCE	787 CE	793	871
The wonderfully named Battle-Axe, Boat-Axe and Funnel-Beaker people, named after the stone tools they used, enter southern Norway from Sweden. They trade amber for metals from mainland Europe.	The earliest account of Norse seafaring appears in the *Anglo Saxon Chronicle* for 787, describing how three ships came to Britain, piloted by sailors who were described as Northmen.	The dawn of the Viking age comes when Vikings plunder St Cuthbert's monastery on the island of Lindisfarne, off the coast of Northumberland in Britain.	Tønsberg in southern Norway is founded around this year, making it the oldest still-inhabited town in Norway. It later serves as a royal court and an important trading town.

very much the forerunners of modern Norway. But who were these ancient warriors who took to their longboats and dominated Europe for five centuries?

Conquest & Expansion

Under pressure from shrinking agricultural land caused by a growing population, settlers from Norway began arriving along the coast of the British Isles in the 780s. When the boats returned home to Norway with enticing trade goods and tales of poorly defended coastlines, the Vikings began laying plans to conquer the world. The first Viking raid took place on St Cuthbert's monastery on the island of Lindisfarne in 793. Soon the Vikings were spreading across Britain, Ireland and the rest of Europe with war on their minds and returning home with slaves *(thrall)* in their formidable, low Norse longboats.

The Vikings attacked in great fleets, terrorising, murdering, enslaving, assimilating or displacing local populations. Coastal regions of Britain, Ireland, France (Normandy was named for these 'Northmen'), Russia (as far east as the river Volga), Moorish Spain (Seville was raided in 844) and the Middle East (they even reached Baghdad) all came under the Viking sway. Well-defended Constantinople (Istanbul) proved a bridge too far – the Vikings attacked six times but never took the city. Such rare setbacks notwithstanding, the Viking raids transformed Scandinavia from an obscure backwater on Europe's northern fringe to an all-powerful empire.

For all of their destruction elsewhere, Vikings belonged very much to the shores from which they set out or sheltered on their raids. Viking raids increased standards of living at home. Emigration freed up farmland and fostered the emergence of a new merchant class, while captured slaves provided farm labour. Norwegian farmers also crossed the Atlantic to settle the Faroes, Iceland and Greenland during the 9th and 10th centuries. The world, it seemed, belonged to the Vikings.

Little is known about the nomadic, hunter-gatherer Nøstvet-Økser people, who were most likely tall, blond-haired and blue-eyed and spoke a Germanic language, the predecessor of modern Scandinavian languages.

BOOKS ABOUT VIKINGS

➡ *The Penguin Historical Atlas of the Vikings* (John Haywood; 1995)

➡ *A History of the Vikings* (Gwyn Jones; 2001)

➡ *The Vikings* (Magnus Magnusson; 2000)

➡ *The Oxford Illustrated History of the Vikings* (Peter Sawyer (Ed); 2008)

➡ *The Viking World* (James Graham-Campbell; 2013)

➡ *The Last Vikings: The Epic Story of the Great Norse Voyagers* (Kirsten A Seaver; 2014)

➡ *The Vikings* (Else Roesdahl; 2016)

872	997	c 1000	1024
Harald Hårfagre (Harald Fair-Hair) fights his fellow Viking chieftains in the Battle of Hafrsfjord and unites Norway for the first time. Some 20,000 people flee to Iceland.	Trondheim is founded at the mouth of the Nid River and is the first major settlement in the country; it becomes the first capital of the fledgling kingdom.	Almost five centuries before Columbus, Leifur Eiríksson, son of Eiríkur Rauðe (Eric the Red), explores the North American coast, which he names Vinland, meaning the 'land of wine'.	Olav II founds the Church of Norway and establishes it as Norway's state religion throughout his realm, a situation that continues to this day.

Harald Fair-Hair

Harald Hårfagre (Harald Fair-Hair), son of Hvaldan Svarte (Halvdan the Black), was more than the latest in a long line of great Viking names. While most Viking chieftains made their name in foreign conquest, Harald Fair-Hair was doing something that no other leader had managed before – he united the disparate warring tribes of the Viking nation.

Harald's greatest moment came in 872 at Hafrsfjord near Haugesund when he emerged victorious from one of world history's few civil wars to be decided at sea. When the dust settled, Norway had become a single country.

The reign of Harald Hårfagre was such an odd and entertaining time that it was recorded for posterity in the *Heimskringla,* the Norwegian kings' saga, by Icelander Snorre Sturluson. According to Snorre, Harald's unification of Norway was inspired by a woman who taunted the king by refusing to have relations with a man whose kingdom wasn't even as large as tiny Denmark. Through a series of confederations and trade agreements, he extended his rule as far north as what is now Trøndelag. His foreign policies were equally canny, and he even sent one of his sons, Håkon, to be reared in the court of King Athelstan of England. There is no record of whether the woman in question was sufficiently impressed. Harald died of plague at Avaldsnes on Karmøy island around 930.

The king who unified the country could do little about his own family, however. He had 10 wives and fathered a surfeit of heirs, thereby creating serious squabbles over succession. The one who rose above them all was Erik, his last child and only son with Ragnhild the Mighty, daughter of the Danish King Erik of Jutland. The ruthless Erik eliminated all of his legitimate brothers except Håkon (who was safe in England). Erik, whose reign was characterised by considerable ineptitude, then proceeded to squander his father's hard-won Norwegian confederation. When Håkon returned from England to sort out the mess as King Håkon den Gode (Håkon the Good), Erik was forced to flee to Britain where he took over the throne of York as King Erik Blood-Axe.

Christianity & the Viking Decline

The Vikings gave Norwegians their love of the sea and it was during the late Viking period that they bequeathed to them another of their most enduring national traits – strong roots in Christianity. However, this overturning of the Viking pantheon of gods did not come without a struggle.

King Håkon the Good, who had been baptised a Christian during his English upbringing, brought the new faith (as well as missionaries and a bishop) with him upon his return to Norway. Despite some early success, most Vikings remained loyal to Thor, Odin and Freyr. Although the missionaries were eventually able to replace the names of the gods with those of Catholic saints, the pagan practice of blood sacrifice continued

HISTORY HERE COME THE VIKINGS

The Haugelandet region of western Norway is considered by many to be the cradle of Viking culture and Karmøy island, south of Haugesund, has a Viking Festival in June (www.opplevav aldsnes.no/viking festivalen/).

The word 'Viking' derives from *vik,* an Old Norse word that referred to a bay or cove, a reference to Vikings' anchorages during and after raids.

1030	1049	1066	1261
After being sent into exile by King Canute (Knut) of Denmark in 1028, King Olav II returns, only to be killed in Trøndelag at the Battle of Stiklestad.	Harald III (Harald Hardråde, or Harald 'Hard-Ruler'), half-brother of St Olav, founds Oslo and uses it as a base to launch far-ranging raids across the Mediterranean.	The Viking age draws to a close after Harald III dies at the hands of King Harold of England at the Battle of Stamford Bridge in England.	Greenland joins the Kingdom of Norway, followed a year later by Iceland, reflecting Norway's growing influence over the affairs of Europe's far north.

unabated. When Håkon the Good was defeated and killed in 960, Norwegian Christianity all but disappeared.

Christianity in Norway was revived during the reign of King Olav Tryggvason (Olav I). Like any good Viking, Olav decided that only force would work to convert his countrymen to the 'truth'. Unfortunately for the king, his intended wife, Queen Sigrid of Sweden, refused to convert. Olav cancelled the marriage contract and Sigrid married the pagan King Svein Forkbeard of Denmark. Together they orchestrated Olav's death in a great Baltic sea-battle, then took Norway as their own.

Christianity was finally cemented in Norway by King Olav Haraldsson, Olav II, who was also converted in England. Olav II and his Viking hordes allied themselves with King Ethelred and managed to save London from a Danish attack under King Svein Forkbeard by destroying London Bridge (from whence we derive the song 'London Bridge Is Falling Down'). Succeeding where his namesake had failed, Olav II spread Christianity with considerable success. In 1023 Olav built a stone cross (p174) in Voss, where it still stands, and in 1024 he founded the Church of Norway. After an invasion by King Canute (Knut) of Denmark in 1028, Olav II died during the Battle of Stiklestad in 1030. For Christians, this amounted to martyrdom and the king was canonised as a saint; the great Nidaros Cathedral (p257) in Trondheim stands as a memorial to St Olav and, until the Protestant Reformation, the cathedral served as a destination for pilgrims from all over Europe. His most lasting legacy, however, was having forged an enduring identity for Norway as an independent kingdom.

Of the kings who followed, none distinguished themselves quite as infamously as Harald III (Harald Hardråde, or Harald 'Hard-Ruler'), half-brother of St Olav. Harald III raided throughout the Mediterranean, but it was a last hurrah for the Vikings. When he was killed in an ill-conceived raid in England in 1066, the Viking air of invincibility was broken.

> According to some linguists, Viking gods gave their names to the days of the week in English – Tuesday (Tyr's Day), Wednesday (Odin's Day), Thursday (Thor's Day) and Friday (Freyr's Day).

Viking Sites

Stiklestad

Tønsberg

Kaupang (Larvik)

Eidfjord

Kinsarvik

Haugesund

Karmøy island

Balestrand

Leka

Lindesnes

No Longer Independent

The Vikings may have been fast disappearing into history, but Viking expansionism, along with the coming of Christianity, planted the seeds – of success, of decline – for what was to come. As Norway's sphere of international influence shrank, Norway's neighbours began to close in, leaving this one-time world power having to fight for its own independence.

Trouble Abroad, Trouble at Home

In 1107 Sigurd I led an expedition of 60 ships to the Holy Land. Three years later he captured Sidon, in modern-day Lebanon. But by this stage foreign conquest had become a smokescreen for serious internal problems. Sigurd died in 1130 and the rest of the century was fraught with brutal civil wars over succession to the throne. The victorious King

1319	1349	1469	1537
Magnus becomes King of Sweden and unites Sweden and Norway. This ends Norwegian independence and the royal line of Harald Fair-Hair, and begins two centuries of decline.	Bubonic plague (the Black Death) arrives in Bergen and quickly spreads throughout the country, forever altering Norway's social fabric.	The Orkney and Shetland islands, along with the Isle of Man, are sold to the Scots, bringing to an end centuries of Norwegian expansion.	The Reformation that sweeps across Europe reaches Norway, after which the incumbent Catholic faith is replaced with Lutheran Protestantism.

Sverre, a churchman-turned-warrior, paved the way for Norway's so-called 'Golden Age', which saw Bergen claim the title of national capital, driven by Norway's perennial ties to foreign lands and, in particular, trade between coastal towns and the German-based Hanseatic League. Perhaps drawn by Norway's economic boom, Greenland and Iceland voluntarily joined the Kingdom of Norway in 1261 and 1262, respectively.

But Norway's role as a world power was on the wane and Norway was turning inward. Håkon V built brick and stone forts, one at Vardø to protect the north from the Russians, and another at Akershus (p55), in 1308, to defend Oslo harbour. The transfer of the national capital from Bergen to Oslo soon followed. When Håkon V's grandson Magnus united Norway with Sweden in 1319, Norway began a decline that would last for 200 years. Once-great Norway had become just another province of its neighbours.

In August 1349 the Black Death arrived in Norway on board an English ship via Bergen. The bubonic plague would eventually kill one-third of Europe's population. In Norway, land fell out of cultivation, towns were ruined, trading activities faltered and the national coffers decreased by 65%. As much as 80% of the nobility perished. Because their peasant workforce had also been decimated, the survivors were forced to return to the land, forever changing the Norwegian power-base and planting the seeds for an egalitarianism that continues to define Norway to this day.

By 1387 Norway had lost control of Iceland and 10 years later Queen Margaret of Denmark formed the Kalmar Union of Sweden, Denmark and Norway, with Eric of Pomerania as king. Margaret's neglect of Norway continued into the 15th century, when trade links with Iceland were broken and Norway's Greenland colonies mysteriously disappeared without a trace.

In 1469 Orkney and Shetland were pawned – supposedly a temporary measure – to the Scottish Crown by the Danish-Norwegian King Christian I, who had to raise money for his daughter's dowry. Just three years later the Scots annexed both island groups.

Buffeted by these winds of change, Norway had become a shadow of its former self. The only apparent constant was the country's staunch Christian faith. But even in the country's faith there were fundamental changes afoot. In 1537 the Reformation replaced the incumbent Catholic faith with Lutheran Protestantism and the transformation from the Norway of the Vikings was all but complete.

Denmark & Sweden – the Enemy

Talk to many Norwegians and you'll quickly find that there's no love lost between them and their neighbours, Denmark and Sweden. Here's why.

A series of disputes between the Danish Union and the Swedish crown were played out on Norwegian soil. First came the Seven Years

Viking Museums

Vikingskiphuset (Oslo)

Lofotr Viking Museum (Vestvågøy, Lofoten)

Nordvegen Historiesenter (Karmøy island)

HISTORY NO LONGER INDEPENDENT

So ferocious were the Vikings that the word berserk comes from 'bare sark', which means 'bare shirt' and refers to the way that ancient, bare-chested Norsemen used to fight.

1596	1612	1720	1814
Willem Barents, a Dutch explorer searching for a northeast sea passage to Asia, becomes the first European to set foot on Svalbard. He names the archipelago Spitsbergen ('sharp mountains').	Commercial whaling begins on Svalbard, with English, Dutch, Norwegian, French and Danish fleets driving many whale and other marine species to the brink of extinction in the centuries that follow.	After 150 years of conflict on Norwegian soil (the Seven Years War, the Kalmar War and the Great Nordic War) Sweden is finally defeated, although Danish and Swedish influence remains strong.	Norway is presented to Sweden in the so-called 'Union of the Crowns'. Disgruntled Norwegians draft their first constitution, an event still celebrated as Norway's first act of independence.

War (1563–70), followed by the Kalmar War (1611–14). Trondheim, for example, was repeatedly captured and recaptured by both sides and during the Kalmar War an invasion of Norway was mounted from Scotland.

In two further wars during the mid-17th century Norway lost a good portion of its territory to Sweden. The Great Nordic War with the expanding Swedish Empire was fought in the early 18th century and in 1716 the Swedes occupied Christiania (Oslo). The Swedes were finally defeated in 1720, ending more than 150 years of warfare.

Despite attempts to re-establish trade with Greenland through the formation of Norwegian trading companies in Bergen in 1720, Danish trade restrictions scuppered the nascent economic independence. As a consequence, Norway was ill-equipped to weather the so-called 'Little Ice Age', from 1738 to 1742. The failure of crops ensured a period of famine and the death of one-third of Norwegian cattle, not to mention thousands of people.

During the Napoleonic Wars, Britain blockaded Norway, causing the Danes to surrender on 14 January 1814. The subsequent Treaty of Kiel presented Norway to Sweden in a 'Union of the Crowns'. Tired of having their territory divided up by foreign kings, a contingent of farmers, businesspeople and politicians gathered at Eidsvoll Verk in April 1814 to draft a new constitution and elect a new Norwegian king. Sweden wasn't at all happy at this show of independence and forced the new king, Christian Frederik, to yield and accept the Swedish choice of monarch, Karl Johan. War was averted by a compromise that provided for devolved Swedish power. Norway's constitution hadn't lasted long, but it did suggest that Norwegians had had enough.

Independent Norway

Norway may have spent much of the previous centuries as the subservient vassal of foreign occupiers and its days as a world power had long ago ended, but not all was doom and gloom. It took almost a century after their first constitution, not to mention nine centuries after Harald Fair-Hair first unified the country, but Norwegians were determined to once and for all become masters of their own destiny.

A Confident Start

During the 19th century, perhaps buoyed by the spirit of the 1814 constitution, Norwegians began to rediscover a sense of their own, independent cultural identity. This nascent cultural revival was most evident in a flowering of musical and artistic expression led by poet and playwright Henrik Ibsen, composer Edvard Grieg and artist Edvard Munch.

Language also began to play its part with the development of a standardised written form of Norwegian known as *landsmål* (or *Nynorsk*).

The mystery behind the disappearance of the Greenland colonies is examined in Jared Diamond's *Collapse: How Societies Choose to Fail or Survive* (2005).

Sweden and Visions of Norway: Politics and Culture 1814–1905 (2002), by H Arnold Barton, offers a detailed analysis of the enmity and uneasy neighbourliness between Norway and Sweden in the pivotal 19th century.

1861	1870s	1895	1905
Fridtjof Nansen, an explorer, scientist, diplomat and winner of the Nobel Peace Prize, is born near Oslo (then called Christiania). He later becomes a symbol for Norway's growing international influence.	Emissaries from London gentlemen's clubs journey to Norway's western fjords to find blue ice for the clubs' drinks. Soon after, Thomas Cook begins the first tourist cruises into the fjords.	Alfred Nobel's will decrees that the interest on his vast fortune be awarded each year 'to those who, during the preceding year, shall have conferred the greatest benefit on mankind'.	Norwegians vote overwhelmingly for independence and against union with Sweden. Norway becomes independent, with its own constitutional monarchy.

Norway's first railway, from Oslo to Eidsvoll, was completed in 1854 and Norway began looking at increased international trade, particularly tied to its burgeoning fishing and whaling industries in the Arctic North.

Norway was still extremely poor – between 1825 and 1925, over 750,000 Norwegians resettled in the USA and Canada – but the surge of national pride and identity would not be stopped.

In 1905 a constitutional referendum was held. As expected, almost 80% of voters favoured independence from Sweden. The Swedish king, Oskar II, was forced to recognise Norwegian sovereignty, abdicate and reinstate a Norwegian constitutional monarchy, with Haakon VII on the throne. His descendants rule Norway to this day, with decisions on succession

ROALD AMUNDSEN

The Norwegian explorer Roald Amundsen played a pivotal role in forging a proud sense of Norwegian identity in the early 20th century.

Born into a family of shipowners and captains in 1872 at Borge, near Sarpsborg in southern Norway, Amundsen sailed in 1897 to the Antarctic as first mate on the Belgian *Belgica* expedition. Their ship froze fast in the ice and became – unintentionally – the first expedition to overwinter in the Antarctic.

Amundsen then set his sights on the Northwest Passage and the study of the Magnetic North Pole. The expedition, which set out from Oslo in June 1903, overwintered in a natural harbour on King William Island, which they named Gjøahavn. By August 1905 they emerged into waters that had been charted from the west, becoming the first vessel to navigate the Northwest Passage.

Amundsen dreamed of becoming the first man to reach the North Pole, but in April 1909 Robert Peary took that honour. In 1910 Amundsen headed instead for the South Pole. In January 1911, Amundsen's ship dropped anchor at Roosevelt Island, 60km closer to the South Pole than the base of Robert Falcon Scott's *Terra Nova* expedition. With four companions and four 13-dog sleds, Amundsen reached the South Pole on 14 December 1911, beating Scott by a month and three days.

In 1925 Amundsen launched a failed attempt to fly over the North Pole. He tried again the following year aboard the airship *Norge*, this time with Lincoln Ellsworth, Hjalmar Riiser-Larsen and Italian explorer Umberto Nobile. They left Spitsbergen on 11 May 1926 and, 16 hours later, dropped the Norwegian, US and Italian flags on the North Pole. On 14 May they landed triumphantly at Teller, Alaska, having flown 5456km in 72 hours – the first ever flight between Europe and North America.

In May 1928 Nobile attempted another expedition in the airship *Italia* and, when it crashed in the Arctic, Amundsen joined the rescue. Although Nobile and his crew were subsequently rescued, Amundsen's last signals were received just three hours after take-off from somewhere over the Barents Sea. His body has never been found.

1911	1913	1914	1940
Norwegian explorer Roald Amundsen becomes the first person to reach the South Pole, highlighting a period of famous Norwegian explorers going to the ends of the earth.	Norway introduces universal suffrage for women, 15 years after men but long before many other European countries, and begins a tradition of gender equality that has become a hallmark of modern Norway.	Norway, Sweden and Denmark announce that they will remain neutral during WWI, thereby sparing Scandinavia the devastation that the war visits upon much of the rest of Europe.	On 9 April Nazi Germany invades Norway. King Haakon and the royal family flee into exile, first to the UK and then to Washington, DC, where they remain throughout the war.

Archaeo-logical Museums

Bryggens Museum (Bergen)

Arkeologisk Museet (Stavanger)

Historisk Museet (Oslo)

Museum of Natural History & Archaeology (Trondheim)

Alta Museum (Alta)

remaining under the authority of the *storting* (parliament). Oslo was declared the national capital of the Kingdom of Norway.

Newly independent Norway quickly set about showing the world that it was a worthy international citizen. In 1911 the Norwegian explorer Roald Amundsen reached the South Pole. Two years later Norwegian women became among the first in Europe to be given the vote. Hydroelectric projects sprang up all around the country and prosperous new industries emerged to drive the increasingly growing export economy.

Having emerged from WWI largely unscathed – Norway was neutral, although some Norwegian merchant vessels were sunk by the Germans – Norway grew in confidence. In 1920 the *storting* voted to join the newly formed League of Nations, a move that was opposed only by the Communist-inspired Labour Party that dominated the *storting* by 1927. The 1920s also brought new innovations, including the development of factory ships, which enabled processing of whales at sea and caused an increase in whaling activities, especially around Svalbard and in the Antarctic.

Trouble, however, lay just around the corner. The Great Depression of the late 1920s and beyond almost brought Norway to its knees. By December 1932 there was 42% unemployment and farmers were hit especially hard by the economic downturn.

Norway at War

Norway chose a bad time to begin asserting its independence. The clouds of war were gathering in Europe and by the early 1930s fascism had begun to spread throughout the continent. Unlike during WWI, Norway found itself caught up in the violent convulsions sweeping across Europe and in 1933 the former Norwegian defence minister Vidkun Quisling formed a Norwegian fascist party, the *Nasjonal Samling*. The Germans invaded Norway on 9 April 1940, prompting King Haakon and the royal family to flee into exile, while British, French, Polish and Norwegian forces fought a desperate rearguard action.

Six southern towns were burnt out and despite some Allied gains the British, who were out on a limb, abandoned Arctic Norway to its fate. In Oslo, the Germans established a puppet government under Vidkun Quisling, whose name thereafter entered the lexicon as a byword for those collaborators who betray their country.

Having spent centuries fighting for a country to call their own, the Norwegians didn't take lightly to German occupation. In particular, the Resistance network distinguished itself in sabotaging German designs, often with the assistance of daring Shetland fishermen who smuggled arms across the sea to western Norway. Among the most memorable acts of defiance was a commando assault on February 1943 on the heavy water plant at Vemork, which was involved in the German development of an atomic bomb.

WWII Books

Assault in Norway: Sabotaging the Nazi Nuclear Campaign (Thomas Gallagher; 2002)

War and Innocence: A Young Girl's Life in Occupied Norway (Hanna Aasvik Helmersen; 2000)

The German Invasion of Norway: April 1940 (Geirr H Haarr; 2012)

1945	1945	1949	1950s
On 7 May the last foreign troops on Norwegian soil, the Russians, withdraw from Arctic Norway, following the devastation wrought across the country by the retreating German army.	Norway becomes a founding member of the UN. This membership later provides a platform for Norwegian foreign policy, with Norway an important mediator in numerous international conflicts.	Norway joins NATO and aligns itself with the USA despite fears in the West that left-leaning Norway would turn towards the Soviet Union.	A Norwegian government commission declares that 'the chances of finding oil on the continental shelf off the Norwegian coast can be discounted'. How wrong it was.

HEADING INTO EXILE

When German forces invaded Norway in April 1940, King Haakon and the Norwegian government fled northwards from Oslo. They halted in Elverum and on 9 April the parliament met at the folk high school and issued the Elverum Mandate, giving the exiled government the authority to protect Norway's interests until the parliament could reconvene. When a German messenger arrived to impose the Nazis' version of 'protection' in the form of a new puppet government in Oslo, the king rejected the 'offer' before heading into exile. Two days later, Elverum became the first Norwegian town to suffer massive bombing by the Nazis and most of the town's old wooden buildings were levelled. By then the king had fled to Nybergsund (close to Trysil), which was also bombed, but he escaped into exile.

The Germans exacted bitter revenge on the local populace and among the civilian casualties were 630 Norwegian Jews who were sent to central European concentration camps. Serbian and Russian prisoners of war were coerced into slave labour on construction projects in Norway, and many perished from the cold and an inadequate diet. The high number of worker fatalities during the construction of the Arctic Highway through the Saltfjellet inspired its nickname, the *blodveien* (blood road).

Finnmark suffered particularly heavy destruction and casualties during the war. In Altafjorden and elsewhere, the Germans constructed submarine bases, which were used to attack convoys headed for Murmansk and Arkhangelsk in Russia, so as to disrupt the supply of armaments to the Russians.

In early 1945, with the Germans facing an escalating two-front war and seeking to delay the Russian advance into Finnmark, the German forces adopted a scorched-earth policy that devastated northern Norway, burning fields, forests, towns and villages. Shortly after the German surrender of Norway, Quisling was executed by firing squad and other collaborators were sent off to prison.

The first Allied victory of WWII occurred in late May 1940 in Norway, when a British naval force retook Narvik and won control over this strategic iron ore port. It fell again to the Germans on 9 June.

The Oil Years

Although there were initial fears in the postwar years that Norway would join the Eastern Bloc of Communist countries under the Soviet orbit – the Communist party made strong gains in postwar elections and took part in coalition governments – the Iron Curtain remained firmly in place at the Russian border. More than that, Norway made a clear statement of intent in 1945 when it became a founding member of the UN. Ever conscious of its proximity to Russia, the country also abandoned its neutrality by joining NATO in 1949. Letting bygones be bygones, Norway joined with other Scandinavian countries to form the Nordic Council in 1952.

Late 1960s	1993	1994	2001
Oil is discovered, transforming Norway into one of the richest countries in the world. Oil revenues provide the basis for an all-encompassing system of social welfare and generous foreign aid.	In defiance of international opinion and contrary to a 1986 moratorium, Norway resumes commercial whaling operations, thereby complicating its claims to be a model environmental citizen.	Norwegians vote against joining the EU. The 'no' vote (52%) draws on the concerns of family farms, fishing interests and the perceived loss of national sovereignty that membership would supposedly bring.	A rare victory for a conservative-liberal coalition after the Labour-led government suffers a massive fall in its vote in national elections; no single party wins enough votes to form government.

There was just one problem: Norway was broke and in desperate need of money for reconstruction, particularly in the Arctic North. At first, it appeared that the increasingly prosperous merchant navy and whaling fleet would provide a partial solution, but in truth Norway struggled along (postwar rationing continued until 1952) as best it could.

That would soon change in the most dramatic way possible. It was the discovery of the Ekofisk oilfield on Norway's Continental shelf, in the North Sea southwest of Stavanger in 1969, that turned Norway into a major oil-producing nation (the world's 15th-largest in 2016, with around 2.75% of world reserves). The economy boomed, transforming Norway from one of Europe's poorest countries to one of its richest.

A TROUBLED MULTICULTURALISM

On 22 July 2011, Norway lost its innocence. That was the day when Anders Behring Breivik detonated a car bomb in Oslo aimed at the nation's political class (eight people were killed), and then, disguised as a policeman, gunned down 69 young political activists on the island of Utøya. When later captured, Breivik claimed that he had acted so as to save Norway and Europe from being taken over by Muslims. Norway's measured response to the most deadly attack in modern Norwegian history was praised around the world and the country united in condemning the attacks and its motives.

And yet, the massacre left deep scars in a country wholly unaccustomed to political violence, let alone terrorism of any kind on its home soil. Breivik was convicted and is likely to spend the rest of his life in prison. But whether the sense of national unity that followed the massacre can survive remains to be seen.

The attack brought to the forefront a debate that had been simmering for a long time. In 1970 just 1.5% of people living in Norway were immigrants. Now, nearly one in six Norwegians were either born overseas or were born to two immigrant parents. This radical demographic shift has changed the way that Norwegians think about their country.

On the one hand, mass immigration is a central pillar in Norway's own national story – in the dark days of the 19th century, Norwegians emigrated in their thousands to escape hardship. Later, the fabulous oil wealth of the late 20th century nurtured the deeply held belief that Norway, as one of the richest countries on earth, had to serve as an example of a responsible and tolerant global citizen, and modern Norwegians are rightfully proud of their tolerance and generosity in assisting troubled countries get back on their feet.

At the same time, there is unease in some quarters about what the rise in immigrant numbers means for ethnic Norwegians and their sense of national identity. At parliamentary elections in 2005, 2009 and again in 2013, the Fremskrittspartiet (Progress Party) – which advocates a crackdown on immigration – polled more than 20% of the vote. In the process it has easily become the second-largest party in the country and, since the 2013 elections, the Progress Party has been part of the coalition government. Its leader, Siv Jensen, who has warned of the 'Islamisation of Norway', is currently Norway's Minister of Finance.

2005	22 July 2011	2013	2014
A 'red-green' coalition wins parliamentary elections, overturning the conservative-led coalition government. They lose power to a centre-left coalition four years later.	Right-wing extremist Anders Breivik kills 77 people in Oslo and on the nearby island of Utøya in protest of Norway's multicultural policies. He is later sentenced to the maximum 21 years in prison.	A four-party, centre-right coalition unseats the red-green coalition of Prime Minister Jens Stoltenberg, winning 96 out of 169 parliamentary seats. Erna Solberg becomes prime minister.	Norway's Major-General Kristin Lund becomes the first woman to command a UN peacekeeping force, heading a 1000-strong peacekeeping force in Cyprus.

At Home & Abroad

Since the transformation of the Norwegian economy following the discovery of oil, successive socialist governments (and short-lived conservative ones) have used the windfalls (alongside high income taxes and service fees) to foster one of the most extensive social welfare systems in history, with free medical care and higher education, as well as generous pension and unemployment benefits. And there looks to be no end in sight for the era of government largesse – its rapidly rising oil fund for future generations soared to around US$958 billion in June 2017. It all adds up to what the government claims is the 'most egalitarian social democracy in Western Europe'.

Thanks in part to its oil wealth, Norway wields a level of influence on the international stage far out of proportion to its relatively small population. Its energetic participation in a range of international institutions, its pivotal involvement in peace processes from the Middle East to Sri Lanka, and its role as a leading player in assisting refugees around the world, in particular, have won international plaudits.

At the same time, Norway remains, by choice, on the fringes of the continent that it inhabits and has yet to join the European Union. Casting an eye over Norwegian history, it's not difficult to understand why Norwegians remain wary of forming unions of any kind with other countries. Having narrowly voted against EU membership in 1972 and again in 1994, despite Norwegian governments pressing for a 'yes' vote, Norway remains on the outside looking in.

In light of Norway's own experiences, when Brexit happened and the UK formally left the European Union (EU) in January 2020, Norway watched with interest. They moved quickly and signed a free-trade deal with the UK in July 2021. Coping with the COVID-19 pandemic was more complicated, although the government's combination of social and travel restrictions with widespread testing and vaccinations was effective in slowing the spread of the virus. By mid-July 2021, there had been 134,000 cases in Norway, with 796 deaths – far fewer than in most other European countries. Neighbouring Sweden, for example, has around twice the population but registered 1.09 million cases and 14,642 deaths at the same stage. By mid-2021, around 30% of Norway's population had been fully vaccinated, while almost 57% had received one vaccine dose.

Modern Norway Travel Literature

Fellowship of Ghosts: A Journey Through the Mountains of Norway (Paul Watkins; 2006)

The Magnetic North: Notes from the Arctic Circle (Sara Wheeler; 2010)

True North: Travels in Arctic Norway (Gavin Francis; 2011)

The Almost Nearly Perfect People: The Truth About the Nordic Miracle (Michael Booth; 2014)

Out in the Cold: Travels North: Adventures in Svalbard, the Faroe Islands, Iceland, Greenland and Canada (Bill Murray; 2017)

2017	2017	2020-21	2021
An unusually warm winter in the sub-polar archipelago of Svalbard causes flooding in the Global Seed Vault, forcing a rethink of the vault's impregnability.	PM Erna Solberg and her Conservative-Progress coalition win re-election four years after their first election win, this time with a reduced majority, taking 88 seats in the 169-seat parliament.	Norway weathers the coronavirus pandemic better than most European nations, with fewer than 800 deaths and 134,000 cases in the first 15 months.	Cementing the country's prominent role in international affairs, Norway takes up a seat on the UN Security Council for 2021–22.

Landscapes & National Parks

Norway's geographical facts tell quite a story. The Norwegian mainland stretches 2518km from Lindesnes in the south to Nordkapp in the Arctic North with a narrowest point of 6.3km wide. Norway also has the highest mountains in northern Europe and the fourth-largest land mass in Western Europe (behind France, Spain and Sweden). But these are merely the statistical signposts to the staggering diversity of Norwegian land-forms, from glacier-strewn high country and plunging fjords to the tundra-like plains of the Arctic North.

The Coast

Seeming to wrap itself around Scandinavia like a protective shield from the freezing Arctic, Norway's coastline appears to have shattered under the strain, riven as it is with islands and fjords cutting deep fissures inland. Geologists believe that the islands along Norway's far northern coast were once attached to the North American crustal plate – such is their resemblance to the landforms of eastern Greenland. Further north, Svalbard is geologically independent of the rest of Europe and sits on the Barents continental plate deep in the polar region.

In the North Sea lie two rift valleys that contain upper Jurassic shale bearing the extravagantly rich deposits of oil and gas.

Fjords

Norway has the eighth-longest coastline on earth and if the Norwegian coast were to be stretched from end to end, it would encircle the earth nearly two and a half times.

Norway's signature landscape, the fjords rank among the most astonishing natural landforms anywhere in the world. The Norwegian coast is cut deeply with these inlets distinguished by plunging cliffs, isolated farms high on forested ledges and an abundance of ice-blue water extending deep into the Norwegian interior.

Norway's fjords are a relatively recent phenomenon in geological terms. Although Norwegian geological history stretches back 1.8 billion years, the fjords were not carved out until much later. During the glacial periods over this time, the elevated highland plateaus that ranged across central Norway subsided at least 700m due to an ice sheet up to 2km thick. The movement of this ice, driven by gravity down former river courses, gouged out the fjords and valleys and created the surrounding mountains by sharpening peaks and exposing high cliffs of bare rock. The fjords took on their present form when sea levels rose as the climate warmed following the last ice age (which ended around 10,000 years ago), flooding into the new valleys left behind by melting and retreating glaciers. Sea levels are thought to have risen by as much as 100m, creating fjords whose waters can seem impossibly deep.

In 2005 Unesco inscribed Geirangerfjord and Nærøyfjord on its World Heritage List because they 'are classic, superbly developed fjords', which are 'among the most scenically outstanding fjord areas on the planet'.

Glaciers

Ranking high among the standout natural highlights of the country, Norway's glaciers cover some 26,092 sq km (0.7% of mainland Norwegian territory and 60% of the Svalbard archipelago) – at last count there were 2534 glaciers. But this is a far cry from the last ice age, when Norway was one vast icefield; the bulk of the ice melted around 8800 years ago.

Not only are glaciers a stunning tourist attraction, they also serve an important purpose in Norway's economy: 15% of Norway's electricity derives from river basins below glaciers.

Concerns about shrinking glaciers and ice sheets in the Arctic have taken on added urgency in recent years as the impact of climate change takes hold. Some of Norway's glaciers retreated by up to 2.5km in the 20th century, and glacial ice is also thinning at an alarming rate. In 2013, for example, northern Norway experienced its hottest summer on record, following on from above-average temperatures during much of the preceding decade, thereby accelerating the melting of Norway's glaciers. Inland glaciers are considered to be at far greater risk than Norway's coastal glaciers and a few Norwegian glaciers have grown in recent decades – the thickness of the ice on the Nigardsbreen glacier grew by 13.8m from 1977 to 2007, although it later retreated by 136m in the five years that followed.

Jostedalsbreen is mainland Europe's largest icecap and it feeds some of Norway's largest glaciers, among them Nigardsbreen, Briksdalsbreen and Bødalsbreen. Another spectacular example is Folgefonn, while central Norway's Jotunheimen National Park is home to 60 glaciers.

Glacier Hikes

Jotunheimen National Park

Hardanger-jøkulen glacier, Hardangervidda

Folgefonna National Park

Nigardsbreen

Briks-dalsbreen

Bødalsbreen

Saltfjellet-Svartisen National Park

Svalbard

Arctic North

If the fjords have drama, Norway's Arctic North has an irrevocable sense of mystery. From Svalbard to the Arctic Highway that carries you north into Arctic Norway, Norway's far north is rich in phenomena that seem to spring from a child's imagination.

The first thing you'll likely notice is the endless horizon that never quite seems to frame a landscape of austere, cinematic beauty. Or perhaps what you'll remember most is the astonishing night sky in winter when the weird and wonderful aurora borealis, also called the northern lights, can seem like an evocation of a colourful ghost story writ large. The midnight sun and seemingly endless polar night can be similarly disorienting, adding a strange magic to your Norwegian sojourn.

BIGGEST & HIGHEST

Jostedalsbreen is continental Europe's largest icecap.

Sognefjorden, Norway's longest fjord at 203km (second only in the world to Greenland's Scoresby Sund), is 1308m deep, making it the world's second-deepest fjord (after Skelton Inlet in Antarctica). Hardangerfjord, at 179km, is the third-longest fjord network in the world.

Galdhøpiggen (2469m) is the highest mountain in northern Europe.

Hardangervidda, at 900m above sea level, is Europe's largest and highest plateau.

Utigårdsfossen, a glacial stream that flows into Nesdalen and Lovatnet from Jostedalsbreen (not readily accessible to tourists), is placed by some authorities as the third-highest waterfall in the world at 800m, including a single vertical drop of 600m. Other Norwegian waterfalls among the 10 highest in the world are Espelandsfossen (703m; Hardangerfjord); Mardalsfossen (655m; Eikesdal); and Tyssestrengene (646m in multiple cascades), near Odda.

LANDSCAPES & NATIONAL PARKS GLACIERS

Also part of Norway's Arctic mix is the lichen-strewn tundra landscape of Svalbard.

Aurora Borealis

There are few sights as mesmerising as an undulating aurora. Although these appear in many forms – pillars, streaks, wisps and haloes of vibrating light – they're most memorable when taking the form of pale curtains wafting on a gentle breeze. Most often, the Arctic aurora appears as a faint green or light rose but, in periods of extreme activity, can change to yellow or crimson.

The visible aurora borealis, or northern lights, are caused by streams of charged particles from the sun, called the solar wind, which are directed by the earth's magnetic field towards the polar regions. Because the field curves downward in a halo surrounding the magnetic poles, the charged particles are drawn earthward. Their interaction with electrons in nitrogen and oxygen atoms in the upper atmosphere releases the energy creating the visible aurora. During periods of high activity, a single auroral storm can produce a trillion watts of electricity with a current of 1 million amps.

The Inuit call the lights *arsarnerit* ('to play with a ball'), as they were thought to be ancestors playing ball with a walrus skull. The Inuit also attach spiritual significance to the lights, and some believe that they represent the capering of unborn children; some consider them gifts from the dead to light the long polar nights and others see them as a storehouse of events, past and future.

The best time of year to catch the northern lights in Norway is from October to March, although you may also see them as early as August.

Northern Lights Books

Northern Lights: The Science, Myth, and Wonder of Aurora Borealis (2002) Calvin Hall et al

Aurora: In Search of the Northern Lights (2016) Dr Melanie Windridge

MIDNIGHT SUN & POLAR NIGHT

Because the earth is tilted on its axis, polar regions are constantly facing the sun at their respective summer solstices and are tilted away from it in the winter. The Arctic and Antarctic Circles, at 66° 33' north and south latitude respectively, are the northern and southern limits of constant daylight on their longest day of the year.

The northern half of mainland Norway, as well as Svalbard and Jan Mayen Island, lie north of the Arctic Circle but during summer, between late May and mid-August, nowhere in the country experiences true darkness. In Trondheim, for example, the first stars aren't visible until mid-August.

Conversely, winters here are dark, dreary and long, with only a few hours of twilight to break the long polar nights. In Svalbard, not even a twilight glow can be seen for over a month. During this period of darkness, many people suffer from SAD syndrome, or 'seasonal affective disorder'. Its effects may be minimised by using special solar-spectrum light bulbs for up to 45 minutes after waking up. Not surprisingly, most northern communities make a ritual of welcoming the sun the first time it peeks above the southern horizon.

Town/Area	Latitude	Midnight Sun	Polar Night
Bodø	67° 18'	4 Jun–8 Jul	15 Dec–28 Dec
Svolvær	68° 15'	28 May–14 Jul	5 Dec–7 Jan
Narvik	68° 26'	27 May–15 Jul	4 Dec– 8 Jan
Tromsø	69° 42'	20 May–22 Jul	25 Nov–17 Jan
Alta	70° 00'	16 May–26 Jul	24 Nov–18 Jan
Hammerfest	70° 40'	16 May–27 Jul	21 Nov–21 Jan
Nordkapp	71° 11'	13 May–29 Jul	18 Nov–24 Jan
Longyearbyen	78° 12'	20 Apr–21 Aug	26 Oct–16 Feb

SVALBARD RISING

Glaciers have a staggering power to shape the landscapes through which they flow. Glaciers, for example, played a significant role in gouging out the fjords. More recently, there is evidence to suggest that as glaciers melt and diminish in size, the weight they exert upon the landscape is similarly reduced – the result is that Svalbard is actually rising by a small but significant elevation (8.5mm per year has been measured at Ny Ålesund) with each passing year. While it may not be enough to combat the problems associated with rising sea levels, it does represent one largely unforeseen consequence of climate change.

Fata Morgana

If the aurora inspires wonder, the Fata Morgana may prompt a visit to a psychiatrist. The clear and pure Arctic air ensures that distant features do not appear out of focus. As a result, depth perception becomes impossible and the world takes on a strangely two-dimensional aspect where distances are indeterminable. Early explorers meticulously laid down on maps and charts islands, headlands and mountain ranges that were never seen again. An amusing example of distance distortion, described in *Arctic Dreams* by Barry Lopez, involves a Swedish explorer who was completing a description in his notebook of a craggy headland with two unusual symmetrical valley glaciers, when he discovered that he was actually looking at a walrus.

Fata Morganas are apparently caused by reflections off water, ice and snow, and when combined with temperature inversions, create the illusion of solid, well-defined features where there are none. On clear days off the outermost coasts of Lofoten, Vesterålen, northern Finnmark and Svalbard, you may well observe inverted mountains or nonexistent archipelagos of craggy islands resting on the horizon. It's difficult indeed to convince yourself, even with an accurate map, that they're not really there! Normal visibility at sea is less than 18km, but in the Arctic, sightings of islands and features hundreds of kilometres distant are frequently reported.

Glacier Museums

Norwegian Glacier Museum (Fjærland)

Breheimsenteret Visitors Centre (Nigardsbreen)

High Country

If you think Norway is spectacular now, imagine what it was like 450 million years ago when the Caledonian Mountain Range, which ran along the length of Norway, was as high as the present-day Himalayas. With time, ice and water eroded them down to their current form of mountains and high plateaux (some capped with Europe's largest glaciers and icefields) that together cover more than half the Norwegian land mass.

Norway's highest mountains are in Jotunheimen National Park, where Galdhøpiggen soars to 2469m. Nearby Glittertind (2465m, and shrinking) was for a long time the king of the Norwegian mountains, but its melting glacier sees its summit retreat a little further every year.

National Parks

At last count, Norway had 44 national parks (including seven in Svalbard, where approximately 65% of the land falls within park boundaries). Thirteen new national parks have been created since 2003, with further parks as well as extensions to existing park boundaries planned. Around 15% of the country lies within protected areas.

National Parks

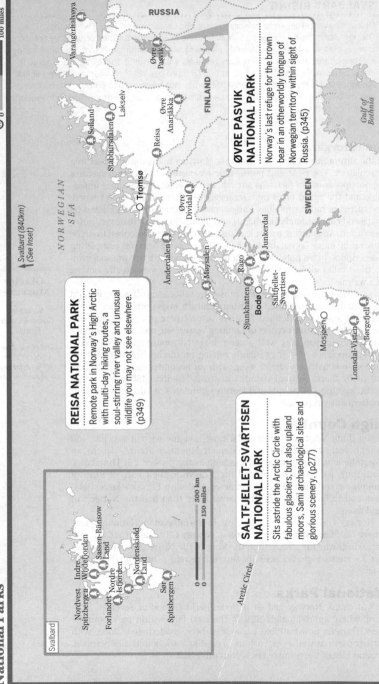

REISA NATIONAL PARK

Remote park in Norway's High Arctic with multi-day hiking routes, a soul-stirring river valley and unusual wildlife you may not see elsewhere. (p349)

ØVRE PASVIK NATIONAL PARK

Norway's last refuge for the brown bear in an otherworldly tongue of Norwegian territory within sight of Russia. (p345)

SALTFJELLET-SVARTISEN NATIONAL PARK

Sits astride the Arctic Circle with fabulous glaciers, but also upland moors, Sami archaeological sites and glorious scenery. (p277)

RUSSIA

FINLAND

SWEDEN

Gulf of Bothnia

NORWEGIAN SEA

Svalbard (840km) (See Inset)

Varangerhalvøya

Øvre Pasvik

Lakselv

Seiland

Øvre Anarjåkka

Stabbursdalen

Reisa

Tromsø

Øvre Dividal

Anderdalen

Møysalen

Rago

Junkerdal

Sjunkhatten

Bodø

Saltfjellet-Svartisen

Mosjøen

Lomsdal-Visten

Børgefjell

200 km
100 miles

Svalbard

Nordvest Spitsbergen

Forlandet

Indre Wijdefjorden

Nordre Isfjorden

Sassen-Bünsow Land

Nordenskiold Land

Sør Spitsbergen

Arctic Circle

300 km
150 miles

JOSTEDALSBREEN NATIONAL PARK

Europe's largest icecap tumbles down into the fjords in a series of glaciers that are among Norway's most accessible. (p224)

JOTUNHEIMEN NATIONAL PARK

The roof of Norway with more than 275 peaks over 2000m, year-round skiing and arguably Norway's best hiking. (p146)

FOLGEFONNA NATIONAL PARK

A year-round taste of winter, with an icecap as ideal for skiing as it is for glacier hiking. (p194)

DOVREFJELL-SUNNDALSFJELLA NATIONAL PARK

Stark upland plateau that's home to wild reindeer, primeval musk ox and eerily beautiful scenery. (p141)

FEMUNDSMARKA NATIONAL PARK

Wild land of lakes, marshes and mountains close to the Swedish border. The hiking is superb, and there are reindeer and musk oxen in residence. (p138)

RONDANE NATIONAL PARK

Home to some of Norway's shapeliest peaks and an excellent park for wildlife-watching and hiking, with some intriguing archaeological sites. (p142)

HARDANGERVIDDA NATIONAL PARK

Vast, pre-Arctic scenery with tundra-like landscape perfectly suited to wildlife (including Norway's largest population of wild reindeer), hiking, mountain-biking and skiing. (p151)

FINLAND

HELSINKI

TALLINN

ESTONIA

LITHUANIA

STOCKHOLM

SWEDEN

Baltic Sea

Gulf of Bothnia

ATLANTIC OCEAN

Grong

Lierne

Blåfjella-Skjækerfjella

Skäckerfjällen

Skarvan og Roltdalen

Trondheim

Forollhogna

Røros

Femundsmarka

Gutulia

Dovrefjell-Sunndalsfjella

Dovre

Rondane

Koppang

Ormtjernkampen

Lillehammer

OSLO

Ytre Hvaler

Larvik

Ålesund

Reinheimen

Jostedalsbreen

Breheimen

Lom

Jotunheimen

Hallingskarvet

Geilo

Hardangervidda

Folgefonna

Bergen

Stavanger

DENMARK

MAJOR NATIONAL PARKS

NATIONAL PARK	FEATURES
Børgefjell	alpine vegetation, Arctic fox
Breheimen	high country
Dovre	every Norwegian flora type present within its borders; highest elevation 1700m
Dovrefjell-Sunndalsfjella	musk ox, reindeer, Snøhetta (2286m) highlands, Fokstumyra marshes
Femundsmarka	glaciers, highlands, musk ox, reindeer
Folgefonna	glaciers, Folgefonn icecap
Forlandet	waterbird, seal & walrus breeding grounds on Prins Karls Forlandet in Svalbard
Hallingskarvet	wild reindeer
Hardangervidda	vast upland plateau, largest wild reindeer herd in Europe
Jostedalsbreen	Jostedalsbreen icecap (487 sq km), glaciers
Jotunheimen	Norway's highest mountains, glaciers
Nordvest Spitsbergen	Kongsbreen icefield, Magdalenefjord, archaeological sights, caribou & marine-mammal breeding grounds
Øvre Dividal	forested Alpine wilderness rich in wildlife, including brown bear, wolverine and Eurasian lynx
Øvre Pasvik	Norway's largest stand of virgin *taiga* (marshy forest), last Norwegian habitat of brown bear
Rago	high peaks, plunging valleys & waterfalls
Reinheimen	wild reindeer
Reisa	Reisa Gorge, waterfalls, wildlife
Rondane	reindeer, Rondane massif, archaeological sites
Saltfjellet-Svartisen	straddles Arctic Circle, upland moors, icecaps, Sami archaeological sites
Sør Spitsbergen	Norway's largest park, 65% ice coverage, seabird breeding grounds
Stabbursdalen	world's northernmost pine forest, lynx, wolverine
Varangerhalvøya	Arctic fox, Sami reindeer herding, ancient Arctic landscapes

Park Focus

The focus of Norway's national parks is the preservation of remaining wilderness areas from development, rather than the managed interaction between humans and their environment, although a few interpretation centres do exist.

Further national park information is available at local tourist offices and from the Norwegian Environment Agency (www.miljodirektoratet. no/nasjonalparker, in Norwegian) in Trondheim.

Park Restrictions

Regulations governing national parks, nature reserves and other protected areas are quite strict. In general, there are no restrictions on entry to the parks, nor are there any fees, but drivers must nearly always pay a toll to use access roads. Dumping rubbish, removing plant, mineral or fossil specimens, hunting or disturbing wildlife, and using motorised off-road vehicles are all prohibited.

National Park Centres

Few of Norway's national parks have interpretation or visitor centres but there are exceptions:

SIZE (SQ KM)	ACTIVITIES	BEST TIME
1447	birdwatching	Jun-Aug
1691	hiking	Jun-Aug
289	hiking	Jun-Aug
1693	hiking, climbing, birdwatching, wildlife safaris	May-Sep
573	hiking, boat trips	mid-Jun–Aug
545	glacier-hiking, summer skiing	May-Sep
4647	birdwatching	Jul & Aug
450	hiking	Jul & Aug
3422	nordic skiing, hiking	Jun-Aug
1310	hiking, ice-climbing, kiting, boat trips	Jun-Aug
1151	hiking	Jul & Aug
9914	hiking, kayaking	Jul & Aug
750	hiking, dog-sledding	Jul & Aug, Dec-Mar
119	hiking	year-round
171	hiking	Jul & Aug
1969	hiking	Jun-Aug
803	hiking	Jun-Aug
963	hiking, wildlife safaris	Jun-Aug
2102	hiking	Jul & Aug
13,282	birdwatching, wildlife-watching	Jul & Aug
747	hiking	Jul & Aug
1804	hiking, birdwatching	Jul & Aug

➡ **Folgefonna National Park Centre** (p194), Folgefonna National Park

➡ **Jostedalsbreen National Park Centre** (p229), Jostedalsbreen National Park

➡ **Hardangervidda Natursenter** (p189), Hardangervidda National Park

➡ **Halti Nasjonalparksenter** (☎77 58 82 82; www.reisa-nasjonalpark.no; Hovedveien 2, Storslett; ☺9am-8pm mid-Jun–mid-Aug, 11am-6pm early Jun & late Aug, 9am-3pm Tue & Thu, noon-6pm Wed Sep-May), Reisa National Park

➡ **Nordland Nasjonalparksenter** (Nordland National Park Centre; ☎75 69 24 00; www.nordlandsnaturen.no; off E6, Storjord; ☺10am-5pm daily Jun-Aug, to 3pm daily Sep & Oct, to 3pm Tue-Sun Feb-May) Covers Nordland's fine collection of little-known national parks.

➡ **Øvre Pasvik National Park Centre** (p347), Øvre Pasvik National Park

➡ **Stabbursnes Naturhus og Museum** (p338), Stabbursdalen National Park.

Wildlife

Norway is home to some of Europe's most charismatic fauna and tracking them down can be a highlight of your trip. While Norway's unique settlement pattern spreads the human population thinly and limits wildlife habitat, Norway more than compensates with its variety of iconic northern European species – from polar bears, walruses and Arctic foxes in Svalbard to musk oxen, reindeer and elk on the mainland. And offshore, whales have survived the best efforts of hunters to drive them to extinction.

Land Mammals

Arctic Foxes

Once prolific throughout Arctic regions, the Arctic fox may be Norway's most endangered land mammal. Numbers of Arctic foxes have scarcely risen in the decades since it was officially protected in 1930; the species' greatest threat now comes from the encroachment of the much larger and more abundant red fox.

The Arctic fox is superbly adapted to harsh winter climates and is believed capable of surviving temperatures as low as minus 70°C thanks to its thick insulating layer of underfur. Almost perfectly white in winter, the Arctic fox can in summer have greyish-brown or smoky-grey fur. In sub-polar regions, it inhabits the sea ice, often cleaning up the scraps left by polar-bear kills.

Elk Safaris

Oppdal

Rjukan

Evje

Andøya, Vesterålen

Musk Oxen & Elk

After being hunted to extinction in Norway almost two millennia ago, the downright prehistoric *moskus-okse* (musk oxen) were reintroduced into Dovrefjell-Sunndalsfjella National Park from Greenland in the 1940s and have since extended their range to the Femundsmarka National Park near Røros. Fewer than 100 are believed to survive in the two Norwegian herds, although their numbers remain more prolific in Greenland, Canada and Alaska; in North America, the Inuit word for the musk ox is *oomingmaq,* which means 'the animal with skin like a beard'. Wherever it is found, the musk ox is one of the most soulful of all Arctic and sub-Arctic species.

From the forests of the far south to southern Finnmark, *elg* (elk; moose in the USA), Europe's largest deer species, are fairly common,

---

NORWAY'S BIG FIVE

There are dozens of wonderful wildlife encounters possible in Norway, but the following five will get even veteran wildlife-watchers excited:

Polar bears, (p355) Svalbard

Walruses, (p356) Svalbard

Musk oxen, (www.nasjonalparker.org) Dovrefjell-Sunndalsfjella National Park

Humpback or sperm whales, (p309) Andenes

Reindeer, (p151) Hardangervidda

WHERE TO SEE ARCTIC FOXES

Svalbard undoubtedly offers the best chance of seeing the Arctic fox, with sightings even possible close to Longyearbyen.

On the mainland, Børgefjell National Park, north of Rørvik and just south of the Arctic Circle, is home to one of mainland Norway's few viable populations. A small population is also believed to survive in the **Dovrefjell-Sunndalsfjella National Park** (p383) in central Norway and a tiny number have been reintroduced onto the Hardangervidda Plateau: Europe's southernmost Arctic fox population. In the far northeast of the country, **Varangerhalvøya National Park**) is an important breeding area.

If you don't see one in the wild, you're almost guaranteed to see the species at **Polar Park** (p325), in northern Norway.

although given the Norwegian fondness for elk meat, they wisely tend to stay clear of people and roads.

Reindeer

Wild *reinsdyr* (reindeer) exist in large herds across central Norway, usually above the treeline and sometimes as high up as 2000m. The prime viewing areas are on the Hardangervidda Plateau, where you'll find Europe's largest herd (around 7000). Sightings are also possible in most national parks of central Norway, as well as the inland areas of Trøndelag. For a fine interpretation centre, visit the Norwegian Wild Reindeer Centre (p141) in Dovrefjell-Sunndalsfjella National Park.

The reindeer of Finnmark in Norway's far north are domestic and owned by the Sami, who drive them to the coast at the start of summer, then back to the interior in winter.

The smaller *svalbardrein* (Svalbard caribou or reindeer) is native only to Svalbard, although some Russian reindeer do occasionally wander onto the archipelago over the sea ice from Siberia.

Other Land Mammals

Like many of Norway's larger mammal species, *bjørn* (brown bears) have been persecuted for centuries, and Norway's only permanent population is in Øvre Pasvik National Park in eastern Finnmark, although sightings do happen from time to time in Reisa, Øvre Dividal and Stabbursdalen National Parks in the far north.

A forest-dweller, the solitary and secretive Eurasian lynx is northern Europe's only large cat. It is found throughout the country but rarely seen.

Lemen (lemmings) occupy mountain areas through 30% of the country and stay mainly around 800m altitude in the south and lower in the north. They measure up to 10cm and have soft orange-brown and black fur, beady eyes, a short tail and prominent upper incisors. If you encounter a lemming in the mountains, it may become enraged, hiss, squeak and attempt to attack!

Other smaller mammal species that are more difficult to see include *hare* (Arctic hares), *pinnsvin* (hedgehogs; mainly in southern Trøndelag), *bever* (beavers; southern Norway), *grevling* (badgers), *oter* (otters), *jerv* (wolverines), *skogmår* (pine martens), *vesel* (weasels) and *røyskatt* (stoats).

Marine Mammals

Polar Bears

Isbjørn (polar bears), the world's largest land carnivore, are found in Norway only in Svalbard, spending much of their time on pack or drift ice. Since the ban on hunting came into force in 1973, their numbers have

Although polar bear numbers have remained relatively stable since 2001, US government scientists estimate that two-thirds of the world's polar bears (now numbering between 20,000 and 25,000) will disappear by 2050 due to diminishing summer sea ice, and that the remainder could die out by the end of the 21st century.

increased to around 3500, although they remain extremely difficult to see unless you're on a cruise around Svalbard – sightings close to Long-yearbyen are extremely rare. Despite weighing up to 720kg and measuring up to 2.5m long, polar bears are swift and manoeuvrable, thanks to the hair on the soles of their feet, which facilitates movement over ice and snow and provides additional insulation.

A polar bear's diet consists mostly of seals, beached whales, fish and birds, and only rarely do they eat reindeer or other land mammals (including humans). Polar-bear milk contains 30% fat (the richest of any carnivorous land mammal), which allows newborn cubs to grow quickly and survive extremely cold temperatures.

Whales

Possibly the largest animal to ever inhabit the earth, the longest blue whale ever caught measured 33.58m; 50 people could fit on its tongue alone.

The seas around Norway are rich fishing grounds, due to the ideal summer conditions for the growth of plankton. This wealth of nutrients also attracts fish and baleen whales, which feed on the plankton, as well as other marine creatures that feed on the fish. Sadly, centuries of whaling in the North Atlantic and Arctic Oceans have reduced several whale species to perilously small populations. Apart from the minke whale, there's no sign that the numbers will ever recover in this area. Given this history, the variety of whale species in Norway's waters is astonishing.

Minkehval (minke whales), one of the few whale species that is not endangered, measure around 7m to 10m long and weigh between 5 and 10 tonnes. They're baleen whales, which means that they have plates of whalebone baleen rather than teeth, and migrate between the Azores area and Svalbard.

Between Ålesund and Varangerhalvøya, it's possible to see *knolhval* (humpback whales), baleen whales that measure up to 15m and weigh up to 30 tonnes. These are among the most acrobatic and vocal of whales, producing deep songs that can be heard and recorded hundreds of kilometres away.

Spekkhogger (killer whales), or orcas, are the top sea predators and measure up to 7m and weigh around 5 tonnes. There are around 1500 off the coast of Norway, swimming in pods of two or three. They eat fish, seals, dolphins, porpoises and other whales (such as minke), which may be larger than themselves.

The long-finned *grindhval* (pilot whales), about 6m long, may swim in pods of up to several hundred and range as far north as Nordkapp. *Hvithval* (belugas), which are up to 4m long, are found mainly in the Arctic Ocean.

The grey and white *narhval* (narwhal), which grow up to 3.5m long, are best recognised by the peculiar 2.7m spiral ivory tusk that projects from the upper lip of the males. This tusk is in fact one of the whale's two teeth and was prized in medieval times. Narwhal live mainly in the Arctic Ocean and occasionally head upstream into freshwater.

The endangered *seihval* (sei whales), a baleen whale, swim off the coast of Finnmark and are named because their arrival corresponds with that of the *sei* (pollacks), which come to feast on the seasonal plankton. They can measure 18m and weigh up to 30 tonnes (calves measure 5m

POLAR BEAR & ARCTIC FOX RESOURCES

➡ *Ice Bear: A Natural and Unnatural History of the Polar Bear* (Kieran Mulvaney; 2011)

➡ *Ice Bear: The Cultural History of an Arctic Icon* (Michael Engelhard; 2016)

➡ Polar Bears International (www.polarbearsinternational.org)

➡ *Arctic Fox: Life at the Top of the World* (Garry Hamilton; 2008)

WHERE & WHEN TO SEE WHALES

Late May to August These are ideal whale-watching months, coinciding as they do with the more hospitable summer temperatures. Sperm whales are the real prize at this time, although pilot whales are also possible. Andenes (p309) and Stø (p306) both have excellent whale-watching outfits.

Late October to mid-January or February Orcas (killer whales), humpback and fin whales are all possible in whale safaris from Tromsø.

at birth). The annual migration takes the sei from the seas off northwest Africa and Portugal (winter) up to the Norwegian Sea and southern Barents Sea in summer.

Finhval (fin whales) measure 24m and can weigh 80 tonnes. They were a prime target after the Norwegian Svend Føyn developed the exploding harpoon in 1864 and unregulated whaling left only a few thousand in the North Atlantic. Fin whales are also migratory, wintering between Spain and southern Norway and spending summer in northern Norway.

Spermsetthval (sperm whales), which can measure 19m and weigh up to 50 tonnes, are characterised by their odd squarish profile. They subsist mainly on fish and squid and usually live in pods of 15 to 20. Their numbers were depleted by whalers seeking whale oil and the valuable spermaceti wax from their heads. The fish-rich shoals off Vesterålen attract quite a few sperm whales and they're often observed on boat tours.

The largest animal on earth, *blåhval* (blue whales) measure around 28m and weigh in at a staggering 110 tonnes. Although they can live to 80 years of age, 50 is more common. Heavily hunted for its oil, the species finally received protection, far too late, from the International Whaling Commission in 1967. The blue whale is listed as Endangered by the International Union for the Conservation of Nature (IUCN), which estimates blue whale numbers worldwide to be somewhere between 10,000 and 25,000; 341,830 blue whales were recorded as killed in the Antarctic and sub-Antarctic in the 20th century. Recent evidence suggests that a few hardy blue whales are making a comeback in the northeast Atlantic and blue whales are occasionally sighted in the waters surrounding Svalbard.

Grønlandshval (bowhead whales), or Greenland right whales, were virtually annihilated by the end of the 19th century for their baleen, which was used in corsets, fans and whips, and because they are slow swimmers and float when dead. In 1679 Svalbard had around 25,000 bowheads, but only a handful remains and worldwide numbers are critically low.

Walruses

The *hvalross* (walrus; *Odobenus rosmarus*) is one of the most charismatic and sought-after marine mammals for wildlife-watchers. In Norway, they live only in Svalbard, most notably on the islands of Prins Karls Forlandet (p363) and **Moffen Island**; summer safaris from Longyearbyen (p356) to the former are the best chance you'll ever get to encounter these behemoths of the sea.

Walruses measure up to nearly 4m and weigh up to 2000kg (most weigh between 800kg and 1700kg); their elongated canine teeth can measure up to 1m long in males. They spend much of their lives in shallow water at sea looking for molluscs, coming to land to rest and bask in the weak Arctic sun. Walruses can live up to 30 years in the wild, and may not breed until they reach 15; gestation lasts 15 to 16 months. Apart from humankind, the only natural predators able to kill walruses are polar bears and orcas (killer whales).

BOOKS ON WHALES

➡ *Marine Mammals of the North Atlantic* (Carl Christian Kinze; 2003)

➡ *A Field Guide to North Atlantic Wildlife: Marine Mammals, Seabirds, Fish, and Other Sea Life* (Noble S Proctor & Patrick J Lynch; 2005)

➡ *North Atlantic Right Whales: From Hunted Leviathan to Conservation Icon* (David W Laist; 2017)

Although once heavily hunted for their ivory and blubber, the Svalbard population has increased to around 1000 since they became a protected species in 1952. The Atlantic walrus subspecies numbers an estimated 25,000 (compared with 10 times that number for Pacific walruses), but the great colonies of up to 8000 walruses are very much a thing of the past. The walrus is universally regarded as a keystone species for the health of the Arctic environment and remains Vulnerable according to the IUCN (www.iucnredlist.org).

Other Marine Mammals

Norway's waters shelter reasonable populations of bottlenose, white-beaked, Atlantic white-sided and common dolphins.

Seals are also commonly seen near the seashore throughout Norway and some inland fjords. The main species include *steinkobbe* (harbour seals), *havert* (grey seals), *ringsel* (ringed seals), *grønlandssel* (harp seals), *klappmyss* (hooded seals) and *blåsel* (bearded seals). Summer tours that take you out to see seal colonies include from Stø (p306) and Tromsø (p320).

Birds

Norway is an excellent destination for ornithologists, with 473 species recorded here. The greatest bird populations are found along the coastline, where millions of sea birds nest in cliff faces and feed on fish and other sea life. The most prolific species include terns, *havsule* (gannets), *alke* (razorbills), *lundefugl* (puffins), *lomvi* and *teist* (guillemots), *havhest* (fulmars), *krykkje* (kittiwakes), *tjuvjo* and *fjelljo* (skuas) and *alkekonge* (little auks). Lovers of the humble puffin should head for Runde, Bleik, Gjesvær or Svalbard.

The standout species among Norway's host of wading and water birds include the *storlom* (black-throated wading birds), *smålom* (red-throated divers; called 'loons' in North America), *horndykker* (horned grebes), *åkerrikse* (corncrakes) and Norway's national bird, the *fossekall* (dippers), which make their living by diving into mountain streams.

Norway is also home to at least four species of owl: *jordugle* (short-eared owls), *spurveugle* (pygmy owls), *snøugle* (snowy owls) and *hubro* (eagle owls).

The most dramatic of Norway's raptors is the lovely *havørn* (white-tailed eagle), the largest northern European raptor, with a wingspan of up to 2.5m; there are now at least 500 nesting pairs along the Nordland coast, Troms and Finnmark. Around the same number of *kongeørn* (golden eagles) inhabit higher mountain areas. The rare *fiskeørn* (ospreys) have a maximum population of 30 pairs and are seen only in heavily forested areas around Stabbursdalen and Øvre Pasvik National Parks, both in the far north. Stabbursdalen is also good for the endangered lesser white-fronter goose.

For Arctic species, both resident and migratory, the Varanger region of northeastern Norway is deservedly popular among birders. Signature species include Steller's eider, red-necked phalarope, tundra swan and eagle owl.

Environmental Issues

Norway and the environment are like everyone's model couple – from the outside, they seem like a perfect match but close examination reveals a darker picture. Indeed, the story of how Norway has been acclaimed for promoting environmental sustainability while being one of the world's largest producers of fossil fuels (oil is the elephant in the room) is a fascinating tale. In short, it's a complicated picture.

Climate Change

Climate change is by no means a solely Norwegian problem, but few countries have committed to doing as much about it as Norway, at least at home. In 2007 the Norwegian government promised to 'be at the forefront of the international climate effort' and announced plans to become 'carbon neutral' and cut net greenhouse gas emissions to zero by 2050. The country aims also to only sell electric cars by 2025. This will mostly involve offsetting its annual carbon dioxide emissions by purchasing carbon credits on international markets. The government also agreed to cut actual emissions by 40% by 2030.

Arcticness: Power and Voice from the North (2017), by Ilan Kelman, is an important contribution to the debate with a focus in some of the essays on how climate change is already affecting Arctic communities.

Already 100% of Norway's electricity supplies come from renewable (primarily hydro power) sources. Norway also has targeted tax regimes on carbon dioxide emissions, and allocates billions of kroner to carbon dioxide capture and storage schemes and climate-related initiatives, both within Norway and overseas.

For all such good news at home, it is worth remembering that Norway is a major exporter of fossil fuels; one study found that in 2017 emissions from the country's oil exports will exceed Norway's domestic emission by 1000%. The Norwegian government continues to promote an aggressive strategy of oil exploration – in 2017 Statoil began work on five new major wells in the Barents Sea. While Statoil claims that its exploration will only take place in ice-free waters – cleaning up an oil spill in ice-bound waters is next to impossible – the fact is that Norway remains committed to, and dependent on, fossil fuels for its prosperity. This apparent contradiction between good environmental citizen and major producer of fossil fuels goes to the heart of Norway's relationship with its environment.

A DANGEROUS ENVIRONMENTAL HAZARD – MOOSE FARTS

Global warming. Fossil fuels. Moose farts... Although it doesn't quite roll off the tongue as a serious threat to the environment, a moose with gas can actually be more dangerous to the environment than your average family car.

According to a report in London's *Times* newspaper in August 2007, by doing nothing more than farting and belching every year a single adult moose releases the methane equivalent of 2100kg of carbon dioxide emissions, equal to about 13,000km of travel in a car. With an estimated 120,000 wild moose roaming the Norwegian wilds – the Norwegian authorities authorise an annual nationwide hunting quota of around 37,000 – that adds up to a disturbingly high output of methane, not to mention a heightened state of nervousness among otherwise innocent moose.

Climate change in Norway is most evident in the worrying signs that its glaciers may be under threat and in the perilous state of Arctic sea ice. Again, Norway's principled position on Arctic pollution is undermined by its production of fossil fuels – the government's strict provisions protecting the environment in Svalbard have won praise, even as it continues to make exemptions for (albeit declining) coal production on the archipelago. At the same time, the Svalbard Global Seed Vault is also seen as an important resource in protecting biodiversity in the event of a large rise in global temperatures.

Commercial Fishing

Fishing and aquaculture (fish farming) remain the foundation of Norway's coastal economy, providing work for an estimated 30,000 people in the fishing fleet, and a host of secondary industries. With an annual catch of around 2.5 to 3 million tonnes, Norway is one of the world's largest exporters of seafood.

Fears over allowing access to Norway's waters by European fishing fleets have been a major reason why Norway has decided to remain outside the EU. In 2013 the country finally signed an agreement with the EU on fishing quotas.

And yet centuries of fishing have severely depleted fish stocks among species that were once the mainstays of the Norwegian economy. By the late 1970s, for example, herring stocks were nearly wiped out. In addition, overfishing depleted stocks of cod all across the North Atlantic. Three decades of conservation measures later, including strict quotas, the herring-fishery industry is recovering. Cod-fishing regulations are now in place, although it will be many years before the numbers return.

It's fair to say that Norwegians usually view the critical depletion of fish stocks in Norwegian waters as much through the prism of economic self-interest as they do a strictly environmental concern. Still Norway's second-largest export earner after petroleum and related products, it was one of the country's few commercial resources in the days before oil – an essential context to understanding many of Norway's environmental policies as they relate to fishing.

Sealing

Norway has a long tradition of seal hunting, and until 2017 the government set annual quotas of between 30,000 and 50,000 harp seals. The government's support for seal hunting – it provided funding for sealing vessels – was mainly driven by the lobbying of the fishing community, which wished to restrict the competition between fishing boats and marine mammals that depend on fish and eat up to 2.5kg per day. Seal meat is also considered a delicacy in many regions of coastal Norway.

To mitigate protests, regulations limited seal hunters to only two tools: a rifle (using expanding bullets) and a hakapik, or gaff; the former was for adult seals and the latter for pups (which could not be hunted while suckling). Hunters were also required to take courses and shooting tests before each sealing season. Such regulations notwithstanding, media reports suggest that the injuring of young seals abandoned during the hunt was widespread.

But for the first time in centuries, in 2017 the seal hunting fleet remained in port and not a single seal was killed. While environmental groups rejoiced (among those to call for an end to sealing have been the International Fund for Animal Welfare (IFAW), the Humane Society and Greenpeace), the reasons behind the failure of the seal hunt had less to do with decades of protests than the very real environmental problem of shrinking sea ice – seals require sea ice to breed and feed; the 2016 Norwegian sealing fleet had difficulty in finding enough seals to make viable their long-distance expeditions from Tromsø.

It was the logical endpoint of years of decline – in previous years, actual culls had amounted to barely 10% of the allocated quota. The removal of government subsidies (which accounted for 80% of sealers' incomes) and a 2009 EU ban on seal-skin products also had an impact.

As is the case with whaling and fishing, many Norwegians have longed viewed the sealing industry in historical and economic (rather than environmental) terms. In 2016, the nostalgic documentary *Ishavsblod (Sealers: One Last Hunt)* was featured at the Tromsø International Film Festival.

Whaling

No Norwegian environmental issue inspires more international fervour and emotion than that of renewed whaling in the North Atlantic.

The International Context

In 1986, as a result of worldwide campaigns expressing critical concern over the state of world whale populations, the International Whaling Commission (www.iwc.int/home) imposed a moratorium on whale hunting. Although it has largely held, two key elements continue to place the moratorium under threat.

The first was the decision by the three major whaling nations – Norway, Japan and Iceland – to resume commercial whaling. The second was a concerted campaign that saw nations with no history of whaling – including Mauritania, Ivory Coast, Grenada, Tuvalu and even landlocked Mongolia, San Marino and Mali – joining the commission. The result of this second has seen a change from nine pro-whaling votes out of 55 in 2000 to an almost 50-50 split among its 88 members currently (a 75% majority is required to change IWC policy). Allegations that pro-whaling votes have been rewarded with development aid have not been denied by the Japanese.

Norway, for its part, sees the moratorium as unnecessary and outdated. It argues that, unlike in the past when whalers drove many whale species to the verge of extinction (in the 17th century alone, Dutch whalers killed an estimated 60,000 whales in the waters off Svalbard), modern whalers have a better and more informed perspective, that they adhere to a sensible quota system and now adopt more humane methods of killing. The Norwegians claim that they support only traditional, family-owned operations and have no intention of returning to industrial whaling.

For a Norwegian perspective on whaling, stop by the Whaling Museum (p98) in Sandefjord, along Norway's southern coast.

The International Whaling Commission (IWC; www. iwc.int/home) is a largely dispassionate resource on whaling and the surrounding politics. There are useful sections, such as the 'Status of Whales', with estimates for current whale populations.

KING CRABS

They may be delicious and a safari to catch them may be one of the more popular ways to spend a winter morning up in Kirkenes and elsewhere, but the red king crab is a rather serious issue.

The world's largest crustacean (its leg span routinely reaches 1.8m and it has been known to weigh 15kg), the red king crab's story is a remarkable one. Seven king crabs were introduced into the area from the North Pacific by Russian scientists in 1961 and they have been multiplying at an astonishing rate ever since. Every year, each female king crab gives birth to around 10,000 surviving offspring and there are now 20 million in the Barents Sea alone.

The problem with this apparent success story is that red king crabs eat everything they come across as they crawl across the ocean floor. Their seemingly unstoppable march westwards along the Norwegian coast and north to Svalbard is expanding their territories by an estimated 50km a year.

Norway's Recent Practice

Norway resumed commercial whaling of minke whales in 1993 in defiance of an international whaling ban, but under its registered objection to the 1986 moratorium. While Norway supports the protection of threatened species, the government contends that minke whales, with a northeast Atlantic population of an allegedly estimated 100,000, can sustain a limited harvest. Despite condemnation by international environmental groups such as Greenpeace and the Whale and Dolphin Conservation Society, the Norwegian government maintains an annual minke-whale quota of 1278, although in recent years whalers have killed less than half their allocated quota.

Japan and Norway resumed trading in whale meat in 2004 and it tends to be the export market that drives the industry rather than domestic consumption, although whale meat is openly sold in fish markets (especially Bergen) and remains on many Norwegian restaurant menus – a good moment to decide where you stand on the issue.

Follow the whaling debate at Greenpeace UK (www.greenpeace.org.uk), the Whale and Dolphin Conservation Society (www.wdcs.org) and the Norwegian Ministry of Fisheries (www.fisheries.no).

Forestry

Forests cover an estimated 38% of mainland Norway, but forests set aside for cultivation account for around 25% of Norwegian territory. Government-protected wilderness areas account for less than 1% of Norway's forests, well below the international standard of 5%. More than 1000 forest-dwelling species are considered to be endangered and areas of old-growth forest are extremely rare.

One remaining stand of old-growth Norwegian forest that has caught the attention of environmentalists is Trillemarka-Rollagsfjell, about 100km west of Oslo and covering 205 sq km. Declared a nature reserve in 2002, it shelters endangered species such as the lesser spotted woodpecker, tree-toed woodpecker, Siberian jay and golden eagle, as well as threatened plant life.

Another important stand of forest is the virgin *taiga* (marshy forest) in the Pasvik River valley south of Kirkenes – it remains largely undisturbed, although it is only an extremely small proportion of a much larger forest across the border in Russia.

Although no forestry operation can be entirely environmentally sound, Norway currently has one of the world's most sustainable forestry industries and much of the visible damage to the forests is due to agricultural clearing and timber overexploitation between the 17th and 20th centuries.

NOT-SO-PERMAFROST

Permafrost is, it seems, not permanent after all. The word 'permafrost' refers to ground (whether soil or rock) that exists at or below freezing (0°C) for at least two years in a row. Much of the permafrost that ranges across Siberia, Greenland and Siberia has, of course, been in a frozen state for much longer than two years, although concerns over climate change have sparked significant anxiety about the consequences of melting permafrost – a 1.5°C rise in global temperatures would be enough to begin the process of permafrost melt. Why this matters is that melted permafrost releases methane that will contribute significantly to further global warming.

Norway's proportion of the world's permafrost is relatively small, but small areas exist around the Pasvik River Valley and the Varangerhalvøya National Park, both in mainland Norway's far northeast. Much of Svalbard, too, is laid upon a permafrost base. In 2017, unexpectedly warm temperatures caused permafrost surrounding the **Global Seed Vault** (p354) on Svalbard to melt, which led to flooding within the vault. It was a serious shock for those who believed the so-called Doomsday Vault to be impregnable.

Wilderness Areas

Norway may have one of the lowest population densities in Europe, but due to its settlement pattern – which is unique in Europe, and favours scattered farms over villages – even the most remote areas are inhabited and a large proportion of the population is rural-based.

As a result, the natural world has been greatly altered by human activities and the landscape is criss-crossed by roads that connect remote homes, farmsteads and logging areas to more populated areas. All but a couple of the country's major rivers have been dammed for hydroelectric power and even the wild-looking expanses of Finnmarksvidda and the huge peninsulas that jut into the Arctic Ocean serve as vast reindeer pastures. As a result, apart from the upland icefields and Norway's impressive network of national parks, real wilderness is limited to a few forested mountain areas along the Swedish border, scattered parts of Hardangervidda and most of Svalbard.

Recycling

Norwegians strongly support the sorting of household waste for collection and recycling, and travellers are encouraged to do likewise. A mandatory deposit scheme for glass bottles and cans has been a success and about 96% of beer and soft-drink bottles are now returned. Supermarkets give money back for returned aluminium cans and plastic bottles (usually 1kr to 1.50kr).

Since the early 1970s, however, the average annual level of household waste generated per person has nearly doubled to around 375kg (or up by 40% since 1995), a rise that coincides with the golden years of Norway's oil-fuelled prosperity boom. Although it took a while to catch on, around 50% of household waste and two-thirds of industrial waste is now recycled, while Norway is a world leader when it comes to recycling electrical and electronics products. Methane from waste nonetheless still accounts for 7% of Norway's greenhouse gas emissions and Norwegians consume more than 130,000 tonnes of plastic packaging every year.

The Future History of the Arctic (2011) by Charles Emmerson is an engaging exploration of the Arctic, with a particular focus on the big issues of energy security, environmental protection and the exploitation of the region's natural resources.

ENVIRONMENTAL ISSUES WILDERNESS AREAS

Norway's Sami

The formerly nomadic, indigenous Sami people are Norway's largest ethnic minority and Norway's longest-standing residents: they have inhabited northern Scandinavia and northwestern Russia for millennia. Of approximately 60,000 Sami, around 40,000 reside in Norway, primarily inhabiting the northern region of Finnmark, with scattered groups in Nordland, Trøndelag and elsewhere in central Norway. Sami, who refer to their traditional lands as Sápmi or Samiland, also inhabit Sweden, Finland and Russia. Encounters with the Sami could become a highlight of your trip.

Sami History

Although it's believed that the Sami migrated to Norway from Siberia as early as 11,000 years ago, the oldest written reference to the Sami was penned by the Roman historian Tacitus in AD 98. In AD 555 the Greek Procopius referred to Scandinavia as Thule (the 'furthest north'), and its peoples as *skridfinns,* who hunted, herded reindeer and travelled about on skis. The medieval Icelandic sagas confirm trading between Nordic peoples and the Sami; the trader Ottar, who 'lived further north than any other Norseman', served in the court of English king Alfred the Great and wrote extensively about his native country and its indigenous peoples.

During medieval times, the Sami people lived by hunting and trapping in small communities known as *siida*. While the 17th- and 18th-century colonisation of the north by Nordic farmers presented conflicts with this system, many newcomers found that the Sami way of life was better suited to the local conditions and adopted their dress, diet and customs.

Around 1850, with Sami traditions coming under increasing threat from missionary activity, reforms were introduced, restricting the use of the Sami language in schools. From 1902 it became illegal to sell land to any person who couldn't speak Norwegian; this policy was enforced zealously and Sami culture seemed to be on the brink of extinction.

After WWII, however, official Norwegian government policy changed direction and began to promote internal multiculturalism. By the 1960s the Sami people's right to preserve and develop their own cultural values and language was enshrined across all government spectra. Increasingly, official policy viewed the Sami as Norwegian subjects but also an ethnic minority and separate people. Their legal status improved considerably and the government formed two committees: the Samekulturutvalget to deal with Sami cultural issues; and the Samerettsutvalget to determine the legal aspects of Sami status and resource ownership.

From 1979 to 1981, an increasingly bitter Sami protest in Oslo against a proposed dam and hydroelectric plant on Sami traditional lands on the Alta River drew attention to the struggle for Sami rights. The dispute saw 600 police – 10% of the nation's entire force – sent to Alta to confront and ultimately remove the protesters. In 1982 Norway's Supreme Court ruled in favour of the government, but while the protest ended in defeat, it significantly raised the profile of Sami concerns on the national stage.

In 1988 the Norwegian government passed an enlightened constitutional amendment stating: 'It is the responsibility of the authorities of

The Sami were formerly known as Lapps and their homeland was (and is still often) referred to as Lapland. However, in recent decades, that term has come to carry negative connotations and is considered insulting by many Sami.

the State to create conditions enabling the Sami people to preserve and develop its language, culture and way of life.' It also provided for the creation of an elected 39-member Sami Parliament (p347) to serve as an advisory body to bring Sami issues to the national parliament (similar bodies also exist in Finland and Sweden).

In early 1990 the government passed the Sami Language Act, which gave the Sami language and Norwegian equal status. Later the same year, Norway ratified the International Labour Organization proposition No 169, which guaranteed the rights of indigenous and tribal peoples.

Although Sami rights are supported by most parties across the political spectrum, the Sami's struggle continues. The right-wing Fremskrittspartiet has called for the Sami Parliament to be abolished.

Reindeer herding, once the mainstay of the Sami economy, was successfully modernised in the 1980s and 1990s and is now a major capital earner; herders are, for example, more likely now to travel between their herds by snowmobile rather than on skis. In addition to reindeer herding, modern Sami engage in fishing, agriculture, trade, small industry and the production of handicrafts.

To be officially considered Sami and (if 18 or over) be able to vote in elections for the Sami Parliament, a person must regard themselves as Sami, speak Sami as their first language or at least one of their parents, grandparents or great-grandparents must have spoken Sami as their first language.

Sami Culture & Traditions

For centuries Sami life was based on hunting and fishing, then sometime during the 16th century reindeer were domesticated and the hunting economy transformed into a nomadic herding economy. While reindeer still figure prominently in Sami life, only about 10% to 15% of Sami people are today directly involved in reindeer herding. These days, a mere handful of traditionalists continue to lead a truly nomadic lifestyle. The majority fish or are engaged in tourist-related activities.

A major identifying element of Sami culture is the *joik* (or *yoik*), a rhythmic poem composed for a specific person to describe their innate nature and considered to be owned by the person it describes. Other traditional elements include the use of folk medicine, artistic pursuits such as woodcarving and silversmithing, and striving for ecological harmony.

The Sami national dress is the only genuine folk dress that's still in casual use in Norway, and you might see it on the streets of Kautokeino and Karasjok. Each district has its own distinct features, but all include a highly decorated and embroidered combination of red-and-blue felt shirts or frocks, trousers or skirts, and boots and hats. On special occasions the women's dress is topped off with a crown of pearls and a garland of silk hair ribbons.

Sami Religion

Historically, Sami religious traditions were characterised mainly by a relationship to nature and its inherent godlike archetypes. In sites of special power, particularly prominent rock formations, people made offerings to their gods and ancestors to ensure success in hunting or other endeavours. Intervention and healing were affected by shamanic specialists, who used drums and small figures to launch themselves onto

---

BOOKS ON THE SAMI PEOPLE

➡ *The Sami People* (Davvi Girji; 1990)

➡ *The Sami: Indigenous People of the Arctic* (Odd Mathis Hælta; 1996)

➡ *The Sami People: Traditions in Transitions* (Veli-Pekka Lehtola; 2005)

➡ *The Sami Peoples of the North: A Social and Cultural History* (Neil Kent; 2014)

➡ *Beneath the Ice: In Search of the Sami* (Kenneth Steven; 2016)

out-of-body journeys to the ends of the earth in search of answers. As with nearly all indigenous peoples in the northern hemisphere, the bear, as the most powerful creature in nature, was considered a sacred animal.

Historically, another crucial element in the religious tradition was the singing of the *joik* (literally 'song of the plains'). So powerful was this personal mantra that early Christian missionaries considered it a threat and banned it as sinful. Although most modern Sami profess Christianity, elements of the old religion are making a comeback.

Sami Organisations

The first session of the Norwegian Sami Parliament was held in 1989. The primary task of the parliament, which convenes in Karasjok and whose 39 representatives are elected from Sami communities all over Norway every four years, is to protect the Sami language and culture.

The Norwegian Sami also belong to the **Saami Council** (☎in Finland 400725226; www.saamicouncil.net), which was founded in 1956 to foster co-operation between political organisations in Norway, Sweden, Finland and Russia. In Tromsø in 1980, the Saami Council's political program adopted principles stating:

'We have an inalienable right to preserve and develop our own economic activities and our communities, in accordance with our own circumstances and we will together safeguard our territories, natural resources and national heritage for future generations.'

The Sami participate in the Arctic Council and the World Council of Indigenous Peoples, which encourages solidarity and promotes information exchange between indigenous peoples.

The **Sami University College** (Sami University of Applied Sciences; Samisk høgskole; ☎78 44 84 00; www.samas.no/en; Hannoluohkka 45, Kautokeino) at Kautokeino was established as the Nordic Sami Institute in 1974 and promotes Sami language, culture and education, as well as research, economic activities and environmental protection.

Sami Sites

- *Varanger Sami Museum (Varangerbotn)*
- *Ceavccageadge (Mortensnes)*
- *Sápmi Park (Karasjok)*
- *Sami Parliament (Karasjok)*
- *Sami National Museum (Karasjok)*
- *Kautokeino Museum (Kautokeino)*

Arts & Architecture

Norway is one of Europe's cultural giants, producing world-class writers, composers and painters in numbers far out of proportion to its size. Norwegian artists and performers also excel in the realms of popular culture, from dark and compelling crime fiction to musical strands as diverse as jazz, electronica and heavy metal. And when it comes to architecture, Norway is as known for its stave churches as it is for the zany contemporary creations that are also something of a national speciality.

Arts

In the late 19th century and into the early 20th century, three figures – playwright Henrik Ibsen, composer Edvard Grieg and painter Edvard Munch – towered over Norway's cultural life like no others and their emergence came at a time when Norway was forging its path to independence and pushing the creative limits of a newly confident national identity. More than just artists, Ibsen, Grieg and Munch are an expression of the Norwegian soul. In the 20th century three Norwegian writers – products of Norway's golden age of cultural expression – won the Nobel Prize for Literature.

Literature

Folk Tales

Nowhere else in Europe does a tradition of folk tales and legends survive to quite the extent it does in Norway. Although many of these tales have been committed to paper, their essence is that of an oral tradition that has passed down through the generations.

Norwegian folk tales, often drawing on the legends of medieval Norse literature, are populated by an impossibly rich imaginary cast

Two success stories on Norwegian television in recent years were also the most unlikely. The first tracked the Oslo–Bergen railway from a camera on the front of the engine...for seven hours. Then, Norway's national broadcaster NRK did the same with the Hurtigruten coastal ferry, this time for six days.

CULTURAL ICON: HENRIK IBSEN

Born in Skien in southern Norway, Henrik Johan Ibsen (1828–1906) became known internationally as 'the father of modern drama', but to Norwegians he was the conscience of a nation. Norwegians are extremely proud of Ibsen, but from 1864 until 1891 he lived in disenchanted exile, decrying the small-mindedness of Norwegian society of the day. The enormously popular *Peer Gynt* (1867) was Ibsen's international breakthrough. In this enduring epic, an ageing hero returns to his Norwegian roots after wandering the world and is forced to face his own soul.

His best-known plays include *The Doll's House* (1879), the highly provocative *Ghosts* (1881), *An Enemy of the People* (1882), *Hedda Gabler* (1890) and, his last drama, the semi-autobiographical *When We Dead Awaken* (1899).

Throughout his life, Ibsen was always more than a chronicler of Norwegian society and saw himself as the reflection of 19th-century Norwegians: 'He who wishes to understand me must know Norway. The magnificent but severe natural environment surrounding people up there in the north forces them to keep to their own. That is why they become introspective and serious, they brood and doubt – and they often lose faith. There, the long, dark winters come with their thick fogs enveloping the houses – oh, how they long for the sun!'

of mythical characters. The antics of these fantasy characters, as well as the princesses and farm boys that managed to outwit them, are as essentially Norwegian as the fjords and Vikings. But it is only due to the work of Peter Asbjørnsen and Jørgen Moe in the early 1800s that they were ever written down at all. Inspired by the popular work of the Grimm brothers, the two men began with what they knew best: the folk tales told in the woods and valleys surrounding Oslo. Comic, cruel, moralistic, ribald and popular from the moment they were published, these stories set the tone for some of Norway's greatest authors, including Henrik Ibsen and Bjørnstjerne Bjørnson.

The tales, most often illustrated with the distinct sketches of Erik Werenskiold and ending with the words 'Snipp. Snapp. Snute. Så er eventyret ute' (a Norwegian rhyme signifying 'The End'), remain popular and easy to find.

The Golden Age

The late 19th and early 20th centuries were the golden age of Norwegian literature. Although most of the attention centres on Henrik Ibsen, it was Bjørnstjerne Bjørnson (1832–1910) who in 1903 became the first Norwegian writer to win the Nobel Prize for Literature. Bjørnson's work included vignettes of rural life (for which he was accused of romanticising the lot of rural Norwegians). His home at Aulestad (p125) is open to visitors.

Knut Hamsun (1859–1952) won the Nobel Prize for Literature in 1920. Hamsun's elitism, his appreciation of Germanic values and his idealisation of rural life led him to side with the Nazis in WWII. Only now is his reputation being rehabilitated and he is widely recognised as belonging to the tradition of Dostoevsky and Joyce. To find out more, visit the Hamsunsenteret (p279), the museum in Hamarøy dedicated to his life.

Sigrid Undset (1882–1949) became the third of Norway's Nobel Literature laureates in 1928 and is regarded as the most significant female writer in Norwegian literature. Undset began by writing about the plight of poor and middle-class women. Bjerkebæk (p125), her former home in Lillehammer, is open to the public.

Contemporary Literature

One of the best-known modern Norwegian writers is Jan Kjærstad (b 1953), whose *The Seducer* (2003) combines the necessary recipe for a bestseller – a thriller with a love affair and a whiff of celebrity – with seriously good writing. It won the 1999 Nordic Prize for Literature among other international prizes. Other Norwegian winners of the prestigious Nordic Prize include Per Petterson (b 1952) and Lars Saabye Christensen (b 1953). Another world-renowned author is Jostein Gaarder (b 1952), whose first best-selling novel, *Sophie's World* (1991), sold over 15 million copies worldwide. Dag Solstad (b 1941) is the only Norwegian author to win the Norwegian Literary Critics' Award three times.

In the crime-fiction genre, Gunnar Staalesen, Karin Fossum, and the master, Jo Nesbø, have devoted international followings.

Music

Folk Music

Folk music is a central pillar of Norwegian music, and the Hardanger fiddle – which derives its distinctive sound from four or five sympathetic strings stretched out beneath the usual four strings – is one of Europe's best-loved folk instruments.

Some of the hottest folk acts include Tore Bruvoll and Jon Anders Halvorsen, who perform traditional Telemark songs *(Nattsang);* the live

Henrik Ibsen Sites

Ibsen Museum (Oslo)

Ibsenhuset Museum (Grimstad)

Henrik Ibsenmuseet (Skien)

National Theatre (Oslo)

Peer Gynt Vegen (Central Norway)

CULTURAL ICON: EDVARD GRIEG

Norway's renowned composer Edvard Grieg (1843–1907) was so disappointed with his first symphony that he scrawled across the score that it must never be performed! Thankfully, his wishes were ignored. Grieg was greatly influenced by Norway's folk music and melodies and his first great signature work, *Piano Concerto in A minor*, has come to represent Norway as no other work before or since.

Two years after the concerto, Grieg, encouraged by luminaries such as Franz Liszt, collaborated with Bjørnstjerne Bjørnson, setting the latter's poetry and writing to music. The results – *Before a Southern Convent, Bergliot* and *Sigurd Jorsalfar* – established Grieg as the musical voice of Norway. This was followed by a project with Henrik Ibsen, setting to music Ibsen's novel *Peer Gynt*. The score found international acclaim and became Grieg's – and Norway's – best-remembered classical work. According to his biographer, Aimer Grøvald, it was impossible to listen to Grieg without sensing a light, fresh breeze from the blue waters, a glimpse of grand glaciers and a recollection of the mountains of western Norway's fjords.

Norwegian performances of Bukkene Bruse (heavy on the Hardanger fiddle; *Spel*); Rusk's impressively wide repertoire of music from southeastern Norway *(Rusk);* Sigrid Moldestad and Liv Merete Kroken, who bring classical training to bear on the traditional fiddle *(Spindel);* and Sinikka Langeland, whose *Runoja* draws on ancient runic music. In 2009 Alexander Rybak, a Norwegian composer, fiddler and pianist of Belorussian descent, won the Eurovision Song Contest.

Sami Music

The haunting music of the Sami people of northern Norway is enjoying a revival. Recent Sami artists such as Aulu Gaup, Sofis Jannock, Mari Boine and Nils Aslak Valkeapää have performed, recorded and popularised traditional and modern versions of the traditional *joik* (personal songs). Boine in particular has enjoyed international air-time and her distinctive sound blends folk-rock with *joik* roots.

Contemporary Music

Modern Norwegian music is about far more than A-ha – yes, they're still around and released their 10th studio album *Cast in Steel* in 2015 – with Norwegian artists excelling at everything from jazz and electronica to that peculiarly Norwegian obsession, black metal.

Jazz

Norway has a thriving jazz scene, with world-class festivals held throughout the year all over the country.

Jazz saxophonist Jan Garbarek is one of the most enduring Norwegian jazz personalities and is one of the biggest names on the international stage, quite apart from his fame within Norway. His work draws on classical, folk and world-music influences and he has recorded 30 albums, some including collaborations with renowned artists across a range of genres. His daughter, Anja Garbarek, is seen as one of the most exciting and innovative performers on the Norwegian jazz scene, bringing pop and electronica into the mix.

Other well-known performers include pianists Bugge Wesseltoft and Ketil Bjørnstad, saxophonist Trygve Seim, guitarist Terje Rypdal and female jazz singers Solveig Slettahjell, Sidsel Endresen and Karin Krog. Supersilent, the Christian Wallumrød Ensemble and the cutting-edge Jaga Jazzist rank among Norway's best-loved jazz groups.

Edvard Grieg Encounters

Edvard Grieg Museum (Bergen)

Open-air concerts (Bergen)

Grieghallen (Bergen)

When it comes to modern DJs, Todd Terje is widely considered among Scandinavia's best, while music producers and DJs Prins Thomas and Hans-Peter Lindstrøm are the country's most dynamic double act – their *Lindstrøm & Prins Thomas* (2005) is a great entry point into their 'space disco' style.

Electronica

Norway is at once one of Europe's most prolific producers, and most devoted fans, of electronica. Although much of the energy surrounding Norwegian electronica has shifted to Oslo in recent years, the so-called Bergen Wave was largely responsible for putting Norway on the world electronica circuit in the first years of the 21st century. Tromsø band Röyksopp (www.royksopp.com) in particular took the international electronica scene by storm with its debut album *Melody A.M.* in 2001. The Bergen Wave was not just about electronica; it also produced internationally acclaimed Norwegian bands Kings of Convenience (www.kingsofconvenience.eu) and Ephemera (www.ephemera.no).

In more recent years Oslo took up the electronica mantle with *Sunkissed*, spun by G-Ha and Olanskii.

Metal

Metal is a genre that Norway has taken to heart and Bergen tends to be the home city for much of the action. Two venues famous throughout Europe are Hulen (p171), an almost mythical venue among European heavy and indie rock fans; and Garage (p171), another iconic rock-heavy venue.

Norway is particularly known for its black-metal scene which, for a time in the early 1990s, became famous for its anti-Christian, Satanist philosophy. A handful of members of black-metal bands were involved in the burning down of churches such as the Fantoft Stave Church near Bergen. Among the better-known (or more notorious) Norwegian black-metal bands are Darkthrone, Mayhem, Enslaved, Gorgoroth and Satyricon.

Painting & Sculpture

Nineteenth-century Norway gave birth to two extraordinary talents: painter Edvard Munch and sculptor Gustav Vigeland, whose work adorns Oslo's public spaces.

Best Art Galleries

Nasjonalgalleriet (Oslo)

Munchmuseet (Oslo)

Bergen Kunsthall (Bergen)

KODE (Bergen)

Stavanger Kunstmuseum (Stavanger)

Museet for Samtidskunst (Oslo)

Astrup Fearnley Museet (Oslo)

Henie-Onstad Art Centre (Oslo)

One lesser-known early-20th-century talent whose work is finally receiving the acclaim it deserves is the mystical/expressionist Nikolai Astrup (1880–1928). A UK tour of his works in 2016 was a popular and critical success and you can see his work at KODE (p157) in Bergen.

Of the crop of contemporary Norwegian artists, Olav Jensen, Anne Dolven, Ørnulf Opdahl, Bjørn Tufta, Håvard Vikhagen, Odd Nerdrum and Anders Kjær have all created a minor stir with their return to abstract and expressionist forms. Their works often feature harsh depictions of the Norwegian landscape. Norwegian sculptors who've distinguished themselves include Bård Breivik, Per Inge Bjørlo and Per Barclay.

Perhaps in a category all his own, New York–based Bjarne Melgaard (b 1967) was described by London's *Evening Standard* newspaper in 2014 as 'the most famous Norwegian artist since Edvard Munch'. Known for his bad-boy, conceptual art, Melgaard shot to international fame with his 2014 fibreglass sculpture *Chair*. Conceived as a comment on the politics of race and gender, it depicted a black woman on her back with the seat cushion on her thighs and created a storm of controversy.

Architecture

Norway's architects have clearly been inspired by the country's dramatic landscapes, while recognising the need to build structures capable of withstanding the harsh dictates of Norway's climate. The results are often stunning: from rustic turf-roofed houses, whose design dates back almost two millennia, to Norway's signature stave churches, soaring religious architecture, and creative adaptations of Sami symbols and some Arctic landforms.

Traditional Architecture

Sami Architecture

In the far north, where both wood and stone were in short supply, the early nomadic Sami ingeniously built their homes out of turf, which provided excellent insulation against the cold. The temporary shelter that the Sami used on their travels is popularly known as the *lavvo* (although it has different names in various Sami dialects). Less vertical (and hence more stable in the winds of the high Arctic) than the North American teepee, the *lavvo* was held aloft by a tripod of three notched poles with a cover of reindeer skins (and later canvas).

The *lavvo* formed at once a centrepiece of Sami life and a refuge from the elements. The *lavvo* also holds considerable modern symbolism for the Sami: in the early 1980s the Oslo police bulldozed a Sami *lavvo* that had been set up outside Norway's parliament building to protest against a proposed dam that would have inundated Sami herding lands. These events provided a catalyst for a reassessment of Sami rights and led indirectly to the foundation of the Sami Parliament. The stunning modern Sami Parliament (p347) building in Karasjok was inspired by the traditional *lavvo* form.

Stave Churches

Seemingly conceived by a whimsical childlike imagination, the stave church is an ingenious adaptation to Norway's unique local conditions. Originally dating from the late Viking era, these ornately worked houses of worship are among the oldest surviving wooden buildings on earth, albeit heavily restored. Named for their vertical supporting posts, these churches are also distinguished by detailed carved designs and dragon-headed gables resembling the prows of classic Viking ships. Of the 500 to 600 that were originally built, only about 20 of the 28 that remain retain many of their original components.

Contemporary Architecture

Due to the need to rebuild quickly after WWII, Norway's architecture was primarily governed by functionalist necessity (the style is often called *funkis* in the local vernacular) rather than any coherent sense of style. Nowhere is this exemplified more than in the 1950, red-brick Oslo Rådhus (p54). As the style evolved, functionality was wedded to other concerns, such as recognising the importance of aesthetics in urban renewal (for example in Oslo's Grünerløkka district), and ensured that the country's contemporary architectural forms once again sat in harmony with the country's environment and history.

Tromsø's Ishavskatedralen (Arctic Cathedral; p315), designed by Jan Inge Hovig in 1965, mimics Norway's glacial crevasses and auroral curtains. Another beautiful example is the Sami Parliament (p347) in Karasjok, where Arctic building materials (birch, pine and oak) lend the place a sturdy authenticity, while the use of lights to replicate the Arctic night sky and the structure's resemblance to a Sami *lavvo* are extraordinary. Alat's Northern Lights Cathedral (p328) is weird and wonderful, and the creative interpretation of historical Norwegian shapes also finds expression at the Viking Ship Sports Arena (p132) in Hamar, while Oslo's landmark new opera house (p49) powerfully evokes a fjord-side glacier.

Kåre Tveter (1922–2012), a Norwegian painter whose work appears in Oslo's Nasjonalgalleriet as well as Galleri Svalbard, was particularly famous for his portrayal of the spare Arctic light of the Svalbard archipelago.

ARTS & ARCHITECTURE ARCHITECTURE

Best Film Festivals

Tromsø International Film Festival – January

Kosmorama, Trondheim – April

Norwegian International Film Festival, Haugesund – August

Bergen International Film Festival – late September

Norwegian Cuisine

Norwegian food can be excellent. Abundant seafood, local specialities such as reindeer, and a growing trend in cutting-edge cooking are undoubtedly the highlights. The only problem (and it's a significant one) is that prices are prohibitive, meaning that a full meal in a restaurant may become something of a luxury item for all but those on expense accounts. As a result, you may end up leaving Norway pretty uninspired by its food, which is such a shame considering what's on offer.

The Basics

Norway has a fairly standard range of eating options, and advance reservations are rarely required anywhere except for dinner in top-end restaurants.

Restaurants From simple diner-style eateries to Indian or Thai outposts to high-end gourmet experiences.

Cafes Open usually for breakfast and lunch only, most serve light meals and pastries to go with the coffee that's the main event.

Hotels Almost all of Norway's hotels have restaurants; many serve evening buffets and most are open to nonguests.

Kiosks Cheap alternatives to sit-down restaurants, serving fast food (hamburgers, hot dogs etc).

Fish Markets In larger towns, with fresh fish on offer.

Staples & Specialities

Meat

Norway is that rare place where signature wildlife species also provide some of the country's most memorable meals.

Norwegians love their meat. Roast reindeer *(reinsdyrstek)* is something every non-vegetarian visitor to Norway should try at least once; despite its cost (starting from around 275kr and often much higher), you'll likely order it again as it's one of the tastier red meats, and that's how it should be ordered – nice and red. In the far north, or if you're fortunate enough to be invited to a Sami wedding, you'll also come across traditional reindeer stew *(bidos)*. Another popular local meat is elk *(elg)*, which comes in a variety of forms, including as a steak or burger.

Other meat-based dishes that Norwegian chefs excel at preparing include *bankebiff* (slices/chunks of beef simmered in gravy), *dyrestek* (roast venison) and *lammebog* (shoulder of lamb). Not surprisingly given the Norwegian climate, meats are often cured, one variety of which is *spekemat* (cured lamb, beef, pork or reindeer, often served with scrambled eggs). Further dishes include *kjøttpålegg* (cold meat cuts), *fårikål* (lamb in cabbage stew), *syltelabb* (boiled, salt-cured pig's trotter), *lapskaus* (thick stew of diced meat, potatoes, onions and other vegetables) and *pytt i panne* (eggs with diced potato and meat).

Surprisingly few Norwegian restaurants offer the kind of meals that Norwegians eat at home, or at least used to when their mothers and grandmothers cooked for them. One such dish is traditional Norwegian meatballs served with mushy peas, mashed potatoes and wild-berry jam.

Authentic Norwegian Cooking by Astrid Karlsen Scott emphasises the practical and has been endorsed by none other than Ingrid Espelid, the Betty Crocker or Delia Smith of Norway. The Norwegian Kitchen by K Innli (ed) brings together more than 350 favourite recipes of members of the Association of Norwegian Chefs.

FOOD IN A TUBE

A Parisian orders a *cafe au lait,* a Londoner kippers. In New York it might be a bagel, in Tokyo rice. Comfort food or culture shock, it's breakfast, and for Norwegians it comes in a tube.

The question mark at hotel breakfast buffets, and nothing to do with dental hygiene, cream cheese and *kaviar* (sugar-cured and smoked cod-roe cream) packaged in tubes have been Norwegian favourites for decades. There are two especially popular Norwegian brands: the Trondheim-based Mills, best known for its *kaviar,* and the older Kavli in Bergen. Going strong since 1893 (its first tube food appeared in the 1920s), Kavli now produces bacon, ham, salami, shrimp, tomato, mexicana and jalapeño flavoured cheeses, all packaged in the familiar tubes.

Though both spreads are good alone and are part of a well-rounded Norwegian *frokost* (breakfast), *kaviar* is especially popular coupled with Norvegia cheese or a few slices of boiled egg.

Seafood

One Norwegian contribution to international cuisine that you shouldn't miss is salmon (grilled, *laks;* or smoked, *røykelaks*). Whereas other Norwegian foods may quickly empty your wallet without adequate compensation for taste, salmon remains blissfully cheap, although this applies only to farmed salmon; wild salmon is considerably more expensive. The quality is consistently top-notch. An excellent salmon dish, *gravat laks* is made by marinating salmon in sugar, salt, brandy and dill, and serving it in a creamy sauce.

Other Norwegian freshwater seafood specialities include brown trout, perch, Arctic char, Arctic grayling, bream and eel.

The most common ocean fish and seafood that you're likely to eat are cod (*torsk* or *bacalao;* often dried) and boiled or fresh shrimp. Herring (once the fish of the poor masses and now served pickled in onions, mustard or tomato sauce) is still served in some places, but it's becoming rarer as wild stocks recover. Norwegians are also huge fans of *fiskesuppe,* a thin, creamy, fish-flavoured soup.

Other dishes to watch out for include *fiskebolle* (fish balls), *fiskegrateng* (fish casserole), *gaffelbitar* (salt- and sugar-cured sprat/herring fillets), *klippfisk* (salted and dried cod), *sildesalat* (salad with slices of herring, cucumber, onions etc) and *spekeslid* (salted herring, often served with pickled beetroot, potatoes and cabbage).

Fish Markets

Bergen

Stavanger

Kristiansand

Trondheim

Narvik

Other Specialities

Potatoes feature prominently in nearly every Norwegian meal and most restaurants serve boiled, roasted or fried potatoes with just about every dish.

The country's main fruit-growing region is around Hardangerfjord, where strawberries, plums, cherries, apples and other orchard fruits proliferate. The most popular edible wild berries include strawberries, blackcurrants, red currants and raspberries; blueberries (huckleberries), which grow on open uplands; blue, swamp-loving bilberries; red high-bush and low-bush cranberries; and muskeg crowberries. The lovely amber-coloured *moltebær* (cloudberries) are highly prized and considered a delicacy. They grow one per stalk on open swampy ground and in Norway some cloudberry patches are zealously guarded. Warm cloudberry jam with ice cream is simply fantastic!

Norwegian cheeses have come to international attention as a result of the mild but tasty Jarlsberg, a white cheese first produced in 1860 on the Jarlsberg estate in Tønsberg.

Roots web (www.rootsweb. com/~wgnorway/ recipe.html) has easy-to-follow recipes of traditional Norwegian foods passed down through generations of people of Norwegian descent.

One scheme worth watching out for in northern Norway is the Arctic Menu, an attempt by an association of restaurants to revive interest in local ingredients and recipes.

Vegetarian & Vegan Food

Norwegians are not the most vegetarian of people. That said, most restaurants offer some vegetarian options. Sometimes this may just be a cheese-and-onion omelette or a pasta with cream sauce, but increasingly you'll find creative salads (although vegans won't appreciate the widespread use of cheese) and a range of crêpes or pancakes to add some variety to your diet. The predominance of potatoes on most Norwegian restaurant menus almost always provides a fall-back option.

In general, the rule is that the larger the town, the wider your choices of vegetarian fare. Tapas restaurants are a recurring theme in larger towns and most have vegetable-only options. Pizza restaurants also always have at least one vegetarian dish.

Every Thursday from September to May, many Bergen restaurants serve *raspeballer*, a powerful traditional meal with salted meat, potatoes and mashed turnip – an acquired taste perhaps, but hearty winter food.

Eating in Norway

Habits & Customs

The Norwegian day starts with coffee (always!), a boiled egg and some sort of bread or dry crispbread (normally Ryvita) topped with cheese, cucumber, tomato and a type of pickled herring.

For lunch, most people opt for an open sandwich, a slice of bread topped with sardines, shrimp, ham, olives, cucumber or egg. In the mid-afternoon Norwegians often break for coffee and one of the highlights of the day, waffles with cream and jam. Unlike the firm Belgian waffles, which are better known abroad, Norwegian waffles are flower-shaped, soft and often strongly flavoured with cardamom.

The main meal is eaten between 4pm and 6pm, considerably later in summer. Usually the only hot meal of the day, it normally includes a meat, seafood or pasta dish, with boiled potatoes, a scoop of vegetables and perhaps even a small salad or green garnish.

Opening Hours

Although lunch is usually served from noon to 3pm and dinner from 6pm to 11pm, many restaurants (and their kitchens) remain open from noon to 10pm or 11pm.

Where to Eat & Drink

Hotel breakfasts in Norway often consist of a gargantuan buffet that is dominated by continental-style choices, with a few hot dishes (usually bacon, eggs and/or sausages) and some Scandinavian options (such as pickled herrings) thrown in. If you're staying somewhere where breakfast

---

TRAVEL YOUR TASTEBUDS

Norway has its share of strong-tasting culinary oddities that the brave among you may wish to try:

➡ Brown cheese (*Gudbrandsdalsost*) – made from the whey of goat's and/or cow's milk and has a slightly sweet flavour despite its off-putting caramel-coloured appearance.

➡ Reconstituted cod, mackerel or saithe balls (*lutefisk*) – more common in homes than restaurants and something of a staple for older folk.

➡ Cod tongues (*torsketunger*) – these are hugely popular in Lofoten and, strangely enough, nowhere else.

➡ Fermented trout (*rakfisk*) – some Norwegians swear by it, but some Lonely Planet authors are happy to leave them to it.

AQUAVIT

The national spirit, aquavit (or *akevitt*) is a potent dose of Norwegian culture made from potatoes and caraway liquor. The name is derived from the Latin *aqua vitae,* the 'living waters'. Although caraway is an essential ingredient, various modern distilleries augment the spicy flavour with any combination of orange, coriander (cilantro), anise, fennel, sugar and salt. The confection is aged for three to five years in 500L oak barrels that have previously been used to age sherry.

Perhaps the most esteemed version of this libation is *linje aquavit,* or 'line aquavit', which first referred to stores that had crossed the equator. In the early days, ships carried oak barrels of aquavit abroad to trade, but the unsold barrels were returned to Norway and offered for sale. When it was discovered that the product had improved with age and travel, these leftovers became highly prized commodities. Today, bottles of *linje aquavit* bear the name of the ship involved, its route and the amount of time the barrels have aged at sea.

is not included, your best bet is a bakery where bread, pastries, sandwiches and bagels are well priced.

If you love fresh fish, any of Norway's fish markets are fabulous places to eat; buy what you want as a takeaway and find a quiet vantage point alongside the water.

Norwegians love to eat out and just about every town in Norway has at least one sit-down restaurant. Although it's more usual to eat a light lunch and save the main meal for dinner, many Norwegian restaurants, especially in larger towns, serve cheaper lunch specials (often around 99kr). These are often filling and well sized for those wanting more than a sandwich. Sometimes these are signed as a *dagens rett* (daily special).

Drinks

Hot Drinks

If Norway has a national drink, it's coffee. In fact, coffee is drunk in such staggering quantities that one can only wonder how people can remain so calm under the influence of so much caffeine. Most Norwegians drink it black and strong, but foreigners requiring milk and/or sugar are normally indulged.

Teas and infusions are also available all over the country.

Alcoholic Drinks

Beer is commonly sold in bars in 400mL (from 60kr) or 500mL (from 70kr) glasses (about 30% and 15% less than a British pint, respectively). The standard Norwegian beer is pils lager, with an alcohol content of around 4%, and it's still brewed in accordance with the 16th-century German purity law. The most popular brands are the lagers Ringsnes in the south and Mackin in the north, while micro-breweries are a growing trend. Munkholm is a fairly pleasant alcohol-free beer. Note that when friends go out drinking, people generally buy their own drinks rather than rounds, which is scarcely surprising given the prices.

Norwegians increasingly drink wine with meals. According to one study, wine makes up one-third of Norway's alcohol intake, compared to just 12% in 1974. Quality restaurants increasingly offer extensive wine lists with wines from across Europe and sometimes further afield. In some cities, wine bars are all the rage.

Island Summers: Memories of a Norwegian Childhood (2014), by Tilly Culme-Seymour, is a memoir of a happy Norwegian childhood, where home-made food takes centre stage.

Glossary

bacalao – cod (see also *torsk*)
bidos – traditional reindeer stew (Sami)
brisling – sardine
brus – soft drink
dagens rett – daily special
dyrestek – roast venison
elg – elk or moose
fiskebolle – fish balls
fiskesuppe – thin, creamy, fish-flavoured soup
frokost – breakfast
frukt – fruit
gaffelbitar – salt- and sugar-cured sprat/herring fillets
gatekjøkken – food wagons or kiosks
grønnsak – vegetable
Gudbrandsdalsost – brown cheese made from the whey of goat's and/or cow's milk
hvalbiff – whale steak
hvitvin – white wine
jordbær – strawberry
kaffe – coffee
kjøtt – meat
kjøttpålegg – cold meat cuts
klippfisk – salted and dried cod
kylling – chicken
laks – salmon, usually grilled
lammebog – shoulder of lamb
lunsj – lunch
lutefisk – reconstituted cod, mackerel or saithe ball
melk – milk
meny – menu
mineralvann – mineral water
nøtter – nuts
øl – beer
oksekjøtt – beef
ost – cheese
potet – potato
pølse – sausage, hot dog
pytt i panne – eggs with diced potato and meat
rakfisk – fermented trout
reinsdyrstek – roast reindeer
reker – shrimp
rødvin – red wine
rømmegrøt – sour-cream variant on porridge and served at Christmas
røykelaks – smoked salmon
salat – salad
sauekjøtt – lamb
sild – herring
skinke – ham
sopp – mushroom
spekemat – cured lamb, beef, pork or reindeer, often served with scrambled eggs
svinekjøtt – pork
torsk – cod (see also *bacalao*)
torsketunger – cod tongues
tunfisk – tuna

Survival Guide

Directory A–Z

Accommodation

Norway offers a wide range of accommodation, from camping, hostels and pensions to international-standard hotels. Booking ahead is always wise in high season.

Hotels Hotels are everywhere. Most have some affiliation with major local and international chains and are midrange to top-end, but there are a few family-run places.

Camping Norway's campsites are widespread, often in stunning locations; free camping is also possible.

DNT & Other Mountain Huts Mountain and wilderness huts, some staffed, others not.

Guesthouses, Pensions & B&Bs Small, more personal options sprinkled throughout the country with some real gems.

Booking Services

Bed & Breakfast Norway (www. bbnorway.com) Has extensive online listings for B&Bs throughout Norway; click on 'Online Catalogue'. The print version of its listings is no longer updated and therefore of limited use.

Hostelling International (HI; www.hihostels.com) Although not all Norwegian hostels belong to the Hostelling International network, many do. HI members pay 15% less than nonmembers. Check the HI website to find its office in your home country so that you can join and qualify for members' prices in Norway.

Norske Vandrerhjem (☑23 12 45 10; www.hihostels.no) The Norwegian hostelling association, Norske Vandrerhjem is HI-affiliated and publishes the free *Hostels in Norway*, which contains a full listing of hostels and updated prices for the 49 hostels on its books; it's available from hostels and some tourist offices.

Best Western (www.bestwestern.no) The Best Western Rewards system operates at all Best Western hotels in Norway and beyond, in addition to occasional summer deals.

Nordic Choice Hotels (www. nordicchoicehotels.no) Covering Clarion, Clarion Collection, Quality and Comfort Hotels, with the Nordic Choice Club you can earn free nights if you stay in enough member hotels. In some of its properties you get a light evening buffet included in the price. Its best properties are its relatively new upmarket, boutique brand, the Clarion Collection.

De Historiske (☑55 31 67 60; www.dehistoriske.no) Although it's less a chain than a collection of historic hotels and there are no membership options, it's always worth checking out the worthwhile De Historiske network, which links Norway's most historic old hotels and restaurants. The quality on offer is consistently high, every hotel is architecturally distinguished and many are family-run.

Fjord Pass (www.fjordpass.no) The Fjord Pass (two adults and unlimited children under 15 years 150kr) enables discounts at 120 hotels, guesthouses, cabins and apartments year-round; no free nights, but the discounts on nightly rates are considerable. Works best if you book in advance through its website, rather than simply turning up and hoping for a discount.

Scandic Hotels (www.scandichotels.no) Scandic, which in 2014 bought the Rica brand, has swish and classy hotels that generally sport a contemporary look. An excellent rewards program that offers discounts and free nights.

Thon Hotels (www.thonhotels.com) Modern, sometimes slightly characterless hotels, but still some excellent properties, reasonable prices and a family-friendly approach. This program has free membership that qualifies you for discounts or free nights.

ACCOMMODATION ONLINE

For more accommodation reviews by Lonely Planet authors, check out http://lonelyplanet.com/hotels/. You'll find independent reviews, as well as recommendations on the best places to stay.

Dansommer (☐in Denmark 39 14 33 00; www.dansommer.com) Privately run Danish agency that acts as a clearing house for hundreds of self-catering cabins and chalets in Norway and elsewhere in Scandinavia.

Reservations

Although it's rare that you'll arrive in a town to find that all of the accommodation is full – festival times are an exception – it's always advisable to book in advance to ensure that you get the accommodation of your choice; the hotel you'd like to stay in may have rooms, but the only available ones probably have a view of the back wall rather than the fjord.

Most places in Norway accept phone or email reservations (you'll often have to leave a credit-card number). Many hostels are happy to book beds at your next destination for a small fee (around 25kr). Note that popular hostels in Oslo and Bergen are often heavily booked in summer.

Many tourist offices can help you find accommodation, usually for a fee of around 50kr to 70kr; apart from in some larger tourist offices, this service usually operates only if you're physically present in the tourist office and not for advance bookings.

Seasons

The main tourist season runs from around the middle of June to the middle of August. Unusually, although this is the high season, it's also when accommodation prices are at their lowest and many hotels offer their best deals. In some areas the season begins in mid-May and/or hangs on until mid-September.

Winter, particularly in northern Norway where travellers come for activities such as snowmobiling and dog-sledding, is also a popular time to visit although, unlike in summer, prices rarely drop as a consequence.

Some hotels and the overwhelming majority of campsites close during the winter months, while that rare breed, ice hotels – there are examples in Kirkenes and Alta – only open in winter.

Prices

Prices at Norwegian hotels vary widely throughout the year. In a few places, discounted high-season prices apply in July or July to mid-August only. The exception to this general rule is the southern Norwegian coast, where beach resorts sometimes raise their prices to cash in on the school-holiday influx.

During the rest of the year, the assumption seems to be that the only people travelling are those doing so for business and on expense accounts, and prices can soar accordingly (by as much as 40%). The exception is weekends (usually Friday and Saturday nights, but sometimes also Sunday) when, year-round, prices can drop to their much more reasonable summer rates. If you're travelling outside the summer months, ask your hotel about special offers to see if discounts are available.

Prices for single rooms are generally not much less than the rates for double rooms. Remember that if you're making enquiries in advance about prices, they're often quoted per person for double rooms, so always check.

Staying within a tight budget is difficult in Norway, and you'll either need to stay at campsites (in a tent or a simple cabin), hostels or guesthouses. Within the budget category, it's rare that

you'll have your own private bathroom. In midrange and top-end accommodation, rooms are usually very comfortable and almost always have a private bathroom.

Accommodation Types
HOTELS

Norway's hotels are generally modern and excellent, although those with any character are pretty thin on the ground. Comfortable, nationwide chain hotels are the norm and the rooms can all start to look the same after a while, whether you're sleeping in Oslo or Kirkenes. The advantage of these chains or hotel networks, however, is that some offer hotel passes, which can entitle you to a free night if you use the chain enough times; some passes only operate in summer.

CAMPING

Norway has more than 1000 campsites. Tent space costs from 100kr at basic campsites up to 250kr for those with better facilities or in more popular areas, such as Oslo and Bergen. Quoted prices usually include your car, motorcycle or caravan. A per-person charge is also added in some places, electricity often costs a few kroner extra and almost all places charge at least 10kr for showers.

Most campsites also rent simple cabins with cooking facilities, starting at around 450kr for a very basic two- or four-bed bunkhouse. Bring a sleeping bag, as linen and blankets are only provided at an extra charge (anywhere from 50kr to 150kr).

Unless you opt for a more expensive deluxe cabin with shower and toilet facilities (750kr to 1500kr), you'll also have to pay for showers and washing water (there are a few exceptions). Normally, cabin occupants must clean their cabin before leaving or pay an additional cleaning charge (around 150kr).

Note that although a few complexes remain open year-round, tent and caravan sites are closed in the off-season (normally early September to mid-May).

NAF Camp (www.nafcamp.no) is an excellent online resource listing more than 250 campsites around Norway.

Norsk Camping (www.camping. no) is a useful resource for general camping info, as well as the comprehensive *Camping* guide, available in book (there's a charge of 98kr for it to be sent) or pdf format (free); you can also pick it up for free from some tourist offices and campsites. It has hundreds of listings, although most entries are in Norwegian.

DNT & OTHER MOUNTAIN HUTS

Den Norske Turistforening (DNT, Norwegian Mountain Touring Club; Map p50; ☑40 00 18 68, 22 82 28 22; www.turistfore ningen.no; Youngstorget 1, Oslo) maintains a network of 460 mountain huts or cabins located a day's hike apart along the country's 20,000km of well-marked and -maintained wilderness hiking routes. Of these, over 400 have beds for sleeping, with the remainder reserved for eating, rest stops or emergency shelter.

DNT huts range from unstaffed huts with two beds to large staffed lodges with more than 100 beds and renowned standards of service. At both types of huts, DNT members receive significant discounts.

Annual membership for adult/senior/19 to 26 years/13 to 18 years/ child 12 and under costs 660/510/340/205/125kr.

Most DNT huts are open from 16 February to 14

October. Staffed DNT lodges also open from the Saturday before Palm Sunday until Easter Monday, with staffed huts along the Oslo–Bergen railway and a few others open for the cross-country ski season as early as late February. DNT can provide lists of opening dates for each hut.

Members/nonmembers who prefer to camp outside the huts and use the facilities will pay 70/90kr.

There are also numerous private hikers' huts and lodges peppered around most mountain areas, but not all are open to the public. Some offer DNT members a discount.

STAFFED DNT HUTS

At staffed huts, which are concentrated in the south, you can simply turn up and pay your fees. In compliance with international mountain hospitality, no one is turned away, even if there's only floor space left; DNT members over 50 years of age are guaranteed a bed, even if it means displacing a younger hiker! Huts tend to be packed at Easter and are consistently busy throughout summer.

Staffed lodges don't normally have cooking facilities for guests, but a self-service section with cooking facilities is available at some lodges when they are unstaffed. Sleeping sheets are often sold or included in the price at staffed huts.

Prices vary considerably depending on whether or not you're a DNT member, the type of accommodation, and whether you want full-board or bed-only accommodation. For the full range of options and prices at staffed huts, see the DNT website.

UNSTAFFED DNT HUTS

All unstaffed huts offer cooking facilities, but in most places you must have your own sleeping bag or hostel-style sleeping sheet.

For unstaffed huts, you must pick up keys (150kr to 250kr deposit) in advance from a DNT office or a staffed hut. To pay, fill out a Once-Only Authorisation slip and leave either cash or a valid credit-card number in the box provided. There are two classes of unstaffed huts. Self-service chalets are stocked with blankets and pillows and have wood stoves, firewood, gas cookers and a wide range of tinned or freeze-dried food supplies for sale (on the honour system). At other unstaffed huts, users must bring their own food. In unstaffed huts, DNT members/nonmembers pay 255/365kr for a bed; nonmember children pay 180kr.

BED & BREAKFASTS

Some places operate as B&Bs, where prices (usually with shared bathrooms) start from single/double 500/700kr and can go up to 700/950kr.

GUESTHOUSES & PENSIONS

Many towns have *pensjonat* (pensions) and *gjestehus* (guesthouses), and some, especially the latter, are family run and offer a far more intimate option than the hostel or hotel experience. Prices for a single/double with shared bathroom usually start at 550/800kr but can cost significantly more; linen and/or breakfast will only be included at the higher-priced places.

HOSTELS

In Norway, reasonably priced hostels (*vandrerhjem*) offer a dorm bed for the night, plus use of communal facilities that usually include a self-catering kitchen (you're advised to take your own cooking and eating utensils), internet access and bathrooms. Some also have single or double rooms with either shared or private bathroom facilities, but these often represent poor value.

While some hostels have quite comfortable lodge-style facilities and are open year-round, a few are used for school accommodation and others are the cheaper wing of a hotel; occasionally prices work out to be more expensive than a cabin or budget hotel. In most hostels, guests must still bring their own sleeping sheet and pillowcase, although most hire out sleeping sheets for a one-off fee (starting from 50kr) regardless of the number of nights.

Most hostels have two- to six-bed rooms, and beds cost from 220kr to 450kr. The higher-priced hostels usually include a buffet breakfast, while other places may charge from 70kr to 150kr for breakfast. Some also provide a good-value evening meal for around 150kr.

A welcome addition to the budget end of the market are chains such as Citybox, Smarthotels and Basic Hotels. These hostel-hotel hybrids are slick and excellent value, but you'll only find them in larger cities.

Several hostel guides are available, including Hostelling International's annually updated Europe guide.

PRIVATE HOMES

Tourist offices in some towns have lists of private rooms, which are among the cheapest places to stay. In some cases they allow you to stay with a Norwegian family. Prices vary, but you'll rarely have to pay more than 450/600kr for a single/double; breakfast isn't normally included. Showers sometimes cost 15kr to 30kr extra.

Along highways you'll occasionally see *rom* signs, indicating informal accommodation typically costing from 275kr to 500kr per room (without breakfast); those who bring their own sheets or sleeping bags may get a discount.

SUMMER HOMES & CABINS

Most tourist offices in popular holiday areas keep lists of private huts, cabins and summer homes that are rented out to holidaymakers when the owners aren't using them; these arrangements sometimes also apply in the ski season. The price for a week's rental starts from around 1500kr for a simple place in the off-season to around 16,000kr for the most elaborate chalet in midsummer. Most cabins sleep at least four people, and some accommodate as many as 12; if you have a group, it can be an economical option. Advance booking is normally required, and you'll probably have to pay a deposit of around 800kr or 20% of the total fee, whichever is less.

Customs Regulations

Alcohol and tobacco are extremely expensive in Norway. To at least get you started, it's worth importing your duty-free allotment: 1L of spirits and 1L of wine (or 2L of wine), plus 2L of beer per person. Note that drinks with an alcohol content of over 60% may be treated as narcotics! You're also allowed to import 200 cigarettes duty-free. Importation of fresh food and controlled drugs is prohibited.

Svalbard is a duty-free zone; many items are considerably cheaper there than in mainland Norway as they're subject to neither MOMS (VAT) nor customs duties.

Discount Cards

A Hostelling International (HI; www.hihostels.com) membership card will get you a 15% discount at youth hostels.

Senior Cards

Honnør (senior) discounts are available to those aged 67 years or over for admission to museums, public pools, transport etc. The discounted price usually amounts to 75% of the full price. You don't require a special card, but those who look particularly youthful may, apart from enjoying the compliment, need proof of their age to qualify.

Student Cards

Student discounts are often available (usually 75% of the normal fee). You will need some kind of identification (eg an International Student Identity Card; www.isic.org) to prove student status. Some travellers have reported being refused access with their normal university cards (unless it's from a Norwegian university), so the ISIC card is a good investment. It can provide discounts on many forms of transport (including airlines, international ferries and local public transport) and in some internet cafes, reduced or free admission to museums and sights, and cheap meals in some student restaurants.

Electricity

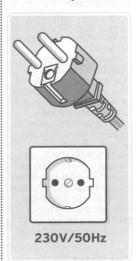

230V/50Hz

The electricity current in Norway is 230V, 50Hz. Norway uses European-style two-pin plugs.

Emergency & Important Numbers

From outside Norway, dial your international access code, Norway's country code, then the number.

Directory assistance	☏180
International access code	☏00
Norway's country code	☏47
Ambulance	☏113
Police	☏112

Health

Norway is, in general, a very healthy place and no special precautions are necessary when visiting. The biggest risks are likely to be viral infections in winter, sunburn and insect bites in summer, and foot blisters from too much hiking.

Availability & Cost of Healthcare

If you do fall ill while in Norway you will be very well looked after as health care is excellent.

Most medications are available in Norway, but may go by a different name than at home, so be sure to have the generic name, as well as the brand name. If carrying syringes or needles, be sure to have a physician's letter documenting their medical necessity. For minor illnesses, pharmacists can dispense valuable advice and over-the-counter medication.

Like almost everything else, medical care can be prohibitively expensive in Norway and insurance is a must.

Tap Water

Tap water is always safe to drink in Norway.

Out in the wilds, it's wise to beware of drinking from streams, as even the clearest and most inviting water may harbour giardia and other parasites. For extended hikes where you must rely on natural water sources, the simplest way of purifying water is to boil it thoroughly; at high altitude water boils at a lower temperature, so germs are less likely to be killed. Boil it for longer in these environments (up to 10 minutes).

If you cannot boil water it should be treated chemically. Chlorine tablets (Puritabs, Steritabs or other brands) will kill many pathogens, but not giardia and amoebic cysts. Iodine is more effective in purifying water and is available in tablet form (such as Potable Aqua). Too much iodine can be harmful.

Environmental Hazards

HYPOTHERMIA

Norway's perilously cold winters require that you take the proper precautions if travelling at this time. And even on a hot day in the mountains, the weather can change rapidly – carry waterproof garments and warm layers, and inform others of your route.

Symptoms of hypothermia are exhaustion, numb skin (particularly of the toes and fingers), shivering, slurred speech, irrational or violent behaviour, lethargy, stumbling, dizzy spells, muscle cramps and violent bursts of energy. Irrationality may take the form of sufferers claiming they are warm and trying to take off their clothes.

To treat mild hypothermia, first get the person out of the wind and/or rain, remove their clothing if it's wet and replace it with dry, warm clothing. Give them hot liquids – not alcohol – and high-kilojoule, easily digestible food. Do not rub victims: allow them to slowly warm themselves instead. This should be enough to treat the early stages of hypothermia. The early recognition and treatment of mild hypothermia is the only way to prevent severe hypothermia, which is a critical condition.

Internet Access

Norway's internet network is fast and reliable. Wi-fi, 3G and frequently 4G are available right across the country, often in surprisingly remote locations.

Public Libraries & Tourist Offices

Free internet access is available in most municipal libraries (biblioteket). As it's a popular service, you may have to reserve a time slot earlier in the day; in busier places, you may be restricted to a half-hour slot. Be aware that some libraries are replacing their internet-access computer terminals with free wi-fi.

Most tourist offices in major towns have free wi-fi, and sometimes an internet terminal as well (for which there's usually a small fee).

Wi-fi

Wi-fi is widely available at most hotels, cafes, restaurants and tourist offices; it's nearly always free nowadays, although you'll usually have to ask for the password. Most of Norway's airports offer free wi-fi; the standard service can be slow, but there's usually an option to pay for faster access.

Several airlines, including budget carrier Norwegian (www.norwegian.no), have also started to offer free onboard wi-fi for its customers, as has the state railway NSB (www.nsb.no) and some bus services.

Language Courses

There are a number of options in Oslo if you want to learn Norwegian (or another language).

Berlitz Language Services
(Map p50; ☎23 00 33 60; www.
berlitz.no; 7th fl, Akersgata 16)
Convenient location in the heart
of Oslo, with an additional school
in Stavanger.

Folkeuniversitetet Oslo (Map
p50; ☎22 47 60 00; www.
folkeuniversitetet.no/eng/
Language-courses; 5th fl,
Torggata 7) Centrally located
language school.

**International Summer School,
University of Oslo** (Map p66;
☎22 85 63 85; www.uio.no/
english/studies/summer
school/; 6th fl, Gaustadalléen
25) Northwest of the centre at
the university.

Oslo Voksenopplæring (☎23
47 00 00; www.felles.oslovo.
no; Karoline Kristiansens vei
8) Language school east of the
city centre.

Legal Matters

Norway has an excellent legal
system and should you fall
foul of the law, you have a
right to legal representation
and an interpreter. As a
general rule, what's illegal in
your home country is likely
to be illegal in Norway; drug
possession, even of small
quantities, is illegal.

One local law that you're
unlikely to be familiar with
applies on Svalbard, where
it is illegal to pick any
wildflowers.

LGBTIQ+ Travellers

Norwegians are general-
ly tolerant of alternative
lifestyles, although this is
less the case in rural areas.
Homosexuality has been
legal in Norway since 1973,
and the country was the first
in the world to pass a law
prohibiting discrimination
against homosexuals. Then,
in 2009, Norway became the
sixth country in the world to
legalise same-sex marriage
when its parliament passed
a gender-neutral marriage
law. The new law granted full

rights to church weddings,
adoption and artificial insem-
ination to married couples
regardless of their sexual
orientation.

All of that said, public
displays of affection are not
common practice, except
perhaps in some areas of
Oslo. Oslo is generally the
easiest place to be gay in
Norway, although even here
there have been occasional
attacks on gay couples hold-
ing hands, especially in the
central-eastern areas of the
capital. You're most likely to
encounter difficulties wherever conservative religious
views predominate, whether
among newly arrived Muslim
immigrant communities or
devoutly Lutheran communities in rural areas.

Oslo has the liveliest gay
scene, and it's worth stopping by **Use-It** (Map p50; ☎24
14 98 20; http://use-it.unginfo.
oslo.no/; Møllergata 3; ☺10am-
5pm Mon-Fri, noon-5pm Sat;
🚇Brugata), where you can
pick up the excellent annual
Streetwise booklet with its
'Gay Guide' section.

Organisations & Websites

FRI (Foreningen; Map p50;
☎23 10 39 39; www.forenin
genfri.no; Tollbugata 24, 4th fl,
Oslo) The Norwegian National
Association of Lesbian and
Gay Liberation; website only in
Norwegian.

Global Gayz (www.globalgayz.
com/europe/norway/) The
Norway page has some interesting background information and
practical information.

Night Tours (www.nighttours.
com/oslo/) A gay guide to the
Oslo night.

Visit Oslo (www.visitoslo.com)
Click on 'Gay Olso' for some
useful links.

Maps

Most local tourist offices
distribute user-friendly and
free town maps.

Country Maps

Bilkart over Norge
(1:1,000,000) by Nortra-
books is one of the best
maps of Norway for general
travellers. It includes useful
topographic shading and
depicts the entire country
on one sheet. *Michelin Norway – 752* (1: 1,250,000) is
also good although the last
update was in January 2007
and the font size can be a
problem.

Hiking Maps

Den Norske Turistforening
(DNT, Norwegian Mountain
Touring Club; Map p50; www.
turistforeningen.no; Storget 3,
Oslo; ☺10am-5pm Mon-Wed
& Fri, to 6pm Thu, to 3pm Sat;
🚇Jernbanetorget) is the best
source of hiking maps. Hikers
can pick up topographic sheets
at any DNT office, although the
offices in larger cities have a
wider selection beyond the local
area. National park centres and
nearby tourist offices are good
sources for the excellent Turkart
or Statens Kartverk (www.
statkart.no) hiking maps. Statens
Kartverk, Norway's official
mapping authority, covers the
country in 21 sheets at a scale of
1:250,000.

Road Maps

The best road maps are the
Cappelens series, which are
sold in Norwegian book-
shops. There are three maps

PRACTICALITIES

➡ **Newspapers & Magazines** The most respected Norwegian-language daily is *Aftenposten* (www.aftenposten.no), while *VG* (www.vg.no) and *Dagbladet* (www.dagbladet.no) are other national mass-circulation dailies. *Morgenbladet* (www.morgenbladet.no) is a Norwegian-language weekly, while the *Norway Post* (www.norwaypost.no) is a good source of news in English.

➡ **TV & Radio** Government-run NRK (one TV and four radio channels) competes with TV2 and TV Norge networks and satellite broadcasts of TV3. Hotels often have cable TV. Numerous private radio stations, mostly with a music focus, supplement the government stations. The NRK Alltid Nyheter station broadcasts the BBC World Service every second hour or so.

➡ **DVD** Norway uses the PAL (Region 2) DVD system.

➡ **Smoking** Forbidden in enclosed public spaces, including hotels, restaurants and bars.

➡ **Weights & Measures** The metric system is used. Watch out for the occasional use of *mil* (mile), which is a Norwegian mile (10km).

---

at 1:335,000 scale: *No 1 Sør-Norge Sør*, *No 2 Sør-Norge Nord* and *No 3 Møre og Trøndelag*. Northern Norway is covered in two sheets at 1:400,000 scale: *No 4 Nordland og Sør-Troms* and *No 5 Troms og Finnmark*. The *Veiatlas Norge* (*Norwegian Road Atlas*), published by Statens Kartverk, is revised every two years.

Money

The most convenient way to bring your money is in the form of a debit or credit card, with some extra cash for use in case of an emergency.

ATMs

'Mini-Banks' (the Norwegian name for ATMs) are widespread and most accept major credit cards as well as Cirrus, Visa Electron and/or Plus bank cards. Check with your bank before leaving about which banks charge the lowest withdrawal fees.

Changing Money

Don't assume that all banks will change money: in some places you may need to shop around to find one that does. Rates at post offices and tourist offices are generally poorer than at banks, but can be convenient for small amounts outside banking hours.

Credit & Debit Cards

Norway is well on its way to becoming a cashless society – you'll find the vast majority of transactions these days are by card. Visa, Eurocard, MasterCard, Diners Club and American Express cards are widely accepted throughout Norway. If your card is lost or stolen, report it immediately.

American Express (☑22 96 08 00)

Diners Club (☑21 01 53 00)

MasterCard (☑80 01 26 97)

Visa (☑80 01 20 52)

Currency

The Norwegian krone is most often represented either as Nkr (preceding the number), NOK (preceding the number) or simply kr (following the amount). Lonely Planet uses kr. One Norwegian krone (1kr) equals 100 øre.

Exchange Rates

Australia	A$1	6.48kr
Canada	C$1	7.00kr
Europe	€1	10.35kr
Japan	¥100	8.00kr
New Zealand	NZ$1	6.20kr
UK	UK£1	12.20kr
USA	US$1	8.80kr

For current exchange rates, see www.xe.com.

Tipping

Tipping on a North American scale is not expected.

Service charges Service charges and tips are included in restaurant bills and taxi fares.

Reward service If the service has been particularly helpful in a midrange to top-end restaurant, 5% is generally appropriate, while 10% is considered generous.

Paying by credit card If you're paying by credit card in a restaurant, space will be left for adding a tip.

Opening Hours

These standard opening hours are for high season (mid-June to mid-August) and tend to decrease outside that time.

Banks 8.15am to 3pm Monday to Wednesday and Friday, to 5pm Thursday

Central Post Offices 8am to 8pm Monday to Friday, 9am to 6pm Saturday; otherwise 9am to 5pm Monday to Friday, 10am to 2pm Saturday

Restaurants noon to 3pm and 6pm to 11pm; some don't close between lunch and dinner

Shops 10am to 5pm Monday to Wednesday and Friday, to 7pm Thursday, to 2pm Saturday

Supermarkets 9am to 9pm Monday to Friday, to 6pm Saturday

Public Holidays

New Year's Day (Nyttårsdag) 1 January

Maundy Thursday (Skjærtorsdag) March/April

Good Friday (Langfredag) March/April

Easter Monday (Annen Påskedag) March/April

Labour Day (Første Mai, Arbeidetsdag) 1 May

Constitution Day (Nasjonaldag) 17 May

Ascension Day (Kristi Himmelfartsdag) May/June, 40th day after Easter

Whit Monday (Annen Pinsedag) May/June, 8th Monday after Easter

Christmas Day (Første Juledag) 25 December

Boxing Day (Annen Juledag) 26 December

Safe Travel

You and your personal belongings are safer in Norway than in most travellers' home countries.

➡ The cities (even east Oslo, which has a relatively poor reputation) are reasonably safe at night, but don't become blasé about security.

➡ Be careful near the nightclubs in the Rosenkrantz gate area of Oslo, and beware of pickpockets around the Torget area of Bergen.

➡ Normally the greatest nuisance value will come from drug addicts, drunks and/or beggars (mainly in Oslo), who can spot a naive tourist a block away.

➡ If hiking out into the Norwegian wilds, Norway's weather can, even in summer, change rapidly.

Taxes & Refunds

Norway has a well-organised system of tax refunds on items purchased at participating shops.

How it Works

For goods that cost more than 315kr (290kr for food items) at shops displaying the 'Tax Free' logo, you're entitled to a 'Refund Cheque' for the 25% MVA (the equivalent of value-added or sales tax) or 15% for food items. (Note that the cost threshold relates to the total you spend in a single shop, rather than the amount per item.) At the point of sale, you fill out the cheque with your name, address and passport number, and then, at your departure point from the country, you present your sealed goods, passport and Refund Cheque to collect the refund; ferry passengers normally collect their refund from the ferry's purser during limited hours once the boat has sailed.

Further Information

For more information, pick up the *How to Shop Tax Free* brochure from most tourist offices and some tourist shops, which explains the procedure and lists border crossings at which refunds can be collected; or visit www.globalblue.com/tax-free-shopping/norway/article117202.ece.

Telephone

Telephone kiosks are still fairly widespread in Norway, but many won't accept cash. Instead you have to use either a credit card or a phonecard, which you can buy at 7-Elevens and convenience stores.

Mobile Phones

There aren't too many places where you can't get mobile (cell) access; there's coverage in close to 90% of the country. This doesn't, of course, apply to wilderness areas and the hiking trails of most national parks.

If you want to use your home-country mobile phone in Norway, always check with your carrier about the cost of roaming charges to avoid a nasty surprise when your next bill arrives. In theory EU phones should have no roaming charges, but do check first. An increasing number of providers now offer packages that allow you to take your minutes, texts and data allowances overseas for a small charge.

If you wish to use your mobile, but with a Norwegian SIM card, check that your phone is unlocked. If your phone accepts a foreign SIM card, these can be purchased from any 7-Eleven store and some Narvesen kiosks. However, as the connection instructions are entirely in Norwegian, you're better off purchasing the card from any Telehuset outlet, where they'll help you connect on the spot. SIM cards start from 200kr, which includes 100kr worth of calls.

There are three mobile-service providers:

Chess (www.chess.no) A relatively new mobile operator.

Telenor Mobil (www.telenor.no) The largest mobile-service provider.

Telia (www.telia.no) Norway's second-largest operator.

Time

Note that when telling the time, Norwegians use 'half' as signifying 'half *before*' rather than 'half past'. Always double-check unless you want to be an hour late! Although the 24-hour clock is used in some official situations, you'll find people generally use the 12-hour clock in everyday conversation.

Norway shares the same time zone as most of Western Europe (GMT/UTC plus one hour during winter, and GMT/UTC plus two hours during the daylight-saving period). Daylight saving starts on the last Sunday in March and finishes on the last Sunday in October.

Note the following time differences:

Australia During the Australian winter (Norwegian summer), subtract eight hours from Australian Eastern Standard Time to get Norwegian time; during the Australian summer, subtract 10 hours.

Finland One hour ahead of Norway.

Russia One hour ahead of Norway.

Sweden and Denmark Same time as Norway.

UK and Ireland One hour behind Norway.

USA USA Eastern Time six hours behind Norway, USA Pacific Time nine hours behind Norway.

Tourist Information

It's impossible to speak highly enough of tourist offices in Norway. Most serve as one-stop clearing houses for general information and bookings for accommodation and activities. Nearly every city and town has its own tourist office, and most tourist offices in reasonably sized towns or major tourist areas publish comprehensive booklets giving the complete, up-to-date low-down on their town and the surrounding area.

Offices in smaller towns may be open only during peak summer months, while in cities they're open year-round, but with shorter hours in the low season.

Tourist offices operate under a variety of names – *turistkontor* and *reiseliv* are among the most common – but all have the information

symbol (i) prominently displayed outside and are easy to identify and find.

Norwegian Tourist Board (Norges Turistråd; 🖉22 00 25 00; www.visitnorway.com) For general info on travelling in Norway.

Travellers with Disabilities

Norway is generally well set up for travellers with disabilities and all newly constructed public buildings are required by law to have wheelchair access. That said, like in most countries, the situation remains a work-in-progress. As a result, anyone with special needs should plan ahead.

Most Norwegian tourist offices carry lists of wheelchair-accessible hotels and hostels, but your best bet is to contact the Norwegian Association for the Disabled. Nearly all street crossings are equipped with either a ramp or a very low kerb (curb), and crossing signals produce an audible signal – longer beeps when it's safe to cross and shorter beeps when the signal is about to change.

Most (but not all) trains have carriages with space for wheelchair users and many public buildings have wheelchair-accessible toilets.

Download Lonely Planet's free *Accessible Travel* guide from https://shop.lonely planet.com/categories/accessible-travel.com.

Organisations & Tours

Mobility International USA (www.miusa.org) In the US,

advising travellers on mobility issues.

Norwegian Association for the Disabled (Norges Handikapforbund; Map p50; 🖉24 10 24 00; www.nhf.no; Schweigaards gate 12, Grønland, Oslo; 🚊34) For information on travel and sites of special interest to travellers with disabilities in Norway.

Society for Accessible Travel & Hospitality (www.sath.org) In the US; offers assistance and advice.

Visas

Norway is one of 26 member countries of the Schengen Convention, under which 22 EU countries (all but Bulgaria, Cyprus, Ireland, Romania and the UK) plus Iceland, Norway, Liechtenstein and Switzerland have abolished checks at common borders. The process towards integrating Bulgaria, Cyprus and Romania has slowed but they may join sometime in the future.

The visa situation for entering Norway is as follows:

Citizens of Denmark, Finland, Iceland and Sweden No visa or passport required.

Citizens or residents of other EU and Schengen countries No visa required.

Citizens or residents of Australia, Canada, Israel, Japan, New Zealand and the USA No visa required for tourist visits of up to 90 days.

Other countries Check with a Norwegian embassy or consulate.

To work or study in Norway A special visa may be required – contact a Norwegian embassy or consulate before travel.

Transport

GETTING THERE & AWAY

Norway is well linked to other European countries by air. There are also regular bus and rail services to Norway from neighbouring Sweden and Finland (from where there are connections further afield to Europe), with less regular (and more complicated) services to/from Russia. Regular car and passenger ferries also connect southern Norwegian ports with Denmark, Sweden and Germany.

Flights, cars and tours can be booked online at lonelyplanet.com/bookings.

Entering the Country

For EU citizens and travellers from countries that don't require a visa, you'll just pass straight through passport control, although you may be asked for an onward ticket (or other proof of how long you plan to spend in the country) if you're not from an EU or Schengen country.

Passport

All travellers – other than citizens of Denmark, Iceland, Sweden and Finland – require a valid passport to enter Norway.

Air

Norway is well-connected with direct flights to/from the rest of Europe and, to a lesser extent, North America. To reach Norway from Asia and Australia you'll probably need to connect through the MIddle East. Oslo receives the largest number of international flights, but Bergen, Tromsø and other airports receive numerous flights from elsewhere in Europe.

Airports & Airlines

For a full list of Norwegian airports, visit www.avinor.no; the page for each airport has comprehensive information.

The main international Norwegian airports are Gardermoen (Oslo), Flesland (Bergen), Sola (Stavanger), Tromsø, Værnes (Trondheim), Vigra (Ålesund), Karmøy (Haugesund), Kjevik (Kristiansand) and Torp (Sandefjord).

Dozens of international airlines fly to/from Norwegian airports. There are direct flights to Norway from East Coast USA and the UK. If coming from Australia or New Zealand, you'll need to connect via an airport in Asia, the Middle East or Europe.

Norwegian (www.norwegian.com) Low-cost airline with an extensive and growing domestic and international network.

SAS (www.sas.no) The longest-established of Norway's carriers with a large domestic and international route network.

Widerøe (www.wideroe.no) Local carrier that predominantly operates between smaller towns and cities, and also provides

CLIMATE CHANGE & TRAVEL

Every form of transport that relies on carbon-based fuel generates CO_2, the main cause of human-induced climate change. Modern travel is dependent on aeroplanes, which might use less fuel per kilometre per person than most cars but travel much greater distances. The altitude at which aircraft emit gases (including CO_2) and particles also contributes to their climate change impact. Many websites offer 'carbon calculators' that allow people to estimate the carbon emissions generated by their journey and, for those who wish to do so, to offset the impact of the greenhouse gases emitted with contributions to portfolios of climate-friendly initiatives throughout the world. Lonely Planet offsets the carbon footprint of all staff and author travel.

flights to the Lofoten Islands and the far north.

Land

Norway shares land borders with Sweden, Finland and Russia.

Train travel is possible between Oslo and Stockholm, Gothenburg, Malmö and Hamburg, with less frequent services to northern and central Swedish cities from Narvik and Trondheim.

Eurolines (www.eurolines.com) The main operator for many international bus services to/from Norway is Eurolines, which acts as a feeder for national companies.

Nor-Way Bussekspress (www.nor-way.no) Nor-Way Bussekspress has a reasonable range of international routes.

Swebus Express (☎0200 218 218; www.swebusexpress.se) Numerous cross-border services between Norway and Sweden.

Border Crossings

Crossing most borders into Norway is usually hassle-free. That's particularly the case if you're arriving by road where, in some cases, you may not even realise that you've crossed the border.

If you're arriving in Norway from a non-EU or non-Schengen country,

expect your papers to be checked carefully. If you're from a non-Western country, expect that you and your baggage will come under greater scrutiny than other travellers at airports and some of the staffed border crossings; this also applies for all travellers crossing by land into Norway from Russia.

Finland
BUS

Buses run between northern Norway and northern Finland.

Eskelisen Lapin Linjat (☎016-342 2160; www.eskelisen.fi) Operates most cross-border services between northern Norway and northern Finland.

CAR & MOTORCYCLE

The E8 highway extends from Tornio, in Finland, to Tromsø; secondary highways connect Finland with the northern Sami towns of Karasjok and Kautokeino – if you're travelling between Kautokeino and Tromsø, it generally works out quicker to take the southern route via Finland. Regular buses serve all three routes.

Russia

Russia has a short border with Norway and buses run twice daily between Kirkenes in Norway and Murmansk in Russia (one way/return

460/750kr, five hours). Once in Murmansk, trains connect to St Petersburg and the rest of the Russian rail network.

To cross the border, you'll need a Russian visa, which must usually be applied for and issued in your country of residence.

Sweden
BUS

Swebus Express (☎0771-21 82 18; www.swebus.se) has the largest (and cheapest) buses between Oslo and Swedish cities.

Among the numerous cross-border services along the long land frontier between Sweden and Norway, there are twice-daily services between Narvik and Riksgränsen (one hour), on the border, and Kiruna (three hours).

There are also less-frequent services between Bodø and Skellefteå, and along the Blå Vägen, or 'Blue Highway', between Mo i Rana and Umeå. Swedish companies **Länstrafiken i Norrbotten** (☎0771-10 01 10; www.ltnbd.se) and **Länstrafiken i Västerbotten** (☎0771-10 01 10; www.tabussen.nu) offer some cross-border services.

TRAIN

Rail services between Sweden and Norway are operated by **Norwegian State**

BUSES FROM FINLAND & SWEDEN

Options for bus travel between Finland and Norway include the following (some in summer only)

FROM	TO	FARE	DURATION (HR)
Rovaniemi	Alta	€101	10
Rovaniemi	Karasjok	€77.90	6
Rovaniemi	Tromsø (Jun-Sep only)	€102.20	8-10
Rovaniemi	Nordkapp	€132.10	10½
Saariselkä	Karasjok	€33.10	2¾

Buses operate to Oslo from the following Swedish destinations

FROM	FARE	DURATION (HR)	FREQUENCY (PER DAY)
Gothenburg (Göteborg)	Skr119 to Skr279	3¾	6
Malmö	Skr169 to Skr469	8	5
Stockholm	Skr309 to Skr449	8-13	4

Railways (Norges Statsbaner, NSB; 🖉press 9 for English 81 50 08 88; www.nsb.no) or **Sveriges Järnväg** (SJ; 🖉0771-75 75 99; www.sj.se).

It's worth noting that some of the Stockholm–Oslo services require a change of train in the Swedish city of Karlstad.

It's also possible to travel from Trondheim to Sweden via Storlien and Östersund, although you'll need to change trains at the border.

Sea

Ferry connections are possible between Norway and Denmark, Germany and Sweden. Most ferry operators offer package deals that include taking a car and passengers, and most lines offer substantial discounts for seniors, students and children. Taking a bicycle incurs a small extra fee.

If you're travelling by international ferry and plan on drinking at all while in Norway, consider picking up your maximum duty-free alcohol allowance while on-board.

Denmark

The following companies operate ferries between Norway and Denmark.

Color Line (🖉in Denmark 99 56 19 00, in Germany 0431-7300 300, in Norway 81 00 08

11, in Sweden 0526-62000; www.colorline.com) Operates two express ferries from Denmark: Hirtshals to Larvik (3¾ hours) and Hirtshals to Kristiansand (3¼ hours).

DFDS Seaways (🖉in Denmark 33 42 30 00, in Norway 21 62 13 40, in UK 0871 522 9955; www.dfdsseaways.com) Copenhagen to Oslo (17 hours, once daily).

Fjord Line (🖉in Denmark 97 96 30 00, in Norway 51 46 40 99; www.fjordline.com) Hirtshals to Kristiansand, Bergen, Stavanger and Langesund (Oslo).

Stena Line (🖉in Denmark 96 20 02 00, in Norway 02010; www.stenaline.no) Fredrikshavn to/from Oslo.

Germany & Sweden

Color Line (🖉in Denmark 99 56 19 00, in Germany 0431-7300 300, in Norway 81 00 08 11, in Sweden 0526-62000; www.colorline.com) connects Norway with Germany and Sweden. Check the website for different fare and accommodation types. From Oslo to Kiel, Germany, there are seven weekly departures (from €327, 20 hours), while ferries (operated by both Color Line and Fjord Line) from Sandefjord to Strömstad in Sweden depart up to 20 times weekly (from €15, 2½ hours).

GETTING AROUND

Air SAS and Norwegian have extensive domestic networks. Widerøe services small towns.

Boat Ferries, many of which will take cars, connect offshore islands to the mainland, while the Hurtigruten sails from Bergen to Kirkenes and back every day of the year.

Bus Services along major routes are fast and efficient. Services to smaller towns can be infrequent, sometimes with no services at all on weekends.

Car Roads are in good condition, but travel times can be slow thanks to winding roads, heavy summer traffic with few overtaking lanes, and ferries.

Train Trains reach as far north as Bodø, with an additional branch line connecting Narvik with Sweden further north. Book in advance for considerably cheaper minipris tickets.

Air

Due to the time and distances involved in overland travel, even budget travellers may want to consider a segment or two by air. The major Norwegian domestic routes are

SWEDEN–NORWAY TRAINS

Train services between Sweden and Norway include the following. Most require a change en route.

FROM	TO	FARE	DURATION (HR)	FREQUENCY (PER DAY)	OPERATOR
Gothenburg (Göteborg)	Oslo	From 576kr/ Skr275	4-6	2-4	Norwegian Railways & Swedish Railways
Malmö	Oslo	From Skr615	7½-9	3-6	Swedish Railways
Stockholm	Oslo	From Skr375	6-7½	5	Swedish Railways
Stockholm	Narvik	From Skr717	20-22	0-3	Swedish Railways

quite competitive, meaning that it is possible (if you're flexible about departure dates and book early) to travel for little more than the equivalent train fare.

Keep an eye out for *minipris* return tickets, which can cost just 10% more than full-fare one-way tickets. In addition, spouses (including gay partners), children aged two to 15, travellers aged under 26, students and senior citizens over 67 years of age may be eligible for significant discounts on some routes – always ask.

Airlines in Norway

Aside from tiny charter airlines and helicopter services, three airlines fly domestic routes.

Norwegian Low-cost airline with an extensive and growing domestic network that now includes Longyearbyen (Svalbard).

SAS Large domestic network on mainland Norway, plus flights to Longyearbyen (Svalbard).

Widerøe A subsidiary of SAS with smaller planes and flights to smaller regional airports.

Bicycle

Given Norway's great distances, hilly terrain and narrow roads, only serious cyclists engage in extensive cycle touring, but those who do rave about the experience.

Assuming that you've steeled yourself for the challenge of ascending mountain after mountain, the long-distance cyclist's biggest headache will be tunnels, and there are thousands of them. Most of these, especially in the western fjords, are closed to nonmotorised traffic; in many (although not all) cases there are outdoor bike paths running parallel to the tunnels. If no such path exists, alternative routes may involve a few days' pedalling around a long fjord or over a high mountain pass.

Rural buses, express ferries and nonexpress trains carry bikes for various additional fees (around 150kr), but express trains don't allow them at all and international trains treat them as excess baggage (350kr). Nor-Way Bussekspress charges a child's fare to transport a bicycle!

The Norwegian government takes cycling seriously enough to have developed an official Cycling Strategy (www.sykkelbynettverket.no), among the primary goals of which is to increase cycling in larger Norwegian cities.

Hire

Some tourist offices, hostels and camping grounds rent out bicycles to guests, while bicycle shops (*sykkelbutikken*) are another good place to ask. Rental usually starts at around 60kr for an hour and is rarely more than 400kr per day, although the per-day price drops if you rent for a few days.

Boat

Norway's excellent system of ferries connects otherwise inaccessible, isolated communities, with an extensive network of car ferries criss-crossing the fjords; express boats link offshore islands to the mainland. Most ferries accommodate motor vehicles, but some express coastal services normally take only foot passengers and cyclists, as do the lake steamers.

Long queues and delays are possible at popular crossings in summer. They do, however, run deep into the night, especially in summer, and some run around the clock, although departures in the middle of the night are less frequent. Details on schedules and prices for vehicle ferries and lake steamers are provided in the timetables published by the Norwegian Tourist Board, or *Rutebok for Norge*. Tourist offices can also provide timetables for local ferries.

DENMARK–NORWAY FERRIES

Ferry services between Denmark and Norway include the following. Fares and weekly departures are for high season (mid-June to mid-August); at other times, fares can be half the high-season price but departures are much less frequent. Depending on the route, there are a range of prices and accommodation types and, in most cases, you can transport your car.

FROM	TO	FARE	DURATION (HR)	FREQUENCY (PER WEEK)	FERRY OPERATOR
Copenhagen	Oslo	From €119	16½	7	DFDS Seaways
Fredrikshavn	Oslo	From €47	12	7	Stena Line
Hirtshals	Bergen	From €48	19½	3	Fjord Line
Hirtshals	Kristiansand	From €27	2¼-3¼	Up to 14	Color Line & Fjord Line
Hirtshals	Larvik	From €29	3¾	Up to 14	Color Line
Hirtshals	Stavanger	From €45	12	4	Fjord Line

Norway Fjord Cruise (☎57 65 69 99; www.fjordcruise.no) and **Fjord1** (☎55 90 70 70; www.fjord1.no) both offer boat-based tours and/or ferries in the fjord region; the former also covers Lofoten and Svalbard.

Canal Trips

Southern Norway's Telemark region has an extensive network of canals, rivers and lakes. There are regular ferry services or you can travel using your own boat.

Hurtigruten Coastal Ferry

There are few better ways to drink in the scenery of the fjords than to hop aboard the iconic **Hurtigruten coastal ferry** (☎81 00 30 30; www.hurtigruten.com), which has been ploughing Norway's waters since 1894. Every day and every night of every year, there's at least one Hurtigruten boat shuttling along the 5200km of Norway's coastline, stopping at 35 ports between Bergen and Kirkenes.

Though it was conceived to provide a vital link between Norway's most far-flung communities, these days the Hurtigruten is a full-blown cruise-ship service, complete with cabins, cafeteria, shops and restaurant – although the 11-strong fleet includes vessels of varying ages (the oldest dates from 1956, but all were substantially remodelled in the 1990s). There are also three 'expedition' ships which voyage all the way to Svalbard and the high Arctic.

Famously, Hurtigruten also provides a 'northern lights' promise – if you take the full 12-day cruise in winter and don't manage to spot the aurora, they'll give you another six- or seven-day cruise free of charge.

FARES

Long-haul Hurtigruten trips can be booked online, while all tickets can be purchased from most Norwegian travel agencies. The Hurtigruten

---

HURTIGRUTEN – SLOW TRAVEL

Although the Hurtigruten route is a marvellous journey, it's worth remembering that the ferry usually only stops in ports for 15 to 60 minutes and these times can be cut shorter if the ferry is behind schedule. It is important to keep in mind that even though the majority of passengers are tourists, the Hurtigruten is a regular ferry service, not a tour.

---

website carries a full list of international sales agents. You can also purchase tickets through **Fjord Tours** (☎81 56 82 22; www.fjordtours.no).

Summer fares, which run from mid-April to mid-September, are considerably more expensive than winter prices. Prices depend on the type of cabin, which range from those without a view to supremely comfortable suites. Sample fares (per person in a twin-bedded cabin):

Bergen–Kirkenes–Bergen From €1750 (November to February) up to €4700 (June and July)

Bergen–Kirkenes €890 to €2800

Kirkenes–Bergen €825 to €2750

It is also possible, of course, to book shorter legs, although you'll probably need to do this once you're in Norway; the Hurtigruten website makes shorter-haul bookings near-on impossible. Cars can also be carried for an extra fee. Discounted fares apply to children aged four to 16, students, and seniors over the age of 67. Ask also about cheaper, 21-day coastal passes if you're aged between 16 and 26 years.

EXCURSIONS

It's possible to break up the trip with shore excursions, especially if you're travelling the entire route. Each of the excursions, which are organised by the shipping company, may only be available on either northbound or southbound routes – there are 24 northbound and 15 southbound excursions,

---

although many are seasonal. Options range from city tours, cruises deep into the interior fjord network, a bus up to Nordkapp, or a trip to the Russian border from Kirkenes to activities such as dog-sledding and snowmobiling. The Hurtigruten website has a full list, with prices.

These excursions offer fairly good value but, in a few cases, you'll miss segments of the coastal scenery.

Yacht

Exploring the Norwegian coastline aboard your own yacht is one of life's more pleasurable experiences, although harsh weather conditions may restrict how far north you go. Almost every town along Norway's southern coast has an excellent *gjestehavn* (guest harbour) where the facilities include showers, toilets, electricity and laundries as a bare minimum, while some offer bicycle hire and wireless internet. Standard mooring fees generally range from 180kr to 300kr per 24 hours.

Bus

Buses on Norway's extensive long-distance bus network are comfortable and make a habit of running on time. You can book tickets and consult timetables for most routes online.

In addition to the larger networks, there are a number of independent long-distance companies that provide similar prices and levels of service. In northern Norway there are several Togbuss (train–bus) routes, while elsewhere there's a host of local buses, most of which are confined to a single *fylke* (county). Most local and some long-distance bus schedules are drastically reduced everywhere in Norway on Saturday, Sunday and in the low season (usually mid-August to mid-June).

To get a complete listing of bus timetables (and some prices) throughout the country, pick up a copy of the free *Rutehefte* from any reasonably sized bus station and some tourist offices. All bus stations and tourist offices have smaller timetables for the relevant routes passing through town.

Lavprisekspressen (www.lavprisekspressen.no) The cheapest buses are operated by Lavprisekspressen, which sells tickets online. Its buses run along the coast between Oslo and Stavanger (via Kristiansand) and along two north–south corridors linking Oslo with Trondheim. If you're online at the right moment, Oslo–Trondheim fares can cost as little as 99kr; even its most expensive tickets are cheaper than those of its competitors.

Nettbuss (www.nettbuss.no) Nettbuss has a big network which includes the subsidiaries TIMEkspressen, Nettbuss Express and Bus4You (Bergen to Stavanger).

Nor-Way Bussekspress (www.nor-way.no) Nor-Way Bussekspress operates the largest network of express buses in Norway, with routes connecting most towns and cities.

Costs & Reservations

Advance reservations are rarely required in Norway. That said, you're more likely to find cheaper fares the earlier you book. Buying tickets over the internet is usually the best way to get the cheapest fare (special *minipris* tickets are frequently offered in summer), and online bookings are often the only option for Lavprisekspressen buses. Tickets are also sold on most buses or in

advance at the bus station, and fares are based on the distance travelled. Some bus companies quote bus fares excluding any ferry costs, so always check.

Many bus companies offer student, child, senior and family discounts of 25% to 50%, so it pays to ask when purchasing. Groups (including two people travelling together) may also be eligible for discounts.

In northern Norway, holders of InterRail and Eurail passes are also often eligible for discounts on some routes.

Car & Motorcycle

There are no special requirements for bringing your car to Norway. Main highways, such as the E16 from Oslo to Bergen and the entire E6 from Oslo to Kirkenes, are open year-round; the same cannot be said for smaller, often more scenic mountain roads that generally only open from June to September, snow conditions permitting.

Fuel is considerably more expensive than in other parts of Europe, so it's important to factor the cost in when planning journeys, especially over long distances.

Vegmeldingssentralen (175, press 9 for English 22 07 30 00; www.vegvesen.no) Statens Vegvesen's 24-hour Road User Information Centre provides up-to-date advice on road closures and conditions throughout the country.

Automobile Associations

By reciprocal agreement, members affiliated with AIT (Alliance Internationale de Tourisme) national automobile associations are eligible for 24-hour breakdown recovery assistance from the **Norges Automobil-Forbund** (NAF; 92 60 85 05; www.naf.no). NAF patrols ply the main roads from mid-June

to mid-August. Emergency phones can be found along motorways, in tunnels and at certain mountain passes.

Driving Licence

Short-term visitors may hire a car with only their home country's driving licence.

Fuel

Unleaded petrol and diesel are available at most petrol stations. Just because Norway is exceptionally rich in oil, doesn't mean that Norwegians enjoy cheap fuel – Norway's petrol prices are some of the most expensive in the world. Prevailing prices at the time of research ranged from around 15kr to 16kr per litre. Diesel usually costs around 1kr per litre less. You can pay with major credit cards at most service stations.

In towns, petrol stations may be open until 10pm or midnight, but there are some 24-hour services. In rural areas, many stations close in the early evening and don't open at all on weekends. Some have unstaffed 24-hour automatic pumps operated with credit cards.

A word of warning for those driving a diesel vehicle: don't fill up at the pump labelled 'augiftsfri diesel', which is strictly for boats, tractors etc.

Hire

Norwegian car hire is costly and geared mainly to the business traveller. Walk-in rates for a compact car (with 200km per day included) typically approach 1200kr per day (including VAT, but insurance starts at 100kr per day extra). Per-day rates drop the longer you rent, and booking through online brokers can bring the price down as low as 600kr per day.

Check the terms carefully before booking – look out especially for extra charges like collision damage waiver and high excesses. Also avoid contracts with limited mileage, as this can rapidly make a cheap deal very expensive indeed. Check the condition of the tyres and the spare wheel (especially if you're travelling in winter); make sure to note any damage to the vehicle before departure, and have it noted on your copy of the contract.

GPS units are usually available to hire, but it's cheaper to bring your own, assuming it has the relevant maps loaded, of course. Many mobile phone companies now offer packages that allow you to use your data allowances overseas, which makes using online map services feasible – although it can be a huge pain if you suddenly lose service in the middle of nowhere.

CAR-HIRE COMPANIES

Avis (☑81 56 30 44; www. avis.no)

Bislet Bilutleie (☑22 60 00 00; www.bislet.no)

Budget (☑81 56 06 00; www. budget.no)

Europcar (☑67 16 58 20; www. europcar.no)

Hertz (☑67 16 80 00; www. hertz.no)

Rent-a-Wreck (☑81 52 20 50; www.rent-a-wreck.no)

Sixt (☑81 52 24 66; www. sixt.no)

CAR-HIRE BOOKING AGENCIES

Auto Europe (www.auto-europe. com) Online rental agency which acts as a clearing house for cheap rates from major companies.

Autos Abroad (www.autos abroad.com) UK-based clearing house for major companies.

Ideamerge (www.ideamerge. com) Motorhome rental and information on the Citroën car-leasing plan.

Insurance

Third-party car insurance (unlimited cover for personal injury and 1,000,000kr for property damage) is compulsory and, if you're bringing a vehicle from abroad, you'll

have fewer headaches with an insurance company Green Card. Ensure that your vehicle is insured for ferry crossings.

If you're renting, it's worth paying extra for comprehensive insurance – in the case of even a small accident, the difference between having to pay 1000kr and 10,000kr is considerable.

Road Conditions

If Norway were Nepal they'd have built a road to the top of (or underneath) Mt Everest. There are roads that can inspire nothing but profound admiration for the engineering expertise involved. The longest tunnels link adjacent valleys, while shorter tunnels drill through rocky impediments to straighten routes. To get an idea of just how hard-won were Norway's roads and tunnels through the mountains, visit the **Norwegian Museum of Road History** (Norsk Vegmuseum; ☑61 28 52 50;

NATIONAL TOURIST ROUTES

The Norwegian Public Roads Administration has 18 specially designated roads (covering 1850km) known as 'National Tourist Routes' (www.nasjonaleturistveger.no/en), each one passing through signature Norwegian landscapes. Many already have regular lookouts and information points along these pre-existing routes, with more such facilities planned. Of most interest to visitors is the easy identification of some of Norway's most scenic routes, and help in planning and making the most of your trip along Norway's most picturesque drives.

In recent years some stunning contemporary structures have been added to various viewpoints along the routes, adding a whole new dimension to the experience of driving these routes.

Of the 18 roads, some of our favourites:

➡ Sognefjellet Rd (Rv55)

➡ Rv86 and Rv862 on the island of Senja

➡ Kystriksveien coastal route between Stokkvågen, west of Mo i Rana, and Storvik, south of Bodø

➡ E10 through Lofoten

➡ West coast road through Vesterålen from Risøyhamn to Andenes

➡ Gamle Strynefjellsvegen between Grotli in Oppland and Videseter in Sogn og Fjordane (Rv258)

➡ Trollstigen, south of Åndalsnes

➡ Two routes through Hardanger from Halne in the east to Steinsdalsfossen (Rv7) and Jondal (Rv550) in the west

➡ Varanger (E75 and Fv341) from Varangerbotn to Hamningberg in the far northeast

TUNNELS IN NORWAY

In November 2000 the world's longest road tunnel, from Lærdal to Aurland (24.51km long, 7.59km longer than the St Gotthard tunnel in Switzerland), was completed at a total cost of 1082kr million. There are no tolls to use the tunnel as it was paid for entirely by the national government. The two-lane tunnel, part of the vital E16 road connecting Oslo and Bergen, reduces the difficulties of winter driving and replaces the lengthy Gudvangen–Lærdal ferry route. It was drilled through very hard pre-Cambrian gneiss, with over 1400m of overhead rock at one point. Motorists should tune into NRK radio when driving through the tunnel (yes, there are transmitters inside!) in case of emergency.

In addition to Lærdal, there's also the Gudvangentunnelen in Sogn og Fjordane (11.43km, also on the E16), Folgefonntunnelen in Hardanger (11.15km, on Rv551 passing beneath the Folgefonn icecap), the Jondalstunnelen (10.4km), which helps connect Odda with Jondal, also in Hardangerfjord, and the Ryfylke tunnel (14.3km), which opened in 2019.

New tunnels under construction at the time of research include the sub-sea Rogfast tunnel in the Stavanger region which, at 27km, will break the record when completed in 2026. It will cut travel time between Stavanger and Bergen by an estimated 40 minutes. Norway also has a number of undersea tunnels, which typically bore over 200m below the sea bed; Eiksund-tunnelen (7.76km long, connecting Eika island to the mainland in Møre og Romsdal) is the world's deepest undersea road tunnel at 287m below sea level.

www.vegmuseum.no; Hunderfossvegen 757; ⏰10am-5pm mid-Jun–mid-Aug, 10am-3pm Tue-Sun rest of year) FREE, outside Lillehammer.

Most tunnels are lit and many longer ones have exhaust fans to remove fumes, while others are lined with padded insulation to absorb both fumes and sound. Motorcyclists must be wary of fumes in longer tunnels and may want to avoid them where possible.

Although the roads are generally excellent, plan on taking longer than you expect to get where you're going, especially in summer high season. Speed limits rarely reach let alone exceed 90km/h and you'll share most roads with trucks, campervans and buses with very few overtaking lanes in sight.

Road Hazards

Older roads and mountain routes are likely to be narrow, with multiple hairpin bends and very steep gradients. Although most areas are accessible by car (and very often tour bus), some of the less-used routes have poor or untarred surfaces only suitable for 4WD vehicles, and some seemingly normal roads can narrow sharply with very little warning. On some mountain roads, caravans and campervans are forbidden or advisable only for experienced drivers, as it may be necessary to reverse in order to allow approaching traffic to pass.

If you're expecting snowy or icy conditions, use studded tyres or carry snow chains.

Vegdirektoratet (🖥️press 9 for English 22 07 30 00; www.vegvesen.no) Vegdirektoratet outlines on a map the restricted roads for caravans; its website also has a handy route planner.

Road Rules

For more detail than you probably need, there's a downloadable PDF of Norway's road rules on the website for **Vegdirektoratet** (www.vegvesen.no); follow the links to 'Traffic', then 'Traffic Rules'.

Blood-alcohol limit The limit is 0.02%. Mobile breath-testing stations are reasonably common, and violators are subject to severe fines and/or imprisonment. Because establishments serving alcohol may legally share liability in the case of an accident, you may not be served even a small glass of beer if the server or bartender knows you're driving.

Foreign vehicles Should bear an oval-shaped nationality sticker on the back. UK-registered vehicles must carry a vehicle registration document (Form V5), or a Certificate of Registration (Form V379, available from the Driver and Vehicle Licensing Agency in the UK). For vehicles not registered in the driver's name, you'll require written permission from the registered owner.

Headlights The use of dipped headlights (including on motorcycles) is required at all times and right-hand-drive vehicles must (in theory) have beam deflectors affixed to their headlight in order to avoid blinding oncoming traffic.

Motorcycle parking Motorcycles may not be parked on the pavement (sidewalk) and are subject to the same parking regulations as cars.

Red warning triangles Compulsory in all vehicles for use in the event of a breakdown.

Roundabouts (traffic circles) Give way to cars coming from the left, which are liable to shoot across your bows 'like a troll from a box', as one Norwegian told us.

Side of the road Drive on the right side.

Speed limits The national speed limit is 80km/h on the open road, but pass a house or place of business and the limit drops to 70km/h or even 60km/h. Through villages limits range from 50km/h to 60km/h and, in residential areas, the limit is 30km/h. A few roads have segments allowing 90km/h, and you can drive at 100km/h on a small part of the E6 – bliss! The speed limit for caravans (and cars pulling trailers) is usually 10km/h less than for cars.

Road Signs

Most road signs are international, but a white M on a blue background indicates a passing place on a single-track road (the 'm' stands for *møteplass*). Others worth watching out for:

➡ *All Stans Forbudt* (No Stopping)

➡ *Enveiskjøring* (One Way)

➡ *Kjøring Forbudt* (Driving Prohibited or Do Not Enter)

➡ *Parkering Forbudt* (No Parking)

➡ *Rekverk Mangler* (Guardrail Missing)

Road Tolls

Around one-quarter of Norway's road construction budget comes from road tolls – you'll soon become accustomed to the signs warning of toll points.

Apart from some smaller country roads, most of Norway's toll stations are automated. If you're driving a Norwegian rental car, they'll be fitted with an automatic sensor – after you return your car, the hire company adds up the accumulated tolls and then charges it to your credit card.

If, however, you're driving a foreign-registered car (including some rental cars from other countries), you're expected to register your credit card in advance online at www.autopass.no (whereupon you pay a 200kr deposit) and the tolls are later deducted. The alternative is to stop at one of the pay stations (sometimes the first petrol station after the toll station) to pay the fee there. If you don't pay, the authorities will, in theory, attempt to track you down once you return to your home country (often as much as six months later) and you'll be expected to pay both the toll and a penalty fee of 300kr.

Vehicle Ferries

While travelling along the scenic but mountainous, fjord-studded west coast may be spectacular, it also requires numerous ferry crossings that can prove time-consuming and costly. For a complete list of ferry schedules and fares, get hold of the *Rutebok for Norge*, a phone-book-sized transport guide sold in bookshops and larger Narvesen kiosks.

Hitching

Hitching is never entirely safe and we don't recommend it. Travellers who decide to hitch should understand they're taking a small but potentially serious risk. People who choose to hitch will be safer if they travel in pairs and let someone know where they're planning to go.

If you're determined to hitch, you'll find Norwegians generally friendly, and they understand that not all foreigners enjoy an expense-account budget or earn Norwegian salaries. Your chances of success are better on main highways, but you still may wait for hours in bad weather. One approach is to ask for rides from truck drivers at ferry terminals and petrol stations; that way, you'll normally have a place to keep warm and dry while you wait.

Local Transport

Bus

Nearly every town in Norway supports a network of local buses, which circulate around the town centre and also connect it with outlying areas. In many smaller towns, the local bus terminal is adjacent to the train station, ferry quay and/or long-distance bus terminal. Fares range from 25kr to 45kr per ride. Day- or multitrip tickets are usually available.

Taxi

Taxis are best hailed around taxi ranks, but you can also reserve one by phone; hotels and tourist offices always have the numbers for local companies. If you're phoning for a taxi immediately, remember that charges begin at the moment the call is taken. Daytime fares, which apply from 6am to 7pm on weekdays and from 6am to 3pm on Saturday,

---

SPEED CAMERAS

The lethargy-inspiring national speed limits may seem laborious by your home standards, but avoid the temptation to drive faster as they're taken very seriously. Mobile police units lurk at the side of the roads. Watch for signs designating *Automatisk Trafikkontrol,* which means that there's a speed camera ahead; these big and ugly grey boxes have no mercy at all – you'll be nabbed for even 5km/h over the limit. Fines range from 1000kr to well over 10,000kr.

If you're in a rental car, the fine will be deducted from your credit card. If you're in a foreign-registered vehicle, you may be tracked back to your home country.

cost from around 52kr at flagfall (more in larger cities), plus 22kr to 32kr per kilometre. Weekday evening fares are 22% higher, and in the early morning, on Saturday afternoon and evening, and on Sunday, they're 30% higher. On holidays, you'll pay 45% more. In some places, you may find 'maxi-taxis', which can carry up to eight passengers for about the same price.

Tours

Norway has some outstanding local tours that enable you to make the most of limited time and which save the hassle of having to arrange your own transport. In every tourist office you'll find an exhaustive collection of leaflets, folders and brochures outlining its offerings in the immediate area.

Train

Norwegian State Railways (Norges Statsbaner, NSB; press 9 for English 81 50 08 88; www.nsb.no) operates an excellent, though limited, system of lines connecting Oslo with Stavanger, Bergen,

Åndalsnes, Trondheim, Fauske and Bodø; lines also connect Sweden with Oslo, Trondheim and Narvik. Most train stations offer luggage lockers for 50kr to 90kr and many also have baggage storage rooms.

Most long-distance day trains have 1st- and 2nd-class seats and a buffet car or refreshment trolley service. Public phones can be found in all express trains and most intercity trains. Doors are wide and there's space for bulky luggage, such as backpacks or skis. Free wi-fi is available on the majority of routes, although the service can be unreliable once you get out into the countryside and start travelling through tunnels.

Reservations sometimes cost an additional 50kr and are mandatory on some long-distance routes. If you book in advance online, look out for cheap *minipris* fares which offer substantial discounts on standard ticket prices.

Buying Tickets

The easiest – and usually cheapest – way to book tickets is online at the NSB website (www.nsb.no/en/front-page). On most routes you'll

be sent an online ticket with a barcode, to be scanned on-board by the conductor.

Alternatively, you can buy tickets from automated machines at most main stations, as well as at customer-service counters. It is possible to buy tickets on-board from the conductor, using either cash or credit card. For shorter journeys this is usually at the standard fare, but for longer journeys you might be missing out on cheap and discounted tickets such as the *minipris* fares, so always try booking online as far in advance as you can.

Classes & Costs

On long-distance trains, 2nd-class carriages provide comfortable reclining seats with footrests. First-class carriages, which cost 50% more, offer marginally more space and often a food trolley, but they're generally not worth the extra expense.

Travelling by train in Norway is (like everything else) expensive. Indeed, the fact that it often costs less to fly than it does to catch a train puts a dint in Norway's impressive environmental credentials. However, if you learn how to work the *minipris* system, or the train passes, train travel suddenly becomes affordable. And think of the scenery...

There's a 50% discount on rail travel for people aged 67 and older, for travellers with disabilities, and for children aged between four and 15; children under four travel free. Students get discounts of between 25% and 40%.

On long-distance overnight routes, sleeper compartments (you pay for the whole two-bed compartment) are additional to the standard fares.

Train Passes

Rail passes are available for Norway (but should be bought before you arrive in the country). Eurail has a pass that includes only Norway.

MINIPRIS – A TRAVELLER'S BEST FRIEND

If you plan to travel on longer routes by train through Norway and you know your itinerary in advance, the following information will save you hundreds of kroner. On every route, for every departure, Norwegian State Railways sets aside a limited number of tickets known as *minipris*. Those who book the earliest can get just about any route for just 299kr. Once those are exhausted, the next batch of *minipris* tickets goes for 399kr and so on. These tickets cannot be purchased at ticket counters and must instead be bought over the internet (www.nsb.no) or in ticket-vending machines at train stations. Remember that *minipris* tickets may only be purchased in advance (minimum one day), reservations are nonrefundable and cannot be changed once purchased. In peak seasons (especially from mid-June to mid-August) on popular routes, you may need to book up to three weeks in advance to get the cheapest fares. That said, the savings are considerable, often as much as 75% off the full fare.

RAIL PASSES

Details about rail passes can also be found at www.rail pass.com or www.railcc.com.

INTERRAIL PASSES

InterRail passes are available to people who have lived in Europe for six months or more. They can be bought at most major stations and student travel outlets, as well as online.

InterRail has a Global Pass encompassing 30 countries that comes in four versions, ranging from five days of travel that must be taken within 10 days to a full month's travel. These, in turn, come in three prices: adult 1st class, adult 2nd class and youth 2nd class. The one-month pass costs, respectively, €844/632/493; children (aged four to 11 years) travel for half the cost of the adult fare. Youth passes are for people aged 12 to 25. Children aged three and under travel for free.

The InterRail one-country pass for Norway can be used for three, four, six or eight days in one month. For the 2nd-class, eight-days-in-one-month pass you pay €300/150/226 per adult/child/youth.

EURAIL PASSES

Eurail (www.eurail.com) passes are for those who've been in Europe for less than six months and are supposed to be bought outside Europe. They're available from leading travel agencies and online.

Eurail Global Passes are good for travel in 21 European countries (not including the UK); forget it if you intend to travel mainly in Norway. Passes are valid for 10 or 15 days within a two-month period, 15 or 21 consecutive days, or for one, two or three months.

The Eurail Select Pass provides between five and 15 days of unlimited travel within a two-month period in three to five bordering countries (from a total of 19 possible countries). As with Global Passes, those aged 26 and over pay for a 1st-class pass, while those aged under 26 can get a cheaper 2nd-class pass.

Eurail also offers a Norway national pass, a two-country regional pass (Norway and Sweden) and a Scandinavia Rail Pass (valid for travel in Norway, Sweden, Finland and Denmark). For these passes, you choose from between three and 10 days' train travel in a one- or two-month period. The adult eight-day national pass (valid for one month) costs €325. Regional passes come in three versions: 1st-class adult, 2nd-class adult saver (for two or more adults travelling together), and 2nd-class youth.

Language

The official language of Norway is Norwegian, which belongs to the North Germanic (or Scandinavian) group of languages.

There are two official written forms of Norwegian, known as *Bokmål* (literally 'book language') and *Nynorsk* (or 'new Norwegian'). They are actually quite similar and understood by all speakers. Both varieties are written standards, and are used in written communication (in schools, administration and the media), whereas the spoken language has numerous local dialects. *Bokmål* is predominant in the cities, while *Nynorsk* is more common in the western fjords and the central mountains. It's estimated that out of the five million speakers of Norwegian around 85% use *Bokmål* and about 15% use *Nynorsk*. In this chapter we've used *Bokmål* only.

In northern Norway, around 20,000 people speak Sami, a language of the Finno-Ugric group. It's related to Finnish, Estonian and Hungarian. There are three distinct Sami dialects in Norway – Fell Sami (also called Eastern or Northern Sami), Central Sami and South Sami. Fell Sami is considered the standard Sami language. Most Sami speakers can also communicate in Norwegian.

Pronunciation

Most Norwegian sounds have equivalents in English, and if you read our coloured pronunciation guides as if they were English, you'll be understood. Length is a distinctive feature of Norwegian vowels, as each vowel can be either long or short. Generally, they're long when followed by one consonant and short when followed by two or more consonants. Note that the eu in the pronunciation guides is like the 'ur' in 'nurse', and that ew is pronounced like the 'ee' in 'see' but with pursed lips.

Most Norwegian words have stress on the first syllable, and sometimes there's more than one stressed syllable in a word. In our pronunciation guides the stressed syllables are indicated with italics.

BASICS

Hello.	*God dag.*	go·*daag*
Goodbye.	*Ha det.*	*haa*·de
Yes.	*Ja.*	yaa
No.	*Nei.*	ney
Thank you.	*Takk.*	tak
Please.	*Vær så snill.*	veyr saw snil
You're welcome.	*Ingen årsak.*	*ing*·en *awr*·saak
Excuse me.	*Unnskyld.*	*ewn*·shewl
Sorry.	*Beklager.*	bey·*klaa*·geyr

How are you?
Hvordan har du det? vor·dan haar doo de

Fine, thanks. And you?
Bra, takk. Og du? braa tak aw doo

What's your name?
Hva heter du? vaa *hey*·ter doo

My name is ...
Jeg heter ... yai *hay*·ter ...

Do you speak English?
Snakker du engelsk? sna·ker doo *eyng*·elsk

I don't understand.
Jeg forstår ikke. yai fawr·*stawr* i·key

ACCOMMODATION

Do you have a ... room?	*Finnes det et ...?*	*fi*·nes de et ...
single	*enkeltrom*	*eyn*·kelt·rom
double	*dobbeltrom*	*daw*·belt·rom

How much is it per night/person?
Hvor mye koster det pr dag/person? vor *mew*·e *kaws*·ter de peyr daag/*peyr*·son

campsite	*campingplass*	*keym*·ping·plas
guesthouse	*gjestgiveri*	*yest*·gi·ve·ree
hotel	*hotell*	hoo·*tel*

youth hostel	ungdoms-herberge	ong·dawms·heyr·beyrg
air-con	luftkjøling	luft·sheu·ling
bathroom	bad	baad
window	vindu	vin·du

DIRECTIONS

Where is ...?
Hvor er ...? vor ayr ...

What is the address?
Hva er adressen? va ayr aa·dre·seyn

Could you write it down, please?
Kan du skrive det? kan doo skree·ve de

Can you show me (on the map)?
Kan du vise meg (på kartet)? kan du vee·se ma (paw kar·te)

at the corner	på hjørne	paw yeur·ney
at the traffic lights	i lyskrysset	ee lews·krew·sey
behind	bak	baak
far	langt	laangt
in front of	foran	faw·ran
left	venstre	vens·trey
near (to)	nær	neyr
next to	ved siden av	vey see·den aav
opposite	ovenfor	aw·ven·fawr
right	høyre	hoy·rey
straight ahead	rett fram	ret fram

EATING & DRINKING

A table for (four), please.
Et bord til (fire), takk. et bawr til (fee·re) tak

What would you recommend?
Hva vil du anbefale? va vil doo an·be·fa·le

What does it include?
Hva inkluderer det? va in·kloo·dey·re de

I don't eat (meat).
Jeg spise ikke (kjøtt). yai (spi·se) i·key (sheut)

Cheers!
Skål! skawl

I'd like the bill, please.
Kan jeg få regningen, takk. kan yai faw rai·ning·en tak

Key Words

bar	bar	bar
bottle	flaske	flas·ke
breakfast	frokost	fro·kost

Sami

Although written Fell Sami includes several accented letters, it still doesn't accurately represent the spoken language – even some Sami people find the written language difficult to learn. For example, *giitu* (thanks) is pronounced *gheech*·too – the strongly aspirated 'h' is not written.

Hello.	Buorre beaivi.
Hello.	Ipmel atti. (reply)
Goodbye.	Mana dearvan. (to person leaving)
Goodbye.	Báze dearvan. (to person staying)
Thank you.	Giitu.
You're welcome.	Leage buorre.
Yes.	De lea.
No.	Li.
How are you?	Mot manna?
I'm fine.	Buorre dat manna.

1	okta
2	guokte
3	golbma
4	njeallje
5	vihta
6	guhta
7	cieza
8	gávcci
9	ovcci
10	logi

cold	kald	kal
cup	kopp	kawp
dinner	middag	mi·da
food	mat	maat
fork	gaffel	ga·fel
glass	glass	glas
grocery store	matbutikk	maat·boo·tik
hot (warm)	het	heyt
knife	kniv	kniv
lunch	lunsj	loonsh
market	marked	mar·ked
menu	meny	me·new
restaurant	restaurant	res·tu·rang
spoon	skje	shai
vegetarian	vegetariansk	ve·ge·ta·ree·ansk
with/without	med/uten	mey/u·ten

LANGUAGE EMERGENCIES

Signs

Åpen	Open
Damer	Women
Forbudt	Prohibited
Herrer	Men
Informasjon	Information
Inngang	Entrance
Stengt	Closed
Toaletter	Toilets
Utgang	Exit

Meat & Fish

beef	oksekjøtt	ook·se·*sheut*
chicken	kylling	chew·ling
cod	torsk	tawshk
fish	fisk	fisk
hake	lysing	lew·sing
halibut	hellefisk	he·le·*fisk*
ham	skinke	shin·ke
herring	sild	seel
lamb	sauekjøtt	sow·e·*sheut*
mackerel	makrell	ma·krel
meat	kjøtt	sheut
pork	svinekjøtt	svee·ne·*sheut*
sardine	brisling	brees·ling
sausage	pølse	peul·se
shrimp	reker	rey·ker
tuna	tunfisk	tun·fisk

Fruit & Vegetables

apple	eple	ep·le
banana	banan	baa·*naan*
fruit	frukt	frookt
grapes	druer	droo·er
mushroom	sopp	sop
onion	løk	leuk
orange	appelsin	aa·pel·*sin*
pineapple	ananas	aa·naa·nas
potato	potet	po·*tet*
strawberries	jordbær	yor·bar
tomato	tomat	too·*maat*
vegetable	grønnsak	greun·sak

Other

butter	smør	smeur
cake	kake	ka·ke
casserole	gryterett	grew·te·ret
cheese	ost	ost
chocolate	sjokolade	sho·kaa·*laa*·de
cold buffet	koldtbord	kolt·bawr
cream	fløte	fleu·te
eggs	egg	eg
ice cream	is	ees
jam	syltetøy	sewl·te·toy
nuts	nøtter	neu·ter
pancake	pannekake	pa·ne·*kaa*·ke
pâté	postei	po·*stai*
salad	salat	sa·*lat*
sugar	sukker	soo·ker
sweetbread	brissel	bri·sel

Drinks

beer	øl	eul
coffee	kaffe	kaa·fe
(orange) juice	(appelsin)jus	(a·pel·*seen*·)joos
milk	melk	melk
red wine	rødvin	reu·veen
soft drink	brus	broos
tea	te	te
(mineral) water	(mineral)vann	(mi·ne·*ral*·)van
white wine	hvitvin	veet·veen

EMERGENCIES

Help!
Hjelp!   yelp

Go away!
Forsvinn!   fawr·svin

I'm lost.
Jeg har gått meg vill.   yai har gawt mai vil

There's been an accident.
Det har skjedd en   de har shed en
ulykke.   oo·lew·ke

Call ...!	Ring ...!	ring ...
a doctor	en lege	en le·ge
the police	politiet	po·lee·tee·ay

I'm ill.
Jeg er syk.   yai er sewk

It hurts here.
Det gjør vondt her.   de yeur·vont heyr

I'm allergic to (antibiotics).
Jeg er allergisk mot   yai eyr a·ler·gisk mot
(antibiotika).   (an·ti·bi·o·ti·ka)

SHOPPING & SERVICES

I'm looking for ...
Jeg leter etter ...   yai ley·ter e·ter ...

May I look at it?
Kan jeg få se på det?   kan yai faw se paw de

I don't like it.
Det liker jeg ikke.   de lee·ker yai i·key

How much is it?
Hvor mye koster det?   vor mew·e kaws·ter de

That's too expensive.
Det er for dyrt.   de eyr fawr dewrt

What's your lowest price?
Hva er din absolutt   va eyr deen ab·saw·lut
laveste pris?   la·ves·te prees

There's a mistake in the bill.
Det er en feil på   de eyr en fail paw
regningen.   rai·ning·en

ATM	minibank	mee·ni·bank
credit card	kredittkort	kre·dit·kawrt
internet cafe	Internettkafé	in·ter·net·ka·fe
post office	postkontor	pawst·kawn·tawr
mobile phone	mobiltelefon	mo·beel·te·le·fon
tourist office	turist-informasjon	tu·reest·in·fawr·ma·shawn

TIME & DATES

What time is it?
Hva er klokka?   vaa eyr klaw·ka

It's (two) o'clock.
Klokka er (to).   klaw·ka eyr (taw)

Half past (one).
Halv (to).   haal (taw)
(lit: half (two))

in the morning
om formiddagen   awm fawr·mi·dan

in the afternoon
om ettermiddagen   awm e·ter·mi·dan

Question Words

How?	Hvordan?	vor·dan
What?	Hva?	vaa
When?	Når?	nawr
Where?	Hvor?	vor
Which?	Hvilken?	veel·keyn
Who?	Hvem?	vem
Why?	Hvorfor?	vor·fawr

in the evening
om kvelden   awm kve·len

yesterday	i går	ee gawr
today	i dag	ee daag
tomorrow	i morgen	ee maw·ren

Monday	mandag	maan·daa
Tuesday	tirsdag	teers·daa
Wednesday	onsdag	awns·daa
Thursday	torsdag	tawrs·daa
Friday	fredag	frey·daa
Saturday	lørdag	leu·daa
Sunday	søndag	seun·daa

January	januar	yaa·nu·aar
February	februar	fe·broo·aar
March	mars	maars
April	april	aa·preel
May	mai	mai
June	juni	yoo·nee
July	juli	yoo·lee
August	august	ow·goost
September	september	sep·tem·ber
October	oktober	awk·taw·ber
November	november	naw·veym·ber
December	desember	de·seym·ber

TRANSPORT

Public Transport

boat	båt	bawt
bus	buss	bus
plane	fly	flew
taxi	drosje	draw·shey
train	tåg	tawg

1st class	førsteklasse	feur·ste·kla·se
economy class	økonomi-klasse	eu·ko·no·mi·kla·se
one-way ticket	enveisbillett	en·veys·bee·let
return ticket	returbillett	re·toor·bee·let

I want to go to ...
Jeg skal til ...   yai skaal til ...

At what time does it arrive/leave?
Når ankommer/   nawr an·kaw·mer/
går den?   gawr den

Numbers

1	*en*	en
2	*to*	taw
3	*tre*	trey
4	*fire*	*fee*·re
5	*fem*	fem
6	*seks*	seks
7	*sju*	shoo
8	*åtte*	*aw*·te
9	*ni*	nee
10	*ti*	tee
20	*tjue*	*shoo*·e
30	*tretti*	*trey*·tee
40	*førti*	*feur*·tee
50	*femti*	*fem*·tee
60	*seksti*	*seks*·tee
70	*sytti*	*sew*·tee
80	*åtti*	*aw*·tee
90	*nitti*	*nee*·tee
100	*hundre*	*hun*·dre
1000	*tusen*	*tu*·sen

Does it stop at (Majorstua)?
Stopper denne på   *staw*·per *dey*·ne paw
(Majorstua)?   (maa·*yoor*·stu·a)

Please tell me when we get to (Oslo).
Kan du si fra når vi   kan doo see fraa nawr vee
kommer til (Oslo)?   *kaw*·mer til (*os*·law)

Please stop here.
Vær så snill å stoppe   veyr saw snil aw *sto*·pe
her.   heyr

first	*første*	*feur*·ste
last	*siste*	*si*·ste
next	*neste*	*ne*·ste

baggage claim	*bagasjeskranke*	ba·*gaa*·shes·*kran*·ke

bus stop	*busstopp*	*bus*·stawp
cancelled	*avbestillt*	*av*·be·stilt
delayed	*forsinket*	fawr·*sin*·ket
left-luggage office	*gjenglemt bagasjes kranke*	*yen*·glemt ba·*gaa*·shes· *kran*·ke
reservation	*reservasjon*	re·ser·va·*shawn*
train station	*stasjon*	staa·*shawn*

Driving & Cycling

I'd like to hire a ...	*Jeg vil gjerne leie en ...*	yai vil *yer*·ne *lai*·e·en ...
4WD	*fire- hjulstrekk*	*fee*·re- hyools·trek
bicycle	*sykkel*	*sew*·kel
car	*bil*	beel
motorcycle	*motor- sykkel*	*maw*·tor· *sew*·kel

child seat	*barnesete*	bar·na·*se*·te
diesel	*diesel*	*dee*·sel
mechanic	*verksted*	*verk*·stey
petrol/gas	*bensin*	ben·*seen*
service station	*bensin- stasjon*	ben·*seen*· staa·*shawn*

Is this the road to (Gol)?
Er dette veien til (Gol)?   eyr de·*tey vai*·en til (gol)

(How long) Can I park here?
(Hvor lenge) Kan bilen   (vor *leng*·e) kan *bee*·len
min stå her?   min staw her

I have a flat tyre.
Jeg har punktert.   yai haar poonk·*tert*

I've run out of petrol.
Jeg har gått tom for   yai haar gawt tawm fawr
bensin.   ben·*seen*

I've had an accident.
Jeg har vært i en   yai haar veyrt ee en
ulykke.   oo·*lew*·ke

GLOSSARY

You may encounter some of the following terms and abbreviations during your travels in Norway. Note that although the letters ø and å fall at the end of the Norwegian alphabet, we have included them under 'o' and 'a' respectively to make things easier for non-Norwegian-speaking readers.

allemannsretten – 'every man's right'; a tradition/law allowing universal access to private property (with some restrictions), public lands and wilderness areas

apótek – pharmacy

Arctic Menu – scheme to encourage the use of the region's natural ingredients in food served by restaurants

arête – a sharp ridge between two valley glaciers

arsarnerit – name given by Inuit (Eskimos) to aurora borealis

aurora borealis – northern lights

automatisk trafikkontroll – speed camera

bakke – hill

berg – mountain

bibliotek – library

billett – ticket

bilutleie – car-hire company

blodveien – literally 'blood road'; nickname given to the Arctic Highway during construction due to the high number of worker fatalities

bokhandel – bookshop

bro, bru – bridge

brygge – quay, wharf

bryggeri – brewery

bukt, bukta – bay

bunad – the Norwegian national costume; each region has its own version

by – town

calving – the breaking off of icebergs from tidewater glaciers

cirque – an amphitheatre scoured out by a glacier

crevasse – a fissure in moving ice, which may be hidden under snow

dal – valley

DNT – Den Norske Turistforening (Norwegian Mountain Touring Club)

domkirke – cathedral

dressin – rail bikes or bicycles on bogies

elg – elk (moose)

elv, elva – river

Fata Morgana – Arctic phenomenon whereby distant features do not appear out of focus

fell, fjall, fjell – mountain

festning – fort, fortress

fiskeskrue – fish press

fjord – drowned glacial valley

fonn – glacial icefield

forening – club, association

foss – waterfall

friluft – outdoor, open-air

Fv – Fylkesvei; county road

fylke – county

fyr – lighthouse

galleriet – gallery, shopping arcade

gamla, gamle, gammel – old

gamlebyen – the 'old town'

gamma, gammen – Sami tent or turf hut, sometimes partially underground

gård, gard – farm, courtyard

gata, gate – street (often abbreviated to g or gt)

gatekjøkken – literally 'street kitchen'; street kiosk/stall/grill

gjestehavn – 'guest harbour'; the area of a port town where visiting boats and yachts moor

gjestehus – guesthouse

gravlund – cemetery

grønlandssel – harp seal

gruva, gruve – mine

hage – garden

halvøya – peninsula

Hanseatic League – association of German traders that dominated trade in Bergen from the 12th to 16th centuries

hav – ocean

havn – harbour

honnør – senior citizen

Hurtigruten – literally 'the Express Route'; a system of coastal steamers plying the route between Bergen and Kirkenes

hus – house

hval – whale

hvalross – walrus

hytte – cabin, hut or chalet

hytteutleie – hut-hire company

ice floe – a flat chunk of floating sea ice or small iceberg

icecap, icefield – a stable zone of accumulated and compressed snow and ice, and a source of valley glaciers; an icecap generally covers a larger area than an icefield

isbjørn – polar bear

jernbanestasjon – train station

jerv – wolverine

joik – 'song of the plains'; religious Sami tradition

jul – Christmas

kai, kaia – quay

kart – map

kerk, kirke, kirkja, kirkje – church

kort – card

krambua – general store

krone – Norwegian currency unit

kulturhus – a large complex containing cinemas, public library, museums etc

kvadraturen – the square grid pattern of streets measuring six long blocks by nine shorter blocks

kyst – coast

landsmål – Norwegian dialect

lavvo, lavvu – tepee; Sami tent dwelling

legevakten – clinic

lemen – lemming

libris – books; indicates a bookshop

lundefugl – puffin

magasin – department store

marka – the forested hills around Oslo

mil – Norwegian mile measuring 10km

minipris – cheaper fares, usually for transport

MOMS – Value Added Tax/ sales tax

moskus-okse – musk oxen

M/S – motorskip or motor ship; designates ship names

museet – museum

MVA – see *MOMS*

nasjonalpark – national park

navvy – railway worker

nord – north

nordlys – northern lights (aurora borealis)

Norge – Norway

Norges Turistråd – Norwegian Tourist Board, formerly NORTRA

Norsk – Norwegian

Norway in a Nutshell – a range of tours that give high-speed travellers a glimpse of the best of Norway in one or two days

NSB – Norges Statsbaner (Norwegian State Railways)

ny – new

Nynorsk – see *landsmål*

og – and

øst – east

oter – otter

øvre – upper

øy – island

pack ice – floating ice formed by frozen seawater, often creating an impenetrable barrier to navigation

pensjonat – pension, guesthouse

plass – plaza, square

polarsirkelen – Arctic Circle; latitude 66°33'N

Pomor – Russian trading and fishing community from the White Sea, which prospered in northern Norway in the 17th century

rådhus – town hall

reinsdyr – reindeer

reiseliv – local tourist office

riksdaler – old Norwegian currency

rom – signs on roads indicating private rooms/cabins for rent

rorbu – cabin/fishing hut

rutebilstasjon – bus terminal

ruteplan – transport timetable

Rv – Riksvei; national highway

schøtstue – large assembly room where employees of the Hanseatic League met and ate

sentrum – town centre

siida – small Sami communities or bands that hunted and trapped together

sild – herring

sjø – sea

sjøhus – fishing bunkhouse on the docks; many are now available for tourist accommodation

skalds – metaphoric and alliterative works of Norwegian court poets in the 9th and 10th centuries

skerries – offshore archipelago of small rocky islets

skog – forest

sla låm – slope track

slott – castle, palace

snø – snow

solarsteinn –Viking navigational tool used when the sky was overcast or the sun below the horizon

sør – south

spekkhogger – killer whale (orca)

stabbur – raised storehouse

stasjon – station

Statens Kartverk – State Mapping Agency

stavkirke – stave church

steinkobbe – harbour seal

storting – parliament

strand – beach

stuer – trading firm

sund – sound, strait

Sverige – Sweden

sykkel – bicycle

sykkelutleie – bicycle-hire company

taiga – marshy forest

tårn – tower

teater – theatre

telekort – Telenor phone cards

tog – train

togbuss – bus services in Romsdalen and Nordland run by NSB to connect railheads with other popular destinations

torget, torvet – town square

turistkontor – tourist office

ulv – wolf

utleie – hire company

vandrerhjem – youth hostel

vann, vannet, vatn, vatnet – lake

veg, vei – road (often abbreviated to v or vn)

vest – west

vetter – mythical Norwegian guardian spirits of the wildest coastline

vidda, vidde – plateau

Vinmonopolet – government-run shop selling wine and liquor

yoik – see *joik*

Behind the Scenes

SEND US YOUR FEEDBACK

We love to hear from travellers – your comments keep us on our toes and help make our books better. Our well-travelled team reads every word on what you loved or loathed about this book. Although we cannot reply individually to your submissions, we always guarantee that your feedback goes straight to the appropriate authors, in time for the next edition. Each person who sends us information is thanked in the next edition – the most useful submissions are rewarded with a selection of digital PDF chapters.

Visit **lonelyplanet.com/contact** to submit your updates and suggestions or to ask for help. Our award-winning website also features inspirational travel stories, news and discussions.

Note: We may edit, reproduce and incorporate your comments in Lonely Planet products such as guidebooks, websites and digital products, so let us know if you don't want your comments reproduced or your name acknowledged. For a copy of our privacy policy visit lonelyplanet.com/privacy.

OUR READERS

Many thanks to the travellers who used the last edition and wrote to us with helpful hints, useful advice and interesting anecdotes: Adam Brewer, Adeel Zafar, Alban Plence, Alessandra Furlan, Claude Gravel, Dirk-Jan Scheffers, Dolores Schech, Don Bollinger, Elisa Orso, Emily Pfeifer, Gemma Graham, James Oakez, Jon Wisløff, Kai Wieland, Katrin Flatscher, Larry Wade, Mark Friedman, Martin Gallmann, Martin Williams, Meg Smith, Mel Farrell, Michael Herbert, Nico Löbner, Nicola Long, Rick Sanders, Roger Horne, Stuart Dowding, Theo Kellner, Vebjørn Enersen.

WRITER THANKS

Anthony Ham

Special thanks to Gemma Graham for sending to the most beautiful country on earth. At Lonely Planet, I'm grateful to the following for their patience and wisdom: Genna Patterson, Joel Cotterell, Sandie Kestell, Elizabeth Jones, Kellie Langdon and Andrea Dobbin. Countless Norwegians were unfailingly helpful – too many to name – and Miles Roddis deserves special thanks for so many shared memories. And to my wonderful family – *os quiero*.

Oliver Berry

As always, thanks to all the people who helped out on my Norwegian adventure this time around, including Magnus Svendsen, Kristina Johansen, Karl Larsen, Nina Hedstrom, Jenny Eriksen and Jon Nordlie. Back home, a hearty thank you to my fellow authors Anthony Ham and Donna Wheeler for their work on this guidebook, and to Gemma Graham for steering the Norwegian ship home to port. And thanks to Rosabella for all the long-distance calls, words of encouragement and keeping my spirits up during the long days (and nights) of write-up.

Donna Wheeler

I'm ever grateful to the city of Oslo, possibly the kindest, most decent place on earth. I am incredibly indebted to Arvild Bruun and to Barry Kavanagh for such inspiring leads, and for the delightful company. Thanks also to dear friend Daniel Nettheim for another weekend wander, Claudia Van Tunen for your hospitality, and to Chris Wareing, Mark Steiner and Hugo Race for the music. And as ever, thanks to Joe Guario in Melbourne for your love through the wires.

ACKNOWLEDGEMENTS

Climate map data adapted from Peel MC, Finlayson BL & McMahon TA (2007) 'Updated World Map of the Köppen-Geiger Climate Classification', Hydrology and Earth System Sciences, 11, 163344.

Cover photograph: Geirangerfjord (p240), Sergii Beck/Shutterstock ©.

BEHIND THE SCENES

THIS BOOK

This 8th edition of Lonely Planet's *Norway* guidebook was researched and written by Anthony Ham, Oliver Berry and Donna Wheeler. The previous edition was also written by Anthony, Oliver and Donna; and the 6th edition by Anthony, Donna and Stuart Butler. This guidebook was produced by the following:

Product Editor Angela Tinson

Cartographer Valentina Kremenchutskaya, Anthony Phelan

Book Designer Katherine Marsh, Mazzy Prinsep

Assisting Editors Nigel Chin, Pete Cruttenden, Melanie Dankel, Andrea Dobbin, Gabrielle Innes, Alexander Knights, Kellie Langdon, Jodie Martire, Anne Mulvaney, Charlotte Orr, Ross Taylor

Cover Researcher Brendan Dempsey-Spencer

Thanks to Sasha Drew, Kate James, Darren O'Connell, Gabrielle Stefanos

Index

441

INDEX G–L

NOTES

Map Legend

Sights

- Beach
- Bird Sanctuary
- Buddhist
- Castle/Palace
- Christian
- Confucian
- Hindu
- Islamic
- Jain
- Jewish
- Monument
- Museum/Gallery/Historic Building
- Ruin
- Shinto
- Sikh
- Taoist
- Winery/Vineyard
- Zoo/Wildlife Sanctuary
- Other Sight

Activities, Courses & Tours

- Bodysurfing
- Diving
- Canoeing/Kayaking
- Course/Tour
- Sento Hot Baths/Onsen
- Skiing
- Snorkelling
- Surfing
- Swimming/Pool
- Walking
- Windsurfing
- Other Activity

Sleeping

- Sleeping
- Camping
- Hut/Shelter

Eating

- Eating

Drinking & Nightlife

- Drinking & Nightlife
- Cafe

Entertainment

- Entertainment

Shopping

- Shopping

Information

- Bank
- Embassy/Consulate
- Hospital/Medical
- Internet
- Police
- Post Office
- Telephone
- Toilet
- Tourist Information
- Other Information

Geographic

- Beach
- Gate
- Hut/Shelter
- Lighthouse
- Lookout
- Mountain/Volcano
- Oasis
- Park
- Pass
- Picnic Area
- Waterfall

Population

- Capital (National)
- Capital (State/Province)
- City/Large Town
- Town/Village

Transport

- Airport
- Border crossing
- Bus
- Cable car/Funicular
- Cycling
- Ferry
- Metro station
- Monorail
- Parking
- Petrol station
- S-Bahn/Subway station
- Taxi
- T-bane/Tunnelbana station
- Train station/Railway
- Tram
- Tube station
- U-Bahn/Underground station
- Other Transport

Routes

- Tollway
- Freeway
- Primary
- Secondary
- Tertiary
- Lane
- Unsealed road
- Road under construction
- Plaza/Mall
- Steps
- Tunnel
- Pedestrian overpass
- Walking Tour
- Walking Tour detour
- Path/Walking Trail

Boundaries

- International
- State/Province
- Disputed
- Regional/Suburb
- Marine Park
- Cliff
- Wall

Hydrography

- River, Creek
- Intermittent River
- Canal
- Water
- Dry/Salt/Intermittent Lake
- Reef

Areas

- Airport/Runway
- Beach/Desert
- Cemetery (Christian)
- Cemetery (Other)
- Glacier
- Mudflat
- Park/Forest
- Sight (Building)
- Sportsground
- Swamp/Mangrove

Note: Not all symbols displayed above appear on the maps in this book

OUR STORY

A beat-up old car, a few dollars in the pocket and a sense of adventure. In 1972 that's all Tony and Maureen Wheeler needed for the trip of a lifetime – across Europe and Asia overland to Australia. It took several months, and at the end – broke but inspired – they sat at their kitchen table writing and stapling together their first travel guide, *Across Asia on the Cheap*. Within a week they'd sold 1500 copies. Lonely Planet was born.

Today, Lonely Planet has offices in the US, Ireland and China, with a network of over 2000 contributors in every corner of the globe. We share Tony's belief that 'a great guidebook should do three things: inform, educate and amuse'.

OUR WRITERS

Anthony Ham

Trondelag; Nordland; The Far North; Svalbard Anthony is a freelance writer and photographer who specialises in the Arctic, Spain, east and southern Africa, and the Middle East. When he's not writing for Lonely Planet, Anthony writes about and photographs Spain, Africa and the Middle East for newspapers and magazines in Australia, the UK and US. Anthony continues to travel the world in search of stories.

Oliver Berry

Central Norway; Bergen & the Southwestern Fjords; The Western Fjords Oliver Berry is a writer and photographer from Cornwall. He has worked for Lonely Planet for more than a decade, covering destinations from Cornwall to the Cook Islands, and has worked on more than 30 guidebooks. He is also a regular contributor to many newspapers and magazines, including *Lonely Planet Traveller*. His writing has won several awards, including The Guardian Young Travel Writer of the Year and the TNT Magazine People's Choice Award. His latest work is published at www.oliverberry.com.

Donna Wheeler

Oslo; Southern Norway Donna has written guidebooks for Lonely Planet for more than 10 years, including *Italy*, *Norway*, *Belgium*, *Africa*, *Tunisia*, *Algeria*, *France*, *Austria* and *Australia*. She became a travel writer after various careers as a commissioning editor, creative director, digital producer and content strategist. Born and bred in Sydney, Australia, Donna fell in love with Melbourne's moody bluestone streets as a teenage art student. She has divided her time between there and her beloved place of birth for more than two decades, along with residential stints in Turin, Paris, Bordeaux, New York, London and rural Ireland. Donna travels widely (and deeply) in Europe, North Africa, the US and Asia.

Published by Lonely Planet Global Limited
CRN 554153
8th edition – January 2022
ISBN 978 1 78701 608 8
© Lonely Planet 2022   Photographs © as indicated 2022
10 9 8 7 6 5 4 3 2 1
Printed in Singapore